The European Heritage: An Outline of Western Culture

The European Heritage

An Outline of Western Culture

A. G. Lehmann

PHAIDON · OXFORD

Phaidon Press Limited, Littlegate House, St. Ebbe's
Street, Oxford

First published in 1984
© 1984 by Phaidon Press Limited

British Library Cataloguing in Publication Data
Lehmann, A. G.
  European Heritage
  1. Europe Civilization
  I. Title
  940   CB401
  ISBN 0–7148–2307–4

Phototypeset by Wyvern Typesetting Limited, Bristol
Printed in Spain by
Heraclio Fournier, S.A. Vitoria

Frontispiece: Donatello, *Gattamelatta* (detail);
see plate 53

Acknowledgements

The publishers have endeavoured to credit all known persons
holding copyright or reproduction rights for illustrations in
this book, and wish to thank all the public, private and commercial owners, and institutions concerned, and the photo-
graphers and librarians, especially Ted Colman, Gordon
Roberton, Tise Vahimagi, and Liz Williams.

The works of Duchamp (Plate 187) and Kandinsky (172, 188)
are © A.D.A.G.P., Paris 1984, those of Klee (176), Ko-
koschka (181, 183) and Schwitters (203) are © COSMO-
PRESS, Geneva and A.D.A.G.P., Paris 1984, and those of
Beckmann (201), Ernst (202), Grosz (192), Lichtenstein (236),
Picasso (186), Warhol (234) and Wols (222) are ©
S.P.A.D.E.M., Paris 1984.

Plates 17, 19, 21, 46, 47, 58, 83: Alinari, Florence; 185, 189,
213: © T. J. Benton; 50, 192: Staatliche Museen Preussischer
Kulturbesitz; 206: Sammlung Ernst Toller, Archiv der
Akademie der Künste; 190, 193: Bildarchiv Preussischer Kulturbesitz, Berlin West; 176 (Paul Klee Stiftung) and 203 (Stif-
tung Prof. Max Huggler): Kunstmuseum Bern; 165: Cour-
tesy, Museum of Fine Arts, Boston; 135: Collection of the Art
Institute of Chicago; 239: © Ted Colman; 205: Theater-
museum des Instituts für Theaterwissenschaft der Universität
Köln; 139: © Country Life; 218: Coventry Cathedral In-
formation Office, photo Roland G. Bailey; 88, 132: National
Gallery of Scotland, The Mound, Edinburgh; 142: Royal
Commission on Ancient Monuments, Scotland; 2, 4, 8:
Photo Alison Frantz; 32, 85, 140: Photo Giraudon; 140: ©
Sylvia Katz; 13, 128: © A. F. Kersting; 183: By courtesy of the
Arts Council of Great Britain; 194, 195, 198, 199, 207, 208,
215, 221, 228, 229, 230, 232: Courtesy of the National Film
Archive/Stills Library; 25, 27, 29, 66, 126: The British Lib-
rary; 1, 6, 67, 137: Reproduced by courtesy of the Trustees of
the British Museum; 118: The Greater London Council as
Trustees of the Iveagh Bequest, Kenwood; 148: By permission of Kensington and Chelsea public libraries; 225: Photo
London Features International; 16, 55, 75, 84, 103, 104, 108,
109, 110, 114: Reproduced by courtesy of the Trustees, the
National Gallery, London; 144, 155, 158, 166, 167, 169: Royal
Commission on Historical Monuments (England); 161, 162,
201, 227, 234: The Tate Gallery, London; 120: By kind per-
mission of the Rt. Hon. Mr. Speaker, House of Commons;
235: © Bruno Barbey, Magnum; 226: Whitworth Art Gal-
lery, University of Manchester; 35, 39, 40: Bildarchiv Foto
Marburg; 214: Mary Evans Picture Library; 125: Bayerische
Staatsgemäldesammlungen; 204: Deutsches Theatermuseum,
Munich; 133: © National Trust; 186: Collection, The
Museum of Modern Art, New York; 146: By courtesy of the
Surveyor to the University of Oxford; 23, 38, 90, 100: Phot.
Bibl. Nat. Paris; 77, 127, 129: Cliché des Musées Nationaux
Paris; 238: Picturepoint London; 124: Photo Pubbli-aer-Foto,
courtesy of Joseph Ziolo, Paris; 86, 87, 112, 136, 151: Repro-
duced by Gracious Permission of Her Majesty The Queen; 9,
10, 48, 52: Photo Ilse Schneider-Lengyel; 153: Courtesy of
Sotheby's Ltd.; 121: © Hildegard Steinmetz; 181: Graphische
Sammlung der Staatsgalerie Stuttgart; 69, 70, 94:
Monumenti, Musei & Gallerie Pontificie, Città del Vaticano;
217: Archiv der Gedenkstätte Mauthausen, Vienna; 138:
National Gallery of Art, Washington.

Contents

For Alastine

Foreword

On the threshold of this essay, a word is due on the place allotted to the pictures within. Briefly, they make up not a gallery of Western achievement in the arts, nor yet a visual archive for the various sections they accompany; more simply, they aim to illustrate—sometimes I hope suggestively—a few, a very few, of the ideals and concerns of the societies brought under discussion in the text. The fact that in their chapter groupings they may also look disconcertingly diverse is not wholly without reason. No doubt anthologies of the written word could serve a similar purpose; but the force of the Chinese maxim has become apparent as I went along—'a hundred listenings cannot compare with one seeing' (baǐ wén bù rú yī jiān).

In so inexhaustible a subject the rich evidence brought within the small compass of a picture seems peculiarly helpful. Most of the illustrations in fact display human beings (and their ideals); some show their perceived environments, or their artefacts or buildings, their communications or their rites or rituals. The brief captions that accompany them are, likewise, unrelated to art history. Barbarous as it may sound (especially in a volume appearing under a Phaidon imprint), even the greatest masterpiece appearing in the pages that follow is there to bear witness to something *other than itself*—though on occasion its splendour may well be a part of the testimony it offers.

It is a pleasure to record something of what I owe to others in the preparation of this volume. To begin with, not a few profound or seminal scholars and writers, past or present: in the absence of footnotes there is a problem of acknowledgement which I have tried to meet (all too incompletely) through the select bibliographical lists at the back of the book and, once or twice, by mention in the text itself. It is even harder to itemize debts to individuals who at one time or another in the past have by a word or query raised a train of thought or provoked a reaction or otherwise guided my steps for the future: a book such as this does not take shape in an intellectual void. Alongside such intangibles, there are more direct forms of help at later stages in my task: in particular I should like to mention kindnesses shown me by Monica Pidgeon, on points of modern architecture, and by numerous friends and former colleagues at the University of Hull in various other fields—among them especially John Bernasconi, Peter King, Edward Page, Michael Robinson, Michael Smith, Christopher Strachan. My debt to Phaidon's staff is no less varied and weighty. Bernard Dod has been generous beyond belief in sharing his time, his learning, and his critical acumen in matters large and small, through every draft. He and his advisers, readers and editors have been selfless in freeing me from clumsy errors and slips, and in constructive suggestions: in this connection I would like also to express my gratitude to Jennifer Speake, who also drafted the chronological tables. Peg Katritzky's tireless efforts in picture research have overcome (I would like to hope) some of my prejudices and blind spots. To Jacky Peters I owe thanks for so patiently and expertly turning a large amount of MS into legible typescript. And throughout every stage I owe to my wife an almost inexpressible debt of gratitude for her unremitting support and for helpful comments on drafts as they emerged.

In sum, what began as an individual exercise owes its completion to the contribution and work of many. At the end of the road it remains for me to claim as mine alone the responsibility—not a light one—for errors and deficiencies which remain.

A. G. Lehmann
June 1983

Introduction

This book attempts an inquiry into ways in which some of the great characterizing features of European culture have come into existence, and then persisted so as to have a place in our heritage.

The task is presumptuous. This European heritage is so enormous, so varied and complex, that there is no one alive who can speak with authority even on the limited range of features of it which are touched on in the following pages (and this author, for one, would not be so foolish as to lay claim to that wide competence).

Curiously, that may well be the strongest reason for undertaking an inquiry of this kind. Someone living in the middle of this heritage may not be at all satisfied by the stereotype images of himself which are reflected back from the eyes of observers in other regions of the world; yet, confronted by Europe's different states and societies, by the baffling diversity of a common pool of ideas, traditions, techniques, values, styles, by the astonishing wealth of works of art made available in concert halls and in picture galleries and libraries, the monumental remains of every age and character which surround him, the reminiscences of antiquity and of yesterday which come to him from television screens and radio loudspeakers, all obstinately refusing to fall together in a tidy picture—how can he possibly *make sense* of this enormous medley?

The fact is that we *do* all carry around with us a more or less vague image or awareness of this heritage; just as without being astronomers we also carry around with us a vague map of the universe with ourselves as a central dot, placed on the surface of the earth, located in a solar system, in a galaxy, in . . . The map is mostly blurs and blanks, but it is there; and whatever shape or order it possesses is necessary to our comfort of mind and always a little better than nothing. Likewise we know that somehow we have arrived today at being different from the much more simply endowed peoples of the neolithic world from whom undoubtedly we descend in a continuous series of generations; that in particular the last two and a half thousand years of human achievements lie around us and mingle also in our awareness and habits; and we are under some kind of compulsion to *make sense of it*, in however sketchy or shadowy a way. Well or ill, we do so.

This locating of ourselves is, nevertheless, problematic. Let us approach it another way. Suppose that the culture we share was one in which all was clear and rationally comprehensible, a kind of science fiction flatland, an impeccably well-organized here-and-now. In such a state of affairs we should have no need (and maybe no chance) to ask ourselves how it came to be like it was. We would grow up by exploring sets of flawless, coherent, *integrated* patterns of living, all ready made (how it all came to be so would be as obscure as the origin of the universe). But that, as we know, is not how we experience life. We are aware of—and used to—customs and arrangements and institutions and traditions which fit together reasonably well; but we are also aware of all sorts of anomalies. We are invited to admire things we would not dream of imitating; we grapple with contradictions between different value systems, incompatible allegiances (in recent times these have been visible in racial equality, women's rights, the claims of religion, conventions of attire, consumerism, environmental protection, radical disturbances in all the arts), and we make what we can of our difficulties. That is to say, we perceive flaws in the patterns of our culture which would be incomprehensible—and very upsetting—were we not ready to see that they are actually there because of antecedent states of the world we live in. No one today would *invent* Greek temples, Gothic churches, or Baroque palaces, nor, for that matter, men's suits with waistcoats or symphony orchestras with their traditional instruments: but we face their presence, and that of a myriad other ingredients in our landscape, because at some moment or other in a world which was not exactly like ours, some of our forebears felt it was extremely important to create these things, and to do so in the particular way they did. Or to change them. And the more we look, the more we find that *every single feature* of our ways of living has been shaped, at some time, by acts of creative innovation or adjustment, many of them quite remote in the past.

The nature of this book, then, begins to take shape. It is an essay in—how shall we call it?—*orientation* in the confusing, because excessively rich, contributions of the past to European culture. An encyclopaedic approach is of course ruled out: an orientation loses its point if it attempts too much. Whatever casts a shadow on the present from the past is, however, of necessity something rather large; if not necessarily momentous at the time it comes into being, it is at least something that has grown to high significance (and we continue to *give* it that significance). We have thus a certain principle of selection, even if the range of choice remains enormous: we are interested in large things.

A question of method

The circumstances in which a major feature of a culture comes into being—Christianity, say, or the Industrial Revolution or abstract art—are never immaterial to its character; the same is true of changes which it may subsequently undergo.

We say '*a culture*', and in so doing imply the idea that a society possesses, or is shaped by, a single overarching pattern of cultural regularities of some kind or other. We have only to migrate from one country to another to find from experience that to some extent this is indeed so. There are laws, presumed binding on all; procedures for reaching major decisions affecting all persons ('political'); codes of morality more or less dependent on the laws. (It is also true that we come upon individuals or groups challenging some of these regularities: sometimes they are relegated to a category labelled 'deviant', sometimes their challenge may reach such a pitch that they claim to stand for an 'alternative culture'—the phenomenon is old, the name fairly new.) In addition to the regularities which may be all-embracing, there are also arrays of customs, rules, beliefs, ongoing traditions, regarding the *right way* for people to conduct themselves in all manner of roles (as parents, or professionals, or policemen, as citizens or as secretaries of clubs) and what to expect of others carrying out *their* roles; the *right way* for institutions and organizations to be conducted (public, religious, pri-

vate, economic, etc.); the *right way* to use language or adornments or other expressive symbolisms; the *right* standards with which to approach works of symbolic import or see beauty in them; the *right kinds* of belief to hold about the universe, religion, science, the relations of these things to one another and to *right* institutions and behaviours (ideologies). In a word, a culture is a society's rule-book, a shared blueprint of values and standards for a way of life. All its contents are *known*, shared, transmitted, learned. Of course, they may also be challenged.

Put in this way, '*a culture*' sounds reasonably clear. Unfortunately, it is also somewhat baffling. A small detail to begin with: the blueprint is much too vast for anyone to know it all, and nobody in fact needs to for living in a complex society (it may have been different for pre-colonial Andaman Islanders or traditional Eskimo culture). This need not worry us: in something like the same manner we may 'know' a language very well without being familiar with all the words in it, let alone all its literature. But then there is also the fact that nobody has actually ever constructed a 'complete' blueprint of a sophisticated culture; and this is more serious. Unlike a complete systematic description of a language, which is perfectly within our means, it is not possible to list exhaustively, let alone arrange in a definitive order, the ways in which the various collections of rules mesh together within a single system. All the categories of rules listed above in fact intersect, and in different cases can have enormously different values. (We have only to think of the possibility for varying the relations between religious beliefs and systems of 'positive' natural science, between authority and personal freedom, etc.) Though there are rules, there is no single way to assemble a general pattern of rules; all the numerous attempts (functionalist, Marxist, evolutionary, structuralist) to arrive at a master formula have in the end been only partially successful. One of the things that gives us pause in reviewing a European cultural heritage is precisely the prodigious variation between the outlines of different blueprints in successive stages of time.

What in fact we normally do, whether in our daily life or in investigating a culture, is to pick on one corner and explore it as if it existed on its own, whether it be painting in oils, or the practice of agriculture, or a political system, etc. In each of these instances there is a 'little'(!) field of meaningful and coherent procedures, a body of tradition to explore on its own. That is how there come to be 'specialists', 'schools' of this and that, 'movements' in the arts, institutionalized professions, corporate identities. But always at a certain point in the exploration we come upon something—a cross-reference, a constraint, a limit, a puzzle—which forces us to take account of other things beyond that field. (Take again the case of a well-charted and reasonably familiar field, that of language. Up to a point we can master an unfamiliar system of grammar and sounds in isolation, but when we want to go further, our task broadens out: we find it subject to all sorts of constraints and full of all sorts of surprising capabilities, discriminations, and odd distinctions, announcing its interrelation with fields which are not 'strictly' language. We notice them because of their difference from our own 'normal' expectations—regarding distinctions of kinship, say, or colour, or politeness, or even logic, where we have assumed that our own cultural formation and usage reflect a 'natural' state of things.) Great cultural achievements in particular exist within a field which has its own autonomous rationale, its own tradition; but never a complete independence. At the same time, outside its field (whatever it is) there is nothing except other fields, other parts of *a* culture which are equally accessible to reasoned inquiry. A culture is the sum of its parts and of their actual and potential interrelations, not some separate mystic entity.

That said, it remains that the interrelations and their results can often be hypnotically impressive and also very prominent; so prominent in fact that on some occasions we are under the necessity of recognizing them as in some sense absolutely typical of a particular society, even if they are not a basis for its full definition. The humanism of ancient Greece comes to mind as an obvious example. And furthermore, results of this kind, to which it is impossible to refuse the term 'style', can on occasion be amalgamated with very deliberate initiatives which we are calling ideologies: attempts to shape an assortment of strands of culture into a particularly compelling composite—it may be Pericles' vision of democracy, or it may be nineteenth-century liberalism, or Mussolini's 'fascist style', or a movement of youth revolt in the 1960s. Again, it has to be said that ideologies, even when dominant, are always partial, one-sided, and never universal representations of the values of a whole society; their particular dynamism gives them away. A culture may very well support an ideology, or even more than one, within it, yet without being comprehensively defined by it or them.

A question of change

It is very convenient, and not always misleading, to visualize the culture of a society as *simply* a loose assembly of various coherent activities being pursued in more or less regular fashion, and with interrelations,

under a common umbrella of an assortment of shared values. In Chapter 2 for instance we shall glimpse a world of medieval kings and barons and farmers and merchants, priests and monks and friars and teachers and writers and builders and sculptor-craftsmen going about their affairs, largely dominated by a framework of beliefs and institutions of a universal Christian Church, and carrying on their various traditions of war, government, crafts, trades, theology, building, sculpting, writing, etc.

A cultural 'picture' of this kind cannot possibly correspond to reality unless we also take account of something that has already been mentioned: namely creativity, novelty. Or more widely still, change of virtually any kind. It may come from outside or from within, it may be well or ill perceived (like changes in population), a discovery or an invention, willed or unwilled, accepted or rejected: any intrusion changes the picture. Perhaps only within a tradition, to begin with (in that medieval world of AD 1200, examples of novelty include a new kind of religious order, the creation of a hybrid corporation of learning, the spread of some newly recovered writings of Aristotle, the windmill, the compass, history writing in the vernacular); but sooner or later, to the extent that there are interconnections, there are repercussions in other areas too. Typically, a 'new' style makes others old; a new grouping of individuals coming together develops its own ideas, different from those already existing; or to take an example fresh in our own memories, changes occurring after 1945 in European societies, aided by inputs from elsewhere, open the way to changes in the 1960s which can be traced in music, clothes, theology, literature, manners, philosophy, drama, work attitudes, sexual mores, politics . . . and these changes are all in some manner interconnected.

The idea is commonplace enough, if difficult to pin down; these complex processes, constellations of change, are never absolutely identical, always unique. At best we can point to one or two invariable, indeed logical, features of them: they are associated with time-lags (the provinces are backward, the old coexists with the new), and they introduce stresses within a culture: resentments, the need for new accommodations . . . Other features we shall return to in a closing section of this book. But for the moment, we have to retain the plain fact that no culture ever stands still, but is changing all the time and therefore subject to stresses always—however much we might prefer to believe that it can also possess a certain stability. That makes it much more difficult to describe at a moment in time; we are dealing not with a picture, but with a kind of huge animated cartoon—such of it as we can see—whose abstract shapes are constantly bulging and melting and transforming themselves into other shapes—changing colour, too, in the process—even though at any particular moment there is no absolute break in the continuity of the picture. There is no convenient way of rendering this in ordinary prose discourse.

On the approach we are following, anyone at all may be the agent, witting or unwitting, by whom some eventually significant novelty enters the culture of a society; there are, however, two kinds of activity which we find especially closely related to change.

One of course is scientific discovery, with or without consequences in technology; for science is by definition concerned with introducing change into 'right' knowledge. In some forms it does this by simply adding, or extending, a habitual approach; in others, by bringing about a veritable Copernican revolution and opening out whole new avenues for further advance. Our own world is so massively aware of this, so well provided with theoretical analyses of the processes, paradigms, constellations of conditions involved, that we are prone to map out the past in terms of 'progress'; progress being defined as solving problems in such a way as to enable further problems to be faced and in their turn solved. This vision is of course quite recent (Bacon, Descartes), and there have been huge tracts of earlier time when such an idea has been entirely absent from 'natural philosophy': ages satisfied with Ptolemy's astronomy, Greek doctrines of the four elements of nature, or the four humours of the body, or astrology, or alchemy. The scientist has not always been a revolutionary, a threat to stability.

The other category is the expressive arts. Artists (by which we mean painters, musicians, sculptors, poets, dramatists, architects, and so on, shading off into those concerned with the applied arts, dress design, media copy-writing, etc.) capture and objectify values and attitudes, collective perceptions and dreams and *intimations*, often with peculiar precision. Sometimes they do this to order, sometimes not; occasionally they convey more than they intend; but at their best they convey the very latest state of feeling, even when they are not out to announce it. It is not by accident that the word 'culture' is often narrowed down to refer to their business of producing expressive objects, the symbols or distillations of much more broadly-spreading patterns of value. By their nature artists are more or less fated to *reflect* change, and in modern European societies they have come to be expected, very often, to herald it, to anticipate it, to be prophets, seers, scouts of the future;

but already in the earliest example of literary criticism known to us—Aristophanes' comedy *The Frogs* (405 BC)—the lately deceased Greek tragedian Euripides is taken to task for going along with what are evidently the then *modern* tastes of his Athenian audience. Creativeness in the arts is either a matter of building forward within an existing tradition or of moving to reflect in some new way the shift of outward circumstance and its bearing on a tradition, or both: and this is as true of Pheidias as of Henry Moore, of Rubens as of Max Ernst, of Euripides as of Samuel Beckett.

And just in case, in a tough-minded age, we should be tempted to think that the prominence being given here to expressive symbolism alongside scientific discovery is disproportionately large, and that the arts are 'only' arts, one might care to have in mind Plato's well-known, and repeated, attacks on poets and his resolve to have all arts heavily censored in his 'ideal' (closed) society of *The Republic*. Careful heed has been given to this recommendation in one way or another in nearly *all* societies of subsequent ages, including some well-known examples in the present day.

These somewhat abstract remarks are enough to supply us with a clue as to how to conduct our 'orientation'. Given that we are interested in 'large' cultural phenomena, we will attempt to see them emerging in their original context: not with a view to investigating them in close detail there, but in order to see what society, what kind of culture, presides over their birth. Since we are interested in novelty as well as pattern, we shall seek to centre attention on each occasion on a relatively short span of time, a clip, so to speak, of one or two generations, and to localize so far as possible on one region or country. (In one instance, this localization is impossible: where we consider the transmission of the heritage of the ancient world to something more properly to be called Europe.) Of necessity we shall be looking at the arts for something more than hints—for rounded-out, *dense* presentations of values clotted together, either in the consensus of dominant parts of a society or in the outlook of quite small groups within it. But we cannot, obviously, confine ourselves to them: for example, if poets in the sixteenth century attempt to capture something of the scientific thought of that age, they are no longer doing so three centuries later. And the cultural life of men in society comprises very much more than just standing back and saying what it is all about, although within the limits of a few hundred pages we cannot possibly reach out to a full-blooded 'anthropology' of culture: we can nevertheless strive towards an *outline* of a balanced picture.

Chapter 1
Roots

The roots of European culture go down into the ancient Mediterranean world of Greece and Rome, together with the origins of Christianity, which are cradled in that world. Few disagree with this view, simply because any alternative looks absurd. Our debt to the Celts, or to various Germanic and other vigorous wandering societies of the past is not negligible, but it is not very considerable either. We owe little to ancient China, to the Persian or Mongol empires, or to the Moguls in India, and so on. Nevertheless there is something breathtaking about it. It provokes the enormous question: 'How can we really imagine classical antiquity having any relationship to our times?' For we seem to be making a claim about continuity which is really rather staggering: we are presuming some kind of durability in traditions and beliefs and ideals handed down through something like eighty generations since the origins of Christianity and nearly a hundred generations since the death of Socrates. With what each of us knows from direct experience about changes in patterns of value between our own generation and our parents', is it reasonable to suppose that *any* tradition or belief or ideal can survive with a definite and recognizable identity through a process of transmission as precarious as that, only a hundred times repeated?

Our problem is simplified by the fact that the world of the ancient Greeks collapsed, and that some features of their culture were absorbed into the Roman Empire. But it is made immensely more complex by the fact that the Roman Empire also collapsed some centuries later in the West, and in an Eastern (Byzantine) continuation slowly shrank to nothing, before being overrun by the Ottoman Turks; that in the Western Dark Ages a Roman-type city life disappeared almost completely, with only vestiges of Roman customs and ideas being absorbed into the fragmented and impoverished societies that took its place; that the Christian Church in the West survived these profound transformations both by shaping them and by adapting to them, and in the end

permeated new institutions largely by transforming herself. We know that, to the south, Arabic expansion spread Islam as far as Spain and the Pyrenees and Sicily, creating traditions profoundly different from those which survive (or are being created anew) within Christendom. Finally, we know that throughout the European Middle Ages the process of *recovering* Roman traditions (and with them snatches of Greek philosophy and medicine) is an entirely learned activity carried out by churchmen, not in any way a 'popular' one. Moreover, the recovery of ancient Greece in the Renaissance is an even more tenuously artificial exercise, undertaken by scholars in a world which until a century or two ago had very little of the knowledge eventually made available by the skills of archaeology, art history, economic analysis, and ethnology.

So when we examine these roots we assume from the start that they have been almost—though not *quite*—severed from the enormous developments of later ages. Because of modern scholarship what we are now in a position to visualize are societies and cultures different from those imagined by medieval monks or Renaissance humanists or even by the antiquarians of six generations ago. To the extent that our understanding is a little less narrow than theirs, we may be even more surprised and impressed that there should be any continuities at all through the successive eras of European society. At the same time we must recognize that our view of antiquity, although more extensive, is considerably more detached than that of a medieval physician, say, peering into Galen to enlarge his understanding of drugs, or of Machiavelli earnestly seeking political lessons for his time in the history of the Roman Republic, or of Palladio measuring Diocletian's palace at Split to discover the secret of the beautiful. We no longer *feel* ourselves to be under the tutelage of the ancients, and in several chapters of this book we shall come upon examples of its vigorous rejection. That does not mean that we are free of it.

Athens

The Greek city-state, the *polis*, achieves its great development in the fifth century BC. It has already been through more changes than its inhabitants understand, and they cloak their past in legends and myths (which it has taken a great deal of labour to unravel in later ages). That remote past is below the horizon of European culture. Archaeology apart, it only concerns us because out of dim echoes of a Minoan world centred on the island of Crete, and subsequently a Mycenaean one centred on mainland Greece, the Hellenic peoples who settle this corner of the Mediterranean have woven marvellous heroic tales and handed down orally through the generations two great epics to which the name of Homer attaches: the first, and still to some the greatest, monuments of European poetry. Homer becomes for them a kind of permanent quarry for poetic inspirations; for great human values which they venerate while knowing them to be archaic; for a sort of traditional wisdom, shared but ever more distant. The siege of Troy, the heroes Achilles and Hector, the great kings Agamemnon, Priam, and Menelaus, the great adventurer Odysseus, are by the seventh century BC totally remote from the business of living, which the Hellenes pursue steadily in what we would see as a much more 'modern' world. There is nothing explosive in the flowering of Hellenic culture, though taken as a whole it is an extraordinary spectacle.

At the period which interests us the picture is relatively clear. The whole Mediterranean is dotted with small communities of Greek-speaking peoples, as far as Spain to the west and northwards into the Black Sea. A minority are ancient settlements—on the mainland which we call Greece today, and on adjoining islands. Many more are 'colonies', self-governing communities set up as long as several hundred years ago from a mother-state, and always near to the coast, trading inland, but also maintaining a constant sea-traffic. We are looking at a *Mediterranean* system, not at isolated minuscule societies: a community of cultures—language, religion, societal conventions, trade and other forms of traffic, common objects of reverence such as an oracle at Delphi and the shared games at Olympia, for which a truce is regularly observed by all the Hellenes.

This system has contacts all around its circumference. To the south lies an incredibly ancient Egyptian empire, with which the Hellenes trade but have otherwise rather few dealings. To the north, beyond Thrace, are peoples whose languages are remote and who have not developed the sophisticated systems of

1   Red-figure storage jar, *c.* 490 BC. London, British Museum

Attic pottery circulates widely throughout the Mediterranean. This stamnos *or storage jar is decorated with a scene from Homer, therefore familiar to all Hellenes—Odysseus bound to the mast of his ship to prevent him yielding to the lure of the Sirens.*

city life which characterize Hellas; they grow plenty of corn, and there are long-standing links with them, of which we catch traces in legend—the tales of Jason and the Golden Fleece, for example, or of Iphigenia. To the east is the Persian empire, a huge multinational state reaching into Asia Minor. Though loosely organized, its Great King's power seems in 500 BC unlimited; it has overrun some of the small cities of the Hellenes (mainland settlements in Asia Minor and offshore islands collectively called 'Ionia'), and further south it controls the Phoenician towns and their naval resources: all this constitutes a formidable threat. With a dubious exception for Egypt, every one of these neighbours is classed as 'barbarian'—outsiders, lacking the advantages and enlightenment of Hellas. Again, this is evidence of the general 'system' to which six or seven million Hellenes feel they belong, alongside their direct membership of the quite small community of a *polis*, or local city-state.

A *polis* is not primarily what we would think of as a *political* unit. It is a *social* unit which cannot be thought of separately from its government; it is a people with its own name ('Athenians', 'Corinthians'); it occupies a

2   Panoramic view of the Acropolis, Athens

After two and a half millennia, the Acropolis is still the unique site which Pericles and his fellow citizens adorned for their own greater glory. The Parthenon (once painted in vivid colours), seen here from the south, was built between 447 and 438 BC; over to the left the Propylaea or gate-house, also begun by Pericles, dates from around 437 BC.

modest area of land around a fortified place where temple-shrines and other buildings and assembly-places are grouped. Despite our use of the word 'city', the *polis* is actually anchored in the use of the land and most of its members live in what we should call the countryside, though as it prospers it does become more urbanized. Athens, which is a very ancient *polis*, with an above-average population of around 50,000 free men, together with women, children, foreigners, and slaves (prisoners of war essentially), covers about 2,000 square kilometers, including the built-up centre itself. Like some other *poleis* it has specialized in wine-growing and olive oil (its grain is imported from the

Black Sea); it has also valuable silver mines and an important ceramic industry, occupying a special quarter named after it, the Ceramicus. Therefore Athens has an unusually extensive trade, a strong ship-building tradition, and even a kind of extension, the Piraeus, specializing as a port and *entrepôt*.

In the course of the fifth century, the urban character of this unusually intense civic life becomes a commonplace. Aristophanes' comic character Strepsiades (in *The Clouds*) harks back to the 'good old life' of healthy country living, unhaunted by debts and settlement days and other worries of the town; Euripides has a considerable nostalgia for the independent smallholder, untouched by urban corruption. In fact Athens stands out among her neighbours in quite a number of respects: size, certainly, and extent of trade, and sophisticated wealth and urbanization and a large fleet—these all go together. But there are two other features which make her unique at the height of her prosperity and are much remarked on. One is democracy and the other is imperialism.

To understand the democracy (rule of the *demos* or people) we must recall that the archaic origin of the *polis* is a tribe following a warrior-king, as in the world pictured in Homer's *Iliad*. This system evolves as a confederacy of tribes, with an oligarchy of leading families and their clans. It is the leading families, the *eupatrids*, or well-born (perhaps 'landed gentry' or 'notable families' is not too misleading), who operate the religious cults and dominate public life, but who also become less and less able to command the allegiance of growing numbers; so that eventually in the course of the sixth century they are overthrown in a number of states by what we might call populist dictators, or 'tyrants' (*tyrannoi*). In Athens around 556, Peisistratus is a rather successful tyrant, building an aqueduct, developing the potteries, expanding trade, and (we are told by Cicero) arranging for the traditional poems of Homer to be written down for the first time. Tyrants do not last, however, and Peisistratus' son Hippias is overthrown (510); there follows the momentous Athenian invention of democracy.

How it is achieved is not too clear; but we know that a certain Cleisthenes, a notable associated with the priesthood at Delphi, induces the Athenians to transform the whole of their social organization. In place of the numerous clans grouped in four tribes, Athens is reformed into ten quite artificial new 'tribes', each divided into sub-groups (*demes*). A further novelty is that families are allocated to *demes* according to where they live, and without regard to old allegiances (which were of course determined by birth); the *demes* of a tribe are not even placed adjacent to one another but dispersed

4   Theatre of Dionysos, Athens, fifth century BC

Immediately below the Acropolis, the great theatre of Dionysos is the setting for the city's drama festivals. Though in use from the early fifth century, what we see today is a reconstruction dating from Roman times. At the centre of the horseshoe of stone seating, a semi-circular space for dance and chorus is conspicuous, backed by what we would call the stage.

around the *polis*, so that tribes cease to be divisive alignments. Each 'tribe' forms a unit of government and sets up its own cult, no longer based on a *eupatrid* myth; each *deme* chooses a tutelary deity (in the event, Zeus or Apollo—gods already associated with the protection of Athens). Furthermore, each male head of a household owning a piece of land, of whatever size, becomes an equal citizen. Aristotle remarks a century and a half later, 'If you want to set up a democracy, do as Cleisthenes did: establish new tribes (. . .), substitute religious ceremonies open to all, confuse as much as possible the relations of men with one another, and take care to abolish all earlier associations.' Democracy is not in any way a 'natural' condition but a very deliberate artifice for avoiding tyranny or oligarchy.

The new state is heavy on 'participation'. Alongside the religious offices which remain in existence, eighty elective posts are created, for the central functions of policy; many of these are further duplicated at the level of tribe or *deme*. Every citizen may thus expect to be an office-holder at some time—many are of course re-elected. A citizen is liable for jury-service (about 6,000 are empanelled every year); he votes in elections to a deliberative Council of Five Hundred (and can be elected to it); he has a duty to attend, and a right to address, an assembly of all the citizens, where high policy is decided. Thus the duties and dignities of office are spread widely; public affairs are indeed public. The citizen listens to envoys from other states, appoints generals, punishes them if they lose battles, and considers all the problems of peace and war and ways and means. Democracy of course has its limits: this is definitely a man's world, and although women are not chattels they have no place in public life; foreigners and slaves are not citizens either; and the *eupatrids* retain special recognition in some of the city's priestly functions, subscribe to the fitting out of ships, sponsor particular performances at the theatre, subsidize public monuments, and influence policy in all the ways usually open to the rich. Nevertheless there is in the early decades of Cleisthenes' Athens a vigour in public affairs (perhaps we hear its echo in Aeschylus) and in later decades a violence (carefully reported by Thucydides) which both stem unmistakably from the practice of democracy.

There is at all times a 'party', or loose alignment, of support for democracy, and a more aristocratic one opposed to it. Regardless of party, however, almost all the great leaders of Athens are *eupatrids*—Cleisthenes himself, Aristides, Pericles, Cimon, Alcibiades. Of those who are not, Themistocles has what we would call 'good connections', while Demosthenes is the son of a once wealthy sword-maker who has fallen on hard times. Perhaps the most grandiose of those just named is Pericles; descended on his mother's side from Cleisthenes, he is aloof and condescending, perhaps at heart sceptical, but at the same time a great flatterer of the common man, even verging on demagogy. It is Pericles who in mid-century introduces the very popular measure of paying citizens an honorarium for attendance at public business; and more than any other Athenian he leads his fellows in a disastrous policy of aggression.

Athenian imperialism has its origin in a life-and-death struggle against Persian expansion. A huge army launched by Darius against Greece is defeated at Marathon (490) by Miltiades with 10,000 Athenian citizen-soldiers. Nine years later Xerxes returns to the attack, and after the Spartan disaster at Thermopylae it is again the Athenians who stem the tide under their general Themistocles, this time by an extraordinary strategy: abandoning their city to be sacked, they 'take to their ships', trap Xerxes' navy and destroy it offshore at Salamis (480), and then in the following year, confront and defeat a weakened Persian army at Plataea. These successes, together with the size of her fleet and army and her strategic position, earn Athens the leadership of an 'Ionian' alliance, the 'league of Delos', which she preserves after the Persian danger has passed; in fact she turns it into a permanent hegemony, and the league's treasure store at Delos, originally for war procurement, is fed by the tribute of weaker client states and used by Athens very largely for her own

purposes. Prominent among these purposes is first the reconstruction, and then the adornment, of the city; the tribute in due course pays for the splendours on the Acropolis as well as the jury-service and all those public duties . . .

Other 'democratic' *poleis* come into existence, though none so conspicuous as Athens. On the other hand there are many states which remain firmly set against this formula, either as oligarchies or as tyrannies; and of these none offers so striking a contrast as Sparta, the leading state among the 'Dorian' peoples of mainland Greece. Unlike Athens, she has oligarchic rule plus hereditary 'kings' for leading her armies. Her growth has been linked not with trade and colonies but with local conquest of her neighbours. In this process her institutions have become so ruthlessly militarized that earlier traditions of technical excellence in the graces of civil life (poetry, crafts) are allowed to languish; priority goes always to war, to repressing her subjugated *helots* (serfs), who actually carry out the tasks of agriculture, and who are rightly feared. Spartan citizens are in effect a military caste; they are *not allowed* to be traders, or even to handle gold or silver. State security requires every male Spartan to be conscripted at seven into a state-controlled military career which ends only at sixty; hence the cult of athleticism, which looks not too different from that of Athens, yet bears a very different and one-sided meaning. The Athenian Thucydides remarks that, if anyone in future ages should wish to judge Sparta's greatness from her ruins, he would be hard put to it: the city has no splendid temples but resembles rather a straggle of villages. And indeed, in a general sense, it is necessary to have Sparta in mind when we attempt to appreciate the meaning of Athenian democracy, and the *choice* actually and collectively effected at the time of Cleisthenes and maintained in the sequel; the two cities exhibit polar extremes of how the Hellenes conceive of possible societies. Sparta represents what we should call the totalitarian option—highly attractive even so to those Athenians who disrelish democracy, and not without charm for Plato. The fact remains that the Spartan citizenry, however formidable, is not numerous; it is already shrinking

5 Poseidon (?), *c.* 470 BC. Bronze, height 83 in (208 cm). Athens, National Archaeological Museum

This magnificent figure, identified as the god Poseidon, or Zeus, is poised to strike with his trident (or thunderbolt). Nothing could more clearly display the humanizing trend in fifth-century Hellenic sculpture: the ideal forms dictate our vision of men and gods alike, without detracting from the majesty of the latter (compare plate 6).

in Pericles' time, and continues to do so; Sparta is in no way able to challenge the hegemony of Athens on her own. As things turn out, she does not need to.

By the middle of the century Athens is widely feared and hated; her democracy is insatiable. She continues to expand the Delian league: on the mainland now and even under the nose of Sparta, making inevitable the alliance of her neighbours against her, and a state of almost endless warfare. After the death of Pericles (429) there are ever more disastrous excesses: first, a predatory expedition to Sicily, motivated by pure greed and in which two fleets and all the Athenian soldiers are lost; then (415), a shocking reprisal against Melos for refusing to join the league—the island is invaded and *all* the inhabitants slaughtered or sold into slavery. At this point imperialism meets its nemesis: Sparta, Corinth, and Thebes combine and eventually crush Athens (404), and thereafter she never recovers the will or the means to dominate her neighbours. Democracy is overthrown, restored, and then carried on in much quieter vein until with all the other *poleis* Athens is subdued by a new power: the Macedonians under Philip and his son Alexander the Great. In this second period of eclipse and eventual subjugation (first three quarters of the fourth century) Athens continues to enjoy a sort of cultural supremacy: now she is the centre to which artists and thinkers gravitate. And as Hegel remarks, the Owl of Minerva takes wing *at dusk*; this now is the great age of philosophers—Plato and Aristotle, gathering up the harvest of the recent past, joined presently by Stoics from Asia Minor and by Epicurus, each with an attendant 'school'.

There is thus a quite gradual unfolding of Athenian greatness—economic power, political innovation, hegemony (which coincides with the development of a great public drama), the creation of a sumptuous 'show-window' for Hellas, and *only then* the consolidation of philosophy. Six generations separate Cleisthenes from Aristotle; when the latter theorizes about Greek tragedy with examples from Sophocles' *Oedipus* he is dealing with something from a century back, already a piece of scholarly revival.

At almost the mid-point in that long unfolding (430) the great leader Pericles (*eupatrid*, as we know, yet re-elected as general fourteen years in succession by a democratic majority) is credited by Thucydides with the text of a magnificent funeral oration to mark the end of one phase of Athens' endless wars. In it he extols her greatness in words of which the following supply the central message: 'The whole city is an education for Hellas. Every individual in our society would seem to be capable of the greatest self-reliance and of the utmost skill and grace in the widest range of activities . . . While the law ensures equality for all alike in their public disputes, the claim of excellence is also recognized. When a citizen is in any way outstanding, he is generally advanced in the public service . . .' Thucydides, writing the history of Athens' later disasters, is no friend of democracy, yet in Pericles' speech he seems to have caught something of an ideal—a lofty and exalting ideal—which we must believe to correspond to widely shared feelings among the Athenians. Pericles' claim highlights the challenge of self-development offered by the freedoms of this particular, and uniquely favoured, *polis*. No one would deny that it seems to have been accepted by the citizens, and with extraordinary results.

Yet *freedom* is not the whole story. What are Athens' unique *productions*? They are, first, her political institutions; then an unequalled standard of public tragedy in the spring festivals (where Aeschylus, Sophocles, Euripides, *compete* for the glory of being performed before audiences of 20,000 men, women, and children); also a surprising vein of comedy, in which, following the tragedy, public affairs are treated hilariously but also quite seriously; a high but not pre-eminent reputation in the quality of her industries; and finally, the outstanding beauty and grandeur of her public monuments (for these last, also, she has one incomparable setting—the Acropolis). But the monumental buildings and their statues and adornments, these symbols of the whole people, are not something in which we can decipher 'democracy' in any direct form. They result from three quite other things: wealth (we have seen how it is acquired), the vision of men such as Pericles (*eupatrids*, with great public works and grand gestures in their bones—what Aristotle later calls *megalopsychia*—magnanimity), and the skills of *all Hellas*, not of Athens particularly.

The Parthenon is begun (447) shortly after the completion of the great temple of Zeus at Olympia; it copies it in its basic conception as a Doric★ monument, using the strong and manly order specially favoured for temples (even if the word Doric refers also to the dialect and customs of Sparta, Athens' chief rival). To design it Pericles brings in his fellow-citizen Pheidias, whose (lost) statue of Zeus at Olympia has been accounted a marvel. Pheidias similarly fashions for the Parthenon a

---

★ Doric, Ionic, Corinthian: three major 'orders' or styles of Hellenic building design, with their own characteristic proportions, repertories of decoration, and associations. They continue to be taught in European architecture schools, down to the twentieth century.

great statue of Athene to form its original focus, and two architects, Ictinus and Callicrates, build the temple itself. The general point need not be laboured: Athens' buildings and sculpture are not parochial, nor the reflection of a peculiar local polity, they are Hellenic. They have their place in the larger culture already noted and in the ready traffic between cities—and in which Athens participates even while she also sets up her own Panathenaic Games (commemorated by a procession of figures in the Parthenon frieze). If an Athenian like Pheidias were not immediately in sight to undertake the assignment, why then the wealth of the city is great enough to attract any other leading master she takes a fancy to: they abound through Hellas—at this moment there is Polyclitus of Argos, Myron of Eleuthera . . . It is often impossible to ascribe a surviving major work of sculpture with certainty to an artist or even to a city. In the world that emerges into sunlight after the Persian Wars the great achievements of sculpture reflect a shared ideal view of the Hellene; very probably the sculptor takes it for granted that it is also the ideal of man. In a word, we can forget 'democracy'.

The figures are themselves eloquent of what that ideal is. They are unsurpassed for grace (Pericles' word), controlled energy and power, natural dignity, excellence. It is as though any excess—bulging muscles, other deformity—partook in some sense of the ugly; even individualization is a form of excess. There is some slight difficulty in understanding Greek expressions for beauty or excellence; perhaps they include overtones similar to those which we recognize nowadays when we talk of the 'beauty' of a racehorse, neither purely functional nor merely formal. Also we remember that at the end of the day Plato is unable to dissociate beauty from truth and moral excellence. Sculptors, fortunately, are not required to be philosophers.

It is not at all obvious that the Athenian tragedy of Aeschylus or Sophocles has to do with the *same* image of an ideal, even though it is strictly contemporary. The tradition, evidently, has a different pedigree. While we still do not know exactly how tragedy has originated, it is clear that it is in some way echoing the cult of Dionysos, god of wine and ecstasy, and that from the start it is nourished by the archaic poems of Homer and Hesiod, myths of religious import, old hero-legends. Its central figures are a little larger than mortal: they confront the gods and are trapped in cruel dilemmas; they suffer great wrong (Prometheus), commit terrible offences (Orestes, Oedipus), fall victim to intolerable retributions (Antigone, Hippolytus). A chorus links by its commentary the high misdemeanours and the suffering of tragic heroes with the life of the *polis*, assembled to

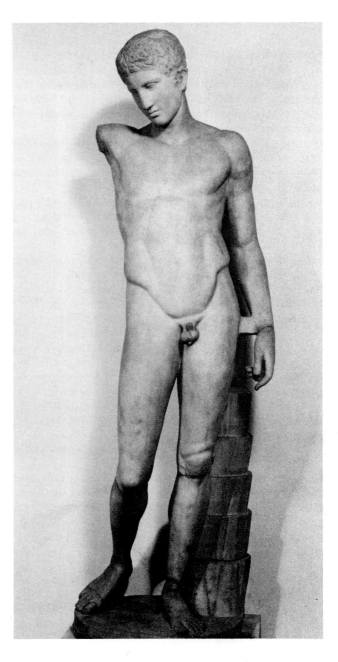

6   Athlete, *c.* 450 BC. **Marble, height 59 in (150 cm). London, British Museum**

Games and athletics are formalized exercises derived from the major skills of war or hunting. As with gods, so with men: the Hellenic sculptor portrays an ideal of human excellence, embodied in the naked youth. Though professionalism enters competitive sport in the fifth century, the ideal is applicable to any well-reared young citizen, or to his affectionate mentors.

watch, to ponder, and be moved. (In this tradition, incidentally, a figure such as Theseus is to Athens somewhat as Charlemagne is to medieval France or King Arthur to Tudor England.) What is the meaning, the lesson of it all? The gods may not be evil-doers, but they rule over a world beset with danger, and there is no safe guidance, except to warn that Nemesis (goddess of retribution) or the Furies await the imprudent, the over-weening, or even the merely unlucky. Tragedy, then, unfolding in the theatre of Dionysos, just below the Acropolis, is the ritualized enactment of a dark world, magnificent indeed, elevated by moving poetry, by dance and music, by actors unnaturally masked and taller than real life; it is a spell-binding presentation, but in no way a complacent one. No wonder that Nietzsche sees in it a fusion of light and shadow, the 'Apollonian' calm of the frieze of the Panathenaic Games with the 'Dionysian' terrors of much older mystery cults. For us, that 'fusion' may seem far-fetched and rhetorical, but there remains the contrast between two *kinds* of vision: one enacted on the stage below, the other carved around the temple above. Yet Aeschylus has fought at Marathon; and Sophocles and Pericles are fellow-soldiers in the same Athenian army.

Behind this duality there are two religious traditions, or even more: that is clear. There is an archaic tradition, that found in the great canon of Homeric poetry, in clan pieties, in an infinity of local cults: the gods of Olympus have left their trace in every sacred grove and every noble family in the land. Another tradition is less obviously shaped by primary social affiliations (such as echoes of tribal loyalties): that of the mysteries, secret cults entered into on a personal basis around the consoling powers of Demeter or Adonis, Cybele or Dionysos, and celebrated by gatherings at Eleusis or at Samothrace or even at the very gates of Athens (one rip-roaring Aristophanic comedy follows an Athenian citizen in drag into the middle of a women's mystery celebration). And there is the tradition which we might call municipal, with temples and offerings and well-connected priests who maintain the service of Athene, Zeus, Hermes, protective deities of the city; Aristophanes, for all his profanity, never makes ribald jokes about *these* divinities. This last-named religion, the municipal one, places a very light burden on the citizen. Piety has to do with ensuring collective good fortune; the destiny of the individual as such is not what it is about.

Perhaps at this point it would be wise to clarify what the Hellenes mean by gods (in the plural) and mythology. Out of a multitude of tribal deities, whether strictly local or with oriental or other connections,

7   Red-figure mixing bowl (*krater*), with Hephaistos returning to Olympus, painted by Lydos, *c.* 550–540 BC. New York, Metropolitan Museum of Art

Another Attic vessel displays a scene of mystery dancers ritually attired—and we note the markedly archaic style of the figures, with their conventionally thickened thighs, vulpine profiles and jutting beards.

Hellas has already by the time of Homer and Hesiod evolved a composite vision of a hierarchy and genealogy of the gods who preside in the world. As told by the old poets, certain deep and primitive powers—Chaos, Gaia, Nux, Ouranos, Okeanos, Kronos, Rhea—loom behind an array presently headed by Zeus, father of gods and of the sky. He is flanked by Hera (his sister and wife), his brother Poseidon (the sea), his children Ares (war), Apollo or Phoebus or Helios (sun, light, begetter of the Muses), Artemis (chastity, vegetation), Aphrodite (love), Dionysos (wine), Pallas Athene (wisdom, olive cultivation), Hephaistos (metal crafts), Hermes (messenger, trade), Hades (infernal regions), and so on and so forth. In turn these deities have peopled the universe with offspring, who are supernatural in varying degrees, and some of these in turn have begotten heroes: the nymph Thetis is mother of Homer's Achilles; leading families claim descent from this or that supernatural intrusion among mortals.

Were this to be all that is needed for an understanding of the gods who are presumed to have their seat on Mount Olympus, Greek mythology would be copious, but simple—too simple to be comprehensible to sophisticated Hellenes. In fact, identifications are infinitely more wide-ranging and nuanced. Thus, as J.-P. Ver-

nant points out, Zeus 'is' sky 'because' he is sovereignty, power; but by the same principle he is also
present in high mountain peaks, or in lightning, in
heavy rain, in gold, in very large trees (Zeus Enden-
dros); and in human relations too—in royalty,
judgeship, clan headships; similarly he protects legitimate marriage, the boundary round the property, the
family wealth (Zeus Ktesios). And so too with all other
gods: they cover between them in principle all powers
and potentialities, and in a manner of speaking *structure*
the universe. They are symbolic links between all the
circumstances in which their power can be seen, or felt,
or appealed to, or surmised. And on a psychological
plane, who has never been gripped by Panic in a lonely
place, by terror in battle (contagious terror being of one
kind with what we sometimes call a 'team spirit') or in a
storm? Who under stress has never muttered a prayer,
'touched wood', felt for a charm or talisman, or sought
to take out *some* kind of 'insurance'? The ancient Greeks
have noted these experiences and carried these procedures, especially rituals, to a high state of elaboration;
they share them very publicly, whether in the family,
the city-state, the particular venture. Between the
rituals, the identifications of power, stretches the web
of mythology which in a manner of speaking is a theology too.

This scheme of belief and supposition is comprehensive; but it has gaps and silences. There is even no
agreed belief concerning what happens after death;
which is baffling when we consider the importance to
Athenians of their burial rites and family ancestor cults.
There are of course myths and gods associated with the
underworld; many are associated with the vegetable
cycle of death and rebirth. In Homer the departed hero
can at best look forward to a shadowy after-life which is
not to be envied of mortals; aristocratic Pindar in his
ceremonial odes consigns the souls of the good to the
Isles of the Blessed; and the various mysteries appear to
offer their votaries a promise of something better than
total extinction. But Socrates, though he improvises
the remarkable myth of a universal Last Judgement,
purgatory, and personal rebirth in human or animal
form according to merit, is still not very sure what, if
anything, is to come when he actually faces his own
death (according to Plato). Pericles in his funeral oration (according to Thucydides) has no word whatever
about the survival of the Athenian dead, otherwise than
in the memory of the living—the good report of those
who die for the *polis*. What a contrast with all that is
revealed to us by Etruscan burial practices in the same
period, or by the Egyptian mythologies and cults of the
dead, a major industry up and down the Nile!

What then have the philosophers to say about man,
the gods, the law of the universe? In Athens at the time
of Pericles—very little. Philosophers are not popular
there, though they flourish all around in Ionia and have
done for a century: Thales, Anaximander, Parmenides,
Heracleitus are all renowned sages of the region but
they have no dealings with Athens that we know of.
Anaxagoras, who does, and who enjoys Pericles'
friendship, is expelled from the city in about 430,
maybe for political reasons. For the time being, public
democracy does not make it fashionable to brood on
fundamentals or theorize about the universe.

Instead, at a less exalted level, more practical forms
of mental exercise are prominent, carried on by the
Sophists. These men, diverse and hard to classify, seem
to have prospered in satisfying a need: they are teachers
of the practical arts of rhetoric and public debate.
Socrates (469–399), a strangely attractive but elusive
figure, who seems to stand aside from public life while
pursuing wisdom in his own way, is reported to mock
the Sophists for offering to teach instant skills—for a
fee!—in practically any field (yet Aristophanes brings
Socrates himself on to the stage, no doubt mischiev-
ously, in the guise of a Sophist). It is hard to estimate
how they *do* influence thought; yet they clearly stimu-
late or focus some kind of reflection, and can hardly
have been as contemptible as Plato would wish us to
think. Thus the itinerant Protagoras arrives with the
very interesting doctrine that every man is endowed
with an innate sense of justice and is fit to carry out the
duties of a citizen—a vindication of democracy. That
raises but does not answer the difficult question: 'What
is justice?' To this question Socrates and Plato later
devote their main energies. For the time being the
Hellenic vision of man is shaped, at least in Athens,
without benefit of deep analytical minds; and (as it
would seem) without benefit of a coherent theory either
of the gods or of the universe or of our place in relation
to these.

Yet there *is* a vision of man, somewhere in the minds
of poets and sculptors, Sophists and citizens. It is
shaped, evidently, in the experience of quite small communities, many of them far smaller than Athens, *poleis*
which seek to pursue their ends in a dangerous world. It
is overwhelmingly marked by the value of self-reliance.
'Small is beautiful?' More than that: 'small is rational.'
The gods may or may not interfere; we must pay them
reverence, consult the oracle, take precautions; none
the less we are 'on our own'. From there it is an easy
step to discovering that 'Man is the measure of all
things', a doctrine also put about by Protagoras. This is
a humanism which admits of democratic overtones:

8 The Parthenon frieze (west IX, 16–17), c. 447–432 BC. Marble, height c. 36 in (91.5 cm). Part of a section still in its original place

The frieze of sculpture surrounding the Parthenon, even after the ravages of history, gives us a glimpse of the delicate balance of energy and form achieved by Hellenic craftsmen in the age of Pericles. These horsemen are part of a solemn procession of Athenians.

institutions can be changed to suit *us*. But it goes wider. It invites us to consider man as he is, rather than be content with a myth of puny origins at the hand of terrifying gods: to dignify his qualities, powers, and skills. His actions, to attain high results, must reconcile conflicting needs, exhibit harmony, proportion. The athlete, the *archon* (chief magistrate), the god—each exhibits his proper qualities; Poseidon's statue shows a formidable but not a nightmarish deity. The temple announces its harmonious proportion, its structural principles—why hide them? Fittingness, excellence, are to be sought in all things. Right laws and fitting behaviour, the avoidance of bravado and presumptuousness (*hybris*), are summed up in one word, *sophrosyne*—we might call it 'wisdom', 'restraint', 'detachment'. *Sophrosyne* is not grounded in a mystery or a revelation; it is the fruit of experience and reflection, of a profound morality (if only we know how that can be explained . . . Plato and Aristotle are not yet there).

And so it comes about that after Herodotus, the inquisitive but not very critical collector of customs and cults and portents and stories, we encounter a truly impressive, very 'modern', historian—Thucydides, the chronicler of Hellas and the fall of Athens: who for the first time seeks to present an account of the wars of the *polis* based on a critical review of the 'facts' which he has painstakingly sought to collect and on a purely human psycho-sociological analysis of the forces at play (one of his methods being to *invent* suitable speeches at every turn to make manifest the thoughts and motives of the various actors). Pericles and Alcibiades, the overweening statesman and the reckless adventurer, are not the pawns of a supernatural destiny, nor are their actions favoured or confounded by mysterious powers: they are *men* whose acts are comprehensible.

The scholars of Athens

Settling in Athens, Plato (427–347 BC) establishes an Academy for citizens of leisure intent on the pursuit of wisdom. It becomes the permanent centre of his 'school' or doctrine. His own writings cast little light on how or even quite when it is set up; they are nearly all exemplary fictitious dialogues, sometimes made vivid by lifelike touches, but also bringing in well-known 'names' from all over Hellas to represent characteristic standpoints, regardless of when or where the speakers have lived. We must suppose that the participants in his Academy are not *too* unlike the Athenian characters who feature in the dialogues, namely gentlemen free from pecuniary care or public duties; some young, others quite old, and all—at least in their discussions—avoiding passion and seeking truth. For all the naturalness and sophisticated elegance of the dialogues, however, the 'message' of Plato is not unambiguously clear. Even the spokesman for Platonic wisdom, Socrates himself, is an elusive figure, and Plato does not go out of his way to make him consistent. Furthermore, we do not know the precise sequence in which Plato writes his dialogues; he *seems* to have changed the emphasis of his thought between earlier and later discussions, though even that is conjectural; also what Aristotle attributes to him (albeit on the basis of taking part for some twenty years in the work of the Academy) is sometimes clearer than what Plato himself *may* have been trying to convey.

Subject to all these cautions, a Platonic philosophy is certainly laid down in the mid-fourth century, and in the sketchiest terms it has the following main features.

1   To begin with, Plato is aware of the great range of speculations and scientific beginnings by now accumulated all around Hellas and especially in Ionia: astronomy, mathematics, medicine, debates on terms like 'good', 'just', 'true', arguments about 'Being', and about the relations between parts of thought and the whole of thought, discussion regarding the chief ends of Man (since 'religion' has no conclusive guidance to offer), and disputes about suitable methods for probing such questions. He sets himself to bring order into selected parts of this tangle, and to outline a general perspective for the whole of it.

2   In this huge task, the attitude and approach will be uniformly one which exhibits *sophrosyne*; indeed it seems to be taken sometimes to extremes in the ferocity of the *Republic* and still more in the *Laws*, where 'ideal' political institutions are under discussion. But *sophrosyne* is also symbolized in Plato's central 'character', the figure of Socrates himself, with his cheerful and courteous manner, his unswerving and fearless search after truth, his questioning of all and every superficial opinion or casual belief, his 'dialectic' of debate; he stands for an unconditional use of freedom to pursue deeper insight, even at the cost of his life.

3   An important triumph of Hellenic thought has been in mathematics: Pythagoras' theorem, for example, is part of a world of truths apparently free from the accidents of life, and profoundly impressive to Plato. Perhaps influenced by this, a recurring theme in many dialogues is the doctrine of 'Ideas': they are models not visible to the eye but grasped by the mind, to which objects in our experience and words in our language stand in some kind of subordinate relation. The *Republic* offers a magnificent allegory of this doctrine in its picture of the cavern, the shadows which men within it perceive, and the sun outside. The Idea of all Ideas may even, we find, be identified with the Good, but Plato also teases his listeners by laying bare in other dialogues some of the paradoxes of a theory of Ideas.

4   Given this preoccupation, Plato exhibits—exceptionally—a quite dogmatic position against Heracleitus, the philosopher credited with the notion that everything is in a state of continual flux. Ideas, and all the more perfect forms of reality, are permanent and unmoving; changefulness in some way denotes inferiority.

5   Since we glimpse regularities all around us and in our ideal conceptions, our thoughts lead us on to glimpse a grander, unfathomable Unity. A single unchanging supreme principle or God (not in any way comparable to a person as we conceive of a person, neither man-like nor Zeus-like) stands 'behind' the universe of all sensible and rational things, and has caused that universe to be created (by some subordinate power or *demiurgos*). Perhaps the latter has delegated to lesser gods, those whom we know by name, particular minor tasks in creation. To do justice to the plenitude of all the power so exhibited there must be, between God and ourselves, and between ourselves and the meanest creature, an array of beings of every conceivable order of perfection—later called a 'great Chain of Being'.

This vision of divinity, an ideal order, a created universe, overrides the cults of municipal gods and the cults of the mysteries; it outsoars Ionian philosophy; it is infinitely more spiritualized than anything yet encountered in Hellas. It also supplies an answer to questions regarding the chief end of man: for what else could man's chief end be but to purify his wisdom and advance towards a view of, or even a union with, that Supreme Being, however little we—or Plato—can express such a consummation? We read simply in the *Timaeus* that the vision of Unity is one of 'indescribable beauty', and this is not elaborated further; it is not clear whether God, the supreme Good of the *Timaeus*, is identical with Plato's Idea of the Good, the ground of all other Ideas, as presented in the *Republic*. On occasions when he wishes to convey a view beyond the reach of argumentative discourse, he switches into the idiom reserved for divine things—allegory, home-made myth. These are *two* such allegories central to his thought: that of the cavern in the *Republic*, that of the creation in the *Timaeus*. And perhaps they are incompatible; we shall never know if Plato thought them so. At all events his followers preserve both; and both the dialogues in which they feature survive the vicissitudes of the next two millennia, and haunt the minds of the ancient world, the Middle Ages, and modern Europe, with a deep-seated mysticism.

Let us be quite clear: these are not matters within the ken of Periclean Athens. Plato's philosophy is worked out in a society which is enjoying (if that is the word) an era of drift, of renewed but unoriginal political activity, not an imperial adventure. Some of its citizens and visitors are satisfying the urge to self-improvement; that is all. To be sure, Plato's 'political' views are by the standards of his time conservative, that is, nostalgic; the *Republic* contains a shocking blueprint for a 'closed society'; against Protagoras he argues the plain fact that not all men are naturally inclined to noble thought (although some can be reared to it . . .). But these ideas do not necessarily dominate his philosophy, nor do they have any practical bearing on the impending fate of Athens.

From Plato to Aristotle (384–322 BC) is barely more than a generation, but it marks the birth of professionalism. Where Plato's Socrates questions, probes, encounters paradox, and passes from dialectic to allegory, Aristotle (who is not an Athenian) develops a fully systematic body of reasoning in his school, the Lyceum. His logic, the precursor of modern logic, has entirely generalized rules for the conduct of discursive argument (syllogisms); a system of 'categories', that is to say those classes of characteristics that can be predi-

cated of a substance—such as genus, species, essence, accident, quantity, quality; the pregnant distinctions of form and matter, of actual and potential; the distinction of different kinds of causes—formal, material, efficient (what triggered it off), and final (that is to say, to what end): this is already a gigantic 'tidying up' by comparison with Plato, and one on which Western thought has been almost continually nourished ever since. We also notice that in direct opposition to Plato, all Aristotle's emphasis is on the real existence of *substances* (individual men, things, etc.), and not on the superior reality of Ideas: indeed these latter have in his considered view no separate being whatsoever. But further than that, Aristotle (son of an eminent physician) surveys with a sympathetic eye all that Greek science has already collected, and continues to collect, by way of information on the natural universe (*physis*) and on man: his books on natural philosophy are an array of essays on the considerable amount of knowledge already built up—from fishes and dreams and physiology to colours and meteors and the stars above; and his *Metaphysics* supplies the physics with a grounding in the ultimate nature of Being itself, a grounding in which the same rigour and coherence are no less searchingly attempted. Again in contrast with Plato, Aristotle *reasons* to the necessary existence of a supreme God, this time as the being who is substance but not matter, who is not caused but who causes: the prime mover of the universe (which is, as any star-gazer can see, in motion); but not its creator, nor indeed concerned to 'interfere' in it at all other than by simply being.

However, nature is not unrelated to God: this universe of changing individuals exhibits an awesome spectacle of regularity and order, of species that survive the death of individuals, of congruent activity, and Aristotle sees in *all* substances signs of their final causes; that is to say, everything seeks to achieve a purpose (*telos*)—its own, that which is specific to it—and all nature together strives towards God, the final cause and final good. In other words, the universe is *purposive*: a noble dream, if a fragile one. Between God and inanimate nature is man: a being with a soul (like all organic creatures), man is also endowed with reason (*logos*), which like God is immaterial and immortal. The doctrine of man emerges from various of Aristotle's physical writings—on generation, on the soul—and includes a well-developed theory of knowledge, of right reasoning by the use of memory, logic, probable inference, and experience. Aristotle does not stop there. He pursues his systematic inquiry into ethics, from the viewpoint of the virtuous citizen of the city-state; into political science, with profound comparisons of different systems of government; even into rhetoric, and poetics and drama: all fields of knowledge can be brought under the appraisal of his great system (it is developed and filled out by his numerous successors).

Aristotle's philosophy is at least as vast as Plato's, but almost totally different both in character and in form: not austerely puritanical but moderate and painstaking, not mystical but down-to-earth; not teasing dialogues, but texts for pupils: an equally astounding achievement, but of a different kind. Parts of Aristotle's encyclopaedic and essentially *tidy* philosophy will prove indestructible as a procedural guide; one day we shall see it dominating European philosophy and science; it will also serve as a launching pad (though some would say an obstacle) for a different kind of science. And even if today its zoological theories are mere curiosities, the field naturalist continues to classify his specimens by the light of principles which go straight back to Aristotle's logic.

And then, a generation younger than Aristotle's school, a third movement or school appears in Athens. This one, the Stoa, is very different from its predecessors because Athens has, dramatically, had its status in the world transformed shortly after the death of Plato. Alexander the Great (356–323 BC, briefly tutored by Aristotle in 342) has put an end to the long history of independent cities, destroyed Thebes, put the states of Attica under military rule, and enlisted Hellenes and others for an extraordinary conquest of the known world. Egypt, the Middle East, Persia, fall to his army; an expedition penetrates as far as India; in the space of a decade a kind of universal state is established—something not previously known. It hardly matters that on the early death of Alexander the Great his lieutenants immediately break up the conquests into three separate, though still very large, empires; in the short time in which the world is turned upside-down, groups of Hellenes have carried their customs and their skills to new settlements far and wide, from the Nubian desert to the upper Indus valley. The congeries of little *poleis* – Athens, Thebes, Sparta, Corinth and the rest—is a curiosity of the past; the Hellenes, now spread over more extensive regions, cannot imaginably disseminate their old forms of government; instead they disseminate those arts in which they enjoy some real superiority.

The universalization of this later Hellas is what we call 'Hellenistic'. It works on Greek thought in the philosophy of the Stoa, brought to Athens by thinkers from Asia Minor to whom Plato's vision of man perfecting himself in a city-state is merely quaint. Zeno (336–264 BC), the most famous Stoic—though not the best recorded figure of the age—is aware of enormously larger horizons than those of the Athenian schools: Asiatics are obviously not barbarians; man is by rights a citizen of the whole (known) world, a cosmopolitan. But how must we think of the world, if not in the old narrow terms? Why, by seeing it in its full extent—as Nature. Beginning with the stars above, the earth and water around us, we are part of one great system animated by laws and regularities, including those already detected by philosophy; a macrocosm not subject to the whims of tyrants or local gods; a majestic order, within which man too must learn to see his place. And the flux and change of things, to which Zeno and the Stoics (unlike Plato) accord special attention, is not random wantonness and imperfection, for there is astrology (the ancient Chaldean science), which treats of the influence of the stars on human and no doubt all other destinies. Within this order, man must learn to live without special favours or supernatural hopes, but simply in accordance with Nature; practise virtue, accept unavoidable suffering 'stoically', and for that matter avoid being carried away by pleasures—or as Cicero later sums it up, 'bow to Time, follow God, know oneself, do nothing to excess.' These are practical lessons of the Stoa as they are picked up in the next century by the conquering Roman Republic and adopted by some of the great administrators of its Empire. It is true that, unlike Plato, Zeno is not prepared to compromise on a 'popular' religion for the ignorant alongside a lofty vision of truth for the select few: since all men should be wise in *his* ideal republic, there is no further place for the superstition of temples, cults, or idols. That is, however, an extreme position to which no patriotic Roman can agree, however enlightened or cosmopolitan he may seek to be. Virtue need not fear to compromise—even while admitting its own hypocrisy; neither Cicero nor the (Stoic) Emperor Marcus Aurelius ever incurs the charge of impiety.

It is otherwise with the *fourth* school set up in Athens, by Epicurus (341–270 BC); for this contemporary of Zeno agrees with him in refusing to allow the old gods (with their narrow little associations and horizons) any place in human affairs, and goes on to show that he has no time either for Chaldean astrology, however venerable. From Democritus, one of the daring Ionian speculators on physics, Epicurus takes over a belief that the universe is made up simply of atoms, following their own regular courses through the void; 'natural' laws are the sole foundation of wisdom; we must attend to what our *senses* tell us of the world we perceive, in calm and in modesty; our organized powers of understanding and control are in some sense the product of a natural

Chronology for Chapter 1

BC

776	First Olympiad (conventional starting point of Greek chronology)		hegemony in Greece after battle of Chaeronea
753	Traditional date of the founding of Rome	c. 335	Aristotle founds Peripatetic school of philosophy at Athens
510	The tyrant Hippias overthrown at Athens; democratic reforms instituted by Cleisthenes	330	Alexander the Great founds Alexandria in Egypt
509	Etruscan monarchs expelled from Rome; foundation of Roman Republic	323	Death of Alexander the Great at Babylon
499	Outbreak of Ionian revolt against Persia	322	Death of Demosthenes
490	Athenians defeat Persians at Marathon	c. 315	Zeno of Citium founds Stoic school of philosophy at Athens
484	Aeschylus wins drama prize for first time	c. 305	Epicurus teaching at Athens
480	Persians burn Athens; their fleet defeated off Salamis by Athenians under Themistocles	c. 300	Euclid active at Alexandria
479	Greeks under Pausanias defeat Persians at Plataea	c. 280	Alexandrian scholars translate the Hebrew holy books into Greek (the Septuagint)
478	Delian league established under Athenian dominance	c. 270	Building of the Pharos at Alexandria
c. 476–460	Pindar's odes	264–241	First Punic War ends in Rome's acquisition of its first province—Sicily
468	Sophocles wins drama prize for the first time	219–202	Second Punic War, ending in defeat of Hannibal
460	Reforms instigated by Pericles secure ascendancy of democratic party at Athens	212	Death of Archimedes in Roman sack of Syracuse
449	First codification of Roman law (the Twelve Tables)	184	Death of Plautus, Rome's first comic playwright
447	Parthenon begun under Pericles' direction	168	Battle of Pydna ends Macedonian monarchy and establishes Roman hegemony in Greece
441	Euripides wins drama prize for the first time		
438	Dedication of Pheidias' statue of Athene in the Parthenon	146	Third Punic War ends; destruction of Carthage
431	Outbreak of Peloponnesian War between Athens and alliance of Peloponnesian city-states	87	Civil strife at Rome between *plebs* and aristocrats
429	Death of Pericles	81	Sulla becomes dictator at Rome and reasserts senatorial authority
c. 425	Death of Herodotus	60	Formation of First Triumvirate (Pompey, Caesar, Crassus)
423	Aristophanes' *The Clouds* produced		
413	Athenian expedition to Sicily ends in total disaster	c. 55	Death of Lucretius; Pompey builds first public theatre in Rome
404	Defeat of Athens by Sparta ends Peloponnesian War	49–48	Civil war in Rome; Caesar defeats Pompey
c. 400	Death of Thucydides	44	Assassination of Caesar sparks off renewed war
399	Judicial murder of Socrates	44–43	Cicero's Philippics against Antony
c. 385	Plato establishes his Academy at Athens	43	Cicero murdered by Antony's agents
c. 360–340	Praxiteles active at Athens	c. 35	Horace's first book of satires published
338	Philip of Macedon establishes Macedonian	33–23	Composition of most of Horace's odes

31	Octavian defeats Antony and Cleopatra at Actium
27	Pantheon begun by M. Agrippa; Octavian assumes title of Augustus
19	Virgil dies, leaving *Aeneid* to be published posthumously

AD
14	Death of Augustus
64	Fire at Rome affords Nero pretext for first persecution of Christians
79	Pompeii destroyed by eruption of Mount Vesuvius; Colosseum dedicated at Rome
106	Trajan conquers Dacia
117–38	Hadrian emperor
161–80	Marcus Aurelius emperor
199	Death of Galen
212	Caracalla extends citizenship to all free adult males in empire
244	Plotinus teaching Neoplatonism at Rome
250	Extensive persecution of Christians under Decius
272	Dacia abandoned to the Goths
293	Diocletian reorganizes the imperial office, sharing power between two Augusti assisted by two Caesars
303–5	'Great Persecution' of Christians
313	Constantine declares official toleration of Christianity in empire
325	Council of Nicaea
330	Byzantium refounded as Constantinople
374	St. Ambrose becomes bishop of Milan
376	Goths enter the empire in large numbers from across the Danube
378	Goths annihilate Valens and the imperial army at Adrianople
378–95	Theodosius emperor, strongly promoting orthodox Christianity against Arianism and paganism
382	St. Jerome begins work on the Vulgate Latin Bible
395	Arcadius and Honorius divide the Roman world into Eastern and Western empires
402	Western emperor's court moves from Rome to Ravenna
409	Roman legions withdraw from Britain
410	Visigoths under Alaric sack Rome
413–26	St. Augustine writing *The City of God*
429–37	Theodosian legal code compiled
444	St. Patrick founds cathedral church of Armagh
451	Romans and Visigoths combine to defeat Attila and the Huns at Châlons
455	Vandals sack Rome
476	Death of Romulus Augustulus, last Roman emperor in the west
481	Clovis becomes king of the Franks
507	Franks expel Visigoths from Gaul
524	Boethius executed by the Ostrogoth king Theodoric at Ravenna
529	Justinian closes the schools of Greek philosophy at Athens; St. Benedict founds his monastic community at Monte Cassino
530–40	Codification of Roman law (Corpus Juris Civilis) by Justinian's jurist Tribonius
538	Church of Hagia Sophia consecrated at Constantinople
563	St. Columba founds monastery on Iona
568	Lombards invade Italy
590	Gregory I (the Great) becomes pope
597	St. Augustine begins conversion of England
732	Arabs defeated at Poitiers
800	Charlemagne, king of the Franks, crowned Holy Roman Emperor

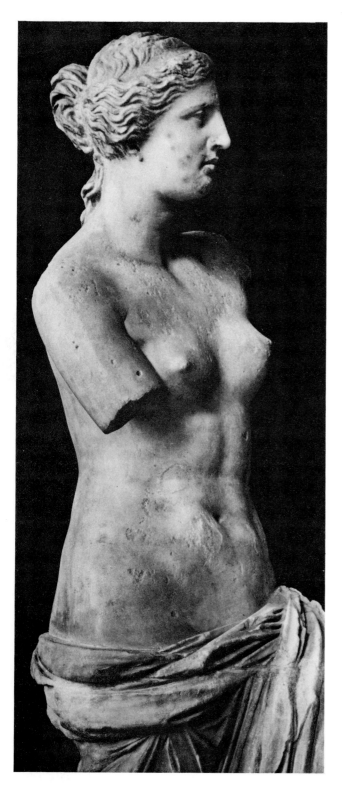

evolution. Our happiness lies therefore in our self-cultivation, not in stern self-torture. Gods no doubt do exist, since the idea of them could not have arisen in the minds of men without some cause or ground, but they have nothing to do with us and we owe nothing to them; and we need not fear them either, in our continuing search for enlightenment and contentment . . . These teachings of Epicurus spread widely among peaceable men of leisure, and like Stoicism reach Rome as soon as Rome reaches Athens; indeed, they win a passionate apologist in the Latin poet Lucretius (98–55 BC). In his *de Rerum Natura* (*On the Nature of Things*) he is not afraid to proclaim that the Greek philosopher has shown a way to escape 'the (crushing) weight of religion'. Such doctrines are for obvious reasons held far more 'subversive' than any other set of ideas put in circulation in Athens and they are regularly denounced and vilified; Epicureans are represented as immoral, sensualist, or slothful. Yet (thanks to Lucretius) Epicureanism is never stamped out, but continues to tempt and challenge European thinkers down to the eighteenth-century Enlightenment (which in fact takes its name from Lucretius' lines, in Book I of *de Rerum Natura*: 'not the rays of the sun, the bright shafts of day, are what are needed to dispel the dread and darkness of the soul, but Nature's forms and rationality'). One thing at any rate Epicurus has in common with all his competitors in Athens: each of their systems seeks out a knowledge of the natural world, of man, of morality, of social relations, and of the gods, as a coherent and *explicit* body of *sophia*, or wisdom. Whatever it is, there is *a* philosophy. When, nearly two thousand years later, particular single sciences begin to make sensational progress in Europe, each in its own direction, this Greek lesson of unity is still present—to be heeded or bypassed or denounced (in fact all three), but never quite disregarded. The staggering fact is that Hellenic, and Hellenistic, science and thought are not lost (or if partly lost, are bit by bit recovered in later ages); their impact, with all the contradictions and variety of which a glimpse has been given, will at certain times be at least as great as that of a face-to-face encounter with some completely separate civilization.

9   Aphrodite, second century BC. Marble statue found on the island of Melos, height 82 in (208 cm). Paris, Musée du Louvre

Familiarity should not prevent us seeing that the famous Aphrodite of Melos, better known as the Venus de Milo, is more a placid than a compelling embodiment of physical perfection; chance, largely, has led to this figure coming to be regarded as an epitome of Hellenic idealism, which in fact it post-dates by about 300 years.

**10   Laocoön and his sons, Roman copy of a Greek
original of the late second century BC by Athanadorus,
Hagesandrus and Polydorus of Rhodes. Marble,
height 7 ft (2.1 m). Rome, Vatican Museum**

*A glance at the Laocoön group should dispel any
over-simplified ideas about calm and reposefulness in Hellenistic
art. Homer's horrifying tale of the priest of Troy crushed with his
two sons by a supernatural serpent is recounted in Virgil (Aeneid
II), but has been anticipated with astonishing power in this
sculpture.*

Alexandria

The coming of Stoicism to Athens is only one sign of
the birth of a new order of things. As Hellenistic culture
is spread vigorously eastwards and into Egypt, its centre of gravity shifts away from Athens and the world of
the old *poleis*, with their fratricidal little wars and by
now merely provincial existence, and comes to rest in a
quite different kind of setting: the literally new city of
Alexandria.

Founded by Alexander the Great in 330 BC and built
up by the dynasty of Ptolemy, the general who succeeds to that portion of his empire, Alexandria is from
the outset not a confederation of tribes but a multinational community: not only settlers from Macedon, but
also a very large contingent of Jews are brought in at
Alexander's direction to join the local Egyptian population. Within a generation Alexandria has 'taken off' and
grows steadily to a size unknown in Hellas. It is the
meeting point of Europe and Asia and Africa, of their
trade and industry, their wealth and luxuries and tastes;
of their religions too—Alexander's own mausoleum,
Greek temples, the Egyptians' temple and ancient cult
of Serapis dominate the city—and of their speculations
and leisures. The first Ptolemy builds the renowned
Pharos, or lighthouse, and endows a museum and
around it a kind of university library. In this setting
scholars collect and edit almost all the written materials
of the Hellenes that have come down to us: it is curious
to think that without the librarian Aristarchus (220–143
BC) we should have only the most fragmentary idea of
what their greatest poet Homer has written. In consequence, while the schools of Athens linger on (indeed,
they are only shut down in AD 529 by the Emperor
Justinian) they gradually become quite undistinguished, merely respectable. In what has hitherto been
'Ionian' science, the greatest advances are now to be
looked for in the new cosmopolis: their fruits are
sufficiently identified by a few names—Euclid,
Archimedes, Apollonius, Hipparchus, and Ptolemy the
astronomer and geographer. Patronage, facilities,
wealth, and prestige supply the spur and the opportunities never before encountered in the ancient Mediterranean world—and for that matter, not subsequently
rivalled.

Other fruits are surprising too. In Alexandria, Judaism becomes hellenized to the point at which the holy
books have to be translated into Greek to remain accessible to the chosen people (the Septuagint, around 280
BC). The 'schools' of philosophy are all implanted, and
one of them in particular, Platonism, becomes more
and more prone to fuse with the very heterogeneous
influences around it. In the lifetime of Christ, the Jewish
philosopher Philo is engaged at Alexandria in an elaborate 'Platonic' commentary on the book of Genesis.
Similarly Platonism becomes highly attractive to early
Christian Gentiles, not only in the doctrines which link
a Supreme Being to a rational principle of *Logos* as well
as to an act of creation (clearly reflected in the Christian
Gospel of St. John), but also through its development
of an overwhelmingly mystic system. This figures a
Supreme Being, a process of 'emanations' from him,
hierarchies of spiritual beings (Plato himself has emphasized only three levels—God, a creative demiurge, and

11   Fresco painting from a house in Pompeii, destroyed by the eruption of Mount Vesuvius in AD 79. Naples, Museo Nazionale

Among the varied manners of Hellenistic painting recovered in the murals of Pompeii, a number recall scenes from Greek myth and hero-legend. In the late fresco shown above, Jason returns from the Argonauts' expedition and confronts King Pelias (who has put his parents to death).

discourse of this style and comparable subtlety, and to produce statements of belief ('creeds') of almost infinite sophistication, in the face of innumerable hybrid cults elaborated around them in Hellenistic Alexandria.

In a cosmopolitan world the arts and crafts of the Hellenes, too, are from the third century BC onwards adapted to a 'world market'. So far as the Mediterranean basin is concerned, this means that sculpture becomes blander and that painted ceramics are prettified; ironically it is these productions which become current in the Roman empire, and later still will be 'rediscovered' by ecstatic Europeans—Winckelmann in eighteenth-century Rome, Lessing confronting a Laocoön group of about 50 BC, or Keats enraptured by a 'Grecian Urn' whose deathless (but also lifeless?) tranquillity is certainly not that of the vigorous designers of old Hellas. The results are unquestionably successful: Hellenistic naturalism is preserved uncannily in the Roman villas of Pompeii, it supplies the forms for the religious art of the early Christians (not without picking up on the way an infusion of that wide-eyed Egyptian style of representation of the dead which is transmitted into Byzantine art), and further afield, spreading eastward, it blends into Persian and oriental styles in central Asia, and beyond.

'Alexandrianism' becomes, eventually, a legend; this extraordinary *entrepôt* at the hinge of the later ancient world is identified by later historians with luxury, decadence, frivolous extravagance, aimless virtuosity in literature, fanatical sects, mob wars, the world of cosmopolitanism. In later ages virtuous idealists will dream of 're-creating' Athens—never Alexandria. From our point of view this is less important than the fact that without such a meeting point of traditions, a focus of Mediterranean cultures for almost eight hundred years, a great deal of the Greek world that has entered our inheritance would not have done so.

Rome

Out of the thousand-year saga of the city founded by Romulus, European culture has extracted two images of Rome. The first one, of course, is the Roman republic, seen as a kind of repertory of moral education, as set out by historians whether Roman or Greek (Polybius, Livy, Caesar, Plutarch). Quite separate from Hellas, at least in the mind of posterity, it is a Rome which has been a vivid, if literary, reality for as long as *all* educated Europeans have had Latin at the centre of their school studies—that is to say until quite recent times. They have either read for themselves or heard from others about the Horatii, Cato, Regulus, the Gracchi, and

the gods of Greece), and a two-way universe of divine irradiations and human aspirations. In what we call Neoplatonism, which in Alexandria in particular grows up alongside the new Christian religion of the second century AD, we find Plotinus (204–269) inviting us to contemplate God: 'He who is the one God and all the gods, where each is all, blending into a unity, distinct in powers but all one God in virtue of that one divine power of many facets.' It is not surprising that the early Christian Church, faced with endless problems of defining a right doctrine for its monotheistic Trinity, and of keeping its own mysteries distinct, should have produced theologians trained to handle

12 The Colosseum, Rome, AD 72–80

Begun by the Emperor Vespasian and completed by Titus, the Colosseum is the largest single Roman building. The builders, working on a vast scale, have used three distinct 'orders'—Tuscan, Ionic and Corinthian—one above another in the superimposed arcades. The top storey is a late addition.

Brutus, or the valour of legions, and the tales of stern virtue, patriotism, self-sacrifice, or heroism in which they feature. Perhaps there is also the image of a city with highly formalized laws and traditions but in which the plebs and the patricians (Roman equivalent of *eupatrids*) seem to engage in an endless conflict. Such names and images and examples have nourished the thoughts of medieval schoolmen, of Erasmus, of Shakespeare, of Rousseau and Garibaldi and countless others.

The *other* Rome is the empire which issues from a republic that has already subjugated the Mediterranean (including the Hellenistic world), but then collapses in civil war at home; an empire inaugurated by the chief of the Julian clan, the only great faction to survive that civil war—Octavian, or Augustus as he comes to be called, the adoptive son of the murdered dictator Julius Caesar. This Rome, if we listen to the stories put about by historians (notably Tacitus and Suetonius) offers nothing like such an edifying spectacle as the other one. The same imaginations that have thrilled to the stories of the old republic and its rough but virtuous manners have also absorbed with relish a whole panorama of wickedness, extravagance, cruelty, and nameless horrors, associated with such names as Caligula, Nero, Domitian, or Decius. It seems odd that an empire with such abominable rulers should have lasted for over four hundred years in the West (and a thousand years longer in the East).

However, realities no less than anecdotes are transmitted down the ages, and the realities of this second Rome, and the ideas associated with them, have had an importance far greater than anything that the first can offer. These realities are large things: the rule of law, civil society, a universal empire, and a universal Church. To which might be added the Latin language and a huge repertory of writings, among them the histories just noted, which preserve a vision of the ancient world and its values, including those of the early days of Rome.

So large are these things that it is often difficult to separate out what remains specifically due to Rome through the ages and what to subsequent mixtures and

13   The Pont du Gard, near Nîmes, late first century BC

The aqueduct over the river Gard in southern Gaul brings water to the provincial city of Nîmes: an example of Roman engineering skills that will not be rivalled in western Europe for more than a millennium. (By contrast, when Charlemagne tried to dig a short canal to join the Rhine and the Danube in 797 the result was a muddy ditch whose banks at once fell in.)

fusions. An example (taken at random) would be the status of women in a male-run civil society. We have precise knowledge of relevant customs and laws in imperial Rome, but in the sequel we have also to take into account the customs and laws of immigrant waves of Franks and Goths and Vandals, of Saxons and Lombards and Norsemen, as these displace or fuse with those of Rome over long ages. For all that, twentieth-century women's liberation has grappled with attitudes and assumptions that go back at least in part to Rome, whether in its civil laws or in the Christian institutions that partly reflect them. By virtue of Latin (which incidentally supplies most of the abstract words on this page) the Roman heritage has this further peculiarity, that at least until the seventeenth century it serves as a constant reservoir of values, examples, models: an alien world and yet a familiar one, a *second* body of experience constantly being consulted, a schooling inasmuch as 'classics' are what are studied in class. And one cannot over-emphasize the significance of this 'double vision'. Alongside the moral teaching of the gospels and the Bible at large, Christian Europe has regularly had held up to it the moral values of pagan antiquity—of Cicero, of Marcus Aurelius—sometimes conformable, sometimes dissonant. Through centuries of 'backwardness' the ancient world's Greek mathematics, astronomy, and medicine, all cradled by Rome, have supplied something at least which would not have developed so fast in their absence. The 'classical' forms of expressive symbolisms remain everywhere: the sky is full of Latin constellations, Latin analysis reaches into the grammars of vernacular languages. If for numbering we have gone to Arabic and for technical jargon to Greek, in only one field has Rome been as dumb to us as the Etruscan tomb: in music.

The Roman empire, as one might see it in its most accomplished form, say around AD 120 under Hadrian, is enormously more diverse than Pericles' Hellenic world, or even Alexander's. Within its huge size (it takes months to travel from, say, York to Jerusalem) it comprises every kind of society. At one extreme is Rome itself: a city of monumental splendours but by now entirely parasitic, dependent on overseas wheat to feed a million mouths, and surpassed only by Alexandria in the cosmopolitan diversity of races assembled there. At an opposite extreme are the barely tamed border-lands on the Danube and in the Low Countries, or wild Britain with a border on the unreduced Caledonians and within it very little Roman presence yet. Between these extremes there are the more settled north of Gaul, the fully Romanized municipal lands of Italy and the provinces of southern Gaul and Spain and coastal north Africa; agricultural Egypt; wealthy Syria; hellenized Greece and Asia Minor.

The central fact about the creation of this empire is that it has taken place, apparently, without that break in continuity which Alexander the Great represents in the east. There is in fact a long tradition of very *deliberate* continuity. The old republic has not destroyed the neighbours she conquers, but linked them by alliance and tutelage in treaties set out with pedantic and legalistic care. By the time she has defeated Carthage (which,

14 The Arch of Constantine, Rome, AD **315**

The victory arch erected by Constantine to mark his conquest of Rome is not a Christian monument at all. It owes its design to a similar arch built by Trajan between 111 and 117, and many of its reliefs seem to have been lifted bodily or copied from that source. 'Decorated with his victories' (as the inscription says), it serves countless times as a model for later imperial pomps.

for once, *is* utterly destroyed) Rome is strong enough to establish whole 'provinces'; these are not assimilated to the city-state, now, but governed by a 'proconsul'— tyrannically no doubt, yet still by an accountable officer of the republic. Throughout the whole process of growth there also grows up an almost obsessive, indeed very definitely superstitious, regard for tradition.

We see it for instance in the constitutional forms of society. When Augustus consolidates what we are calling an 'empire', he in fact insists he is restoring the republic after a long period of civil war and chaos. All the old institutions and the complicated system of magistrature and government are meticulously put back: the patrician senate, the elected posts of consul (chief officer of government), praetor (high court judge), censor (controller of civic status), tribune (watchdog of the people). There is just one little difference: Augustus either holds these top posts himself, or controls them. He attends the senate like any other senator, not as king or tyrant but simply as 'leading citizen of the city' (*civitatis princeps*). The *imperium* is strictly speaking a form of overriding authority conferred for a limited time on a general in the field: clearly the *princeps* is always going to hold that, and Augustus has it conferred on himself over and over again. Eventually it gives rise to the title 'emperor', though he and his successors are normally identified as either 'Augustus' or 'Caesar' (whence *Tsar* and *Kaiser*).

There is only one respect in which the empire departs very significantly from the visible institutions of the republic. This is the practice of recognizing as a god the emperor when he dies: a custom imported from the east, applied to Augustus at his death, and then to all his successors. (Some of the latter cannot wait to die before they assume the formidable attributes.) Alongside the traditional objects of piety, the array of gods of the ancient world, there will from now on be a particularly *imperial* cult, a symbol of political unification.

With this one exception there is all the *appearance* of continuity; Augustus even has to be tolerant of Livy when he extols the great days of republican history. But in fact the empire has entirely outgrown the old system.

15   The Arch of Constantine, Rome, detail of reliefs, AD 315

The reliefs of the Arch of Constantine offer 'high' Roman examples of monumental sculpture which, adorning a memorial to the first Emperor associated with Christianity, will stand as models to artists for over a thousand years. What we also notice is that (unlike costume or customs) the sculptured idiom has become arrested, frozen.

Party politics plus the wealth of distant provinces equals civil war: so party politics are abolished, and the *princeps* establishes a centralized bureaucracy. In every province there is a proconsul, or governor, and a military commander; they are flanked by the separate *procurator* or emperor's fiscal representative. The legion keeps the peace, the procurator sees that taxes are raised; behind both is the imperial headquarters in Rome. One result of this arrangment is that whereas legions are normally kept in one location, the great administrators can be and are moved regularly from one country to another and may be recruited anywhere

(as in any efficient modern organization), and not only in Rome or in Italy. This applies also to emperors: Vespasian is a provincial, and Hadrian will have had 'experience' in half a dozen different regions.

But whether Augustus or Vespasian or Hadrian—in fact down to the end of the third century—the emperor maintains the forms and fictions of a vanished republic while exercising a virtually unfettered authority. If he is overthrown another emperor will take his place, the great machine will continue, consuls will as usual be *elected*, the *imperium* will be voted, and so on as before.

Together with the continuity of government, and its overall unifying effect, there is that of the laws of Rome. In their origins they are the quaint little laws of a small inland city-state (contemporary with Cleisthenes' Athens), a network of contracts covering citizenship and its rights and duties and important social relations—inheritance, property, family discipline, and the like. They protect the citizen, his life and limb; they guarantee him fair legal procedure, public recognition of his marriage contract, redress of certain wrongs, an appropriate share in political decisions, etc. Growth brings home the fact that it is not convenient for neighbours and client cities to be brought under these laws. Two results flow from this.

First, for political reasons, Roman citizenship is granted sparingly to important individuals domiciled outside Rome. This is unlike the practice of the Hellenes; nevertheless it is a key to the future. In the coming-on of time citizenship comes to be seen as a most valuable privilege; it is a condition of any sort of public career, and it is also a protection against arbitrary acts by proconsular officials. Everyone is familiar with the case of St. Paul, a native of Tarsus in Asia Minor: brought before a provincial tribunal, he reveals himself to be a Roman citizen and appeals to Caesar. In the century following that incident, the privilege is more and more widely shared (legionaries, for example, are citizens, though they are simply professional soldiers and have long ceased to be the old farmer-citizens that formed the first armies of the republic). Eventually, in AD 212, Caracalla, wishing to increase the revenue from property taxes paid by the *civis*, extends citizenship—and therefore the reach of the civil law—to every free adult male in the empire.

Alongside the extension of citizenship, expansion of the republic and recognition of other states' laws forces the development of a new branch of the legal system: that which has to do with people of different nationalities such as traders or citizens of allied states. This, again unparalleled in the Hellenic world, is the Roman *ius gentium*, the law of peoples; it has its own courts and a specialized judiciary. The development of this law, furthermore, comes under the influence of Greek Stoicism (which is very widespread among cosmopolitan citizens) and its doctrine of natural law; Stoicism, advancing a high ideal of justice, insists on human and not sectarian standards, equity, or 'fairness', emphasis on the spirit rather than the letter of an agreement. *Ius gentium* is absolutely essential to a rule of law in a universal state; it is not superseded by Caracalla's edict, but indeed comes eventually to be identified with natural law (in the legal system drawn up by Justinian); and natural law and the ideal of justice continue to confront positive laws down to this day.

That brings us to a final characteristic of the rule of law for which we are indebted to the Roman Empire. Under the republic the elected *praetor*, or judge, has each year announced the principles on which he personally intends to judge cases during his tenure of office, and he does so by displaying his 'edict' to the public on a white notice-board (the *album*). Under the empire, where the real judicial authority is the emperor, such a practice is obsolete, and Hadrian (who has no intention of going out of office at the end of a year) replaces it by a 'perpetual edict'—a permanent codification of the laws of Rome, despatched to all corners of the world. This is a first model for the great codes of civil laws drawn up later under Theodosius and then Justinian: in a *codified* form Roman law, its terminology, principles, and logic, will be passed down to the jurists of medieval and then modern Europe. In being codified, it is made coherent, fixed; raised above the hazards of caprice, case law, or change in the world.

Uniform administration—extended citizenship—the law of peoples—codification—these things may not mean much to an Egyptian peasant or a Batavian tribesman, and they mean nothing at all to a slave. But they are crucial to the administration of a large and diversified empire. The framework of *imperium*, they allow almost every imaginable society and culture to be brought within the universal state. They are as it were the minimum programme of Romanization.

Civility

But not the limit of that programme. Rome is a *city* (*civitas*), and where she rules there she implants a political culture based on the citizen (*civis*) and civil laws, and city life, civility. The process of doing this is called, obviously, civilization.

Wherever the legion conquers, there the administration seeks to find or adapt or establish something corresponding to a city, a *municipium*, with citizens and local self-government on the Roman 'republican' model. The Greek cities, to be sure, hardly need anything doing to them; they are already highly advanced. Elsewhere, new enclaves of civil life are created. Time-expired legionaries are encouraged to set up colonies, with grants of land. New citizens are assimilated to the language, the law, Roman attire . . . And, evidently, new towns are *built*. Their ruins everywhere bear witness to an almost standard ideal of what city life should be: often a rectangular lay-out of streets, always a forum for public meetings, municipal baths for the citizen's very characteristic Roman pastime and his social exchanges; temples for municipal and imperial cults; in more prosperous centres a theatre, and in great cities an arena for public games or animal fights (gladiatorial contests are an expensive speciality virtually confined to Rome); and naturally palatial houses for imperial administrators, and mansions for the rich and powerful (in Rome and Ephesus they are in profusion, in remote Britain more typical are modest residences of timber on a stone base). In the greatest centres of all, there are not only a bewildering number of temples, but also monuments by which each emperor (and often too a great subject, a proconsul or a magnate) is fittingly commemorated: a column, an arch, a palace, a specially grandiose temple. Augustus has given the lead here in Rome, but there are other exceptionally energetic builders: Hadrian adorns Athens by completing the huge temple to Olympian Zeus and adorns Rome by building (among other things) a mausoleum so enormous that it has survived eighteen centuries, as ruin, fortress, papal residence, and prison.

Finally, mention must be made of one other institution to which emperors give repeated attention: the endowed school or local academy where ambitious citizens can study 'liberal' arts (grammar, rhetoric, 'dialectic' or elementary logic, arithmetic, geometry, astronomy, and music) and, more importantly, can acquire skill in the eloquence needed for law and success in the big world. Without the prestige of Athens or Alexandria, such schools are none the less an essential part of civility.

The culture of cities is a kind of barometer of imperial prosperity. For over two centuries it rises continually. And in that age is formed an image which time fails to destroy: that of the universal society, stable and orderly, where not only officials, but ordinary citizens as well, can travel safely from one end of the 'world', or *oecumene*, to the other, under the Roman Peace, *pax romana*. The trader can carry his wares from Alexandria to Gaul, the legionary his cult from Syria to Britain, the apostle his creed from Asia Minor to Rome. Wherever he arrives there is something approximating to civility.

Rome does not re-invent all the amenities that fill up this civility. She supplies a political and social framework, to be sure, and engineering skills of a tremendous order to build cities, aqueducts, roads, frontier walls. (One is constantly aware that civil engineering is also one of the major skills carried from land to land by the army.) Her monumental art of building is different from the Hellenic. Monuments are *imperial*, massive, round-arched, barrel-vaulted, colossal as required, seldom elegant. But Roman arts and crafts recall that the legions have conquered Greece at a rather early date (200–168 BC), and many of the superior Hellenistic achievements are simply absorbed into the Roman way of life. This is most notable in statuary, ceramics, and painting. At best, the Roman comes to depend on the finest models he can import: in Pompeii (destroyed AD 79) there are even copies of older, Hellenic, vintage paintings (in other places there is an abundance of kitsch too). The first theatre in Rome is built because Pompey has imported the idea from Greece. The hippodrome in Rome bears a Greek name; so does Marcus Agrippa's Pantheon, though an ultra-patriotic Roman monument. In language, eloquence, and letters, political conquest followed by symbiosis has noteworthy results. Latin of course should be the language of government, but in the East it is Greek, and in the West the two actually co-exist. The Roman Empire is bilingual. Latin is admirably suited to jurisprudence, with its roots in an age-old Roman tradition; Greek however becomes the preferred language of civilized exchanges, the daintier medium. In the schools, eloquence draws on both. And in *belles-lettres* the eminence of Greek is plain. There come to be great monuments of Latin literature, but behind each stands a Greek: Lucretius latinizes Epicurus; Cicero is nourished by Plato's *Republic*, the Stoics, and Demosthenes; Virgil by Homer; Horace by the Greek lyric; Plautus and Terence by the Athenian New Comedy. Under Augustus, patronage and patriotism encourage the production of great Latin masterpieces, but the standards of excellence—dare we say it of Virgil?—are still Greek.

Nowhere is the Greek pre-eminence more clear and revealing than in philosophy. In this sphere, Athens and Alexandria rule; Rome has virtually nothing to add to what their thinkers have put into circulation, and the stock of ideas in Cicero or Seneca is borrowed (not that that stock is trivial). The empire's most considerable natural philosopher is undoubtedly Pliny the Elder (died AD 79). All his writings that survive show him to be an indefatigable *compiler*; his *Natural History*, he tells us, contains 20,000 statements drawn from other scholars. On the one occasion when Pliny is moved to add to the store of delivered wisdom by making an original investigation, the result, reported by his nephew, is unfortunate: witnessing from his boat the start of the great eruption of Vesuvius, he goes ashore to get a good look and perishes along with Pompeii. Such curiosity is not typical. In contrast, the Hellenistic world continues to supply the intellectuals (see p. 31), nurture the best doctors (of whom Galen will become legendary), and will soon hatch the last great innovation in Greek philosophy—the Neoplatonism of Plotinus and others in Alexandria, already mentioned.

Decline

If a barometer can rise, it can also fall. From the third century AD we observe signs of what will eventually, five or six generations later, be experienced as the collapse of empire in the West. We are not concerned here with the causes, which are undoubtedly internal and social and include a profound disorder of the economic system; it is rather the symptoms which are of great importance to the future of European culture because they determine the *form* in which antiquity will be transmitted to later ages.

First, cities all over the empire decline, their economic life and trade in ruins, and, despite ferocious edicts, there is a large-scale exodus of their despairing and over-taxed inhabitants. Some become ghost towns, squatters' settlements. Imperial institutions survive, of course; great villas and estates flourish; but international trade and intercourse decline.

As a sign of the latter, the Greek language loses its hold in the West. Around the middle of the third century, western Christian congregations change to a liturgy in Latin; Greek goes out of fashion in the eloquence of the schools; soon Jerome will be moved to retranslate the Holy Scriptures from Greek into Latin; St. Augustine will learn some Greek at school, but hates it, and in effect acquires his knowledge of Greek philosophy from Latin sources; the Christian Church in the West will be a Latin Church.

There is also the beginning of a kaleidoscopic population change. The legions, already, recruit Germans for service in the Rhineland and in Britain; but in the third century there is as well the beginning of immigration across the *limes*, or frontier. The Franks filter into Gaul, and other tribes move in along the Danube; over the following century the trickle will grow into a flood, with wave upon wave of Franks, Goths, and Alemanni. They will form tribal enclaves, at first nominally subordinate to Roman authority, even if they have no use for cities and not much time for procurators. But presently as client states, or uncontrollable kingdoms, they will sweep through ill-defended or quite undefended regions: Goths will overrun Pannonia; Franks, Goths, and Vandals will rule in Gaul and conquer Spain and Africa; Alaric sacks Rome (410); Saxons overwhelm Britain. Later still, Attila and his Huns launch their devastating (though short-lived) assaults, from the Rhine to the Black Sea; the Avars on the Danube and the Lombards in large parts of sixth-century Italy blot out almost all that is left of the Romans' way of life. Here and there an old estate survives, a corner of the old society; but mostly there is local tribal dominion, and a rural subsistence economy prevails, very much the order of things that existed before the legions conquered their territories. One point catches the eye: where Roman manners have been weakly implanted, as in Britain, Latin disappears in the face of invasions; in lands where they are strong, as in Gaul up to about the middle of what is today Belgium, the newcomers wrestle with the language, and it survives and evolves; Gallo-Roman becomes, eventually, Old French—and in other places analogously. But civil Latin itself becomes a 'learned' tongue.

Lastly, in the age which sees the cities fade, central government has also become entirely erratic and unstable; at the end of the third century the ruler gives up even the pretence of old 'Roman' institutions. Diocletian, who 'stops the rot' around 295, does so by establishing no fewer than *four* emperors—two senior Augusti and two junior Caesars, with himself supreme—to govern and defend each region of the empire as a kind of despotism. He himself adopts eastern manners and symbols of authority more typical of the Persian Great King of old than of a Roman magistrate, and his subjects prostrate themselves before him; he ceases to bother to recognize Rome as a capital or Italy as different from any other province (for retirement he builds his tremendous palace at Split (Salona) on the Adriatic, in his native Dalmatia, but also mid-way between East and West). In his wake the soldier Constantine, proclaiming himself western Caesar and conquering Rome with his share of the legions (306–313), carries the new political vision to its logical end. To re-establish an empire he knocks out his eastern co-emperor and in 330 founds an entirely new capital city, *New Rome* (Constantinople) on the best possible site from which to govern: close to the most immediate danger-spots, namely his threatened Danube provinces, and close to the main reservoir of wealth and soldiers, namely his eastern provinces. Though he starts his career in York, he sees the West as of minor

16 Funerary portrait from the Fayum, 2nd–4th century AD. Wood, 11¼ × 7½ in (28.6 × 19.1 cm). London, National Gallery

A haunting wide-eyed funerary portrait from the Fayum shows the influence of Hellenistic painting in Egyptian art. Such intricate exchanges between seemingly contrasting traditions around the Mediterranean form the background to the birth of a Christian religious art in the 4th and 5th centuries, and a breakaway from 'classic' Roman models.

importance; the various Caesars who may be proclaimed thereafter in Rome are in fact of no significance, and what eventually comes about there has already been noted; after 475 there are no further attempts even to pretend that Rome is a seat of imperial power.

17   Painting from a catacomb in the Via Appia, Rome, 4th century AD

At the time of this unique painting, Christianity is above ground and legal, but not yet the Empire's sole religion. In it we see a stately Roman matron, Vibia, of whom we know nothing but her name, being inducted into a scene of heavenly rejoicing. Quality apart, there is not much to separate this scene from some that have been buried in Pompeii: a distinctive style of sacred imagery has not yet arisen.

There are of course two further details about Constantine which concern us. He has shed the customs and dignities of old Rome and stepped into Diocletian's shoes: from now on the emperor rules in his Greek not Latin court as *basileus*, king, despot. Also he licenses the worship of the Christian God (313) and on his deathbed (337) is baptized a Christian.

The Christian Church

Until the arrival of Constantine, the outlook of Rome on matters of religion is, with one exception, not very different from that of the Hellenic world. There are cults of every sort, multiplied through every province: those of Rome herself, of Hellas, of Egypt, of Syria. Reasonable men can glimpse fragments of pattern—perhaps an equivalence between Jupiter and Zeus, Minerva and Athene, and so on—but no unifying conclusions; Platonists explain cults as allegories, glimpses of deeper things; Stoics put up with the host of supernatural entities as a concession to human weakness. Augustus has set an example of 'piety' and to follow that example is prudent—towards the tutelary gods and the many other powers, of clan and hearth, countryside and sea and elements . . . up to a reasonable limit. The Sibylline centre at Cumae replicates in a sense the oracle at Delphi; divination is a specialized art; generals consult the auspices before battle. The tolerance of the authorities allows sects and mysteries to spread from the east across the empire; true-blue Romans regret the 'effeminacy' of some, or their reputed immorality, but tolerance prevails.

The great exception, where the empire differs from Hellas, regards the one cult which enshrines the identity of the state itself: the cult of the late emperor, already mentioned. Manifestly, no one is ever in much awe of the most recently enrolled divinity; yet his rite has a strong political significance, very much like saluting the flag. Men of standing are glad to be associated with it: in a tolerant world there is no sense in being derisive. On the other hand, to stand aside or reject it would be subversive, treasonable. This creates a problem for any community or any sect so eccentric as to believe in One God to the exclusion of all others and therefore to reject the emperor cult—which is precisely the situation of the Jews and the Christians.

Imperial treatment of Jewish monotheism (and nationalism) is both consistent and brutal. The *pax*

**18 Marble sarcophagus of an unknown Roman,
mid-fourth century AD. Vatican Museum**

*The sarcophagus is an expensive stone coffin available to the
well-to-do in Rome; its sides invite sculpture. For the interment of
a leading citizen who is also—now—a Christian it is natural that
Bible scenes should replace pagan subjects. The defunct, idealized,
is shown surrounded by reliefs which include (top row right)
figures of Abraham and Isaac, Adam and Eve, and (below, from
the centre rightwards) Jonah, Daniel and the lions, Moses smiting
the rock.*

romana must be upheld, and various expedients are tried
to make it operable; but when religion sparks off violent resistance to the symbol of authority—an imperial
cult in Jerusalem—stern repression and the sack of Jerusalem follows (AD 70), and eventually the sanguinary
and total destruction of Jerusalem and the dispersal of
the Jews (AD 135). Jewish communities in the diaspora
can thenceforward only survive by keeping a very low
profile.

Christianity is more puzzling for the authorities. It
starts as a sect within Judaism, alongside others, and
spreads to Damascus, Antioch, and northwards. By the
time of Paul's conversion or of the martyrdom of James
in Jerusalem (AD 62) it has a distinctive name. In Rome
the historian Suetonius reports some Christians to be in
dispute with the Jews, and they may have been made
scapegoats for the great fire that occurs in the city in AD
64 under Nero. But Paul's conversion and labours in

the Greek world transform the sect, removing many
Judaic prescriptions; Gentiles no longer see an apparent
conflict between the Gospel's moral teaching (at any
rate) and that of Greek philosophy; the Christians'
claims for their divine Founder and Mediator are not
totally unlike those of other 'redemption' or mystery
cults already widespread (Dionysian, Mithraic,
Orphic); its monotheism is close to that of many educated Greeks. Christianity is a highly original creed but
its components are not startlingly unique, except for
the fervent expectation of an imminent Second Coming
and the end of the world which colours the belief of its
early adherents. Paul is obliged to warn the (Greek)
converts in Corinth to set their minds against the philosophers' ideas of wisdom; St. John's Gospel presup-
poses a Greek readership attuned to philosophic discourse and accessible to a new way of thinking about
Logos.

Opened to Gentiles and Jews, men and women,
slaves and citizens, the gospel of love and salvation
spreads fast around the empire; by AD 100 it is common
in the Hellenistic world and has a hold in Italy; a century
later it has followers up the Nile, in Hungary, Gaul,
North Africa, Spain, and is still on the move. Its characteristic congregations grouped around a presbyter or
bishop are not at all checked by the difficulties that arise
over their absolute rejection of the imperial cult or by
their martyrdoms: their minds seem distracted from the
'natural' concerns of citizens. The emperor Trajan is an

enlightened, very thorough, and sometimes temperate ruler; we find in his correspondence with Pliny the Younger (nephew of the unfortunate scholar) a certain puzzlement on their account. Are they subversive? Apparently not; unlike the Jews they do not aspire to a state of their own. But they are disaffected . . . They will continue to fall foul of emperor worship, and especially under Decius (around 250) and Diocletian (around 290) there will be many glorious martyrdoms. But by the third century in most towns their missionar-ies have been active, and they are very numerous and highly organized, with hierarchies of bishops, priests, deacons, acolytes, a more or less agreed 'rule of faith', and an agreed canon of Holy Writ (New Testament writings as well as the Septuagint). In a time of mount-ing chaos they include in their numbers ranking impe-rial bureaucrats, they have their own graveyards, the Church in Rome itself gives charity to large numbers of the poor and starving, and Christianity is beginning to look something like an 'alternative society' (less so in

19   Church of Santa Pudenziana, Rome, apse mosaic, early fifth century AD

This mosaic depicts a mild, benign Christ enthroned— neither classically Roman nor yet severe—with a gallery of pious and holy followers, against a background of sacred and profane buildings and (in the sky) mystic winged figures: the junction of earthly and supernatural.

20   Hagia Sophia, Istanbul (Constantinople), AD 537

The splendour of Justinian's great church derives not a little from the prodigious dome floating effortlessly overhead; but the Hagia Sophia is also a repository of architectural subtleties, rich materials, and treasures of art which embolden the Emperor to compare himself to the biblical Solomon building the Temple.

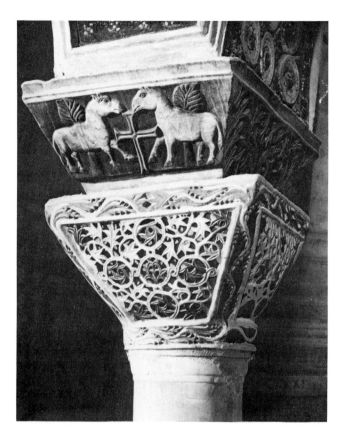

21   Carved capital in the church of San Vitale, Ravenna, AD 525–47

At Ravenna, Byzantine art appears in all its elaboration in the church of San Vitale. This capital is only one detail showing skills that cannot now be matched further west; the mystic animals framing the Cross attest the beginning of what will eventually develop into a luxuriant Romanesque fauna.

statue of the sun-god. The festival of Christmas is aligned on the latter's feast-day, and the imperial law-courts close every week on the Sunday, *hēmera hēliou* (which is also the Christian Lord's Day, *dies Dominica*, and definitely not the Jewish sabbath.) Authorized Christianity is brought under imperial control: it is Constantine who, exasperated by theological dispute among its branches (over difficult questions of the nature of Christ and the mystery of the Trinity), summons a great council of bishops at Nicaea (325) to settle once for all on a standard creed. And if not Constantine himself, then at any rate his successors are invested with *priestly* status, and in proportion as they can control their subjects they also govern the Church. 'Orthodox' Christianity becomes the state religion, a 'Caesaropapism', and the Eastern patriarchates are indelibly stamped as such.

The contrast with the West is very marked. There, over a century and a half, imperial authority becomes fragmented, eventually invisible. From 313 till its disappearance there is just time for a Latin Church to put down deep roots of its own: Theodosius in 391 abolishes paganism (if not the loyalties of aristocratic families to their ancient cults), and in the West as in the East temples are either converted to houses of Christian worship or torn down, some supplying materials for the basilicas (originally royal, then simply public, halls) now also built. The bishops acquire additional functions as district magistrates: when this is joined to their spiritual authority we find that in a city like Milan the great Bishop Ambrose (340–397) is not only the pastor of his flock, but also, by their support, a considerable force in imperial politics. The question of the 'priority' of the Apostolic See of Rome, if not its supremacy, appears to be resolved in further councils.

But above or underlying these shifts, the Church offers, in place of a fast-vanishing *pax romana*, its own spiritual security. When Alaric and his Goths actually sack the city of Rome in 410, Augustine, the bishop of Hippo in Africa, responds with his tremendous book, the *City of God* (the *civitas Dei*, not that of the *princeps*): in it he argues that the whole secular history of the pagan world can be written off (except perhaps for the religious intuitions of Socrates and Plato), and that the 'People of God' form a different, imperishable city of the elect, the true Society. And when the Vandals over-run Augustine's Africa, this and other writings of his are spared, just as Alaric has spared the Christian sanctuaries in Rome, and the apparatus of a universal Church proceeds onward through decades and then centuries of social disruption and cultural upheaval, carrying with it in the West the relics and fragmented

the countryside, which is harder to penetrate—hence the rural population, living in the *pagus*, supplies the term 'pagan'). There is no doubt that the numerical strength of Christianity has political significance to Constantine: though his own tastes incline him personally to worship a sun-god, he agrees, once Rome is captured, to legitimize the cult of this quite large proportion of his new subjects. The decision transforms the operations of Christianity in the world; within three generations the old polytheism will have been disestablished, and then proscribed.

New Rome, when Constantine builds it, is consecrated by priests and contains churches, but also a new temple to the fertility goddess Cybele and a colossal

22 Church of Sant' Apollinare, Classe, apse mosaic, AD 547

At the port of Classe near Ravenna, the apse of the basilica of Sant' Apollinare displays the patron saint gathering in the mystic flock of Christ. The art of mosaic, transmitted from Byzantium, has a foothold from which in due course it will pass to Venice, Sicily, and wherever Byzantium retains links with the west.

learning of the ancient world. Goths, Franks, even eventually the Lombards, will have to be, and are, Christianized or tamed by the Church on the territories of the old empire which they now rule.

The Church in the East has a quite different destiny. It is part of an 'oriental' despotism of imposing power, hellenized; its immediate background swarms with confusing and hybrid mysticisms—Gnostics, Neoplatonists, magicians, Manichees. The struggle over Christian 'Orthodoxy' in Constantinople, Alexandria, and Antioch is also an extremely murderous power struggle. Eventually, at a time when Pope Gregory the Great presides in Rome over a city of vast ruins and hovels, ghosts and squatters, Justinian builds his stupendous church consecrated to the Holy Wisdom (Hagia Sophia), exulting that he has equalled the biblical Solomon and his temple at Jerusalem: in style it is already proceeding from the basilica towards a new architectural repertory of hieratic majesty, which invests God Himself with the splendours of the emperor. And at the same time, while in the West the old traditions of Roman citizenship and magistrature become mere recollections or less, the emperors in the East—first Theodosius, then Justinian—put their jurists to work to update and perfect Hadrian's example of a comprehensive body of Roman law, the *corpus juris civilis*. Justinian, uniquely, has the power to reconquer the Balkans, Hungary, southern Spain, North Africa, and Italy—many of these lands for only a brief spell. But he leaves his mark, and more than a mark, to contribute to the puzzling continuity of empire. In north Italy, the powerful Ostrogothic king Theodoric (*Dietrich*) finds it convenient to accept from the eastern emperor the title of exarch and military commander; and there we find, in the town of Ravenna over which he rules, both a small replica of Rome's own monumental style in Theodoric's mausoleum, and also the implantation of what by now it is proper to call a Byzantine★ symbolism of power and religion—in the three churches of San Vitale, Sant'Apollinare Nuovo, and Sant'Apollinare in Classe.

Survival

Apart from a few privileged enclaves such as Ravenna, the 'Dark Ages' are a period when the institutions of a settled 'civil' existence—towns, roads, trade, the use of money, specialized skills and crafts, building in stone, laws, eloquence, and education—simply cannot survive the shocks of invasion and the interruption of regular customs. They fade away. Even the ruin of a Roman town affords no certainty that it will be used as a settlement by chieftains and populations habituated to simpler modes of life. Overall, it is doubtful how far everyday skills in agriculture, livestock tending, leatherwork, textiles, and metallurgy benefit from the earlier Roman achievement. Certainly the arts of war owe nothing to it. Gaul, where the transition has in a sense been gradual, preserves the art of building in stone; at any rate for the Church's basilicas, though not apparently for the upkeep of urban societies.

★ The use of this adjective (from the name of the old Greek city of Byzantium that antedates Constantine by a thousand years) has this advantage, that it reminds us of the Greek character of the imperial headquarters.

23 Pages from the Godescalc Gospels, written in Germany, c. 781. Carolingian. Paris, Bibliothèque Nationale

One result of the surge of teaching prompted by Charlemagne and Alcuin of York is the production of Bibles, many of them beautiful work. Alongside the development of a characteristic script, pages are—as at Lindisfarne—devoted to elaborate illustration: here, St. Mark with his symbol the lion confronts St. Luke and the bull. In each the art of writing is emphasized.

After the age of Ambrose, Jerome, and Augustine, who have lived in settled civil societies, comes that of Benedict, founder in Italy of a great monastic rule; it is the monks, even more than the bishops and priests, who now preserve and spread the faith and the literacy which goes with it. Monasteries are retreats out of the world; they are also self-supporting. They recruit very simple men; they are also repositories of all manner of books and manuscripts; and copying is, like work in the fields, a task which features in the well-regulated daily routine. Within their walls, pious hands assemble what is going to be the survival kit of Latinity: grammar books by Donatus and Priscus, a mediocre rudiment of the liberal arts by one Martianus Capella (around 400), the writings of Boethius including his Latin translation of two texts on logic by Aristotle (Boethius is a philosophic Christian imprisoned and executed for obscure reasons by Theodoric at Ravenna in 524), a plan of studies for liberal arts by Cassiodorus (a Roman aristocrat also from Ravenna who has founded two monasteries on his own estates in the south of Italy). It is worth itemizing this job lot of writings, for they are destined to be the basic teaching materials of the Church, still in use eight hundred years later, along with a few profane Latin texts by Virgil or Ovid, the writings of the Latin Church Fathers, and Holy Writ: but there are *no* Greek works, except Plato's *Timaeus* in a Latin translation and presently a Neo-Platonist theology wrongly ascribed to the Dionysius whom Paul is recorded as encountering in Athens. This, then, at the fall of the empire, is the 'heritage of Rome'! (In fact it amounts to very much less than what the monasteries *have* collected and *could* deliver, were it felt to be necessary: a striking example of this is the *de Architectura* (*Of Architecture*) by Vitruvius, a unique survey which some pious monk in the monastery of St. Gall (see below p. 47) copies during the tenth century, and so preserves for rediscovery half a millennium later.) Beyond the 'survival kit' all the rest of Latin and Greek antiquity will have to be recovered slowly, hazardously, bit by bit, over a long millennium that follows. This is one reason for the enormous value and significance in the meanwhile of religious works which like Augustine's *City of God* happen to plot out for pious eyes a very considerable number of allusions and references to the Roman world, its history, its authors (Augustine in his argument also includes a potted history of Greek philosophy). Through the Church, the men of the Middle Ages will have a considerable *awareness* of an ancient world which they sense to be more sophisticated than their own, and of standards and values, ready to hand and often very striking, which they could not possibly have imagined for themselves even if they had been so minded.

At the nadir of confusion and dislocation in the West, the Church sets out to reconvert the peoples of the eclipsed empire and then to carry its faith further afield. Under a manic pope, the monk Gregory the Great, monks and missions are sent out to France, England, Germany, to convert chieftains, baptize their followers, set up new sees and churches and monasteries. These efforts are strikingly different from those of two centuries earlier (and indeed from those of the Eastern empire; Gregory never sees Ravenna, but he has been to Constantinople and observed for himself the splendour of Hagia Sophia and the crushing opulence of public life—the lessons of the East are simply irrelevant to the tasks he faces). Whereas in the lifetime of Augustine the task has been to confront and confute the pagan traditions of the old Roman families and strike down their temples, now things are less straightforward: to 'convert' the pagan means to persuade a tough and illiterate chieftain, not a lawyer, of the value to him of the gospel, as well as of its truth. The missionaries are briefed to face realities, turn local customs to advantage, and *christianize* the pagan cults they come upon. What Gregory has to say by way of guidance to them about demons and miracles and the magic of the Eucharist is in a different key from the enlightened discourse of Ambrose or Augustine. The learning of antiquity has no longer very much part in missionary work; Gregory's Latin can afford to be defective—he brushes aside Donatus if grammar interferes with the outpouring of Spirit. Yet he is 'Gregory the Great', and more than any other man sums up the way the Latin Church has now to go about its business: self-directing, ardent to appropriate all things to its ends, which are divine *and* practical; relying on secular clergy *and* on the spread of monastic establishments; and insisting on Rome as the dominant see.

It is interesting to compare this spirit with that of an Irish Church set up by St. Patrick a little earlier, in the mid-fifth century. Patrick (a Briton) is reputed to have studied in the pre-Benedictine monastery of Lérins, off the south coast of Gaul; he introduces to Ireland a monastic organization and an outlook untouched by the later counselling of a Gregory—its grouping of a dozen or a score of holy men in little cells established here and there, each more or less on its own, as well as the Irishmen's tonsure and their calculation of Easter, attest their relative isolation. Yet the Irish monks are learned men, at least as impressive as their contemporaries on the continent, and, interestingly, they are familiar with the Greek Fathers as well as the Latin ones; in their calligraphy and their decorated Bibles too, they eventually combine Byzantine and Italian inspiration

24 Ivory book cover, French, tenth century. Paris, Musée de Cluny

The centre panel of this ivory book cover displays the Crucifixion, with the Virgin and St. John on either side of the Cross. In this early example of what later will be called Romanesque art, we are looking at sophisticated stylization; but in the service of a western Church (Pope Gregory and St. Benedict, both on the right, feature among the great figures commemorated).

with their own original invention and with Celtic abstract forms carried to the highest level of sophistication. Their missionary fervour, also, is admirable: after spreading across Ireland, they reach over first to Iona, then the Scottish mainland, then Northumbria. Even after they encounter Roman missions in England and stand down in that country, they pass on eastward – Columbanus and others found monasteries in Switzerland (St. Gall) and northern Italy.

Gregory's rewards and those of his successors in Rome are of course spectacular. In the north-east corner of re-Christianized England there is a sudden flare-up of piety, monastic building, and learned schooling, recorded in Bede's history. From this well-established centre Boniface leads missions across the water to convert the Germans. Presently the Frankish kingdom (officially Christian) rises to commanding military heights; under a series of great warlords it grows to stretch from the Pyrenees to Germany, its host conquers the Lombard kingdom in northern Italy, and its leader Charles the Great (Charlemagne) resolves on a policy of strengthening the Church throughout his lands. He is himself, like other outstanding kings in early medieval Europe (Alfred, Knut), a *personal* leader of tremendous energy. But with vast territories to be controlled, more is needed than endless campaigning, now at this boundary and now at that: only the Church can supply a consolidating influence, and for that matter also something approaching a regular administration. In consultation with Rome, he summons Alcuin from York to reform the Frankish bishoprics; he confesses a duty to bring salvation closer to all his subjects and peoples, and although he himself can read but not write, he particularly charges Alcuin to set up in every see a school for the training of clerks (clerics). At the start there is a shortage of books—hence the labours which produce a marvellous flowering of Carolingian Bibles.

One innovative feature of the Church's relations with Charlemagne is both more and less momentous than contemporaries would be able to perceive. In 800, at the height of his power, Charles consents to a ceremony of coronation at Rome, thus adding to his numerous kingships a different kind of title, that of *Imperator Caesar Carolus Rex Francorum*. In such a title there is no definite claim to the supremacy over a Roman empire, if only because there already exists a perfectly good and legitimate Roman emperor (or at this particular moment an Empress Irene) in Constantinople, and both Charles and papacy avoid a head-on political confrontation. The imperial style is, even so, suggestive. Charles becomes a 'Caesar' (and, presently, an 'Augustus'); the greatness of the past is being revived in modern times. But the past with a difference: that Charles should *receive* his title from the pope in Rome is an absolute novelty, one whose meaning will become a problem looming over all the politics of medieval Christendom. For the present it consolidates both the monarch's authority and the status of the Church.

In two other respects the coronation of Charlemagne is much less full of meaning than might be expected. To begin with, the new empire does not last. Two decades after Charles' death (814) it is divided up; East, South, and Middle go their separate ways, and in turn are further fragmented. In the course of this process also an entirely new social system—feudal land-tenure, a complex hierarchy of subordination—begins to make its appearance in different regions, responding to new invasions, new challenges. Despite the memories it leaves behind, the Carolingian Empire is not a new beginning for Europe but rather, if anything, an epilogue of antiquity. It is the Church, not the empire, whose continuity is now assured.

And then in a second respect the fragility of the whole transaction really does rather strike the eye. In this early ninth century, at the other side of the world, a Japanese emperor is about to lay out his spacious capital of Kyoto, with great palaces and broad streets; in Baghdad, Haroun-al-Rashid rules over a huge city and a brilliant society; in Constantinople, the great churches and other splendours attest a power and wealth not yet too noticeably decaying. By contrast, Charles' dominion, though very extensive, is military and rustic; his court is often on the move; he leaves hardly any memorials in stone. Of the numerous Gallo-Roman basilicas in his Frankish kingdom, many are by his time in disrepair and he commands—that they be put in order! The great church at Aachen, which remains his chief monument, is copied from Ravenna's San Vitale, in its plan, adornment, even its mosaics. Carolingian art and the art of the religious book rely on the skills of Byzantium; although Christian Rome can supply some venerable models, it is in the East that craftsmen abound, where supernatural realities and their worldly images and derivatives have come to be given authoritative form in mosaics and icons, carved stone and ivory, the repertories of sacred figures and appropriate patterning. If we can reasonably speak of a 'Carolingian Renaissance', it is from England that the learning comes, and from Byzantium, not Rome, that men seek a hieratic language to link them to the city of God. And this latter fact will continue to prevail when Charles the Great is in his sarcophagus and his 'empire' dissolved.

25   Decorated page from the Lindisfarne Gospels, *c.* AD 698. London, British Library, Cotton MS Nero D. iv, fol. 27

The monk Eadfrith makes his pious and sumptuous copy of the Gospels around AD 698 at the Northumbrian monastery of Lindisfarne (founded originally by St. Aidan, coming from the Irish monastery at Iona). The opening page of St. Matthew's Gospel (using the Vulgate text) shows something of the prodigious expenditure of labour and precious materials applied to the vellum; and the merging of Celtic and other decorative invention in the opening letters (spelling LIBer—the book). The tiny writing in the margin is a tenth-century translation into English.

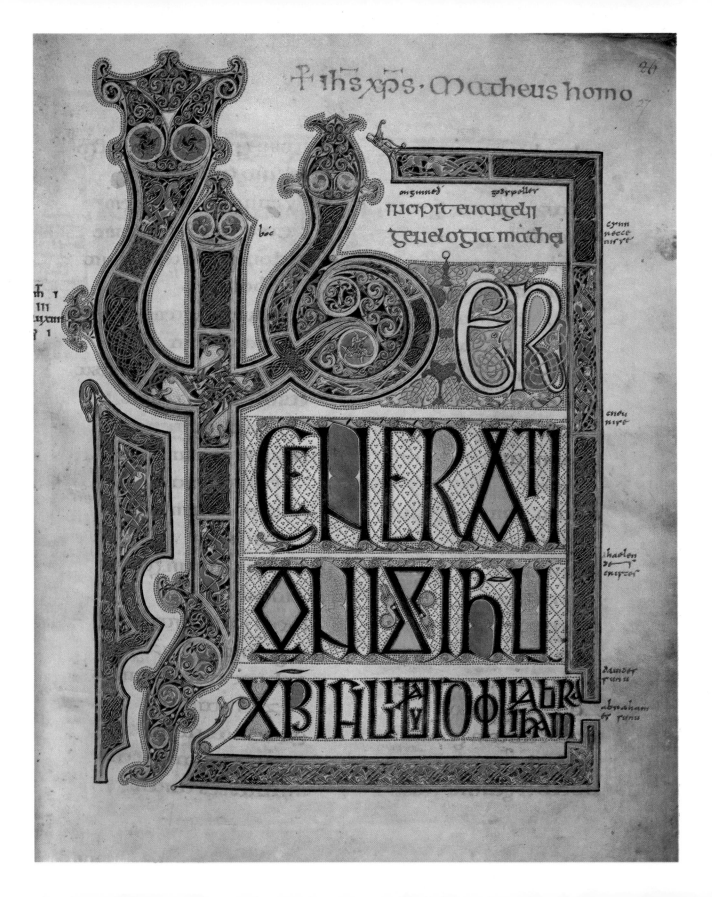

✝ ihs xps . Mattheus homo

incipit euangelii
genelogia matthei

Liber
generati
onisihu
xбihlufilioiabrhim

Chronology for Chapter 2

1118	Order of Knights Templar founded
1122	Suger becomes abbot of St.-Denis (Paris)
1130–54	Roger II King of Sicily
1141	Abelard condemned by Council of Sens
1142	Death of Abelard
1144	Suger's new church of St.-Denis consecrated
1147–9	Second Crusade
1153	Death of St. Bernard of Clairvaux
1155–90	Frederick I Barbarossa emperor
1163	Building of Notre Dame (Paris) begun
c. 1167	English scholars expelled from Paris and found university at Oxford
1170	Murder of Thomas Becket, archbishop of Canterbury
1175–85	Rebuilding of Canterbury cathedral in Gothic style
1176	John of Salisbury becomes bishop of Chartres
1180–1223	Philippe Auguste king of France
1187	Saladin defeats Christians at Hittin and takes kingdom of Jerusalem
1188–92	Third Crusade
1191	Order of Teutonic Knights founded
1198–1216	Innocent III pope
1200	Philippe Auguste recognizes university of Paris and grants it certain privileges
1202–4	Fourth Crusade
1204	Constantinople sacked by crusaders
1208	Innocent III allows Paris university to frame its own regulations
1208–18	Crusade against the Albigensian heretics in France
1209	Franciscan order founded
1210	Gottfried of Strasbourg's *Tristan*; ecclesiastical ban on recently recovered Aristotelian texts
1212	Children's Crusade
1215	Fourth Lateran Council
1217–21	Fifth Crusade
1220	Dominican order founded
1220–50	Frederick II Hohenstaufen emperor
1226–70	Louis IX (St. Louis) king of France
1228–9	Sixth Crusade under Frederick II
1231	Papal bull grants charter to Paris university
1232	Imperial edict against heretics inaugurates Inquisition
1235	Guillaume de Lorris' *Roman de la Rose*
1247–59	Vincent of Beauvais writing his encyclopaedic *Speculum Maius*
1248	Ste-Chapelle (Paris) completed; St. Bonaventura begins teaching at Paris; St. Louis leads Seventh Crusade to Egypt
1265–74	St. Thomas Aquinas writing his *Summa Theologica*
1268	Conradin executed by Charles of Anjou
1274	Death of Aquinas
1275	Jean de Meung's continuation of the *Roman de la Rose*
1275–92	The Venetian Marco Polo at the court of Kublai Khan
1280	Death of Albertus Magnus
1282	'Sicilian Vespers' break the power of Charles of Anjou in southern Europe
1292	Death of Roger Bacon

Chapter 2
A Medieval Crossroads

We use the expression 'Middle Ages' for no better reason than that four hundred years ago eager men of learning chose to dismiss all that went between the Roman Empire and their own times as barbarous and uncouth. The 'middle' ages coincided with what they had decided were 'dark' ages. The point of view changes, the old term survives; we might as well use it, while remembering that this so-called 'middle' lasted a thousand years.

During that immensely long period, from the fifth to the fifteenth century, the cultures and civil societies that succeeded and overlaid one another in Western Europe were at least as diverse as anything in the Mediterranean in the millennium up to the fall of Rome. There is no way in which they could be described satisfactorily here; but we see more clearly than the Renaissance humanists that even when they were destroyed, or dissolved, or merged into new patterns, they left durable traces—whether the Visigothic kingdoms of Spain, the exarchate of Ravenna, early Irish Christianity, the scores of different continental peoples and war-bands migrating and mixing between the steppes and the Atlantic, the Viking and the Norman settlements, the short-lived empire of Charlemagne, the Norman conquests north or south . . . One reason why a humanist like Rabelais could speak of 'dark' ages is, quite simply, that it was for him—and for us still is—impossible to trace any unifying progression, any one master institution, shining through so prodigious a confusion, century upon century—except, evidently, the Christian Church, through all vicissitudes. Another reason is that very many features of high civility in Roman times did either vanish or decay in the two centuries after the fall of Rome: cities, roads, trade, education, arts and crafts and skills, uniform laws, the reality of the *imperium* and most of the expectations it supported. The re-creation of all these things was slow and fitful and uncertain.

Looking at Western societies in, say, the tenth century, one might well judge them to be 'under-developed' by the standards of much more advanced Islamic societies to the east and in Spain, or by those of Constantinople. Only two centuries later, however, such a judgement could no longer be sustained. For now, there are all the signs of what we crudely call 'development'—in populations, settled habits, communications, trade,—and an enlargement of cultural horizons. Historians speak of a twelfth-century 'renaissance'. They perceive it in the visible traces of the age, in church architecture and styles, in sacred learning and profane letters, in the courtesy and chivalry spreading as ideals in noble society; they perceive it through comparisons not available without benefit of hindsight—in the larger and firmer political institutions at last emerging, however tumultuous these still are, and in the slow crystallization of a 'continental' pattern of things. By the end of the twelfth century we confront a world, the world of the 'High' Middle Ages, which no one in his senses could today dismiss as 'backward'. It is a meeting-ground of old and new, past and future; a conglomerate of many inheritances, many of them interacting strongly: a veritable 'Europe', in more senses than a geographical one.

By this we mean to imply that the fruits of 'development' and cultural activity are noticeably diverse. There is no one centre to match Constantinople or imperial Kyoto in Japan at the same period. Rome is the nerve-centre of the Church, but no longer a metropolis. The picture seen from one corner of the map emphasizes features quite different from those to be seen from the opposite corner. Venice, trading with the east, has not very much in common with Durham, in the Norman kingdom of England; neither gives a helpful lead-in to what we should find in Toulouse at the heart of a brilliant 'feudal' culture or at Lübeck with its new trade on the Baltic, or at Palermo in the cosmopolitan king-

26   The month of June from the *Très Riches Heures* of the Duc de Berry, c. 1416. Chantilly, Musée Condé, fol. 6v

There survives no contemporary view of Paris in the early thirteenth century, though at a later date illuminated manuscripts offer a choice of more or less fanciful renderings. Among them, the most famous is the Book of Hours commissioned by a royal prince from the leading Flemish miniaturists of the day, the Limbourg brothers; they enliven their hay-harvest scene with a glimpse of the Palace on the Île de la Cité and the Sainte-Chapelle.

dom of Sicily . . . Nevertheless, if already at this 'plateau' in time there is no one European model, no single centre to epitomize all the rest, we can still recognize a broad synchronic picture of underlying generali-

ties around the year 1200 and then observe at one crossroads—in Paris, at the centre of a thriving French kingdom—the emergence of several striking cultural achievements that have since entered the common European heritage, at the same time 'medieval' and very close to us.

Christendom

In speaking of the High Middle Ages we should copy the usage of the times and use the term Christendom, not Europe. For we are looking at a part of the world where the Christian Church, more exactly, the Western Church, is the dominant institution, certainly the only unifying one. Christendom has here a unity which later ages will lose; a unity partly due to the Church and partly to the absence of other (political) forces strong enough to disrupt that unity. No doubt life in the medieval village is the humble lot of the huge majority—an unimaginably tiny world of local customs and restricted horizons. But on the other hand there are few obstacles in the way of those who are able to venture abroad on a pilgrimage, to follow their lord·to a crusade, to study at a distant centre of learning, to carry out the bidding of the Church, or in some cases to bring their skills to a town or seek trade in a new centre. For the villager, Christendom is simply the way the world is; for the more fortunate, Christendom is a *spacious* experience.

For men may—and do—see themselves as Gascons or Lombards or Saxons or Yorkshiremen, *and* as subjects of this king or that lord; but the two perceptions are not fully merged. There are nations, in the sense of ethnic families, and local patriotism is real; yet it falls short of being a political force. Fortune may—and frequently does—bring a change of lord (and for those not directly involved in his service, to be his subject may not evoke any very obvious gratitude). More importantly, there is no transcendent myth to focus a nation's ideal. As to kings and great personages, for all the legal or hereditary titles which secure them their lands, and therewith rank, wealth, and power, they are on the whole not tied by local horizons, but are on the lookout for new lands, or richer ones, to be acquired by marriage or by brute force. Norman adventurers win kingdoms in England or Sicily or the Holy Land, or duchies in Greece, and like others are entirely ready to leave one home to settle in another. So too are their vassals and knights and retainers. How often, in a medieval tale of chivalry and romance, are we not introduced to a knight-errant riding across a strange land and inquiring, 'Who is the lord in these parts?'

meuly admuset-et ſi remerchie
de voſtre delmrance monſeigneiz
de bourbon et monſeigneur de
couey car ilz ont moult-fort en
tendu pour vous. Et auſſi la
conteſſe de ſamct pol car la bon

ne dame ſen eſt moult gruude
ment acquuttie de vous aydier
Le ſeigneur de clary reſ
pondy en telle maniere et dist
grans merciz a meſſeigneurs
mais ie cuidoie auoir bien fait

27   Medieval tournament from a fourteenth-century illuminated manuscript. London, British Library, Harley MS 4379, fol. 23v

The cult of 'chivalry' is exhibited at the courts of kings, where tournaments are sumptuous occasions for feudal lords to gather around a suzerain and display heraldic emblems, retinues, equipment, and personal prowess in jousting. In this picture, the plate armour, helmets, caparisoned war-horses, and tented pavilions are of a dazzling magnificence.

Romance is of course a world of make-believe, and this detail may appear trivial; but it hints at a certain reality. The reality is an absence of sharply defined moral frontiers of the kind later taken for granted.

The outer boundaries of Western Christendom are, on the other hand, mostly quite clear. For the Church, they are the perimeter of an area within which bishops obedient to the pope govern the spiritual life of the people. The frontiers, at present, are in Spain confronting the Moorish culture of the south, on the Baltic, on the marches of Hungary, in a corner of Palestine (the crusader kingdoms). For a time, following the scandalous happenings of the Fourth Crusade which, instead of pursuing its declared aims, sacks Constantinople in 1204, the frontiers take in that city and southern Greece, an embarrassing extension. These are all, it should be noted, fighting frontiers—Christendom is growing.

Alternatively, we can arrive at a political definition of Christendom by observing how its ruling princes are expected to behave. The boundaries would still be the same. Ready to make truces with an Islamic ruler in Spain, or to come to terms with pirates on the Barbary coast, they never form dynastic unions with a non-Christian family, nor do they seek to win Islamic frontier lands other than by force. They cannot, even if they wished to, accept the lordship of a 'heathen' ruler. The great Emperor Frederick II Hohenstaufen (like his Norman forbears) is felt to be blurring these frontiers by assimilating Muslims in his kingdom of Sicily, even negotiating with a sultan the safety of Jerusalem (instead of leading a proper crusade to slaughter the infidel). This is no posture for a Christian monarch; and as his power constitutes in any case a severe threat to the papacy, he is excommunicated and his heirs will be hounded to destruction. On the other hand, what is reprehended in princes may well be subject to other standards where trade is concerned. In 1200 the richest individual centres of Christendom are in Italy; they include the city-states of Pisa, Venice, and Genoa. All have benefited from special advantages offered recently (1173–77) by Christendom's arch-enemy, the great ruler Saladin, to induce them to route their import-export activities through his port of Alexandria instead of using the rival ports of the crusader kingdoms, where they have also invested, or Constantinople, where they likewise compete for privileges. On issues of this kind faith may sometimes take a back seat.

What then of Constantinople itself, the ageless Eastern empire? Although it is in schism with the Western Church, it is in a sense a Church of Christians, and a Roman empire to boot, not sharply cut off from the West. It is both fearful and disdainful of Latinity, yet seeks help against the heathen; its power and influence are on the wane, yet there are Western princes eager to marry a daughter into an imperial dynasty or receive a wealthy bride from it. The Eastern emperor makes treaties with Western princes. His patriarch tours the West to arouse crusading ardour. Constantinople is not exactly a foreign culture—it is ambiguous though, strange, even exotic, with its alien tongue, contrasted political institutions, oriental costumes, ancient and immobile traditions, and prestigious art forms from which the West will increasingly distance itself.

Feudal society

Within these limits of thirteenth-century Western Christendom live not more than twenty-five million souls, thinly spread over a patchwork of small 'lands'. At its heart is a 'Holy Roman Empire of the Germans', simply a congeries of territorial princes who recognize one of themselves as elected 'emperor' but seldom obey him. The next largest population is that of what we now call France, though it too is only a loose patchwork. Why is this so? Across almost the whole extent of Christendom the organizing principle of society is a feudal system (more exactly, several varieties of such a system). The 'system' is barely two and a half centuries old, and the 'serfdom' associated with it can barely be traced back to Charlemagne's land settlements; yet it all seems anchored in timeless custom. At its apex is the elected emperor, or a hereditary king, with his own land, or domain; around him are usually some great landowning vassals who owe him service and counsel (chiefly a defined amount of military service) as a condition of holding their lands from him; beneath them, further vassals or lesser nobles or knights or lords of estates similarly bound; and at the base a rural population, servants of the manor, tenants, copyholders, serfs, share-croppers, sometimes freemen—always owing *something* to a lord, producers but underlings (or in technical phrase, 'servile'). At each stage in this pyramid there is a title to land or a relationship to land, and a contractual relation to a superior—strenuously enforced and no less strenuously contested.

Seen from outside, feudal institutions are adapted to just two principal functions: government and war. Great lords, indeed all owners of land, retain the closest connections with the arts of war and their mystique. The profession of arms is reserved to them and to their households (the rustic is not a warrior). Fighting on horseback is not only a technique, but also a mark of their rank and status. Hunting is their martial exercise, and similarly reserved. Tales of military deeds and knightly prowess are fit matter for their ears. The education of their sons is a training for war. Their feudal ties invariably bind them to military duties.

As for the other function, 'government', this is directed, first, to the enforcement of domestic justice according to the custom of the land; but secondly and more importantly to the endless struggle in which a lord, great or small, seeks to uphold his claim to property and patronage, to enhance it at the expense of others, to bestow fiefs on supporters who have served him well, or to enlarge his domain and with it the roll of followers who will answer his next call to arms. One might judge that a feudal system thus defined could only be a formula for pandemic civil war, and so in a sense it is: a condition in which peace breaks out only when a successful predator quells all likely rivals and imposes *his* order on the neighbourhood; but only for so long as he remains active and vigilant, for the first sign of weakening leads to new danger. Eventually, as we know, a few powerful princes will prevail over all other rivals and build united kingdoms such as France, England, Portugal, and Spain; the process is long drawn out in Germany, never quite accomplished in Poland. All that, however, is far in the future. In the thirteenth century neither kings nor emperors can take power for granted. Fortunately, there is another power on the scene – the Church.

The Church

The endowments and lands of bishoprics and abbeys take up a large share of all European territories; bishops and abbots are great feudal lords. Hence the Church has strong practical interests—aside from spiritual ones—in damping down lawlessness, civil strife, and the sacking of villages. From the twelfth century in fact its force has been exerted on behalf of a sort of generalized peace movement. To channel that profane expansionism of which the Normans in their conquests provide so startling an example, a new outlet comes providentially to hand: the crusades. What better way to harness warlike energies and land-hunger than in fighting distant enemies of Christendom and winning new allotments of land (fiefs) from the commanders of these expeditions? More remarkable still has been the effort of the Church to spiritualize the ideals of Christendom's war-thirsty landlords, in a word, the invention of chivalry: a code of honour, a moral ideal, even an established order (complete with religious fasting, vigils, initiation rites, rules for courteous behaviour between members and towards the fair sex, discouragement of violence against the downtrodden poor). How it begins is hard to detect, but the spread of chivalry under lordly patronage owes much to the huge literature of courtly romances, a great deal of it from the pens of tonsured clerks. After epics around the figure of Charlemagne there follow now the tales of Arthur and his knights, built up no doubt from even more shadowy names and legends; even when psychological finesse peeps through there is a heavy dose of edification. The disturbing story of Tristan and his uncontrollable passion

for Iseult might not seem too promising a theme for improving the mind of a scrupulous Christian knight; yet that too is in a measure tamed and brought into line (1210) by the urbane poet Gottfried of Strasbourg.

Between the ideal and the reality there remains, evidently, a huge gap: barons continue to raid their neighbours, hold one another to ransom, allow their followers to plunder villages and burn crops; medieval chronicles abound with massacres, barbaric outrages, dark villainies of every kind. Yet the ideals are there, at least as between the well-born, and not without some kind of validity. Thus in far-off Byzantium it is commonplace, in fact a more or less recognized procedure, for deposed monarchs to be garrotted or at any rate blinded by their sons or brothers; in the West a quiver of universal indignation and horror greets Charles of Anjou when he coldly and publicly puts to death Conradin, grandson of Emperor Frederick II.

The Church has, naturally, more coercive means to hold together the anarchic sprawl of murderous feudal powers. In the thirteenth century we see it at the height of its authority, exercised with extraordinary vigour by Innocent III. Pope, successor to St. Peter, and—a title first assumed in this pontificate—Vicar of Christ, Innocent is also the lord of central Italy and suzerain of Provence and Sicily. He is deeply involved in high feudal politics. He condescends to crown the king of Aragon in Rome; he withholds recognition of Norman ambitions in Italy; he accepts new powers and titles (thus when John of England looks like succumbing to an alliance of his nobles with the French, submission to Innocent as his suzerain is an ingenious defensive ploy in which the pope acquiesces). For that matter, Innocent excommunicates the king of France's son on this latter occasion for seeking to invade England, and at other moments of tension makes no difficulty about excommunicating the kings of both countries.

If the pope can invoke religion to control force, he is also apt to invoke force to support religion. Thus he summons kings to go on crusades, excommunicating the emperor when he fails to keep his vow to do so; he influences local affairs through his legates or bishops or great abbots; at the worst, when his commands are ignored, he places lands under an interdict (that is to say, suspends the performance of all religious services whatever). There are, it is true, limits to the exercise of this 'plenary power' (*plenitudo potestatis*). It is easier to launch a crusade than to control its outcome, and the knights of the Fourth Crusade are not deterred by the free use of excommunication from sacking Constantinople. Nor are all the papal summonses effective: the king of France holds back prudently from Innocent's

28 Sainte-Chapelle, Paris, window bay A south, 1243–8

One bay of Saint Louis' sumptuous Gothic stained glass windows is given over to displaying how the precious Crown of Thorns has been brought to Paris. In the lower of the two scenes shown, messengers bearing it arrive at Venice; in the upper, Louis himself welcomes it reverently to his kingdom. Although the stained glass of the Sainte-Chapelle has been extensively restored, the king's head which we see here is exactly as it was seen by his contemporaries.

29 A *Bible Moralisée*: page showing Christ's miracles of healing, French, c. 1240. London, British Library, Harley MS 1527, fol. 27

In an elaborate teaching aid, or Bible moralisée, the painter-scribe has a task like that of the Romanesque sculptor—namely to fill a very small space with the essential figures of his stories (in thirteenth-century costume, be it noted). Even so, they are apt to spill out over his 'frame'.

call to march against heresy in Languedoc, and his place has to be taken by an abbot; later appeals for crusades against disobedient princes gradually lose their force. The high politics of the Church are hampered above all by a bitter rivalry between papacy and empire over the control of Italy, a struggle in which eventually both powers are disastrously weakened.

It is evident that the Church's power in great affairs of state depends upon its control over the minds of men. From birth to death the Church guides, or seeks to guide, every soul in Christendom. Its rites and sacraments are everywhere the same. It regulates the institutions of kinship, family life, marriage; performs baptisms, weddings, burials (whence the awful power of the interdict). It controls standards of behaviour, teaches and offers salvation, absolves the penitent, casts

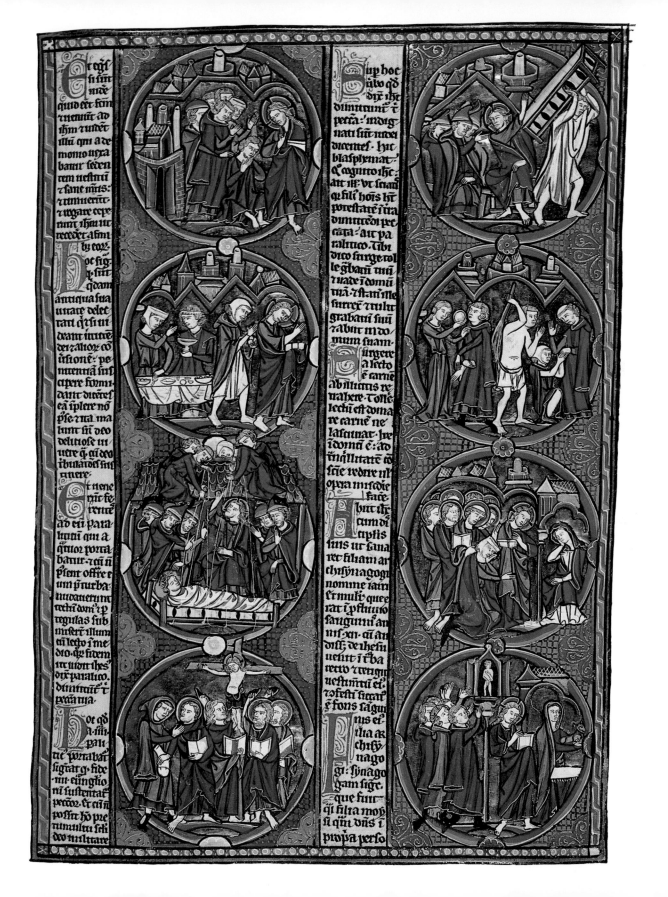

out the unregenerate. It has converted to its use old routines and habits of mind, in fact 'christianized' them. The Christian calendar is an example so obvious that we tend to overlook it: superimposed on pagan days of the week and months of the year, its days of rest or fasting and its holy festivals are a continuous symbol of religion. The priest blesses the fields and the harvest and the fisherman's boat; the intercession of saints, and especially of the Virgin, is invoked in time of drought, famine, plague, sorrow, perplexity, or danger, by great and poor alike. Local cults are converted by the overlay of a saint's legend. All else failing, old witches' lore, fairies, and other obstinate survivals are classed as work of the devil and his crew. The host of the Church Triumphant is enlarged by papal canonization of holy men—even including one or two kings, but more commonly a cleric, increasingly a member of one or other of the great regular orders—and a new shrine is added, a new cult of veneration. Well-organized pilgrimages to the shrines of the most popular saints, such as James at Compostella and Antony at Padua, take on huge importance: every year, thousands seek relief from past sins by journeys which are often arduous and long (the longest is to Jerusalem); for such voyagers, monasteries offer a night's shelter along well-charted routes. And by the same token, relics are eagerly sought: the remains of St. Mark are said to have been stolen in Alexandria and smuggled triumphantly to Venice; a relic of Mary Magdalen is the pride of Vézelay; the Saviour's Crown of Thorns, bought by St. Louis in 1239 from the impecunious Emperor Baldwin, is housed in Paris in the exquisite Sainte-Chapelle (completed 1248).

The regular orders

All this is under the eye of bishops and the secular priesthood, an immense and varied host of churchmen. But alongside them, and steadily increasing in importance, are the regular orders, no less numerous and varied: Benedictine monks, Augustinian canons, 're-formed' Benedictines—the tenth-century Cluniac network in Burgundy and Germany, the Carthusians, the Cistercians of the twelfth century . . . Monasticism is almost as old as the Church; it has survived barbarian times, offered refuge to seekers after salvation, converted the heathen, transmitted the surviving skills of writing and Latin and ancient learning, even spread the arts of husbandry. Nor should we forget that a monastery is apt to have the care of a parish at its gates. Together, the diocese and the monastery supply the only schooling that exists, originally for the Church's own recruits; they maintain the universal language used

30   Bonaventura Berlingheri, Saint Francis Altarpiece, 1235. Panel. Pescia, church of San Francesco

This early representation of Saint Francis features scenes from his life – in Italy, the Holy Land, etc. As extensive as any originating in the Middle Ages, his cult leaves its trace in painting, stained glass, decorated chests, and other church furnishings.

within the Church—Latin; and in an illiterate world they provide the only medium of mass communication and guidance, namely the pulpit.

The bishops of some great dioceses and the heads of a few monastic orders are, under the pope, figures at least as powerful as kings or great nobles. Abbot Suger of St.-Denis is chief adviser to the king of France; the influence of Archbishop Thomas Becket in England is well known; St. Bernard of Clairvaux preaching the Second Crusade is probably the most influential voice in Christendom; the abbot of Cîteaux actually takes the field to command a crusade against the Albigensian heretics in Languedoc. For duties relating to crusades in the Holy Land, too, several imposing (though to our eyes rather strange) orders have come into existence. Part monastic, part military—communities of fighting monks, as one might say—they are dedicated to protecting the Temple of Jerusalem (Knights Templar), providing hospital service (Knights Hospitaller or Knights of St. John), or simply smiting the infidel (Teutonic Knights). The first of these orders is extremely rich and consorts with the greatest in the land: in its house in Paris it is even entrusted with the royal treasure until the king of France can build himself a suitable castle in which to store it. But it is doomed to be dissolved a century later, in a storm of scandal and horror. The second, after a long and heroic history in Rhodes and Malta, including centuries as a sovereign power, subsides into the modest role that can still be seen in some countries' voluntary first-aid services. The third, transferring its attention from the Holy Land to the Baltic (in 1228) conquers and holds huge territories there until one day its leader adopts the reformed faith of Luther and assumes the title of Duke of Prussia; his successors eventually submit (together with their lands) to the neighbouring Elector of Brandenburg, which is one reason why *his* successors can become kings of Prussia; the order drifts away.

These examples of Church vitality suggest more a concern with power than with spirituality. In contrast, two remarkable new orders present themselves to the generation of 1200, founded respectively by the Italian St. Francis (1209) and the Spaniard St. Dominic (1220). Both have this novelty, that they address themselves not to a withdrawn life (let alone to warfare) but to preaching; and that in place of the endowed wealth necessary to a monastic order they embrace the poverty of Christ, a life of begging. Their work is in the midst of men, therefore in towns, and the papacy quickly encourages them to take on the duties of a task force (even against the prudent instinct of St. Francis) in meeting new needs; evidently they are capable of a greater impact on growing city populations than the secular clergy or the monastic orders. To help them in their missions the friars (brothers) are exempted from the local control of bishops. Within a mere twenty years Franciscans and Dominicans have spread right across Christendom, with huge recruitments (especially to the former), hundreds of 'houses' in all important centres, large supporting circles of 'second' and 'third' order followers (nuns and novices living 'in the world'), missions, and teaching centres. The Dominican Friars Preachers also furnish a specialized Inquisition, or ministry to combat heresy. A new 'mass movement' has been born.

This profusion of institutions and organizations of the Church and its enormous if varied membership form a society within a society, all the more noticeable for the relatively small global population of Christendom. Every order, whatever its nature, is open to control by the papacy. Regulars, like secular priests, take vows of celibacy: for celibacy is a mark of dedication, a convenience in the running of a great supranational system, and also a wise precaution to prevent the properties of a see or abbey from being claimed by a lineal descendant of the last incumbent; and in an age passionately attentive to the inheritance of land, great lords cannot prolong their line through and beyond a great ecclesiastical office.

There are however many degrees of ordination: Dominican friars are ordained priests, Franciscans not necessarily so. It is not unknown for a papal officer or a regular to be elected pope, *then* quickly ordained a priest so that he may be installed as bishop and pontiff (such indeed was the case with the great archdeacon Hildebrand, known to history as Gregory VII). On the fringe, a tonsured clerk or a Franciscan novice, though regarding himself as an ecclesiastical subject, may hardly have any actual function in the Church at all. Yet he is governed by its canon law, which is administered in Church courts and is quite distinct from whatever system of laws may govern the laity around him.

In sum the Church through its myriad forms and agencies acts within the world while yet in a peculiar sense being not quite *of* the world. As Thomas Becket reminded Henry II, the whole Church of God comprises two orders, the clergy and the people—the latter including kings, princes, dukes, and counts. And kings obtain their authority from a religious source, precisely as the prophet Samuel anointed Saul. On this view, if the Church hands over civil authority to a prince, it is because it has other and more pressing duties of its own.

The world

How, in a society permeated at every point by the Church's guidance, values, horizons, should men visualize the world as a whole? Put in this crude way, the question is not as difficult to answer as it will become in later ages. There *is* a standard picture, and the only problem is to know how widely it is perceived. Christian culture in 1200 offers a single, if not a totally simple, 'world view', along something like the following lines.

The world and everything in it are God's creation, and man's understanding is aimed at grasping its spiritual sense. As shaped by its Creator, and described by

Ptolemy and the Psalmist and other authorities, earth is at the centre, girded by ocean. In its depths is hell; above it, air, then a set of concentric spheres in which the moon, the sun, planets, and stars revolve; beyond these, heaven. Between God and man there are angels, spirits not imprisoned in mortal bodies, who do their Master's bidding; similarly, there are fallen angels in hell. The stars on their courses, the succession of the seasons, the four elements, the natures of living things and their spirits and humours, the rebirth of seed in the ground, the properties of matter, the map of distant places, are details which the learned may study. The authorities may differ, as on the number of spheres above us, and whether earth rests upon the waters—as the Psalmist claims—or upon nothingness. In such cases an attempt is made to reason out the 'best' view, but always the end of such study is to manifest and glorify the works of the Creator.

The very dimensions of this emphatically *closed* universe are spiritual—not an abstract space, not space-time, not a great void, but God's thought and will, a *plenum* of his purposes. Within it the small purposes of men are closely linked to the drama of God's love for the world. From creation to Last Judgement there is a continuous and meaningful sequence of occurrences, known to us through Holy Scripture, old historians, St. Augustine and the Church Fathers, as well as more recent chroniclers. At the centre of time, radiating its dazzling significance, is the incarnation of Christ and his passion, the crucial link between the divine and created man, the ineffable means of spiritual salvation.

On the one hand, therefore, there is a pervasive spirituality, not easy for us to recapture; but on the other a concreteness, a matter-of-fact simplicity which is perhaps even more elusive. The imaginative span does *not* confront vertiginous infinities or eternal silences (beyond the spheres is simply heaven); it confidently produces collections of information regarding all known created things (for those who can read, Vincent of Beauvais's *Universal Mirror* is one such compilation in the 1240s). The monk sitting down to chronicle last year's events sees himself as adding a supplement to the chronicles of the Bible, the pagan historians, and early Christian historians such as Eusebius: a puny duplicate of that greater record accumulating steadily on high against the Day of Judgement. Only perhaps when we look at the sculpture of the Middle Ages can we recapture the disconcerting concreteness of this medieval world view.

'Understanding' the world is thus a task which has to do not so much with how things work as with what they mean: the purposes of God, the place and duty of man in a scheme of purposeful occurrences. The scene is fixed and stable: the creation being a once-only event, history with one single exception (the Incarnation) does not advance or change its sense. The Word of God 'endureth for ever'; there is nothing to add to the Ten Commandments. Short of the Second Coming and the Last Judgement, the Church has no dogma of secular change; it has 'only' its mission to glorify God, guide souls, expand, and spread the Word.

Yet there is change in Christendom: the growth of the mendicant orders of friars, if nothing else, attests it. And within this feudal world, and rural society, shaped in its beliefs by the Christian Church, a new type of social entity has, in the previous century, begun to acquire prominence: the town.

Paris

Towns do not fit at all happily within a feudal system. What man-to-man relation does lordship imply in a community of fifty thousand, as compared with a village of fifty or five hundred? What can chivalry mean to a butcher? What charm has war for a trader? Who should control the new concentrations of wealth? It is not surprising that town populations should over time develop new values and outlooks not at all suited to the concerns of feudal barons—though quite endurable to far-sighted kings. The example of Paris, if not entirely typical, will illustrate these matters.

Paris, a very ancient pre-Roman settlement, later a Roman camp, is in 1200 the flourishing centre of a royal domain. The king of France is its lord; it is a considerable asset to him. Its townsmen create all sorts of useful wealth by producing artefacts or carrying on trade; they merit protection, even a certain regard, and may therefore be allowed their own organizations—subject to supervision. Philippe Auguste (1165–1223) is a less chivalrous figure than his contemporary Richard I of England, but very much more attentive to these practical matters. He gives his city strong stone walls and a new fortified castle—the Louvre, long since vanished. (It also catches our notice that a day's ride to the north a *very* much larger and more menacing castle is built by a vassal, the lord of Coucy.) He subsidizes a new water supply, paves several streets, licenses new city corporations, ensures law and order. In return the townsmen supply 300 foot-soldiers on call, pay taxes, and keep the peace. Only a century later do we find them in revolt against their lord over a matter of inflation and the doubling of rents.

Within the walls of Paris live about fifty thousand inhabitants, much above the average for Christendom as a whole. (For comparison, London is much smaller, Rome about the same, and the most typical town has perhaps three to four thousand inhabitants; the really large cities are very far away: Cairo, Baghdad, Constantinople, with a million each.) Of this Parisian population, about four thousand are burgesses; their self-administered guilds and corporations are growing rapidly, under royal favour. By mid-century there will be some three hundred such groupings of special crafts and trades: watermen, butchers, mercers, apothecaries, drapers, weavers, locksmiths, bakers, chandlers, and so on. Recent arrivals are a number of 'Lombards' (money-changers from Italy, useful to raise loans for the crown and able to get around the Church's ban on usury by executing long-distance transactions which justify an interest charge). Only by 'incorporation' on terms agreed by the king can traders obtain secure rights, and all trades, even acrobats and actors, seek that privilege. Though the king encourages markets and trade fairs, Paris has not the commercial importance of the Flemish towns or great Italian cities. Instead, however, it enjoys an unusual source of prosperity and an unusual prestige—as a centre of learning. For this it has to thank neither the king nor its townsmen, but the Church; yet the influence of the town, surprisingly, is decisive in one respect which we shall soon come to.

To get an idea of the presence of the Church in thirteenth-century Paris, and in the surrounding region of the Île de France, we have only to look at what survives of the work of a great industry which is not strictly urban: building in stone. In this age town houses are built of wood, with thatch or shingle roofs. None survives. There is no archaeology of the early city corporations of Paris. City walls, though, and palaces, castles, and especially churches, are made of stone. In the century from 1150 to 1250, in this quite small royal domain, not only does the king fortify and adorn his city (while vassals do the like around him), but parish churches are being rebuilt or enlarged, and no fewer than *ten* really enormous edifices are erected or rebuilt: first the great abbey church of St.-Denis, and then in swift succession the cathedrals of Sens, Noyon, Senlis, Paris, Laon, Chartres, Reims, Amiens, and Beauvais. At any one time, five or six of these are under construction; tens of thousands of hands are involved in quarrying, carterage, digging, scaffolding, masonry, glass making, carving . . . It is hard to imagine the unprecedented scene, with building-sites at every important centre of population, and impossible to gauge the economic and social 'spin-off'; but here an intriguing new profession makes its appearance: that of the master-builder or general contractor and architect. Out of this prodigious upheaval, also, there emerges something else, quite new—Gothic architecture.

The Church in fact is all around: visible not only in the surge of new building, but in the work of its existing parishes, its monasteries (St.-Germain, the Benedictines of Montmartre, St.-Victor, Ste-Geneviève), its hospital for the infirm (the Hôtel-Dieu), its leper house, its Templars' house, and its schools.

University

The university originates in the cathedral school and in the two monastic foundations of the Left Bank. Over the previous century they flourish greatly, and two exceptional teachers, the Breton Peter Abelard and the Italian bishop of Paris, Peter Lombard, attract pupils from far and wide to study, in particular logic and theology. But law is also taught, and a start is made on medicine. (Most of the graduates continue in the Church; but increasingly there is a demand for literate clerks in royal offices, even noble households. We are told that of Abelard's pupils twenty become cardinals, and fifty bishops. One of the latter, a poor boy who goes through great hardships to sit at Abelard's feet, has been a recent bishop of Paris, Maurice de Sully, the mastermind behind the new cathedral of Notre-Dame. Another, later, student of the schools is Innocent III. With such alumni success is understandable.) By 1200 probably five thousand students are crowded into the town, a surprising ten per cent of the total population! The great majority have come from far away; Germans, English, and Picards are attested by the names of their student 'nations' or organizations. And because these extra mouths bring prosperity to the city, Philippe Auguste in 1200 grants important privileges to the schools. Teachers and students are tonsured clerks. Being nominally under the control of the bishop's 'chancellor' (and to some extent in practice also), they have some immunity from the civil police.

From the privileges granted by the king there flow some unexpected results. The masters of the schools, who include monks and diocesan teachers, but also a large majority of immigrant clerks, now press for an organization of their own, not as a typical Church community, which would hardly suit, but as a recognized corporation on the model of the city's trades corporations—with elected officers, statutes, induction rituals, discipline, regulations defining the role of masters and apprentices (that is, students). Indeed they proceed forthwith to set up their own statutes, in defiance of the bishop, who in 1210 excommunicates them all for disobedience!

Fortunately for them, a greater patron has his eye on the scene. Innocent himself has conceived the idea that Paris should become a great centre of learning for all Christendom. He sends the schools encouraging messages, forwards a request to supply teachers for the Catholic schools being set up in a hurry in Constantinople, and in 1215 authorizes them to develop a corporate self-governing body. His legate Gerson (another graduate) smooths over problems with the diocese, intervenes in a town-and-gown fracas over lodging shortages, and takes the opportunity to lay down rules for the curriculum. These rules are in fact extremely cramping and conservative, and are followed up by a very revealing ban on the teaching of civil law, in order to give greater emphasis to the teaching of the Church's own canon law. The new Franciscan and Dominican orders are urged to open houses in Paris and join in the teaching: they comply promptly, and in very little time occupy a large place in the theology school. A charter is granted by papal bull; the *universitas* (or collectivity) of masters and students receives informally a name which eventually comes to supersede its proper title (*studium*); successive popes confirm the validity of its academic degrees for teaching throughout Christendom.

In all this process the university (as we shall call it) becomes a quite new species of institution; it achieves a certain freedom both from the king and from its local bishop. All in all, it is a momentous invention: if not the first to be established (that honour goes to the civil law school of Bologna, protected by the pope's rival, the emperor), nor the last (in quick succession there now follow Oxford, Naples, Toulouse, and many others), it is at any rate the most important so far as papal policy can influence its fortunes; and by the standards of the age it is large.

We would do well, however, not to lose sight of its limitations.

As an ecclesiastical body, the *studium* of Paris exhibits the high achievements of a strictly Church culture. To most townsmen its doings (conducted entirely in Latin) are a mystery. They lodge and feed the students while resenting their liberties; and unbend only so far as to set up *commercial* book-copying workshops to supply their needs (this innovation is, all the same, noteworthy). To a baron in his castle a hundred miles away the activities of the university are of no moment whatever, if he has so much as heard of them. It is quite certain that few of his retainers or serfs could form any idea about them for some time to come. We may suspect too that very many parish priests are hardly touched by the zeal for learning exhibited in the growing university; and to judge by the standards of copying carried on in monas-

teries we may have grave doubts about the level of Latin teaching or even literacy throughout the Church. We know from the (unique) Inquisition records for a remote little village in the Pyrenees—Montaillou—that once one strays any distance from town centres, a countryman's grasp of Christian belief becomes decidedly vague, and indeed not fully distinguishable from an amiable paganism. In short, though the Church is vast and expanding, and though its threads penetrate into all walks of life, its high culture is nevertheless what some today would call 'elitist', and has a deep effect on re-

31   The computist, the astronomer, and the scribe, miniature from the Psalter of Louis and Blanche of Castille, French, *c.* 1220. Paris, Bibliothèque de l'Arsenal, MS 1186, fol. iv

In this miniature from a Psalter made for the king of France's son and his bride, the clerical artist has included practitioners of the liberal arts: (left to right) a mathematician, an astronomer holding up an astrolabe, and a young clerk. Two are shown tonsured, the third may be presumed to be. The Church's monopoly of learning is plain to see.

latively few people. With that caution we may yet trace in the new Paris university an extremely important aspect of its cultural orientation.

Scholasticism

The tradition of the schools goes back to what the monasteries have rescued from antiquity: Holy Writ, Latin grammar and some Latin authors, passages of Aristotle translated by Boethius, some commentaries. These still form the *trivium*, or first liberal arts, inherited from Rome—grammar, rhetoric, dialectic (see p. 37) They lead on to the *quadrivium* of arithmetic and geometry, astronomy and music, again based on ancient learning. Beyond that are the 'higher' professional studies, theology, medicine (based on Galen and Hippocrates) and law—to which the Church is adding its own canon law. All teaching, all texts, are in Latin.

An originality of Paris is the famous 'method' established by Abelard, a general technique for reasoning. In essence it is simple: to introduce into dialectic the thorough procedures used already by lawyers for reviewing their precedents and written authorities; to align *all* relevant propositions, for or against a given point of view, apply logic to them, and then to decide on the most coherent. This technique of *Sic et Non* (for and against) comes to be regarded as a powerful weapon for handling virtually any subject. Abelard, who is an 'arts' teacher, has made himself unpopular by looking too closely at awkward texts and problems in ethics and theology and by discussing inconsistencies in Holy Writ. The technique supplies the format for public examinations, conducted orally as 'disputations'; indeed the clerks of Paris attain notoriety as exponents of this art of ritualized debate. The method of *Sic et Non* is an attempt to discover the rationale of things by a kind of logical detective work. Even of sacred things? St. Bernard abominates Abelard's intellectual detachment: 'virtues and vices are discussed with no sign of moral feeling, the sacraments with no indication of faith.' And he is not alone in that view. But even had Abelard not developed this approach, there is every possibility that some other interdisciplinary hybrid would have come about in this milieu of scholars pursuing their various subjects. At a distance we may judge it a rather ponderous routine for supplying verbal consistency to what is known (or believed) rather than for arriving at new knowledge. As a method it is liable to lapse into hair-splitting, or even to become a game; from time to time outsiders are invited in to join in a jocular debate on some non-academic topic, in which arguments 'for'

and arguments 'against' succeed one another in chains of logical distinctions and syllogisms.

This weakness is familiar to critical spirits outside Paris. From nearby Chartres the scholar John of Salisbury complains that 'Logic is still the only thing they [the Parisians] talk about . . . It distracts attention from all else . . . They compile every opinion . . . because they have no opinions of their own.' Likewise Friar

32   Heloïse and Abelard, from a manuscript of *La Roman de la Rose*, French, fourteenth century. Chantilly, Musée Condé, MS 482, fol. 60v

In Jean de Meung's continuation of the Romance of the Rose *(see text, page 73), the star-crossed love of the scholar Abelard and the nun Heloïse enters the realm of literature.*

Bacon, from Oxford, is scathing in the thirteenth century about the Parisians' ignorance of Greek and Hebrew and mathematics, all pushed to one side in favour of disputation.

A crisis of belief

Abelard's intellectual heritage has however a graver implication. It harbours, deep down, a claim for inquiry to recognize no bounds. And this pretension, tolerated for a time, becomes intolerable at the very moment of birth of the 'university'.

The chance cause of the crisis is a major discovery, or rediscovery: Aristotle's writings on physics and metaphysics, newly translated from Greek and from Arabic, and arriving in Christendom via Constantinople and Toledo. Why from Arabic? Simply because the great philosopher's writings have, in the Middle East, been translated into Syriac; and have then survived the spread of Islam and come to the attention of generations of Arabic scholars. Aristotle is of course the prince of learning in the Western schools, and fragments of his logic are already woven into Christian belief. For example, the dogma of transsubstantiation, affirmed at the Lateran Council of 1215, rests on his theory of 'substance' and 'accidents'. But the new and very exciting texts that have come to hand are found to clash in part with Christianity. For example, they acknowledge (it appears) a supreme God—a Prime Cause—yet assert that the world has existed from eternity, which denies to God the role of Creator. Likewise, in his theory of 'forms', Aristotle teaches that the soul is a living man's form, and hence (broadly) denies its immortality. Worse, the only imperishable feature in the soul is that of 'active intellect', which Arabic commentators take to be a power distinct from individual persons, a sort of collective entity: this stultifies the whole idea of a Last Judgement. Three major heresies in an author almost as venerable as the prophets . . .

From about 1170 onwards, the distant translators have made all this available to any clerk able to lay hands on their manuscripts; but around 1200 there are masters in the Paris schools who begin to share the new learning with groups of their students, publicly. This is a much more serious matter, and the Church reacts. A council of bishops held in Paris in 1210 bans the teaching of the new texts and their Arabic commentators; the ban is renewed ferociously by the legate Gerson in his curriculum of 1215, and by the pope. The issue is nevertheless too grave to be left at that: it proves impossible to suppress interest in the dangerous writings; translations of the Arabic commentators continue to be made, read, and circulated (notably Averroës); after some years the papacy authorizes a review and revision of the contentious texts.

In Paris, three positions crystallize. The monks of St.-Victor, firm in the tradition of Augustine and Plato, discourage or at least play down rationalist enthusiasm; so also do the Franciscans, whose greatest teacher, St. Bonaventura, will shortly appear in Paris. For them, steadfast contemplation of the divine mysteries far surpasses the merit of intellectual adventure. An exactly opposite tendency spreads in the arts faculty, where the forbidden texts are eagerly pored over, not without confusion, since apart from Averroës (whose commentaries reach Paris in Latin in about 1230) Arabic scholarship has not been unduly faithful to Aristotle, and some of the texts ascribed to him are not in fact his at all. By mid-century the ban on 'new' Aristotle is so far relaxed that he features prominently in the arts curriculum. There are plenty of indirect signs that the dangerous speculation has in fact become fashionable; eventually in 1277 one of the masters of arts, Siger of Brabant, is brought to trial before the bishop and condemned for teaching heresy. Even then, 'Averroism' is not stamped out.

Midway between these two extremes, the Dominicans take up their own characteristic position. One of their number undertakes to retranslate Aristotle; they devote intense effort to trying to see how far the 'new' Aristotle can be reconciled with received doctrine. Albert the Great of Cologne (Albertus Magnus), leading encyclopaedist of the age, covers all the texts in his surveys of natural philosophy, while conceding that some of their reasoning is erroneous. And his Italian follower, Thomas Aquinas, who likewise teaches in the Dominican house in Paris, proceeds between 1254 and 1274 to a profound, even definitive, synthesis of philosophy and faith. In almost every chapter of his *Summa Theologica* he refers to Aristotle, but in order to arrive at a new compromise, something as follows.

Theology is, for Thomas, the 'higher' science. Divine truths (for example, the Creation, the Trinity, the Incarnation) descend to us by revelation, while the 'natural light of reason' ascends from created man towards God; and reason cannot in any way originate or explain divine truths. This distinction is not quite so simple as it sounds: Thomas in fact offers lengthy philosophic 'proofs' of the existence of God and immortality, which a believing soul might well judge needless. He argues however that philosophy can be valuable to combat erroneous arguments which might lead the faithful astray; and it can represent a definite advance in our understanding of some objects which we already

33   Part of a page from a 13th-century English textbook containing Aristotle's logical works. Paris, Bibliothèque Nationale, MS Lat. 16599, fol. 70v

Aristotle's Posterior Analytics *(logic) in Latin translation form a standard Arts Faculty text; on this opening page the margins are used for commentaries, or 'glosses'. The glosses are in fact the substance of the lectures (that is, 'readings') dictated by masters in the schools of Paris, Oxford, and other centres: already, by the mid-thirteenth century, the teaching method is fully institutionalized.*

believe in. An example would be the phrase in Holy Writ by which the Deity defines Himself: 'I am that I am' (Exodus 3:14) can be understood philosophically. To be sure, a reasoning creature who studies the sense of these awesome words is still infinitely below his Creator. Even so, it is not inconsistent, or heretical, to accept the idea of two kinds of theology, the 'revealed' kind and the 'natural' kind (as exhibited in this example, or in proofs of the existence of God). The latter, or natural, theology is inclusive of what we call metaphysics or the science of Being; it proceeds by reason, and it underlies and controls other branches of natural

wisdom. The order of created things is after all endowed by God Himself with its own forms of knowledge, beginning with the senses and other natural faculties; such 'lower' knowledge can be consistent and valid, it requires its own kinds of special study, and it affords legitimate delights. It is even possible that one day we may come to extend such knowledge beyond the limits reached in antiquity. At the same time it is wrong to expect that such knowledge could ever extend to our having a natural 'understanding' of the nature and thought of God. For that, we are absolutely dependent on what He judges fit to reveal to us. Thus, when natural reasoning *does* contradict revealed truth (as may just possibly be the case in Aristotle's *Metaphysics*) the former is simply wrong; careful study is then needed to see where and how error has crept in.

No thumbnail summary can convey an idea of the thoroughness, richness, and sheer breadth of Thomas Aquinas's writings. In the *Summa* he proceeds by careful definition, by a series of *quaestiones* (631, to be precise, covering about 10,000 opinions), and by argument based on the method of *Sic et Non* (for these writings derive from his teaching in Paris). In carefully ordered sections he embraces not only theology and metaphysics but also a great amount of the subordinate 'natural' knowledge—psychology, ethics, politics. No medieval philosopher will surpass him in the sheer majesty of the resulting construction, even if many dislike its ruthless intellectual rigour, even aridity, and some claim to find errors in it. The fact of its achievement suggests something of the intense importance which not only Thomas and his order, but many others as well, attach to the task of establishing the integrity of an unchanging Christian belief without turning aside from a seemingly changeable world. Evidently, the *Summa* is not the last word in scholastic philosophy, any more than it is the first. Perhaps though it is the climax of a controversy set in train in Paris fifty years earlier, under the novel conditions of a university.

Long before the *Summa* is composed, learned men are, we know, brooding on Aristotle's *Physics*, and looking into natural phenomena for themselves (as Aristotle did). More complete texts of Euclid's *Geometry* arrive from Spain—including now his proofs!—and likewise fuller versions of Ptolemy's *Astronomy*: in mid-century they too enter the arts curriculum in Paris. Albert the Great includes in his writings *his own* direct observations in biology. Scholars in England and Germany harvest Arabic science and consider problems in

optics or the effects of glass lenses, attempt to explain the rainbow and formulate a theory of colours, even adventure into astrology (a science despised, as it happens, by Aristotle). Natural philosophy *is* on the move, however slightly. It is stimulated, as we may conjecture, by three factors: the nudge and shock administered by Aristotle (itself part of an increase in traffic with the non-Latin world); the very large increase in the number of men turning to scholarly tasks; and the creation of this new kind of institution, the university, in step with the growth in numbers. Paris to be sure is wedded to logic and disputation, less curious about physical facts than Roger Bacon in Oxford or the learned alchemist Michael Scot in Palermo: it is still very much the obvious place for Aquinas to hammer out his compromise and make room for, and as it were legitimize, natural philosophy alongside the search for

34   Apse of the church of St.-Paul, Issoire, France, mid-twelfth century

A really large Romanesque church is apt to be built up out of a large number of assembled features; as with this apse and crossing, surmounted by its octagonal tower.

35   St.-Denis, Paris, *c.* 1140

Despite much later restoration, the novelty of the choir and east end of St.-Denis remains clear—the explicit buttresses, impression of great height, vast windows to admit a flood of light, regularity, symmetry.

God. In the end, these clerks and monks and friars, in the semi-freedom of more and more universities throughout Christendom, accomplish a rickety beginning to European science.

The Gothic

We have noted the curious link by which a Church institution, the university, takes on the typical form of organization of secular town life, the corporation. The facts are clear, if we cannot show the borrowing process in detail, and the dynamic results are surprising. Is there a further link or interaction of any sort between the intellectual arts developed in the schools and that other outstanding cultural labour developed in the same re-gion at much the same period, namely Gothic architecture? Some scholars have thought so.

The origins of Gothic are well known. Abbot Suger in 1140 commissions the rebuilding of the choir of the royal abbey church of St.-Denis, on an enlarged scale. The result is that a set of techniques and forms (pointed arch, ribbed vault, free-standing buttresses, greatly en-larged windows, rigorous symmetry, strict regularity of elevation), which are all in existence already, though separate, are brought together into a near-miraculous synthesis, unlike anything achieved before. Almost at once, the style is taken up for all the nine cathedrals mentioned above (p. 61), and elaborated. In 1163 a start is made on rebuilding the choir of Notre-Dame in Paris, to accommodate the swelling train of diocesan

36 Laon Cathedral, west front, c. 1160

A feature of early French Gothic cathedrals is the aspiration, alongside all else, to build high towers (and if resources allow, cap them with steeples). Laon, shown here, has in all five towers, visible for many miles around. That over the crossing (just glimpsed) is topped with a modest pyramidal shape; but in most cases they are left unfinished.

clergy; consecrated in 1182, the whole cathedral is complete by 1235 in more or less the form in which we know it. By then also, the whole of St.-Denis has been rebuilt to harmonize with its choir. There, and elsewhere, the result is a triumph of spatial organization: a spacious ground-plan is matched by soaring height (it encounters a vertiginous limit at Beauvais); light replaces the subtle modulations of the much more enclosed Romanesque; the structural forces of the building are brought out frankly into the open; a new symbolism of the kingdom of God is disclosed—vast, exultant, and comprehensively articulated.

The consequential changes are legion. Whereas Byzantine churches convey their lessons through mosaics, and Romanesque through painting and—mostly—sculpture carved in the structure, Gothic teaches mainly through stained glass and statuary, much of it free-standing (Chartres displays almost ten thousand figures in glass or stone, Notre-Dame not much fewer). The symbolic relation of choir to nave and transepts is modified. The passage of devout souls from west to east, from portal to high altar, takes on a new sense.

What is curious is that none of this revolutionary novelty is discussed in the recorded thought of the age. Abbot Suger gives a careful account of the treasures, richness, and size of his church, and claims to have been inspired by the thought of emulating the glories of Hagia Sophia. Apart from that, what we do find are grumbles from St. Bernard that the extravagance of Suger is an outrage to the principle of Christian humility, and a similar criticism, by Peter the Cantor, of the height of the new choir of Notre-Dame. There is no recognition, anywhere, of any *new* meaning, or possible meanings, of the style as a Christian symbol. This deafening silence should not be overlooked, when we consider how attentive churchmen can in fact be to the significance of great masterpieces; Geraldus Cambrensis, for example, rhapsodizes in 1185 on a beautifully illuminated Irish bible, calling it 'the very shrine of art'.

What then of the builder's art, the extraordinary achievement of a handful of master-builders who interpret their ecclesiastical clients' desires and arrive at the magic synthesis? It has been suggested that these well-travelled (if not clerically trained) men, observing the public disputations of the Paris schools, the fashion for argument proceeding by *Sic et Non*, the construction of a regular edifice of reason, the new orderly setting out of chapters one after another, the insistence on logical *clarity*, have taken a hint—more than a hint—from the schoolmen and put together a coherent, intellectually

38 Page from the sketchbook of Villard de Honnecourt, *c.* 1235. Paris, Bibliothèque Nationale

The earliest sketchbook of a secular master-builder known to us (Villard de Honnecourt) reflects his endless practical curiosities: on this page models for depicting a sculptor, a fish-like design, sundry figures, a face, a boar's head. On other pages he tries out rib-vaulting patterns, wrestling figures, etc.

37 St.-Denis, Paris, choir, *c.* 1140

Within St-Denis, the Gothic choir is seen in a view from the nave (rebuilt in the thirteenth century to harmonize). The disciplined unity of the church is manifest; as also the soaring vaults—we recall Abbot Suger's ambition to emulate the splendour of the Hagia Sophia—and the flood of light flowing in from Suger's 'splendid variety of new windows'.

39 Autun Cathedral, tympanum, c. 1130–5

The Romanesque tympanum at Autun depicts the Last Judgement, the damned (right) being committed to the hands of terrifying devils, the saved to felicity. The Judge sits in a formalized (in fact oriental) pose in a central lozenge, His robes heavily stylized. The supporting capitals, the band of medallions surrounding the tympanum, are further surfaces to fill with angels, men, monsters, symbolic creatures, a vast repertory.

satisfying *Summa* in stone. And in detail, too: the problems of rib-vaulting for an ambulatory with a ring of shrines, the problems of inserting a rose-window in the west elevation while retaining a truthful rendering of the pitched roof end-on behind it: these problems they examine by a methodical sifting of all technical possibilities, a veritable *Sic et Non*, ending up with the decisive *determinatio* (decision) of the master.

The schema is attractive, and has been brilliantly argued by Panofsky. It does however encounter great difficulties of chronology. When Suger sets about his choir (which is the decisive point), no great *Summa* is yet in existence to serve anyone as a suggestive example; Abelard's 158 *Quaestiones* hardly fit the specification, being an anthology and not a monumental edifice of reason. The architect in fact antedates the schoolman. It thus remains a complete mystery what process has occurred in the mind of Suger's master-builder (his name even is unknown): how he comes to integrate the wide technical repertory at his disposal, whether he fully recognizes what he has achieved— though he must have recognized it to be unlike any earlier Romanesque solution, even Durham. It is an open question whether considerations of strength and cost play an important part (Suger is not worried about cost, but the saving at least on stone and on scaffolding for the vaults may have been appreciable), or whether the builder simply elects to do something amazingly *new* for this very special client. At all events St.-Denis is

40 Notre-Dame, Paris, west front, c. 1170

A very early part of Notre-Dame is the portal of St. Anne, presided over by the Virgin and Child in a pose which is both majestic and intensely human. Adorning her throne (as also below it) it is worth noting that the sculptor has carved conventional church buildings as yet innocent of any 'Gothic' features such as this new cathedral displays.

copied, and copied again; the idiom is found to be practicable, lends itself to enlargement, elaboration, accentuation. The rest follows without too much surprise. By the time Albert the Great and Thomas Aquinas embark on *their* huge intellectual cathedrals, the new style is a full century old. And if later masters in their sketchbooks (one survives from the 1230s) play with all the theoretical possibilities of complex vaulting patterns, that may show an awareness that these exercises have something in common with the explora-

tory reasoning of the schoolmen in their disputations; but it casts no light on how the builder *first* came to be integrating and exploiting the stylistic resources of the Gothic. In short, there is no convincing evidence that the two greatest cultural phenomena of the age (in our perspective, at any rate), radiating from one and the same corner of Christendom, have any more intimate relation to one another in their origins than that both are produced in the bosom of a single huge and many-faceted institution—the Church—at a time of great expansion and great confidence.

A 'Naturalist' age?

What then of an even more tenacious and challenging idea—that this early thirteenth century exhibits a deep unifying trend, in the shape of a growing awareness of Nature, a new 'naturalism' springing up in a dozen diverse fields? In other words that the typical, spiritual world-view outlined earlier is in fact being infiltrated by a different, even discordant, style of thought?

The obvious starting-point for this idea is early Gothic sculpture, the statuary with which craftsmen in stone adorn the shining new cathedrals of the Île de France. Like the master-builders, the craftsmen are un-

known to us by name, but they are, like the former, carrying out a revolution in their art. Not quite overnight, but rather suddenly even so, statues begin to look different. Up to now, the conventions of church sculpture (for all their variety in different parts of Christendom) have a general family likeness to which

41   Basilica of Ste-Madeleine, Vézelay, carved capital, *c.* **1130**

The theme of this carved column at Vézelay is the milling of grain: but it is a mystic handmill, worked by beings who for all the fresh liveliness of their pose have still the 'Romanesque' attributes of swirling robe and patterned hair. Compare the next picture.

42   Notre-Dame, Paris, relief figures on west front, *c.* **1170**

On the left portal of the west front at Notre-Dame, the reaper sharpens his blade and the harvester stacks his sheaf, tunic tucked back for work. The figures may be 'ideal' but they are straight replicas of the everyday. And in the larger figure glimpsed to the right, note the tendons of the hand and the entirely 'natural' fall of drapery.

we give the name of Romanesque. This style has its ultimate origins in Constantinople; it spreads into the West via sixth-century Ravenna and the ninth-century Carolingian revival. Whether in the stylized gesture of a figure, the rendering of facial expression, the stiff posture of a divine judge, the patterning of drapery, the near-abstraction of elaborate foliage or of mystic creatures adorning a pillar, it is a heavily loaded *language*, hieratic, symbolic, not quite of this world: it is telling us supernatural things, and the terms it uses are formalized, and never let us forget their sacred import. The things of this world are in fact *transformed* into mystic symbols, and representation is subordinated to significance.

But now, within the space of a few decades around 1200, something different appears in the new statues, which are standing out freely from the fabric of the church. The angel's face at Chartres bears a movingly human expression; gesture loses its stiffness; the folds of a robe flow not only beautifully but (it might almost seem) in obedience to the laws of Nature. A leaf is recognizably a leaf of a known species of tree and not an elaborate part of mystic ornamentation. This change is a very great miracle. And of course one would like to 'explain' it. Unfortunately the one thing we may not do is to infer that craftsmen have suddenly been inspired by schoolmen and natural philosophy, that their sense of a 'real' world has been quickened by the new ideas, that Gothic sculpture is 'Averroist'. Because once again the work in stone antedates the ideas known to be in the minds of the schoolmen.

These poses, faces, draperies, leaves, are evidence that someone (a craftsman) is capturing the forms around him in a new way, and there are more and more craftsmen following the fashion and developing it; but it is not obvious that the revised language is intended to express a new 'balance of power' between the mystic reality of a sacred meaning and the visible creation. And undoubtedly the craftsman gradually turns his back on an age-old tradition, adventuring into new language; but chronology forbids us to say that the turning away is due to the dethronement of an old Byzantine authority or to the sack of Constantinople. Of course it is possible for the new sculpture to have the effect (however marginal) of nudging beholders into new kinds of experience: in all ages art has had this power. As a matter of fact we have some evidence that the statuary of Notre-Dame does just that. There is a Parisian fabliau in which two zanies up from the country are described gawping at Notre-Dame and the statues of kings which adorn it. One says to the other in his *patois*, 'Look! That's Pepin! There's Charlemagne!' and as they

stand absorbed, gazing upwards, a cutpurse relieves them of their savings. Such a glimpse of a scene, which looks trivial, is in fact quite revealing. To begin with, the 'sightseers' in Paris are carrying coins in a purse: a hundred years earlier the money economy is so little developed as to make that detail unlikely. More to the point, before the thirteenth century no one, clerk or rustic, would have been expecting to look up at a church and see on it a row of historical figures identifiably depicted (not quite the same thing as working out that *this* stylized figure is Christ, *that* one the patron saint, or David, or Peter, etc.). The kings to our eyes may look rather alike, but they do look like kings of the age, and not merely symbolic figures.

Let us turn for a moment from sculpture to literature. In contrast to the increasing refinements of 'courtly' romances, the fabliau—since we have come upon one—is a free and easy form for story-tellers: perhaps satirical, often merely saucy, but always accessible, popular. (In a later century, Chaucer's *Reeve's Tale* is a superior example of a very smutty fabliau which has strayed into mixed company.) As a recognized 'kind', it too antedates by at least a decade the public study of Aristotle in the light of his Islamic commentators. Jean Bodel—and he is not the first—produces half-a-dozen well-known fabliaux in the neighbouring town of Arras before 1200. Some modern editors have called him 'Averroist', but without cause: merely because a fabliau is cheeky or disrespectful, or does not pay elaborate homage to Higher Values, it is not necessarily a piece of philosophical subversion. 'Popular' tales in all ages tend to be free of lofty idealism; but their 'realism' need have nothing to do with a more deliberate 'naturalism'.

The first piece of profane literature which does advertise naturalism in a very remarkable way is Jean de Meung's prodigiously famous continuation (1275) of the *Roman de la Rose*—a poem written by Guillaume de Lorris in Paris in 1235, and in its original form a singularly beautiful and etherialized allegory of love. The continuation, hugely long, ostentatiously 'philosophical', sophisticated, does most certainly reflect an 'Averroist' cult of Nature; indeed it even goes beyond that. Jean de Meung transforms the original intention of the poem when he adds his fourteen thousand extra lines. Instead of an allegory of refined courtesy, he gives us a philosophy in which 'Nature' is personified as really the creator and mover of all things. The potency of Nature is closely woven in with the theme of generation—sexuality—in a way which seems to have affinity with earlier eccentricities of 'Platonism' rather than with Aristotle. Since Jean de Meung also plays on a very popular theme of the Middle Ages, namely misogyny, the *Roman* has an unusually wide success, and must not be taken as evidence that 'philosophy' is a craze of thousands of readers. But even so, by the time of its appearance, there are signs of a conscious, or self-conscious, intellectual fashion in Paris, something like the existentialism or other 'isms' of a later age on the same Left Bank of the Seine. The schools even exhibit by then a certain libertine recklessness, which, as noted earlier, attracts wholesale counter-attack by the bishop of Paris in 1277. But that is not the kind of trend we are trying to pin down as a deep and pervasive 'naturalism'. In any case, it is half a century too late.

At a critically early date, probably around 1220, St. Francis of Assisi, far away from Paris, composes his unforgettable rhapsodies to 'Brother Sun' and to the birds and beasts and beauties of God's creation. We must suppose that an echo of this joy is carried across Christendom by some at least of Francis's followers, the *Fraticelli* (while not forgetting also that a decade or two later one of them, Thomas of Celano, almost certainly composes the *Dies Irae*, the formidable verse sequence evoking not the beauties of the earth but the terrors of the Last Judgement, a quite different tonality). How far does Francis's outpouring of love and joy reflect the same regard for the world that the sculptor's hand betrays, or the story-teller's wit? Evidently not at all. The very large Franciscan Order includes a wide array of talent: not only Thomas of Celano, but also the serene and spiritual Bonaventura in Paris, the confirmed philosopher and naturalist Roger Bacon in Oxford. The founder himself, Francis, is unique; his followers are awake to learning, and reach in many directions; but not, in the main, to 'new' Aristotle, or to Averrroës.

Where else then should we be looking for signs of 'naturalism'? A little earlier than Francis's hymn, a quite different kind of person, Geoffroy de Villehardouin, writes his chronicle of the *Conquest of Constantinople* (between 1205 and 1213). He has of course been an eye-witness. His book is not a narrative poem, but the first great work of historical prose to be written in French instead of Latin (its author is a minor nobleman from Champagne who settles and dies in Greece). It is a very intelligent and 'detached' piece of political writing—there is after all a good deal for a Christian apologist to explain away in the shocking tale he has to tell—and the sophisticated tone has been contrasted with that of the monk Otto of Freising, who was writing a chronicle of the not dissimilar acts of his nephew Frederick Barbarossa, only a generation or two earlier. Whereas Otto follows the best tradition in seeing at all points of his theme the will of God, Villehardouin is very much more matter-of-fact and circumstantial; in fact one would judge him thoroughly secular in outlook, addressing an equally secular (and hypocritical?) audience. Is this narrative, then, evidence that public affairs are beginning to be seen in a more 'naturalist' way than formerly? If so, does this mean that Villehardouin has given up attaching too much emphasis to the providential guidance of human affairs? Or is it not more likely that in common with many others of his day, he is prepared to stand his ground and offer his own reading of the will of God—more favourable to himself, obviously, than that of some critics (including Pope Innocent III)? And, as a general question, does supernatural meaning *have* to be incompatible with coolly described facts 'as they actually happened'? Does the angel, by exhibiting human beauty, cease to be angelic?

This and other riddles have no plain answer. By the age of Albert the Great (mid-thirteenth century) there is nothing to argue about: the Dominicans, and others as well, have made it respectable to take a curious interest in Nature. The trend is, at it were, public, even consensual. Vincent of Beauvais can popularize all 'natural knowledge', exultantly; extremists compromise themselves; the bandwagon is on the move. But if the historian considers instead the early years of the century, he may *sense* that the things of this world are already coming to be accorded a more weighty attention *for their own sake* than two generations previously—though in ways he cannot easily generalize. If we were to proceed year by year, the first major symptoms of 'naturalism' would be early Gothic statuary; and then (misleadingly) popular fabliaux contrived in the streets of Paris or neighbouring towns for down-to-earth (but emphatically urban) audiences. Then we have noted Villehardouin's rather unusal chronicle. After that, and only then, comes intellectual ferment in the schools, and all that flows from it. This sequence shows that university philosophers, at any rate, are not the cause of all these novel developments of the age. Overall, the high cultural achievements do not explain one another, on their own. They do not even hang together.

Is there any *other* way in which they can be related? Consider the persistent social and economic developments of Christendom in the twelfth and thirteenth centuries. They include the well-known growth of towns (most of all in Italy, but very markedly in other lands too, not least in France), and the foundation of *new* towns in the north—Lübeck, Rostock, Berlin, Riga, Stettin, Danzig, Stockholm, Frankfurt, Königsberg, Cracow, all between 1150 and 1257. Along with that

manda par iiii le parcon vel vie
uer dirai. Tuit al qui se auissero
ient et feroient le pinse deu un an
en lost seroient quittes de tor lor pe
chiez que il auoient fait dont il se
roient confes. porce q al pardons
fu issi granz. si sen esmurent mult
li cuers des gens. et mult sen aui
sierent porce q li pardons ere si granz.
l'autre an apres q al preuell
folques parla en si de dieu ot

pert ses freres. Gautiers de ouill
gnori. Gautiers de mombeliart.
Eustaices de chonelans. Guis
de plaissie. ses freres. henris dar
sillieres. Ogiers de saincheron. vi
lains de nuilli. Joffroi de vilehar
doin. li mareschaus de campa
igne. Joffroi ses niers. Guillel
mes de nuilli. Gautiers de sinl
simes. Curaz de montcingni. m
anassiers de lisic. Mach.....res

**43   The Crusaders attacking Constantinople:
miniature from a manuscript of Villehardouin's
Chronicles, 14th century. Oxford, Bodleian Library,
Ms Laud Misc. 587 fol. 1r**

*A 'realistic' depiction of the assault on Constantinople is hardly
to be expected of an illustrator ignorant of that city. The prow of
his galley is unmistakably Venetian, though; and the knights and
nobles (listed in the text) offer him no problem.*

there is the steady enrichment of the countryside as
well. For the land is not stagnating, even if its secular
lords mainly specialize in fighting one another. The
watermill, for example, is a recent supplement to animal power, introduced to several countries of north-
west Christendom by the Cistercians and followed
shortly by the windmill. The techniques of metallurgy
and mining advance. In many regions, feudal control of
the peasantry is shifting, losing its force. The steady
development of trade, both south and north, in Italy
and Flanders and on the Baltic coast, distributes textiles
and rare commodities and resources, and enriches and
knits together the lands touched by it. A growing
money economy in the towns is one condition of that
progress. Almost the only lands that are in decay are
southern Italy and southern France, both ruined by
endless violence. Elsewhere, enough new wealth is created to provide for all manner of crusades and wars,
with enough over to allow of that extraordinary building of cathedrals (for example) that we have noted
around Paris. Slowly growing populations support
the drain of banditry and wars and *still* provide recruits
to the towns and to the new mendicant orders.

This picture as a whole is not grasped by anyone,
change itself being not a perceived dimension of society. But Mammon *is* on the move, regulated maybe in
all sorts of ways, including Aquinas's and others' rul-
ings on financial usury, but also protected by secular
powers, which on occasion find it convenient to turn to
bankers and money-changers to mobilize wealth for
some extravagant enterprise. And, last but not least,
these secular powers, whether king or baron or municipality, are in fact becoming stronger, and larger. The
papacy has recently seen a need for new kinds of
Church organization. The world is tilting. Though
imperceptible, its drift cannot fail to have *some* bearing
on the myriad reflexes which go to make up human
experience, most of all where the fruits of development
or novel encounters or social conjunctions are at their
most visible.

Villehardouin's *Conquest of Constantinople* is evidence
(at least) of the existence of a purely secular audience for

whom it is written. The fabliaux are the profane amusements of growing urban communities. Awareness of an audience is itself part of a cultural outlook, and has its place in the process by which men establish or adjust their identities or values, and express them, for example in writing. Secular values in the thirteenth century's Christian frame are, on this argument, as much as anything else a function of collectively perceived identities of social groups.

Could this approach be extended to early Gothic sculpture? That is much less easy to argue. We have really no knowledge of the world of those late twelfth-century craftsmen in stone, of their relations with one another or with the people who they know will pass by and look at their finished products. But it is possible that if we had that knowledge, we might glimpse a situation not too different from the one we are advancing for their near contemporary Villehardouin, or for the writers of popular tales.

In brief, whereas some historians have claimed to detect a pervasive climate of cultural awareness which they call 'naturalism', seeping into the life of the 1200s, we are inclined (on the same evidence) to see something slightly different. In a world which is, and remains, dominated by Christian ideals and ideologies, there are segments of society, unrelated and different from one another, which are all growing into and arriving at half-awareness, or even a full awareness, of themselves as secular institutions; and they are 'talking to themselves' in ways which they develop because such ways make the most sense to them in each case. The segments do not keep in step with one another; but over the decades the process, however slow, is cumulative—and irreversible. And the cultural novelties we observe are (seen from this angle) made possible by the steady underlying accumulation of populations and/or their resources; and virtually forced into light by the slowly changing patterns of interrelation.

44   Cloth Hall, Ypres, 1260–1380

The great increase in wealth of thirteenth-century towns and their guilds allows a spill-over into municipal building, often on a grand scale, of Gothic styles and motifs. The textile centres of north-west Europe offer many examples: over the course of a century the Cloth Hall at Ypres becomes more and more palatial. Such buildings will provide models for the Gothic Revival public works of a history-minded nineteenth century (compare plate 166).

Chapter 3

Renaissance in Florence

The Renaissance: a milestone in the fifteenth century, a turning point in art and attitudes to art, in learning, in science; a new vision of the individual and his worth; a 'rebirth'; the beginning of a new world. This view is commonplace and hardly to be overturned—it is in fact how men of the late Renaissance, such as Vasari in Italy and Rabelais in France, have themselves advertised what they and their like have been doing; and we have continued to listen to their testimony and still use the very suggestive name they have put into circulation.

Yet we recognize it to have been a tendentious name. It focuses our attention on a particular range of their concerns; it disregards the discovery of a New World (named after a Florentine); it bypasses a European transformation which many would judge of central importance (the Protestant Reformation); it crowds out Copernicus's revolution in astronomy and actually obscures the process by which modern science slowly begins to emerge from ancient beliefs. Its claim for novelty, even, in recovering the ancient world and through it so many occasions for pride, is disproved by history; there is not *one* Renaissance, there have been numerous earlier occasions on which a cultural 'rebirth' has been sparked off by partial returns to antiquity. The century immediately preceding the great fifteenth-century refulgence in Florence is, in particular, an age of 'Renaissance', with Petrarch at the centre of a quickening of attention to ancient Rome; while in the sequel there spreads out from Florence a whole ripple of 'Renaissances' of various degrees of deliberateness, in other lands, lasting well into the 1530s and even beyond. In short, we no longer see the world as Rabelais did.

For all that, the Renaissance, if not an absolute novelty, yet forms part of a set of changes so striking in their outcomes as to warrant our attention, and our retention of the name—if not quite in the sense propagated by its sixteenth-century adherents.

Republicans and traders

Florence in 1400, setting the stage for the coming innovations, contrasts strongly with the little town of Paris in 1200. It is one of a number of prosperous and economically advanced city-states, a republic governed by its leading citizens, who are all merchants: that is the first large difference. In Italy, the richest region of Europe, it is a focal point of an international economy; it has become great by dominating the textile industry, which is a complex flow of transactions that starts with English wool exports, passes via the Flemish weavers and trade fairs down to the dyeing and finishing workshops of Tuscany, and then continues in the shape of high-grade finished goods outwards to Europe and the eastern Mediterranean and beyond, in exchange for flows of imports—spices, silks, rare objects—that arrive from Asia and the Middle East via Tabriz or Alexandria or Constantinople. The scale of this Florentine trade is five or ten times larger than that of comparable towns in the Low Countries, and in Europe is matched only by Venice.

The chief merchant houses of Florence (as of other Italian cities) have also used their wealth to develop financial services—banking—with sophisticated branch networks throughout Christendom, especially along the axis of their major trade. Among their customers the Florentines have, in addition, one particularly important and steady client, not all that far away—the Church in Rome. For the Church is now run by a very advanced and elaborate curia, and its international financing needs are huge: the transmission of ecclesiastical taxes from far and wide to Rome or elsewhere, transfers of funds involving distant benefices, advances to travelling prelates, the supply of money for large international councils. This traditional connection is highly lucrative, and commands good interest rates; no questions about 'usury' arise in matters of this kind . . .

Chronology for Chapter 3

1378	Ciompi revolt in Florence under leadership of Salvestro de' Medici
1401–24	Ghiberti making his first set of bronze doors for the Florence Baptistery
1420	Brunelleschi commissioned to build dome of Florence cathedral
1421	Giovanni de' Medici elected gonfalonier (chief magistrate)
1425–52	Ghiberti making his second set of Baptistery doors
1429	Death of Giovanni de' Medici, succeeded by his son Cosimo (the Elder)
1436	Alberti's *Della Pittura* contains earliest account of perspective construction
c. 1438–43	Donatello's *David*
1439–42	Council of Florence
1446	Death of Brunelleschi
1453	Constantinople taken by the Ottoman Turks
c. 1455	Gutenberg prints the 42-line Bible at Mainz
1462	Florentine Academy established under Ficino
1464	Death of Cosimo de' Medici
1466	Death of Donatello
1469	Lorenzo de' Medici (the Magnificent) assumes power in Florence
1470	Completion of Santa Maria Novella with façade by Alberti
1471–84	Sixtus IV pope
1472	Death of Alberti
1473	Building of Sistine Chapel begun in Rome
1483–4	Ficino's translation of Plato published
1492	Death of Lorenzo de' Medici; Columbus discovers America; expulsion of the Jews from Spain
1492–1500	Alexander VI pope
1494–8	Savonarola in power in Florence
1500	First edition of Erasmus's *Adagia*
1501–4	Michelangelo's *David*
1503–13	Julius II pope
1508	Raphael in Rome to decorate Vatican *stanze*
1508–12	Michelangelo's frescoes for the Sistine Chapel ceiling
1513	Giovanni de' Medici becomes Pope Leo X
1514	Raphael succeeds Bramante as chief architect of St. Peter's
1517	Luther posts his 95 Theses on the door of Wittenberg church
1519	Magellan sets out on circumnavigation of the world; death of Leonardo da Vinci in France
1520	Death of Raphael
1523	Giulio de' Medici becomes Pope Clement VII
1527	Charles V's troops sack Rome and imprison Pope Clement VII; Medici expelled from Florence and republic established there
1530	Alessandro de' Medici restored as duke of Florence
1537	Alessandro de' Medici murdered; succeeded by Cosimo de' Medici (Cosimo I), founder of grand duchy of Tuscany

One Florentine house that is conspicuously committed to the business is that of the Medici; it has branches all the way from Bruges (originally for the cloth trade) to Naples (financing imports of corn from Sicily) and Rome (banking). Its head, until his death in 1429, is Giovanni, banker to Pope John XXIII (the first of that number) and his successors; Giovanni is also 'prior', or head, of the guild of money-changers in Florence. His son Cosimo, who succeeds him, continues these policies.

The city is strategically placed, then, for all that concerns its prosperity: astride international trade, with a large manufacturing resource, and a happy position for benefiting from its proximity to a major 'power'. It is also vulnerable. Florentine business houses are apt to be ruined when they lend large amounts to foreign princes, as happens when Edward III of England defaults on his debts in the 1340s. The Black Death is a disaster which over a period of thirty years from 1348 more than halves the population of Christendom. The Hundred Years' War, the Italian wars between Milan and Genoa and Venice, the downfall of the French ruling Angevin dynasty in southern Italy, the removal (twice) of the papacy to Avignon, are all major hazards. More ominously, the Ottoman Turks are slowly crushing the Eastern empire and by 1357 have arrived at Gallipoli. Ten years after that, the Mongol general Tamerlane arrives from nowhere to devastate the Middle East: these distant catastrophes begin to tilt the balance of world trade. Worst of all, the rise of textile industries in north-western Europe itself has begun to undermine the foundation of Florentine wealth.

Florence survives, and even prospers. Its policies are prudent; it annexes some of its small neighbours, including Pisa (1406), and thereby acquires a valuable sea-going capability. Yet there are internal stresses. The republic does not escape the wave of trouble that passes through many fourteenth-century European towns in the wake of depression. In 1378 she has her own revolt of the *Ciompi* ('clogs', that is, the artisans in the cloth-finishing workshops). The merchant guilds and local nobility aided by mercenary bands fairly quickly overcome it by force and 'attrition', but it leaves its mark in a constitution to all appearance highly 'free' and democratic in that it provides for representation on the governing *Signoria* of both the 'major' city guilds, or corporations, and a number of 'lesser' ones alongside. There are also strains between what one might call the cosmopolitan magnates, who comprise the leading members of the wool and finishing and silk and money-changers' and law guilds (the *popolani grassi*), and at the other end of the citizen scale the 'small man' (the *popolo*

45   Filippo Brunelleschi, dome of Florence Cathedral, 1420–36

Brunelleschi's octagonal dome—seen here from the east—completes an edifice begun a century earlier under the auspices of the Florentine Wool Guild, and with Giotto as superintendent. Its bold and individual shape, rising above an ornate Tuscan structure, completes an ensemble where we observe details of Romanesque, Gothic, and now also a revived Roman style.

minuto) or workshop masters with no inkling of world affairs or high finance, too 'selfish', it is said, to consider the republic's interest as a whole. There are also the 'ancillary' members of lesser guilds (*sottoposti*), whose rights and protections are limited, and livelihoods precarious; or, again at the other end of the scale, a landowning country gentry, which on occasion is aligned with one or other faction in the town. A 'Guelf party' (originally pro-pope, anti-emperor) tends to serve as one coalition grouping of magnates and also middling citizens (*mezzani*), with conservative aims. But there are also one or two great houses which allow it to be felt that they have strong sympathy for the lower guilds; the Medici are a notable example. The

46   Fra Filippo Lippi (*c.* 1406–69) and Fra Diamante (*c.* 1430 – after 1498), *Madonna del Ceppo*, 1453, detail showing Francesco di Marco kneeling before the Virgin. Tempera on panel. Prato, Museo Comunale

By an established practice, the donor of a religious picture to a church or monastery is able to appear in person in a corner of his offering. The merchant of Prato is here shown in the simple – though good quality – attire of his calling; his pose is reverend, and he stretches a protective arm around several deserving fellow-citizens. Compare this simplicity with plate 62.

1410), the merchant of Prato so brilliantly evoked by Iris Origo. Francesco, a self-made man and a native of the little satellite town of Prato, migrates to papal Avignon and strikes out in general trade on his own; he returns to Prato, and then becomes a citizen of Florence, only when the revolt of the *Ciompi* is safely over. Once settled in the big city he assimilates; he is a *mezzano* with ambitions. He joins the silk guild (suitable for those intent on general import and export business); through agents and factors he trades profitably in Aragon, Venice, Naples; he also joins the money-changers' guild and embarks on a banking venture (interrupted by a recurrence of the plague in 1400). Because his correspondence and books of account survive, we have an extremely accurate view of his daily life and outlook. Like greater men, he invests his surpluses in land around Tuscany and builds a private house in Prato. He keeps a low profile for fear of heavy taxation, and though rich, lives frugally; but like all merchants, he has a certain fastidiousness in clothing. To welcome an old friend he orders a good chicken and a bottle of wine, and notes down the outlay. He works from dawn to night, and demands the same from his score or so of employees, chides inattention to detail, records everything in his double-entry books. A good Christian, he judges the monks and friars very unsatisfactory custodians of charity; at his death he wills his fortune to good works, but not at their hands. His house, which is well equipped, boasts several sacred pictures and frescoes, supplied by local talent; this is as normal as owning silver forks or painted store-chests, and in any case while in Avignon Francesco has dealt in religious pictures specially imported from Florence. But—and here is the point that catches the eye—he is not remotely interested in what these pictures represent (he leaves that to his factor), and to him they are not even an investment: like other chattels he values them simply at cost, and Iris Origo notes that cost is chiefly accounted for as the price of materials consumed. He treats the painters he hires as the artisans they in fact are; he even sacks them on the job on one occasion, and is sued by their guild for unpaid wages. This quite wealthy citizen is no worshipper of the arts; he is, though, very close to the ideals of austerity, money-seeking, and level-headedness, which dominate Florence and which are similarly exhibited by another run-of-the-mill Florentine, Giovanni Morelli (1371–1441) who leaves behind him a chronicle of his times for the edification of his son. In this world, art is artefact and artists are artisans. Yet as early as 1446 Brunelleschi will be given a state funeral in the Duomo, the dome of which he built, and by the end of the century the

republic, for all its wealth and prestige, is thus in 1400 politically unstable and its social stratification is under a number of strains arising both from the international economy and from its own constitution. In the course of the century the former become more serious; but the latter are disguised or transformed entirely to the benefit of a coalition of magnates dominated by Giovanni's son Cosimo and (in time) his great-grandson Lorenzo the Magnificent.

It is essential to see the Renaissance in this setting: at the outset it concerns only a tiny sector of the population. To perceive this we have only to look at the life and world of one particularly well-documented middling citizen in Florence—Francesco di Marco (1335–

Florentine-trained Michelangelo and Leonardo will behave, and wish to be treated, as though they are no less to be respected than their exalted patrons. From a starting-point in this down-to-earth, indeed rather philistine, world of Florentine business life, what path leads to Michelangelo?

Modern Romans

The Florentine Renaissance has its first point of departure in book-learning, that is, the study of classical Latin. This learning is channelled in particular ways. At the start, there is the motive of patriotism. The city claims to be a *Roman* foundation: independent, it takes pride in being heir to the Roman Republic and its liberties. This is not a matter of indifference to diplomats dealing with the pope or emperor, or to lawyers who look to Roman law when elaborating the civil codes of the republic, or even to the prosperous merchants: unlike Francesco, who has come up the hard way, Morelli does urge his son to read Virgil and Seneca. Further, learning chimes in with the cult of that virtuous republican lawyer Cicero, a cult already advanced by Petrarch and now taken up in a big way by Florentine lawyers and municipal officers. One of their number, Poggio Bracciolini, outlines a republicanism for virtuous citizens (which is also anti-noble) at the same time as he promotes the rediscovery of Plutarch and Stoic philosophy and selected Roman institutions: all portray and sanction an (ideal) democracy, a dream to guide the citizen. Leonardo Bruni (died 1444) touches on a fruitful extension of the idea when he claims to see Florence as a 'modern Athens'. Rectitude and austerity are marvellous ideals for city magistrates to adopt and recommend to disgruntled sections of the community (to say nothing of tax-avoiders like Francesco). They can even be applied in a practical way. When Cosimo de' Medici prematurely builds himself too fine a palace, it is a pretext for rivals led by a faction of the wool magnates to have him banished as a threat to the republic (1433). A new Alcibiades? A dictator in the making? (How right they are . . .)

The city's ancient roots have thus a practical value; they are ideologically useful. They also authenticate the secular nature of the regime. At the same time, cultivating the classics need not imply any hostility to the established institutions of the Church. (In Florence this is for obvious reasons important. By contrast, in the kingdom of Aragon which is at loggerheads with the papacy over southern Italy, classical learning can be pointed in other directions, and one of Aragon's leading scholars, Lorenzo Valla, applies his command of Latin to show that the pious 'Donation of Constantine', by which the Church claims secular authority, is based on a text which is, to put it bluntly, a gross forgery.)

Above all, the cult is 'modern', fashionable among Florentine magnates, their entourage, the legal officers of the republic; and once this fashion sets in, it takes on a momentum of its own and a character it has not had before. Niccolo Niccoli (1346–1437), son of a wealthy merchant, amasses a large library of classical manuscripts; in his later years he advises Cosimo de' Medici on the creation of an even more magnificent one. Leading citizens set up discussion groups—prominent are Bruni, Niccoli, Filelfo from the university, Toscanelli the mathematician, the learned Traversari (in whose monastic school Cosimo studies Latin and Greek texts). From these divers activities there slowly emerges the conclusion that ancient learning must be rebuilt anew. The medieval university is hardly suitable for this job though it has its share of sound scholars, and indeed the first chair of Greek in the West. So the self-appointed lay scholars set to work to translate Plutarch and Plato into Latin and to retranslate Aristotle: more carefully than ever before, and from carefully sought-out 'good' manuscripts. When in mid-century Cosimo de' Medici creates his library and academy he is simply following—but with spectacular resources—a trend that has already set in strongly.

From this (still quite narrowly based) turning to classical antiquity a number of connected trends branch out—one is tempted to say, 'logically'. For example, the élitist taste for fine literary style, already visible in Petrarch's admiration for Cicero and scorn for medieval, and especially French, Latinity, is much extended, and Florentine ambassadors are urged to study and adopt the eloquence of Cicero, as though this were in some sense a badge of republican virtue. From the schools, mathematics makes a different kind of contribution to the search for classical regularity and principles: optics, mechanics, natural philosophy are not neglected. The search for ancient science also unearths surprising treasures: Poggio rediscovers the old treatise *de Architectura* of Vitruvius in the faraway monastery of St. Gall, Niccoli locates a virtually 'complete' Pliny. But even more importantly, under the eye of what we shall from this point on call 'humanists'—devotees of the humane studies, the *bonae litterae* (*belles-lettres*) of antiquity—new kinds of impulse to *science* encounter and partly merge with the *arts* of the workshop. To this we now turn.

The typical painter of fourteenth-century Florence makes *religious* pictures: for Francesco di Marco, for churches and monasteries, for the guilds or *Arti*. The

47 Filippo Brunelleschi (1377–1446), Foundling Hospital, Florence, 1419

The elegant portico of Brunelleschi's Foundling Hospital, with its slim Corinthian pillars, roundels, discreet pilasters, and classical fenestration, is offered as a model of 'Roman' style. But is it truly that? Nikolaus Pevsner has argued that beneath the apparent novelty is a more profound fidelity to Tuscan Romanesque (compare plate 45).

painter is himself an ancillary in the city's guild of apothecaries (sculptors are attached to the bricklayers and architects to the carpenters); he has a workshop, apprentices, and a rather lowly status. He confronts a range of patrons who tell him what they want, and what to put in the picture. From *some* great commissions he can however acquire a reputation; there is even a tiny chance, perhaps one in a thousand, that he may become really celebrated, like Giotto in the past, commanding a large workshop and notable rewards. Now

one effect of the new passion for antiquity is to subvert this relation of patron and obedient artisan. Poggio, for example, compiles a *descriptio*, or list, of ancient Roman monuments, the imposing ruins of the Eternal City; Brunelleschi and Donatello even make special visits to Rome to study them. But who can apply their lessons to Florence? And how? Not the patron. It turns out that new ways of thinking by the artist himself, not just imitation or dexterity, are involved.

We see this very clearly in the case of Brunelleschi. For this educated goldsmith cannot be told simply to go and copy a Roman temple. Commissioned to rebuild the Foundlings' Home in Florence (1419) he does indeed provide elegant Corinthian pillars and arches and pediments, but the result is not a copy of anything seen in Rome. The dome of the cathedral, which he undertakes in 1420 (with a fine gesture of independence in refusing to explain to the commissioning wool guild how he proposes to do it), is not in the least a Roman feature, for all his much vaunted study of the great dome of the Pantheon; nor could it very well be. It is an original invention with an unforgettable profile; and the remarkable double shell (a Gothic device) solves the engineering problem of span in a way unexampled in antiquity. Again, when Brunelleschi builds Santo Spirito in 1436, he designs it as a basilica, with Corinthian columns and classical motifs; but what causes it to be hailed as a masterpiece is the application of the old in a new rationality and spatial harmony overall: this is what is unprecedented, and it is not the result of copying ruins. Brunelleschi has nothing of the compliant artisan about him; he is an inventor.

Furthermore, as a talented engineer and all-round creative artist the new challenges encourage him to exchange ideas within the intellectual circles of the day; for example with Toscanelli, regarding the wonderful science of perspective, in which geometry, optics, construction, design, and, yes, painting too, are all implicated. And from such discussions the whole new discipline or dimension of perspective enters into the art of Donatello, and Masaccio, and Paolo Uccello, and Ghiberti himself, and is put to the service of 'classicizing' patrons—in Masaccio's frescoes of the Brancacci Chapel (1425–27) and Uccello's in the Chiostro Verde (1430s), or in the reliefs of the new (third) set of doors made by Ghiberti for the Baptistery (1425–52).

This kind of emergent novelty has not been bargained for by Florence's officials and magnates: how could they possibly anticipate it? The point is that it is artists who by their attainments can now distance themselves from the common artisans, of whom no such things are expected.

Though we have offered Brunelleschi and architecture as a first instance, similar features characterize sculpture and painting. The visual arts may not yet have joined the liberal arts; even so, they are on the way to being distinguished from the mechanic arts. Thus Donatello, aside from being one of the early enthusiasts of perspective, is the first man since the fall of Rome to master the process of casting an equestrian statue in bronze, and in his representation of the human figure captures the noblest forms of which Roman naturalism is capable. Uccello's experiments in per-

48   Donatello (1386?–1466), *David*, 1430–2. Bronze, height 62¼ in (158 cm). Florence, Museo Nazionale del Bargello

To the modern eye a helmeted nude is a trifle disconcerting. Nevertheless, Ghiberti's ex-pupil Donatello has clothed the Bible's most secular hero with something already approaching a classical grace.

49   Giotto (1276–1337), *The Return of the Virgin*, fresco in the Scrovegni Chapel, Padua, 1305–10 (?)

Giotto, the giant who opens a great age for Florentine painting, executes commissions for some of the city's trading magnates, and eventually receives the post of superintendent for the Cathedral project. In this earlier work he decorates the entire interior of a small chapel in Padua with frescoes of the Gospel, Saints' lives, and a Last Judgement, where he contrives to fuse reverence and humaneness with an amazing freshness.

50   Antonio Pollaiuolo (1433–98), *The Annunciation* (detail), *c.* 1470. Oil on panel, 59 × 68½ in (150 × 174 cm). Berlin (West), Staatliche Museen

Framed in a classical window, Pollaiuolo has inserted a panoramic view of Florence, identified by Giotto's campanile and Brunelleschi's dome, in a setting of the Arno valley. What also catches the eye is a highly conscious application to this corner of a much larger composition of the 'new' perspective, as codified by Alberti.

52   Lorenzo Ghiberti (1378–1455), *The Meeting of Solomon and Sheba*, **1425–52. Detail of second bronze door. Florence, Baptistery**

This panel from Ghiberti's second pair of doors for the Florence Baptistery, depicting Solomon and the Queen of Sheba, has a new disciplined monumentality that is derived from the lately introduced 'classical' science of perspective; the ageing master shows himself fully 'up-to-date'.

51 (left)   Masaccio (1401–28?), *The Expulsion of Adam and Eve from Paradise*, *c.* **1425–7. Fresco. Florence, Santa Maria del Carmine**

The enigmatic and short-lived Masaccio, decorating the Brancacci Chapel in the Carmine church of Florence, develops a standard of monumental and austere classicism whose grandeur will not be equalled by three generations of painters in Florence (many of whom, including Piero della Francesca and Michelangelo, nevertheless study his work attentively).

53 (right)   Donatello, *Equestrian statue of the Condottiere Gattamelata*, **1447–53. Bronze, height 122 in (310 cm). Padua, Piazza del Santo**

Executed some 20 years after his David, Donatello's statue of the mercenary commander Gattamelata is the first life-size equestrian bronze to be cast in Europe since pagan antiquity. Its influence is prodigious and in an age to come, the equestrian statue will be a highly prized symbol for the expression of personal power.

spective become so absorbing to him that they seem to have ended up as a most uncraftsmanlike theoretical obsession. Ghiberti, at heart a most traditional if outstanding master, will write a Latin treatise on sculpture, leaning heavily on antiquity. From 'the other side', the distinguished humanist Alberti will not disdain to do the same for painting and architecture at the same time as he tries his hand at designing a 'Roman' church exterior at Rimini and a palazzo in Florence.

The first generations of the Florentine Renaissance thus feature a comprehensive programme for the revival of antiquity, and in the process they actually liberate powers of artistic creation and bring about shifts in the identity and status of intellectuals and artists and workshop masters—and also a shift in the balance between secular and religious in things of the spirit. Taken all together, this movement is already one of broader significance than earlier appeals to antiquity.

From wool to silk

No sooner is the new revival of things Roman fairly under way, however, than the society in which it is hatched undergoes a rather crucial change: the failure of Cosimo de' Medici's opponents to enforce his exile marks the start of a new era, in which he and his clan and friends completely dominate the city. On his return, to great popular acclaim, in 1434, the traditional wool industry is already in decline; the Medici have no great interest in trying to reverse the trend. We notice though that the silk industry prospers. This contrast is both political and symbolic. Florence is dominated less and less by the old key trades and related crafts that have founded her greatness, and, over time, their workshops are ruined; more and more she lives by less indigenous trades and international connections and banking. And symbolically, silk stands for a less humdrum way of life, more gentility—a gentrification of the magnates. Cosimo is careful never to accept a special dignity or outstanding public office, and his manner is studiously unassuming; but, like Augustus in ancient Rome, he is the real governor of the republic, acting through a broad coalition of business and adherents (some devoted, some bribed) and popular support against typed 'pro-noble' groups. When he dies, the city votes him the title of *Pater Patriae* (Father of the Fatherland). While he lives, he conducts the republic's foreign policy and also shapes, with outward blandness but real firmness, its internal affairs, subtly narrowing the scope for anything approaching true 'republican liberties', while putting his family in a position of unassailable power. The earlier balances within oligarchic government, against all appearances, are eroded. The visible sign of this is, precisely, an irresistible temptation to 'gentility': an increasing splendour in high life, the style of a prince surrounded by parvenu supporters.

It is not the case that these social pretensions, and the lavish display that accompanies them, are necessarily or even solely channelled into giving a further hoist to the cults of classical antiquity. Cosimo's father Giovanni, it is true, has been somewhat closer in style to Francesco di Marco than to his own son; the Medici now pour their wealth into public works and private commissions on a grand scale, and much of what issues from this, though not all, undoubtedly bears the mark of classical lessons. Cosimo has Donatello sculpt a *David* for his palace; he commissions Brunelleschi for the churches of Santo Spirito and San Lorenzo (the latter being eventually taken over for a Medici family shrine); he puts work in the direction of Fra Angelico, Fra Lippo Lippi, Domenico Veneziano, Paolo Uccello, Antonio

54   Jacopo da Pontormo, *Portrait of Cosimo Medici*, 1519. Panel, 35⅜ × 28⅜ in (90 × 72 cm). Florence, Galleria degli Uffizi

Carved on the monumental chair is his name, with the letters 'P.P.' (pater patriae, 'father of his country'), the Roman style bestowed by a grateful (or compliant) Florence at his death. With only that hint and a symbolic laurel to alert us, this striking portrait dwells on the 'simplicity' affected by the greatest of the Medici. The face attentive, deeply thoughtful; the old man's hands unaffectedly clasped; even his attire is that of any other Florentine merchant.

Pollaiuolo. With such patronage no wonder that masterpieces are forthcoming! And within his palace, the *cortile* becomes virtually a classical museum—the first such museum—crowded with busts and medallions and sarcophagi. And it will be the same with his son and his grandson, in the second half of the century.

But at the same time, the Florentine élite is strongly aware of the tastes and values favoured by other European élites, and especially those with whom it deals:

55 Paolo Uccello (1397–1475) *St. George and the Dragon, c.* **1460. Oil on canvas, 22¼ × 29¼ in (56.5 × 74.3 cm). London, National Gallery**

This small painting, about which little is known though it seems to date from about 1460, reminds us that until this period secular subjects are rarely depicted except in manuscripts and tapestries, or on furniture (and particularly the sides of chests – cassoni). It may also serve as a corrective, here, to the idea that Florentine painters are taken up with a craze for antique themes and forms. However, even in a scene of chivalry, with its Gothic 'damsel in distress', strangely juvenile hero, conventional rocky cavern, crescent moon and bubbly cloud, Uccello's devouring passion for perspective manages to peep through.

those of Burgundy and of the Low Countries, a brilliant aristocracy and a wealthy bourgeoisie respectively. Not only does Ghiberti's work exhibit at the start an infiltration of classical motifs—and perspective!—into the essentially international 'Gothic' idiom in which he has grown up; Uccello's *St. George* attacking the dragon (in two separate treatments) is in no sense a classical but a chivalrous theme; Gozzoli's magnificent adornment of the Medici palace chapel relies upon an entirely 'Gothic' conventionalized background of jagged mountain. Again, for great celebrations the most aristocratic kind of entertainment is a tournament, the typical form of display by European, and especially French, nobilities: in due course the Medici regale the city with a magnificent tournament (1465), in which Cosimo's short-lived grandson Giuliano plays a brilliant and gallant role, more befitting a prince's son than the heir to a

56   Leone Battista Alberti (1404–72), Tempio Malatestiano, Rimini, 1450–5

The learned Florentine expatriate Alberti is not content to write Ten Books of Architecture *(1435), but also designs a number of edifices and has executed at any rate one strictly uncompromising Roman monument (begun 1450). The Tempio Malatestiano (it owes its name to the local tyrant of Rimini) results from encasing an existing church. The exterior is never finished.*

banking house. Most tellingly of all, Aby Warburg has demonstrated that for all the classical exhibition in the *cortile*, when it comes to furnishing their private apartments the Medici lean rather towards the tastes of a European market, not a classical revival at all. They have Flemish tapestries, for preference, and other equipment similarly inspired, without any objection to the medieval figure representations that adorn them; the secular portraits of donors in the religious paintings they commission have a down-to-earthness more strongly evocative of the realities of trade in present-day Florence (or Bruges) than of Roman senators.

Ancient Rome, in short, is not allowed to block the nobiliary pretensions of the triumphant magnates; nor does it exclude a taste for luxuries brought in from the lands with which the Medici have the most mundane relations. But at the same time it does provide a continuing challenge for artists to assimilate and hybridize and blend the pagan and the practical, chivalry and antiquity, religious and secular values: and down to the generation of Botticelli this process is ever present.

Florence in mid-fifteenth century becomes a very brilliant city indeed. The greatest families follow the Medici example and build superb palaces; even if they

57   Leone Battista Alberti, Palazzo Rucellai, Florence, 1446–51

A 'humanist' is 'universal' by transgressing the demarcation lines of the guild. For the Rucellai family, Alberti also tries his hand at designing a graceful and well-proportioned town mansion. Noticeable features are the pilasters (recapitulating the classical orders) and a significantly elaborate cornice to emphasize the compositional unity of the elevation.

58   Story of Alexander (detail), tapestry woven in Tournai, c. 1459. Rome, Palazzo Doria

The Medici involve themselves as bankers to the Duke of Burgundy. This brilliant (but eventually disastrous) link is reflected in their taste for Burgundian tapestries of the richest quality—an aristocratic adornment for palace walls. 'Noble' subjects are often hunting scenes or sequences from medieval romance: here, the widely known Romance of Alexander.

cannot match the scale of Cosimo's spending, earlier frugality goes by the board. Critics have gibed that Florence embarks on a programme of extravagant 'high culture' just at the time that her economic power is fading, and this is true. But the programme does serve two practical purposes. There is obviously an internal political one—to dazzle and delight the crowd. But there is also an external one. Cosimo conducts a very active foreign policy which affords the republic advantages greater than her economic power warrants; and his efforts in this field are backed by what today would

be called cultural diplomacy. The first major example of this comes in 1439, with his success in bringing to Florence the adjourned Council of Ferrara: a summit conference for which (not for the first time, but, sadly, the last) the Eastern emperor has journeyed west to seek help against the Ottoman threat and to hold out the prospect of union between the Eastern and Latin Churches. The pope, Eugenius IV, has already taken refuge in Florence from civil disorders in his own city; now by bringing the whole council across Italy to Florence, Cosimo treats the world and the man in the street to the

59   Benozzo Gozzoli (1420–97), *The Journey of the* *Magi* **(detail),** *c.* **1459. Fresco. Florence, chapel of the Medici-Riccardi Palace**

In the chapel of the Medici Palace, Gozzoli's huge Journey of the Magi *celebrates the cultural achievements of his patrons. Recalling the Council of 1439, the first two kings (not shown here) are represented as the Eastern Patriarch and the Emperor John Palaeologus; the third king, a beautiful youth, is Lorenzo the Magnificent, attended on horseback by (left to right) his brother Giuliano, great-uncle Lorenzo, grandfather Cosimo and father Piero. Behind them are supporters, artists, learned men: Ficino, Pulci, Bessarion, Plethon . . . Gozzoli identifies himself in the throng (between two bearded Greeks) by printing his name on his cap.*

sight of an emperor, a patriarch of Constaninople, and their attendant train, as well as the pope and a host of Western prelates, accepting his hospitality, honouring the republic by their presence, and assembling to debate a momentous world issue in the city's newly completed Duomo. The immediate triumph is great—an apparent reunion of all Christendom—even if Palaeologus' submission is promptly repudiated by his subjects, and (in the absence of any help) Constantinople eventually falls to the Turkish conqueror in 1453.

The secondary effects of the council are no less triumphal. Painters like Fra Angelico and Benozzo Gozzoli are struck by the sight of the exotic Eastern robes parading through the streets, symbols of an unchanging high antiquity. The scholars too are excited, by the coming together of Greek specialists, by the contact with men so close to the world of antiquity: Rome in her Eastern form, and behind Rome, Hellas. Among the patriarch's delegation one Gemistos Plethon is a characteristically intriguing figure: Platonist, Neoplatonist, Pythagorean, theosophist, polymath, his conversation excites respect. He seems inclined to make his home in Florence, *the new Athens*, as he styles it; all that lacks here is a Platonic Academy . . . Cosimo takes up the idea, ponders it, decides to create one. It will require a central organizing personality, to bring gentlemanly students together and conduct studies: who is available? His choice falls on Marsilio Ficino, a talented young priest in his own household, and Ficino is put on to learn Greek at once (the detail is instructive—there is not a ready choice of suitable candidates, Greek being still a rare accomplishment). In due course, evidently, the Academy is formed.

Platonists and humanists

At this point we may ask, why a Platonic Academy? One answer that has been given is that Plato expounds social reaction and an obscurantist metaphysic, that reactionary rulers prefer their philosophers to encourage contemplation rather than an active role for citizens, and that thoughtful men who give up hope of influencing events are prone to become Platonists. (Certainly the swing of attention away from a 'Roman Republic' ideology of civic virtue has been noticed in Florence after 1440 or so.) Another attempt to clarify the choice would dwell on the fact that compared with the severe Aristotle, who still dominates all faculties of the university, Plato seems to promise much more excitement, more to be discovered, and at first sight more profundity—besides being much more aristocratic and appealing in style and manner. Whatever the deep motives (if any), this much is certain: that Cosimo is not deliberately restricting the options for his friends. At any rate he shows himself entirely eclectic in another typical Medici venture stimulated by the great gathering of the council: his library. Launched on the idea by Niccoli, Cosimo proceeds to use all the new contacts, the international network of his agents, and almost unlimited wealth, to found a collection (1444) that will materially aid knowledge of the ancient world—knowledge in any and all of its aspects, a grandiose gesture. For a collector, he lives at a fortunate moment. Early manuscripts of Cicero's letters, of the *Commentaries* of Caesar, two manuscripts of Aeschylus, a tenth-century copy of Pliny, the *Pandects* of Justinian; these are only a few of the extraordinary treasures brought together. Since the great library at Alexandria there has been nothing to equal this as an instrument for scholars. Pope Eugenius IV, returning to Rome as the project starts, is fired by the dream of doing the same thing; his dream is eventually realized by the creation of a Vatican library (1475) under Sixtus IV. With such instruments, what we recognize as standards in critical scholarship begin at last to be possible, and new editions begin to be produced, of a quality (from now on) that earlier generations have never aspired to, or even conceived.

The Church's dominance over learning, it is clear, is radically undermined in this process of academy and library development. Not overtly or at once: Ficino is an ordained priest; the papal Curia is not averse to humanists (the great Alberti is in fact a papal official); even the venomous, but talented, Valla is appointed an Apostolic Secretary in Rome in 1447. But by implication secular learning has made a large hole in the monopoly. As part of the transformation, there has also come into shadowy existence a new class of person— the humanist, the dedicated scholar. He is not identified with any particular profession; most emphatically he is not a guildsman. As time goes by, he may be noble or base, native or foreign, clerk or layman, but his learning becomes a kind of membership card to a respectable fraternity that transcends such barriers. Only up to a point, of course; a man who can withhold your living or put you in prison, or worse, is not truly your brother, even if he collects libraries. Yet even so, alongside the great Benedictine or Franciscan orders of the Church, there is now something even wider and looser, a confraternity that furthers the cult of Greek and Roman antiquity, and the values quarried from it, uniting men of goodwill—and in due time also dividing them. And this is certainly a second great novelty that marks off the Renaissance from its predecessors.

Where Cosimo founds, his grandson Lorenzo builds. He is just as unassuming as his grandfather, and no less lavish. He commissions a *David* from Verrocchio, and the *Boy with a Dolphin*; he puts Ghirlandajo to work on the frescoes of Santa Maria Novella and Santa Trinita. His bedroom is adorned with Uccello's *Battle of San Romano*. He founds a new university at Pisa. Deeply committed to public affairs, he is also extraordinarily well-educated, a cultivated poet, enthusiastic to raise the Tuscan language to brilliance and prestige; he finds time to surround himself with learned and brilliant men of all descriptions: Politian his close friend, writer, humanist, Pulci, who produces an ambitious epic poem *in Italian* (*il Morgante Maggiore*), Landini, Ficino, and

60   Piero della Francesca, *The Flagellation of Christ*, 1455. Tempera on panel, 23¼ × 32⅛ in (59 × 81.5 cm). Urbino, Galleria Nazionale delle Marche

Piero della Francesca has little contact with Florence, apart from a short stay in early life; he never comes within its circles of patronage. Yet his work, like that of Uccello in Florence, is permeated with the intellectual fascination of that city's speciality, perspective; and his Flagellation, *among other things, exhibits an extraordinary virtuosity in the use of the new 'science'.*

many others. *Belles-lettres* are a new dimension of this evolving Medici patronage, and also a new start in self-conscious vernacular literature, dignified by the attention of a cultivated élite, and soon to be copied all over Europe.

At this summit of the power and patronage of the Medici clan, the same remark applies as in the generation of Cosimo: there is nothing simple in the blending of rediscovered antiquity into the culture of this central-ized city élite. In painting there remain all the traces of the northern connection: Ghirlandajo can marry religious themes and Roman settings and gestures, and pious figures borrowed from Flemish devotional art—*and* also figures which are strangely evocative of perhaps Roman models. We shall never know exactly how they are perceived by their first observers—whether as syncretist masterpieces or as works having the character, style and richness of shot silk. But in this process of fusing the antique with the cosmopolitan present, there are stranger things than the composition of diversely inspired art styles on a single canvas.

Lorenzo and some of his relatives and friends keenly support the academy, from which great things begin to emerge. Publication is no problem: Lorenzo has brought together a large squad of copyists, pays for all . . . After due preparation, Ficino translates Plato into Latin. This is a large task, and also an epoch-making one; Plato at last becomes available in all his inscrutable richness to a western readership. Ficino proceeds then to weighty commentaries on Plato, and on Plotinus too, and the pseudo-Dionysius. Our humanist no more distinguishes between their various doctrines than Plethon has done: indeed his picture of Platonic ideals is elevating and very beautiful and mystical, more Alexandrian than Athenian. Allegorizing is carried to extremes of ingenuity. Ficino also manages to weave into his Platonism a firm belief in planetary powers, Pythagorean harmonies, and practical astrology. Because of this, a charge of heresy is actually preferred against him in Rome, and only averted by powerful friends there; he is left undisturbed to carry on his clerical duties, correspond with all and sundry, attend the Medici, and their friends—and cast their horoscopes. He also takes part in the joyous little parties and country picnics where initiates of the academy celebrate Plato's 'birthday' and indulge in like pieties of a not very obviously religious nature.

Sandro Botticelli is just as good a Christian as Ficino, and a no less devoted admirer of the Medici clan (as we see from a famous *Adoration*). It is hardly any wonder then that this great religious painter turns to producing work to reflect the academy's tastes; though it is surprising to see the way that influence sometimes operates. For example, there is the strangely stark and allegorical *Minerva and the Centaur*, whose allusiveness we may well not fully fathom; at least it is plain that the goddess of wisdom is pacifying the mythical being who is half-brute, half-man, enigmatic. More remarkable still is the *Primavera* which, thanks to the researches of E. H. Gombrich, can now be seen as quite strictly 'Platonic': this is the artist's working-out of a task evidently prescribed to him by Ficino and his friends—a canvas devoted to the edification of Lorenzo di Pierfrancesco de' Medici in his country house. The popular title is of course misleading; the meaning of the painting is much deeper. What it exhibits is Venus (symbol of humanity, not of carnal love) presiding over an extensive and not particularly composed allegory of Graces, Hours, Flora, Mercury, Zephyr: but what are they all assembled for? We have to know that Botticelli is evoking a scene taken from the late Latin author Apuleius, who describes this court; and only initiates of this Platonizing literature will know that in the painting Venus is represented as awaiting the arrival before her of Paris (completely absent from the scene). As such, the work commissioned of Botticelli is 'really' a hymn to spiritual beauty: even the features of Venus' very beautiful head are subordinated to that allegory. Is this spirituality Christian or pagan? Ficino would certainly say 'both Christian *and* pagan (or rather, Platonic)'. At all events

61   Piero della Francesca (*c.* 1416–92), *Resurrection*, late 1450s. Fresco. Sansepolcro, Pinacoteca

We may doubt (but never know) whether the climate of taste around the Medici would have encouraged the disposition in which Piero conceives and executes his greatest religious masterpiece, in his native town. Here the majesty and visionary power of the central figure rise clear away from the lower part of the composition and its sleeping soldiery (partly Romanized); and if the torso of Christ owes something to classical modelling, the pose does not; nor does the head.

Botticelli has produced something which belongs to no conventional style or genre—and is certainly not anchored in the antique tradition. Indeed, the *Primavera* has challenged scholarship not only because of its recondite allusiveness, but because in style—once again— Botticelli seems to be elaborating a very peculiar fusion; the classical sources are perhaps being rendered by details echoing Roman models, but it is equally possible that the animation of gauzy drapery and hair flowing in the breeze (so very unnaturally) are following a manner of late Gothic stylization.

What are we to make of the Platonic Academy? It would not merit prolonged attention here were it not that in the century to come 'Platonism' develops as a

**62   Sandro Botticelli
(1444–1510),** *The Adoration
of the Magi,* **c. 1477.
Tempera on panel, 43¾ ×
52¾ in (111 × 134 cm).
Florence, Galleria
degli Uffizi**

*The same theme as in plate
59, and the same clan; but a
different art. While Botticelli's
Cosimo kneels before the Holy
family, with Piero in front and
Giuliano in rapture on the
right, Lorenzo (extreme left)
leans on a sword disregarding
both the scene, the embrace of
his friend Politian, and the
addresses of the picture's donor:
his attention is directed to his
father. Is this a late allusion
(1477?) to Lorenzo's prowess
at the time of the Pitti
conspiracy ten years earlier?
Following an even graver
conspiracy in 1478, Botticelli
will be commissioned to paint
effigies of the hanged
conspirators . . .*

**64   Sandro Botticelli, *Minerva and the Centaur*, c. 1488.
Tempera on canvas, 81½ × 58¼ in (207 × 148 cm).
Florence, Galleria degli Uffizi**

*This allegory is an altogether experimental treatment of a
Neoplatonic theme. Disregarding landscape and cornice-like
architecture of rock, we see a by no means 'classical' Minerva,
entwined in garlands and with flowing tresses framing a face of
other-wordly compassionate beauty; the enormous weapon cradled
in her hand cannot be innocent of meaning. The Centaur, bow at
rest, has the doleful head of a biblical prophet. This conflict of
wisdoms – is it pagan? Christian?*

**63 (left)   Sandro Botticelli, *La Primavera*, 1478.
Tempera on canvas, 80 × 123½ in (203 × 314 cm).
Florence, Galleria degli Uffizi**

*For Lorenzo di Pierfrancesco and the Platonic Academy
Botticelli paints one of his most disconcertingly memorable works
(see p. 95). Memory (left) and Zephyr (right) cannot but distract
from the harmony of the scene; more strikingly, neither the
dancing Graces nor the dignified Flora belong to the same stylistic
world as Venus. A highly intellectual argument, not picture
composition, is what unites the free-standing figures or groupings.*

precious cult in high circles of society far outside
Florence. From an early date the academy attracts attention, even visitors and students from abroad. It is not a
quest for salvation in the next world—rather, it expresses an ideal of personal perfection in this one, very
much as Plato has appeared to recommend to his Hellenic pupils. As such it undoubtedly tends to be 'aristocratic'. It is somewhat elastic, too: if Ficino is eclectic,
what must one call his young friend the noble Pico della
Mirandola (1463–94)? Pico sets out to develop an elaborate philosophy-cum-theology of his own: Platonist,
certainly, and devoutly religious, but this time with
infusions of cabbalism picked up from study with
learned Hebraists. (The Cabbala, or Kabbalah, is the
name given to a body of Hebrew speculative and mystic
writing of Middle Eastern and Spanish origins, especially developed in Europe from the thirteenth century
onwards; the doctrine of the soul as presented in one of
its books, the Zohar, would have a peculiar appeal to
Neoplatonists.) Having satisfied himself of the solidity
of his insights, Pico makes his way to Rome to bring
about the required changes in Christian doctrine. Saved
from the charge of heresy, this time by the personal
intervention of Pope Alexander VI, and gravitating
towards new friends in Florence (Politian, Ficino), he
dies young; his name and doctrine immediately become
identified with humanism itself. In Florence the austere
Savonarola venerates him; in Germany the humanist
scholar Reuchlin (who has studied Greek in Italy) calls
him his 'master'; in England Thomas More translates
the *Life* written by Pico's brother and praises in him the
qualities of a saint . . .

Florence's spectacular outburst of antique culture
under Medici patronage arouses emulation. Where
bonae litterae are already cherished, an extended world
of scholars becomes welcome. In the wake of Ficino's
academy, educational initiative thrives. Vittorino da
Feltre's academy is set up at Mantua under princely
patronage to open the benefits of humanism to an élite
of boys *and girls*; new colleges are erected by favour of a
prince or prelate alongside the older universities, or to
form new ones—in Louvain, Milan, Alcala, Heidel-
berg, Vienna, Paris, Oxford . . .

In the face of this 'new' learning, it is interesting to
observe the frequent outbursts of hostility from the
'entrenched' corporations of learning, set in their rigid
mould. In a sense, it is the story of Abelard all over
again: what arouses mistrust is precisely what gives the
revived studies a unique character. This time, under
pretext of teaching pure Latinity and Greek language,
humanists claim as their province virtually *all* knowledge: philosophy, physics, poetry, biology, geo-

graphy, history, rhetoric, law, theology, mathematics, medicine, politics . . . Dilettantism? Mere stylistics? But many of these new men are giants of learning.

More insidiously, the breadth of the classics encourages the idea not only of a 'universal knowledge', cutting across the recognized divisions and faculties, but also of a new humanity—*humanitas*. All man's aptitudes, greatnesses, powers, come under review; and at this point the philosophy of Plato is seen to carry a dazzling further lesson: it is a call to integration. In Plato, all 'goods' are (in some manner) related to a supreme Good. In the order of the world we seek a harmony. So likewise in man: the ideal of man towards which one must strive is the harmonious integration of all that of which he is capable. This is Plato's ideal, and if it can be enacted into reality, we can begin to talk of aristocracy—rule by the best. These principles recur in most humanist aspiration. Lorenzo is 'Magnificent' because he is accomplished in so many ways: in poetry and management, philosophy and physical prowess, public life and friendship. His 'magnanimity' is not just a matter of spending. (Undoubtedly it is this many-sidedness which in retrospect puzzles Machiavelli, the Florentine chronicler of the republic and student of princes: he cannot quite see Lorenzo as a typical wielder of *power*). It is likewise admirable for men to be versatile, able to turn their attention creatively to any skill that may lie within them. The examples of Michelangelo and Leonardo as 'universal' men are familiar. By the same token, though we cannot demonstrate it *in extenso* in this place, the liberation of energies and curiosity which demonstrates the admirable powers of man is a *background* excitation to the tasks of scientific knowledge; such tasks are apt to break the mould of custom—it is no longer trivial or impious to wrestle with Nature, even if some of the forms taken by scientific exertion are (to our way of thinking) misconceived, as in astrology or alchemy. Sooner or later the watertight barriers between different branches of science, reinforced by medieval social custom on the basis of traditions taken over from Aristotle, are *bound* to be broken, as for example in medicine and anatomy.

Platonic too is the form given to the extraordinarily intense *friendship* between so many humanists; it appears effusive, almost sickly (to say nothing of possible overtones of Athenian homosexuality), until we perceive in it a conscious, even self-conscious, *moral* note: an exalted spiritual love for the friend's excellences. In this sense the humanist is at least an intellectual 'aristocrat', regardless of his birth. But the highest love is reserved to those who like Lorenzo succeed in combining their attainments in a 'beautiful' harmony.

That is not so easy to do; where it is achieved the highest moral value is actually an *aesthetic* one—again a Platonic theme. And a further level of beautiful integration is ideally to be expected when a devout Christian disposition is combined with the humane excellences: such at least will be the implication of Erasmus' broad humanism when added to that of Ficino. It will be movingly evoked in the sixteenth century in—of all unexpected places—Rabelais' *Fourth Book*, where the fabulous Pantagruel evolves from being a farcical giant's son into a noble, eloquent, and *pious* prince, a paragon of courtesy, a wise judge of men and manners, and yet also moved to a devout and reflective tear by the classical legend of the mariners hearing the voice calling out 'Great Pan is dead', a presumed echo of the sacrificial death of Christ.

Humanism in the age of printing

Besides patronage, two resources come to assist humanism powerfully. At the very moment that Lorenzo is mobilizing an army of copyists in Florence, printing with movable type is being invented—possibly in Mainz, where Gutenberg eventually prints his Bible. Within a generation there are printers in all major European cities. Their involvement with learning is extremely close, and their labours become as much a part of humanism as the critical study of old manuscripts. One of the first and most famous of them, Aldo Manuzio (1458–1515), is a scholar of Greek and Latin and tutor to Pico's nephews; it is Pico who finances Aldo's first steps in a great enterprise of printing (and so rescuing permanently) all the great works of Greek literature. Settling in Venice, Aldo assembles Greek-speaking assistants, perfects elegant type-faces, sets up an academy (another!) which among other things serves him as an advisory council and includes such friends as Erasmus. Again the confraternity, the network . . . In subsequent generations the direct involvement of printers in scholarship continues to be visible: in Paris and in Geneva the Estienne family combine the two interests (dictionaries, editions of Plutarch and Plato, an introduction to Herodotus); a little later still, in Protestant Leyden, Louis Elzevier will follow a similar course, assisting Hebrew scholarship and publishing a Greek New Testament (1624), Latin texts, and a whole library of chosen French and Italian 'classics' (how far we have come by then from Lorenzo's eagerness to *establish* a respected vernacular literature!). And these are only three among the most distinguished new breed of printer-humanists: there are scores of others. And obviously, printing embraces very much more than just the publication of scholarly books; its history mirrors almost the whole of European culture from the time of its invention. Yet its arrival is particularly timely for the new world of learning. Without printing, it is hard to conceive of the rapid sharing of all advances in learning (including the natural sciences) among scholars widely separated across Europe. Furthermore, with its much higher volume of production, printing gives humanism a penetrative force not hitherto imaginable. This is seen in the humanist's second resource, which this time is a living exemplar—Erasmus of Rotterdam.

Erasmus, like very few individuals in history, is a power by virtue of his personality as well as of the ideas he disseminates. An Augustinian canon, not too concerned with his vows, he towers as a scholar: his classical learning and theological acumen are both of the first order. He travels extensively and maintains, like Ficino, a huge correspondence with humanist friends in every land. But what gives him pre-eminence over others is that he is very widely known and admired; and the source of his fame (as distinct from superiority) is something actually quite modest: a collection of *Adages*, a handy little anthology of excerpts from the classics (Cicero, Homer, Plato, Plutarch), really very unpretentious—but *printed*. First issued in 1500, and then expanded and reissued over and over again in subsequent years, this work is exactly what the not very learned require to give their conversation a more educated or fashionable tone: a digest of humanism, a mass-consumption product like cookery books or travel guides in later ages. Through it Erasmus becomes a household name, a force in his own right; this is something quite new for a modern. And it is entirely due to printing.

Both in these *Adages* (which grow into short essays) and in his other, also very popular, writings, Erasmus carries a humanist's message into all corners of Europe where Latin is read. But also, on the way, he expands it slyly (the word is used advisedly) into something like a campaign of hints for the renovation of morals and, perhaps, religion. Yet another use for Greco-Latin antiquity! At this point we arrive at some sensitive issues.

On the confrontation between the ancients and the Christian faith, to begin with, Erasmus shares Ficino's belief that they *can* be fused. At the very least, the one prepares the way for the other. In one of the *Colloquies* a character comes out with the astonishing and much-quoted phrase, '*Sancte Socrates, ora pro nobis*' ('Holy Socrates, pray for us'), which in fact is only a rather

65   Albrecht Dürer (1471–1528), *Erasmus*, 1520. Charcoal, 14¾ × 10⅝ in (37.3 × 27.1 cm). Paris, Musée du Louvre
Dürer's fine sketch, executed when the much-portrayed Erasmus is at the height of his powers, shows a more tranquil—and certainly a less sly—physiognomy than other renderings of the great humanist.

striking way of expressing a view common to several of the early Church Fathers confronting Platonism. But having taken up this position, Erasmus does not, like some readers of Ficino, become imprisoned in it. He is not an intellectual snob: for him, piety and charity and prayer are more important than deep learning. And the supreme Good, whatever the doctrines of Plato or the wisdom of Socrates, is the Peace of God; knowledge is a means, not an end. It just *happens* that Socrates is an admirable guide for us to listen to, along with other virtuous and great men of ancient Greece and Rome.

But then, like Valla and unlike Ficino, Erasmus has also a combative side to him, and many hard things to say about the Church. The Vulgate Bible contains errors of translation (Erasmus's own Latin version of

ΘΕΟΚΡΊΤΟΥ ΘΎΡΣΙΣ Ἤ ὭΔΗ
ΈΙΔΎΛΛΙΟΝ ΓΡῶΤΟΝ.
ΘΎΡΣΙΣ Ἤ Ὡ̂ΔΉ.

the New Testament is also decidedly controversial); the scholasticism of the schools is ridiculous; the mendicant orders are gross and greedy, besides being obscurantist when they launch attacks on true and devout scholars like Pico's follower Reuchlin. We see the embattled humanist lending the weight of his reputation to airing religious grievances which are beginning to be especially deep-felt north of the Alps. To be sure, he never suggests a revolt against Rome; but he goes to the limit of what is 'safe' in the not very devout age of Alexander VI (Rodrigo Borgia), Julius II (the irascible fighting pope, always at war), Leo X and Clement VII (the two Medici popes). And in speaking out as he does, Erasmus links the humanist image with the aspirations of a much more straightforward and down-to-earth humanity: he expresses his horror of war, his concern for a more humane and sensible attitude to children and their education, and above all the passionate conviction that theological wrangles should not be selfishly interposed between the message of the gospel and the needs of simple uneducated souls—who, moreover, should be able to pray and worship in a tongue they understand, that is, their own vernacular, not Latin. As a result, when Luther's protest inaugurates a wave of violent dispute, reform and schism, Erasmus is blamed by some for subversion, by others for hanging back: it is the usual fate of rather subtle and inwardly detached spirits of his kind. But his evangelical humanism has had time to spread, even so.

Consummations

At a certain point in time, 1494 to be precise, Florence ceases to be the focus and origin of all the novelties that come out of the transformation of learning. With the fall of the Medici in that year, what we have called their cultural diplomacy ceases to have an object; to follow its repercussions, we have to shift our attention to other places, and we shall do so in the next chapter. But before we do so it would be well to see that when the Renaissance is taken up in other parts of Europe it is already disintegrating, and ceasing to be the relatively coherent adventure that can be traced in Florence.

What is commonly called the 'High Renaissance' is, to begin with, something that concerns art historians; and in the last analysis one must say that it concerns *only* art historians. Its central subject is the range of achievements in painting and sculpture (especially) of what appear to have been some of the most prodigiously gifted individuals who have ever lived: Leonardo da Vinci, Michelangelo, Raphael. Each displays a power of invention and skill that already dazzles contempor-

67 Leonardo da Vinci (1452–1519), *Bust of a Warrior in Profile*, c. 1478. Metal-point on paper, 11¼ × 8¼ in (28·5 × 20·8 cm). London, British Museum

Leonardo's consummate virtuosity with brush or pencil serves a restless and needle-sharp mind: even in his profile of an elderly soldier the nature of physiognomy seems to be being questioned. In other sketches he has explored the idea of animal affinities in human characters; is the lion-head on the breastplate, here, hinting something about the face above?

aries; each is sought out by the greatest patrons to do precisely that—dazzle the world—and his reputation is measured by the greatness of the patron who solicits him—the duke of Milan, the republic of Florence (still), the popes Julius II or Leo X or Clement VII, or Francis I, king of France. Each is, almost indifferently, recognized as eminent not in *one* craft but in almost any that he cares to turn his hand to: Leonardo as engineer and sculptor, Raphael as architect, Michelangelo as painter, or, again, as architect, or indeed as poet, or sage. Humanism has opened the door wide.

But for all that, not very many pass through that door, except in Italy; nor are they necessarily humanists. Leonardo regrets at times his lack of Latin and Greek, for all his lofty magician-like posture. Platonism as described above does not invariably bring into existence a general category of omnicompetent artists like those just mentioned, or like old Alberti. Moreover, neither Leonardo nor Michelangelo, for all their apprenticeships in Florence under the eye of Lorenzo or Politian or Verrocchio or the aged Toscanelli, are any longer in the thrall of ancient Rome. Michelangelo can (somewhat scornfully) make statues that are passed off as antique, even in Rome. He is no doubt also stirred by the rediscovery in Rome in 1506 of the extraordinary Laocoön group referred to by Pliny—if only because for once it offers such a very *un*classical model of huge effort and tortured contours, in keeping with his own very personal tastes. But his explorations of human form, of anatomy, of suggestive forms half-emerging from the marble block, of *giant* forces, and of technical problems for their own sake, are in no ordinary sense 'classical'; his *David*, which (coming after those of Donatello and Verrocchio) the Florentines hail as surpassing any other sculpture, old or new, is already a symbol of new kinds of freedoms; and almost half a century after the *David*, his Dantesque *Last Judgement* in the Sistine Chapel is largely enfranchised from both Christian iconography and pagan example: it is unconditionally *his*.

In the case of Leonardo, the whole cast of his mind is an adventure in pitting himself against natural phenomena—in pictorial representation, in the nature and use of materials under the craftsman's hand, in the study of clouds and animals, in mechanical devices and inventions. Such exercises are often remote from the demands of patrons or the appreciation of bystanders, except when he condescends to render human forms in paint with his marvellous technique and powers of composition; these do compel astonishment and applause. Antiquity is again left behind.

The example of Raphael is different in this, that in his greatest works he appears to stand at the very summit of all that antiquity has been prompting the fifteenth

68   Michelangelo (1475–1564), *David*, 1501–4. Marble, height 171 in (434.3 cm). Florence, Galleria dell' Accademia di Belle Arti

Acclaimed by the Florentine Republic as superior to any other work of sculpture, past or present, and erected in triumph as a public monument, Michelangelo's David is—apart from its name—completely free of religious feeling, a pure embodiment of something like sculptural humanism.

century to learn. Ideal forms in their faithfully natural incarnations; eloquent composition; grandeur in a human guise. Freedom, too, from the eccentricity of Michelangelo or the lurking perversities of Leonardo, from mannered effort or persistent indulgence (however inimitable) in *sfumato* and the manipulation of shadow. It is not for nothing that for four hundred years Raphael, and not his peers, has occupied a unique position in European art as a universal yardstick.

Yet in this perfection of the classical there is built in a characteristic which, passed on from Raphael, becomes a feature which we can never believe to have troubled Donatello or Botticelli. It is eloquence. What Petrarch has admired as a controlling principle in Cicero, Raphael's contemporaries admire in him; an effortless if not spontaneous principle. But eloquence for its own sake can be singularly unconvincing. It is also hard to bring into conformity with religious expression of any devout kind; Raphael's adornment of the Vatican Palace is much more magnificent than devout. In lesser hands it becomes apparent that the Roman repertory of eloquent gesture, once mastered from statues and ornate sarcophagi, can lead on to displays of rhetoric of the most gratuitous kind. This is one of the more dangerous bequests of those models that Cosimo and others are so keen to collect—overemphatic gesture. Indulgence in it for its own sake is still regarded by Vasari (the first art historian, around 1550) as a high virtue; yet it is one of the forms of a saga of restlessness which we today are more inclined to call Mannerism; Michelangelo's deliberate dislocations of classical proportion constitute another strand of the same tendency. Mannerism with all its ramifications is on this view the other side of the hill that has been climbed in Florence by artists from the time of Donatello up to that of Botticelli. Its outcome, or one of its outcomes, will call for attention in another context.

With the death of Lorenzo, the expulsion of the Medici, and the four extraordinary years of Savonarola's domination of Florence (1494–98), the artistic preeminence of that city collapses. In consequence the centre of patronage passes to Rome and to the papacy's incomparable resources—from Sixtus IV's commencement of the Sistine Chapel (1473), on through the rebuilding and decoration of the Vatican by Raphael and others under Julius II (who also tears down the old basilica of St. Peter), and down to the painting of Michelangelo's *Last Judgement* (1533–41), commissioned by Clement VII, the same artist's eventual completion of the tomb of Julius (1542–47), and his redesigning of the new St Peter's (1546–64) for Paul III. Even so, these great works of display are not part of a

'Renaissance' as we understand that term in Florence. Leo X is indeed indulgent towards all gracious pagan things, provided they are grand and rich; but the terrible Julius II laughs at Michelangelo's suggestion that his statue should show him with a book in his hand ('a sword, rather!'). Presently all the cultural leadership that is expected of the second Florentine pope (Clement VII) is nipped in the bud by the comprehensive sack of Rome by troops of Emperor Charles V in May 1527. And in any case, by then already the vicissitudes of the papacy are tied in with a much more momentous preoccupation than any that has hitherto intruded: namely the Reformation of the Church itself, so long evaded but now forced on it by events outside Italy.

Echoes of Florence in Mantua, in Ferrara or Venice, in Milan or elsewhere are by no means inconsiderable; for all that, they are marginal to a great political upheaval which is essentially the new rivalry for domination in Italy between Charles V and the king of France. Courtly imitations of the Medici, codifications of aristocratic behaviour, patronage of the arts, the sixteenth-century revival of classical drama in these élite settings, are examples of the onward momentum of cultural ideals in a world vaguely aware of new great polarizations, both political and religious, for which there is no clear precedent. It is for this reason that the High Renaissance is not part of a larger, ecumenical, vision in which all symbolisms are marching in step. There is no 'High Renaissance' in letters—only a diffusion in which in different centres remarkable echoes can be traced to the initiative of humanists and princes.

Alongside the great symbolisms of the Vatican and St. Peter's, therefore, the adventures of thinkers take directions which are all more or less remote from the labours of artists working for the pope. One early and ill-fated example is that of Savonarola in Florence: for four years he attempts a populist retreat to religious strictness, with public bonfires of pagan frivolities. This species of Reformation within Catholicism ends with his own overthrow and death at the stake. Another line of advance we have seen in what Erasmus stands for—an evangelical humanism which echoes for a time across Europe (in Venice, Alcala, Paris, London, but not in Rome). And a third, the most jarring, has its starting point in the visit to Rome of the German monk and theologian Martin Luther, in 1511 to 1512.

Luther, still a devout Catholic, is stunned by the lack of religious fervour surrounding the Vatican and its pomps and pilgrim spots, the apparent cynicism and ostentation and pagan self-indulgence. His cultureshock is very great. In the following year is launched the campaign of 'indulgences' to raise money through-

out Europe for the further glorification of the Eternal City, strenuously marketed through what we might call franchises and direct sales forces and official launch parties. In the year (1519) that Leonardo spends his last days as an honoured guest of Francis I at Amboise, and Michelangelo is working on the sacristy of San Lorenzo (to house the last great sad Medici tombs), Luther is back in Wittenberg, refusing to withdraw his controversial topics for disputation (the 'theses') or recant his imprudent position on the theology of faith and works, his resistance to papal policy and the vanity of indulgences. Driven into a corner by local Dominican fanatics over obedience and submission to Rome, he finally resolves to kindle German patriotism and local resistance to Roman authority by an *Appeal to the Christian Nobility of the German Nation*; the *Appeal* is

69 Raphael (1483–1520) *The School of Athens*, **1511. Fresco, base 308 in (770 cm). Vatican, Stanza della Segnatura**

Called to Rome by Pope Julius II in 1508, Raphael first displays his mastery there with great paintings for the Vatican apartments. The School of Athens portrays an ideal antiquity centred on Plato and Aristotle, in an insistently 'Roman' environment, with a whole repertory of eloquent but seemly figures and bodily gesture.

70 Michelangelo, *The Last Judgement*, **1536–41. Fresco, 48 × 44 ft (14.63 × 13.3 m). Vatican Palace, altar wall of the Sistine Chapel**

In the Sistine Chapel Michelangelo's painting for the papacy culminates in a Last Judgement where his bent for the strenuous and 'terrible' is given full rein. Nowhere before has a Judge dominated by His violent gesture so spine-chilling a dies irae, and with so little of Giotto's beatific vision to compensate.

71   Lucas Cranach (1472–1553), *Portrait of Martin Luther*, 1529. Oil on panel, 14½ × 9 in (36.8 × 22.9 cm). Florence, Galleria degli Uffizi

Cranach's portrait of Martin Luther tells us little about the character of the sitter; in the simplicity of the clerical garb we see an individual, undoubtedly, of formidable obstinacy, perhaps, and with brooding eyes, but not of any very obvious spirituality. It is at least plausible to suppose, though, that the portrait of the reformer is done with a view to the curiosity of a large – and not unduly sophisticated – public. Cranach is being unusually guarded.

printed in 1520, and at once achieves an enormous circulation. Three years later a new Holy Roman emperor, Charles V, sets up the Inquisition in the Netherlands to repress followers of this excommunicated schismatic.

The beginning of the Protestant Reformation is not in any conceivable sense part of a 'Renaissance' (and it is hardly necessary to say that it has not been prefigured in any of the adventures of Florence). To humanism Luther owes the critical nose that causes him to denounce the (forged) 'decretals' on which the Church has based part of its claims to authority: that is a debt to Valla. To humanism also he partly owes the inclination to put all the emphasis of his teaching on Scripture and not on tradition, to return to authentic sources, to the undiluted testimony of a primitive state of Christianity. These lessons are convenient to his way of thinking; but in 1519, and even before, national feeling against a remote *secular* authority is much more important than humanism in articulating the powerful response of Germany to Luther's call. And when we look at the inspiration of the Reformation in the person of its originator, we see a man far more old-fashioned, far closer to medieval institutions, than Ficino or Pico or even Erasmus; a man trained in the disciplines of an old university, untouched by the influence of any academy; a member (presently ex-member) of a regular order of the Church; a teacher in a medieval university; a man who appeals to the authority of medieval powers (princes, nobles, universities) to put right the abuses he denounces in religion, rather than turn his back on them (as does his senior, the ultra-modern Leonardo); a man, finally, who taxes Erasmus with lukewarm faith.

Renaissance, humanism, and then reform: these movements are obviously not unrelated. As presented in the preceding pages, the first two are inseparably linked in their origins, though when considered in their development humanism carries a far broader range of incitements than the expressive symbolisms of Renaissance visual arts—so much so indeed that from the time of Erasmus it can be considered without reference to them. Likewise, humanism and reform are somewhat intricately interconnected; yet we do well to remember that Luther has had his antecedents within Christendom who are not dependent on the lessons of Valla, and have not had to wait for the tide that bears Erasmus, or even for the invention of printing. The relationship and the overlap are thus not tidy ones; and in the early sixteenth century each has its own constellation of ideals, which become more and more distinct, as well as its own trajectories and sequels, which we shall pick up in the next two chapters.

Behind them, though, the experience of Florence is unique; through it, as through a prism, more than through any other single place or collectivity, comes the stream of ideas, or ideals, which animate a whole century and more of cultural innovation.

Chapter 4
The Prince

'The sovereign power, whether placed in one man as in monarchy, or in one assembly of men, as in popular, and aristocratical commonwealths, is as great as men possibly can imagine to make it. And though of so unlimited a power men may fancy many evil consequences, yet the consequences of the want of it, which is perpetual war of every man against his neighbour, are much worse'. Thus the philosopher Thomas Hobbes, writing in 1651, two years after the execution of Charles I of England. Individual and uncomfortable in his views, Hobbes is in a position to look back over six generations' experience of absolutism in Europe; the period in which unified states are brought into existence under the authority of absolute monarchs. By the time he comes to write these words in his *Leviathan*, this world is so firmly established that he can imagine no alternative to absolutism save anarchy and chaos.

'Absolute' power continues to this day to raise problems for Europeans. It has its origins in the emergence late in the fifteenth century of a class of (let us be frank) predators, who exhibit a peculiar appetite for conquering their neighbours or reducing their vassals and establishing very coercive forms of rule (and notably *direct* rule) over their subjects—over and above whatever traditional powers and institutions they may find in existence from one province or duchy to another. In that process the political states of Europe take their first modern shape, with momentous consequences. One could of course imagine all sorts of alternative scenarios: a plausible one might have been a steady evolution and advance of the cities and communes of the late Middle Ages, a kind of generalization of the culture of the Netherlands (rather than of the Florentine example). But one would be wasting one's time. That is not what occurs. What does occur is the advance of a massive centralizing rule by a handful of predators.

To describe these men we shall use the general term of the age, 'prince' (an echo of the Latin title, *princeps*). The prince appears not just in one place, but all over Europe. Other names for him are: king of France, king of Aragon (later, 'Spain'), king of England, duke of Tuscany (a Medici, of course, back in power after a *coup*, and no longer the bland fellow-citizen that Lorenzo has been). Further away, there is the tsar of Russia, or—by far the greatest of all—the sultan of the Ottoman empire. Less purely autocratic (though not for want of trying) are the Holy Roman emperor, the king of Sweden, the king of Denmark . . .

In his essence, the prince is simply power incarnate in a person of tremendous determination, a machine for exercising power in as absolute and unchecked a way as he can, with all the exaltation and the 'glory' that attend such a programme—and also the dizzy risks and dark shadows: no absolute Prince, no assured state. And where he triumphs, his heirs seek to stabilize and enlarge his power.

In this process, it is not merely a weight of authority that changes. The prince creates new executive systems; he gives a twist to old laws and customs. Along with these there follow other transformations which impinge on all manner of expectations of society: new tasks to be done, therefore new groups of royal servants, new avenues for promotion; mobilization of resources—land and men and money—for royal needs (costly and conspicuous government calls for much greater revenues than those with which earlier lords have had to be content). There is ideological mobilization too: a near monopoly of prestige, the harnessing of religious morality, 'divine right', display of force, medieval precedent . . . And emphatic forms of symbolism: the display of power in monuments and public celebrations, the propaganda of the arts, the control of communication—books, the pulpit . . .

This centralizing process, easy to see now, is much less obvious when it takes place over a period as long as a century. But it has persistent features; there is a pattern; and the centre-piece is a single, dominant, focus of power.

72   Jean Clouet (d. 1540), *François I, c.* 1525. Oil on panel, 37¾ × 29⅛ in (96 × 74 cm). Paris, Musée du Louvre

To open a gallery of princes, what better representative than the urbane and magnanimous king of France, portrayed here in lavish court attire by a leading Parisian painter who – a sign of the times – comes to specialize in this line of work? The later years of the reign will be darkened; but for the moment liberality, open-handedness are the order of the day.

73   Raphael, *Pope Leo X with Cardinals Giulio de' Medici and Luigi Rossi, c.* 1518. Oil on panel, 60½ × 47 in (153.7 × 119.4 cm). Florence, Galleria degli Uffizi

Secular portraiture, as distinct from portrait-faces in religious painting or on coins or medallions, becomes fashionable in mid-fifteenth century. Rendering the most lavish and 'pagan'-inclined of the Renaissance popes, Raphael tactfully shows Leo X with a sumptuous book and magnifying lens (as befits a Medici patron).

The will to power

At the dawn of the age, an ex-secretary of the Florentine Republic records one peculiar feature of this patterning, scandalous or simply factual according to how you care to view it: the absolute prince cannot afford to be bound by the laws of private morality and Christian conduct. By the nature of his place in the world he must follow a 'reason of state' which obeys other imperatives; when need arises he must be cruel in order to be benevolent, make promises knowing that he will break them, practise hypocrisy, put appearance before reality, subordinate private virtues to that *virtù* or, as we may call it,

prowess and vigour (including ruthlessness), which is a condition of his conquering and retaining power over others. While Machiavelli fills the empty hours of his exile writing his essay on *The Prince* (1513) he has before him already the example of two extremely ruthless and successful, 'virtuous', state-building princes. He has nothing but admiration for the controlled but measureless ferocity of Louis XI of France, and equally for the consummate hypocrisy of Ferdinand of Aragon. These are true princes. With the guile of foxes and the violence of lions each had unified (more or less) a large kingdom: in Spain, Castile and Aragon are united, Granada conquered; in France, Louis brings Brittany and Burgundy

74   Hans Holbein (*c.* 1479–1543), *Henry VIII*, 1537. Oil on panel, 10 × 7¼ in (25.4 × 18.4 cm). Lugano, Thyssen-Bornemisza Collection

The 'bluff' Henry VIII seeks to play a role among the most powerful princes of the day. Holbein no doubt does as much justice to this aspect of his subject's character as he can. However, he is far too truthful to display Henry with attributes of real personal distinction or magnificence.

75   Diego Velázquez (1599–1660), *King Philip IV of Spain in Brown and Silver*, 1631–3. Oil on canvas, 78½ × 44½ in (200 × 113 cm). London, National Gallery

Of Velázquez's many portraits of his prince, Philip IV, that shown here comes close to the ideal of a court portrait by a great master-painter – the fine but not too idealized face and character, the sumptuous attire, the pose of authority . . .

into his 'web'. In England likewise, Henry Tudor is no more scrupulous in the means by which he puts an end to the barons' warring and cuts down his rivals; and in Rome, Pope Julius II turns out to be probably the most ferocious and 'virtuous' of all princes of the age.

It is commonplace that gunpowder and *artillery* have tilted the odds against baronial castles and in favour of the central power which deploys this new technology. Yet without *policy*, artillery means really very little. In England, the earl of Warwick's private military estab-

lishment has made him a threat to earlier kings; for this reason Henry VII enacts a 'Statute of Liveries' to ban such establishments in future. At the same time German cities retain their freedom in the sixteenth century

76   Titian (1477/89–1575), *Charles V*, 1533. Oil on canvas, 75⅝ × 43¾ in (192 × 111 cm). Madrid, Museo del Prado

The Emperor Charles V, master of half Christendom, has an especial admiration for the Venetian artist. In this portrait, Titian succeeds in masking his patron's somewhat small stature, and brings out the truculent man of action at the expense of imperial majesty.

77   Philippe de Champaigne (1602–74), *Cardinal de Richelieu*, late 1630s. Oil on canvas, 8⅞ × 6⅛ in (225 × 155 cm). Paris, Musée du Louvre

If there is an ample gallery of princely portraiture, that of the great servants of the Crown is three times vaster. In picking out Philippe de Champaigne's Richelieu we bring to attention an unusual career; for this prelate, serving an ineffectual master (Louis XIII of France), pursues an unswerving policy of centralized monarchical power.

by possessing strong walls and *municipal* cannon (which can also be hired out to allies). Charles VIII of France, parading an army through Italy (1494), attracts fear and wonder for his train of artillery, yet it wins him no battle. It is the business of the prince to ensure—by whatever means—that he *alone* possesses overwhelming force, a monopoly, whether in guns or soldiers or the money to hire soldiers. By itself, one piece of technology does not 'explain' the emergence of the prince or the basis of his power.

Government

Once established, by whatever means, the prince has unending labour to make good his monopoly. He delegates key duties not to illustrious vassals (that is, rivals) but to outstanding ministers whom he can raise to great

authority, yet can always control. Sometimes a minister's origins are obscure and his rise spectacular—and often, too, his fall. Such in England are Thomas Cromwell (a student of Machiavelli), Burleigh, Somerset, and Strafford; in France Sully, Fouquet, Colbert, Louvois. The Church with its pool of talent supplies Wolsey and Laud to England, Granvelle to Spain, Richelieu and Mazarin to France. The real eminence and stature of these ministers, clerical or lay, should not blind us to their true position. Louis XIV in his Testa-

Chronology for Chapter 4

1513	Machiavelli completes *Il Principe* (*The Prince*; published 1532)	*c.* 1590–9	Shakespeare writing his history plays
1515–47	Francis I king of France	1598	Edict of Nantes grants religious liberty to French Protestants (Huguenots)
1519–56	Charles V emperor	1605	First part of Cervantes's *Don Quixote* published
1520	Francis I and Henry VIII meet at Field of the Cloth of Gold	1609	Rubens appointed painter to Archdukes Albert and Isabella
1521	Diet of Worms	1611–32	Gustavus Adolphus king of Sweden
1525	Charles V defeats Francis I at battle of Pavia	1618–48	Thirty Years' War
1526	Battle of Mohacs leads to Hungary's submission to Ottoman rule	1629	Bernini appointed architect to St. Peter's; Rubens in London on diplomatic mission
1527	Charles V's troops sack Rome	1632–3	Callot's *Les Gueux*
1528	Castiglione's *Il Cortegiano* (*The Courtier*); Francis I begins building of Fontainebleau	1635	French Academy founded by Cardinal Richelieu
1532	Primaticcio begins work at Fontainebleau; Rabelais's *Pantagruel* published	1641	Descartes's *Meditations* published
1532–43	Holbein working in England under court patronage	1642	Mazarin succeeds Richelieu as chief minister in France
1540	Formal establishment of Jesuit order	1642–9	Civil War in England
1545–63	Council of Trent	1643–1715	Louis XIV king of France
1556–98	Philip II king of Spain	1648–53	Fronde uprisings in France
1558–1603	Elizabeth I queen of England	1649	Charles I of England executed
1562–98	French Wars of Religion	1651	Hobbes's *Leviathan* published
1563	Construction of Escorial begun outside Madrid	1660	Restoration of English monarchy under Charles II
1567	Netherlands revolt against Spanish rule	1661	First enlargement of Versailles by Le Vau
1568	Vignola begins building church of Il Gesù (Rome)	1667	Le Vau appointed chief architect to work on the Louvre
1571	Naval victory by combined Christian forces over Ottomans at Lepanto	1675	Mansart appointed architect to Louis XIV
1572	St. Bartholomew's Day massacre of Protestants in Paris	1683	Siege of Vienna by Ottoman Turks
1580	Philip II annexes Portugal	1685	Revocation of the Edict of Nantes
1588	Spanish Armada launched against England	1693	Couperin appointed organist to Louis XIV
1589–1610	Henry IV king of France	1701–14	War of the Spanish Succession

ment explains very frankly how he chooses his ministers: 'It was not in my interest to seek men of more eminent station . . . it was important that the public should know, by the rank of those whom I chose, that I had no intention of sharing my power . . . and that they themselves, conscious of what they were, should conceive no higher aspirations than what I chose to permit.'

Together with these powerful and always much hated agents, the prince executes his will through various new species of council, or cabinet. The Emperor Maximilian, though 'absolute' only in his own lands, uses a privy council and an 'aulic council' to manipulate the cumbersome machinery of an archaic empire. Francis I's council brings together a dozen great nobles of France, but also some lawyers who, by the reign of Henry IV, come to predominate. The Tudors have their privy council, and also a legal sub-committee of it, the court of Star Chamber by which the monarch's will can be enforced without delay or hindrance from the traditional processes of law. Philip II of Spain begins his reign with a council of grandees, or great nobles, but by the end has reconstituted it, adding special committees to supervise the various parts of a vast empire (Flanders, Italy, America, Portugal . . .); and to all these he appoints not grandees but mostly churchmen and lawyers.

In short, while elaborate old institutions of consultation and government continue to exist—the Imperial Diet, the English Parliament, the States General of France, the Cortes of Castile—they are as far as possible bypassed, or summoned only in time of dire need to vote taxes or 'aids' for war. If (as they are prone to do) they attempt to express a will of their own on such occasions, they are challenging the prince. Granvelle and Strafford repeatedly warn Philip II and Charles I (respectively) to avoid such encounters as much as possible, the former with more success than the latter.

And because the monarch's policies are more incisive than ever in the past and his authority as direct as he can make it, he cannot make do with existing 'grass-roots' administrations. He enlarges to an unprecedented extent the army of royal employees; their recruitment, again, disturbs the mould of custom. In little Florence, a new Cosimo de' Medici re-establishes the family fortunes by a forceful tyranny (1537). To effect his ambitions he requires an army of obedient clerks, so he sets to work to find men of 'humble origins' from all over Italy—not from the ranks of old Florentine families. In Spain Philip appoints minor 'nobles' (who in Castile is *not a hidalgo?*) to municipal posts, but has even more use for the *letrados* (law graduates, often from Naples, usually commoners). The case of France is more com-

plex because of the institution of *parlements*, the assemblies of lawyers who register royal edicts and administer courts in the provinces. The monarchs of the sixteenth century seek to establish one such assembly in each province, to consolidate their power. In each of them the leading posts carry noble status, and the crown has a further interest in this arrangement: it raises revenue by constantly putting additional posts up for sale. By the seventeenth century this has made the *parlements* seriously concerned at the devaluation of these posts; but in the meanwhile the crown has gone on to create further networks of its 'own' servants, its provincial intendants or commissioners, its central ministries and court of *requêtes*, to say nothing of a large household of royal officers.

In short, the prince subtly transforms the position of all his subjects, (always to his own direct advantage) and to effect this result requires all the foxy abilities celebrated by Machiavelli. He flatters his nobles or picks on scapegoats, as required. To the magnates of finance he pledges future revenues in return for cash now. To his cities he promises protection, perhaps advantages of trade. For some in every class there is a dream of particular favours. To the many there are promises of 'justice', often hollow. But what is it all for?

War

What the prince *demands from* his subjects is on a different scale from earlier exactions. For from the moment he has to exert his will, from the moment his power is truly a monopoly, all the costs of maintaining it fall upon one central treasury. If like Elizabeth of England the monarch can live for even a few years within a customary budget he is certain of his subjects' praise, even adoration. But that is a rare occurrence, primarily because of the costs of war.

War, not peace, is the normal condition of the Europe of these sovereign states. For a century and a

78   Pieter Brueghel the Elder (d. 1569), *Dulle Grete* (detail), 1562. Oil on panel, 45¼ × 63¾ in (115 × 161 cm). Antwerp, Museum Mayer van den Bergh

Among Brueghel's handful of elaborate moralizing or visionary compositions, this allegory of war is the most horrific. Dulle Grete ('Mad Meg') stalks through the world, sword in hand, stirring up madness and destruction of every imaginable (and unimaginable) kind—from the murderous soldiery (right) to the maw of Hell (left). Nightmarish eggs, imps, shrimps, fishy monsters, animated barrels sprout here and there, mingling with unspeakable acts of human savagery. All pure fantasy? Compare plate 102.

79 Jacques Callot (1592–1635), *Fruits of War*, 1633. Engraving, 8⅛ × 11¼ in (20.5 × 28.6 cm). Oxford, Ashmolean Museum

Callot's ambiguous engraving of the 'fruits' (i.e., miseries) of war exhibits the rounding-up of bandits by a regiment of musketeers—the fate of such infamous 'thieves', according to the caption, is proof that 'crime never pays'. The priest on the ladder offers absolution.

half from 1500, there is hardly a year when war is not threatening to bankrupt one or more of its princes. There are the French king's invasions of Italy, and imperial campaigns in Italy to expel the French; there are wars between Denmark and Sweden; the Ottoman invasion of the Balkans, the collapse of Hungary (1526), and the Hapsburg emperor's long struggle to ward off Turkish threats against Vienna (from 1529 down to 1699); wars in the Low Countries for Hapsburg supremacy; civil strife and religious wars in Germany; the French wars of religion; annual expeditions of Italian and Spanish navies up and down the Mediterranean, at any rate until the battle of Lepanto (1571); imperial and Spanish and Portuguese campaigns in North Africa; the Netherlands' liberation struggle against Spain; Anglo-Spanish naval wars; the expulsion of the Moriscos from Spain; the reduction and settle-

ment of Ireland; Gustavus Adolphus's wars against Muscovy and Poland; presently the Thirty Years' War across all of central Europe (1618–1648) . . .

The direct costs of all this are incalculable. A standing army's wages, a season's hire of Swiss mercenaries, the fitting out of an artillery train like that of Charles VIII (thousands of horses, a mile-long convoy of wagons, fortunes in gun-barrels and shot and powder), even the rebuilding of a fortress: these outlays call for extraordinary financing. A French army of 20,000 men lost at Pavia, an armada of 150 vessels destroyed off Britain, a stream of regiments funnelled from Naples to Antwerp to reinforce the king of Spain's authority: extravagances such as these ruin a prince's credit. Only the sultan can afford them. There is all the more need therefore, in propaganda, to insist upon the *glory* attaching to war: a peculiar and interesting idea, when one thinks about it. It kindles very particular ardours in would-be participants, especially adventurers or nobles eager for loot or a sovereign's gratitude; perhaps it helps to intimidate or encourage money-lenders; it means less to traders and least of all to peasants. However that may be, in pursuing royal glory (attack) or in surviving someone else's glory (defence) the king's treasury is invariably emptied. Louis XI of France and Henry VII of England cannily fill their vaults: their successors

Charles VIII and Henry VIII promptly empty them in the pursuit of glory.

The indirect costs of war are very much more grievous. The interruption of trade and supplies, the destruction of crops and villages, the sack of cities by famished regiments (Rome, Florence, St.-Quentin, Maestricht, Antwerp are among the victims), the slaughter of untold thousands by famine and the sword (Germany actually decimated between 1618 and 1648) . . . we cannot measure the place in men's minds of these horrors, nor the drain of such destruction upon the real wealth of Europe. The aftermath is just as bad. 'Peace' generates a fresh flood of misery: disbanded armies and homeless fugitives, the darker side of glory. In sixteenth-century Spain vagrancy reaches enormous proportions—Madrid is a sink of destitutes, of a human detritus fit only for the galleys, the *tercios* (military establishments), or the colonies. Jacques Callot's later engravings of this same detritus (*Les Gueux*) evoke a similar picture on the fringe of the Spanish wars in the Netherlands. And along with vagrancy, there is that much more elaborate form of alienation—banditry, which is an aggravated effect of the shortcomings of princely power. Wherever there are inaccessible hills or mountains, banditry is universal. In whole areas of France the king's law disappears: at the height of the religious wars the Duc de Lesdiguières operates a kind of *maquis* on the borders of Savoy. In Campania Pope Sixtus V launches a full-scale military campaign to try and reconquer his papal lands from the brigands—fruitless. In Catalonia highways are impassable, except to armed convoys. At sea the word is not brigandage but piracy: in the Mediterranean 'grey areas' it is a way of life that resumes every time the galleys withdraw to harbour. A little later, in the Caribbean—the 'Spanish Main'—the boundary between piracy and the rule of law becomes ambiguous, the stuff of legend.

Brigands, pirates: this is a world of *outlaws*—that is to say, of non-beings, men with no legal existence. It has no place on the map, or in the ordered system of the state. It does not feature in the portrayal of the prince. No tragedy, no epic, stoops to give such things a glance; the forces of (political) darkness are simply not for discussion. And yet the reality cannot go unnoticed. In Spain, of all places, even before the death of her great architect Philip II, the squalor and chaos of town and highway supply the backcloth to a new and 'alternative' kind of literary diversion, the picaresque novel. This form reaches its highest achievement in Germany, in Grimmelshausen's *Simplicissimus*, portraying the worst disorders and destructions of all, those of the Thirty Years' War. There are limits to princely influence . . .

80   Beggars and cripples; detail of drawing by Pieter Brueghel (d. 1569), 1558. Brussels, Bibliothèque Royale

The mangled detritus of war is an everyday sight in the sixteenth century, as this horrifying page of sketches by Brueghel sufficiently attests.

Liberality

Along with the costs of war the prince has the costs of reigning. His household has to eat; his great servants of state have to be gratified. The wealth heaped by Henry VIII on Cardinal Wolsey allows the latter to build two palaces, endow a college, support a lavish court of his own, and aspire to the throne of St. Peter. Other monarchs are apt to be less prodigal when the purse is empty: Walsingham is ruined in the service of Henry's daughter Elizabeth; Philip II is totally unscrupulous in forcing ministers to pour out their wealth on his behalf. Nevertheless, patronage is a monarch's duty, the carrot to go with the stick. If the lawyers and *robins* (French legal officials) and *letrados* can live by charging fees to the public, their masters need something better. The privy purse requires constant replenishment. As Hobbes tersely puts it, 'Riches joined with liberality is power.'

81 Château de Chambord, Loire, France, begun 1519

The profusion of features on the skyline of Francis I's Château de Chambord, for its era an immense pleasure palace, illustrates both a peculiarly French synthesis of forms and also that enviable lavishness which moves lesser monarchs like Henry VIII to seek to emulate such symbols of royal liberality.

And there is representation. Monarchs require permanent symbols of their presence: palaces. Colbert reminds Louis XIV: 'Your Majesty knows that, aside from dazzling feats of war, nothing more clearly displays the greatness and spirit of a prince than buildings; and that posterity will judge him by the splendour of the mansions which he has erected in the course of his life.' From Fontainebleau and Nonsuch (to say nothing of the Vatican) down to the superlative folly that is Versailles, together with all its successors and imitations for a century more (Schönbrunn, Drotningholm, Sans-Souci), the prince imprints his magnificence on the imagination of his subjects. Pleasure palaces replace castles, but both are too cramped for the needs of a central government or the lodging of a large court. The

Vatican, the Pitti palace in Florence, the Escorial, the projected seventeenth-century palace of Whitehall, the Hofburg, Versailles, all have this in common: they are enormous because in them the prince identifies his residence with the functions of the state, and these functions constantly expand. Versailles in the eighteenth century ends up the largest, simply because France comes to concentrate the largest government functions there. It grows from a hunting lodge (1643) to a pleasure palace (1660) to a government headquarters (1683), with the usual chapel, galleries, guard-rooms, stables, suites of living quarters, official and unofficial cabinets, lodgings for dependants and officials; presently even an opera house; and then, as well as all that, a foreign ministry, and huge paraphernalia of other facili-

82   The Palace of Versailles, 1668–78

At its greatest extension, the Palace of Versailles is hardly recognizable as the building originally converted for royal pleasures by Le Vau (compare plate 100); Mansart's virtual rebuilding and additions by Gabriel and others (the chapel left of the central building, the opera at the end of the same wing) transform it virtually into a small city, with all the amenities (and attendant problems).

ties. Supply problems become acute; simply to provide water a special aqueduct has to be built, costing not much less than a year's campaign in Flanders. Evidently, Versailles becomes an intolerably inconvenient place to *live* in: Louis XIV and his successors build within close reach of it no fewer than four satellite pleasure palaces to retire to.

Buildings are only a start, though an important one: a décor for magnificence, essential to policy. Every royal journey is also a progress, a display of the prince's most cogent justification of his rule—liberality. All that is new in this is its manic intensity. Surrounded by his courtiers, he is fêted in an unceasing round of pageants, triumphal entries into towns, firework displays, masquerades, tournaments, *spectaculars*. Henry VIII and Francis I turn a summit conference into the 'Field of the Cloth of Gold'. Duke Ferdinand welcomes his bride Christine of Lorraine to Florence (1589) with a three-day series of fêtes that include a mock storming of a castle and a battle at 'sea' (complete with thundering salvos). Charles V and his son Philip, and later the king of Spain's representatives, a duke of Alva or a Don John of Austria, are welcomed by colossal and propitiatory pageants in the Low Countries towns they tyrannize.

Ingenuity, to be sure, can make up for lack of money or of cordiality on the part of the host: thus Queen Elizabeth takes a lively pleasure in court entertainments offered at no cost to her by the loyal subjects whom she visits. Catherine de' Medici on tour in the south of France has her own maids of honour sent ahead to spring out from the roadside at various stages of her progress, costumed as nymphs, and to recite welcoming addresses to herself. In general, though, heavy distributions of largesse are the monarch's best form of self-advertisement. The effects of this on the arts will occupy us presently.

Oppression

The convergence of these costs—war, building, patronage, liberality, and magnificence—drives the prince into a very obsessive attitude regarding money. Traditional taxes he may take for granted. Unfortunately they are not much use, being already committed; therefore they must be supplemented. When we look at some of the extra sources developed by the English Tudors and Stuarts, the Emperor Charles V and Philip II of Spain, the house of Valois, or the new dukes (presently grand dukes) of Tuscany, we see how widely the prince casts his net. At different times he has recourse to: borrowing from bankers (the magnates of Augsburg, Florence, Genoa, Venice); forced loans from cities; 'benevolences', or forced gifts, from individuals; special 'aids', or one-off taxes, for war; taxes on the Church; taxes on industry or trade; farming-out taxes (receiving fixed sums while shifting the work and odium of later extortion to other shoulders); debasement of the coinage; sale of annuities, or letters of nobility, or crown offices, or trading licences, or trade monopolies; confiscation of estates or other property (of criminals, heretics, rebels, etc); confiscation of Church property; creation of 'nationalized' (monopoly) industries; exploitation of mines, quarries, treasure, especially bullion from the New World; piratical interception of such bullion on the high sea; and (fortunately not often) directing mutinous armies to sack a city in lieu of pay.

All these ploys are exercised by a category of person who, among other dignities, presents himself as the 'fount of honour'! But throughout the centuries in which the prince acts as the focus of the centralized state, he is never free for any length of time from the diabolical pressure to extort and exact. Nor should we forget the ecclesiastical princes, and in particular the papacy, whose needs are also great. Whether before or after Charles V's infamous sack of Rome, the ordinary expenses of the Church are dwarfed by the extraordinary cost of making the Vatican into the most sumptuous palace, and then St Peter's into the most imposing church, in all Christendom. It is common knowledge that the extra exertion this calls for, 'services' from wealthy sees, taxes on benefices, intensified sale of indulgences—extortions of Rome as they are perceived in distant provinces—help to provoke in 1519 the schism of the Western Church.

We recall that challenge which William of Orange hurls at Philip II, echoing the Athenian Demosthenes denouncing Philip of Macedon: the strongest fortress of a free people against the tyrant (he says) is *distrust*. In distrust Pope Clement loses Luther, King Philip loses the Netherlands, King Charles I loses England, and King Louis XVI loses France. To protect himself against distrust and its consequences, the sovereign prince displays his 'majesty,' goes to battle, builds more palaces; he leans also on venerable sanctions, and first and foremost, on supernatural ones. The Bible to begin with contains some helpful support. According to the Psalms (generally attributed to David the king speaking of course the Word of God) kings are in some sense divine: 'I have said, ye are gods: and ye are all the children of the most Highest.' The king on earth, at the very least, replicates the king in heaven, and the French clergy declare in 1614 that 'kings are the true lieutenants of Almighty God,' and 'by imitation of his divine Majesty represent his image here below.' As Marc Bloch reminds us, a prince's sacred character does seem to be attested by the age-old ritual for curing scrofula through the laying-on of hands. In England and France the ceremony takes place annually: even the apostasy of Henry VIII does not appear to weaken his power to heal, while Henry IV, an uncertain convert from Calvinism, proves just as successful at it as his Catholic predecessors. Other kings try their hand in emulation, with excellent results: in Denmark curing epilepsy, and in Hungary jaundice; in Castile, curing demonic possession becomes Philip II's speciality.

Is there some special divinity that 'doth hedge a king'? Or at least a peculiar and quite unusual nature attributable to kingship? It would appear so; even if it rests only in the beliefs of a large majority of men. For all his advocacy of 'distrust', William of Orange judges that even if the yoke of Philip of Spain is thrown off by patriotic Dutchmen another prince will be needed: 'it is hardly possible to dispense with a head or a superintendent.' Oliver Cromwell refuses the crown of England

83   Escorial Palace, 1563–93

Philip II's Escorial provides its master's royal residence, government headquarters and court accommodation (hence the need for great size, being a day's ride from Madrid) and also—uniquely—a monastery and, beneath its enormous chapel, a royal mausoleum. The union of Throne and Altar is nowhere more emphatically symbolized than in this advertisement of the Most Catholic King.

offered him by Parliament; earlier though, in justifying his dictatorship, he has a curious slip of the tongue: 'I called not myself to this place . . . God and the peoples of these kingdoms have borne testimony to it.' *These kingdoms?* What then has the English civil war been about? Following Cromwell's death, Parliament votes the Restoration 'according to the ancient and fundamental laws', and Charles II returns to take up something less than absolute power, yet still on his own terms (those of the Declaration of Breda). James II is presently sent about his business, and again his place is filled by a monarch; this time Dutch, not 'absolute', though still powerful. And gradually, in one country, an accommodation is arrived at, a formula to preserve the symbolism while evaporating much of the substance of an autocratic head of state. But that is another story, in almost another world.

Throne and altar

The attractions for the prince of Luther's Reformation, or something similar to it, are plain: it ends the need to share a corner of princely power with another sovereign (the pope); in other words it means extension of political power, perhaps unfettered control over the bishop and the preacher, and the enormous windfall of Church lands. Henry VIII is not an admirer of Luther's theology, yet has urgent reasons for wanting to become head of his Church and dictate to its bishops, not forgetting the wealth of the country's monasteries. The prince who remains a dutiful son of Rome, on the other hand, must forgo loot, endure papal taxation of his clergy, and continue to face the essentially political difficulties of nominations to bishoprics.

Yet there are compensations. This Church, moved at long last to hold a great council at Trent, sets in train a major programme of self-renovation. One sign of this is a wave of new religious orders: the Oratory, the Friars Minor, the Capuchins, or reformed Franciscans, and most significantly the Company of Jesus, founded in 1540 by the Spanish soldier Ignatius Loyola. To be sure, the Jesuits' outright self-dedication to the pope makes them suspect to some princes; Philip II in Spain is

84 El Greco, *The Allegory of the Holy League* (detail), 1576–8. Oil and tempera on panel, 22⅞ × 13¾ in (58 × 35 cm). London, National Gallery

It is ironic that the great master of religious art in Spain should fail to find favour with Philip II, for all the latter's keen eye for painting, and the piety of both. In this allegorical composition the King addresses his devout gaze to the heavenly host above and the Church Militant below, his back turned resolutely to the jaws of Hell and the gruesome feast of reprobate heresy.

not displeased when the Dominican Inquisition directs unfriendly attention to its new rival. But in general the Jesuit order is a prince's best friend; not only does it supply missions, martyrs, and saints for every continent, renew moral theology, combat heresy and dis-

affection, it supports the prince unyieldingly, provided he shows himself a pious son; and most valuably of all, it establishes schools for the children of his well-to-do subjects, the decision-makers of the future (as we might say). The Jesuits' curriculum is thoroughly modern: sound rudiments, reliable worldly morals, the acting of plays in Latin—a useful training for public service. By 1600 there are a hundred Jesuit colleges spread across the map of Europe, as far afield as Poland, in every land where the prince will admit them. Some of their number display outstanding spirituality (St. John of the Cross) or fearless devotion to a cause (Edmund Campion), and others exert tremendous influence in the moral work of the Counter-Reformation (Suarez, Molina): whatever the admiration or fear evoked by the order, no one can tax it with mediocrity. More than any single work produced in the Counter-Reformation, Ignatius's *Spiritual Exercises* disseminate an attitude, a tone of spirituality, of the highest importance in shaping the values becoming in the ideal Catholic: intensity, self-discipline, self-abasement, subjugation of the body to the spirit. Yet in the Jesuit college there is also imparted a highly practical decorum and confidence of bearing, a certain *savoir-faire*, fitting in those not destined to be martyrs or missionaries. Without these colleges, the Catholic prince—provided he be strong—would be far less well served by his subjects. And if Philip II prefers to surround himself with Dominican theologians, there is no doubt whatever that the only prince who can outdo him as an absolute ruler, Louis XIV, relies heavily upon the support of Jesuit advisers and prelates for more than half of his long and crushing reign in France.

The estates of the realm

By long habit we picture the prince's rise to supremacy in terms of the support of 'his' commons against a feudal nobility whom he subjugates. This does less than justice to the variety and complexity of states and the foxy versatility of the prince himself.

Obviously, old nobilities (the *second* estate of the realm, clergy being the *first*) resent the erosion of their power, the new proliferation of crown servants, encroachments of a central authority on their rights, and, quite simply, the caprice of a ruler—any ruler—placed over them. Only in Poland however, and briefly in Hungary, do they prevent the establishment of an autocrat, and there is hardly an instance in which they show themselves able to throw off his yoke once it is there (Sweden is a peculiar case). At the same time, though, they retain immense collective power—sometimes inert, often aggressive, always immovable. They all claim exemption from poll taxes, on the grounds that they are subject to a higher calling, the call to arms, which implies constant readiness to pay a 'blood tax' to the suzerain. Because of this real or imaginary ancient duty, they are debarred from the distraction of trade or commerce, or other 'baseborn' ways of gaining wealth, often on pain of absolute loss of 'noble' status. Great or poor, therefore, they despise the prudence of the counting-house and parade the innate superiority of 'blood', honour, rank, and title. It is a mistake, no doubt, when the Medici finally dissociate themselves from the banking which has made them rich; but this sacrifice is undertaken as a necessary preliminary to contracting dynastic (and therefore political) alliances to help

preserve their duchy of Tuscany; and even then, Catherine de' Medici, queen and regent of France and mother of the King of France, is sneered at in that country as 'the tradesman's daughter'.

The 'real' privileges of the nobilities are undoubtedly economic—tax-exemption, rents and dues and services (such as remain) from tenants or share-croppers, old monopolies or powers in the land, seigneurial courts. But they attach no less importance to other privileges which are symbolic and conspicuous: armorial bearings, exemption from sumptuary laws, hunting rights, the right to bear arms, and, perhaps above all, precedence, which is recognition of their 'blood' and also, in a manner of speaking, a banker's reference, a public attestation. In a word, they are lords, by virtue of some mystic quality. At the States General of France in 1614, a spokesman for the French nobility proclaims that his estate stands in relation to the third (the commons) as a master to his servant.

Land-ownership, also, is a necessary attribute of nobility, as it has been since the dawn of feudalism. It is the foundation of all noblemen's claims to authority, to a voice; it is 'real'; that is to say, durable. Even in an age when fixed rents are falling, or their yield tails behind inflation, it confers on them, *vis-à-vis* their monarch, a particularly massive kind of reassurance; it carries with it the support (however reluctant) of a certain number of subordinates, dependants, servants; at the limit land makes it easier to conceive of disloyalty, to risk revolt—always of course in the cause of true religion, or of a higher justice. Without land, no nobility; and no power, or belief in power.

Since the prince cannot entirely transform his kingdom, he must compound with his nobles. He is, after all, still the greatest of them, not of another order. A mixture of flattery, bribery, violence, intimidation, and evasiveness is therefore, without exception, his strategy. For much of the sixteenth century he is ceaselessly on the move, visiting provinces, not from curiosity but from policy. If he is poor, his nobles' hospitality saves money; if rich, he can affirm his authority the more forcibly. Always by his presence he confers 'honour'. Sometimes such honour is ruinous; at others it is accompanied by 'liberality'. Honouring a favourite is universal; but others also share in the spoils the prince can distribute: as viceroys (of the king of Spain), lieutenants of provinces, ambassadors, commanders of armies, great officers of the court; all these things can lead to elevation of rank or grants of land, or wealth, even—very occasionally—a royal alliance. The prince is attentive to his nobles' vanity, their envy of one another: he founds new orders of chivalry—orders of the Holy Ghost, of the Golden Fleece—or gives new prominence to existing ones (the Order of the Garter) as a potent instrument of policy.

There are few variations on this style of surveillance; among them, the most conspicuous is Philip II of Spain. This monarch, once he returns from the Low Countries to establish his capital at Madrid, lives a peculiarly withdrawn existence; indeed he only ventures forth to take possession of the kingdom of Portugal. It is not surprising that his lieutenants such as the duke of Alva, the duke of Medina Sidonia, the viceroy of Naples, pick up so many honours that they shine with a brilliance superior to his. But he has other ways of exerting his power. It is natural that great lords everywhere should emulate a royal style of life—in display, palace building, entertainment, patronage of the arts, a private court. Yet, except where the monarch is weak (Henry III of France, for example), the reality of power is unambiguous: an overweening favourite can be cast down, an Antonio Perez imprisoned, a duke disgraced, a son executed.

From the third estate, or commons, of Europe, the prince fears no such overshadowing. Yet here too there are degrees of dignity. Great wealth, or great status in a city, confers a kind of blason; and at the apex a few dynasties are international powers. In Augsburg the Fuggers, deeply into all manner of trade, finance, and mining investment, are as prominent in the service of Charles V as the Genoese financiers who collectively mobilize vast credits—at a price—in the service of the king of Spain. (A hundred years later it is the same story: near the end of Louis XIV's reign, when the French treasury is empty, the financier Samuel Bernard is invited to Versailles and publicly received with endless flattering marks of distinction by the monarch himself. The Duc de Saint-Simon derives intense amusement from the royal performance . . . the expedient is classic.) In the time of the Fuggers as in that of Samuel Bernard, the echelon of European high finance is an equivalent to the Euro-dollar market of a more recent age. It can mobilize a line of credit far in excess of any prince's wealth (except perhaps that of Philip II, most of which however is still under the ground in Mexico and Peru). It is indispensable to every great royal enterprise. What we tend to overlook is that for the same reason that makes high finance essential to the prince (the sheer scale of his requirements, whether for war or peace), the prince on his side is no less essential to it: he alone can be a client for the really large operations which it is in a position to mount, and he alone can be expected, somehow, not to become a bad debt on its books. There *are* financial disasters of the first magnitude:

85 Claude Perrault (1613–88), east colonnade of the Louvre, Paris, 1661–78

Before the Prince moves definitively out of Paris to Versailles, Perrault's east colonnade of the Louvre embodies a definitively French 'classicism': in contrast to the rejected 'baroque' symbols of Bernini, it presents an example of measured stateliness (with all that that word connotes).

Charles V produces one, and Philip II three, virtual bankruptcies of the state. Yet the prince knows he will have to pay dearly for his default. He and his financiers are, at bottom, partners who require one another.

Behind this unblasoned aristocracy of commoners stand the towns and their corporations of merchant capitalists—in London, Antwerp, the Hansa ports, Frankfurt, Nuremberg, Lyons, Seville, Lisbon, Milan, Florence, Venice, Genoa, and other centres. The Italians are not so prominent now as a century earlier; in the sixteenth century, even disregarding the eastern barrier erected by the Ottoman empire, Europe as a whole becomes a dynamic part of a larger world trade system.

Portuguese, Spanish, English, French, and presently Dutch venturers form new links and colonies on the coasts of three continents, following up the path-finding expeditions of Vasco da Gama and Columbus. Thanks to the vision of Henry the Navigator, Portuguese ships ply from Lisbon to Brazil and on to Africa, Goa, Macao (a six-month journey). By mid-century a Spanish galleon sails annually across the Pacific from Manila to Acapulco and back, linking the two extremities of Philip II's empire. Most notable of all, the Spanish empires of America, pioneered by adventurers but settled as royal territories and partly supplied from Europe, yield—from 1545 onwards—the huge silver treasure of Potosi, shipped back to Seville and funnelled onwards to feed an already chronic European price inflation.

Naturally the prince must, if he can, have a finger in such ventures. Spain is the great exemplar; two viceroys preside over the Americas, and their duty is to fill a treasure fleet every year for the king. But venture capital can operate in alliance with the monarch, and one way to the queen of England's favour lies in putting together successful ventures. Drake, a pirate, is rewarded and knighted. This acts as a spur to vigorous explorations towards Persia, to Russia, or to discover a northern sea route to the Indies, or a north-west passage. Hence the anthologies of travel, narratives such as Hakluyt's *Voyages*, and the rapid development of cartography: they are an attempt to put together bodies of knowledge relevant to trade, to replicate for new regions the deep experience that the Italians have already developed in their established eastern commerce. Naturally there are mishaps: the sad tale of Sir Walter Raleigh is that of a venture promoter, fertile in ideas but unlucky in execution, who is driven in the end to stake his shirt on discovering the fabled gold of El Dorado somewhere in Guyana—and loses. Spain, for the time being, has an unbeatable start, and consolidates it in 1580 by Philip's annexation of Portugal. By the time Portugal regains her independence (in 1640) this huge empire is on the wane; but others are taking shape.

Princely Forms: *the monarch*

For the prince entering on his inheritance, there exists ready to hand a repertory of models, manners, forms, which he can mould to his requirements: Italy, the heritage of Florence and its Italian emulators, and whatever he chooses to favour from the productions of the humanists. After the Florentine Renaissance there follows an almost indefinite series of 'Renaissances' up and down the courts of Europe. The most conspicuous is that of Francis I, seeding a royal and therefore a national

French style (associated with the name of Fontainebleau) by bringing together illustrious masters from Italy (Primaticcio, Serlio) and ambitious artists within France. In the process he lays the foundations for a specifically 'classical' French idiom, neither heavily Roman nor, eventually, subject to extremes of Mannerism. In the visual arts this is a privileged example; in proportion to distance from Italy such borrowings (and hybrids) become weaker and more scattered or delayed in Spain, or in England, or north of the Alps.

Buildings and decorations apart, the courts of Europe, with their increasing size and intrusive importance, have also the means and opportunity to emulate Italian civility or develop their own equivalents of Castiglione's image of courtly life: this again is as much a symbol of the monarch's favoured circle as the livery of his household. Grace and personal accomplishment is a useful, if not infallible, way to catch the sovereign's eye: and the range of accomplishment becomes a good deal wider than is usual in the preceding century.

The prince himself may not be a more versatile individual than his ancestors, but his attainments, when he has them, are now much more widely advertised. He must, evidently, have the martial skills—riding, hunting, fencing, jousting—for he is certain to take the field at some time, and sumptuous tournaments, however archaic and dangerous, are an occasion for him to show off. Deportment, too, and Latin, are useful, and then whatever else may raise him above the common run of mortals. Not all will match Lorenzo the Magnificent, but Francis I and the Emperor Charles V are notable patrons of the arts, Henry VIII a considerable athlete and musician, the morose Philip II an astonishing connoisseur of painting (but he refuses to learn any language but Spanish and devotes his entire life to government and to religion); Charles I of England is likewise a great art collector, as compared with his father James, who shines in learning and disputatious theology; even the ineffectual Cosimo II of Tuscany is a keen experimental scientist (and earns a place in history for protecting Galileo in an evil hour). Princesses are often more surprisingly accomplished than princes: Marguerite of Navarre is a gifted author and centre of a lively circle; Catherine de' Medici is a first-class Latinist (in verse too) and passes on these skills to her protégée Mary Queen of Scots; Elizabeth of England handles Latin and Greek with ease, and is also a talented musician; Maria of Portugal is credited with Latin and Greek and also much philosophy along with her chastity; the elector of Bohemia's daughter Elizabeth conducts learned exchanges with her adored, and admiring, Descartes; Christina of Sweden devours philosophers

**86   Unknown artist, *The Field of the Cloth of Gold*,
c. 1520. Oil on canvas, 66½ × 135⅞ in (168.9 × 347.3 cm).
Hampton Court, Royal Collection**

*That a summit conference should occasion princely display is no
novelty; Henry VIII's elaborate meeting with Francis I in 1520 is
in fact less important diplomatically than his less widely advertised
discussions, shortly before, with the rival Charles V; but (as with
later summit conferences) it serves to enhance the image of the
Prince.*

for breakfast, including that same Descartes. In addition, all princes and princesses of the reformed faith are
wise to have a tincture of theology. And finally, it
becomes a prince or his consort to patronize learning,
found colleges and academies—whether as a part of
'liberality' or for political or confessional reasons—and
gratify favoured writers with a purseful of gold.

If models for all these princely attributes come from
Italy, it is also striking to see how, transplanted into
other contexts, the inevitable hybridizing brings diversity. The 'Fontainebleau' school is a case in point;
another is the cult of Platonism transposed from
Florence to Paris, where it takes shape in attempts to
invent a wholly new style of incantatory music (the
'academy' of the poet J. A. de Baïf) or in festivals of
court ballet with curiously magical overtones.

Or take the case of secular portraiture. In a century of
great achievement which goes from Masaccio to
Raphael or Leonardo it has been completely 'liberated'

both from a religious Gothic tradition and from Roman
tutelage. Simultaneously now, in the 1530s, we find
Charles V sitting to Titian and Henry VIII to Holbein.
Though the former rules over a vast empire and the
latter a quite small kingdom, both share a very similar
political culture; yet it would be hard to credit this by
looking at their respective portraits. Holbein may be,
north of the Alps, the greatest practitioner of the art of
human likeness; he is the friend of the humanists Erasmus and More, but that does not override a certain
stiffness (relatively speaking), an austere economy
even, reminding us how much closer he stands to a
continuing Gothic tradition than does the great master
of the Venetian school. Not for the first time, then—
nor for the last—we encounter in the culture of the
prince, notably in his display symbolisms, the entirely
European phenomenon of diversity and unity. And if
this is especially noticeable in the visual displays of the
prince, enough has already been said to show that each
individual prince has entered on an inheritance which is
slightly different from that of any other—in the social
structures of which he forms the apex, the machinery of
government he lays his hands on, and so forth. The
unity has its sources either in similar institutions or in
deliberate emulation; the diversity arises from there
being different traditions affecting the way innovation
is taken up, or from the manner in which it undergoes
subsequent change.

Princely forms: *the image*

We must not press this argument too far. If humanism, for example, takes on particular colourings depending on whether it is being pursued at an Italian court or in a German university, Latin grammar at any rate is the same everywhere, and so is a common reverence for original texts. And there is another feature of humanism in which we perceive an almost standardized resource for the culture of princes. In its canon of study, it always includes a proportion at least of the great literary monuments of antiquity; and because of this it bears with it, wherever it reaches, an awareness of at least one central object indispensable to the reading of those texts: that object is Greco-Roman mythology, or at least a simplified digest of the pagan Olympus. So much is this the case, indeed, that an understanding of Renaissance art and literary allusion is almost inseparable from familiarity with the two anthologies most used as convenient 'cribs' by the age—Ovid's *Metamorphoses* and Boccaccio's *Genealogy of the Gods*.

The Olympian gods and their derivative relationships, powers, adventures, hero myths, are known to every student of the ancient languages. Allegorized after the mode of Neoplatonism, they furnish an illimitable store of complimentary allusion. The gods are of a *higher order* than mortals; tales told of them attest their peculiar *liberties*, not to say licences; they control the forces of nature and the *destinies* of peoples; they form a hierarchy of *power* (Jupiter at the apex). Each of these features is highly congenial. What prince would refuse identification with the semi-divine Hercules, unless it were to prefer the role of Apollo (patron of the Muses) or even, on occasion, of Jupiter? What princess could disdain the attributes of wise Minerva, or of Venus, or, if appropriate, of Diana, chaste goddess of the hunt?

Setting aside here the more extreme and learned syncretisms of the humanists (Noah identified with Bacchus, Hercules or Pan with Christ) as well as the more coquettishly profound or obscure allusions to little-read authors (humanistic 'showing-off'), we find a new general language of attributes, as unambiguous as the Roman arch, and as easy to decorate, brought into general use in the sixteenth century. If Philip of Spain is more or less immune to it, and the Genevan and Dutch republics averse (for reasons we shall see later), no such obstacle arises elsewhere, for instance among the Lutheran rulers of the north. The Olympians and a selection of their more creditable offspring become a stock-in-trade for flattery. And like every language which becomes frozen in a mould, this one survives in

87 Henry Gissey (1621–73), *Louis XIV as Apollo,* *c.* 1654. **Watercolour with gold on vellum, $11\frac{5}{8} \times 8\frac{1}{2}$ in (29.5 × 21.6 cm). Windsor, Royal Collection**

The young Louis XIV discovers an early vocation for dancing the role of Apollo in sentimental ballets devised for his entertainment: in which he shines no less for his fleetness than for his handsome chestnut hair and other advantages. At a more mature age he stops dancing in ballet and cuts off the hair in favour of a wig; but retains the symbolism.

the icons of the prince (down even into the eighteenth century, in fact) at the price of becoming more and more stilted and incongruous. Ultimately it is swept away—along with the general use of wigs—by the French Revolution, that first 'Twilight of the Gods'. But there is no sense of incongruity in the age of Rubens; nor, a generation later, in that of the young Louis XIV of France, the Sun-King: Louis is not the first to claim that identity, but he is the most insistent, even from a quite early age, presenting himself and being presented as Apollo, victor over powers of darkness, patron of the Muses, pursuer of innumerable Daphnes, life-giving source of joy and comfort.

Princely Forms: *the stage*

'All the world's a stage', and especially is this so for the prince, living symbol of his own power, constantly on display, always at the centre of the scene. His battlefield is a 'theatre of war', his court a prolonged rite, whether sombre and devout in the black attire demanded by Philip, or dashing and brilliant elsewhere. The festivals already referred to structure the important occasions of the sovereign; taken only a little further in stylization they become the court ballet of the Valois, not uninspired by Florentine entertainments but now halfway between pure entertainment and pure ritual, on occasion charged with a grave import. But more significant than masques or court ballet is the emergence of modern drama.

It will not escape the eye of any student of Shakespeare that the score or so of masterpieces which he leaves are not exactly 'courtly' productions (even if his sonnets are). At the same time, they are not exactly 'popular' either. They stand at a point of convergence of several kinds of audience, actual or potential; if nothing else, the large number of playhouses in Elizabethan London, as compared with anywhere else in the same period, points to this fact. In the enormous diversity of his writing, we observe both an unusual vein of patriotism—the history plays, tracing the English monarchy through to its established Tudor dynasty (with the aid of that dynasty's apologist Polydore Vergil)—and also a fascination for the problem of monarchy as such: Macbeth the flawed usurper, Richard II or Hamlet the *weak* prince, Lear the irascible, Richard III the monster . . . He also considers the moral issues arising from abuse of power (*Measure for Measure, The Winter's Tale*) or from its mere possession (*Coriolanus*) or political imperatives (Henry V's repudiation of Falstaff). Within this copious treatment of the vicissitudes of power, there may be a central affirmation of the just and right monarch (Henry V or the murdered Duncan) but it is of infrequent occurrence. Prospero in *The Tempest* is absolute and benign—but a magician; Duke Senior in *As You Like It* is an exile . . . What is certain is that for Shakespeare's world the right patterning of society rests on kingship, authority, degree—well ordered and moral—and that this lesson can be drawn from legend, from chronicle, from antiquity, for the diversion of a highly mixed audience. To arrive at this flowering is not a short process.

Under a direct inspiration of classical models, the strict business of the stage, theatre proper, is first an offering from humanism to Italian courts of the sixteenth century. Aristo, Trissino, Aretino, Giraldi,

Tasso, each with one eye on Seneca or Sophocles or Plautus and the other on Aristotle's *Poetics* (of which no fewer than ten scholarly editions or translations are printed between 1498 and 1576), provide a lead in refined entertainments which are exciting and accessible (in the vernacular) and open to astonishing development the moment their possibilities spill over from the palace hall to the public place. European sixteenth-century theatre history is too complex and too varied to be mapped out here. It involves the survival of traditional mystery plays, and moralities and farces, but also Latin play-acting in the schools (greatly boosted by the Jesuit curriculum); surviving medieval guilds, but also travelling troupes of entertainers; pedantic scribblers and brilliant adaptors of romances and historical stories; courtly and plebeian audiences. On the broad view, however, the older popular traditions are generally in process of being edged out in favour of a more professional and increasingly 'regular' stage, and the establishment of suitable fixed locations for performance. By the generation of Marlowe and Shakespeare, and Corneille's immediate predecessors in France around 1600, the wide gap between rude and gentle entertainment is being rapidly closed; only in Spain does their contemporary Lope de Vega shrug his shoulders at the unpolished character of Church-sponsored *autos*, or edifying stage shows, for which he supplies literally hundreds of ephemeral compositions. And as this professionalizing of the stage advances, with regular companies of players, regular places and seasons for performance, so too the prince sees it in his interest to control—that is to say, to license and to censor—the new industry, with all its potentiality for mischief, for scandal, or for propaganda.

Transferring into the vernacular, and then to popular audiences, a complete and ready-made form of *literary* entertainment has endless repercussions, not the least memorable being the elusive Shakespeare. But almost as remarkable is the attempt to go much further and revive Greek tragedy *integrally*, that is to say, produce a combined art of text and action, dance, spectacle, and music. There being no direct knowledge available of how Athenian or Roman drama was actually presented, the task is not beset with too much difficulty; in 1597, to mark the extremely important dynastic wedding of King Henry IV of France and Marie de' Medici at the court of Duke Ferdinand in Florence, the poet Rinuccini and the musicians Corsi and Peri are commissioned to produce what we today would recognize as the first opera—*Dafne*. The same team, joined by the musician Caccini and his daughter, returns three years later with an *Euridice*, and Rinuccini then proceeds to write fur-

88   Antoine Caron (*c.* 1515–93), *Aquatic Fête at Fontainebleau,* **1564. Watercolour over drawing, 12⅜ × 18⅜ in (31.5 × 46 cm). Edinburgh, National Gallery of Scotland**

The highly political Catherine de' Medici offers court spectaculars on the model of those of her own family, now reigning in Florence. At Fontainebleau in 1564 a marine display borrows from classical antiquity and also from the no less artificially preserved tradition of knightly chivalry. This sketch by Caron will form the basis for a commemorative tapestry—all to advertise the glories of the House of France.

ther librettos for another musician, Monteverdi, at the nearby court of Mantua (*Ariadne* 1607, *Orfeo* 1608). At once the marvellous new entertainment scales the heights. The subjects are classical—naturally; but they combine the dignity of myth with lyric beauty; also, what enables opera to take its place during the next half-century as a highly esteemed form of entertainment at court (or before the aristocracy of Venice,

where Monteverdi settles) is easy to see—it is extremely lavish, and it combines an appeal to all the 'senses', an almost hypnotic appeal. And that is what opera has remained ever since: a spectacular, an expensive enchantment. At first too, it is an enchantment peculiarly linked to Italy; in particular Italy has engineers skilled in arranging the most difficult theatrical device of all—a god descending from the sky in his 'machine' (chariot or cloud). Cardinal Mazarin, to overcome local hostility to his ministry in France, brings the engineer Torelli and an Italian opera troupe to Paris (1645) and has the satisfaction of seeing the amazement aroused by their painted sets, their machines, and their music; for some decades yet, other countries' efforts are pale in comparison. Only the most rigorous pedant would criticize the opera for never coming near the power of Sophocles, for lapsing into conventional prettinesses: the satisfactions of sound and eye have taken over, a new formula of lavish and sensuous artifice replaces the humanist's more austere ambitions.

89 Sebastiano Serlio (1475–1554), stage settings from
Architettura, Venice, 1545

Serlio's version of Vitruvius (1545) includes reconstructions of classical stages, of which two are shown here – the 'comic' (left) and the 'tragic' (right). The distinction lies chiefly in the style of building depicted: more 'municipal' for the commoner art of comedy, as against the palaces, temple, obelisk, suitable for the nobler art of tragedy. Common to both, however, is perspective and the illusion of depth.

90 Jacques Patin (d. before 1604), *Le Ballet Comique de la Reine*, **1581. Etching. Paris, Bibliothèque Nationale**

One of the best-known French court festivals, the Queen's Comic Ballet *(1581), celebrates a dynastic wedding and weaves in allegorical and political messages. In Patin's engraving we see Ulysses imploring the King, and in the far depths Circe the enchantress surrounded by her victims (turned into beasts). Though Pan in his grotto (right) has not a major role, in the sequel Mercury, Minerva and Jupiter will make appearances, in harmony with the King's saving power.*

One consequence of putting music in the service of the classical 'spectacular' is of course bound to be a momentous transformation of music itself. It is one thing for lyric poetry to be normally sung (as is the case): now on the stage action intrudes, and with it the need for new kinds of contrast: action with dance, chorus with solo, recitative with aria. And the aria becomes a prime vehicle for the solo, male or female, to dominate a complex musical structure, a new form of privileged melody, as brilliant as may be desired, and sooner or later bound to lead to the displacement of

91   Andrea Palladio (1508–80), stage scenery in the Teatro Olimpico, Vicenza, 1580, completed by Scamozzi

At the purpose-built Teatro Olimpico, the set for Oedipus *(1585) provides three avenues in exaggerated perspective, receding back from Palladio's elaborately classical frons scena. Miraculously, this piece of theatrical extravagance has escaped the usual fate of theatres built in an age before electric lighting—destruction by fire.*

polyphonic music by monophonic. Caccini makes no idle claim when he offers as 'new music' the songs he proceeds to write for his gifted daughter. The aria confronts the madrigal, and ultimately triumphs. Henceforth the soloist will establish his distance from the accompanying music, virtuosity will be accommodated in new forms, the violin will after a lapse of time supersede the blander viol because it lends itself better to a brilliant solo role; and the way is open to a new era in music which comes of age in the work of Handel, Scarlatti, and Rameau.

If the culture of the prince owes so much already to the long-ago inspiration of genuinely classical (that is to say, Greek and Roman) forms, there is yet one further feature of this debt that is at least as revealing as any other. It has to do with representation, and perception, and space.

We have noted that humanists know little about ancient stage performance. On the one hand they can inspect the ruins of several Roman theatres; on the other, Vitruvius' *Architecture*, which includes a section on the stage, fascinates them, especially after Serlio publishes his edition of it. There is still no clear view of the original décor of a classical play, but Serlio enlivens his treatment with elaborately illustrated sets for 'tragic', 'comic', and 'satiric' stages (respectively, rows of palaces, rows of street houses, and silvan glades). And the most prominent feature of these reconstructions is that they all exhibit an extreme emphasis on *perspective*. Indeed, Serlio brings into use the most orthodox and 'classical' procedure for rendering it, that of the *costruzione legittima* worked out long since by Brunelleschi and Alberti; his stages appear to be squared out in a series of regular receding planes, with a vanishing point plumb in the centre of the backcloth. Now, this perspective transferred to the stage supplies an illusion as powerful in its day as, say, stereo sound in a later age. Such an application is of course no part of Alberti's thinking, but late in the sixteenth century it becomes a veritable craze. And happily we can see exactly how it makes its impression, in one especially grandiose realization: the wealthy notables of Vicenza are so gripped by its charms that they commission Palladio to design, and Scamozzi to complete, a Teatro Olimpico where to this day survives the sumptuous perspective set of Thebes constructed not on canvas but in wood, and in fantastic detail and elaborate perspective, for a revival of Sophocles' *King Oedipus*. Not the least arresting feature of it is the fact, still exhibited to tourists, that when Oedipus makes his first entry backstage and advances slowly down the central 'royal entrance', the actor (who cannot be shrunk to the scale of the furthest away parts of the fixed sets) appears at first gigantic, superhuman, looming over the city roofs. It must have been an awesome moment in 1584 when the set was first shown.

Such elaborate bits of engineering are far beyond the means of a popular performance; but where a prince builds a hall for entertainments he can always offer these illusions to his guests by the use of painted flats; and he can make them the more compelling by framing the whole in a proscenium arch (as Scamozzi does). Then indeed the spectacle is fully under control. *Velut in speculum* (as into a mirror) is written over the arch of old Covent Garden: what we observe through the enchanted mirror is ourselves idealized, or more exactly the prince beholds his kind—the heroes and princes, Orpheus, Xerxes, Rhadamanthus, the god descending on a cloud . . . Moreover this architecture gives theatrical space a *double* focus: beyond the arch, on stage, an orderly scene with vanishing point, but on this side the prince's chair set centrally to face it, being as much the focus of attention as the perspective business of the image world opposite. His own display is no less a spectacle than the illusion confronting it—and no less ordered.

The insidious flatteries of the 'mirror' stage—the symmetrical throne-room scenes, the hero revolving great dilemmas, the god descending, the wonderful *peripeteia*—become lessons in style to haunt the prince's dream and shape his acts. The king of France appears ceremonially before his *parlement* of Paris to dictate his will; the emperor before his Diet . . . even down to that day, much later, in 1771, when the young king Gustavus III of Sweden, appearing before his Estates (a most surprising *deus ex machina*), berates their selfish factions in a magnificent oration and calls for a return to patriotism. What need of stages? The prince conjures up a theatre wherever he goes. *And its perspective ordering is that of his authority.*

Baroque

'Our revels now are ended. These our actors,
As I foretold you, were all spirits and
Are melted into air, into thin air:
And like the baseless fabric of this vision,
The cloud-capp'd towers, the gorgeous palaces,
The solemn temples, the great globe itself,
Yea, all which it inherit, shall dissolve,
And like this insubstantial pageant faded,
Leave not a rack behind. We are such stuff
As dreams are made on; and our little life
   Is rounded with a sleep. . .'(*The Tempest*, 1611)

The prince's own vocabulary has no name for it. Scholars nearly three centuries later label a certain trend in building and the visual arts 'Baroque' (the word originates in late seventeenth-century Italian with the sense 'mis-shapen'). Presently critics of literature transfer the term to *other* trends in poetry and *belles-lettres*; and musicologists follow suit (these last with no shadow of justification, a 'me-too-ism' in the use of fashionable jargon). It is as certain as anything can be that there is no more an 'age of the Baroque' than there is an age of 'naturalism' in the early thirteenth century; yet the expression is used, and challenges our attention.

When we consider two centrally placed and very great artists, Bernini and Rubens, supplying in their work the expressive symbolisms sought by the Church and by princely patrons in the decades after 1600, what strikes the eye unfailingly is their presentation of *power exerted*. Whether the power of supernatural ecstasy ravishing St. Teresa, or of restless and extravagant dynamism bearing aloft the huge bulk of St. Peter's baldachin, or of sheer insolence in the sweep of a façade; whether the aristocratic *hauteur* caught in the bust of a king, or the power of prancing horses lifting human frames quite clear of the ground on which we ordinary mortals are obliged to plant our feet, or of grandiose superpositions of masonry and statuary and decoration and sun-bursts and trophies (or their painted simulacra) in a crushing display: always, and both absolutely and comparatively, power is the central message of these inventions. But power means an overcoming of resistance, a dynamic force; not a simple brute force, indeed, but, if need be, an elaborately assembled and expensively concerted one. Manners and decorum have little place in such effortful display, and less still has modesty; defiance, yes, the challenge to withhold admiration (if we can!) of ostentation or daring, vertigo or illusion; but at all events transcendental forces.

Transcendental? Where are such forces to be found? In the Church, of course—the post-Tridentine Church, renewed and embattled, confronting the world with its militancy, its processions, its missions, its new orders, its Inquisition. But also in the heart of the prince, and for that matter in the hearts of his great nobles and viceroys, of those who attach themselves to his peremptory ideals, if not his humdrum administration.

Power—dynamism—transcendence. No single prince has a monopoly of these values, no one place assembles a complete and tidy array of Baroque formulae. Lands of the Hapsburg or of papal rule, Italy north and south, the Spanish Netherlands, and to a degree Spain itself, are centres (Germany will exhibit its own architectural forms, but somewhat later and mostly

92 Aerial view of St. Peter's, Rome, 1607–14

St. Peter's, worked on for more than a century by a succession of great artists—Bramante, Michelangelo, Fontana, Maderna, and Bernini—represents an extraordinary synthesis of styles: classical, Mannerist, and eventually (with its dynamic colonnades) Baroque. In this aerial view there can also be seen, some way away alongside the Tiber, the round bulk of the Castel Sant' Angelo—originally Hadrian's tomb.

after the end of the Thirty Years' and Turkish wars); strands and wisps will be carried across other frontiers too. Most coherent, evidently, are the particular dynamisms of the Counter-Reformation. Art in the service of the Church becomes a species of higher pro-paganda: magnificent, deeply pious, inspired even, but for all that propaganda in a sense not known before Luther. One fruit of the council of Trent is the setting up in Rome of a new agency, or Congregation for the Propagation of the Faith—hence the term here used, not yet sullied by later associations. It is not by chance that Dominichino, Ribera, Zurbarán, and Rubens in their religious painting, represent with insistence just those holy objects of belief which have been most vehe-mently repudiated by the Protestants, and which are therefore the more passionately and dramatically to be reaffirmed by Catholic art: the Assumption of the Vir-gin, the veneration of the Eucharist, the efficacy of saints, the pre-eminence of St. Peter; martyrdoms too, visions, ecstasies, to illustrate the heroism of the servants of Christ. Faith costs effort, demands not less than all, and transfigures the willing soul.

Along with St. Peter's, on which for over a century the greatest masters work and which eventually stretches out its immense colonnades (by Bernini) to welcome and embrace the whole world, Vignola's Il Gesù in Rome is the first of a new network of Jesuit churches less important for their profile than for what they symbolize. The bracketed façade and single nave and domed transept are outward badges of identity; wealth of adornment inside is an indirect symbol of power; but the intensity of Jesuit action, the specific loyalty of an élite and militant organization, are as limitless as the perspective breaking *upwards* through the vault of heaven to ineffable power on high. At the height of the Jesuits' achievement late in the seventeenth century, this Baroque perspective, this *trompe-l'oeil*, is triumphantly recorded in one of their churches by Andrea

93 Giacomo Vignola (1507–73) and Giacomo della Porta (c. 1537–1602), Il Gesù, Rome, 1575

Vignola's church of the Gesù, its façade completed by della Porta around 1575, is a first architectural contribution by the Jesuit Order to what will presently become the Baroque; its distinctive outline—here still restrained, but also energetic—with bracketed façade and cupola over the crossing, will be echoed and vastly elaborated across three continents.

Pozzo. As it develops and proliferates, Baroque religious architecture will display not only all possible forms of pomp but also an unparalleled range of examples of this boundless aspiration; and well beyond the reach of Jesuit control—in Austria, in Franconia, in Spain, in Mexico—its monuments survive.

Central to Ignatius's spiritual training, already referred to, is the violence to be done to human frailty by systematic routines, the dramatization of an extreme contrast between spiritual destitution and the infinite power of salvation. In forcing the will to submit to the masterful will of God, the soul is poised between blackness and ineffable light. Such drama is part of an unprecedentedly emphatic style in religious feeling, and it is not peculiar to the Jesuits—processions of flagellants through the streets are another and more public witness, judged not unseemly in religious affirmation, and the *auto-da-fé* is a no less striking display of the will to overpower darkness. For a whole wing of the Catholic Church this is a new age of saints and martyrs, of all or nothing.

At the level of the purely human, not only the visual arts illustrate the will to transcendence. Literature too bears its traces. How else indeed can one view the poet's elaboration of the conceit, the *concetto?* Its extraordinary development in Italy (the *Marinisti,* following Marino), in Spain (Gongora and his imitators), to some extent in France (Sponde, unquestionably Malherbe, behind the smooth diction), and even in England (Donne, the 'Metaphysicals'), attests the bravura of image and figure carried to the threshold of excess, dizziness even; dizziness being the mark of extraordinary, perhaps totally unreasonable, striving and strain upon the faculties. To turn away from Greek or Latin models of seemly rhetoric, to build an elaborate figure of speech for ten or forty lines, capture in its hyperbolic logic the sun, the beloved's eyes, divine love, the muse, a dozen disparates: here is a folly and a recklessness no less prized for being so visibly contrived, a tension between will and stubborn matter, a grappling with transcendence.

And on the stage, with all respect to Aristotle and regularity, a different set of possibilities still tends to tension and disturbance of soul. If high tragedy stands broadly on the firm lines laid down by antiquity (as Richelieu sharply reminds Corneille when the latter plunges into a rhapsody of aristocratic heroics—*The Cid* of 1636), what marvellous openings remain for ravishment or vertigo—the clemency of Augustus or Titus, the *peripeteia* (turn-around in the plot) opening chasms before us! Or in tragi-comedy, the marvel of a statue come to life (in Shakespeare's *The Winter's Tale* or in Molière's *Dom Juan*). And in the comedy, what licence to tease us by wavering on the borders of being and not-being! Were we for a moment charmed into illusion? Prospero's actors on the London stage retreat into their roles, dispersed by the magician; the illusion vanishes; the Globe theatre itself is put in doubt. In Corneille's *Comic Illusion* (1635) a play within a play ends—or rather, fails to end, since no satisfactory ending seems possible to its fanciful imbroglio—with the actors trooping on to the stage to draw their pay, for all the world like a Pirandello trick. In comedy the effort of transcendence is recognized—but renounced; comedy is only comedy—a low form, not the *other*, 'real' thing . . .

So far so good: the stage itself can be set upon a stage, credulousness mocked; the ordinary is far below the great or heroic. That is one of the great lessons of antiquity: the epic and the tragic poem are noble, comedy and satire are base-born. But what if the mirror which the stage purports to be is turned around? What if we raise, with Calderon (in his *La Vida es Sueño*, published in 1636), the thought that life itself is but a dream, 'a fitful dream'? We should then, as a matter of fact, be into a fashionable, insistently recurring *topos* of the early literature of the century: again, no chance encounter. This theme—like Baroque art itself—is not schizophrenic, not uncontrolled, but self-conscious and deliberate; everyone knows that God exists, the prince exists, the world exists in the way that God and the prince affirm that it should. These questionings of reality are themselves but conceits. It just so happens that in 1637, Descartes' *Discourse on Method* begins the argument for a wholly new philosophy with the procedure of methodic doubt: *all* suppositions and beliefs about the existence of a world may be challenged, all without exception, down to that last, unchallengeable 'I think' which is *not* in doubt.

The fame of Descartes rests today upon his rational philosophy and his *cogito*. Yet he also grapples (as his metaphysics oblige him to) with the question of human self-direction and the passions, and in his late *Treatise on Passions* he elaborates the thesis that 'there is no soul so weak but that, properly conducted, it can acquire absolute power over its passions.' The will can be ruler—*absolute* ruler—of the impulsions of the body no less than of the mind. And what is this but the reflection of a fashion of moralizing about glory, will-power, transcendence, heroism, royal and aristocratic values, all prevalent in the country of Descartes' early years (he being a pupil of the Jesuits of La Flèche) under the regency of Marie de' Medici—when Rubens adorns her palace and Guez de Balzac writes his treatise on *Glory*—

94   Gian Lorenzo Bernini (1598–1680), column with entablature from the baldacchino, 1624–33. Dark bronze, partly gilt. Rome, St. Peter's

As a feature to dominate the interior of St. Peter's, Bernini designs a canopy or baldacchino *to surmount the traditional burial-place of the patron saint. Though its enormous size cannot easily be conveyed in a photograph, its profuse and weighty ornament can, and this symbol of a claim to authority calls for no additional comment.*

all congenial to the prince who, like God or Corneille's Augustus, rules by the *mere motion* of an untrammelled will? Or would dearly like to . . .

Baroque, then, as we can see it, is not *only* a repertory of particular styles in painting or architecture, nor yet merely a family of kinds of rhetoric. It links these things, certainly, in a ghostly and general way; but at the same time it appears most meaningful as a concept if we observe it in terms of the actual people, actual societies, between whom its meanings are actually exchanged. In a 'directory' of the Baroque, first, we find who its customers are: they are the papacy, the Roman

95   Gian Lorenzo Bernini, *Saint Theresa in Ecstacy*, 1645–52. Marble, life-size. Rome, altar of Santa Maria della Vittoria

For those familiar with the very down-to-earth correspondence of Saint Theresa of Avila, there is something of a shock in confronting the monument which Bernini has entitled Saint Theresa in Ecstasy. *It epitomizes, however, the Baroque vision of ravishment by supernatural agency: very much not down-to-earth, under the rays of a sunburst and posed on a swirl of immaterial substance . . .*

96   Bartolomé Esteban Murillo (1617–82), *The Immaculate Conception*, 1656–60. Oil on canvas, 8⅛ × 5⅝ in (20.6 × 14.4 cm). Madrid, Museo del Prado

The Immaculate Conception of the Virgin (an article of belief upheld by the Council of Trent) is celebrated here by a benign vision of the Virgin poised between heaven and earth and surrounded by a host of angels.

Catholic Church, great prelates; they are princes, and especially those most particularly associated with the exertion of absolute power and with the Counter-Reformation (but not exclusively the latter); and of course their adherents, apologists, suppliers. Baroque is very definitely *not* a style associated with 'small' men, nor with measured outlooks, and it *never* comes cheap: it is only for those for whom the folly of heroism is a great ideal, and power a unilateral declaration. Its extreme affirmativeness matches the mood of the post-Tridentine Church—not of the easier days of Renais-

sance popes and pagan classicism. It attracts and admirably suits the ill-starred English monarch Charles I, married to Marie de' Medici's daughter and not too humbly inclined towards his mean and puritan subjects: but it has no place in the culture of those who most strenuously repudiate both pope and prince—as we see in the next chapter. Even in France, despite the short interregnum of Marie de' Medici, Baroque has little attraction, either for the church which is resolutely Gallican (that is, anti-Jesuit and tending towards independence from Rome) or for a monarchy whose poli-

97   Peter Paul Rubens (1577–1640), *The Triumph of the Catholic Church*, 1628. Oil on canvas, 33⅞ × 41⅜ in (86 × 105 cm). Madrid, Museo del Prado

The great master of Antwerp (in the Spanish Netherlands) is cosmopolitan in his connections and prodigious in his output. Among his contributions to the art of the Counter-Reformation, this 'baroque' allegory is exceptionally outspoken: Mother Church, in triumphal chariot, holds aloft the Sacrament, a papal mitre poised over her; angels bestride the horses (one bears an ensign of Peter's crossed keys); and as the procession advances irresistibly onwards its loathsome adversaries are simply ridden down.

tical rulers, especially Richelieu, keep their distance from the Counter-Reformation, and whose artists work at a measured 'classicism' congenial to local magistratures and, eventually, the crown. It is consistent with this scene that Bernini himself, journeying to Paris to redesign the royal palace of the Louvre for an ambitious young king, has his plans rejected by the minister Colbert. His prancing equestrian statue of Louis XIV is rejected too: it is even off-loaded into a ditch at the bottom of the gardens of Versailles. The French monarch seeks an absolute grandeur; but not with such overtones of brio and fiery exaltation as have inspired his recent enemies, the aristocratic rebels of the *Fronde*. Thus it is not Bernini but Perrault who builds at the Louvre; and Le Vau and then Mansart at Versailles.

98   Andrea Pozzo (1642–1709), *The Triumph of St.*
Ignatius Loyola, **1691–4. Fresco. Rome, nave ceiling of**
Sant' Ignazio
The painted ceiling of Sant' Ignazio celebrates the entry into
Paradise of the founder of the Jesuit Order. In this prodigious
trompe-l'oeil, where painted structures reach towards the opened
heavens, other martyrs and heroes of the Order float upwards from
four continents, assisted by heavenly beings.

Absolute rulers: (i) *Philip of Spain*

By far the largest concentration of power of any ruler of
the west is that of Philip II of Spain. His reign is devoted
to the huge task bequeathed him by his father, the
Emperor Charles V: to govern Spain, to hold Milan and
Naples against the French, and the Mediterranean and
bridge-heads in North Africa against the Turk, to defend the Netherlands obstinately against rebellion and
heresy, and to exploit his American viceroyalties and
other colonies. To this he adds Portugal (1580) and *her*
vast dependencies in Brazil, Africa, India, the Far East
. . . Absolute in his rule in Spain, in the harrying of
Moorish minorities, the suppression of revolt in Granada, the persecution of Jews and heretics, he is above all
absolute in his tragic endeavour to *will* the obliteration
of heresy from his lands, from his Netherlands provinces, from England and France. His only obedience is
to the Inquisition, which he has confirmed on his accession; his public appearances grace from time to time its
burning of unbelievers. He appoints his great officers—
Margaret of Parma, Granvelle, Ruy Gomez, Garcia de
Toledo, Alba, Antonio Perez, his bastard half-brother
Don John of Austria, Alexander Farnese, Medina
Coeli, Medina Sidonia—and dangles the cleverest of

them like puppets on a string, sets them one against another, directs their actions, reproaches the slightest departure from orders, keeps them waiting for new instructions, recalls or dismisses them, even assassinates one of them. He builds his peculiar palace outside Madrid, the Escorial: it is not at all a pleasure palace, more a convent, chapel, government block, tomb. Then he lives and works there, and there only. Not for him the triumphant self-display of lesser monarchs: every day is spent in reading, annotating, dispatching mountains of documents, letters, memoranda, acts, charters, orders, with minute attention. His councils and his bureaucracy we have referred to; the instructions which set them to work all come from him personally. Coldly impervious to the human effects of his policies, the ruin of cities or of whole provinces, the insurrection of Granada, the loss of armies or fleets, the ruin of families or the hatred of victims—none of which he ever confronts—he suffers uncertainties only on points of theology; his advisers are able to reassure him on issues which seem to us strangely pedantic, such as how to break a promise of safe-conduct or how to exculpate the murder of a favourite.

This bizarre reign is not that of a Renaissance prince. Philip has literally no time for Italian splendours; he surrounds himself with inquisitors rather than men of profane learning; lives frugally (for all the rumours of debauchery); interests himself in but one art, painting, to adorn his palace and the kingdom's monasteries and churches. But his taste is solitary: although he has an odd weakness for the old Flemish eccentric Hieronymus Bosch, he rejects the work of arguably the greatest religious artist living in his kingdom—El Greco.

It is just as well that his authority is unshakably strong, and buttressed by the Church as well as by an army of spies. For no ruler is more effective than the efficiency of his agents allows. And in Spain, as in other lands in his time, efficiency is rather low. The annual treasure fleet arrives by order at Seville; between its original loading and the receipt of treasure unaccountable losses occur. Early in Philip's reign, the traditional provincial Cortes resist his will; later there are towns which simply cannot pay their—his—taxes, or remain at best unenthusiastic about collecting them. Great nobles impose their own private levies on their lands before the king's men can get their cut. The 'privileges' of Aragon resist his rapacity; those of Portugal he dare not challenge. Such abatements of his resources are kept quiet, but foreign ambassadors report them.

We have noted the disorder and vagrancy of the times. At Philip's accession Spain is bankrupt, and for all his power and empire, for all the wealth and treasure of America and Italy and the Low Countries, the state is bankrupt again at his death. But not all within it are equally impoverished. There are in Spain two estates whose wealth is prodigious: the Church and the great nobility. Both compensate themselves for the deficiencies of liberality of the morose prince, and on a scale the more stunning for the contrasting poverty of the country. At the death of Philip the court bursts into a blaze of glory—at last—even while Spanish sea trade is being destroyed and plague and brigandage spread unchecked. With huge resources of patronage, of which we see something through the eye of Velázquez, Spain becomes the exporter of style and fashion and etiquette and—less predictably—literary fashion to the courts and nobility, even the commonalty, of Europe. The poet Gongora and his contorted virtuosity (again a trace of the Baroque?) casts a longer shadow than the Italian Marini on the poetry of conceit; Spanish music (fed also by talent from the Low Countries and Naples—Comes, Morales, Victoria) sets the standard of excellence in church music; Spanish rule in the Low Countries shares with Rome the patronage of Baroque painting—Rubens alongside Bernini—and in devotional writing, pastoral theology, and Christian apologetic she dominates Catholic Europe. All these superiorities pour from the Spain of Philip II.

There is another side to the coin, to which we may be sure he would have been even less attentive, since it commemorates the costs of his rule. From the start of the reign, in contrast with the official, and therefore important, forms of art which reflect the universe of order, there comes into being another literature which recognizes the reality of disorder. Of course reality has been present all along in popular anecdote and burlesque, picked up in tales or alluded to in sermons, but now it dictates a more elaborate form of its own and not in the least a classical one. We do not know the author of the very first 'novel' to be centred on the life of a vagabond, *Don Lazarillo de Tormes* (1554), nor what exactly he has in mind when he evokes around this dubious 'hero' a panorama of low life. His 'invention' lies not in conceiving all the incidents which are strung together—these are simply lifted from popular repertory—but in framing them in a loose sequence of adventure, shocking mishaps, and repeated fresh starts, a sequence which does not need, and does not have, an Aristotelian beginning or end, so long as it keeps the reader in the mood for the next episode . . . and the next . . . 'Don' Lazarillo is the pimping offspring of a whore and a thief, begotten on the banks of the river Tormes: that is a sort of beginning. The end—one assumes it to be the end—sees him married off to the concubine of the archpriest of Toledo and appointed towncrier, to keep him quiet. In between, the world of misrule throws up beggars as vindictive as Satan, priests as hypocritical as any prince, and Lazarillo no better than the worst. Naturally this tale of a rogue, or *picaro*, is a parody: confronting the romances of chivalry, the *picaro* takes a burlesque title to key us in, and the adventures thereafter pursue their wayward story-line in mockery of the would-be order of the world. This, together with a certain verve and elegance, is enough to account for *Lazarillo*'s huge success in its time: there is not an atom of sermonizing or 'social criticism' in the anonymous author's message.

Half a century later, however, when Philip's reign has run its course, the *Buscon* (1626) of Queveda y Villegas (this time we know our author: a minor noble, courtier, and politician) pulls the picaresque novel out of its ambiguities. As before, there is the wayward string of adventures and shocking basenesses and treacheries. But the scene has been extended; the rogues and vagrants are joined by tradesmen and barbers, usurers and tailors and doctors and hangmen, by reprobate bureaucrats too, *letrados* and *arbitristas* (financial advisers to the crown). All these are now venal, corrupt, strangers to faith and truth and loyal service. The *déclassé hidalgo* among them is no better either: he has decayed into a grotesque, a horror. Away with them all! 'Ship them to America, which is the land for truants and *picaros* and adventurers.' That is, clear them out of Spain, which is in terrible disorder, almost beyond repair. The cause? Bad policies urged on the prince by his unworthy servants. Who alone might stop that drift to chaos and disgrace? Only the noble, the idealist, the representative of an order pledged to duty and justice. Say a Queveda . . . Should we call this another *Baroque* dream? Hardly; the aspiration may be there, but it is futile; and further, what is noble in the picaresque scenes?

At about this same time, there is another *hidalgo*, a veteran of the wars and of Lepanto, the adventurer Miguel de Cervantes, whose greatest literary composition is not picaresque but yet evokes a parallel theme of disorder. Don Quixote makes his first sally from the backward province of la Mancha (1604) to tilt at windmills; driven by illusions and noble dreams as archaic as those of Queveda, he too affirms a vanished world of faith and justice against the drift of society which is meaningless to him and can only appear ordered (if at all) to much commoner, lowlier spirits. It is by no means clear that Cervantes intends us *only* to laugh: if Don Quixote provokes the amazement or contempt of innkeepers and shepherds, cynics and rascals, he re-ceives a touching loyalty from the curate, the bachelor, and the servant. And Sancho Panza too, stands for something solid, if commonplace, which has no place in the picaresque. We therefore do not sell Cervantes short, as most of his early admirers seem to have done (including Philip III) when they savour the Don's side-splitting misadventures, his lucid and edifying death scene, his recognition of the illusion of romance and chivalry in the face of a less inspiring reality.

Just as later in Japan the samurai, so in sixteenth-century Spain the *hidalgo* finds himself at the rough end of a process of social change (and partial disintegration): to the last he affirms his ideal, at least in literature, even as the necessities and indifference of the prince makes them more and more irrelevant—and pathetic. In retrospect, the grandeur of the Spanish prince may have earned no more lasting honour than this: that out of these *minor* forms of literary entertainment, a handful of picaresque tales and *Don Quixote*, there emerges in time something else quite unimagined, even unimaginable four hundred years ago—the modern novel.

Absolute Rulers: (ii) Louis XIV

Like Philip, Louis of France has the issue of personal authority won for him before his reign begins; he then rules for a very long time; and dies leaving a realm prostrated by war and bankruptcy. There is also a distant parallel in the fact that Louis faces religious schism and, like Philip, deals with it with absolute arbitrariness and extreme brutality, with no apparent benefit either to the faithful or to the persecuted. In each case, Spain in the sixteenth, France in the late seventeenth century, the greatest power in western Europe is terribly weakened through policies which flow from the will of one man.

There the parallel tails off. Louis' reign commences not with an *auto-da-fé* but with extravagant profane festivities, jousting and liberality, fashionable jollifications. Pensions are distributed to a swarm of writers (the carrot to go with the stick of censorship); the Louvre is refronted pompously; a little hunting-lodge is rebuilt, partly with the spoils from a fallen favourite's palace (this is the beginning of Versailles, and the work goes on for half a century). A 'golden age' has dawned. In the artificial wonderland of the hastily constructed Versailles and its spreading gardens, royal fêtes are mounted (1664, 1668, 1674): in these occasions we find a whole anthology of a hundred years of courtly self-advertisement, assembled in one deliberate effulgence. On the very first, the *Pleasures of the Enchanted Isle* celebrates not a dynastic marriage, but simply the rape of a pretty lady; it features martial cavalcades and knightly displays and dancing, actors royal and otherwise taking on the dashing roles of Rinaldo and his companions to enact an Ariostan fairy-tale. The grandee Duc de Saint-Aignan is master of ceremonies, the comedian Molière is sergeant-major, fireworks are let off by the Italian engineer Vigarani, there are marine displays, parades of wild animals, pompous mythological addresses of loyalty, stage performances of lyrical-heroic fantasy, copious banquets, and a final blowing-up of the sorceress Alcine's island. All this conjured out of a swamp and a hunting park! What can the prince's will and liberality not bring about? That the lesson should not go unheeded, the narrative of this first festival is carefully recorded by Molière, and a volume of magnificent commemorative engravings distributed to the courts of Europe. These lavish pleasures of the king are propaganda, even if they are held rather a long way out of Paris. Everything is in them, except opera. However, in a repeat performance in 1674 that omission is remedied: to mark the prince's victorious return from war, the composer Lully contrives the inclusion of his *Alceste* and secures a *monopoly* for the performance of this kind of enchantment throughout the kingdom. Opera has been naturalized in France.

The monarch grows up. He abandons the peculiarly French custom of dancing, cuts off his hair and puts on the Spanish wig (already fashionable), introduces more and more of the Spanish *hauteur* into court behaviour, damps down the scandals of his harem, builds the chapel in his pleasure palace, settles down to control all the doings of his servants and ministers, much like Philip: every morning shut up in his cabinet, he superintends appointments, financial problems, diplomatic exchanges, preparation for war or peace, buildings, suppression of heresy or Jansenism. Under a heavy tyranny, the 'golden age' of literature tails off—the creative days of La Fontaine and Molière, Boileau and Racine and the aged Corneille are over by the time Louis settles at Versailles, and he forgets his 'French Academy' of writers; in compensation though there is the academy of music (and every day the royal chapel is supplied with fresh music by Couperin or others); the Academy of Sciences is founded, and patronage of the decorative arts is nourished with every enlargement of Versailles, or Trianon, or Marly. Without Louis, it is an open question whether French 'classicism', as we call it, would have been less parochial than say Tudor architecture or Franconian Baroque; thanks to Louis and his long reign, it becomes the model to all Europe.

There develops here a remarkable consistency of styles, embracing architecture, decoration, painting,

99 Hyacinthe Rigaud, *Portrait of Louis XIV*, 1701. Oil on canvas, 10⅞ × 7⅜ in (27.7 × 19.4 cm). Paris, Musée du Louvre

The ne plus ultra of personal majesty, and a face of absolutism to be copied by lesser princes: Rigaud's Louis XIV, in robes of state, sword of office, and court wig. But is the expression of the face benign, or merely implacable?

sculpture, furnishings, garden landscaping: 'classical' (though of course no longer 'Roman'), and rather heavy in its pretensions. Its artisans are Le Vau, Le Nôtre, Mansart, Lebrun, Rigaud; a prodigious cohort of submissive talent. Its increasing uniformity symbolizes an order, that of the prince *and his state*: not brio, not Baroque, but a settled majesty (elegance is for another time). The organizing theme is naturally that of the 'Sun-King': Louis-Apollo, patron of Muses, god of life and light, a 'Renaissance' theme applied with absolute thoroughness. The performer at the centre is indeed a sun-god to his courtiers—and to all others, as his dis-

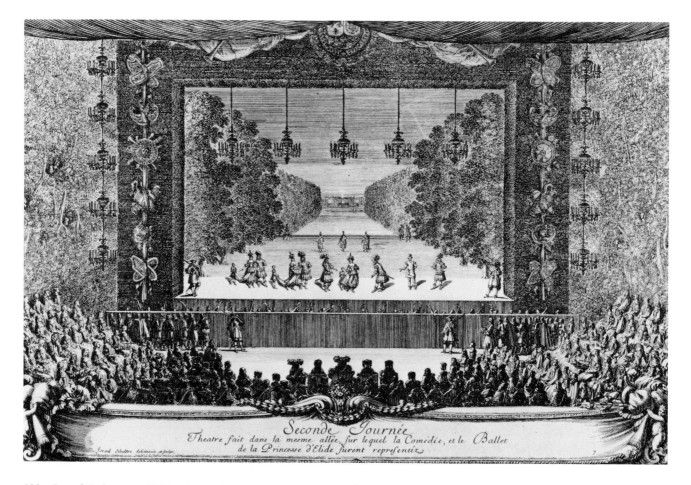

Seconde Journée
Theatre fait dans la mesme allée, sur lequel la Comédie, et le Ballet
de la Princesse d'Élide furent representez.

100   Israel Sylvestre (1621–91), Carlo Vigarani's setting for *La Princesse d'Élide*, **staged at Versailles as part of** *Les Fêtes de l'Île enchantée*, **1664. Engraving. Paris, Bibliothèque Nationale**

On the second day of the Fêtes *of the Enchanted Isle at Versailles (1664), the comedian Molière, on a stage astride Le Nôtre's new central avenue (most of the greenery consists of hastily planted shrubs and cut branches) performs a new play,* La Princesse d'Élide, *with ballet* intermezzi. *The set itself offers a certain piquancy: we, and the spectators of 1664, are looking not at a painted perspective backdrop but at a real avenue leading to the real pleasure-palace just completed for the young monarch.*

gruntled subject the Duc de Saint-Simon observes: presence at court is essential to catch a ray of patronage or favour, absence is certain disfavour; merely to be noticed by the prince as he takes the air is a triumph. The unity of the style, the unique polarity of the monarch himself, the silencing of open discord—this is all one huge accomplishment of the absolute will.

It would be an exaggeration to say that from this

hypnotic example Europe learns to dream of an integrated culture, a pre-established harmony of forms and feelings and perspectives, an integrated society. For of course there have been other, humbler, examples; princes have their liveries, artisans merge their efforts, generalized leitmotivs iterate a propaganda line . . . And moreover this integration is purely superficial; it marks out what is in fact an entirely *artificial* capital; it ignores perennial religious discords outside—the repression of Protestantism, endless obstinate (and eventually political) wranglings over the puritanical tenets of Jansenism; it ignores too obscurer rumblings—vagrancy, rural distress, famines. The lesson goes out to lesser courts of Europe, but it is a treacherous one. Not least because by the end of Louis's reign it is quite clear that in a kingdom as great as his the precarious unities of Versailles will not survive. And in the regency which follows the death of the monarch the pomp itself gives place to prettiness, dignity to comfort, and absolutism to expediency.

Chapter 5

A Reformation Culture
in the Netherlands

'Should anyone be about to set up a Republic, he should consider at the start whether it is to expand (like Rome) in extent and power or to be confined within narrow limits'?
Machiavelli, *Discorsi*

Reforms and republics

At the opening of the seventeenth century, a small republic stands almost alone in the north-west of Europe, repeatedly at war with the princes of a Spanish empire which threatens its existence. It survives; and for a hundred years it flourishes as no other state in Europe. At last its small size proves too much of a handicap, and it slowly sinks back to a role more proportionate to its real resources. But in the meanwhile it has made unique contributions to European statecraft, arts, technology, exploration, thought, and law; and although its particular tensions do not enter into a European heritage, the achievements do. We are looking, evidently, at the Dutch Republic.

Machiavelli, one imagines, would have been intrigued by this society, had he lived to see it; for the ex-secretary of the Florentine Republic, as well as writing a monograph on the prince, also writes a longer monograph on republics, the *Discourses on the Histories of Livy*. He would have been fascinated to see, for example, how a society which remains 'confined within narrow limits' nevertheless achieves a quite extraordinary growth and extension, and that in a manner not achieved by his own Florence. He would also find this republic in several respects different from the Roman Republic which he has studied so diligently: in its diffused constitutional arrangements, for example. And above all, no doubt, he would have been surprised by its religious institutions; for he dies several years too soon to take account of a major cultural change, very important for the Netherlands, which is still called the Protestant Reformation.

Between 1517 and 1520 the revolt of Martin Luther is a decisive crisis in the long build-up of dissatisfaction within the Church. His attack on the spiritual authority of the Roman papacy is a many-sided one: theological, but also institutional and political; and of course economic and social too in its outcome. Luther's success in northern Europe does not, it is true, undermine the *principle* of authority itself, either religious or secular; he is no enemy of princes, for he sees them as called upon to correct errors or abuses which may arise in the Church; he is himself powerfully shielded from his adversaries by a German prince; and the Confession of Augsburg (1530) is a doctrinal statement subscribed by a dozen German princes. They, no less than 'the cobbler, the smith, and the peasant', have their 'calling and duty', in the station in life to which it has pleased God to call them. Indeed, Luther has no sympathy at all with the starving or the oppressed when they rise against their appointed masters: the peasants' revolt of 1524 evokes from him the most unbridled call for its repression. In short, the Evangelical Church as it comes into being is compatible with an unchanged political order in Germany; the ruler even has a more direct control over his bishops than before, as well as an interest in the dissolution of monasteries and the arrest of flows of money to Rome. By a change of doctrine, it is only an *alien* authority which has been abolished; why should this overset other political arrangements?

The Lutheran Evangelical Church is not, however, the only form of Protestant Church to issue from the wave of resistance to papal authority. There are other sects as well: 'Anabaptists' of varying complexion, followers of the Swiss evangelical reformer Zwingli, and in particular the 'reformed' Churches associated with the name of the Frenchman John Calvin. A principle guiding all of them is the search for the 'primitive' purity of the early, simple Christian Churches; this in effect implies small, self-governing, localized con-

Chronology for Chapter 5

1566	Calvinist iconoclasm in Antwerp and other Netherlands cities
1567–73	Duke of Alva Spanish governor of Netherlands, briefed to repress Protestantism
1575	Leyden University founded by William of Orange (the Silent)
1576	Antwerp sacked by mutinous Spanish troops
1579	Union of Utrecht effectively marks beginning of independent Dutch Republic
1584	Assassination of William of Orange
1587	Earl of Leicester withdraws from Netherlands; Leyden University botanic garden founded
1592	Elzevir family begin printing at Leyden
1593	William Barentz sets out to seek north-east passage to East Indies
1595	Cornelius Houtman leads first Dutch expedition to Java
1602	Dutch East India Company founded
1606	Dutch ship makes first landfall by European explorers on Australia; death of Lipsius
1609	Twelve-Year Truce signed with Spain; Dutch establish trading station in Japan; Hudson explores east coast of North America for Dutch East India Company; Amsterdam bank founded
c. 1610	Microscope invented, probably by Zacharias Janzoonz
1618–19	Synod of Dort imposes strict Calvinist orthodoxy in Dutch Republic
1618–48	Thirty Years War in Central Europe
1619	Execution of Oldenbarnevelt
1622	Calvinism becomes state religion of Dutch Republic
1623	Dutch massacre of English merchants at Amboyna in the Moluccas
1624	Dutch colonists found New Amsterdam (New York)
1625	Death of Maurice of Nassau, prince of Orange; Grotius's *De Jure Belli ac Pacis* published
1636	Descartes's *Discourse on Method* published
c. 1637	'Tulipomania' at its height in Holland
1641	Dutch establish control over Malacca
1642	Tasman discovers Van Diemen's Land (Tasmania); Rembrandt's *The Night Watch*
1646	Death of Grotius
1648	Treaty of Münster ends Thirty Years War and confirms sovereignty of the Dutch Republic
1650	Death of William II of Orange; birth of William III
1652	Permanent Dutch settlement established at Cape of Good Hope
1652–4	First Dutch War with England, caused by shipping and commercial rivalries
1656	Christian Huygens applies pendulum to regulate clockwork
1661	Rembrandt's *Conspiracy of Julius Civilis*
1664	English seize New Amsterdam
1665–7	Second Dutch War with England
1672–4	Third Dutch War with England
1675	Death of Vermeer
1677	Spinoza's *Ethics* published; William III of Orange marries Mary, daughter of the future James II of England
1689	William of Orange and Mary accept English crown

101   Nicolas Visscher I (*c.* 1550–*c.* 1612), Engraving of the Amsterdam Bourse, 1612. Amsterdam, Gemeentelijke Archiefdienst

Not by any means the first building to serve the needs of trade, but certainly the first Stock Exchange as we understand the term: where modern transactions of commerce and speculation can be conducted year-round, in all weather. This early engraving, which conveys the necessary message of wealth and solidity, is further adorned by laudatory verses taken from Amsterdam's illustrious citizen P. C. Hooft.

gregations. As with Luther, Calvin teaches that the faithful soul must face his Maker and Judge armed with trust and faith, not with propitiatory works; he has no need of a specially privileged priesthood, and he cannot benefit from the intercession of a hierarchy of saints or pious souls. Calvin goes beyond Luther in a number of respects, however, and nowhere more visibly than in placing at the centre of his creed a doctrine of predestination—that is to say, a belief that God bestows his grace on those whom he chooses, and that they alone are destined to be saved: all others are damned. This is a new kind of exclusiveness, but also a new kind of fellow-feeling. Established in the little state of Geneva around 1538, Calvin's reformed Church develops a system of self-government of a form curiously close to that of the municipality itself—authoritarian, certainly, and also woven into the secular structures of society: the 'consistory' which heads the congregation even has its meetings chaired by the town syndic. Evidently, no need is felt for bishops or similar established figures of authority: instead there is an equality of citizens, of the elect before God. Republican in spirit and in form, Calvinism reserves no special place for princes, though there is no prejudice against them either, and in a practical way their protection is very acceptable: Henry of

Navarre, later king of France, grows up a Calvinist, and so do other hereditary rulers, but without in any way determining the nature of this new style of ecclesiastical organization.

Lutheran Evangelical Churches take a hold in Saxony, Brandenburg, Prussia, Scandinavia; the southern lands—Spain, Italy—and most of the Hapsburg lands in Germany hold the reforming movements at bay; in England, the Tudor monarchy secures the material and political advantages of reform while attempting no more than a compromise with Lutheran doctrine. At the same time Calvinism spreads out of Geneva through France from the mid-century (giving rise to a series of frightful civil wars), and into the Palatinate, Scotland, parts of England, and the Low Countries.

It is in the midst of the turmoil of religious dissensions, repressions, wars, and reformations on all sides that the United Provinces of the Netherlands rise up in a bid for freedom from the rule of the Most Catholic King of Spain, Philip II, who has inherited these lands from his father, the Emperor Charles V. The revolt of the Netherlands bears the mark of the age in this respect, that it is hard to say whether economic or religious 'causes' are the more important in provoking it. As in the earlier case of Geneva, which throws off the rule of

102   Hendrick Vroom (1566–1640), *The Explosion of the Spanish Flag Ship during the Battle of Gibraltar on 25 April 1607*. Oil on canvas, 54⅛ × 74 in (137.5 × 188 cm). Amsterdam, Rijksmuseum

A republic whose survival depends on control of the sea takes readily to views of naval achievement. Vroom leads the way in a new specialism, combining seascapes with historical reportage. His view of a naval action in the Gibraltar roads shows a Dutch boarding party coming alongside the Spanish galleon which has been rammed and in this instant explodes. All the interest is in detail: collapsing masts, drowning figures, a pennant blown skywards, men and ladders flying in the air from the force of the explosion . . . Compare plate 78.

103   Jan van Goyen (1596–1656), *A Windmill by a River*, 1642. Oil on panel, 11½ × 14½ in (29.4 × 36.3 cm). London, National Gallery

Everybody's image of a Dutch country scene—the unending flat countryside, weather-beaten windmill, scattered figures, water, distant villages, low skyline and huge cloud-filled sky . . . an atmosphere, undoubtedly; but also a moral climate?

**104   Pieter Saenredam,
*Interior of the Buurkerk,
Utrecht,* 1644. Oil on
panel, 23⅝ × 19¾ in (60.1 ×
50.1 cm). London,
National Gallery**

*Saenredam, a specialist in
depicting public buildings
(compare plate 105), has subtly
dramatized the proportions of
this great church while
rendering it with an otherwise
chilly precision. The figures in
the foreground are children,
those further off are reduced in
scale, as though to emphasize
the echoing space within an
unadorned place of worship.*

the duke of Savoy, the two grounds of revolt are inter-woven: resistance to extortionate taxation by a distant prince, resistance to an autocratic attempt to suppress heresy. In the event, a wave of (Calvinist) iconoclasm in 1566 stings Philip into appointing one of his most formidable lieutenants, the duke of Alva, to suppress resistance *and* heresy. Within two years revolt is widespread; by 1574 Alva is rejected by Holland and Zeeland (two most strongly Calvinist states), and, by the time

Amsterdam joins in, all the main towns north of Antwerp are included in the uprising, and the states that comprise them are persuaded by a Calvinist prince, William of Orange, to form a confederacy to fight for their complete freedom. The two decades of war which follow, in which more states join the revolt (including for a time Antwerp, which is predominantly Catholic) illustrate that freedom from Spain is more highly prized than either confessional purity or republican rule. We see this when an attempt is made by the rebels to replace Philip as their lawful ruler by installing the French (and Catholic) duke of Anjou as titular duke of Brabant and count of Flanders—a disastrous experiment, since Anjou has ambitions of his own, wantonly attacks Antwerp, and has to be expelled. Following the assassination of William of Orange, a further experiment brings the English earl of Leicester (another disaster) and then an invitation to the French King Henry III (declined). It is only after these experiments in the search for a titular sovereign that the United Provinces settle down to accept that their traditional Estates-General can do duty as a collective and sole sovereign—or perhaps that the individual states have each a residual sovereignty: the detail of the question is not fully resolved. At all events, the realization comes slowly; it is only from the end of the century that we can confidently talk of a Dutch Republic. Even then, there is *de facto* a representative of one princely family, descended from the great William of Orange, who enjoys a special status—that of 'lieutenant', or *Stadhouder*, of most of the individual states; this is combined with the nominated post of captain-general of the republic's armies whenever war impends. For a prince's competences lie in war and in international diplomacy, and the republic cannot conveniently do without these competences. At least, in such an anomalous arrangement, the prince is not very likely to make a bid for sole and autocratic power. Many of the nobility of the Netherlands, having either sided with the king of Spain or stood aside from the recent struggle, are by now of almost no political account in the community that has emerged; this means that they are incapable of intervening strongly to support a would-be autocrat. This is visible in the pattern of government of Holland, the largest state: its estates comprise representatives for each of the large towns, and reserve exactly one seat for a noble to represent the countryside and smaller places.

Narrow limits

It is essential to hold in mind the very small size of the Dutch Republic. Its territory is small; the 'remoteness' of a town such as Groningen or Franeker is a purely relative term. Communication poses no real problem: distances are short, the network of rivers and canals and ports unequalled. And the population is tiny—in all, some 750,000 souls. Of these, 100,000 are in Amsterdam, a town which a century before was barely a tenth that size; the next largest town, Leyden, has 45,000 inhabitants; and apart from Utrecht all others are much smaller—The Hague, which is the seat of the Estates-General and also of the *Stadhouder*, has barely 15,000.

Yet more than half the Dutch population live in towns: and this is a staggering concentration for the age. Moreover, the nation, though tiny, is growing fast, not least by a flow of refugees and traders from the Spanish-held southern provinces. Thus in 1600 we find Amsterdam's citizens building six hundred new town houses; and in the ensuing century the population of the town doubles again. By contrast, Antwerp, which has been Europe's busiest city in 1550, suffers a series of disasters. Sacked by Spanish soldiery in 1576, then on joining the revolt besieged and taken again by the duke of Parma in 1585, then losing many exiles to the north, and—worst of all—cut off from its main trading routes by the new republic: it is not surprising that a once thriving population sinks by half to around 45,000.

The republic, then, is small and compact and very urbanized, and growing. It has preserved and shaped to its new freedom a political and social system which, taken with the new independence, is uniquely significant for its culture. To begin with, each small state is self-governing. Its traditional governing body or estates, and the municipal councils too, raise only those taxes to which their members freely consent; sometimes even a town, especially Amsterdam, stands out against what is regarded as the general interest. The 'regents'—burgomasters and town councillors and jurors (*schepenen*), as well as the delegates to the estates (and beyond that to the Estates-General of the republic)—are recruited from solid families in good standing, that is to say, well-to-do merchants or sons of merchants, members of really rather small social groups. To all intents and purposes they form a bundle of small oligarchies; each co-opts its new members, who often serve for life, the while dispensing patronage to friends or hangers-on and combining to decide key issues of policy. One might expect that a class of patricians would soon emerge, combining wealth with immovable power as in Venice, and equally haughty and remote. This does not quite happen, because internal disagreements within the republic produce in almost every generation a crisis, a shift of power, and at least some turnover of official appointments; in the crisis of 1618, shortly to be discussed, a quarter of the regents deputed to the state of Holland are replaced. And there is also some social mobility: expansion brings newly enriched families within reach of public office. For both these reasons, the regents are not quite a closed class. Even so, their political rights are not in practice open to individuals who may come up on the outside of the network of their families or by sheer talent attract attention. Some of the most outstanding figures of the re-

105   Pieter Saenredam (1597–1665), *Amsterdam Town Hall*, 1657. Oil on panel, 25⅜ × 32⅝ in (64.5 × 83 cm). Amsterdam, Rijksmuseum

This painting of the Old Town Hall conveys a clear idea of the modest status of Amsterdam before the city's prodigious growth makes it the chief financial centre of Europe. Compare the next plate.

106   Gerrit A. Berckheyde (1638–98), *The Cathedral Square of Amsterdam with the New Town Hall and Exchange*, 1668. Oil on canvas, 21 × 24¾ in (53.5 × 63 cm). Karlsruhe, Staatliche Kunsthalle

The New Town Hall, commissioned in mid-century by the Regents of Amsterdam, may not be as ornate or dashing as a Baroque palace, but its restrained classicism (pilasters, swags over the lines of windows, pediment, cupola) conveys a sense of cosmopolitan dignity—and also reveals the penetration of standards of 'taste' from neighbouring (and hitherto allied) France.

107   Jan Porcellis (*c.* 1584–1632), *Sailing Boats and Rowing Boats*, 1629. Oil on panel, 10⅝ × 14 in (27 × 35.5 cm). Leiden, Stedelijk Museum 'De Lakenhal'

Porcellis's seascape off the Holland shore portrays a huge sky, lowering clouds driven by the wind that stirs the waves, and the ubiquitous Dutch sailing vessels; one of these is loading merchandise inshore. A factual and undramatic record whose veracity any Dutchman can check for himself.

public (Oldenbarnevelt, Grotius, Cots) rise in this way, and rapidly—but to bureaucratic appointments. As city advocates or 'pensionaries', with influence and standing to be sure, they serve the regime of the regents without ever being quite assimilated to them.

In the middle of this confederation of little oligarchies of commercial wealth, active in their city and state organizations and the Estates-General which is the overall co-ordinator and ultimate authority, the position of the *Stadhouder* remains peculiar. The princes of Orange are men of extraordinary ability: William of Orange (who really founds the republic), Maurice (the most famous general in Europe), his brother Frederick Henry (a subtle diplomat with dynastic ambitions, and wealthy enough to assemble around himself a little cosmopolitan court at The Hague), William II (who dies in the middle of an unfinished coup in 1650 and discredits the dynasty), and of course William III, who recovers the lost ground in 1672 and later succeeds to the throne of England. Inevitably the *Stadhouder* has patronage and influence; he also polarizes allegiance. There is an Orange party, both aristocratic and populist; and there is an opposite faction favouring the municipal regents if tension arises between them and the prince. (Only in 1650 do we begin to notice a third, more radical, democratic strain of thinking, similar in

its ideals to the radical dissent faced by that other, much more dictatorial '*Stadhouder*', Oliver Cromwell, in England in the same decade: then Johan de la Court spells out arguments for more extensive kinds of freedom.) In the meantime, there can—and will—be *Stadhouder*less interregnums, in time of peace; and against that there is always the possibility that the prince will find occasions to rally a mass of support to his side against the regents.

The real business of the republic is in any case not one in which a prince is expected to be proficient. It is business. In the Estates-General, Holland is the dominant state; and among the eighteen towns of Holland, Amsterdam wields by far the most power. What does she use it for? Increase of trade. There is a large volume of existing traffic with Germany, Denmark, the Baltic, and beyond, on which the Dutch economy heavily depends; also with France, and, paradoxically, with the enemy Spain (which needs to import northern grain); interests edge even further afield to the Mediterranean and Turkey and the Levant. With independence and the eclipse of Antwerp, though, come boundless new possibilities: and they are pounced on by Amsterdam, leading the Estates-General along with it.

Expansion

In the summer of 1593, while the issue of independence is still very much in doubt, Amsterdam venturers led by Moucheron (a refugee from Antwerp) and William Barentz set out to discover a *north-east* passage to the East Indies. A heroic idea, but of course doomed to failure; in consequence the Dutch traders accept the inevitable alternative, which is to confront Portugal (and therefore the king of Spain) by capturing a southern route for their trade. Accordingly, Cornelius Houtman's little fleet, financed by Amsterdam, is the first of several expeditions that set out in 1595 and the years following to round the Cape of Good Hope; four or five venture companies are set up. In 1602 they are all merged into one United East India Company, a national institution set up with a huge share capital open to subscription by any Dutch citizen; thousands buy shares, with Amsterdam merchants taking up a good half; of the company's five 'chambers' that in Amsterdam is the most important. We are looking at the first publicly quoted joint-stock company in history, permanent and with transferable shares. Fortified with a monopoly from the Estates-General, its expeditions proceed to set up trading posts at Bantam and at Amboyna in the Moluccas, where spice plantations are developed; a colony in Java; posts in Formosa, Ceylon,

108   Hendrick Avercamp (1585–1634), *A Scene on the Ice near a Town*, c. 1610. Oil on panel, 23 × 35½ in (58 × 90 cm). London, National Gallery

A steady demand for this type of compendious winter scene in Dutch art must derive in part from pleasure felt in observing the transformations wrought on familiar scenes and their tonalities, as well as the characteristic postures of skaters and other holiday-makers on the ice.

India, the Gulf, St Helena, Mauritius, eventually a fortress at the Cape (1652). The Dutch alone survive the exclusion of Europeans from Japan, retaining a trading post in the bay of Nagasaki by a signal favour of the shogun. In Batavia a local governor comes to preside over a large colony. To achieve all this they shoulder aside (and not at all gently) any rivals (Portuguese or English) already in the field, and in half a century the company has created a vast if sketchy trading empire with complete and secure communications. It has 50,000 men in its employ. The main beneficiaries of its trade are Amsterdam businessmen who buy up the imported rarities, such as cloves, mace, and Chinese ceramics. But other benefits are not negligible: this activity swells the demand for ships at yards outside Amsterdam (the company's great Indiamen are far too large ever to get near the port) other procurement needs and commerce at large.

Two rather specialized non-commercial kinds of spin-off might be added. The first is exploration. In seeking to develop the business of Batavia, William Janszoon discovers Australia by accident (1606), landing on the west side of Queensland in the Gulf of Carpentaria. In 1615 the independent-minded Jacques Le Maire, not to be put down by exclusion from the company's routes, sails westwards round Cape Horn, pioneering a new route to the east. In 1623 Arnhem Land is discovered and named. In the 1630s, Dutch captains chart the long coast of Western Australia which they call New Holland. Tasman attempts a southerly route to America and comes upon New Zealand. Others will take up and carry further these discoveries; though like the Portuguese a century earlier, the Dutch are simply not a numerous enough nation to build on every discovery—especially on those which are judged to be marginal to commerce.

109 Jan Treck (c. 1606–52), *Still-life with a Pewter Flagon*, 1649. Oil on canvas, 51⅛ × 43¾ in (130 × 110 cm). London, National Gallery

A still-life offers both truth of rendering and virtuosity—here for example the lights on the pewter mug, or the hop-stem entwining it—and also pride of possession: the two Chinese (Ming) bowls, readily identified by the time this picture is painted, are among the valued trophies of a Dutch East India trade.

The second by-product of overseas trade is of course cartography. The greatest map-makers of the Netherlands, Gerhard Kremer (Mercator) and Abraham Ortelius, are both dead by 1598; but Wagenaer, who engraves charts of the coasts of Western Europe and the Baltic, is given a pension by the state of Holland, and with his great productions Leyden becomes a major centre for the engraving of maps.

Alongside the epoch-making East India Company, a second milestone achieved by Amsterdam is also crucial to business: the *Amsterdamsche Wisselbank* (exchange bank) of 1609. Already of course there are in use the usual techniques and facilities of commercial credit, needed and used by traders in exactly the same way as in Antwerp or Florence or anywhere else. There is also an unusual institution, the *bourse*, where sophisticated speculation has been carried on among businessmen for at least twenty years, in the open or in a handy church, and for which the city erects a very handsome new building, brought into use in 1611—the world's first stock exchange. The originality of Amsterdam's public bank, now, stems from the fact that it receives a monopoly for currency exchange, in which therefore something like an organized and orderly market is created. It also has a monopoly for the deposit of high-value commercial paper; wealthy merchants must therefore open accounts with it if they are to be involved in large-scale transactions. And while the bank does not make advances to small clients, it does make loans to the town, to the East India Company, to the states of Holland. Perhaps the symbolic significance of all this is even more important: the municipal bank is performing publicly and visibly the most crucial function of capitalism—the mobilization of funds, and their profitable application. One result of this mobilization, and of the efficacy of financial practices as a whole, is a low rate of interest (often 3 per cent), the envy of Europe.

In 1609 also, the year in which a twelve-year truce with Spain is at last signed, and serves as a spur to new ambition, the merchants of Amsterdam turn their attention westwards: to girdle the globe, no less. The English explorer Hudson is hired by the East India Company to go off and discover a *north-west* passage. This turns out to be another mirage, but at least we cannot fault the company for not framing grand conceptions. In discovering the Hudson River, which the explorer hopes may yet be the desired waterway to the Pacific, the effort is in any case not wasted. A New Netherlands Company is promptly formed to exploit a trade monopoly in fur, granted of course by the Estates-General; by 1624 a Dutch colony is established on the Hudson (New Netherlands); and New Amsterdam is of course the original name of a small town which, after capture by the English in 1664, will come to be better known under a substitute name—New York. A start is made to recruit and settle Dutch colonists up-country too, though not very many respond to the opportunity.

Most daring and speculative of all the Netherlands expansion projects is the West India Company, planned in Amsterdam but prudently blocked by policy until the twelve-year truce shall have come to an end (1621). This project is seen from the outset as a head-on confrontation with Spain and her colonies. Once again there is a public subscription of shares. A colony is set up in northern Brazil and the Angolan coast is wrested from the Portuguese (both to gain access to African gold and to control the slave trade which supplies the Brazilian sugar plantations). Further footholds are secured in Guyana, in Curaçao. But the real *raison d'être* of this company, its really exciting feature, is piracy; or perhaps one should call it spoliation. The Spanish treasure fleet which sails every year from Cartagena is to be systematically intercepted: in a good year a huge dividend can then be declared. Unfortunately, not many years are 'good'. Also, when Portugal recovers her independence (1640), Brazil too stirs, the Dutch colony is given up, and in the second half of the century the over-ambitious West India Company fades out of existence.

Arguably, these stupendous achievements of a few dozen shipfuls of Dutchmen going out to set up a global colonial empire are out of all proportion to the actual results for their home economy. It is still the European commerce which makes Amsterdam and her sister towns rich, though the spice trade adds a valuable supplement. What is striking, however, is that the republic, like no other state in Europe at this time, has put its economic life at the centre of its policy and is able to carry it forward without any inhibitions at all (except for the delay in commencing piracy in the West Indies). The results are startling, and appear even more so to contemporaries. Dutch poets celebrate with some complacency the bustle of Amsterdam's life, but foreigners regard it as miraculous. Here is a French observer in 1650 describing the city: 'The town of Amsterdam has recorded the weight of its merchandise this year: 6,000 pounds a day. It has laid out twenty-two bastions for enlargement, they will cost half-a-million each. Its town hall will cost eight millions before it is finished. In the port, the masts of 6,000 vessels stand up constantly like a great forest, though sometimes as many as six hundred ships set sail in one day. The bank has always a few millions in minted silver in its vaults, besides what the town uses . . .' Given the pace of this world of business, Sorbière's breathlessness is not to be wondered at. And the might of the city, and in particular the size of the Dutch fleet, is regularly overstated. But this is clearly because business interests have taken over as the central force in the running of the whole system of the state; energies and ships and money are mobilized with virtually no government impediment, and of course no royal predator. A striking small detail: bookkeeping is a respectable thing for boys at school to learn—no contempt anywhere in the land for these prosaic skills! Something of the same spirit appears to pervade not only large-scale enterprises of the breathtaking kind, but also the multitudinous smaller activities of economic life as well. Horticulture is specialized,

110 Jan Steen (1625/6–79), *Skittle Players*, *c*. 1662–3. Oil on panel, 13½ × 11 in (33.5 × 27 cm). London, National Gallery
Through and beyond the extreme of fidelity of execution in this famous picture, the artist seems to affirm the goodness of the plain things of life, caught in a moment of peace and repose outside a country inn.

and intensive; ship-building highly advanced; land use and engineering works unmatched anywhere in Europe . . . In consequence the tiny republic *appears* to outsiders much larger than it is, and far more powerful: which effectively *makes* it more powerful. The Lord favours his people . . .

Calvinism and tolerance

With the exception of the twelve-year truce with Spain (1609–21) the republic is at war for most of the first eighty years of its existence, and under constant threat of destruction. It escapes by alliances, especially with Spain's enemy, France; but also by valour, by its own large fleet, by hiring mercenary soldiers from abroad,

111   Meyndert Hobbema (1638–1709), *Road on a Dyke*, 1663. Oil on canvas, 46½ × 50½ in (108 × 128.3 cm). Private Collection.

Another highly characteristic 'Dutch' scene, destined to exercise great influence two centuries later; and once again refusal of high drama, an unemphatic yet tenacious exploring of the ordinary, with by now a certain weakening of the moral eye. Trees, cattle, tracks, human beings are a pleasure to recognize but not necessarily a challenge to ratiocinate.

and by hard-headed prudence. When in 1609 peace is possible, the regents are for it—against the *Stadhouder*'s instinct to go on fighting. When later an alliance with France is vital for survival, and the French minister Richelieu imposes conditions that include Dutch naval help against their fellow Calvinists the French Huguenots, resisting Richelieu in the port of La Rochelle, the regents squarely accept this betrayal of their faith. And unity survives. Nevertheless, in the middle of the truce the unity is put under a very severe strain; and it is typical that the issues leading to the execution of Oldenbarneveldt (advocate, or chief administrator, of the Estates-General) are a complex mixture of theology and politics.

Theology first: and here we encounter the Calvinist doctrine of predestination. Within the municipally run reformed Churches, there is (and probably always has been) a strong minority sentiment that this particular doctrine is, frankly, rigid and odious. The minority's leading Dutch exponent is a kindly theologian, Arminius, a pupil, no less, of Calvin's successor Bèze (Beza) in Geneva. He more and more insistently proclaims that salvation is open to *any* sinner who heeds the call of Jesus Christ. The strict Calvinist view is upheld by a theologian named Gomar, with a wide and popular following; he mounts a very violent attack on the backsliding faction. Arminius, under the weight of years

and virulent controversy, dies in 1609, but the dispute continues to grow, up and down the land. It is fanned by a movement of 'Remonstrants'—'Arminian' followers seeking a change in the teaching of the Churches—and by a campaign of 'anti-Remonstrants', whose preachers use their pulpits for highly inflammatory denunciations of laxity. No doubt the Gomarists see themselves emulating Calvin himself, who in 1551 has expelled from Geneva the preacher Bolsec for likewise arguing against predestination. Here in the Netherlands things are more complex: the states of Holland are appealed to, and being generally favourable to Arminius they seek to ban the carrying-on of the divisive dispute; Oldenbarneveldt himself favours this position, which would be consistent with his old master William of Orange's injunction to tolerance; only the regents of Amsterdam put on a show of puritanism and oppose it. Eventually the doctrinal issue is settled,

112   Rembrandt (1606–69), *Portrait of Agatha Bas*, 1641. Oil on canvas, 41⅛ × 33¼ in (104.5 × 85 cm). London, Royal Collection
Rembrandt's portrait of a rich burgher's wife conveys a suitable seriousness in the sitter, while it also gives prominence to her lace, jewellery, fan and costly black gown. Yet in sumptuary terms, this is far from being ostentatious by the standards of patrician Amsterdam.

113   Michiel Jan van Miereveld (1567–1641), *Portrait of the Stadhouder Maurice.* **Oil on canvas, 46⅞ × 37¼ in (119 × 94.5 cm). Hague, Mauritshuis, Foundation Johan Maurits van Nassau**

The Stadhouder Maurice, though he esteems himself the greatest general of the age, is shown in this careful though dull portrait against a marine, not a military, background. Allegory in fact prevails: the Stadhouder guides the ship of state through stormy times.

in favour of Gomar, by the Estates-General (and the *Stadhouder*) agreeing to summon a general synod, or council, of the reformed Churches, which at Dort in 1618 denounces Arminianism, decrees the dismissal of all Arminian pastors, and reaffirms the complete Calvin. From then on every pastor and teacher and civil servant in the republic is required to subscribe to the synod's articles of faith, including predestination.

Before the synod, however, the near-schism over religion is overtaken by a political crisis. Put simply, during the truce many towns are reluctant to support a military force at the disposal of the *Stadhouder*, and presume instead to make do with their own local militias. This is in the last analysis an issue of sovereignty: who decides about the necessary defence of the republic? On the dubious pretext of authority from the Estates-General, Prince Maurice in 1618 goes on a

lightning tour of the towns, dismissing many of their regents, replacing them with more docile ones, and arresting three chief civil servants, including Oldenbarnevelt, known to support the regent oligarchies against him. In a special court rigged with Orange supporters, Oldenbarnevelt is condemned to death and promptly executed; his two fellow-victims are imprisoned for life. All three are Remonstrants; one of them, Grotius, has drafted the Holland resolution against pulpit factionalism. By this one very shocking act, therefore, the *Stadhouder* Maurice has checked separatism in the towns, cut short the theological dispute, and added to his own authority.

It might seem surprising that a *coup de main* of this sort should go unresisted in the republic. In fact all risk for the *Stadhouder* disappears from the moment that the regents of Amsterdam distance themselves from Oldenbarnevelt over the Remonstrant issue: the prince's adversaries are divided, and the moderate statesman is vulnerable. Why then do the Amsterdam regents break rank? No one would suppose them to be either deep theologians or pure and austere in their daily lives. Personally they are more likely to incline to tolerance, if they care at all. But they do preside over a large city where they know the supporters of Gomar to be numerous among the artisan classes: they have no wish to stand out against the mass and to provoke riots. In addition to the motive of prudence, they harbour a particular grudge against Oldenbarnevelt himself—not as architect of the truce (which they favour), but as the chief obstacle to their West India Company project (at a time when its launching would prejudice Oldenbarnevelt's chances of clinching peace with Spain). The venerable advocate harangues and warns them in vain; and Maurice duly arrives in Amsterdam and expels those regents who are thought insufficiently keen on predestination (the *Stadhouder* himself supports that doctrine for political reasons).

Oldenbarnevelt, at the end of a long and glorious career, predicts that 'other maxims will now apply in the state than those by which (he) has lived.' He is, fortunately, wrong—at least until much later in the century—and the *Stadhouder*, however strengthened, can never quite grasp at autocratic power. There are no more judicial murders; and though the republic adopts as its own a very strict Calvinism, the tolerance which William of Orange and Oldenbarnevelt have always sought does, in fact, survive.

This is not surprising. Both internally and in her foreign relations, the republic has to deal with such diverse peoples and confessions that it is inconceivable for a narrow view of 'election to salvation' to prevail.

Arminianism in fact is not to be blotted out by a synod. In the country of Erasmus the extremer forms of Protestantism turn out no more practicable than in little Geneva—rather less so, indeed. In addition, the Jews who have sought refuge in Holland from persecution elsewhere continue to enjoy wide tolerance; lesser Protestant sects are not disturbed, except the Socinians, that is, Unitarians, who are judged too abominable to be endured. In parts of the republic, especially in the south, Catholics remain very numerous, and though the practice of their faith is officially illegal, they secure a sort of tolerance by paying bribes or hush-money to officials who might otherwise denounce their attendance at Mass. This is common sense and sound politics. When Prince Henry follows Maurice as *Stadhouder*, his entourage includes numerous French friends, both Huguenot and Catholic. Two French regiments are on almost permanent loan to the republic; Catholic visitors (especially French) come and go without hindrance, some making prolonged stays or enrolling in the universities, even though the teachers there are of necessity Calvinist.

In spite of the crisis of 1618, therefore, the Dutch Republic is already a haven of tolerance; and it remains so. Precisely in the winter of 1618, a French gentleman of no means and small expectations, a pupil of the Jesuits, by name René Descartes, visits Holland on his way to seek military service. He likes what he sees well enough to return nine years later and settle down to spend almost the whole of the rest of his life in the Netherlands: in Franeker first, then Amsterdam, Leyden (where at his father's death he buys a small castle a few miles outside the town), Deventer, Utrecht . . . Why this self-imposed exile? Descartes' answer is famous: 'In what other country can one enjoy so complete a liberty?' Descartes has in mind to pursue some quite original speculations, but he is no hero; the recent death at the stake of the atheist Vanini in Toulouse, the menace of the Paris theological faculty, alarm him; so does the condemnation of Galileo by Rome in 1633. He protests his Catholic orthodoxy in all his writings (and nobody in the republic objects to this); yet while he holds back his *Treatise on the World* (too chancy, because too near to Galileo), he does publish his *Discourse on Method* (1637) and his *Metaphysics* (1640)—from the safety of the republic. When he proves to be finding disciples for the new philosophy at the university of Utrecht, Cartesianism is attacked by theologians on the spot; Descartes ceases to be left alone, and in his last years he faces acrimonious legal disputes. But his personal safety is never in question. No doubt this is partly because what he has to say is of interest—for the time being—only to a tiny handful of leisured scholars and *literati*.

Dutch tolerance is even-handed. Besides Descartes there are exiles of all complexions: Puritans from England, then fugitives *from* Puritanism (Charles II himself, Hobbes his tutor, his cousin Rupert of the Rhine, whose unlucky mother Elizabeth of Bohemia has lived under the protection of the *Stadhouder* at The Hague). Later there are fugitives from James II's England and from Louis XIV's France, then after that also Jacobite fugitives from William III's regime; to say nothing of free-thinkers and others who scandalize all creeds— Sorbière, the Rosicrucian mystic Robert Fludd, the subversive journalist and critic Pierre Bayle. In this climate, as perhaps nowhere else in Europe, the dissident Jew Spinoza can publish an upsetting treatise on politics and theology, and then an even more profoundly subversive *Ethics*, odious alike to Cartesians and Judaists . . . In days to come, this tolerance will be one of the republic's principal glories; it is also the basis of an exceedingly prosperous book trade. Trade in goods and trade in ideas go well together; in the last resort the business of Amsterdam and the novelties of learning are neither of them held under control by theocratic sectaries of Gomar or by the secret police of an autocrat.

The art of the republic

In contrast then with the concentration of its trading activity, the political authority of the republic is decentralized. Maurice and Frederick Henry at The Hague have their circle of followers and make bids for popular support, but by the nature of things they cannot dominate the state like a German margrave or a king of Spain. The Estates-General is a faceless collectivity, open to challenge. State and municipal governments are collective, and multiple. Sovereignty is not focused on a single individual, or even on a single institution like the Venetians' Grand Council. This political diffuseness has reverberations throughout Dutch culture.

First, in this republic, there is no dominant magnetic field radiating from a prince: no place for adulation, for boundless devotion, for the ethos of superhuman striving, for the cult of hereditary excellence, for heroic and exhibitionist will-power; no symbolic display of that ethos of ostentation, extravagance, literary conceits, Baroque sculpture.

Between Amsterdam and Antwerp, around 1600, a gulf opens. To the south, princes, absolutism, Rubens; to the north, the small republic with an insignificant nobility and rapidly growing wealth, a world of citizens and peasants and merchants and fishermen—

114   Gerard ter Borch (1617–81), *The Swearing of the Oath of Ratification of the Treaty of Münster*, 1648. Oil on copper, 17⅞ × 23 in (45.4 × 58.5 cm). London, National Gallery

The Treaty of Münster (with the parallel Treaty of Osnabrück it constitutes what history calls the Treaty of Westphalia) is a European landmark and by any standards an important event for the Dutch Republic: the general settlement ends 80 years of war and confirms the sovereignty of the Republic. Yet how prosaic is this rendering of a great scene! A couple of score burghers signify ratification as though voting on a municipal improvement.

and *their* painters. Frederick Henry at The Hague would be happy to assimilate to the south, but as a good patriot supports local talent; so along with his Van Dycks he commissions work from the local school which has most echoes of Rome, of cosmopolitan fashion: Utrecht, where Honthorst comes nearest to the mark. The grand manner still has its adepts, and there will shortly be Rembrandt. But it is in decline. According to classical theory, the highest art is that which handles the highest themes—epic, heroic, mythological, historical, or biblical. But there is no autocrat or lavish nobility to commission it; Frederick Henry's circle is a rather small and inhibited outpost. And there is something else, still more important. The other patron of the grand and the sublime, the Church, has been transformed in the Dutch Republic. Calvinism is a very plain creed, and the house of God is as plain as the creed: no 'idols', no images of God are allowed; indeed no pictures at all are commissioned for it. A painter seeking the means to fill a great canvas must look to committees of citizens refurbishing their town hall (infrequent) or adorning their corporate offices or their own homes; this may be done proudly, perhaps, even opulently, but in such places the grandiose or the staggering novelty would look jarringly aggressive, or simply silly.

What then is left? The painter must look principally to portrait commissions (lucrative) or simply to the market. Fortunately that market does exist, is large (in this very small country), and becomes more buoyant every year. It embraces not only the regent class but also the middling tradesman, the artisanate, even well-to-do peasants, who are never very far away from a town or its art guild; we may call it a popular market, and its vigour surprises foreign observers. It is supplied by the traditional guilds of painters in the towns—Delft, Haarlem, Utrecht, Leyden, Amsterdam. Most of these painters are themselves more artisan than 'bourgeois', often sons of inn-keepers or weavers, mostly untouched by study in Rome or advanced education or humanistic theory, and innocent of the idea that a painter is an artist, a great man, a teacher. What they possess, and are carrying on, are the high skills already developed in a previous century (Brueghel after all is only two generations back).

It is important to see the values of any cultural tradition, including painting, as tending towards (if never quite reaching) an overall economy or coherence at a moment in time. The peculiarity of Dutch art arises from a negative circumstance: the down-grading of the heroic, which has the effect of causing all other values in

115 Rembrandt, *The Sampling Officials of the Drapers' Guild*, 1662. Oil on canvas, 75¼ × 109⅞ in (191 × 279 cm). Amsterdam, Rijksmuseum

For a typical group commission Rembrandt has devised a composition of remarkable power, lowering the spectator's plane of view and conferring on each dignified sitter a uniquely individual pose—and character. Compare plate 114.

the economy to be shifted, to a greater or lesser extent. Alongside the historical subject, the moral allegory, the portrait, we find that the less 'noble' forms—less noble because to the humanist they carry a slighter message—can expand into extraordinary new possibilities. *Things* become interesting, especially landscape; also the still life, the composition put together from homely objects, or prized objects, or from flowers (echoing the intensive and specialized horticulture of the land). Because neither Church nor prince is pre-empting prestige work in the studio or riveting the painter's ambition, the latter is free to turn his eye to observe Holland's more prosaic achievements and specialize in one or other branch to celebrate them. A church is now a municipal monument, not a shrine, which is partly why it begins to be painted in a new and meticulously factual way. The observed realities which the painter shares with his fellow citizens (his market)—the artefacts such as ships and windmills or the elements about him, waves, wind, cloud, and storm—these are free to carry a weight of attention and a weight of meaning without precedent in artistic tradition. These two things taken together, the weight of attention and the weight of meaning, are what we understand by the realism of the Dutch school. It is a product both of earlier achievement and of a present configuration of values concentrated in the society of the republic; a heightened esteem for artefacts and natural objects 'as

they actually are', whether at the waterfront or indoors or on the table, whether the alignment of houses on a well-known skyline, or a windmill standing on an inlet of water or a familiar vista of lonely dunes under a huge sky or a quality of cloud and atmosphere and light . . . These things, no longer crowded to the side, are reconciled in the painter's compositional discoveries for their own sake.

Or very nearly so. 'Realism' still has problematic aspects. The depiction of even a flower implies awareness of all sorts of assumptions to do with botany (the botany of the seventeenth century) and how things grow. The nature of things is after all open to rational appreciation: scholarly humanists pursue just that science in the university of Leyden's *Hortus academicus* (botanic garden). Indeed there is in the seventeenth century no other way of imagining reality. Triangles, tulips, laws, or ships all exhibit their nature. The painter and the scientist are not looking at two *different* realities, one concrete and the other abstract, or even at two different *aspects* of a reality, one visual and the other rational. They are looking at exactly the same object, except that the painter will record its surface rather than its dissected innards, while the scholar may sometimes wish to explore the latter. Even then, the appearance of an object to the painter, under determinate conditions, is still a part of its nature—a point taken for granted by any naturalist. There is thus no need for a special artistic

116   Johannes Vermeer, *View of Delft* (detail), *c.* 1661. Oil on canvas, 38⅝ × 46⅛ in (98 × 117.5 cm). The Hague, Mauritshuis

Not only civic pride but also (we must surmise) some deeper feeling give this view of Delft a quality that has haunted many admirers. If it anticipates the tourist agency photograph, it is also something else; though we cannot be sure the seventeenth century saw it in this light.

philosophy to justify realism: no excuses are required.

It is tempting to suppose that because the republic's patrons of art are plebeian (in the sense of 'not noble'), down-to-earth people who can tell one grade of cloth from another, flower-fanciers attentive to the curl of a petal, artisans and craftsmen similarly conscious of the values of precision, *therefore* the art of the republic is bound to reflect what is common to all such dispositions—the various embodiments of 'realism'. There is also the fact, already emphasized, that this is a small country; little in it is unknown or mysterious; there is no call to introduce wayward distortions or breathe transcendental qualities into scenes familiar to everyone. Indeed it could be ridiculous. And on the same line of argument, architectural fantasies, composite pictures of town scenes made up of buildings known to everyone but assembled in a grouping which could never actually occur—such fantasies have little market here.

But it is always imprudent to suppose that 'the consumer is king', and leave it at that. Why, for example, among chattels collected in a home, should pictures feature so largely anyway? Is it in part because the painters are there creating the 'need'? (We know that many of them are also dealers in paintings.) Can it be that the painter guilds and the numerous individual painters are an important motor in developing a situation where some citizens buy literally dozens of seascapes just as others buy hundreds of plants or bulbs or shrubs for their newly laid-out gardens? As in the notorious case of speculation in tulips, is there not an element of *investment* in works of art, unusually widely diffused? (And this incidentally says much about general levels of prosperity.) It would be hard to dismiss any of these aspects of the scene: but they lead us to the further point, that if the buyers in the market 'know what they like', they still have no option but to choose from what is available. It is the painters who feel their way forward, in Haarlem no less than in Rome, experimenting and testing their powers, initiating and branching out on their special interests within a general tradition which, as it also shapes expectation, escapes the ultimate control of any one of them individually. Even though we shall see how the citizens of Amsterdam partly reject Rembrandt, we cannot 'explain' either Rembrandt or for that matter Vermeer purely in terms of the social predispositions of a Netherlands public. At most these last can be reckoned to make life easy for a Vermeer and difficult for a Rembrandt.

The case of Rembrandt is very noticeably that of an artist who is not really suited by this small world. He sets out with the deliberate aim of specializing in the

117 Rembrandt, *The Conspiracy of Julius Civilis: the Oath*, 1661–2. Oil on canvas, 77⅛ × 118½ (196 × 309 cm). Stockholm, Nationalmuseum

Contemporary with plate 116, Rembrandt's tremendous evocation of national striving in a remote past is in its way too historically vivid—the one-eyed hero-giant, barbarous following (was that the Batavian élite?), threatening light and shadow, pulsating colour—not to jar on his patrons in the New Town Hall.

grand style. The son of a miller and a baker's daughter, he is apprenticed to a craft—painting. No humanist learning here! After a first apprenticeship he goes on to study under Lastman, a painter who has been to Italy and has a name for historical and biblical scenes: ambition and the challenge of the Baroque are aroused. True, Rembrandt's early work in Leyden is careful and precise, and when he moves to Amsterdam in 1632 it is in order to be able to paint portraits for wealthy clients, in which his success is great. But although he has left hardly any clues to his private thoughts, his canvases reveal a dilemma. He has the good fortune to be commissioned for some work for Frederick Henry, and there at least his treatment of religious subjects shows an unhampered abandon to the Baroque. But the heroic tradition has little else to offer; he is more and more unsupported, alone, and idiosyncratic in the further development which produces his greatest works. Charged in 1642 to paint a group portrait of a town militia band and its leader (at 100 florins a head plus more for the captain), Rembrandt departs from the conventional: he takes their muster for a routine night patrol and composes that into a huge, portentous epic scene. Very good, very fine; but not quite what is being expected. Called on to produce a patriotic *historical* canvas for the stately town hall which the regents of Amsterdam decide on in 1650, inviting van Kempen to build it in the *classical* style (how cosmopolitan and proud of itself this city is now becoming!), Rembrandt opens his Tacitus and reads of the old Batavian rising

against the Roman *imperium*, and the taking of a 'barbarous' oath by Julius Civilis and his conspirators. He then transforms his subject into a vision of explosive power—the Batavian patriots become the rugged barbarians that Tacitus suggests they were, menacing, anything but civilized. That is too much for the regents: they reject the canvas. Rembrandt's self-portraits, again, tell a different tale from the commissioned portraits; they take us into a region of spiritual realism—brooding, unfathomable, and by the standards and tastes of his world, unaccountable. In sum, he goes his own way, because there is not really a royal road in Holland; even his heavy paintwork is more and more at variance with the style of the times, and one of the very greatest artists of modern Europe is rewarded by his fellow-countrymen with a mixture of admiring awe (for his colossal technical powers) and outright condemnation (for his eccentricity).

By contrast, in the quiet little town of Delft, Vermeer works so completely within the range of art conventions established in mid-century Holland that among his contemporaries he arouses neither surprise nor curiosity. This modest guildsman has studied closely what others are doing in townscape and genre painting, and concentrates on the latter, reducing it to the simplest yet at the same time the subtlest compositions: an ultimate refinement of the moralizing scene, where the human figure barely hints at what it may all be about, and the domestic interior is freed to engage our whole attention: a still, muted life.

118   Rembrandt, *Self-portrait* **(detail),** *c.* **1660. Oil on canvas, 45 × 37 in (114 × 94 cm). London, Kenwood House, Iveagh Bequest**

In later self-portraits Rembrandt has taken leave of the 'realism' of his earlier Amsterdam commissions; painting purely to please or understand himself, the emphasis has shifted to a brusque search for tones and masses, interpretative light and shade, essential character, a vision in the mind's eye, a different reality.

Even in Vermeer we perceive traces of the wide and often ambiguous moral appeal which makes *genre* pictures so much a part of Dutch seventeenth-century tradition in general. What is harder is to recognize how far that tendency reaches. It is easy enough to sense in a meticulous view of a Dutch town something of pride in civic achievement; or in a portrait, the character ascribed to the sitter, whatever it may be. It is less easy to accept that both painter and public recognize in the humblest depicted object a *meaning* of some sort; that this meaning relates to the moral order of the universe; that a flower, to an Amsterdammer, is seen as an object *which dies*, that a country scene is both a familiar record and a commentary on human vanity. It does not follow that Dutch sea scenes or landscapes shout crude slogans at us. But it does account for a rather pervasive seriousness in their seventeenth-century landscapes. This is no country for 'wit'.

What part might religion play, alongside social promptings, in the development of this school? One might be inclined to guess that painters in general are more likely to be Arminians than Gomarists, simply because (to us) it appears more natural that they should find innocence and beauty in the scenes they render than that they should be haunted by a pitiless dichotomy of 'saved' and 'damned' lurking around every corner of God's creation. We have absolutely no means of supporting that kind of conjecture. It would of course be very bizarre to try and read into the portraits that look out at us from canvasses minute shading of theological persuasion, though the sobriety of a general style of life is more than evident in the countless heads of municipal worthies, and in the conventional seriousness of their poses—which precisely because it is conventional is a powerful reminder of prevailing values.

There are however two further angles to this question. Calvin himself has laid down quite definite guidelines on art. He specifically forbids all attempts to depict God (idolatry, etc.), but at the same time he expresses approval for the fine arts as a purely secular activity. Painters are not reprobates. Beyond that general permission there is a more subtle orientation, perhaps more interesting for us. Calvin has also taught most emphatically that in reading the Bible the Christian must seek out its plain and literal meaning, and set aside the whole paraphernalia of mystical and allegorical concordance beloved of the Middle Ages. The *literal* sense: that is what the preacher offers week by week and day by day as indispensable to his flock; that alone supplies all the moral and practical lessons of Scripture. No flights of intellectual ingenuity, no secret meanings, no speculative allusiveness; only the plain truth is requisite to salvation. Genre painting, evidently, is conformable enough to that stance: however elusive its symbols (to us in a later age), the moral messages are in fact always a little—shall we say—straightforward; and if the symbols disconcert us, it is precisely because they *are* often presented in a literal and matter-of-fact way. But the same value applies in portraiture, in landscape, in still life . . .

There is no question but that religious values of this kind must influence the painter's choice of desirable ways of developing his art, and that there is a very strong conformity of biblical teaching and painterly representation. Sober distaste for obscurity, for the far-fetched, or the extravagant is a value instilled from the pulpit no less than from the routine of daily work or practical self-government. It is matched by representation of the real in the atelier. Fortunately it leaves intact the possibility of exploring the resources of eye and composition, nuance and colour, technique and insight, in arriving at what is 'really' and truthfully 'real'.

Sciences

In a 'reformed' republic, learning and the Church are still as close together as elsewhere in Europe. A learned Calvinist is (like any other learned man) a humanist; the classical tongues open the way to the proper study of history, law, philosophy, medicine, and religion. The same trunk supports all the branches, and the only peculiarity is in the status of biblical study, which is heavily stressed. Literacy may spread (it is not universal—in Amsterdam perhaps a third of the population are literate, a goodly proportion even so for the age) and the Bible may be translated and read in the vernacular; but to study it deeply means to go back to origins, a main theme of Protestantism. That implies ancient languages. Also, if worship is conducted in the vernacular, the language of the scholarly community everywhere, naturally enough, remains Latin. That is sufficient, incidentally, to create a shadowy barrier between science strictly and properly defined as natural philosophy and most kinds of technology—or as they are commonly styled, 'arts'. We can detect various new 'arts' in the seventeenth century, for example agricultural economics or social statistics, being developed outside the tradition of the universities simply because the earliest books about them are written in French or English or Dutch rather than in Latin. Descartes' use of French for his *Discourse* is actually a pugnacious gesture, an appeal away from the learned to the laity.

The political institutions of the republic are in fact very intimately tied in with those of education. Public servants, as elsewhere, are drawn from the university schools. And the universities are to all intents and purposes town institutions, and prized by their citizens. They also benefit from links with the reformed communities of other countries. Huguenot humanists are prominent in the early years of Leyden university, the world-famous scholars Lipsius and Scaliger are attracted to it by research chairs, and some of their pupils are among the great scholars of the next generation—the classicist Heinsius, the lawyer Grotius. The intellectual world of Leyden, as of all the other teaching centres, is firmly that of humanism, now in its fifth generation.

This humanism of the Reformation is even, if anything, a little *too* successful: even in Holland it resists challenges. Thus the universities' contribution to new natural sciences is for that reason at first marginal: in Holland, as elsewhere, the experimentalists are outside its walls, 'amateurs', not serious; and when Descartes' new philosophy is taken up by one or two admirers at Utrecht it is violently resisted by an 'Establishment' led by the theology professor Voet (Vossius). Descartes' dream of a universal science embracing medicine and astronomy, optics and physiology, appears altogether too disturbing because it implies an upheaval of the present perfectly successful arrangements and opens the door to outlandish novelties. The French philosopher, it is rumoured, has been seen calling at a butcher's shop to buy an ox-head for dissection, to prove his theory that all animals are automata. What will he turn to next? Would he have scholars set to work polishing lenses? Make their own telescopes?

Tolerance, therefore, is one thing; a take-over in the colleges quite another. Accordingly, when Christian Huygens, the son of a great Dutch humanist and civil servant, discovers a vocation for these new curiosities, we find he has settled in Paris (1655); it is there that he discovers the rings of Saturn by the use of a *home-made* telescope, studies the phenomena of light, improves the clock by fitting a pendulum to it (and sends one of these new devices back to his homeland). To be sure, experimental sciences *do* then take off in Holland; thanks to a lens-making industry, the simple microscope is invented there, with momentous results later; we simply note an initial resistance.

In the traditional fields of learning, the most impressive and influential product of the republic's scholarship is also the work of a man not cherished, but utterly rejected from the community: the jurist Huig van Groot, recognized throughout Europe under the Latinized form of his name, Grotius. Grotius is a brilliant and precocious student of classical humanities at the University of Leyden under the great Scaliger, and he is only fifteen when he is seconded to Oldenbarnevelt for an embassy to France; on his return he studies law and then enters practice. He also writes poetry and plays in Latin, and one of these, *Adam Exul*, one day awakes an echo in Milton's *Paradise Lost*. At twenty he is appointed historian to the republic. A typical humanist's career then takes him on to be advocate for the fisc of Holland and Zeeland, and at thirty, pensionary of Rotterdam. It is in that capacity that he drafts the fateful edict by which Holland seeks to end the violent Arminian quarrel, and when Maurice carries out his punitive strike, Grotius is arrested and put on trial along with Oldenbarnevelt. He escapes the fate of the older man, with the more 'lenient' sentence of life imprisonment. Were it not for a resourceful wife and a romantic gaolbreak, that would presumably have been the end of this official. As it is, he escapes to France, where old and new friends among the men of law welcome him; and it is there that he writes the first great modern work on the law of nations, the *de Jure Belli ac Pacis* (*On the Law of*

War and Peace), printed in Paris, dedicated to the king of France, and published at Frankfurt in 1625.

This gigantically learned book, loaded with quotations from every known classical legal authority, is not just the foundation of modern international law. It is also the fruit of long thought about some quite precise and typical problems encountered in Holland. In 1604 Grotius has been retained by the East India Company to defend one of its captains against charges of piracy which are being levelled at him by the Mennonites of Holland. The gallant sailor has captured a Portuguese ship off Malacca, laden with treasure. Has he, or rather his employer the company, any right to behave in this manner? Grotius writes a short treatise on the questions at issue. He argues that the Portuguese cannot, to begin with, claim to own the high seas as if they were lands under their jurisdiction: the ocean cannot be anyone's property, it is free to all. He next goes on to argue that the capture is lawful, to the extent that war is lawful (the Mennonites being pacifists, a proof that war can be lawful is also necessary). These same issues, twenty years later, are very fully explored in the *de Jure*. The lawfulness of war is argued by treating it as a species of law-enforcement—a view basic to later international organizations, though in 1625 not novel. The theory regarding the high seas, on the other hand, is a political bombshell. The 'haves' execrate it, the more predatory states greet it as Solomonic wisdom. Though law has never stopped a war (at least until very recent times) Grotius' arguments feature repeatedly in the coming quarrels between England and the Dutch Republic. They also inaugurate a wholly new branch of learning.

Grotius may have hoped that the success of his treatise will soften his fellow-countrymen and induce them to invite him home. In this he is disappointed; the condemnation stands, and though some of his theological writings receive the honour of publication in Amsterdam, he dies an exile. The reason is that he remains anathema to the Gomarists. His earlier pleas for tolerance among the sects are not forgotten; and later writings in which he goes on to outline a simple and uncontroversial form of Christianity are taken by his enemies as proof that he is virtually a convert to Rome. Though that is not true (*de Jure* being placed on the Roman index of prohibited books) Grotius is singularly detached and coolly statesmanlike in his approach to the fearsome schisms of religion: a Protestant Erasmus, perhaps, quite close in outlook to those French middle-ground jurists who, in the wake of Jean Bodin, attempt to calm religious fanaticism in their own country.

There is, moreover, a further aspect of *de Jure* which is bound to offend any puritan with a nose for heresy.

Grotius is so deeply versed in his classical authorities that he ends up appearing to base the foundations of natural law entirely outside the Word of God and the Bible. For example: 'freedom of trade is based on a *primitive right of nations which has a natural and permanent cause.*' Law turns out to be ultimately grounded in the nature of things: like logic, it cannot originate in an arbitrary act of will. God Himself cannot change it, therefore, even though he has also laid down his divine laws. Grotius does not go to the point of sharply separating religion from moral law: that is for the future. But he clears the road.

The spirit of capitalism

The Dutch Republic in the early seventeenth century is the epitome of a 'capitalist' society. Its merchant class controls the country in a manner entirely—or almost entirely—convenient to itself; it has created all the organizations judged necessary for dominating long-haul trade; its policies are seldom turned aside from the business of business. Even pictorial art has been touched by the way this society has adjusted to freedom and applied its wealth—and we could equally point to analogous forms of 'liberation' in Dutch technology, land reclamation, the harnessing of the pump, the advance of specialized agriculture and horticulture, the application of middle-class wealth to town-house building, and much else.

This same republic is a state whose official religion is that of the Reformed Church of Calvin. This, together with its wealth and achievement, make it a unique case. For that reason if for no other we can hardly avoid reference to Max Weber's classic study of *The Protestant Ethic and the Spirit of Capitalism*, where the relation of the two things is examined, and in our turn ask, 'How crucial is the dominance of this Protestant ethic to the emergence and prosperity of the republic's capitalism?'

The 'spirit of capitalism', for Weber, means a set of traditions helpful to the rational conduct of a business enterprise: sober and disciplined procedures, such as accurate book-keeping on which rational evaluation and investment can be based, systematic thrift and the ploughing back of surpluses, stable market institutions, a settled labour market. Without these, the whole complex of systematic business cannot be imagined—piracy, yes, and opportunism of all sorts, and greed, but not the methodical and deliberate conduct of a bank or a trading company, which are peculiarly European inventions.

Confronting this 'spirit', Weber's 'Protestant ethic' refers to the seriousness of a man's conduct in life, based on Luther's idea of a calling (see p. 141 above); the idea that in daily life a disciplined self-scrutiny and self-denial, an everyday severity towards oneself, can be as sanctified as the asceticism of life in the cloister. There is also the peculiar sanction of Calvinist predestination—the man of faith has no certain evidence that he is chosen for salvation, but he can at least know from self-scrutiny that he has incurred damnation (even if he prospers, he may yet not be one of the elect, but if he goes to the wall by idleness or inexcusable personal shortcomings, he knows who is to blame).

At a superficial level, there is little to suggest that Calvinism is a decisive motor or supercharger of capitalism in the Dutch Republic, and a great deal to suggest that it is not. Double-entry book-keeping (even if taught to schoolboys) is older than Protestantism; Francesco di Marco has used it. Amsterdam merchants have learned to run their successful businesses by imitating Catholic forerunners in Antwerp, Genoa, Florence, and elsewhere; a whole body of 'capitalist' practice goes back far before the Reformation. Many of the leading Dutch entrepreneurs are anyhow supporters of Arminius, that is to say, not Calvinists in any strict sense; among the wealthy, who have time for such things, literary tastes are by no means confined to the Bible, and 'thrift' is not quite the word to associate with their town-houses, surburban villas, and handsome gardens adorned with statues—though 'careful' is a description which does fit them. As to religion, there is not much of a gap between their evangelical tolerance and that of the Catholic admirers of Erasmus. This is no surprise: magnates everywhere are little given to fanaticism. The strength of Gomarism is at a less exalted level, in point of fact in the artisan or popular classes.

Then there is the disturbing fact that the republic has a reputation (at least among foreigners) of being not a republic of virtue but of corruption; one where venality and bribery are more common than anywhere else in Europe, where money can buy anything whatever. French observers note the judicious expenditures which help the republic turn a blind eye to the exercise of their Catholic faith. What hypocrisy! But that is only part of the picture. The East India Company is a great public institution: its profits, and therefore its dividends, are eaten away by corrupt practices at every level and its business strategy—to keep monopoly prices always as high as possible—is of dubious morality. In its collusion with Amsterdam's leading merchants (where it helps them to corner particular markets) the company arouses such furious public indignation that it is forced in the 1640s to amend these abuses. Yet its directors are gentlemen of high standing, dignified pillars of society, in some cases no doubt the same who benefit in property deals during Amsterdam's explosive growth. Or again, the company's shares may not be owned by foreigners—yet everyone knows that there are always citizens who for a price will help out the foreigner as his nominee. As for the *West* India Company, earning one half of its income from capturing other people's treasure ships and the other half from slaving (the slave trade stirs no consciences in Europe, and Protestants are still no less and no more sensitive about it than anyone else), what particularly disturbs the public at large is not the morality of the American business but its high risk.

There is a further contrast that is regularly drawn between the Catholic and the reformed faiths in their bearing on business enterprise: it concerns the question of usury. Under Catholic canon law, the charging of interest on money loans is prohibited; but in Protestant lands canon law is no longer recognized. Is this not surely an advantage to capitalism? Contrary to a still widely-held belief, it would appear that it is not. In the first place, though usury is in canon law sinful, there are so many distinctions and let-outs (for risk, for loans at a distance, for clever forms of contract, and so on) that the effect of this injunction on Catholic opinion is more to create confusion or reinforce prejudice in places where money-lenders are hated (among peasantries up to their eyes in debt, for example) than to inhibit capital accumulation or discourage the use of credit in trading. It is true that wealthy Catholic bankers and businessmen have always taken out insurance against damnation by willing important endowments to charity or the Church, and have often commissioned large numbers of Masses, just *in case* they may prove to have offended. But in any country where a Church is reformed and nationalized—or municipalized—and where salvation comes from faith alone, not from works, such a gesture entirely loses its meaning. Pious conventions of this nature do not seem to have exerted any noticeably damping effect on the fortunes of, say, the Medici, so long as they have stayed in business. In any case, however, by the time the Dutch Republic comes into being, charging interest on loans is absolutely general; in 1540 Charles V legalizes it for money-changers and others by an imperial edict; in the Spanish Netherlands the Catholic Church itself invests in municipal pawn-shops set up to advance cash against pledges and to charge interest, generally at the rate of 15 per cent. What one can note, and emphasize, is that in the republic the highly organized state of the money-market produces a very advantageous *low* prevailing rate of interest. But the same is true of Genoa.

Overwhelmingly, when one considers Dutch culture in the seventeenth century, one has the impression that it is neither the presence of Calvinism nor the absence of Catholic canon law which accounts for the triumphs of capitalism, but the fact that the state is to all intents and purposes identical with the servicing of practical, that is to say business-like, or simply business, operations. And this identity is *morally* important. It means that there is no aristocratic caste 'lording it' over society and setting an example of contempt for the 'lowlier' tasks which produce practical results like polders or fleets; it means that the wielding of power is made largely identical with the creation and custody of wealth, not with its dissipation; it means that the municipal leadership is proud to accomplish its public projects hand in hand with its private initiators, and that the institutions of an advanced economic system— *bourse*, bank, insurance, harbours, communications, land reclamation—are procured with a minimum of political obstruction.

It is true that elsewhere in this age the Catholic Church, with its organization, its possessions, its militant new purposes, is inextricably bound up with autocratic regimes; such regimes are themselves very ill placed to produce the kind of unfettered development which the Dutch Republic enjoys in its golden age. (In this period, though not at a later date, attempts to transfer Dutch methods into a different social scene are often unsuccessful: Vermuyden's attempted transfer of land-reclamation know-how to England, for draining Hatfield Chase and the Cambridge fens, is hampered by mistrust, political in-fighting, and civil dissension there; while the 'export' of East India Company know-how to an eager Denmark—in 1616, by a couple of enterprising Amsterdammers—produces nothing of note whatever.) From that point of view, the Protestantism of the states is a favourable circumstance—in a roundabout, negative sense of offering no obstacle— for capitalist development; it remains that the positive favourable circumstance is actually the republicanism which almost by an accident of the independence struggle has developed out of the claims of ancient municipalities resisting the king of Spain.

119　Johannes Vermeer (1632–75), *The Art of Painting*, 1662–5. Oil on canvas, 51⅛ × 43¾ in (130 × 110 cm). Vienna, Kunsthistorisches Museum

How much does this allegory of Painting owe to the moralizing genre scene? The model, robed and garlanded, holds a trumpet and a book. The artist has begun work on his canvas—painting in the garland. And what a curious studio: the elaborate chandelier, inconvenient lighting, colossal curtain, roll-map of the United Provinces edged with views of 20 principal towns . . .

What golden age?

A lesson to all Europe? Undoubtedly. The Dutch inventions in the large-scale organization of business, overseas trading corporations, banking, stock exchange operations, are strikingly in advance of anything elsewhere in Europe. If not immediately, then over time, they will be studied and, inevitably, copied at least in part. In France, copying first takes the form of a prince's own corporate system for overseas trade, directed by Colbert, when peace and stability return to that country. In England, copying will be wholesale: first a Dutch king will be imported (William III, the *Stadhouder* of that name), and then overseas trading and a central bank *and* a stock exchange, and even its attendant coffee-shops, along with the tell-tale traces of Dutch domestic architecture and—far more important—ambitions for agricultural 'improvement', the basis of further large advances in the eighteenth century. One could go further: the Dutch experience of compromise arrangements with a prince, the *Stadhouder*, who is neither authoritarian nor yet quite without power, will also be a key, in a sense, to the solution of the problems of absolutism in England: confronting an immovable landed interest which hankers for an absolute monarch (English 'Tories'), the new ingredient personified by William III opens the way to a constitutional alternative, a 'Whig' coalition of land and trade and money, slightly less distant than the Tories from Calvinism and 'small men', more receptive to undignified forms of wealth creation, more *liberal* ('Liberal' not in the sense of Aristotle and Hobbes, but in a larger frame of ideas, shortly to take coherent form). In a word, the Dutch Republic passes on the torch, and a much larger flame is kindled.

It is interesting to reflect, though, that the 'golden age' of the republic lies in the years we have been considering, when all is yet discovery and expansion and innovation from that amazingly small base, and before the limits of scale bring it face to face with forces which it simply cannot overcome or circumvent: namely, overseas competition, the English fleet, and, perhaps most serious, the shading off of internal growth. (When 50,000 Huguenot refugees from Louis XIV's persecution arrive in the republic in the 1680s they effect little change there; a smaller number migrating to Prussia transform Berlin.) Holland's golden age is its heroic age.

Exactly the opposite is the case with the republic's main adversary, Spain. There, it is only after the death of Philip II and in the beginning of a long retreat from political heroism that what is likewise called an 'age of gold' (in exactly the same period as the Dutch) begins to be noticed across the frontiers of southern Europe: in manners, in literature, in music. By the side of Cervantes, Calderon, Gongora, Victoria, and their fame, the spread of the Spanish wig, the guitar, and aristocratic costume are all indicators of that cultural presence.

The point of this contrast—which from every point of view is extreme—lies surely in the nature of the Dutch achievement: its entirely practical nature. And this in turn brings to mind its overwhelmingly prosaic character: beginning with sieges and dikes and ending with sermons and paintings. 'Prose' is not a term of contempt or denigration: there can be a poetry of prose. But consider: is it even imaginable that this society should, like Spain, produce a picaresque novel? (In 1600 Amsterdam is indignantly suppressing vagrancy, if necessary, by shutting up the offenders.) Or a *Don Quixote*? There are no two ways about it: there is no context in the life of the Dutch Republic in which Don Quixote, with his strain of lofty and pathetic idealism as well as his ridicule, could have a *meaning* in relation to perceived reality around Holland: whether in his capacity as the socially aimless, crazed *hidalgo* subject to endless delusion (forget the unfamiliarity with windmills) or as a symptom of some deep cultural want.

Everything under these north-western skies, or almost everything, suggests on the contrary an orientation towards reality, reality unclouded by perplexity. Certainly there are strains (discord over salvation and hell is enough to sharpen political divides to crisis point in 1618), but also a rather emphatic dismissal of anything suggesting unfathomable complexity. We have seen Calvinism and realism marrying with some ease; also Calvinism and republicanism, and small-town government; we have suggested there is no awkward gap between the forms of government and the aspirations of business, between arts and crafts and their market, between town and country, faith and work. Foreign perils have ensured cohesion, though at some risk of political instability. *It is possible*, at the price of realistic vigilance, to hold the sea beyond the dikes, the enemy beyond the frontier; and no one is too far from sea and frontier to escape that awareness or fail to understand the task. In such a world Don Quixote is certainly impossible: there is no room and no need for those symbols of misplaced impulse, of misdirected longing. In such a world, too, if Rembrandt dreams, he dreams alone.

Chapter 6
Enlightenment

'A century which will become more enlightened day by day, so that all previous centuries will be lost in darkness by comparison'—Fontenelle, Preface, *History of the Renewal of the Royal Academy of Sciences*, 1702

Fontenelle is the modish popularizer of science, a kind of Bronowski of the Paris salons. Though he lives under the shadow of a tyrannical prince, in no way agreeable to change, he is deeply impressed by the feeling that around 1700, throughout Europe, something is stirring. In the confident prediction quoted above, he is by no means alone, either; his views are shared by the philosopher Clarke in England, by the great Leibniz in Germany. None of them would be able to appreciate that what is being prophesied includes the following:

—A doubling of Europe's population during the century
—A large expansion of trading empires and a quadrupling of international trade
—Continual advances in sciences of observation and experiment, including
—Evolutionary biology, chemistry, medicine
—A significant displacement of Christianity as the authoritative source of beliefs, morals, wisdom, in several strata of society in southern Europe
—A revolution in aesthetics and literary taste
—A new ideology of liberalism
—The birth of modern economics and social sciences
—An industrial revolution in one country
—The creation of the United States of America
—A social revolution and republic in France
—A near glimpse of democracy in that republic, and the birth of a new nationalism
—Twenty years of generalized war.

Who should blame a prophet for selling his listeners short? In 1700 history does not yet display the fearsome acceleration that marks a later age: kings and their kingdoms pursue their pompous course, peasantries everywhere their unchanging narrow lives, the 'orders' their privileged existences. Our prophet bases his forecast only on what is closest to him, namely natural sciences and philosophy. Aware of change, he merely fails to anticipate some of the repercussions. Or, putting it another way, it is manifest that a new institution has lately surfaced, after long preliminaries: a loose community of scholars and learned men, who make observations, conduct experiments, communicate the results to one another, and between them cause learning to *advance*, in fulfilment of the earlier dream of Francis Bacon. In the eyes of a majority of men, around 1700, such activities are marginal, by comparison with large matters such as fitting out a fleet or building a palace—at best they lead to ingenious devices. But the majority are not necessarily the key opinion-formers; a more privileged minority are coming to see the devices in another light: the English Parliament offers a large prize to whoever can invent an accurate chronometer to aid navigation; academies under royal protection—a Royal Society, academies of Sciences in Paris and Stockholm—applaud even advances which seem to hold no immediate promise of useful application—gravitation, for instance, or animalcules under a microscope.

What Fontenelle is calling 'Enlightenment' is the process by which during the next fifty years the balance tilts, the admirers of new things establish an ascendancy over the indifferent, and in conjunction with other motors of change weave together a great ideology of movement—of 'Progress'. In this, hardly any facets of culture are left untouched: certainly not the arts, symbols of new identities.

Chronology for Chapter 6

1711	Charles VI becomes Holy Roman Emperor
1712	Handel settles in England
1713–14	Treaties of Utrecht end War of Spanish Succession
1716	Death of Leibniz
1721	Montesquieu's *Persian Letters* published
1725	Death of Peter the Great of Russia
1727	Death of Isaac Newton
1732–4	Pope's *Essay on Man* published
1734	Voltaire's *Philosophic Letters on the English*
1735	Linnaeus's *Systema Naturae* published
1739–40	Hume's *Treatise of Human Nature* published
1740	Frederick II (the Great) becomes king of Prussia; Maria Theresa becomes Archduchess of Austria; Richardson's *Pamela* published
1740–8	War of the Austrian Succession
1742	Handel's *Messiah* performed for the first time (in Dublin)
1748	Montesquieu's *Esprit des lois* published
1749–77	Pombal chief minister in Portugal
1749–1804	Buffon's *Natural History* published
1750	Diderot takes on editorship of *Encyclopédie*
1751–77	*Encyclopédie* published
1754	Rousseau's *Discourse on . . . Inequality* published
1755	Lisbon earthquake; Johnson's *Dictionary* published
1765–63	Seven Years War
1757	Death of Fontenelle; Soufflot begins building of Panthéon (Paris)
1758	Helvétius' *De l'esprit* published
1759	Voltaire's *Candide* published
1761	Haydn appointed kapellmeister to Esterházy family
1762	Catherine the Great seizes power in Russia in a coup; Rousseau's *Du contrat social* and *Émile* published; Gluck's *Orfeo*
1764	Voltaire's *Dictionnaire philosophique* and Winckelmann's *History of Ancient Art* published; death of Mme de Pompadour
1765	Walpole's *Castle of Otranto* published
1766–73	Aranda chief minister in Spain
1768	Royal Academy founded in London
1768–71	Cook's first voyage
1770	Bruce discovers source of Blue Nile
1772–5	Cook's second voyage
1773	Jesuit order suppressed by the pope
1774	Turgot appointed comptroller-general in France; Goethe's *Werther*
1776	American Declaration of Independence; the Six Edicts bring about Turgot's fall from power; Adam Smith's *The Wealth of Nations* published
1776–80	Cook's third voyage
1778	Deaths of Voltaire and Rousseau
1779	Lessing's *Nathan the Wise*
1779–81	Mozart in service of Archbishop of Salzburg
1786	Mozart's *Marriage of Figaro*
1789	Outbreak of French Revolution

Discovering progress

Progress is, to us, both a familiar and an elusive idea: at different times of the day it connotes widely differing things. At one moment, it means increase in the wealth of the community, enabling us to obviate famines in which people actually starve to death (still an occurrence in eighteenth-century Europe); at another moment, it stresses a widened enjoyment of the amenities or opportunities of life. It represents an elevation of standards of behaviour—more benevolence, less cruelty —or a levelling-up of 'rights' (that is, reasonable expectations) not just of special groups but of individual human beings, rational and sentient; however uncertainly, it entails some overcoming of age-old servitudes, and enhanced opportunities to expand the enjoyment of life. Another aspect of this is a heightened yearning for—or at least tolerance of—individual choice in self-realization. Also therefore there is implied a generally enlarged control of the world about us, either by the discovery of resources in the ground or by exploration of new regions or by better techniques and understanding ('improvement', invention, positive science); and certainly the rearrangement of social conventions when they obstruct advance. Finally, no limit is assigned to the changes which men may bring about to improve their condition: concepts such as environmental protection, 'limits to growth', are alien to the eighteenth century.

'Progress' is an optimistic creed. All its strands come together in a general idea, forming an attitude, supplying an ideology, an outlook on the world, to which the name *liberalism* ('making free') is attached; a reminder that the freedom to enact that progress is something that must be wrested from an older, stationary, order of things. It rests on the assumption that we can do better than our ancestors—something already proved by natural science, and incidentally also claimed for literature and the arts—and that 'therefore' in other respects too we are not condemned to go round in a fixed circle, like the constellations in the sky.

By the time the men of the Enlightenment have firmly established themselves—and this comes to pass in the generation that spans the years from around 1750 to 1776, chiefly, but by no means solely, in France (or more exactly Paris)—ideas of progress and change are established firmly in a new polarization of European culture. Depending on our standpoints we may see this as the most momentous transformation since Athenian democracy, or as the most obstinate curse ever inflicted by Europe on the world; in no way however can we disregard its originality.

120   A. Fogg (after Hogarth and Thornhill), *House of Commons,* **1730. Stipple engraving, 17½ × 14½ in (27 × 21 cm). London, Palace of Westminster**

The English Parliament, a legislature which excites the envy of some French liberals, is actually the preserve of great noble families (Lords) and their Whig or Tory clients (Commons—with restricted franchise and seats mostly under patronage). Its dignity is recorded in this view of minister Robert Walpole (left) in conversation with the Speaker; its less edifying qualities such as corrupt electioneering—which Hogarth sketches later—are not so well known abroad.

Nature and knowledge

It is natural philosophy, without a doubt, which wittingly or unwittingly sets the example, somewhat as Epicurus (see p. 30) has recommended that it should.

The word 'Nature' bears dwelling on. Since antiquity it has been assumed that everything has *a* nature, that is to say, an essence accessible to human reason. The majestic essences of geometry have dazzled Plato; and since those long-distant times, advance of knowledge by the light of reason, *lumen naturale*, has illuminated more and more of the world.

'The world'? In 1700, just as now, it includes the invisible realm of mathematics, in which impressive progress has been made in the last hundred years: in

121   François Cuvilliés (1695–1768), Residenztheater, Munich, 1751–3

Not a high altar, but the theatre box of an Elector of Bavaria. Ostentation and decorative effect reach their limits (often brilliantly elegant) in central Europe precisely at a time when a different climate of tastes is coming into being further west.

has been opened spectacularly to reason by Kepler, Galileo, and Newton, whose grand vision of order (*Principia Mathematica*, 1686) works on educated imaginations more powerfully than any previous discovery in history. To some, the evidence of divine purpose is made more overwhelming; to others, Lucretius has a new justification.

Or again, there is the knowledge that is being acquired regarding small things: thanks to his improved microscope, Leeuwenhoek in Holland communicates to the Royal Society in London and to the Academy of Sciences in Paris a wholly new account of corpuscles in the blood, animalcules in a drop of water, spermatozoa, the generation of mussels and eels (oversetting Aristotle's belief that such creatures are generated out of mud or water); he traces putrefaction to maggots, describes the life-cycles of the weevil, the flea, and the aphid. The universe is being peopled with a new and marvellous range of living things . . . Likewise an experimental science of medicine is coming into existence, through the labours of the celebrated Boerhaave at Leyden (again a much-delayed weaning from Aristotle) or of Tronchin in Geneva, slightly later: the crowning triumph of this science is a method of inoculation against the smallpox, finally consecrated by the 'operation' performed on Louis XVI in 1774 (his illustrious predecessor having just died of the disease). Or again, there is a thorough study and comparison of plant life, culminating in Linnaeus' great classification of plants on what he claims to be his *natural* system. Or entomology; or physiology; or chemistry . . . All around, the experimental sciences, conducted by gentlemen or scholars or noble dilettantes, and consecrated by academies, patronage, in some cases practical application, gain a foothold in their politer aspects; the visible sign of this being ingenious brass models of the solar system, 'grandfather clocks' incorporating Huygens' pendulum, chronometers in ships, and presently thermometers (another collective achievement by Renaldini in Pisa, Newton in London, Fahrenheit in Holland, Celsius in Stockholm). A scientific revolution is not only a long way into its stride, it is beginning to be recognized—and as an extension of our grasp of the *nature* of things.

But the enlightenment of reason is not confined to *things*. Analogy is a powerful motor of speculation; if reason uncovers the nature of things, why should it not do the same for human affairs? The most widely accessible field for a 'nature' in human affairs is in law: in every society there are jurists, they have studied Roman law, they are aware of natural law—that body of self-evident principles dating from the Stoics, built into the

co-ordinate geometry, in logarithms, in the handling of infinitesimals, and in the calculation of change, in probability, in the properties of curves. This is a collective achievement: for instance, the cycloid, unknown to the Greeks, has been studied by scholars in five countries—Galileo, Descartes, Pascal, Huygens, Wren, and Leibniz. More conspicuous is progress in the visible realm of rational physics. To take the obvious example, the system of the sun and the planets and their regularities

Justinian code, appealed to in almost every fight against tyranny or anomalous custom, and (as already noted) copiously expounded by Grotius. In his turn the English philosopher John Locke (another Arminian, as it happens) appeals to the authority of 'natural law' for the liberation of England from the authoritarian Stuart monarchy (1688); in his influential *Two Treatises*, or *Essays on Civil Government* (1690), he argues that it is in the *nature* of human relations, once the institutions of society and property are admitted, to *require* that individual freedom be preserved from the threat of 'arbitrary or absolute power'. Safeguards of the kind Locke preaches here have, up to a point, come to England with his Dutch patron William III; but they are by no means universally accepted, and in other countries views which are modest 'whiggery' in England are seen as rank subversion. When in France an already famous playwright and publicist, Voltaire, introduces Locke to a large circle of continental readers in his (anonymous) *Philosophic Letters on the English* (1734), he alludes only indirectly to liberties and the safeguards of law; even so, his book is condemned by the courts and burnt by the hangman. Nevertheless, Voltaire and later admirers of the 'constitution' of the (only very moderately) free Britons spread the belief that laws *can* be made reasonable, and that reasonableness lies in simple safeguards to protect the persons, property, and dignity of all subjects (or, as Voltaire calls them, 'citizens'); and this becomes a large part of an 'Enlightenment' credo, the more cogent for its echo of ancient natural principles. 'Progress', here, means simply giving effect to what we clearly understand and some of us desire.

Civil laws prescribe, and natural philosophy arrives at laws which explain. But why should reason not be yet further extended, why should not human nature itself also be brought under scientific principles? A young Scots philosopher, David Hume, sets about the task, inspired undoubtedly by Newton (and a little by Locke, too). Reckoning that 'human nature is everywhere the same', that 'the same motives always produce the same actions', and that 'the same events always follow from the same causes', he announces an ambitious project in his *Treatise on Human Nature* (1739–40). Here is its programme: 'We must glean up our own experiments from a cautious observation of human life, and take them as they appear in the common course of the world, by men's behaviour in company, in affairs, and in their pleasures. Where experiments of this kind are judiciously collected and compared, we may hope to establish on them *a science*, which will not be inferior in certainty, and will be much superior in utility, to any other of human comprehension.'

That 'science' will in the first instance be what we today might call 'psychology', though it is still extremely ill defined. But what of the more general relations between human beings, customary or civil, which lie behind the civil laws? If we turn from the young Hume to the writings of a quite different thinker, the French jurist Montesquieu, we find in his *Spirit of the Laws* (1748) an inquiry of an equally 'natural' kind: this time into the forms of different states and their relation to the customs and values of their inhabitants. Once again, a programme of collecting and comparing, a science both certain and useful; Montesquieu is in fact a fore-runner of what today is called 'sociology'.

Alongside the large 'set-piece' projects of Hume and Montesquieu, moreover, a number of other branches of applied reason in human affairs can be, and have already been, developed piecemeal for ends whose 'utility' is plain: the calculation of probability (to clarify gambling or insurance risks), 'political arithmetic' (to give administration a clearer view of what it is doing), 'political economy' (to serve the economic interests of society). Not just yet, but at the end of the century, impressed by the array of these branches of reasonable inquiry, a French administrator, Mollien, will give them all one generic name: 'social sciences'.

Finally, there is 'natural' religion. Though religious wars have ceased (the last could be said to be Louis XIV's expulsion of the Huguenots from France in 1685), there are still plenty of reminders of intolerance, bigotry, cruelty, even judicial murder, carried on in the name of religion. Such sights are profoundly offensive to 'reason', to say nothing of intellectual scepticism at large. Just as in the past Erasmus and Arminius have sought conciliatory creeds, so now there are 'deists' who go much further in the search for a less divisive, because more 'natural', form of belief. What, they ask, is the *irreducible* nature of religion? They review the facts to unearth a consensus. They find that the best opinions of the Greeks, those of Judaism, the two chief commandments of the founder of Christianity, and indeed also whatever else is now being gleaned by way of information about the Chinese, the Incas, ancient Egypt, Persia, Islam, India, show that man everywhere acknowledges a divinity (Supreme Creator, Architect, or First Cause) and also mostly recommends benevolence towards his fellows. Just two principles; all the rest is divisive, unsupported by reason. Let these two simple principles then be the sole basis of faith: no more complex than Newton's grand laws of the universe, and no more divisive!

In Faith and Hope the world will disagree,
But all Mankind's concern is Charity.

What Alexander Pope expresses in his *Essay on Man* will be repeated by Voltaire over and over again in letters and pamphlets and satirical tales (*Zadig, Candide*), by the 'enlightened' German writer G. E. Lessing in his great parable-play *Nathan the Wise*, and by a multitude of others.

As well as a 'natural' view of the divine, deists—or for that matter, free-thinking atheists—can point therefore to the more positive dictate of a natural ethic. Along with mutual benevolence ('do unto others'), the 'Charity' of Pope and kindred spirits turns out to be a principle singularly easy to understand because it is grounded in self-interest. Enlightened self-interest conduces to the common good:

> God and Nature link'd the general Frame,
> And bade Self-love and Social be the same.

This attractive thought will reappear more weightily in the great liberal edifice of political economy. For the time being it is more a generality for the polite saloon than a programme for action.

Yet these currents of thought are not purely decorative or gratuitous. As if in illustration of them, there is created a new form of cult entirely distinct from the various existing creeds of Europe: freemasonry. Starting in London in 1717, and spreading rapidly to Paris, Florence, Rome, Berlin, everywhere, its deliberately syncretist rituals and décor (Solomonic 'temple', signs, symbols) make it thoroughly cosmopolitan and religiously 'neutral'; it celebrates benevolence, a higher order of spirituality within reason. Its leaders seek to preserve a standard ritual in all its lodges. Nothing could better catch the early spirit of Enlightenment.

Fashions for natural religion or morality look mild enough in retrospect. However, they carry a plea for liberty, which is different from that of the natural philosopher: their plea is heretical. The Roman Catholic Church insistently denounces them, as it also condemns freemasonry. This is not an insignificant gesture: in the early part of the eighteenth century heresy against an established religion is in almost every state a *penal* offence. Much of the time the law is not enforced; nevertheless it is there in reserve, and in Paris the wealthy 'philosopher' and tax-farmer Helvétius, and in Madrid the administrator Pablo Olavide, have cause to regret their free-thinking when the Paris faculty of theology (in 1759) and the Spanish Holy Inquisition (in 1775) are set in motion to cut the blasphemers down to size and force them into grovelling recantations.

It would be absurd to attribute solely to natural religion in its various expressions one very appealing feature of the eighteenth century, which is its eagerness to 'civilize' (that is to say, make less brutal, more humane) the customs of European societies: to reform penal codes, abolish or mitigate barbarous forms of punishment, 'rationalize' prisons and hospitals and asylums for the poor (not always with happy results), and seek ways to help the handicapped. If 'enlightened' spokesmen are prominent in many such causes, they have no monopoly of benevolence; it does seem however that a challenge of new values brings to conscious attention old neglects and abuses too long taken for granted; and a large majority of progressive thinkers profess either indifference to the (Catholic) Church, which they associate with obscurantism and connivance at old ills, or downright detestation of it.

Enlightenment, then, can be described in abstract terms as an outline programme of scientific philosophy (both rational and empirical), constitutional 'freedom' (drawing on natural law), intellectual dissent from established Churches, philosophic rationalism, and echoes of classical antiquity, all brought together under the heading of Nature—a multiplicity of natures, one for each class of object—and also a grand total of ascertainable Nature, the rational universe. It emphasizes simplicity, which makes it easy to spread and congenial to polite manners; and it appears connected to 'improvement', to a forward march of humanity. It also appears to recommend itself to victims of tyranny, or of mere stupidity. A kind of family 'merger' of some or all of these strands of learning from Nature brings about something slightly reminiscent of the humanism of three centuries earlier: a set, or perhaps simply a chance collection of value changes, but brought together with all the appearance of an independent evolution of thought under its own power, a collective spirit of the age. That, at any rate, is how it is presented to the age, and to posterity, by many of its advocates.

Philosophers and despots

So who then are the advocates? Who is 'enlightened'? It is not too easy to supply a standard answer for the whole of Europe. But fairly generally, we find a good proportion of 'intellectuals', attracted towards what by mid-century is being called 'philosophy' with a new and tendentious connotation. And who are these intellectuals? We can identify a quite large, and growing, range of persons. A writer living from his earnings, to begin with: Grub Street is a new feature of expanding rich societies, a vague assemblage of scribblers and young hopefuls and publicists and printers and booksellers, especially in Paris, London, and the Netherlands; a world which rulers feebly seek to control by censorship or 'privileges', or newly invented copyright laws. A few such writers achieve independence and fame, commonly with the help of patronage, one or two by commercial acumen: Voltaire (a unique case) amasses considerable wealth, becomes a capitalist, invests in industries; but Pope, Goldsmith, and Johnson, Lesage and Diderot, Grimm and Lessing, are all 'independent' men of letters too. And none will be more ferociously independent than J.-J. Rousseau, even though he ends his days copying music. Some writers are already 'publicists', producing journals or periodicals for quite small readerships; before the end of the century there will be more or less modern-style newspapers, and the press will play a huge part in the French Revolution, though in mid-century that cannot yet be glimpsed. As well, intellectuals continue to be found where they have long existed. They secure their leisure and opportunity as retainers in great households—tutors, secretaries, chaplains, factors; some also are professional men, especially men of law, and holders of sinecures and public offices; to these one must add untenured clergy in Catholic lands and virtually all men of the cloth in Protestant ones, and some at least of the teachers in universities. For most of them we can say that intellectual capital is already perceived as an intangible asset which with luck may be converted into government stock or even real estate. In short, the 'republic of letters' (the phrase has existed since late in the previous century) offers a career if not a status; as in the earlier case of the humanists, it is free from the regulations that govern every other trade and profession; and therefore compatible with the latter, and especially attractive to the disinherited. But this freedom also has a negative side: the extraordinary character profiled in Diderot's sketch, *Rameau's Nephew*, is a study in the contradictory states of mind of an intellectual who has failed to capitalize on his native brilliance.

Throughout Europe, it is less easy to identify the supporters of Enlightenment, because although in a sense coherent it is also highly diffuse. What is known of the membership of masonic lodges offers an illustration of this. Predominantly we glimpse merchants and financiers, notaries and lawyers, doctors, diplomats, gentry; men of substance or sound reputation. By the mid-century they have been joined also by members of the French royal family, by Frederick the Great, by Maria Theresa's husband Francis of Lorraine and her son Joseph, the next Hapsburg emperor, by a scattering of other princes and great nobles. To judge from this, 'Enlightenment' must claim the allegiance of a huge cross-section of respectable society! At the same time it

122   Louis-Michel van Loo (1707–71), *Denis Diderot,* **1767. Oil on canvas, 31⅞ × 25⅝ in (81 × 65 cm). Paris, Musée du Louvre**

The pose is the pose of genius, undergoing inspiration: wigless, open-necked, undisturbed by formality or conventional pettiness, Denis Diderot is seen going about the special business which underlies his claim to consideration.

is not too easy to see what commitment that involves: it may not even amount to disaffection from established religions. Voltaire confesses in his *Philosophic Letters* of 1734 that the views he advances are held by no more than one man in twenty. By the time he is admitted with great pomp into a publicity-hungry masonic lodge in Paris, forty years later, the appearances are different, mainly due to the fashions of princes. Even so, has anybody ever supposed that these latter would grant favours or enact great 'improvements' which were not in their own direct interests?

Nevertheless there is, rather surprisingly, a category of allegedly 'enlightened' person comprising some of the more despotic *princes* of Europe. Undoubtedly they have quite different motives for favouring 'progress', when they deign to do so. But whenever they oppress an ignorant landlord, disperse a mob, override a superstitious priest, they can be certain of the applause of philosophically minded intellectuals. Hence, against all apparent logic, the bizarre link between intellectuals eager to preach freedom and those absolute rulers whom they are pleased to call enlightened.

Frederick II of Prussia is the prime example. A Calvinist prince in a Lutheran state, a first point in his favour is that he insists vehemently on religious tolerance, be it for Catholic or Turk. Determined to increase the power and stature of his little kingdom, he also reforms his bureaucracy and his schools, with the same high-handedness that his dreadful parent has shown in recruiting grenadiers. He admires all things French (France being an 'advanced' society), builds his own version of Versailles outside Berlin (Sans-Souci), summons a French scientist to head a new academy, and invites Voltaire to join his court. How can a freedom-lover refuse? In the sequel it becomes clear to Voltaire that he is purely an adornment, a trophy, without influence on his host; their parting is bitter. The brief flirtation is nevertheless well publicized, and its effect outlasts those treacheries and aggressions by which Frederick becomes 'the Great'.

We observe, in fact, a regular trickle of intellectual publicists being retained as consultants by canny despots. Denis Diderot, subversive journalist, brilliant polymath, anticlerical and no doubt also 'materialist', answers the summons of Catherine 'the Great' to her new capital of St. Petersburg. The 'Semiramis of the North' has murdered her husband, conquered the Crimea, and plans to annex and share Poland with her neighbours; but she is a great modernizer, with a strong sense of public relations: she even sets up bogus 'Potemkin villages' in the Crimea to dazzle foreign observers. In addition, she calls in German experts to carry on the work of Peter the Great, reforms education, and goes through the pantomime of consulting her subjects on a possible 'constitution' for her empire. Diderot enjoys private conversations with her, has no serious duties to perform, is sent home well rewarded. Not all such assignments are equally happy: Dupont de Nemours is invited to Poland by King Stanislas Poniatowski to set up a modern school system, but his task is hopeless because the country is falling into anarchy (he does rather better by having a son whose American powder company confers a more lasting glory on his name).

Despots are, when it suits them, quite capable of modernizing their lands without aid from imported Enlightenment 'philosophers'. Indeed, they are rather apt to strike spectacular blows against the enemies of 'progress', if not of freedom. In Spain, where the Bourbon Charles III relies on an energetic minister, Aranda, to manage the kingdom for him, two royal measures catch the eye: one is a reclamation scheme for the wastelands of the Sierra Morena in the south, something a good deal more positive than 'Potemkin villages', and effected (since the prince's own subjects seem slow to respond to Enlightenment) by importing a few thousand diligent German labourers; the other is the expulsion of the Jesuit order. In imperial Tuscany, Archduke Leopold, freemason and improver, seeks to abolish 'idolatry' and wayside shrines, a rehearsal for the time when, as emperor in Vienna, he will embark on a surprisingly wide programme of reforms, including a sort of Jewish emancipation, secular schooling, expulsion of Jesuits (again). And there are other autocratic improvers in smaller states—in Parma, in Naples . . .

Most startling of all is the march of progress in Portugal, where the king's minister Pombal outshines all contemporaries in the vigour of his statecraft. The lasting memorial of Pombal's labours is, of course, modern Lisbon, rebuilt with the greatest magnificence after the earthquake of 1755; the new city epitomizes his close alliance with docile commercial classes, who (along with the Jewish community, persecution of which is abolished) benefit enormously from the 'enlightened' opportunities for investment and the promotion of trade. That this master-building in Lisbon costs the ruin of Portuguese agriculture (usually a target for improvement) does not bother Pombal one bit: he has silenced opposition from an old land-owning nobility by several spectacularly gruesome public executions for treason, and for safety's sake he too expels the Jesuits; and by appointing his brother head of the Inquisition he has the even rarer satisfaction of seeing one of their number, Father Malagrida, brought to trial for heresy and publicly burnt at the stake. Europe watches: amazed, admiring, and slightly disturbed . . .

If such is 'Enlightenment', it is evidently not quite what the amiable Fontenelle would have had in mind; this is however not the last occasion on which 'progressive' ideas are turned around in a disconcerting manner. What is afoot is made perfectly clear when we consider how happy the despot is to be rid of the Church's most energetic arm, the Jesuit order. The Jesuits are in no obvious sense obscurantist, though their political and commercial activities are neither popular nor, it seems, under any very firm control. During the 1760s, they are expelled from so many countries (Portugal, Spain, Naples, Austria, France) that the Holy See eventually yields to pressure to abolish the order altogether (1773).

Everywhere hailed as a triumph of reason, this papal act merely illustrates the subjection of an ancient spiritual power—now—to new aggressive political interests. For 'reason' read (the prince's) 'reason of state'.

Frustrations of progress: France

In several lands improvement is in the hands of despots. In England it is patronized by a small nobility and a large 'gentry', a parliament not inattentive to the interest of trade and money, and a king whose powers are anything but absolute: the English play a peculiar game of Whigs and Tories, not readily imitated. So what of the very centre of the European scene, France? Here is a kingdom which sets an example to all lesser societies in polite manners, refined pleasures, luxurious living, and sheer wealth and size. She dominates Europe, hardly affected by setbacks in war or loss of colonies.

Internally, though, 'progress' is not marked. It has too many enemies. The royal family itself, and its several households, officers, hangers-on; the great nobility; the aristocracy of the robe and its *parlements*; a tenacious Gallican Church and aristocratic bishops—all hold the country to a condition of inactivity. Society appears on the surface to be stagnant in the embrace of 'feudal' custom, the numerous different administrations, a cat's-cradle of legal systems, bafflingly varied traditions of land tenure and seigneurial rights and special competences, grown up over centuries. Irrational too are the disabilities of Protestants and Jews, the insolence of privilege, universal nepotism. Here, if anywhere, is scope to combat outrages, the dead hand of clerical tradition, 'arbitrary power', and encourage merit to seek and win its fair reward. These are all natural and reasonable causes. And facing them, considerable margins of tolerance and inefficiency. Here if anywhere is the place for Enlightenment to work most earnestly and purposefully.

In France there is both the greatest mass of inertia and the largest audience for new ideas, in fact by far the largest educated public in Europe. A small 'upper' bourgeoisie, first, of men of law, legal officers, rich doctors, property-owners. Such men are by no means 'conservative'; excluded from high posts, military commissions, and the *parlements*, they are in fact receptive to a great deal of the Enlightenment's programme. There is a large number of middling bureaucrats and employees in administrations, and an even larger number of traders, merchants, contractors. At the centre of 'civilized' living also, two groups have influence out of all proportion to their numbers—a sprinkling of 'liberal' nobles of the sword or the robe (of whom Montes-

123 Allan Ramsay (1713–84), *David Hume*, 1766. Oil on canvas, 30 × 25 in (76.2 × 63.5 cm). Edinburgh, Scottish National Portrait Gallery

The benign philosopher, agreeably portrayed in the formal attire of a Secretary at the embassy during his stay in Paris— not for Hume, be it noted, the disorderly attire or other badges of genius or original inspiration. If his writings subvert metaphysics his actions do not challenge the world.

quieu, Mirabeau, and Lafayette are notable examples), and a number of financiers and bankers, including farmers-general, all hugely wealthy. By the middle of the century, a generation into the reign of Louis XV, this last group's patronage of 'enlightened' letters is as noticeable as the ostentation of its life-style; in fact it has changed the political complexion of salon society in Paris. Rousseau is happy to be entertained by Mme d'Epinay; Helvétius himself is a centre of downright subversion, as Baron d'Holbach will be with his circle of 'materialist' cronies; the sceptical David Hume, arriving as embassy secretary in Paris, is fêted in this milieu as few of his fellow-countrymen have ever been. In pursuit of amusement polite society contrives to

124   Aerial view of Lisbon
In a magnificent square of the rebuilt Lisbon, Pombal erects (1775) a pompous equestrian statue of his monarch Joseph I. To the prince his due . . . However, a Latin inscription on the base commemorates not Joseph but his minister, and also the city's 'collegium negotiatorum' (assembly of traders) who have enabled the redevelopment to be carried through.

make daring thoughts fashionable even when forbidden, provided they be witty; subversion is an indulgence of the great. And all around this focus there is the reading public, a market whose size enables a Voltaire, or a Diderot, to picture his words exercising real power on the minds of men. The proofs of this influence will undoubtedly be seen in 1789; although Enlightenment will by then be merged in with the expression of all sorts of other hopes and interests—including those of ten million peasants quite untouched by fancy ideas—the third estate of 1789 has the huge advantage of an articulate, developed, and familiar set of general opinions. It inherits the ready-made armoury of 'progress'.

Before that fateful year, there are in France two false dawns. The first is when Mme de Pompadour conquers the royal bed, and commands at Versailles: a millennium for the philosophic, because their financier patrons have now a unique ally, and if the king still backs his bishops, the royal mistress backs philosophy. Accordingly the years 1750–51 see the launch of two very large publishing projects, each a landmark: Buffon's *Natural History*, and the collective venture of an *Encyclopédie* master-minded by Diderot. The former is a first summing-up of the great conquests of zoology;

smooth but not without originality, for Buffon is not only cataloguing all forms of life on earth, with a grand manifesto on science, but also addresses the problem of *change* in Nature and takes up earlier conjectures about the evolution of species. The second project, in which almost all the 'philosophers' have a hand, is a comprehensive survey of all the recent lessons of nature, in physics and the analysis of poverty, constitutions and sects, economics and free-will, together with a rewriting of the past in a piquant and critical spirit to refute adversaries. Its preliminary *Discourse* is from the pen of a leading academician (d'Alembert), but even so, without favour at court such a vast project in subversion would be impossible; *with* such favour, after a brief scuffle, it is allowed to go ahead. Under the very nose of

125   François Boucher (1703–70), *Madame de Pompadour*, 1756. Oil on canvas, 79⅛ × 61¾ in (201 × 157 cm). Munich, Alte Pinakothek
Patroness of arts and royal pleasures, Boucher's Mme de Pompadour is shown at ease with what looks suspiciously like a volume of Diderot's Encyclopédie *lying on the ground beneath her escritoire, along with drawings, sheets of music, a map; in her hand she holds a no doubt lighter piece of reading.*

126   Industrial plate of the stocking-maker's workshop from Diderot's *Encyclopédie*, Vol. II, part I, 1751–72. London, British Library

The eleven supplementary volumes of Plates and explanatory articles which Diderot provides for the Encyclopédie *make up a general anthology of arts and crafts as these are practised in the wealthiest and best endowed state of the eighteenth century. Such an anthology has not been seen before; it shows us a huge range of technologies on the eve of the 'industrial revolution'. The plate shown here is followed by others to show the production process in detail.*

Church and state Diderot and his collaborators are free to toil away at the thirty-five volumes which reach out all over Europe and constitute the new *Summa* of Enlightenment and Progress.

Apart from its sheer size, there is one innovation which distinguishes the *Encyclopédie* from earlier compilations of the 'critical' sort. It contains articles on what we today call technology—information on the mechanic arts and crafts, the skills to which 'society' has never thought fit to give polite attention. Diderot (himself the son of a cutler) particularly wishes to emphasize technology and arranges for volumes of handsome plates to illustrate it. The story is put about that one day when Mme de Pompadour is curious to know how rouge is made, a volume of the *Encyclopédie* is sent for and duly supplies the answer: this sparks off quite a little fashion in the very highest society for 'looking things up'—in a work which in the meanwhile has been banned by the Church.

Improvement, in the sense of technical advance, is of course of central importance to Diderot, as it is to those of his friends who are pursuing the study of economic questions (they include Quesnay, who happens to be physician to Mme de Pompadour), and to men of progress generally. They are quite aware that 'improving' has made Dutch agriculture famous and is now the rage in England (notably in the Enclosure Acts, which permit landowners to appropriate common lands and convert them to lucrative pasture); by contrast, such improvement is retarded in France. They are also aware that manufacturing crafts can be greatly extended: but again, not in France. In either case, old social institutions and obscurantism stand in the way: land tenure (mainly) in the case of agriculture, traditional craft corporations in the case of manufactures. Popularizing technology in the *Encyclopédie* is in this perspective not simply a matter of giving amusement to great ladies; it carries a political lesson.

Such lessons become entirely clear in the *second* false dawn of the French Enlightenment, a quarter of a century after the first. Mme de Pompadour is dead, Diderot is ageing and Voltaire extremely old when Louis XVI in the opening month of his reign (1774) appoints Anne-Jacques-Robert de Turgot, an experienced crown official, to be his financial controller. The excitement among philosophers, liberals, economists, is again tremendous: Turgot, a known friend of enlightened ideas, has already shown reforming zeal. As hoped, he embarks on a programme of change: he has, after all, urgent need to raise taxes for his royal master. Prominent among his measures is one to reduce the old guilds and their monopolies and restrictive practices, and enable rural industry to expand—which at present these guilds are preventing. A blow for freedom! Things are not so simple, however; the crown's edict arouses huge opposition in 1776, and not only from the guilds. It is sabotaged, disregarded. And it is the same with a whole succession of other reforms which Turgot puts forward or plans: they enchant his admirers, but horrify one or other of the power groups who form the regime. As well they might; for if we set them out in a list they read very much like a programme for a revolution, a reshaping of society in the light of liberal convictions and ideals. Turgot of course never puts them forward in that way; each proposal is to benefit the crown, assist the autocrat (to be sure, other categories of person are likely to benefit in the process too, and usually not those who already hold monopolies or special advantages).

Thus, on the one hand, we find proposals to end the corvée (traditional forced service to the landlord), abolish various transport monopolies and sundry transit dues, and do away with state control of the grain trade (this proposal, when enacted, produces fearful price speculation, riots and looting, and eventually the minister's downfall). On the positive side, Turgot has ideas for a rational network of canals and cheaper freight costs, for a uniform system of weights and measures (later the metric system), and a discount bank to assist trade. He also has plans of a humane tendency: medical associations to promote public health (for instance by vaccination), regulation of pharmaceuticals, modernization of prisons and hospitals, 'charity workshops' to relieve the huge population of beggars and vagrants (and at one blow also reduce the Church's hold on social charity), a state education system (the same implication), replacement of the unpopular tax-farming by government tax collectors . . . Turgot even puts to the monarch a sketchy idea for a 'constitution', with an electorate of property owners and a representative chamber to vote taxes; and—alas—he has endless proposals for checking the extravagance of the royal households. Taken all together, this range of concerns sums up rather succinctly what Enlightenment means in the eighteenth century when translated into a programme of actual changes to be made to some of the institutions of the old régime.

It would, however, take an extraordinarily resolute despot to carry through such a programme in eighteenth-century France; or else, perhaps, a super-Pombal. Louis XVI has not the character of Frederick of Prussia, and Turgot is no Pombal. In consequence Turgot is dismissed in 1777 (and, just to remind us of some of the archaisms of this immovable regime, banished from the capital). A programme of similar nature, though very much more all-embracing, *will* be started in France, in 1789; but it will not then be to further the interests of the crown. Before that happens there will have been the very striking example, across the Atlantic, of enlightened ideals being used in the definition of an entirely new sovereign state, erected on natural rights and without any kind of compromise with a crown; that process has already begun while Turgot is in office, with the American Declaration of Independence and Benjamin Franklin's mission to France—two resounding and unexpected pieces of encouragement to true philosophers,

and an illustration of the way in which, failing an enlightened despot, a more imposing force can work its will (its collective, or as Rousseau puts it, its General Will). In France, this translates into the later actuality of a class war carried out in the name of universal principles and natural justice by the third estate, beginning in 1789.

Further light from nature

The Enlightenment centred in Paris, as we see from the foregoing, is clearly a hybrid of English and French intellectual inspirations: deism and scepticism, the science of Bacon and Descartes, Newton and Buffon, the liberalism of Locke and Voltaire, the commercial ideology of Turgot, the anticlericalism of Voltaire and Diderot supported on a wave of restless secularism. It has a certain loose coherence. But along with these things, there are other, less coherent, zones. How (if at all) is the kind of elegance we associate with Mme de Pompadour to be related to what has just been traced out? Or the urbane wit of *Candide* related to the triumphs of a quite new vein of literature—*Pamela, La Nouvelle Héloïse*, presently *Werther*? 'Nature' has not yet given us all her lessons.

That the 'nature' of things can be grasped by reason is a supposition of the arts no less than of science. Indeed it is a canon of taste or judgement. 'What we rightly conceive we can clearly express', says the seventeenth-century critic Boileau, and Pope comes at the same idea: 'True Wit is Nature to Advantage dress'd.' Literature and art are concerned with general truths of nature. Even a century after Boileau, this lesson is being firmly repeated by Joshua Reynolds in his *Discourses* for the Royal Academy of Arts, newly founded (1768) in London. Emphasizing the generality of truths of nature he says: 'The whole beauty and grandeur of the art consists . . . in being able to get above all singular forms, local customs, particularities, and details of every kind'—to approach, in other words, an 'ideal beauty', *le beau idéal*, which is inherent in the nature of things. This principle is attributed to all the arts which can be related to (or carried beyond) classical example, and others too; it has been exhibited in the precision and controlled deliberation of Perrault's Louvre colonnade, in the inexorable tidiness of a tragedy by Racine, and (why not?) in the clear formal architecture of a garden laid out by Le Nôtre. In each, a 'nature' is exhibited, and there is a manifest attempt to approach the status of a model. What else, indeed, is 'a classic', or 'classical'?

It remains possible, unfortunately, to disagree as to the 'best' models. That the nature of a thing should be

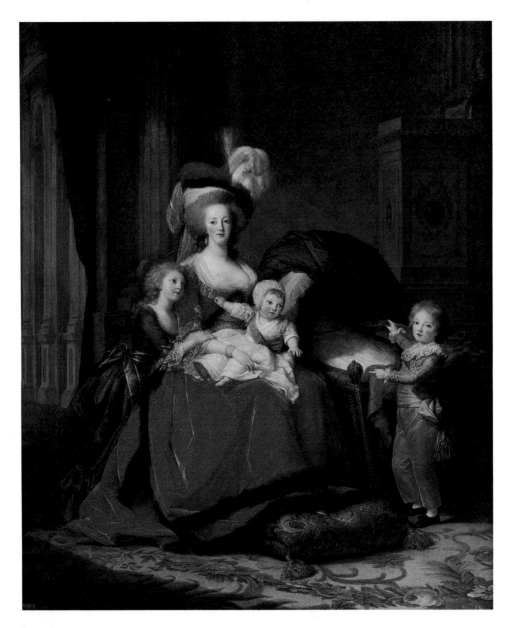

127   Marie-Louise-Elisabeth Vigée-Lebrun (1755–1842), *Marie Antoinette with her Children*, 1787. Oil on canvas, 102¾ × 80¼ in (260 × 205 cm). Versailles, Musée National du Château de Versailles

Unkind though it may be to compare the mistress of Louis XV (plate 125) with the royal Consort of Louis XVI, it is interesting to note how Marie Antoinette has consented to have herself depicted by her artist-friend. Is it to silence malicious tongues that she is surrounded, here, by her children? And the face of the Austrian Emperor's sister—is it not surprisingly ordinary—not to say bourgeois?

rationally exhibited does not prevent a different account of that thing (or of one like it) being equally compelling. Philosophers can disagree—Locke with Malebranche, Clarke with Leibniz, Hume with all of them. A model of the Palladian style in England is no less (symbolically) rational than the classicism of Mansart and Gabriel in France, Chiswick no less 'enlightened' than Trianon. Worse, the French gardens of Versailles serve undoubtedly as a symbol of order (and thus of rationality) in the affairs of that kingdom; before

them, the formal gardens of Dutch regents have no doubt expressed a similar orderliness; but (as N. Pevsner remarks) what if the king of France's enemies see in that orderliness a symbol also of absolutism and overbearing power? 'Natural' can then prompt a more informal alternative, and in 1720 Lord Burlington surrounds his Palladian villa with an 'English' garden: no less artificial, as it happens, still a 'Nature to Advantage dress'd', but Nature nonetheless. And throughout the kingdom, on improved estates, there is space and scope

128 The gardens at Stourhead, Wiltshire (1740–60), planned by Henry Hoare, with architecture by Henry Flitcroft

To accompany the bland Palladian villa of the Whig, the 'English garden' is first created by Burlington's protégé William Kent, then generalized in great parks up and down the land. No more natural than any other, Stourhead is a monument to a wealthy banker's dream: its informality carefully controlled, this time classical in inspiration, liberally sprinkled with grottoes, and laid out for the prepared visit. In short, 'Nature to advantage dress'd'.

129 Jean Cotelle (1642–1708), *Versailles. Les Trois Fontaines*. Oil on canvas. Versailles, Musée de Versailles

But it is hard, now, to find anything very 'natural' in the gardens originally laid out by Le Nôtre, with their vast symmetrical Parterres, fountains, and 'canal' stretching to the skyline, flanked by other artifices and elaborate formal displays. This water-garden (1677) is only one of many; if it lacks a fringe of statues, it is none the less extravagant, because of the huge outlays involved in bringing water to its varied features.

and money to echo, advance, and develop that idea.

At some point, we notice, the semantics of Nature also change subtly. The 'Nature' (of things) is over-taken by, simply, 'Nature' (the sum of things, a collective entity). It is only a matter of emphasis in usage, to be sure, but portentous. 'Nature' becomes, in use, the proper name of the visible universe, of the environment all around, pristine, not yet tampered with, unspoilt by human error (whether or not created by God's design); and by implication a teacher—whether viewed by a devout or a profane eye. In his very celebrated long poem, *The Seasons* (1726–30), James Thomson apostrophizes:

> Oh Nature! all-sufficient! over all!
> Inrich me with the Knowledge of thy Works!

and then proceeds to give a list of what he understands to constitute those 'works': 'Motions, Periods, Laws . . . the mineral Strata . . . the vegetable world . . . the rising System, more complex, Of Animals . . . and higher still, the Mind.' His poem is not anything so

130   Lord Burlington (1694–1753), Chiswick House, Middlesex, c. 1725

A new king, a new oligarchy, a new style: George I, the Whig ascendancy, and 'Palladianism' come to England after 1715. Lord Burlington's house at Chiswick, designed by himself, illustrates the last-named. A cultivated nobleman brings back from Italy architectural ideas to inform domestic buildings with a spirit of – as Summerson calls it – moderation and good breeding.

sophisticated as an echo of Plato or Zeno or Lucretius; Nature is not a goddess, and Thomson is not a pantheist. What brings *The Seasons* a European reputation (many translations, imitations, echoes—in music too) is its naïve panorama of climates and landscapes, conventionalized species, and of course villagers adorning the landscape: all represented as innocent (the rustics are not quite Arcadian, but they are not degraded or despicable peasants either: a classical tradition of Virgil's *Eclogues* and *Georgics* has been replaced by a homespun ideal). On reviewing Nature with Thomson we confront not a research programme in the sciences but an opportunity to exercise our powers of appreciation, develop our feeling, in the face of naturalness: innumerable scenes of simplicity and beneficence, all pleasing or

edifying—except for occasional ugly reminders of the lust-blinded hunter (Thomson detests blood-sports), the insensate barbarous trade of war, and a few other corruptions of civil society.

Here is another 'export' to European culture from the land which has already offered Locke, and the image of a gentleman who does not have to be 'noble', and other novelties simplified and reduced to parables and relayed by Voltaire in challenging form. This one too has the attractive feature that it can be associated with benevolence and merged into denunciations of tyrants, cruelty, aristocratic hauteur, as required. Only this time the great spokesman and European distributor will be not Voltaire, but Rousseau. And the lessons of Nature take a new turn.

Jean-Jacques Rousseau makes his name and mark by a prize essay (1749) *condemning* progress in the 'Arts and Sciences': it is an original and striking paradox to address to the enlightened Academy of Dijon which awards the prize. His argument is crude: the arts can be identified with all that is most vicious in society—war, vain artifice, immorality in the big city, depravity. On the other hand simple and sincere behaviour and customs are favourable to virtue and morality. This

131   Ange-Jacques Gabriel (1698–1782), façade of the Petit Trianon, Versailles, 1762–7

The retreat built for the use of Mme de Pompadour in the vast grounds of Versailles owes its charm to extreme simplicity and the most careful proportioning and detail. It epitomizes yet another stage of French 'classical' tradition—and on the eve of a much more widespread 'neo-classicism'.

awakes echoes of the Roman Republic and its rugged values; or of the purity of the 'Peasant of the Danube' as told by old La Fontaine in his fable of decadence confronted by manliness; to say nothing of Thomson's *Seasons*. Polite society is enchanted: such virile eloquence! There follows a second essay, this time on *Inequality* (1754). Here Rousseau avows his deep uncertainty about the character of Nature, of man, of law—the three great themes on which Enlightenment has come to be so sure of itself. By looking into himself, Rousseau finds only *two* principles: self-preservation, and sympathy for others. Both are deeper than, and prior to, reason. According to this view, the 'first expansion' of the human heart (the only natural one) is family life; that is the point at which man issues from a

state of nature into sociability. And he goes on to rewrite and overturn Locke: property is not a human right but the 'original theft'; civil society *should be* (but is not) a means to redress natural inequality by civil equality . . .

The ideas of Rousseau are by no means simple, nor are they free of contradiction; in particular, what he seems to mean by 'Nature' is full of difficulties and shifts and ambiguities. Nevertheless, with or without misunderstandings, he wins celebrity as a new prophet of—precisely—Nature, interpreted now as meaning 'back to the simple life'. Voltaire may mock him (who would *really* envy the Happy Savage, the Red Indian shivering in his skins by the shores of the Huron, without benefit of modern medicine?) but he proceeds to further triumphs of natural feeling, both in his wildly successful novel *La Nouvelle Héloïse* and in his semi-fictional treatise on education, *Émile*; even his campaign to make music and opera more 'natural' is treated respectfully. Rousseau is by no means a barefoot philosopher or Ivan Illich of the eighteenth century, though he would undoubtedly qualify as the founder of an 'alternative philosophy' (he also repudiates the title 'philosopher'). On the other side, there are limits to

of breaking the confines of a local community and capturing the attention of a large audience. In this peculiar situation, the northern community makes a more than average contribution to the progress of Enlightenment. One of its sons we have met already—James Thomson; a generation later two more, close personal friends, stand out on their own: David Hume and Adam Smith.

Entering on life without the prospect of a settled place in his homeland, Hume addresses his attention to philosophy; specifically, to rational philosophy and the English brand of empirical reasoning epitomized by Locke. It takes the optimism of youth to undertake the two things which he essentially does: put in question the fundamental validity of confident reasoning about what we perceive around us, and then trace out a new blueprint for the science of human nature, its sentiments and passions, along with its processes of understanding. After a certain delay the first achievement gives him fame as a sceptic (not a handicap in polite French society but damaging in Scotland) and the second makes him a hero; in a career which includes a famous History of England and some notable essays (on miracles, on economics) he becomes as admired a figure in France as any local *philosophe*.

Adam Smith, who professes moral philosophy at Glasgow, is not only one of those who attempt to expound the fashionable question of sentiment on a reasoned basis (his *Theory of Moral Sentiments* appears in 1759); he is also the codifier of a new science—political economy, exactly matched to the experience of traders and their freedom-loving interests. *The Wealth of Nations* (1776) appears in the last year of Turgot's administration in France; it also coincides with the revolt of the king of England's colonies in America.

Unlike Hume, Smith does not frighten or horrify the elders of his native kirk: he says nothing heretical. In his great book there is in fact nothing offensive to religion in any of its forms: political economy is neutral with respect to great metaphysical questions. He concentrates on demolishing the old 'mercantilist' view of wealth as a store of gold amassed through control of trade by governments, and he goes beyond the 'physiocratic' theories of Quesnay and the recent arguments of French *économistes* for abolition of guilds and their privileges. Whereas in France it is understandable that one should be tempted to find arguments for the unique importance of agriculture (the *sole* source of wealth—products taken out of the ground) Smith is exposed to no such pressure: new wealth comes out of the ground, but also from transforming metal into pins, wool into cloth; in fact, in any transformation effected by human

132   Allan Ramsay (1713–84), *Jean-Jacques Rousseau*, 1766. Oil on canvas, 29½ × 25½ in (75 × 64.8 cm). Edinburgh, National Gallery of Scotland

By the accident of his journey to England, Rousseau's portrait is painted by order of David Hume. It is a bland and friendly picture, and betrays no hint of the ravings and persecution mania to which Rousseau treats his well-wishers on that occasion. In later years, however, Rousseau will claim that it shows 'the face of a Cyclops'.

what public opinion is prepared to imagine: feeling, yes, but progress too! Enlightenment is not refuted; it has an 'add-on', however difficult to integrate.

It is not only from within England and France that a stream of progressive and liberal ideas enter into circulation at the high tide of the Enlightenment. A suggestive supplement is offered by another, much smaller northern country—lowland Scotland. Here, within the loose and whiggish connection with the south (but strong political dominance from England), there is a severe Calvinist tradition to mark the conduct of local affairs. In Edinburgh and Glasgow, also, there are schools and universities to foster young talent, the need for energy to overcome London's condescension towards provincialism, and the encouraging possibility

agency, value is to be measured by the amount of industry applied. And once the product is put into circulation no government can reasonably lay down what price men will actually attach to what they presently desire: as at the weekly market, each decides for himself. In the absence of government interference or other barriers, a myriad individual decisions over a whole society will see to the matching of demands and efforts; and the development of the economy, the totality of such transactions, will be seen to be guided by a 'hidden hand'—whether this be regarded as the hand of providence or the hand of no one. Two further points: in a free society's economy, progress is a built-in feature; the merchant, the enterpriser, the capitalist, will seek to supply wants where he can discover them, and to introduce 'improvement' or capital where this will increase the yield on his investment. What could be a stronger recommendation for a 'hands-off' policy? And lastly, this whole system rests ideally on a thoroughgoing individualism, the free choice of the subject (or citizen): *any* combination, whether created by government and monopoly, or by guilds, or even by capitalists, is bound to be a 'conspiracy' against the rest of society.

Smith is an Enlightenment doctrinaire: of that there is no question. His political economy which purports to deliver obvious truths is also quite elaborately based on reports and surveys of empirical data—prices and costs and fluctuations of supply and other prosaic matters, worthy of the undertakings of any other empirical science in which facts are being discovered, regularities traced, theories framed. One thing alone in the long chapters of *The Wealth of Nations* is not so obviously grounded in a deep consideration of the 'facts', though it is crucial to the whole argument: Smith's assumption that in making economic choices man is guided by rationality. This very central feature of the new science is another tribute to the power of Enlightenment, and it would no doubt be absurd for Smith to make any different assumption; it suits the description of how traders actually go about their affairs. But it is, even so, open to gross abuse. In particular, Smith has nothing to say about the rationality of the desires men do in practice seek to satisfy (what for example is rational about wearing a wig?): only about their propensity, given a set of desires, to get best value for money, if they want to stay in business. Also he has nothing to say about a different class of situations exhibiting dubious rationality: what of the case of the despairing and starving Paris labourer who on 3 May 1775 refuses to pay out his entire week's wage for a small bag of flour in a time of sudden shortage and decontrolled prices (Turgot's

doing), but instead plunders the bakery and is hanged a week later? Smith's *Moral Sentiments*, in which the theory of 'self-interest equals social' translates into '*laissez-faire*' and thence passes into his outlook on economics, would seem to countenance strange departures from reason. In the last resort, one might venture the thought that the author of *The Wealth of Nations* fails to distinguish between *analysing* economic reality and *making models* which may or may not adequately fit the reality.

'One great republic'?

Edward Gibbon, gentleman historian, cosmopolitan, more at home in Paris than in London, who has seen Italy and retreated to Lausanne to write his *Decline and Fall of the Roman Empire* (1776–88), looks around him and remarks in his closing volume that all Europe is 'one great Republic, whose various inhabitants have attained almost the same level of politeness and cultivation'. If he were speaking of royal courts, there might be some plausibility in this; had he in mind (shall we say) public executions he would undoubtedly be right—in every great city the barbarous ceremonies of hanging, strangling, quartering, breaking, or burning of criminals still excite the keen appreciation of crowds as well as the horror of men of sensibility. Were he referring to the lot of the least endowed of society, the landless labourer in the countryside, again it would be difficult to fault him. But of course Gibbon is not thinking of such things. He is conjuring up a vision of a republic of letters, urbane and as far as may be comfortable, where Horace Walpole corresponds with Mme du Deffand and Voltaire with Frederick the Great, where the journalist Baron Grimm reports on Parisian literary events for a German readership, Gibbon's own *Decline and Fall* is fêted for its elegant periods and ironic detachment from religion, and ideas are a great deal easier than acts (as Turgot has found).

The 'great republic' is almost identical with the world of the Enlightenment. It is fairly secure and privileged; it is reasonably optimistic. Just one year after Gibbon puts down his pen it is true that the Enlightenment is launched in France on the wave of a revolution which goes far beyond anyone's power to understand what is afoot; but for the moment, after the quarter-century which runs from Mme de Pompadour to the American Declaration of Independence and then for a further thirteen years, the precarious balance of despots and intellectuals, of stasis in France and elegant exploitation of arts and crafts (*pace* Rousseau), seems to be edging the established order of Europe steadily along the road of inexorable improvement.

It would take a more observant witness than Gibbon to draw a different lesson from the various signs of change which are in fact already present. We can follow these signs in literature, quite clearly, and in the fine arts, and to a certain extent in other arts too; up to a point they mesh with the trends of the times. But if we wish to have some impression of the limitations of the Enlightenment it would be wise, also, to have a glimpse of one or two cultural developments which are both contemporary and virtually quite unrelated.

'Genius'

It is not only the word 'Nature' that receives a significant twist, consecrated by Rousseau. From the doctrine of feelings duly expanded—and we simplify by fixing our attention on Rousseau and his world—there is another expression which is revolutionized at the same time: genius. To the educated (those who have sat in the Latin class) genius means 'spirit', something impersonal or at least disembodied which is immanent in a place or an object. But for those with a little less Latin, or none, that quality is transposed: as Nature shifts from being a characteristic of things to an entity in itself, so 'genius' shifts from being an immanent spirit and comes to designate an actual live person, a flesh and blood human, vibrant with a unique, original, and natural power. For all the attention which early Enlightenment thinkers may previously devote to such matters as sublimity, or enthusiasm, or the like, 'genius' is in fact an expression and an idea which takes root in the eighteenth century's lower middle classes at their juncture with the republic of letters. Rousseau, for example, has scamped his education but has a marvellous gift—'genius'. This development is not arbitrary, not a quirk of idle intellectuals. And it is the contrary of rational.

Consider some of the outstanding literary success figures of the mid-century. In England Samuel Richardson elevates the art of writing love-letters for the semi-illiterate into exemplary romances for thousands of cobblers' wives and chambermaids; Oliver Goldsmith pitches *The Vicar of Wakefield* at almost exactly the same level; and of course in France Rousseau himself, the eternal underdog and whiner, under the guise of edification fills the thoughts of tens of thousands of young ladies of modest fortune with fantasies of guilty love. A new and amazingly tearful literature attests one development that has escaped the prediction of Enlightenment thinkers until quite late in the day: the growth of a large reading 'market' of intellectually unambitious persons. Each of the writers named, and hundreds of lesser practitioners, is 'selling' original genius (and the virtues of sentimental effusion) to readers who, whatever their other characteristics, are delighted by the lyric ejaculation, the exaltation of the ordinary, within which may lurk their own unique spark under the lineaments of feeling.

How universal is genius! How mysterious the powers which move him! And who knows on what child the fairy godmother (or chance, or providence) will bestow this new passport to achievement? Some such wild conjecture is detectable in the early careers of some of the most prominent figures of the next generation: Marat and Danton and Robespierre all harbour it while they wait for their day; to say nothing of Robespierre's admirer and (briefly) follower, the young artillery officer Napoleon Buonaparte. About the time the latter is born, the men who have created the *Encyclopédie* begin to perceive the new phenomenon. Diderot apostrophizes Richardson as a 'singular Genius'; d'Alembert, who is a respected academician but started life as a foundling, writes an essay precisely on the need for the republic of letters to adjust its relations with its earlier patrons, 'the great'—a new wind is blowing.

Directly connected with the arrival of genius as a supernumerary class in society is a profound, albeit a slow, revolution in aesthetics. The lesson of the ancients and the classics—and Boileau and Pope and Reynolds—comes down to this: that the themes which art and verse and song celebrate, the great truths which they feature, are accessible to the whole of mankind through the exertions of reason; painter and wordsmith being but superior performers when they translate to sense and understanding the shared commonplaces and truths. Such a doctrine now becomes an unacceptable limitation for the genius. Enlightenment is a machine for discovery; but the science of man and his feelings has hardly yet been adequately explored; genius is a discoverer too, and will soon be an inventor. There is more to discover than yesterday's commonplaces.

In letters this revolution is most clearly and swiftly reflected: in the new fictions of sentiment, for example, already noted. But also, and very strikingly, in another field—that opened up by Rousseau's *Confessions* and, most unexpectedly, in biography. Boswell's *Life of Johnson* is the first biography to break out of the commonplaces of formal eulogy and 'ideal beauty', a sprawling portrait of greatness in carpet-slippers, with a profusion of precisely those 'singular forms . . . peculiarities and details of every kind' that Reynolds dismisses; a realm of insights and irregularities which is compelling by sheer quantity and diversity, not by any 'ideal' portraiture of Samuel Johnson. Whatever the old critic may have desired, Boswell's writing makes him great by idiosyncrasy, not regularity.

Without the enfranchisement available to a genius, it is hard to imagine all this. The genius stands for a new approach to change, one in which he is constantly challenging 'taste' (consecrated values). 'Every great poet is a teacher,' says Wordsworth, 'I wish either to be considered as a teacher or as nothing.' 'Let the age continue to love its own darkness,' he adds, 'I shall continue to write with, I trust, the light of Heaven upon me.' Genius appears to win handsomely in the age of Napoleon and Beethoven, and the 'commonplace', from being a term of strong approval, is turned into its exact opposite, a withering dismissal of banality. To Rousseau, and not to Voltaire, we can trace back this beginning of a very great divide in European literature and thought: on the one hand, science and the social sciences pursuing the Enlightenment project of reason and *generality*; on the other, *belles-lettres* turning away to attend to felt experience, sentiment, the unique exploration, the *individual*.

Varieties of the Rococo

We associate the culture of the Enlightenment, its mixture of gaiety and deep seriousness, with the furniture of Louis XV, the elegances of Mme de Pompadour, the luxury spending of princes and great financiers and nobles—a supremely tasteful and mannerly environment in which the *philosophes* come and go—Voltaire, Diderot, Hume, Helvétius, and the rest—and Rousseau cuts his ungainly and incongruous figure. The image is of a polite and urbane world. And it is not a misleading image, though it focuses our attention on only a tiny minority of humanity. Yet when we look more closely, we find our attention straying outward from the centre of the picture; we discover intricacies and elaborations.

At the start, it is typical of a 'philosophic' view surveying the world, in Johnson's phrase, 'from China to Peru', that first expectations should be to find in far-off peoples the same traces of reason and Nature that adorn the nearer scene. Is not human nature everywhere the same? Seventeenth-century Jesuit missionaries in China have identified Confucian doctrine with Christianity, the rule of the mandarin with the best models of the West. A century later (1777) the popular writer Marmontel finds it plausible to write a history of the Incas of Peru in which their 'mild' and 'interesting' customs are held up as those of the 'most enlightened and *sensible* nation of America' (what do we know of

133   Jean-Henri Riesener (1734–1806), roll-top desk, *c*. 1773. Waddesdon Manor, Buckinghamshire

An exceptionally precious roll-top desk (a recent invention) suggests an order executed for an exceptional client (in this case, Louis XV's daughter). But when we consider the quantity and variety of 'Louis XV' furniture surviving, it becomes manifest that these elegant artefacts are not confined to royal and aristocratic use (the French nobility as a whole does not exceed 80,000 persons) but that they define the self-consciously refined taste of a very much wider range of well-to-do ranks of society.

Incan sensibility?). In the intervening decades a panorama of other exotica, real and fictitious, is assembled for display: from the narratives of missions and explorers, the reports of colonists, and, not least, the fancy of playwrights or satirists. The imaginary 'Persia' of Montesquieu's satirical *Persian Letters*, the 'Indian' gallantries of Rameau's opera, the voyages around the world of Bougainville and Cook, the suave barbarism of the *Thousand and One Nights* (translated first into French in 1707), Bruce's travels in Abyssinia: these are all contributions. It is of very little moment whether they paint things seen or imagined, accurate or fanciful or simply extravagant pictures of faraway places: they

134 Johann Gregor Herold (1696–1775), Meissen tankard, 1725. Cleveland, Cleveland Museum of Art (on loan from a private collection)

On the side of this handsome piece of Meissen pottery a Chinese scene is represented – or what purports to be Chinese: a drooping moustache, an embroidered robe, a pigtail, broad flat hats, seem to be about all that is required to convey a characteristic 'exotic' intention.

fill out the imaginative world of a society undisturbed by what they have to tell. If the age is optimistic, it is precisely because the pictures threaten nothing. Evidently they provide an enormous range of variety as compared with the by now stilted icons of classical antiquity. Yet, being without danger, they are theatrical flats, innumerable cardboard flats for an immensely wide stage.

If rococo is a term to designate a family of styles marked off from its predecessors by a certain degree of self-conscious refinement and good-mannered ele-

gance, a turning-away from extremes of self-assertiveness or stiffness, then it is hard to restrict it to the pictures of Boucher and Fragonard, or to the furniture of Boulle and Chippendale or the decorative inventions of Robert Adam. For the patrons of such men are also attracted by *chinoiseries* and all manner of exotica: at the middle of the century Kew Gardens offer an extraordinary medley purporting to represent the civilized symbols of every continent (only the Chinese pagoda survives); the cardboard flats are *also* examples of the rococo. The final monument of these indulgences

135   J. Mornand, clock with ormolu-mounted porcelain group of 'The Harlequin Family' by J. J. Kändler, *c.* 1740. 13½ × 7¼ × 7 in. (34.2 × 18.4 × 17.8 cm). Chicago, Art Institute of Chicago

Clockwork may serve practical needs (mariners' chronometers, etc.) or it may be incorporated in luxury objects for display. In this example, a relatively simple French timepiece is combined with porcelain figures (Columbine and Harlequin, from the traditional Italian commedia dell'arte*) and mounted to form an elegant salon adornment.*

will be a highly fantastical 'pavilion' erected in Brighton for an English prince in a composite Moorish-Hindu-Gothic idiom; seeming to promise the enchantments of a veritable Aladdin's cave, it echoes the obstinate belief that beneath picturesque oddities of custom and costume human nature everywhere goes through a usual repertory of motions—of benevolence and envy, liberality and greed, love and treachery. In this sense, the rococo—whether French or English or German, or in its Chinese, Hindu, Incan, or even Gothic extensions—announces a certain bland and universal benevolence towards mankind at large.

It is not quite the same with that other faraway world which the Enlightenment has no reason not to go on calling (with sublime imprecision) the 'Middle Ages'. It is an era of barbarity, no doubt, for Gibbon, but for his contemporaries it merges into a misty timelessness (rather like the Egyptian-Solomonic aura of freemasonry) which brings together all sorts of half-remembered ancestral oddities: primitive border ballads in Britain, Villon's decidedly sophisticated fifteenth-century ballads in France, druids glimpsed

136   Canaletto (1697–1768)
London: the Thames from the Terrace of Somerset House, the City in the Distance (detail), 1750–1. Oil on canvas, 41½ × 73½ in (105.5 × 186.5 cm). **Windsor, Royal Collection**

Canaletto, one of the eighteenth century's two great suppliers of scenes of 'picturesque' Venice to what is essentially a market of aristocratic tourists, achieves here a curious effect by seeing London under an unmistakably Venetian light. Such a transposition, though piquant, is minimal compared with others that Rococo taste will discover.

137   Plate of the Temple of Hercules from *Vedute di Roma* by Giambattista Piranesi (1720–78). London, British Museum

Rome can only be made interesting, to a man of enlightened sensibility, by seeing it in different ways from formerly; no longer venerated as the birthplace of his beliefs and knowledge, it is a marvellous collection of ruins – 'picturesque'. Piranesi's renderings are wilfully extravagant because his subject is the awesomeness of ancient ghosts – and this chimes in with the perspective of Edward Gibbon's great History. For the generation immediately following, it will be the turn of Gothic ruins to form the most widely favoured décor for romantic effusion . . .

Veduta del Tempio di Ercole nella Città di Cora, dieci miglia lontano da Velletri

138   Jean-Honoré Fragonard (1732–1806), *Blind Man's Buff,* **c. 1765. Oil on canvas, 84⅝ × 77⅞ in (215 × 197 cm). Washington, National Gallery of Art, Samuel H. Kress Collection**

Nineteenth-century historians liked to evoke a wistful, elegiac strain in French Rococo painting: mindful no doubt that Marie Antoinette, having played at Arcadian shepherdesses, ends her life on the scaffold. Fragonard, however, blends a landscape of 'natural' sensibility with clear traces of elegance (fountain, picnic furniture), sentimental flirtation, and an appealingly 'domestic' game of blind man's buff. La dolce vita: but no one here is dancing on the edge of a volcano . . .

through Caesar and Tacitus and speculated on by the antiquary Stukeley, the curious fabrication of Ossian's bardic odes by the patriotic Scot Macpherson. In all these, the exotic has a sentimental attraction for the dilettante; it leads him perhaps as far as good taste permits him to stray in that direction. But as compared with the Inca or the mandarin, the medieval brings him close up to the awkward frontier of that embarrassing literature of undistinguished effusion, a frontier which in many cases he would rather not cross. Not only is society sharply divided over the authenticity of Ossian; Horace Walpole, who indulges his fancy by Gothicizing his mansion at Strawberry Hill (another piece of cardboard), is at pains to make his equally Gothic romance, *The Castle of Otranto,* anything but an effusion: highly original, indeed the first of its kind in the blood-curdling mystery genre, no one could possibly mistake it for anything but an extravagant piece of fantasy. The Gothic revival, at the outset, with its ruins and follies, its crenellations and pointed archways, is only the outward and visible sign of gentlemen at play, and not the serious and laborious business that we observe when, fifty years later, governments and municipalities set to work to recapture their links with the Middle Ages.

It is against this background—a cautionary background—that we should consider a new classical revival which is launched by a few choice spirits in the 1760s

140 Germain Soufflot (1713–80), Ste Geneviève (later the Panthéon), Paris, 1757

At a time when 'taste' is beginning to run riot after novelties gathered in from other eras and continents, Soufflot's church in Paris re-asserts a kind of 'great tradition'; and is here seen in its most classical aspect (transformation into a national monument is a later effect of the French Revolution). Even so, there are traces of self-consciousness, of renewed formalism: that entrance elevation (partly masked by the colonnade), or the block-like austerity of the transept . . . Within a decade, architects will 'revive' the Doric.

139 (left) Horace Walpole (1717–97), Strawberry Hill, Twickenham, Middlesex, 1748–77

The witty and self-indulgent dilettante Horace Walpole makes his residence at Strawberry Hill into a kind of neo-Gothic shrine. Although he carefully instructs his friends, architects and workmen with patterns copied from authentic models, the general result is utterly unreal – Walpole calls it 'my toy castle'; nevertheless, much of the detail is charming, as in the gallery shown here, designed by Walpole's friend Lord Camelford in 1759–62. A miniature, no doubt, in the margin of history; but one which, taken alongside a host of other elegant novelties, pre-figures a coming anarchy of 'taste'.

and 1770s. Unlike earlier and greater renaissances this is not a search for a new way of living that is being attended to by modern progress, but simply for a new style, or at least a purified one, to set alongside the proliferations of the rococo (in the widest sense).

In Paris, first, there is a yardstick; the architect Soufflot is constructing the largest single building project in train in that city: the church of Ste-Geneviève (today the Panthéon). As it slowly rises, it can be seen to be based on an idiom almost severely grand and timelessly classical. This is no revolution (or it appears not to be). But by contrast, the English dilettantes Stuart and Revett who venture to Athens, or others who travel to southern Italy or Sicily, do in fact rediscover Hellas, or at any rate Doric architecture in its authentic forms—the strongest of the ancient orders, largely lost sight of—in the Parthenon and at Paestum. Spelled out with great accuracy in the engravings of the English dilettantes, the contrast with the classicism of Gabriel, or for that matter, of Soufflot, is very pronounced. And contemporaneously, not long after the dramatic unearthing of Roman Pompeii, the German scholar Winckelmann settles in Rome, rediscovers Greek art, in fact Hellenistic art, and with passionate enthusiasm seeks to distinguish what he takes to be Attic purity from the subsequent debasements of the Roman.

Both these ventures, entirely distinct, have one thing in common: the search for purity, for the *original*. The originality of the ancient Greeks is as worthy of attention as the originality (the *primitive* originality) of Ossian. There is no question now of cramming all the jinns and exotica back into Aladdin's jar; if Hellenic antiquity is recovered, it is in order that it should be added to the range of available techniques and manners at the disposal of a world of leisure and caprice. There is no grand simplifying doctrine of Nature to be vindicated now by measuring up old stones. Let us admit that by 1770 already, with wealth, travel, caprice, and expansion, 'untidy' variety has entered European taste. It is there to stay; from the variety now being amassed there will come a mania for diversity, an eclectic appropriation of styles which is one of the peculiarities of the nineteenth century.

Enlightened music?

If the neo-classicism of art in the 1760s results from chance, curiosity, and caprice, the abrupt appearance of a severe neo-classicism in music at the same time is no less an accident. There is of course no binding reason why styles of music should always march in step with those of other arts; in fact they have often followed their own rhythm. It just happens that at the same time as Winckelmann strikes gold in Rome, Gluck does the same in Vienna; labelling both of them 'neo-classical' obscures fundamental differences of intention.

Gluck's music is a deliberate departure from the strait-jacket of so-called 'baroque' opera, whether Italianate *à la* Alessandro Scarlatti or French *à la* Rameau; that tradition looks every year a little more stilted and old-fashioned. In its place, Gluck's ambition is to achieve a more direct, a simpler, impact. The result looks neo-classical, indeed, since he takes up the old operatic themes of *Iphigenia* and *Orpheus* and *Alcestis*, but that is incidental; what matters is that he endows his action on the stage with a depth of feeling, of pathos, that is quite unexpected; that the successions of contrast are more dramatic than elegant, and yet contrive to be sublime, sometimes extraordinarily moving. There is no sense in which one could call them 'antiquarian': on the contrary, they are very modern.

Gluck is acclaimed in Vienna in the 1760s, in Paris in the 1770s. His admirers include the enlightened Leopold II and Marie Antoinette (loyal to her Austrian family)—but also Rousseau, the farouche prophet of Nature, which is less to be expected. Rousseau judges Gluck to have achieved what he believed impossible in opera—the natural! For all that, Gluck is something of a freak; his sublimity is disconcerting, like the real Doric temples. Neither of them is for everyday use.

What music then *is* for everyday use in a polite and cosmopolitan Enlightenment world? There is certainly no shortage of choice: Dr. Burney's *Voyages* of musical exploration in France and in Italy attest the liveliness of the art in those countries; to say nothing of the court orchestras retained by scores of self-respecting German princes and archbishops in the Holy Roman Empire. But its highest and most amiable achievements can of course be epitomized in two names: Haydn and Mozart. Like Gluck, they have a background in the very partially enlightened Hapsburg Empire, not in the world of the *philosophes*. Imperial Vienna has attachments both with Germany and with Italy, and at least in its music is a far more exciting centre than Paris. Also we notice that each of these immensely versatile musicians fastens on, and carries to perfection, a decisively important musical form that has first made its appearance in Paris in the 1750s, the sonata. One's first impulse is to ask 'why?', while knowing that to such a question there can be no simple answer.

In itself, sonata form is no more than a convention which unites 'sonata'-movements, minuets, slow movements, and rondos—pure formal constructive

adventures of themes and modulations, courtly echoes, lyric interludes, and joyous romps. Unlike suites and other earlier forms of instrumental music for general occasions, it has an in-built dynamic character—a 'programme', so to speak, of contrasts of tempo, of tonality, of mood—and this character is present even in the simplest of realizations. It is also capable of great elaboration; it lends itself to the keyboard, to the chamber ensemble, to the orchestra. In the symphony, there is hardly any limit to its structural development. In the instrumental concerto, it allows of endless possibilities. In these embodiments, the sonata form becomes the great work-horse of an age in which music, as no other art, is truly a universal language without barriers, and conformable both to the enlightened and the not-so-enlightened. It is a language of feeling, but without an overt ideology.

For both Haydn and Mozart, the sonata and the symphony are a perpetual adventure, leading to achievements which we call 'classical' (that over-used word) because they span a complete and settled repertory of musical resources with effortless mastery—and occasional surprises. But to see them as composers of the Enlightenment, it is perhaps to their non-symphonic work that we should turn. Haydn's visits to England encourage him to enlarge his palette in emulation of Mozart and produce his most mature and elaborate symphonies. But the same occasion calls forth *The Creation*, in emulation this time of Handel and the tradition of oratorio established by the latter. If we compare Handel's somewhat stiff and evangelical *Messiah* with *The Creation*, the evolution is striking. The later work, without being in any sense profane, is certainly not pompous, and it would be difficult to call it devout. It rehearses its sublime theme with an easy good-humouredness, from the early *fiat lux* to the entry of the beasts of Creation and arias and choruses of praise to divinity—a blend of relaxed benevolence and an ultimate in tastefulness. Let us retrace the story of Genesis without fanaticism; with reverence, certainly, but tempered with a benign familiarity.

In the case of Mozart, the salient feature is a consummate technical skill which allows him to absorb and refashion whatever the tonalities and styles of the age can offer to his attention; he never forces the note of pathos, however, or loses a peculiarly elegant reticence. Aristocratic or popular—what does it matter? Grace and effortless ingenuity also mark the flow of operas: grand lyric (*Idomeneo*), 'Turkish' jollities (*Seraglio*), comedy of intrigue (*Figaro*), of mock-parable (*Così fan Tutte*), of the supernatural (*Don Giovanni*)—and not without a passing spice of refined curiosity for the lineaments of suffering ('sadism' is far too strong a word to apply to *Cosi*). The musical vitality of *The Marriage of Figaro* may cause us to lose sight of the fact that its libretto is adapted from a play by Beaumarchais which, when performed in Paris, is seen as the height of insolent subversion, a political gesture of unbridled 'liberalism'; it is all the same to Mozart.

His relation to an 'enlightened' world is however more apparent in his masonic funeral music, and very plain indeed in the strange *Magic Flute*. This absolutely unprecedented opera is 'masonic' from its portentous opening trombone chords (just as *Seraglio* is given a 'Turkish' flavour by cymbals and brisk military pomps); it is bizarre beyond belief in its obscure allegory, condescending in its two-tier plotting of Tamino (serious) and Papageno (serious too, but 'popular', irresponsible, childish). Above all, *The Magic Flute* is unconcernedly 'secular' in its bland offering of mystery, morality, and venerable tradition, uplifted out of any known time or place, hovering no doubt over the oriental locus of an original wisdom. Even recalling that the Hapsburg emperor is a freemason, and that that vein of progressiveness is as acceptable in officially Catholic Vienna as it is in Paris, the precise status of this fairy-tale opera is anything but clear. Understandably it is not a fashionable public of the capital, but Mozart's 'dear people of Prague' (a lively but nevertheless provincial audience) who welcome as a pure spectacle, as a pretext for brilliant vocalizing, this unusual product from their adopted darling.

Frontiers of enlightenment

The vision offered us by Voltaire and Haydn, Walpole and Mozart, is an amiable and seductive one. It corresponds to the existence of a few thousands of articulate and cultivated individuals, not all of them insignificant in the eyes of posterity; most of them—and this is striking—are animated by some belief in progress. What sort of progress, it is not always easy to show: for Gibbon, undoubtedly, little further change is necessary—perhaps somewhat less attention to religion. Under the shadow of the guillotine, the marquis de Condorcet, Turgot's former lieutenant, will write by way of testament a moving *Outline* of human progress, in which to the end he continues to believe—he has the advantage over Fontenelle of nearly a century of remarkable developments to console him.

Nevertheless, Enlightenment does not have the same powerful attractions everywhere. In Germany, quite simply, it never acquires the tinge of subversion that characterizes its French supporters; instead it is the preserve of university philosophers and theologians, followers of a 'rationalist' impulse whose message inclines to deism rather than anticlerical secularism. In that guise it attracts and influences Lutheran and Jew, the critic Lessing and the philosopher Mendelssohn. But in the hundred or so little states of the fragmented empire social reformers simply do not exist as cohesive groups. There is a further point: despite the efforts of Frederick the Great, the bulk of Enlightenment thinking is under the disadvantage of being seen as foreign, a sign of French hegemony. Deism no doubt can cross this frontier; but on opposite sides of the Rhine the pursuit of taste assumes more and more contrasted forms.

What does cross into Germany is English literary taste and sentimentality, Richardson and Goldsmith; these come to rest in thousands of pious—or pietist—middle-class hearts, along with Rousseau's novel (but not his political writings). To the citizens of Hamburg Lessing, the enlightened, recommends the more 'natural' Shakespeare in place of 'unnatural' French drama; a new 'middle-class' tragedy makes it appearance, and proves far more acceptable than efforts in the same vein by Diderot and Beaumarchais in Paris; and presently an almost unbridled cult of enthusiasm under the name of 'Sturm und Drang' (Storm and Stress) takes Germanic literature off on a tack which owes almost nothing to the Enlightenment. In the background one of the most seminal figures of the day, the Lutheran Herder, goes out of his way indeed to challenge the Enlightenment, crossing swords with Voltaire when he propounds an 'alternative philosophy of history': in place of universal progress, or even Lessing's progressive *Education* of humanity, he affirms the life of unique peoples and nations and their special characteristics; in defiance of reason he sets an example of collecting old folk-songs from the countryside, the voices of popular tradition, folklore; others around him turn to picturesque relics of past superstition, witches, ghosts . . .

Passing through Strasbourg and encountering Herder, young Goethe, barely out of school, is fired by these enthusiasms, is 'into' Rousseau and *The Vicar of Wakefield* and Ossian. It is in that frame of mind that he encounters the Gothic. Whereas at the coronation of George III at Westminster and that of Louis XVI at Reims enlightened eyes can gaze at great 'original' monuments for hours on end without seeing anything in them, Goethe at Strasbourg in 1773 is enraptured by the cathedral. Gothic is the inheritance not of an abstract humanity but of a real and 'natural' tradition; through its testimony the Middle Ages cease to be a time of barbarity and instead vibrate with life . . .

141   Ironbridge, Shropshire, 1779

The first large iron structure in the world, this bridge owes its existence to the use of coke for low-cost extraction of the metal, to the provincial development of cast-iron 'voussoirs' (note however the French terminology!) assembled in a lattice to replace the immensely heavier and more costly and laborious stone arch, and—not least—the unimpeded collaboration of practical engineers and local developers.

Goethe apostrophizes its builder, 'Master Erwin', as a brother and a genius; the tracery of the great vaults overhead is the branching of mighty primal forest trees, growing, organic. And just as he writes a German *Werther* to outdo Rousseau, and a German *Götz von Berlichingen* to outdo Shakespeare, so from the encounter with Strasbourg comes a first draft of that most 'Gothic' of subjects, not yet fully clarified, an adventure into uncharted regions—*Faust*.

In an occasional poem celebrating a journey by coach in company with Lavater the illuminist and Herder the patriot, Goethe coins the semi-ironic formula 'Prophets to the left, prophets to the right, the *Weltkind* ('world-child', that is, himself) in the middle'. *Weltkind*: this is not a creature of reason but of enthusiasm, even delirious enthusiasm. With his prodigious facility, this rather insolent, and also slightly cold-blooded, young man has all imaginable materials around him to feed his creativity, and exults in opportunities quite alien to those of *Rameau's Nephew* (a work for which in later life however Goethe will express unlimited admiration). Even on the banks of the Rhine we are indeed far from the influence of the Enlightenment. And if that influence can be bounded by a river, it can be bounded also by frontiers of a more intangible kind—those of cultural communication between segments of the same society.

Almost unbelievably, the main stream of Enlightenment pays virtually no attention to the first phases of what everyone now knows to have been the largest single 'revolution' the world has ever known, at least since neolithic man mastered the use of fire: the Industrial Revolution, already visible in England in the 1760s.

142   Industrial mill at Dean Village, Edinburgh

While the purpose-built workplace is no novelty, the industrial revolution brings with it very large numbers, and presently hideous concentrations, of new manufactories or 'mills'. Few indeed show signs of loving attention or pride, and with the more general use of steam power they will become an ever uglier and more disturbing feature of the new society.

The reason is simple enough. The men who make the first iron bridge in an out-of-the-way county of England, who harness artificial power to textile manufacture (water first, presently steam engines fired with coal), who devise a flying shuttle, spinning jenny, water frame, spinning mule, and other crucial devices, are not academicians publishing reports for the entertainment of polite society. If the engineer John Smeaton corresponds with the Royal Society, Newcomen, Telford, Kay, Arkwright, Crompton, Watt, Trevethick, are not members of the republic of letters. They are active in a world of artisans and working masters; they transform their techniques and those of others without benefit of official attentions.

If the Industrial Revolution as it occurs in England can be reduced to a loose paradigm, it represents a conjunction of circumstances and aptitudes no less unusual than the results that flow from it. Thus it includes the replacement of charcoal by plentiful cheap coal for fuel, for iron-making, and later the puddling of iron; an expanding mass trade in textiles (with available supplies of wool and cheap cotton to process); an adequate network of transportation to bear expanding trade; merchants ready to put new and more advanced equipment into a piece-worker's cottage (not from philanthropy) and then also to promote a change from cottage work to mill-work (hired labour to work machinery throughout a long day in the factory); it includes the construction and development of a steam engine to pump out the coal-mines as they are pushed further underground and meet increasing hazards of flooding; the application of the steam engine to the mill and the readiness of mill-owners to invest in moving from water-power to steam. At a later stage there is the application of steam engines to locomotion.

That is one segment of the revolution: engineering and textiles. Already it shows how, with or without sophisticated interference from natural philosophy, there is presupposed a social system remarkably free from (or able to obliterate) the restrictions and habits that go with earlier forms of industrial organization and skills. Such a society exists or can be adapted in England as in no other European country of the time; it offers few obstacles to the advance of technology—in other words, to changes in an array of interconnected work-cultures. Furthermore, without any far-sighted intention, the eighteenth century's 'improving' land enclosures throughout Britain may help in driving hundreds of thousands of agricultural poor to seek new livelihoods, a convenient if inhumane way of meeting the mill's demand for labour. This again would be an example of Adam Smith's 'hidden hand': as to whether it is providential or not, opinions are divided. But in Turgot's world it is unimaginable.

The social part of the Industrial Revolution has been an irreversible flood for over a generation, and the steam engine is on wheels and competing with the horse, by the time polite society (as distinct from provincial bankers, traders, and preachers) decides that what is afoot has a significance so profound as to merit attention. That is in another century, however, and in the meanwhile a different sort of revolution will have distracted the thoughts of Europe's élites.

Theory into praxis

The revolution that shakes France in 1789, and then shakes almost the whole of the rest of Europe for a quarter of a century more, has nothing to do with the English Industrial Revolution. Its occasion is a financial crisis of government, and its background includes sharpening conflicts in the countryside, but the forms in which it takes shape are at the outset purely and simply a programme of the liberal Enlightenment. Or, as one might say, the revenge of Turgot with accrued interest. Hence the rights of man, a constitution, civil equality for Protestant and Jew, abolition of hereditary and social privilege and all 'medieval' institutions—nobility, guilds, corporations, universities, seigneurial courts, legally binding monastic vows: these changes have been in the dreams of *philosophes*, and a few of them have been anticipated by the so-called enlightened despots. The 'modernization' of an ancient state, once in train, leads on to modern taxation and local government, a large central bureaucracy, uniform weights and measures, the creation of uniform legal codes, penal reform, a new breath in medicine and public hospitals, reorganization of scientific research, plans for a national education system . . . All of this would have delighted Turgot. But alongside the earliest of these measures, already contentious, there also features an attempted nationalization of the Church: financially tempting, it marks the start of a European conflict between organized religion and liberalism (and its offspring republicanism) which will last a hundred years and more in continental Europe.

The men of 1789 are for the most part sober lawyers, businessmen, property owners, merchants, professional men and journalists, some liberal nobles, a sprinkling of radical clerics. These are the men who most welcome new simplicities, and the rules they draw up, which happen to fit their own interests rather closely, are based on 'universal' principles. It takes them two years to set in place something rather more modern than the 'constitution' of their British neighbours. Is all then complete? By no means. Through a succession of crises, it becomes clear that rational and 'universal' principles are not after all seen in the same way by every group in society. Disagreements arise over all manner of boundaries. Who comes within the class of 'citizen'? What is antisocial? How far do equal rights extend? Where are the limits of the government's power to direct the private individual? A new casuistry is born, and crystallized in the symbolism of a 'left', a 'right', and a 'centre' in politics: this symbolism is still in general use.

And with its conflicts of group interests the new system turns out *not* to have the kind of inbuilt stability which its prophets and leaders assume would crown their reforms. Instead, the revolution in France generates several dynamic processes of its own. One is the backlash made inevitable by the fact that not everyone is prepared to accept new rules and sever old loyalties. From this comes class war, and civil war, and international war—war which is no longer the sport of princes but the mobilization of a whole people. And then follows a whole series of new experiences: mass conscription, and emergency rule, price controls, regicide, mass executions, terror; and also a political evolution going from constitution to dictatorship and then, skirting a democratic movement in the heart of Paris (sternly put down), onwards to military autocracy and then empire. And also the invention of nationalism—a pattern of new loyalties and emotive symbols (flags, uniforms, anthems, conquests, 'natural' frontiers) which is to prove extraordinarily potent, and very exportable, in the nineteenth century.

These lessons to Europe form both a case-book and a supplement to the Enlightenment. In their way they are on all fours with the innovations of Athens which Pericles claims as an education to all Hellas: but they go very much further—to the National Convention, Robespierre, Napoleon and his Caesarism (he too has a 'senate' and 'consults' it, he summons the pope to his coronation to echo Charlemagne) . . . Such things enter into political mythology, and in retrospect make the bad old days of the struggles of the Enlightenment look indeed idyllic.

Chapter 7

The Triumph of Progress

Three revolutions

Nineteenth-century Europe is marked off from anything the world has seen before not by one but by three very large and pervasive transformations, all beginning within the relatively short space of eighty years (1760–1840). Their extent and implications justify in each case the name of 'revolution'.

First, the French Revolution of 1789–1814 exhibits its dizzy sequence of political experiment, creation of a secular nation-state, modernization of a dozen or more institutions in something like the spirit of Turgot: citizenship, laws, secular education, penal reform, medical science, scientific patronage . . . a huge repertory of lessons for other societies to follow, or resist.

Secondly, the Industrial Revolution is stumbled on, as one might say, between 1760 and 1830 in Britain, taken up by France and Belgium and Prussia, and then by other states and regions. This overthrow of the primacy of agriculture and the servitudes of rural life opens a way, perhaps, to enlarged visions of self-fulfilment and well-being, certainly to an enormous enlargement of urban populations.

And then thirdly, and much less obviously, there is the discovery of history. In the most general sense this is an intellectual revolution; it follows from the Enlightenment's ideals of progress, but also from rejection of those ideals, and it is seen in half-a-dozen strands at once: in German discovery of the Middle Ages, a national makeweight to Enlightenment; in revivals of not only medieval and 'Gothic' tastes, but also further 'neo-classical' interests, even in an 'Etruscan' craze; in more persistent contacts with China; in the French expedition to Egypt, and the resulting flow of scholarly labour crowned by Champollion's decipherment of the Rosetta Stone (1822); in the progress of studies in Sanskrit, and their relation to other branches of ancient scholarship; in new and diverse philosophic systems (of Saint-Simon, of Hegel, presently Auguste Comte) all addressing universal history in one way or another; in comparative religion, with all its possibilities for heretical novelty—mystical syncretisms, 'progressive revelation' (Lamennais), or extreme Protestant individualism (Schleiermacher). And the trend spills over into historical jurisprudence (Savigny), which is a further German counter to the French Revolution; into political debate, sparked off by that revolution; and—a time-bomb—into the creation of the science of palaeontology in Paris by Cuvier (1795 onwards).

The weightiness of this intellectual transformation is less easy to gauge than that of the other two revolutions: it can be symbolized, though, if we care to set side by side the cardboard of Walpole's Strawberry Hill Gothic and the gigantic labour needed—and undertaken—to complete Cologne Cathedral in the nineteenth century. Between these two monuments lie the careers of Goethe and Walter Scott and a total change in attitude to the seriousness of the past, and its plenitude. Instead of the kind of reverence shown by men of the Renaissance for Greece and Rome as teachers, the past is now offering an apparently indefinite range of models, examples, justifications for eccentricity or novelty—even if at any one time or place only a limited segment is actually picked on to serve as antecedent. (It is against this background that in a Europe split by the convulsions of states and wars, and national resurgences, experimental writers in Germany come to name themselves 'Romantic', new ideal forms enter English poetry, revolutions of style outdistance public tastes, and what in the loosest way is called 'Romanticism', an accelerated loosening of formal expectations in the arts, begins to make its way. One outcome, much as we may wish to speculate on the 'nature' of the Romantic, is that the nineteenth century will be exposed to a more formidable range of temptations to eclecticism in the arts than any other age of which we have knowledge.)

Chronology for Chapter 7

1811	Prince of Wales becomes regent for his insane father, George III
1811–18	Jane Austen's major novels published
1813–20	Building of Regent Street to Nash's designs
1815	Final defeat of Napoleon at Waterloo
1817	Cuvier's *Le Règne animal* published
1820–30	George IV king of England
1821	Hegel's *Philosophy of Right* and James Mill's *Elements of Political Economy* published
1825	Stockton to Darlington railway opened
1827	London University founded
1828–42	Thomas Arnold headmaster of Rugby
1829	Emancipation of Roman Catholics; successful trial of Stephenson's locomotive The Rocket; Mendelssohn's first visit to England
1830	Cobbett's *Rural Rides* published
1830–7	William IV king of England
1830–42	Comte's *Cours de philosophie positive* published
1830–48	Louis Philippe king of France
1832	First Reform Act passed
1833	Slavery abolished throughout British empire; start of Oxford Movement
1834	Tolpuddle Martyrs transported for trade union activity
1835	Municipal Reform Act passed
1836–65	Dickens's major novels published
1837–1901	Victoria queen of England
1839	First Chartist petition
1841	*Punch* magazine founded
1843	Carlyle's *Past and Present* published
1844	First telegraph line laid in England
1845–6	Irish potato famine
1846	Repeal of the Corn Laws; first production of Mendelssohn's oratorio *Elijah* (at Birmingham)
1847	Marx and Engels publish *The Communist Manifesto*; Ten-Hour Act limits working day of women and children
1847–55	Thackeray's major novels published
1848	Revolutions in France, Germany, Austria, and Italy; Third Chartist petition; Liszt retires from playing in public; J. S. Mill's *Principles of Political Economy* published
1848–52	Pre-Raphaelite Brotherhood active
1849	Marx settles in London
1850	Death of Wordsworth; Tennyson succeeds him as Poet Laureate
1851	Great Exhibition at Crystal Palace (London); Louis Napoleon (Napoleon III) seizes absolute power in France; Landseer's *Monarch of the Glen* painted
1855–67	Trollope's Barsetshire novels published
1859	Darwin's *Origin of Species* and J. S. Mill's *On Liberty* published
1859–76	George Eliot's major novels published
1861	Death of the Prince Consort
1864	Building of the Albert Memorial
1865	William Booth founds Christian Revival Association (Salvation Army)
1866	Atlantic cable laid
1867	Second Reform Act; Marx's *Das Kapital* published

143   M. W. Ridley,
London Bridge at Noonday,
engraving from the
Illustrated London News, **16**
November 1872

In ancient Rome already the satirist Juvenal has complained of the noise, traffic, and other disagreeable features of city life; Boileau imitates him in similar denunciations of Paris in the 1660s; but in nineteenth-century London the street traffic reaches a quite new—and largely uncontrolled—volume and intensity: a matter for pride (as here) or patient resignation.

Each of these three revolutions has a profound effect upon that ideal of 'liberalism' which has already been put into circulation in enlightened circles before the French Revolution. It is in fact this liberalism which, in the nineteenth century, will become a quite central and dominant ideology and cultural inspiration, but permeated everywhere by ideas to do with industrialism, or constitutional change, or the development of a historical 'tradition', however selected, or a mixture of these. No one nation-state of nineteenth-century Europe is, however, exactly like another; their societies steadily diverge, and this is reflected in the different profiles of liberal ideology which we encounter if we pass from say Spain to Prussia, England to Italy, France to Austria. From one place to another we come upon nationalism, anticlericalism, economic aspiration, democratic movements, industrialization, or 'progress'; but such things not only feature in differing combinations in the minds of men, and with differing force, but even have quite different meanings according to context. Rather than compare this endless diversity, it is yet possible to have an impression of what liberalism stands for, and with it the associated idea of progress, by looking at its emergence in the first European society to be exposed in depth to it—that is to say, of course, England. If the example is telling, it is—once again—not typical of its time.

The liberal society

At the close of the wars of the French Revolution and Napoleonic Empire in 1815, the position of the United Kingdom (of Great Britain and Ireland) is unusual. Alone among the large states of Europe she has been isolated from the political upheavals, her political system frozen 'for the duration'. The duration turns out to be not much less than thirty years. During this same period, though, the population of Britain has grown by a third (from ten million to thirteen million—by 1851 the figure will top twenty million). Her industries— cotton textiles, iron, machinery, coal—have grown by even more and these likewise will go on increasing: in 1851 each of the sectors named will supply *more than half of the known output of the whole world.* An industrial revolution has already taken place, and a totally new landscape is emerging in some parts of the country: explosively growing industrial towns, each with its huddle of mills, foundries, and smoke-stacks, canal wharves, and spreading leprous slums. These towns are quite unlike the older market towns; other differences apart, they are enormously larger: in the first half of the century Manchester swells from 90,000 to 400,000 inhabitants, even little Bradford from 13,000 to 104,000. London is already twice the size of any other European city and still expanding. Presently all these large towns

144   Benjamin Dean Wyatt (1775–1850), Apsley House, London, 1828

The London houses of great noble families attest the latter's unshakable status. The Duke of Wellington has achieved eminence in an unusual way (military success), and dominates the 'Tory' aristocracy at least up to the early years of Queen Victoria's reign: Apsley House is thus also an unofficial political headquarters and—sometimes—the object of stone-throwing by hostile crowds.

will be connected by railroad, in a first scramble of company promotions and navvying and building of bridges and tunnels and stations (1835–42). By 1850 more than half the nation's population is urbanized, a concentration equal to that of the Netherlands in 1600, but with this difference: it is fifteen times larger, and quite unlike the latter inasmuch as the towns now become entirely separate from the country and many of their inhabitants are entirely cut off from the rural communities and the open fields.

In the countryside, life remains, relatively speaking, stable—indeed, overwhelmingly so. The lord, the squire who is also the local justice of the peace, his ally the village parson, the tenant farmer, the blacksmith, the labourer, make up their traditional society. Yet the enclosure of common lands, started in the preceding century, is still being carried on by all but the most high-minded and philanthropic landlords, up and down the country, and on 'improved' estates cottages are being pulled down and there is less and less work for casual labourers. The gentry, if less astonishingly rich than the titled lord of great estates, nevertheless dominate the counties, deeply rooted, living close by their lands rather than in London, a real and peculiar 'upper class' of the realm. Under the protection of the 'big house', the local hunt streams across the fields—a conspicuous symbol of hierarchy and values, hardly touched by the industrial developments taking place elsewhere. This life, or a corner of it, has been por-

trayed by Jane Austen, whose novels are certainly not Arcadian fantasy; it still seems unchangeable, even if here and there cottage industries are in distress from the competitive growth of machine-based industries. Order and tradition, old patterns of life and death, and sowing and husbandry and harvests and rents, misfortunes and modest rejoicings, horizons bounded by the local market town—little or no awareness of the world 'outside', except when a son goes away to be a sailor or a gang of labourers arrive on the other side of the hill to dig the embankment for a railway line.

Since this is the world of the country's real 'governing classes', government is slow to perceive and attend to emergent novelty in the cities. Jane Austen's ignorance of the world of 'dark satanic mills', which she never sees, is not unique; until the coming of the railways they are almost a world unto themselves. Yet the grouping together of new industries in the new urban sprawls has brought to birth a quite new double society, which having expanded for two generations under the most complete principle of *laissez-faire* (or, from another point of view, gross neglect) begins in the third decade of the century to confront the rest of the kingdom with its pressing demands, its problems, and its power. In one and the same landscape of factory and slum and suburb-building, of grime and improvisation, of wealth and poverty, there are increasingly numerous and self-assertive middle classes (that is, not gentry), and an increasingly large and scandalously un-

145 Gustave Doré (1832–83), *Over London—By Rail.* **Illustration for** *London: a Pilgrimage,* **by Doré and Blanchard Jerrold, 1872**

Gustave Doré's visionary composition of viaducts—the over-pass of the 1840s—catches the eye not for its theme of movement but rather by its casual glimpse of working-class tenements with their hideous congestion and uniformity: the squalor of new slums.

cared-for concentration of working people (that is, not middle class); both are entirely different in their frame of life from the 'old England'.

The process has not been an abrupt one, or it would have obtruded sooner; for all that, the expansion of the towns is extraordinary, and this same theme of stealthy enormousness characterizes the emergence of *both* the new populations in them. We begin with the more self-assertive half. As compared with the orderly framework of a medieval town and its corporations, or the well-established relations of the countryside, the self-discovery of town society is very much an improvisation. Established commerce and finance and banking families, the newly-arrived mill-owner or industrialist or entrepreneur or successful craftsman, the lawyer, doctor, publisher, retail trader, the clerical or subordinate ranks, the universe of small workshops, and down to the chimney-sweeps and cab-drivers and dustmen and the million or so (and ever increasing) domestic servants: in this rapidly expanding world, with its suburbs stretching, new shops opening, dames' schools and church congregations and philosophical society and every manner of service constantly growing, each individual is intent on staking out his own place, measuring up his neighbour, discovering or in-

venting the important distinctions of social category ('class') and ranking order. For being evolved without a formal framework, class gradations are not lessened but sharpened; the scramble for status is the more critical, and so is the display of credentials—wealth, manners, style of speech, taste.

An endless, and revealing, casuistry comes into existence as to *class*, with new distinctions and sub-distinctions—lower-middle, middle, upper-middle . . . If the same is also happening in France, there is here, as the language reveals, an additional complexity: the existence of a 'gentry' that is not noble gives rise to problems as to who, or what, is a 'gentleman'. Throughout all this, one distinction at least is firm and unbridgeable, namely that between 'middle' and 'lower' classes: it is defined by the old commandment, 'thou shalt not work with thy hands', reinforced by the less absolute distinction between literacy and illiteracy, and a notional income level below which no one could begin to live 'respectably', that is, employ a servant. But above that great divide there are still grey zones of indeterminacy, and the possibility of rising or falling, while below it the labouring (or 'working') classes also stratify themselves endlessly, in emulation it would seem: the engineer, the workshop foreman, the typog-

146   Oxford, neo-Gothic town house, 1860s.

Middle-class town houses or villas, for which there is an immense and unending demand in nineteenth-century England, are as pretentious as the purse allows. If they can be 'Gothicized' (a largely cosmetic affair) so much the better: convenience is secondary. Size, incidentally, is also quite important because well-to-do Victorian families typically comprise numerous offspring.

147   Augustus Egg (1816–63), *The Opera Mantle*, 1851. Oil on canvas, $13\frac{1}{2} \times 11\frac{1}{2}$ in (34.3 × 29.2 cm). Private collection

Among the dreams of genteel display, an evening at the opera has a large place. This young lady (in case we should be in doubt) is studying a programme which clearly names a work by the fashionable composer Meyerbeer; the painter's care is lavished on coiffure and costume, and his title suggests that that is what may really be in her mind.

rapher ('aristocrats of labour') distancing themselves from more menial, less skilled, categories at the bottom of the heap.

In their respective ways the novels of Charles Dickens and (in France) of Honoré de Balzac are saturated with details of every kind of ascriptive middle-class symbol and 'bourgeois' pretension; for both, as for Thackeray in due course, a good part of the 'Human Comedy' is built on the articulations of class distinction—endlessly fascinating, sometimes almost unbelievable. A noticeable amount of Victorian middle-class humour consists in making rather cheap fun of those, especially among the servants, whose social pretensions appear unusually incongruous to their 'betters'. There is of course nothing very new in this—comedies and fables in the past have regularly featured

braggarts, impostors, 'bourgeois noblemen', and the like. But in this society the subject is ever present, and the humour betrays the anxieties.

We move from one quarter of the town to another, across a vacant lot perhaps, and from the human comedy of the middle classes and their auxiliaries we pass into another world. This one has come into being almost, we might think, by inadvertence; and it can hardly be called a comedy. The sprawl of mills, clattering and smoking late into the night, ghettos thrown up by a developer, row upon row of ramshackle tenements without sanitation, often no water supply, the streets a river of filth and slime, no amenity, no parks or open spaces. This part of the town is a hellish prison for its population of workers; they are now being born into it, spending their entire lives in it, never escaping. It may

148 Solomon J. Solomon (1860–1927), *Conversation Piece,* **1884. Oil on canvas, 40 × 50 in (101.6 × 127 cm). London, Leighton House Art Gallery**

We may wonder whether this view of society life—the good life—is as full of virtue as it should be; commonplaces such as these (not to say vulgarity) may nourish dreams but also prove depressing to the sensitive in mid- and late-Victorian England.

be Manchester or other cotton centres, or Birmingham with its engineering, or Liverpool growing up around a great port, or London itself with its ragtrade and engineering workshops spreading east or north, its mile upon mile of warehouses and tenements and seedy docks: everywhere the scene is unspeakable. So for as long as possible it shall not be spoken of . . .

Especially since no one is 'responsible'. The kingdom's old laws provide for *rural* charity, concerted action by the parish, not for this scene. In the new textile industries especially, the large mill-owner's chief concerns are—not universally, but typically—dictated by Adam Smith and that 'liberal' philosophy of the 'hidden hand'. *He* invests in his plant, takes on labourers at the 'going' wage, pays them; after that it is for *them* to survive as they may, in cellars or bare attics, fed or unfed, clothed or in rags, healthy or sick, or dying. Industry is not *all* large mills: there are tens of thousands of little workshops, but even there the same hard rule prevails. And likewise in the coal-mines, whether on the edge of the town or in a green valley.

This 'freedom' of the spirit of enterprise and self-advancement, seen in classical form in an early nineteenth-century England whose government and administration are even more primitive than anything

the Enlightenment has joined battle with in France, provides undoubtedly the chance for many to rise and prosper, but for others—many more others—a degradation as complete as that of any slave system. It is not Karl Marx who coins the expressions 'cash-nexus' and 'wage-slave' to describe the capitalist's callousness or the plight of cotton operative or coal-miner. 'Cash-nexus' first appears in the conservative writer Thomas Carlyle's denunciation of industrial liberalism (*Past and Present,* 1843—a very arresting case of idealized visions of the Middle Ages being brought in to deliver a moral lesson on the degradations of the day). 'Slavery' is already denounced by Wordsworth, however obscurely, in his great poem *The Excursion* (1814):

Oh banish far such wisdom as condemns
A native Briton to these inward chains,
Fixed in his soul, so early and so deep . . .
He is a slave to whom release comes not,
And cannot come. The boy, where'er he turns,
Is still a prisoner . . .

Thirty years later it has become the leitmotiv of the Tory politician Disraeli's extremely shocking presentation of working-class life in his novel *Sybil* (1845). Here

149 Victorian photographic portrait of Mrs Basil Martineau. Oxford, Bodleian Library, John Johnson Collection.

The invention of photography makes possible an immense proliferation of what has hitherto been a relatively restricted art – that of commemorative portraiture (in oil, water-colour, or engraving). The middle-class family album is a compact and inexpensive form of portrait gallery; for posterity it displays the conscious or unconscious claims to status of the sitters.

the profiles of young girls harnessed to tubs of coal crawling through underground workings, starving handloom weavers idle and hopeless in their slums, apprentices living like brutes in an industrial jungle—all these are scenes which Disraeli has taken care to document fully, from public inquiries and reports. He sums up: 'The capitalist has found a slave . . . once he was a craftsman.' 'Freedom', as preached by improvers and economists and enjoyed by the capitalist as never before, has brought terrible things: in a gradual build-up

of industries, of competition, of falling prices and wages, it has brought amazing wealth but also deprivation; destitution far too widespread for the country's ancient system of poor relief to cope with it; and oppression of the weak (long hours, helplessness in times of depression) to which no compassionate man can be indifferent.

It is nevertheless the cause of freedom, and not compassion, which dominates attention on the political stage. An 'old' regime of crown, Church, and Tory landowners has resisted sharing government with the commonalty, but by 1830 the frame of politics allows, in fact compels, the great liberal families and their clients to receive the support of industrialists and commerce, of radical agitators and other enemies of entrenched landowners, in a bid to overset the Tory supremacy. A 'progressive' coalition, first, forces through a reform of Parliament (1832) to enfranchise the great new cities (or at least some of their property-owners); a similar movement then forms to attack the artificial protection of land by repeal of grain tariffs (the Corn Laws keep up land values, but also the price of bread, and therefore wages in towns). After a campaign no less bitter and threatening than that for reform, repeal is finally voted (in 1846, at the height of the dreadful Irish potato famine). For these two successive crusades, huge popular support has been aroused; they convey a very strong sense that progress is the directing ideal of the land.

In fact these full-dress political battles are less than half the story, and taken by themselves are misleading. It would be true to say that up to the middle of the century Britain has all the appearance (if not the reality) of a dangerously threatened society, almost as near to disintegration as France in 1792, rather than of one advancing triumphantly to the millennium. Each of the two great public movements, reform and repeal, is attended by demonstrations and violence, and here and there military repression. In 1830–32 and again in 1846, there are lively fears of 'revolution'. And in the background are other kinds of disturbance. In 1812 already, scattered 'Luddite' riots (outbreaks of machine-smashing by craftsmen and cottagers facing ruin from the competition of modern industry) cause tremors of panic, and they recur in the countryside in the 1820s with rick-burning and sporadic smashing of agricultural machines. An insignificant combination of country labourers is pounced on in the south by local justices, and the culprits (the 'Tolpuddle Martyrs') sentenced to transportation (1834) for 'illegally taking an oath'; this despite the fact that it is legal to form trade unions. The incident is only one of many in which vague and often quite naïve gestures by the 'lower classes' arouse an extraordinarily severe reaction from their 'betters' (in this case a bench of country squires). Above all, there is the diffuse movement of political radicals and literate working-men all over the country—'Chartism'—which seeks to go beyond the reform of 1832 and introduce a vote for every adult male: clearly a threat to society, perhaps inspired by the French example, a move to 'democracy', and made more alarming by the republican overtones that creep into its oratory. An intelligent French visitor, Tocqueville, judges in 1833 that 'democracy is like a rising tide.' In fact the Chartist movement dissolves in 1848, after the presentation of a monster petition to Parliament shows its support to be by no means as strong as its leaders have hoped or others feared; but once again widespread fears of a revolution have been aroused, and a large military force put on stand-by in London under the duke of Wellington.

Despite the alarms, there are no revolutions; apart from a small lunatic conspiracy or two, none is ever planned by anyone. As the country has been untouched by the French Revolution, so in this half-century it escapes the kind of uprisings that preoccupy Metternich in Vienna, and the overthrow of the regime that occurs in France in 1830, and the wave of revolutions which in 1848, almost all over Europe, express a vehement intellectual demand for democracy. And the reasons for this uncanny stability, in the transition from an old regime of society to a strikingly different one, are political and social *and* ideological.

Progress, politics, and the Gospel

Political: there is an already existing parliamentary system, however archaic, which is modified; and then not dramatically. Tocqueville, having noted the 'tide of democracy', also remarks that 'aristocratic privilege is being attacked, but indirectly; public opinion is not hostile, not ready to abolish the Lords.' Then, while liberal middle-class interests clash with the landed Tories, the latter are by no means defenceless; their greatest leader, Robert Peel, is the opposite of a purblind reactionary, and they too can find popular causes to take up against the liberals. Further, if there is no disaffected 'working-class movement', despite scattered radical pioneering which some historians judge portentous, this is in part because the most inhumanly exploited groups, though they are very concentrated and highly visible in particular towns and areas, are still quite few compared with the populations who continue

in traditional trades and livelihoods. The economy, despite slumps, is actually growing very fast. Furthermore, a fraction of the 'lower classes' are glimpsing and attaining the expansion of opportunities—the dream of progress and advancement held out by the liberal creed is up to a point valid, while among the opponents of that creed there is a steady stream of reforms also being put forward. Finally, the peculiarity of religion in England has an unusual impact on the process of bringing about social change, because it affects strongly—for good or ill—the patterns of behaviour of almost everyone in the land.

Liberalism, first. It has both a narrow and a broad connotation. The narrow one is all to do with theory: it is the intellectual doctrine of 'utility', the view that narrow self-interest is bound to add up to public interest overall, provided there is no interference by governments; it is the political economy of Adam Smith, developed now by Mill and Ricardo, demonstrating repeatedly that present satisfactions forgone (saving) procure greater future satisfactions; it is the doctrinaire theory of Malthus arguing that the poor must not be helped too much lest their numbers outrun society's ability to feed them. The broad message of liberalism has on the contrary to do with opportunity, the dissemination of benefits to all who merit them. It is seen not only in the outlook of the mill-owner and banker, but also in the cult of self-help conveyed from the Quaker master to his foreman, from the teacher to the child, from Miss Harriet Martineau to the readers of her edifying stories; it fires the clerk in the counting-house or the apprentice in a good trade, who dreams of rising (like the hero of Mrs. Banks's novel *The Manchester Man*) to become his master's partner and marry his daughter; it reaches even the scullery maid who dreams of becoming cook and marrying the butler in a great household. One of the nineteenth century's great bestsellers, after the Bible, is *Self-Help* (1859) by Samuel Smiles; this is a manual setting out for those on the lower steps of the ladder all the strategies necessary to social promotion, namely thrift, prudence, diligence: it is an epitome of the Protestant work ethic, the same message basically as that of Benjamin Franklin, and before him, of the Calvinist divines preaching to their artisan congregations—except that it can now serve as a practical ideal for literally millions of steady young aspirants, provided they do not aspire to a career in railway promotion or political carpet-bagging. All around are the proofs of opportunity—newly formed partnerships, companies, ventures, products, suburbs, expansion. By contrast with France in these same years, there is no sharp break in the spectrum between the

150   George Cruickshank (1792–1878), 'A Young Lady's Vision of the London Season', c. 1850. Reproduced in *Four Hundred Humorous Illustrations by G. C.*, Simpkin, Marshall, London

The social standing of the dreamer is quite unclear, her ambitions plain—the dizzy round, operas, routs, presentation at Court, fashionable Westminster, perhaps even a wild elopement? Undoubtedly there is an Emma Bovary in every town . . .

fence of experience and old ways or simply on patronage, and a scattering of writers (Coleridge, Carlyle) with hankerings for a harmonious ideal order, whether inspired by German philosophy or by dreams of an imaginary past (a new myth of Merrie England is in the making, alongside the far more poetic one of a wondrous Gothic Middle Age: both Carlyle and Charles Dickens are keen Merrie Englanders). In the Anglican Church itself Pusey and Keble develop an 'Oxford Movement' of especially anti-liberal sentiment, to combat laxity and indifference, and reaffirm old patterns of clerical authority. Among these varied strands there is no lack of voices to denounce the ills which liberals think inevitable and great Whig political leaders (who have become the liberal leaders) would rather not bring into the open; and although the Tory party has its die-hards it also has its opportunists.

In consequence, the transformation of the country is by no means a one-sided affair; and in Parliament itself we observe an interestingly balanced set of contributions from liberals and their opponents. To begin with, in a reformed chamber, a liberal majority goes to work to put the country to rights—at last. Municipal government is reformed to put the cities under a more adequate system of administration; a first Factory Act is passed (largely ineffectual); the Poor Laws, above all, are reformed, in the face of mounting destitution. This last measure is typically 'utilitarian', almost one might say doctrinaire: workhouses are instituted, partly to relieve but partly also to deter the great numbers of decrepit old people, the unemployed, the orphans, with that mixture of Malthusian calculation and callous hypocrisy that Dickens pillories in *Oliver Twist*. Beyond that, liberalism finally abolishes slavery in the colonies, abolishes the (English) East India Company's monopoly, abolishes the Anglican Church's monopoly of marriage registration (to please its Nonconformist supporters), sets up a central civil register, and makes a small gesture to encourage the growth of elementary education. But for Lord Melbourne, the prime minister, that is quite enough.

In contrast it is the backward-looking Carlyle who starts the protest against industrial 'slavery', against the 'motive-Mill-wrights'; and presently it is the conservative movement and the 'Young England' Tories, joined by Disraeli, who take up the cause of the poor in the mills and the mines. The result is a succession of official inquiries, the appointment of factory inspectors, the publication of reports. Certainly in the political arena this is good strategy; but also there is a large measure of consternation and outrage. The inspectors' reports on mines and mills reveal shocking facts; the report of the

well-to-do and the frustrated grocer, such as to drive the latter to democracy (the flaw which brings down the French monarchy in 1848); and there are few 'radicals' who, like J. S. Mill, work their way through political economy and utilitarianism and come out thirsting for systematic state intervention, a profound revolution of authority, and socialism.

Alongside the broad alliance of progressives and liberals, capitalism and self-help, is the country's traditional mass of conservatism. It includes much of the landed gentry and aristocracy, the Anglican Church almost solidly, those who stand on Burke's great de-

parliamentary commission of inquiry into the plight of depressed handloom weavers is a no less powerful condemnation of *laissez-faire*. Both kinds of official revelation are drawn on by radicals, by the young German immigrant F. Engels in his review of the 'condition of the working classes' (and in turn by his friend Karl Marx); but also, as we have seen, by *Sybil*, a much more widely read book, and by many others beside Disraeli. In the 1840s (the 'hungry forties', a time of economic slump and suffering never before seen, capped by the Irish famine), a series of further Factory Acts gradually checks the most heartless forms of labour exploitation; children, then women, are banned from working in mines; enslavement of young children in the mills is made illegal; in 1847, after continuing agitation which brings together Tories and Chartists, a Ten Hour Act is passed, to limit the working day of women and children in textiles (and this movement will continue after the demise of Chartism: more general reductions, free Saturday afternoons, public Bank Holidays). At any rate up to mid-century the Tory party is making *its* contribution to progress.

This 'interventionism', in the name of progress, but against the liberal doctrine of 'freedom', is carried out by politicans seated in a parliament. But its motive power is something more formidable: the wide prompting of Christian consciences.

It is a peculiarity of Britain that long before the Industrial Revolution—in 1739, to be precise—the piety of Wesley breaks out of the complacencies of the Anglican Church. Since that time he and his followers have built up a great movement of evangelical Protestantism ('Methodism') across the countryside and towns of England; the movement grows not only by supplying the deficiencies of the official Church, but also with the dynamic of a formidable population increase. Yet it is neither a 'closed' dissenting sect nor in any way identified with the great in the land. Furthermore the Anglican Church itself develops a rival 'evangelical' wing of its own. In strong contrast with other European countries, the resultant blurring of outline of creeds (Anglican, Methodist and Wesleyan, Presbyterian, Baptist, Unitarian, Quaker) allows Christian belief to be moulded to all manner of class and sectional viewpoints without any major discontinuity.

All these groupings, either in competition (missions and Bible classes) or in coalition (anti-slavery agitation), work on the attitudes of middle- *and* working-class populations. If Methodism is at loggerheads with Anglican divines and brewers over temperance, for example, there are other occasions on which the combined force of the Churches can be irresistible: precisely over slavery, William Wilberforce arouses at the turn of the century a campaign so powerful that a reluctant government is obliged to adopt abolition as one of its major peace aims at the Vienna settlement of 1814. By the early nineteenth century an evangelical puritanism is very firmly dominant in middle-class life, and in the years up to 1840 the fact is exceptionally visible: during this period more churches and chapels are built, all over England, to keep up with or catch up with the phenomenal growth of towns, than at any other time in history, both by the established Church and—even more noticeably—by the non-established ones. Sunday church-going is to all intents and purposes universal (except in the industrial slums); the Bible is compulsory and familiar reading to everyone who knows his letters. This new puritanism only awaits Queen Victoria to become the norm for the whole nation, its morals, its leisure, and its work.

The coming together of dissenting and Anglican evangelicals over human dereliction in towns is thus of huge political significance. The industrial 'slavery', whatever else it is, is a threat to morality. The mill-owner may plead, and does, that by keeping children occupied for twelve hours a day he keeps them 'out of mischief'. But he has no answer to the charge that by so doing he deprives them of all religious instruction, condemns them to grow up—or die—as little pagans. And how can a religious conscience fail to be moved by concern for these exploited children, for sickness in the slums, prostitution in the mill, total and abject ignorance—whether of the gospel or anything else? Time and time again an evangelical philanthropist heads a movement of protest. The most notable, perhaps the most humane, is the seventh Earl of Shaftesbury, a high Tory and an anti-democrat, but an austere and dedicated evangelical. For a lifetime he campaigns for factory legislation, for the Ten Hour Act, just as he campaigns for the reform of lunatic asylums and for the banning of the inhuman practice of sending little children up chimneys to sweep them. But there are many others who work, especially in the dissenting Churches, on the minds of both capitalists and craftsmen, liberals and Chartists—Methodists confronting slums, Quaker businessmen acting on a 'concern' for their work-people. And the range of such causes extends to an almost infinite number of philanthropic objects, and in particular to the furthering of morality by abolishing barbaric customs and cruelty: cruelty to children, but cruel sports also, and cruelty to animals—putting dogs in treadmills, driving pit-ponies or cab-horses to death. Even in the preserves of the well-to-do, the already existing 'public schools', an evangelical concern of strictly Anglican flavour spills over into the reform of a few mindless barbarities—and Dr. Arnold of Rugby wins himself a reputation as a great man. In short, Christian moralities (or more exactly, Protestant moralities) work not only as a powerful social agent across boundaries of political and class interest but also as a pervasive *civilizing* agent in both the new sections of society and the old. The two effects are, of course, not separable.

When therefore Karl Marx announces that 'Religion is the opium of the working-man', he is being unusually doctrinaire. Religion does most undoubtedly blunt the sharpness of conflict between workman and master in England, to the extent that this a conflict for a share in the proceeds of industry. Liberal economists never cease to argue that in dynamic societies competition must drive wages down to the level of bare subsistence, and that is what mill-owners regularly seek to do; and it would be convenient if religion would assist them by preaching outright submission. But that is not quite what the evangelicals are doing in the 1840s (that is, before Marx has a chance to familiarize himself with the scene); and over the long view it becomes increasingly unusual for concerned Christians to be content with the passive role Marx proposes for them. Hence the fact that although there are Chartists and radicals eager for political confrontation and democracy, there are also Methodist Chartist preachers, even Chartist 'Churches'. The aged anarchist and atheist William Godwin (a left-over from French Revolutionary times and the poet Shelley's father-in-law) dies almost without intellectual posterity; the liberal ideologist Jeremy Bentham bequeaths to his followers his 'felicific calculus', but not his dismissal of religion. It is precisely the evangelicals whose great influence (without equivalent in countries known to the young Marx) prevents a disastrous polarization between God and the establishment and the great on the one hand, and a huge mass of disaffected interests and hopelessness on the other; or between a heartless *laissez-faire* carried to its limits and a revolutionary proletariat.

There is a further implication in all these reforming movements. Government intervention is demanded for particular causes, not because of any desire for a strong 'state' (even in 1850 there are not much more than about 40,000 government servants, many of them excisemen or clerks). The doctrines of 'freedom', 'private initiative', 'cheap government' remain intact, alongside the many-faceted gospel of 'personal responsibility'. Decade by decade, it is true, the state in Britain accepts new tasks of control or interference, and imposes others on local government; but only slowly and undogmatically, as agent of last resort. This is the approach to Factory Acts and to public health, and equally to the supply of positive services (postal, police, sewerage, public education, parks and open spaces) or other desirable public goods: always tentative in the face of the more 'natural' course of things, whereby philanthropy and self-help should be expected to supply whatever is wanted, whether race-courses or mechanics' institutes, hospitals or railways, housing or libraries, orphanages or accident insurance (Friendly Societies), scientific research or music academies . . .

A pyramid of taste

A sketch of this kind is necessary to remind us of the circumstances in which Victorian society takes shape and without any real break in continuity transforms itself into a society receptive of liberal ideals and wedded to the grand notion of progress. Britain is neither one kind of state nor another, neither an old regime nor yet a post-revolutionary one, but an amalgam of monarchy, aristocracy, and liberal-tinged parliamentary rule, not in the least a 'democracy'; with a 'state' Church, but also very large and energetic free churches; an incompletely faced-up-to industrialization, a rather small proletariat (but in process of rapid expansion), a very large artisanate, and a proportionately enormous pyramid of 'middle classes'. These middle classes grow larger and wealthier with the passage of each decade, and come in practice to dominate the whole of society and its standards, while yet recognizing some enviable superiority in the 'upper' gentry classes, which are left still very largely in possession of their prestige and what appears to be a disproportionate share of power. In sum, an all-round set of compromises, supported on a continuously rising tide of wealth whose distribution is entirely uncontrolled, and which remains overwhelmingly in the hands of individuals rather than of the state. All these circumstances are relevant to the peculiar hybridization of culture which attains its classic form by the middle of the century and inaugurates a middle-class hegemony of enormous solidity.

The whole society is manifestly a pyramid, with at the apex, as ever, a monarch. But by 1830 the monarch is no longer George III, nor even a wild and eccentric Regent waiting to become George IV; the dynasty has become unremarkable, and it will be some time before a young Queen begins again to influence the style of life and values of her subjects. Nearest to the monarch, a tiny aristocracy (almost half Whig) and a rather large gentry and squirearchy together form an élite. As an élite class, they supply officers for Guards and cavalry

151 Franz Xavier Winterhalter, (1805–73), *The First of May, 1851*, 1851. Oil on canvas, 42 × 51 in (106.7 × 129.5 cm). Windsor, Royal Collection

Winterhalter's canvas contrives to look like a Nativity scene. But the Family is Royal, not Holy—the demure young Queen, her angelic infant Prince Arthur, her noble Consort Albert a discreet facilitator (the new Crystal Palace is just visible far left), and the Duke of Wellington offering a casket with avuncular reverence. What courtly tact, what flattery! What attention to well-rounded forearm, Garter insignia, brocade, marbled column . . .

regiments, hunt over their estates, dip a finger in industry (mining royalties, canals, brewing, property development), provide an upper house in the legislature, live lavishly, and generally present foreigners with a quite misleading stereotype of the Byronic, athletic, gambling, horse-racing, reckless Englishman. Yet it is not easy to distinguish what particular contribution they make to the culture, other than the distinctive and very important one of handing down an *idea* of élitism, and a pervasive attitude of superiority well caught by Thackeray in his *Book of Snobs* (1846).

Below them on the pyramid are the many levels of middle-class emulation and ambition. At the top, ennoblements are exceedingly rare; short of that the possibilities are legion. The self-made mill-owner may be snubbed by the gentry, but he demands that his wife be a 'lady', and that his children be educated to start life as 'gentlemen'; time will see to the rest. Meanwhile he can consolidate his status, with all that it takes. More and more dynasties of finance and industry—especially bankers—who come to match the wealth of the highest in the land will intermarry with them; the scenario is not new. But as we have noted, the scenario is being repeated at any and every level, on every step, and at least often enough to remove it from the realm of fairy-tale. Its enactment is, in fact, being assisted by a barely perceived but in fact very large (80 per cent) expansion in middle-class incomes, in a generation of slightly falling prices (to 1848).

We thus confront a society which is emphasizing both 'achievement' values and 'ascriptive' statuses: social mobility and elaborate class distinctions. Different observers insist on one or other aspect, but neither on its own does justice to the ambiguities and intricacy of the resulting pattern.

Social climbing and achievement represent movement up the pyramid. The correlative of this upward movement is a downward flow of a different kind—'example', and something unkindly called 'apeing one's betters'. A gentlewoman in high society, for example, carries out an elaborate set of rituals: she sends courtesy cards by the footman, has her daughter presented at court, entertains elaborately for her husband or to amuse herself. So too then shall the suburban lady: calling on the 'right' neighbours and leaving cards, holding her 'at home' on a fixed evening in the week,

152 John Tenniel (1820–1914), 'Horrible Suspicion', *Punch*, 1852

The humorous periodical Punch is in 1852 a thoroughly 'safe' reflection of middle-class manners—and tastes. The theme of snobbery has lately been given a vogue by Thackeray, and Punch is happy to illustrate it (as in Tenniel's cartoon, shown here) by poking fun at lower-class foibles.

HORRIBLE SUSPICION IN HIGH LIFE.

Scene—Belgravia.

First Aristocratic Butcher-boy. "HULLO, BILL! DON'T MEAN TO SAY YER'VE COME DOWN TO A PONY?"
Second Ditto Ditto. "NOT DEZACTLY! OUR CART IS ONLY GONE A-PAINTIN'."

entertaining at afternoon tea (an aristocratic invention, this, and nothing to do with temperance campaigns), displaying her daughter in the social round, retaining a suitable pew in church, keeping up with the 'right' reading, or aspiring to all these good things. The protocol and formality that attend social exchanges in all strata become astonishing, even if in modest households the occasions are simple: Dickens has a pitiless eye for it, standing as he does in the thick of the lower middle classes. But even aside from the evidence of literary portraiture—and how do we evaluate the reliability of a fiction like *Dombey and Son*?—the relics of the age testify to these graded emulations: its visiting cards, bookbindings, costumes, qualities of top-hat, even the public transport offered to those who do not own a carriage (first-class for gentry, second for tradespeople, third for servants).

The clearest visible account of the two-way exchanges up and down the pyramid can be read in nineteenth-century domestic architecture. For demographic reasons, there is a gigantic amount of building, as yet entirely 'unplanned'. At the top, nobility and wealth indulge their fancy with a large variety of styles in their country seats (Palladian, Doric, neo-Gothic, picturesque, rustic) and splendour in their town houses. Nash's recent development of Regent's Park (1819–26) is intended as a grand setting for George IV and his

court: large villas for the great, terraced town houses behind stucco façades for the not-quite-so-great. By contrast with that unusual venture, the subsequent sprawl of London features mainly suburban estates catering for every grade of middle-class purse: villas and terraces generous or mean, and also a new invention, the semi-detached villa, first seen in St. John's Wood around 1823. Compromising between thrift and genteel privacy, such villas always have much the same ideal layout: 'public' rooms on ground or first floor, servants lodged under the roof, a piece of garden if possible. The upper classes' styles, such as they are, are echoed, however tight the builder's budget; or at least, bits of them. When Gothic Revival really takes hold—at the start it is an extravagance of the rich—that too is replicated down the steps of the pyramid: with pointed windows and turrets and stained-glass lights to suit a moderate purse, or without turrets for a more straitened one.

Within the villa and the terrace home, grand reception rooms must evidently be scaled down; but a separate 'drawing-room' supplies the setting for self-respecting ritual (the ladies can 'withdraw' to it just as those of the upper classes do). Even further down the pyramid, a working-class terrace will boast its front parlour, a sacred place for formal visits, never otherwise used (since no one here enjoys ladylike leisure).

153   Abraham Solomon (1824–62), *First Class – the meeting*, 1854. Oil on canvas, 27 × 38 in (68.5 × 96.5 cm). Private collection

The railway carriage, rapidly improved in the 1830s, is superior to the horse-drawn coach in speed, safety, comfort, and above all spaciousness. This sentimental 'conversation piece' reveals a décor as close as possible to that of the well-upholstered private coach, and as distant as possible from vulgarity and machinery. But public prudery has compelled the artist to give the young lady a fatherly escort.

154   Honoré Daumier (1808–79), *The Third-class Railway Carriage*, c. 1860. Pen, crayon, watercolour and ink with white heightening, 9 × 13 in (23 × 33 cm). Winterthur, Oskar Reinhart Collection 'Am Römerholz'

The railway not only replaces the mail coach on trunk routes, it supplies very cheap travel for labouring populations whose only way of leaving their local surroundings has hitherto been on foot or by wagon. They travel 'hard', as the democratically inclined artist Honoré Daumier observes in France—but they travel.

155   The drawing room, Osborne House, Isle of Wight, 1845–9

Queen Victoria is both a leader and a prisoner of middle-class eclectic taste, including interior decoration; at her private holiday mansion there is so little room to move for all the furniture and mementoes that one can barely imagine how voluminous female attire can be conveniently manoeuvred in their midst.

Beyond that, the emulation of gentility is less easy to follow. Plaster mouldings, of course, and joinery, of a standard regulated by cost and the builder's pattern-book; generally speaking, the cheaper the nastier, and the more expensive the more incongruous. It is noticeable that in Nash's terraces, underneath the stucco, building structures are already amazingly shoddy and crude, even if the craft standards in visible adornments are high. In the ensuing decades, technical performance of the craftsman remains high but his designs become more and more variable, perfunctory in many cases, and imitative, more a display of labour than of creativeness. Why should speculative development breed a new Robert Adam, or the northern plutocrat find time to study form? Expansion in a rush is imposing its own logic . . .

And as to the contents of these tens and hundreds of thousands of new dwellings, here it is inevitable that sheer quantity and profusion prevail as the rule of taste; it would be hard to pick out any particular 'styles' being handed down from the upper classes. The central facts are obvious enough. In each cell of the ever-spreading world of terraces and villas, there comes to be such an accumulation of domestic paraphernalia, of *things*, as humanity has never before heaped upon itself. Textiles, the great industry, lead the way: in the soft furnishings and carpets and table-cloths, the double or triple arrays of curtains over windows and doors, the innumerable screens and drapes. But every other kind of impedimenta is crowded in too: fire screens and coal-scuttles, tables and rocking-chairs, jardinières and pianos and book-cases, pictures (as many as possible) and mementoes and clocks and barometers and candlesticks and footstools and vases and mirrors, gas-mantles and busts and statuettes (copied from the two or three most renowned masters) and knick-knacks to fill every remaining corner of space. A superlative example can be glimpsed in Queen Victoria's private drawing-room at Osborne. In all this, we cannot speak of a 'Victorian' style (though when we do it is self-evidently a middle-class one) except to suggest plenitude and absence of any guiding style: perhaps there is a connotation of solidly heavy and graceless items of furniture (in contrast with the elegant lightness of Regency 'gentry' furniture), alongside quite inconsequential oddities (for example bamboo chairs which are not bamboo at all but painstakingly carved imitations in less exotic woods); fussy attention to comfort, and diligent exclusion of sunlight (it fades the fabrics); innumerable knobs on brass bedsteads, laborious mouldings on picture frames from the hands of craftsmen pressed into service as markets escalate . . . Without a doubt, 'more is worse'.

Beyond that, 'Victorian' connotes unbridled eclecticism, excess of things as an index of well-being. There is also, as one would expect, a certain contrast between the plenitude of this exhibitable décor and the frugality of the 'offices'. Flush sanitation only begins to be general in the better suburbs in the 1850s, the bathroom much later still; servants carry bathwater in jugs to the bedroom tub; the coal fire heats one side of a draughty room, for which reason the voluminous layers of Victorian clothing have a practical, as well as a symbolic significance; and the spartan conditions in the kitchen are nobody's business.

The Victorian accumulation, as we might call it, has for long been the starting-point for derision and vilification of liberal bequests to culture. It suggests complacency, and of course materialism. Nevertheless it is the setting for activities of extraordinary and explosive vigour, even if it fails singularly to express them. The same weight of numbers and money that builds Victorian suburbs and their stifling décor is also channelled into exploring new worlds of opportunity and meeting a growth in demand of a whole new order of magnitude for almost any product of man's ingenuity. Not every such product is a piece of imitation bamboo. And the expression of middle-class cultural hegemony, strongly shaped in its social symbolism by the pyramid of classes, also gives rise to surprising novelty.

In the written word, for example, newspapers turn to the rotary press to multiply their copies; by mid-century several of them are large enough to acquire a certain status, never previously enjoyed, as responsible institutions. Helped by low costs and price competition, book publishers energetically step up their output to seven or eight hundred new titles each year. Magazines and periodicals, whether general or quite specialized, to say nothing of the humorous *Punch*, reach ten or twenty thousand readers each, and it becomes quite respectable to be an editor: Thackeray is happy to edit the *Cornhill Magazine* and Bagehot *The Economist*. A writer, if he can sell his manuscripts, is freed from want, is almost a gentleman. This is perhaps the only time in modern history when an English poet can aspire to live for a while on the proceeds of his verses.

And novel-writing above all becomes a great industry. The three-decker novel can reach a hundred thousand readers, either through shops or through lending libraries. And it is not limited to comforting romances of what the age styles the 'silver-fork' variety; it can support all manner of critical and moralizing messages from its practitioners who, like leader-writers in the press, are now buoyed up by something like a sense of power: Dickens and Mrs. Gaskell are two conspicuous examples of lay preachers in fiction. There is room for the very astonishing achievements of the Brontë sisters; and perhaps even more typically for the historical novelist. Headed by Bulwer Lytton, who takes over the succession from Walter Scott, Victorian society takes very seriously its duty to become familiar with the past—the last days of Pompeii, the last of the Barons, Rienzi the last of the Tribunes . . .

Travel books no less than historical novels furnish the minds of diligent self-improvers all over Europe; in fact, the 1830s and 1840s are a great time for 'Walks in Rome', 'Mornings in Florence', 'Journeys to the Harz Mountains', 'Voyages to the East', 'American Notes', books flowing from the most professional pens, as well as from the most unpractised. Above all, in the absence of formal education in any developed form, reading is the natural, if strenuous, road to self-improvement, catered for by publications of every shape and size, handbooks and digests, encyclopaedias and collections of sermons, tracts (hence the wide diffusion of the Oxford Movement's proposals on Church reform), pamphlets on free trade or knotty points of economics—a huge flood. Not every terrace house has a library that can stand comparison with an eighteenth-century gentleman's collection; yet the motivations of progress combined with ladylike middle-class leisure bring about a no less formidable range of curiosities.

What is true of the written word has its analogue in other fields. Thus the gentry have for long been in the habit of sending their sons with a tutor to round off their education by a Grand Tour on the continent; and here is a lay-preacher, one Thomas Cook, who, having organized a temperance outing in 1841, sees his way to offering something a little less aristocratic than the Grand Tour and a little more daring than the trip to Brighton—but for many, many people. The cultivated person, or better the person in search of cultivation, shall actually realize that dream of Paris or Florence. And thus is born the tourist industry, a very characteristically middle-class institution, ideally suited to the pyramid . . .

The stuffiness of the Victorian house interior is, in short, only one part, one dimension, of its culture; and

156   Joseph Paxton (1803–65), Crystal Palace, London, 1851

The Great Exhibition of 1851 is a modern trade fair. With heavy emphasis on new industrial marvels, its most striking feature is the Crystal Palace built to house it in Hyde Park: an advertisement for the construction material iron, as used both in garden conservatories and in the modern railway stations.

polite conversation: it is simply 'not done' to discuss the price tag on a house or on a trip to Florence. Where status, not purchasing power, is a dominant principle, symbols of status must speak for themselves. Here is a very central feature of Victorian culture, a constant reminder of its stratification, and as revealing as the fact that the first appearance of advertisements in respectable newspapers arouses indignation.

And there is a further revealing area of awkwardness: how is wealth-creating technology to be absorbed into the good life?

The short answer is that it is not; or only to a very limited extent. Undoubtedly the wealth which flows from coal and cotton, blast-furnaces and steam engines, supports the immense expansion of society. Undoubtedly too, the most successful manipulators of these forces, great engineers for example, are seen as great men. This is, indeed, their heroic age: their energy and practical application, sometimes their demonic vision, are celebrated in volumes of their *Lives* by Samuel Smiles (no less!) and in their own day they are honoured: the scientist Humphry Davy, inventor of a safety lamp for miners, the Stephensons with their railway engineering, and, most typical and imposing of all, the masterful Brunel, who runs a great railway from London to Bristol (1840), designs the iron-framed stations at either end, builds spectacular bridges, and achieves the impossible in three gigantic steamships at the limit of technology's means to launch and propel them. As well as such heroes there are hosts of less romantic figures, initiators and experimenters, groups of interested entrepreneurs prepared to listen to an inventor expounding his new design for a pump or formula for cheap soap; not a few artisans set up on their own and become prosperous masters, even considerable capitalists, on the strength of a lucky device; and all this receives encouragement from a forward-looking Prince Consort (who is aware of government initiatives in such things in Prussia and Saxony and lends his support to public lectures, scientific demonstrations, practical applications of science).

The culmination is to be seen in the Great Exhibition of 1851, when the Crystal Palace, built on a cast-iron frame in the middle of London, houses a prodigious display of the mechanic arts and products of the world (but more especially, those of British manufacture). It is the first event of its kind, opened by the monarch in person, attended by all the famous and the great. Is it not interesting that this nineteenth-century celebration of progress should be mounted in an outsize greenhouse? The greenhouse's designer, Joseph Paxton, happens to be the duke of Devonshire's head gardener, and

it certainly does not tell a tale of complacency or stagnation. One thing it does associate with, however, is pretentiousness. It is noticeable that manners require one to behave as far as possible as though one does not have to stoop to anything so vulgar as actual work: the gentleman does not work. This is of course preposterous, and not at all easy to square with long hours in the bank, in chambers, or even in the shop; yet it is a fact, and a tribute to the powerful magic of the gentry. And by the same token, money, or anything to do with commercial transactions, is sedulously banned from

157 Philip Hardwick (1792–1870), the Adelaide and Victoria hotels, 1839. From an anonymous lithograph, 1840.

Railways and large-scale travel give rise to modern 'hotels'. Euston Station, the first metropolitan railway terminus in the world (1838), lies beyond the stately 'Doric Arch'; within a year of opening, an amazing 500,000 passengers use it, and it is flanked already in 1839 by two hotels—one cheap (left), the other more elegant (right).

158 Isambard Kingdom Brunel, (1806–59), Temple Meads railway station, Bristol, 1839–40

The problem of roofing-in the tracks and platforms of a large and smoky railway terminus is solved by Brunel by the use of iron and glass; but there is no question of using such materials for the more 'monumental' parts of the building—entrance, booking-halls, waiting rooms— which, by relying on traditional materials and styles, rejoin 'architecture'.

159 Isambard Kingdom Brunel, *Great Western*, 1837. Engraving after a painting by Joseph Walter. London, Science Museum

Brunel's first ocean-going steamship bears the same name as the railway company linking London with Bristol, and is intended to carry passenger traffic onwards to North America. Astern is a conventional wood-and-sail warship; though this is soon to be made obsolete, large sailing vessels have another half-century of life before them.

the duke himself is a leading personage in the iron industry; apart from that, to commission an architect would imply erecting far too costly and permanent a building in brick or stone. The fact remains that this palace of marvels, this Crystal Palace, is in its materials and its form very unmistakably an *add-on* type of structure; an annexe, an outhouse to the 'real thing' (later, to be sure, the South Kensington Museum and its successors will be solid, 'real thing' buildings, while the Crystal Palace, resited in south London, turns out to last as well as any of them). Brunel's railway stations, likewise using iron and glass, require monumental masonry frontages to anchor them in public reality. How *real*, we may ask, is engineering and mechanic ingenuity?

In a very curious manner, raw machinery and curtain-draped comfort rub shoulders in this age, under the banner of progress. They rub shoulders, but remain distinct. The design of a railway carriage (as distinct from the locomotive) is modelled on that of the horse-drawn coach—not surprisingly, since the universal means of getting about is still the horse, or in town the horse cab or omnibus. Leaving aside the great entrepreneur or fashionable lecturer, 'engineer' in 1851 evokes a man in an apron standing respectfully at the doorway, tugging at his forelock. Some engineers it is true can become gentlemen by virtue of a new professional association or 'institution', in much the same way as architects (from 1834) or accountants (1854); on the other hand education, to the despair of the Prince Consort, hardly recognizes technology. If the Royal Institution, the British Association, and many other privately launched societies exist in London and the provinces to further science and experiment, and Michael Faraday (to name but one) is making sensational advances in physical sciences and expounding them to large audiences, it is still the case that for many in these audiences Faraday might as well be a conjuror. The great and expanding field of applied science, the inventors, entrepreneurs, investors, energetic railway-builders and shipbuilders and iron-masters, the flow of investment in plant and machinery, the toiling of thousands, the extraordinary volume of exports, in a word the economy of the first industrialized nation: all this has made no mark on the cultural symbolisms of its agents and beneficiaries. We have already spoken of the separation of the slum and the suburb. Who needs to make a factory beautiful? At the meridian of the century, in the year of the Great Exhibition, art and beauty, grace and excellence—whether in private or indeed in public life—have nothing whatever to do with machines or iron ships or industrial design. That, at least, is what the evidence shows.

Beauty

If the good life is not the pursuit of money (or not too avowably), nor making things (except to make money), then what is it for which all the sacrifice of effort and hardship is being made, the saving and investment, the satisfactions postponed and the severities accepted? One very general answer must be 'self-improvement'; that is to say, a Christian preparation for salvation, striving in innumerable good causes, with repression of wickedness in others and control of it in self; including, especially, vigilant effort to suppress all reference to carnal weakness (that is, sex), lest it should lead to loose thoughts, or worse. For the most austere souls that is already quite a programme; but for those seeking a more gracious adornment of life there can also be the cultivation of refined feeling and the taste for whatever is innocent and good and beautiful; which means excluding from the record whatever might be impure or evil or ugly. 'Beauty is truth, truth beauty,' says Keats, but the Platonic message has to be interpreted. Some truths are very upsetting. Those slums, for example. Those truths alone which conform to what is 'ideal' will be admitted; they must be gracious or edifying or both.

Hence the repertory of roses and nightingales and unsullied maidenhood and love in all its purity (not the Other Thing) and, of course, Nature: Nature in the sentimental sense, abounding in scenes of comfort, of moral uplift: the pretty butterfly, the sunset presaging a beautiful passage to a better life, the countryside, the enchantments of moonlight . . . The purveyors of all this gentle beauty are in the first instance the poets, but judiciously selected: Wordsworth, certainly for 'Daffodils' (as the age calls his poem) but not for *The Excursion*, however sublime the morality; Shelley for his 'Ode to a Skylark', though not for his subversive philosophy; Keats—here, for once, is a poet who can be recommended without restriction. The heir of these and others also now dead is Alfred Tennyson, the mellifluous poet of Arthurian *Idylls*, of 'The Lotos-eaters', of 'Ulysses'. Acclaimed repeatedly and appointed Poet Laureate in 1850, even Tennyson however must keep within a decorous range: if he strays too far towards unpleasant truths, or macabre feelings, as happens in *Maud*, the Laureate himself is open to attack by critics as 'bloodthirsty'. By the side of Tennyson, it is a grave thought that the great flowering of English poetry in the age of Wordsworth, Coleridge, Byron, Shelley, Keats, seems to have come to an end; Victorian England's most characteristic and undoubtedly admired talent is that of Mrs. Felicia Hemans (died 1835): in-

160 'Professor Faraday
lecturing at the Royal
Institution before H.R.H.
Prince Albert, the Prince
of Wales, and Prince
Alfred'. Engraving from
the *Illustrated London
News*, 16 February 1856

*The Royal Institution is one
of the more prestigious outcomes
of private initiative in
promoting scientific knowledge;
the Prince Consort indicates his
strong support by taking one of
the Royal princes to attend
Professor Faraday's lecture.*

effably lachrymose, pious, it is hard today even to begin
to understand her appeal. Elizabeth Barrett Browning
is a little closer to us, perhaps, only because she is a trifle
more idiosyncratic and aware of painful stresses in the
morality of her day. Each of these ladies conveys rather
strongly the literary consequences of maudlin individualism and self-pity in the drawing-room; and a
Robert Browning becomes interesting only when he
neglects to flatter those tastes.

A similar picture comes to us from the musical
preferences of the 1840s. To be sure, England creates
only a profusion of hymns and some Anglican anthems;
the genius that marks out a great composer or singer or
pianist has (like sheet music) to be imported from
abroad, where temperament is more conducive, perhaps (or, simply, because England has no *conservatoire*,
no state opera, no official patronage). That said, music
is unquestionably the art which most closely reflects the
temper of the Victorian household, domestic entertainment, the 'at home'. And it may be the songs of
Schubert rather than Beethoven (not forgetting that the
latter's Ninth Symphony has been commissioned by
the Philharmonic Society in London): there is a huge
market for lyrics and ballads, and this is also the climate
in which the nocturne comes into its own (a short piece,
suitably vapid, or as perfected by Chopin, exquisitely
melancholy). Perhaps we have said all when we remark
that the most completely and unreservedly admired

musical genius is that of Mendelssohn, author, at
seventeen, of the *Midsummer Night's Dream* overture,
and Queen Victoria's favourite composer. His *Songs
without Words* are a complete anthology of all that
suburban sentiment can best respond to: the bees' weddings, lullabies, spring songs, barcarolles, even the not
too painful gloom of a short funeral march, exactly
define the bounds of accepted sentiment. And in the
larger arena of the concert hall, very much the same
profile of taste appears: Mendelssohn again, of course,
with his astonishingly fluent symphonies and concer-
tos, or the Handelian *Elijah*, beloved of choral societies;
and alongisde him, omitting lesser figures, the greatest
lion of the day, Franz Liszt, conjuring into existence on
a grandiloquent scale very much the same universe of
beautiful things as Mendelssohn, only a little more
unbridled—namely the *Evening Harmonies* of sunset,
the wild exultation of the Hungarian dance, the sphinx-
like declamatory adventures of sonata or concerto.
Rehearsing one, the great actor-maestro shakes his
locks and chants at the keyboard, in time to the leitmotiv, *'Alles das versteht Ihr nicht'* (This you do not understand); very likely true, but happily there is nothing
there to disturb or offend, only sublimity and rapture,
sorrow, the devout hush, the ethereal tinkling, an ever
more resonant keyboard yielding up ever more brilliantly varied tonalities . . . And of course a 'programme', a kind of great cosmic battle in the skies, an

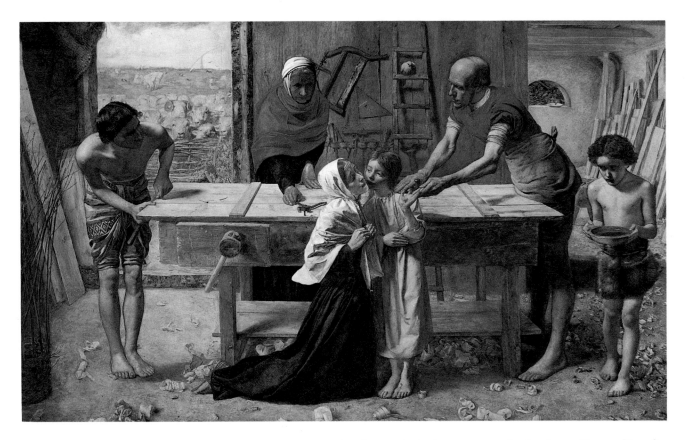

162   Sir John Everett Millais, *Christ in the House of His Parents*, 1849–50. Oil on canvas, 34 × 55 in (86.5 × 139.7 cm). London, Tate Gallery

When is it outrageous to depart from conventional images of the sacred? Millais's canvas is aggressively anti-academic in its realism, but its hostile reception (by Dickens and others) can only be explained in terms of middle-class prejudice. It remains that ridicule lurks around the corner whenever the Pre-Raphaelites venture into symbolism (here the rows of penned sheep visible through the doorway).

161 (left)   William Holman Hunt, *The Awakening Conscience*, 1853. Oil on canvas, 29¼ × 21⅝ in (74.3 × 55 cm). London, Tate Gallery

A parable? To abolish all possible doubt, a glove lies discarded in disorder, and the cat on the carpet has caught a poor little bird. Those drawing-room songs and ballads can be dangerous . . . Providentially though the window is open; a wall-mirror shows us the pristine green and innocent Nature outside, and those promptings no doubt tip the balance in favour of Virtue. It would be unthinkable even to suggest that the outcome could be different.

abstraction of a story, no doubt, but still storylike; for all music now, without exception, depicts or narrates something.

It is in pictorial art, in visual sensibility generally, that the shortcomings of this expanding, rich society are most clearly apparent. For here, unlike music, there has been patronage (the Royal Academy), and there is a tradition. Academic portraiture is of a very high standard: Lawrence at the start, and then the endlessly fluent and accomplished Landseer, equally painstaking over dignified humanity or noble animals—a great favourite at Windsor, though by mid-century Queen Victoria will have developed a taste also for the safe court painter Winterhalter. In landscape both Constable and Turner have produced incomparable work, and Turner in his maturity is advancing magnificently into uncharted impressions of spectral light and composition.

Were that but all! Unfortunately there are also imitators of Canova and Flaxman, and the ripest, even the most luscious fruits of neo-classicism; and Gresham's Law interposing in the realm of taste, a supply of sentimentalized banality pours into the market. Around 1840 the acme of 'beauty' would be represented by

LE GRAND HOMME

163   Alexander (after Bertrand), cartoon of Liszt, 'the Devil of Harmony', at the piano. Lithograph, 1845. Paris, Musée du Carnavalet

The 'great man' virtuoso of the nineteenth century dazzles large audiences by spectacular novelty of performance: none more than Liszt. The flowing locks and gaunt figure too betoken a 'genius', plaything of daemonic forces; to say nothing of the rumoured irregularity of his restless and cosmopolitan life-style. As much as anywhere in Europe, Victorian society cannot do without such a figure, however reprobate. Liszt accepts the rôle with reasonably good grace.

truthful representation, and they are attracted to pre-Renaissance Italian art; beyond that, some are not afraid to elaborate quite garishly naturalistic genre scenes, others to delineate a new streak of 'fay' feminine beauty (supplying a link from Tennyson to a much later exotic vein in Art Nouveau), others again to explore with gusto the decorative possibilities of a sultry medieval-ism. There is not too much in the way of common interests to bind them lastingly together: Hunt's *Light of the World* becomes a revered icon of Oxford Movement sensibility; Millais's *Christ in the House of his Parents* outrages even socially progressive consciences, though he too can slide into breath-taking sentimentalities. It is only when we consider them in the light of Ruskin's advocacy that we can glimpse in them a collective signi-ficance.

Ruskin, born in grimy London but growing up in a leafy suburb, discovers a vocation to correct the artistic vision of his fellow-citizens; and first of all to teach them to admire England's greatest living painter, Tur-ner. This leads him into spelling out a huge new course in aesthetics (*Modern Painters*, 1843–60). If you stand by the side of Turner, there can be no question of seeing art in the way the great new public does: as Ruskin deli-cately tells his readers at the start, 'Public taste seems plunging deeper and deeper into degradation every day'. What then must they grasp, these eager protestant amateurs? Centrally, that painting is an intense disci-pline, a discovery of truth; and in that sense a moral experience, 'a witness to the omnipotence of God'. Study this leaf, this light, this rock-face; do not settle for the stereotype. Hence Ruskin's warm applause for the Pre-Raphaelites, and their regard for him.

But going deeper, Ruskin's doctrine becomes some-what disturbing. By 1853, when he writes the second volume of *Stones of Venice* ('On the Nature of the Gothic') he has learned so much from study of the past that he now sees even the reverent apeing of the Gothic in England as a lesson which has been taken up all wrong; and he is well on the way to a radical rejection of industrial society and its products on moral-artistic grounds. Of the new technologies, railway bridges, machines, he has of course nothing to say; he fixes his attention on the artist, on the integrity which for him is grounded in scrupulous observation, and which can be, must be, *is*, revealed in labours with brush and chisel and trowel. The artist is a craftsman, first and always; only through his craft may he become a Giotto or a Turner; genius is not a short cut; the craftsman can never replicate the dead precision of machines, nor of course would he ever want to. The medieval craftsman has built Pisa's cathedral front with every arch a slightly

some sort of cross between Raphael and Monsieur Ing-res: what Clive Bell disdainfully calls 'grocer's art'. At the end of the road there lurk the soap advertisement 'Bubbles' and the chocolate-box illustration. Halfway down that road we come upon what might be identified as the first-ever movement of artistic revulsion against the tastes of a society—the Pre-Raphaelite Brother-hood—and the first great prophet of artistic integrity against the corruptions of the age—John Ruskin.

The Pre-Raphaelites are not in any clear sense a school, and their association is brief (1848–52). They start from a common ambition, one of meticulous and

different size (Ruskin has measured them all); supporting the doge's palace at Venice every pillar is a different work of art (he describes each one). True Gothic is the collective monument of many *individual* efforts, behind each pious pair of hands a living soul—hence its asymmetries, which like all else in it are 'moral', through and through. That is the lesson of Venice. 'Sermons in stones', says Ruskin. How stands it then with England?

The answer, 'very badly indeed', is no surprise. It never occurs to Ruskin that there could be a sermon in a suspension bridge or integrity in engineering. He hardly looks that way: when he does, his eye is caught by an abomination—a gasholder squalidly disguised as a Roman temple, a monument masquerading as something it is not, a lie. Another abomination: to take a builder's pattern book and throw up a terrace or a row of villas, uniform or trivially varied, mean, shabby, Gothicized or not, a gross symbol of commercial greed, and of the workman's degradation. The stark ugliness in England reflects moral ugliness—in the slums, in the pretensions of Mr Newly-Rich.

Most of the second half of Ruskin's life is taken up in trying to put the clock back; in preaching and teaching (when magazines reject his articles he finds other ways to spread his message, using a considerable inherited fortune); in launching an old-world type of guild; in proselytizing workmen with beautifully produced newsletters; in exemplary projects (road-making, museum-building, endowing collections). Evidently he has an impossible task: he must teach right seeing from the ground up, convert a few million consciences to a different and humbler view of brother-craftsman (working with one's hands is no shame), put into reverse all the iron laws of wages and profits and property development, overturn the entire pyramid of snobberies (while continuing to share some of them). This is no less of a revolution than anything dreamt of by his contemporary Marx, though in an opposite direction: where Marx notes with a shrug the passing of the craftsman, Ruskin would rehabilitate him; where Marx looks to an overthrow of social conventions and liberation by violence, Ruskin looks towards a common humanity realized in joyous work. Both however are haunted by the 'alienations' of the world they live in. And no wonder.

To look around, one would say that Ruskin does not make much more of a dent in Victorian culture than Marx. Yet neither prophet entirely wastes his breath. Ruskin sharpens the attentiveness of Victorian architects to the models which inspire their town halls, railway stations, colleges—sometimes. The Pre-Raphaelites undoubtedly kindle new ambitions in art

164 Sir John Everett Millais (1829–96), *John Ruskin at Glenfinlas*, 1853–4. Oil on canvas, 31 × 26¾ in (78.9 × 67.9 cm). Private collection

One of Millais's more attractive works is the painting of his then friend Ruskin. The setting is 'romantic', but not too starkly so—the rocks on which Ruskin lavishes attention in Modern Painters *are rendered with Pre-Raphaelite care. The critic's pose too is dashing and 'noble' (in a moral but no longer a social sense): Ruskin is almost a Monarch of the Glen.*

(though less strikingly perhaps than their contemporary Courbet in France); in the early 1860s Burne-Jones's young friend William Morris founds a craft movement which is the start of quite new standards of design in Victorian artefacts (and in so doing discovers in his turn the promptings for a 'socialism' very different from that of Marx). Thereafter there has scarcely been a time when groups of artists have not stood forth as a sort of conscience against debasements of industrial mass-production. Ruskin, in his perverse way, would seem to have stumbled here upon a rather deep-seated predicament in modern culture, rooted in the divergence of art and industrial production; it is not until the turn of the century that solutions begin to be offered—solutions which no doubt he would have deeply disliked.

165 Joseph Mallord William Turner (1775–1851),
Slavers Throwing Overboard the Dead and Dying, **1840.**
Oil on canvas, 35⅞ × 54⅜ in (91 × 138 cm). Boston,
Museum of Fine Arts, Henry Lillie Pierce Fund

*This is the first of Turner's 'difficult' later works to be
exhibited (1840—recent abolition of slavery makes its cruel subject
topical). The public is disconcerted, and Thackeray and others
dismiss it as mad. Ruskin, however, (in* Modern Painters*)
acclaims it as 'the noblest sea that Turner has ever painted, and, if
so, the noblest ever painted by man'.*

Philosophers of progress

Victorian society, unlike continental societies in the
same period, is not aware of anything remotely re-
sembling an 'intelligentsia'. It has not the public institutions which could help to shape a category of individuals regarding themselves as in some sense intellectually 'special'. This is apparent the moment we consider how almost all the most remarkable creative
figures of the day arrive at their eminence: purely by
self-help. Ruskin's *Modern Painters* reveals one auto-
didact; Carlyle's *Past and Present* another; John Stuart
Mill receives a formidable education, but it is at the
hands of his father and family friends; the sociologist
Herbert Spencer educates himself by working in a railway company and then as a journalist; Faraday is a
brilliant assistant trained up by Davy; Darwin, who is

166 Alfred Waterhouse (1830–1905), Owens College, Manchester, drawing by the architect.

By mid-century, private wealth and initiative are being applied to the creation of universities in many of the great centres of industrial growth. In Manchester, Owens College is set up in 1851 to be part of a new Victoria University; and neo-Gothic style of building is felt to be appropriate to a large monument of public importance (the same is true of innumerable 'public', that is to say, private, schools set up in the same period —see p. 229).

sent to Cambridge, benefits not from his formal exercises there but from contact with a botanist and a geologist retained on the margin of that university's establishment; and the great physicist Kelvin, a graduate of a Scottish university, begins his self-education on returning to a professorship at Glasgow at the age of twenty-two.

If moreover in almost all branches of learning a large proportion of talent comes from dissenting circles, this is in part because, as noted already, they form the core of the middle classes, taken as a whole; one has an impression of earnestness and application, of a drive to 'achieve' in the face of exclusion from the established seats of learning (Oxford and Cambridge still refuse to admit any but Anglicans), a more natural acceptance of the idea that knowledge and industry and progress are somehow parts of the same great programme of moral duty. From 1827, it is true, there is access to a quite new university, founded in London by liberals and radicals and dissenters (and on modern lines) for those who are debarred by creed from the ancient universities— though a Priestley or a Dalton has not waited for that opportunity, and naturally the philosophical societies of provincial towns impose no religious exclusions.

In the second half of the century, not only will the ancient universities reform themselves, but new colleges and institutions will be created, always of course through private initiative; the free society takes its time, but does apply its wealth to worthy causes. But by then the cultural pattern has set firmly in its mould. In the meantime the lack of state institutions in no way inhibits scholarly-minded individuals from launching into detailed experimental or factual inquiries on the one hand, or into the most ambitious and awesome general systems on the other—when they feel so moved. Indeed, there seem to be ideal conditions for intellectual adventure: absence of constraints, not too vast a burden of tradition to be embraced or refuted. There are also, in the background, very low living costs for those private persons ready to accept frugality as the price of the opportunity to develop their thoughts at full length.

John Stuart Mill is reared by his father with the most extreme thoroughness: he studies the classics, science, law, as well as the pure milk of political economy and utilitarianism; so much so, in fact, that he breaks down under the strain, but recovers. It is clear that he is intended to carry the torch as a liberal thinker; but that is not quite the way things work out. To begin with, the doctrine of political economy is becoming, with every passing day, rather less cheerful than in the days of Adam Smith. Malthus's gloomy teaching now forms an integral part of it; from the 1820s to the 1840s a cycle of business slumps calls for explanation, and with them has come a steady depression of wages, periodical mass unemployment; the economist David Ricardo has come to the conclusion (confirming Luddite intuition) that machinery must in general conduce to gradually fewer jobs. Mill's recovery from his breakdown is accompanied by a developing interest in what England's great poets, Wordsworth and Coleridge, have recently had to say and he responds to the growing gloom of liberal doctrine by moving to a very critical style of thinking about utility and the 'greatest happiness of the greatest number'; he criticizes Bentham's 'Enlightenment' view of self-love; and alongside support for the radicals, addresses himself to rethinking the great doctrines in which he has been brought up. He studies logic again, and the conditions of generalizing from particular cases (induction); he studies the power of 'natural laws' in science; and then commits himself to a *Political Economy* (1848), which he sees as replacing that of Adam Smith.

His central novelty is the view that within the constraints of economic science—which he accepts in full—it is still possible to change the values and conditions of social life. He says:

I confess I am not charmed with the ideal of life held out by those who think that the normal state of human beings is that of *struggling to get on*: that the trampling, crushing, elbowing, treading on each others' heels, which form the existing type of social life, are the most desirable lot of human kind, *or anything but the most disagreeable symptoms of one of the phases of industrial progress*. (emphasis added)

From there it is a short step—he takes it—to framing ideas for a better future, and for what we would call a 'welfare society': in which the state will have duties to interfere in distribution of wealth, to open schools, to lead in the education of the mass of the population by encouraging co-operatives and mixed partnerships of capital and labour, to break the 'iron' laws of exploitation. Were this last not possible (he adds in 1852) it would be better to adopt Communism and abolish private property rather than face an indefinite future of the 'present state of society with all its sufferings and injustices'. But it *is* possible: competition is only a quite recent ideal; and if, in the future, economic society by the abatement of competition arrives at a 'stationary state', there is still much to be done in redefining liberty, in striving against the subjection of women, in creating a new social science of which economics is only a part, in short, still scope for progress. Mill is in fact a tenacious reformer, indelibly marked with Bentham's rational hostility to old prejudices, but also ready to attack new prejudices; and intent on a more humane culture in which the enjoyment of poetry and leisure, Nature and botany (Mill is a great botanizer) shall be, like material wealth, more available to the 'greatest number'. And he trusts instinctively that this may be brought about without tyrannical direction.

The 'Communism' to which Mill alludes in so modern-sounding a way is, like socialism, regarded in the England of the 1840s as a definitely 'foreign' invention—something that has come out of the French Re-

volution; well-informed persons vaguely know that it has been mooted by extremists in France and advocated in 1848 by revolutionaries in Paris and Brussels . . . In 1849 Karl Marx arrives in London to spend the rest of his life there (he dies in 1883). His arrival arouses no more attention, indeed rather less, than that of earlier fugitives such as Mazzini or Louis Napoleon. And if England pays no attention to Marx, he on his side has not come there to pay much attention to it: certainly not to learn important lessons, or, like Tocqueville, to give special attention to instructive local conditions (despite his friend Engels's connections with the Manchester cotton industry, Marx never sets foot inside a factory). Because, of course, the country of his adoption has no new lessons to teach him; his philosophy is in essence complete, and has already been published in the *Communist Manifesto* (1847), from which he never budges. Marx's principal contact with Victorian society in the following decades is through groups of working-men, whom he seeks to guide in the development of their trade unions and mutualist institutions (including the formation of an international working-men's organization), always in pursuit of the ideas of the *Manifesto*. He keeps alive by writing for Horace Greeley's *New York Tribune*, and toils at a vast critique of political economy: *Das Kapital* (1867). Were it not for the tolerance, he could as well have lived anywhere else.

Marx is, in effect, an outsider. Almost everything about him separates him from others in England who are no less preoccupied than he is by the effects of progress on society and its relations. He is, to begin with, cosmopolitan; his background is in the Rhineland, Berlin, Paris. He is an intellectual several times over—the grandson of a rabbi, a student of philosophy and law, a journalist on the 'outside' of the 'official' world from which his wife comes, and by now a fugitive from the political police of several countries, living on the margin of an indifferent host society. Hegel has opened his mind to grandiose speculation, German radicals to critical subversion, and French republican groups to action theory. Taking ideas from each and putting them together, he has arrived at the truth, the 'scientific' (that is, philosophical) definitive truth about man in society: a philosophy of social development grounded in axioms, framed in laws, articulated by Hegel's special 'dialectical' logic, and confirmed by events all around. It remains to clothe this philosophy in *praxis*, that is to say, in revolutionary action to release the inevitable future. Apart from this last idea—that is to say, doing something about things—this rootless, 'free-floating' intellectual could hardly be more different from anyone actively concerned in Victorian culture.

167 Sir Robert Smirke (1781–1867), British Museum, London, 1828–52
Smirke's immense edifice with its Ionic portico is erected between 1828 and 1852 to house collections of every kind except painting, and also the national library. When the Library is first founded (1759) David Hume has used it for historical research; now, in its domed Reading Room, the exile Karl Marx has the run of 350,000 volumes—at this time, the world's largest collection.

And yet, if Marx has no place whatever in Victorian life, he has a very central place in the wider scene of which England is a part (albeit a slightly eccentric part). In the wider scene, he is *the* critic of liberalism, of capitalism, of all other contemporary ideologies, the dogmatic founder of a system which in the generation following his death captures allegiances all over Europe, and beyond. And his great strength lies in having concentrated all his attention on one issue, and one issue only, which is crucial and controversial in all the countries known to him: that of the relations between social classes.

'Class' (rather than 'estates' or 'orders') is an obsessive preoccupation in the early nineteenth century: in England for reasons we have noted; in France, for slightly different ones; and for yet others in Prussia, and in kingdoms haunted by memories of the French Revolution. Marx is quite intelligent enough to distinguish the differences when he chooses; but his great doctrine requires him to group all 'bourgeoisies' together, to see the ideal type of a factory system wherever one is coming into being (the labour market) as a 'law' behind the facts. It is at a very deep and abstract level that 'classes' are ultimately to be defined (ironically, Marx dies before he can completely refine this theme of the *Manifesto*); but from all around him he extracts clues for his system, in which power relations are based on *class* control of wealth production, that control is fortified by *class*-based law and ideological hegemony, and challenges to it are offered only by new *classes* being brought into being by wealth-production itself. It happens that this simplified account, this 'structural' analysis, is more adequate to the description of European social change in the 1830s and 1840s than any other single simplified schema. Marx also builds upon it a singularly corrosive critique of other people's ideologies; these are always inspired, as he sees it, by the kind of bad faith that Voltaire ascribes to priests, and are designed to hoodwink the victims of the ruling class into accepting their subjugation as inevitable or natural or desirable. When he projects this analysis backwards in time, it tends to be less and less helpful, though often suggestive; when he projects it into the future, it loses much of its cogency, precisely because it is so closely moulded to the state of Europe at a particular period that, as the decades go by, the realities of 'pauperization', 'industry', 'capitalist', even of 'class', will become more and more remote from the simplicities of the early nineteenth century. The prophecies turn out simply wrong. But for the year 1847, and with the levels of intellectual sophistication then available, and on the basis of what can be perceived or surmised about development of industrial structures, and the continuing failure of attempts to establish democratic control in European states, the system of Marx is, as a system of interpretation, unsurpassed for profundity and even for a certain intellectual grandeur, not matched since Thomas Aquinas.

In nature too!

According to Charles Darwin's own account, the illumination for the doctrine which bears his name comes from political economy. Having as a very young man spent five years on an exploration around the world, observing and collecting plants and insects and animals and geological specimens, the still unknown naturalist settles down to private life, far from the turmoils of politics or business, devoting entirely to research his prodigious mental alertness and diligence. Even so, society breaks in. In October 1838 he picks up Malthus's *Essay on Population*, 'for amusement' as he says; its argument (that populations tend to grow faster than their means of subsistence) suddenly conveys to him a revelation, a clue to the puzzling diversities of species he has observed at different occasions on his travels. The general thesis is of astounding simplicity and generality. In competition, some creatures survive, others not; by this 'natural selection' a very slow and gradual series of changes, or evolution, comes about, shaping every species of organic life. 'Here then I had got the theory by which to work.' Darwin then spends twenty years incubating his grand argument. It assumes of course an age-span of the universe immeasurably longer than that to be inferred from biblical tradition, and a scenario hard to reconcile with God's creation of fixed families of living creatures; it is bound to attract violent opposition in England. In fact Darwin only announces his views, in something of a hurry, on finding that another naturalist has written an essay offering the same theory; he then follows up a learned paper (1858) with his book *The Origin of Species* (1859).

Evolution is not strictly a novelty. Buffon's conjectures, Cuvier's work, the zoological speculations of Darwin's own grandfather, those of the French naturalist Lamarck, are in some degree familiar to learned men; fossils are accumulating in museums, palaeontology is a science, geology grapples with disturbing problems of time-span. Darwin is an intellectual giant, but he is working on problems that exist already; and if he adds to them by his own collections of field material it is not there that his fame lies. His decisive addition is that of 'natural selection'. And it is less important to our purposes to consider how he puts his grand system together than to observe its effect on his public.

The Origin of Species is the first ever scientific bestseller—in the same year, we notice, as that other bestseller, Samuel Smiles's *Self-Help*. A first edition is sold out on the day of publication; a reprint is rushed out; demand is intense—copies are even asked for on railway bookstalls—and for the rest of the century new editions are constantly required.

This is a very striking phenomenon. Darwin is not a public figure in 1859 (he quickly becomes one). Few readers in England probably expect, or are attuned to, a gesture of dethroning God the Creator (Marx is one—and a great admirer). The book itself is long; though admirably lucid, it takes the reader through the full rigour of lengthy analyses of special cases; by its nature it offers no dramatic excitements, and the implications for faith are barely hinted at. In the months and years following its appearance attention is of course excited by hostile reviews and attacks, weighty rejoinders, and a notorious public clash between the bishop of Oxford and the eminent T. H. Huxley at a scientific conference (which highlights the unpleasing implication that man could have descended from apes and not from an ideal Adam). By then few literate persons can be ignorant of the mild naturalist's challenge to dogma. It is the immediacy of the interest which is instructive.

Failing a list of the 1250 first-day purchasers of *The Origin of Species*, one point to bear in mind is that botanizing is a very widespread leisure pastime in Victorian society (that is not to say that every young lady is as diligent or professional as Darwin, or even J. S. Mill). Then there is the further point that Darwin is ascribing to Nature a process which, in the stud or on the farm, is perfectly familiar to any animal breeder or 'improver'; only instead of 'artificial' selection he claims the process is being carried on by a 'hidden hand'. Then again, though at first blush less important, the mechanism invoked by Darwin is extraordinarily familiar in a general sense: competition, the 'survival of the fittest', is precisely what all are braced to expect and value in Victorian life. Why not in the fields and jungles of the world as well? Finally, if economic competition and the hidden hand are presiding over social progress, refinement of culture, 'The Ascent of Man', why should change and progress not occur also in Nature, whose species we spend so much time identifying and comparing? And why should Nature not be getting *better*?

Darwin's theory, a revolution of thought hardly less startling than that of Copernicus, is thus received by his contemporaries without any great intellectual difficulty (that tells us something about the age's appetite for serious reading and grand synthetic revelations). Its implications are evidently in some ways appalling: it makes the spectacle of Nature a good deal less edifying than poets would have had it (though Tennyson in a glum moment has already glimpsed that); it gives uncomfortable prominence to the topic of procreation; it challenges the English theologian to reinterpret the nature of his age-old sacred statements (unless like Edmund Gosse's father he is prepared to believe that God planted fossil remains in the rocks in order to test men's faith later on). Intellectually though, evolutionism has a magnificent simplicity; it reinforces the claim for a vast historical space, where fossils and geological process can begin to be given a grand coherent meaning

168 Photographic portrait of Charles Darwin

The author of The Origin of Species *devotes some attention (in* The Descent of Man, *1870) to the beard; he believes it to have originated in primitive man 'through sexual selection, as an ornament'. Culturally, the Victorian 'beaver' remains a problem: if it can symbolize sagacity, or Bohemian wildness, or a life at sea, can it also be simply a badge of male supremacy, like the top hat (though without the latter's social overtones)? Darwin is discreetly silent.*

in relation to human affairs; it shifts, by an amount which it is hard to measure, the relative standing of natural science and of authority, new discovery versus traditional belief; and above all it adds a *missing link*—not that of man's descent, but of the nineteenth century's sense of challenge and change, of onward movement, whether destiny or treadmill. Nature too is on the move.

Recessional

Hardly is a great liberal society solidly established, at the middle of the century, than cracks and flaws and disappointments begin to appear. The Great Exhibition marks its triumphal arrival. Thereafter there will be a continuing flow of energetic individualism, a growing population, swelling middle and working classes, free trade and economic expansion, an overseas empire (earlier prejudices against colonies fading to extinction), philanthropy. New institutions multiply at an ever faster rate—'public' schools, universities, professional associations, academies, even municipalities and their modest public works and state schools—and not least, the friendly societies, co-operatives, trade unions, which both create a 'working-class' identity and mark a progressive reduction in social tensions. Throughout, respectability will reign in the person of the indestructible queen. Indeed, liberal society will reach such a pitch of self-satisfaction (self-help accomplishing its tasks) that in 1865 William Booth is moved to go forth and set up a Salvation Army to bring the gospel of conversion and practical charity to the poorest districts, its hymn-singing a standing reproach to the smugness of all those earlier reformers.

It is not only William Booth who bears witness to the flaws in this society. Just as we have seen Mill and Ruskin turn already against complacencies, so the middle classes will find more and more of their sensitive sons becoming restive under the great commonplaces. These are in England so huge, so pervasive, that there can be no early assaults on the heartlands of hypocrisy; only symbolic skirmishes over articles of religious faith. Elsewhere though, the assaults are under way. In France one Gustave Flaubert is brought to trial (1856) for a startling send-up of complacency (allegedly under the chapter of morals): *Madame Bovary*, which he has commenced writing in the very year of the Great Exhibition. In 1866 Henrik Ibsen, with his *Brand*, begins to probe into painful human truths behind the comfortable middle-class picture.

Yet even in liberal England there are signs that conscience and questioning and criticism cannot be frozen, and that freedom leads to other things beside free trade. After the evangelical headmaster Thomas Arnold, here is his son Matthew voicing a new mood of despondency at 'Philistinism' and 'Barbarism' (in *Culture and Anarchy*, 1869). Another Victorian, Walter Pater, unobtrusively slips sideways out of 'progress' into 'aestheticism' (his essay on 'Aesthetic Poetry' appears in 1868). A generation after Tennyson, the verse of Swinburne by no means seeks to capture the spirit of the age, but seems rather to be emigrating to the Lotos-Eaters' land which Tennyson has been at pains to skirt round. The poetic cry of 'Excelsior' must be losing its charms.

And even as these song-birds are beginning to droop in their over-furnished Victorian comfort, one or two painters, under a different sky—Monet, Bazille—are venturing out down the Seine and discovering impressions of a kind undreamt of by liberal respectability, a new world of—dare one call it?—democratic humanism. Can it be that in the rather different circumstances of France the hegemony of 'middle-class' dreams of progress, the hold over past and present in a familiar universe of well-controlled symbolisms, is being undermined from within? Outside Britain, indeed, not only French Impressionists, but also Zola, are breaking new ground; in Germany not only has Richard Wagner written off the whole strange history of wage-slavery (or simply slavery, capital accumulation) in the cosmic allegory of the *Ring of the Nibelung* (written 1856–74), but the young scholar Friedrich Nietzsche launches into his own—very violent—denunciation of all things liberal in Germany. There seems to be a rare coalition of instincts against what should have been going to be a scheme of sustained and unending progress, industrial optimism, satisfaction for all tastes; it is already becoming evident several years before a prolonged general depression (1873 onwards) takes the glitter out of free trade and some of the cogency out of belief in progress.

It is, in fact, only Britain among the great European states that effects both a complete and a relatively durable transition to a liberal beatitude in the nineteenth century, and that by reason of peculiar circumstances, and also of her precocious Industrial Revolution. It would be hard to claim that the results in the arts are fully proportionate to the enormous resources available; though against that it might reasonably be asserted that in intellectual vigour and political achievement the dreams of an earlier Enlightenment are left far behind. There are legacies typical of a society which is thoroughly afraid to enjoy itself, or which, when it does, is apt to lapse into strange barbarities; but also of stern seriousness and devotion, from which it would be unreasonable to expect cities of transcending beauty or elegance. There is a legacy of ferocious puritanism (not mitigated by the disposition of an extremely strait-laced queen), which to this day has not disappeared; and also of an abiding, but hypocritically concealed, commercialism. In sum, the balance-sheet of a culture built on coal and cotton, but not quite able to face that fact.

169   Sir George Gilbert Scott (1811–78), the Albert Memorial, London, 1863–72, with the Albert Hall in the background

To mark the nation's irreparable loss on the death of the Queen's Consort, a public monument is erected in the form of a somewhat large Gothic reliquary. In its iconography are set the past and the present, history and science, the sacred (in Anglican tradition) and the secular. Also traces of an imperial geography. Eclectic over-decoration is not felt to be a problem here.

Chapter 8

La Belle Époque

On the lips of those who survive the Great War (1914–18) the phrase '*la Belle Époque*' is a general expression of nostalgia. It evokes gaiety and brilliance, in the public scene; also a lost sense of well-being, security, and peace (for the Viennese, a *Friedenszeit*). Nostalgia is nothing particularly new in the shared feelings of societies: we meet it in the dawn of European literature (Hesiod's 'Golden Age'), and very commonly it crops up in the outlook of social groups who are on the losing side in some tilting of the balance: medieval peasants petitioning for a return to 'the good old days' in Sicily when Good King William taxed them less unfairly, or French aristocrats recalling *la douceur de vivre* in times before the deluge of 1789. What catches the eye in *la Belle Époque* is that its passing is mourned by so many: not only by fortune's pampered few, but by almost all—the railway clerk and the intellectual, the merchant and the cobbler. Such unanimity is rare. Can it be more than simply a sign that in the catastrophe of 1914 and its aftermath *all* classes have been losers? And is the testimony of the age as emphatic as that of its survivors?

Nations and empires

To live in Europe in 1900 means to owe allegiance to the institutions of one of a score of nation-states, each slightly different from the others, and consciously so. It is not that the continent has fallen into fragments; it is simply that most of the prominent features of modern culture are recognized as due to the existence of political entities called France, or Belgium, or Germany, or Italy, and the political unification of these last two (1860–71) has set a seal upon this trend. The sovereign state (following mainly the early example of France) has etched in, and deeply, all the implications of its controlling authority: national laws and currencies, national tariff barriers, and education systems, and standing armies, and citizenship . . . Passports may not yet be necessary to cross most frontiers; but modern national censuses, which in France and Britain begin to be collected in 1801, are now universal; social statistics begin to abound—always national. Where 'national' interests are transcended, as in cross-frontier postal services or—at the turn of the century—the Hague Conventions on the conduct of war, a treaty is required between officials of the sovereign states. And through education and patronage and public works the state imposes a patriotic vision of its glories, its heritage, its *identity*. The refurbishing of Versailles, the completion of Cologne Cathedral, the cleaning up of the Colosseum, are pious acts to preserve symbols of the French, German, and Italian peoples, organized in nations. So too with the written monuments and archives of the past: the scholars of the nation-state quarry and edit and publish these in profusion. To every nation its ancestry.

In the four generations to 1900, also, the overall population of Europe doubles. This may be a smaller increase than the startling earlier one in Britain; also it is quite uneven (in France the population stabilizes around mid-century); nevertheless, sheer number is the compelling fact behind the development of almost everything in the nineteenth century: cities, wealth, enterprise, industry, trade, railways, and government itself. The institutions of the state have expanded from being the apanage of a monarch to quite large bureaucratic systems, and they take on new functions in almost every decade. As this happens, the state becomes a moral reality, almost a spiritual entity: no longer open to serious challenge, unmoved (though growing) in the middle of shifts in everything else. Authority accumulates. Even in utilitarian England, utilitarianism goes somewhat out of fashion by 1900 (except in provincial Manchester, which lives by free trade), and in its place idealist theories of the state begin to be prominent. It turns out that 'liberal' ideas (with a small 'L'—expectations of freedom, more individual self-realization,

170 Henri de Toulouse-Lautrec (1864–1901), *Moulin Rouge—La Goulue*, **1891. Poster (coloured lithograph), 76¾ × 48 in (195 × 122 cm). Paris, Musée des Arts Décoratifs**

Dancing the can-can stands for all that is jolly and 'daring' for visitors to the most famous of all European night-spots in la belle époque; *but we have become so used to Toulouse-Lautrec's poster that we take for granted its silhouette of odious rapacity.*

171 (right)   Berthold Löffler (1874–1960), poster advertising the Cabaret Fledermaus, 1907. Vienna, Albertina

As compared with Toulouse-Lautrec's Moulin Rouge (plate 170), Vienna's Cabaret Fledermaus is strongly in key with the 'modern' in art and decoration. Löffler's poster is almost a programme. The de-prettified female form (how can one escape old servitudes and images of the 'feminine' without transforming appearance and flouting convention?), the dress, the calligraphy, all indicate a haunt of 'intellectuals' and artists 'in the swim'.

where there will be opportunities for social promotion, though under widely differing conventions; and for new groupings and tensions. Urbanization, the arrival of new industries alongside old crafts, a gamut of new services, secular organizations, subtly twist the older patterns of expectation. A peasant's son may now more often become a primary school teacher, a tax official, or a postman; his grandson may become—anything. Similarly it takes but two generations for a novelty to become a tradition: between 1850 and 1890, station-master goes from being a novel to a respected role; between 1860 and 1900 primary school teachers in France become a large and dependable pressure group for radical anti-clerical democracy. Industrial populations, with large concentrations of working-class wage-earners segregated in unbeautiful suburbs, develop their own characteristic organizations—as they have done in Britain—and also that sense of identity which Marx has judged to be a necessary condition for a 'class' to exist; they stake their claims also in political parties (socialist, social democrat, labour) represented in the liberal parliamentary systems; in Germany and in France such parties become very prominent, elsewhere less so. At the same time, something of the concentration of economic ownership that Marx has also predicted takes place in some fields: small ironmasters disappear entirely, for example, large corporations become prominent, and great 'bourgeois dynasties' now command tens of thousands of employees—not simply traders, or bankers, but industrialists.

A myriad such shifts, each with its own preconditions and logic, its unpredicted consequences, have by 1900 brought about changes so extensive that the simple old regimes of a hundred years earlier could not conceivably satisfy the requirements of political control, guidance, adaptation. This is plainly to be seen in France, with its full-blooded republican system, its confrontations of large popular forces alongside liberal interests which are now, relatively speaking, very staid and 'conservative'. By contrast, in two great central European states, the German Reich and the Hapsburg Empire, all the apparatus of archaic old regime monar-

progress) are quite compatible with centralized state initiative. Elsewhere, in France and Italy and Germany, that issue has never been in question.

Thus it is under a tutelage very different from anything we have seen in the last chapter that the second half of the nineteenth century exhibits its kaleidoscopic transformations. In step with the tide of numbers, the great or middling states one after another follow in the tracks of Britain's precocious Industrial Revolution; in the process their social structures diversify and stretch (and this will have extraordinary results in the expressive symbolisms we shall shortly encounter). Every-

Chronology for Chapter 8

1848–1916	Franz Josef emperor of Austria
1852–70	Louis Napoleon (Napoleon III) emperor of the French
1854–6	Crimean War
1858–60	Construction of the Ringstrasse (Vienna)
1861–5	American Civil War
1861–9	Building of Vienna Opera house
1861–78	Victor Emmanuel II first king of united Italy
1862–90	Bismarck Minister-President of Prussia
1864	International Red Cross founded
1866	Austro-Prussian War
1867	Dual Monarchy (Austro-Hungarian) created
1869	von Hartmann's *Philosophy of the Unconscious* published
1870–1	Franco-Prussian War
1871–88	William I of Prussia first emperor of united Germany
1871–90	Bismarck first chancellor of united Germany
1872	Nietzsche's *Birth of Tragedy* published
1873–83	Building of Vienna *Rathaus*
1874	First Impressionist exhibition in Paris
1878	Paris Exhibition
1880	Split and 'Sezession' of radical liberals in Germany
1880–1	First Boer War
1882	British forces occupy Egypt
1883–92	Nietzsche's *Also Sprach Zarathustra* published
1884–5	Berlin conference on partition of Africa between European powers
1888–1918	William II emperor (Kaiser) of Germany
1889–99	Viennese Sezession artists active
1895	Freud and Breuer publish *Studies in Hysteria*
1897	Queen Victoria's Diamond Jubilee
1897–1907	Mahler director of the Vienna State Opera
1898	Herzl's *Der Judenstaat* published; retrial of Dreyfus
1899	Boxer Rising in China against spread of European influence; Veblen's *The Theory of the Leisure Class* published
1899–1902	Second Boer War
1900	Freud's *The Interpretation of Dreams* published
1900–13	Schönberg's *Gurrelieder*
1901	Thomas Mann's *Buddenbrooks* published
1901–10	Edward VII king of England
1903	Wiener Werkstätten established to promote Art Nouveau ideals
1904	Anglo-French *entente cordiale*
1905	Einstein's Special Theory of Relativity published; first 'Fauvist' exhibition in Paris
c. 1905	*Die Brücke* group of artists formed in Dresden
1906	Algeciras Conference on the division of Morocco
1907	Anglo-Russian entente
1908	Austrian annexation of Bosnia; first international congress of Psychoanalysis
c. 1909	First Cubist paintings produced
1910–36	George V king of England
1911	Agadir crisis; Diaghilev forms his *Ballets russes* company in Paris; Blue Rider group of artists formed in Berlin; Richard Strauss's *Rosenkavalier* produced; Gropius designs Fagus factory
1912	Sinking of the *Titanic*
1913	First volume of Proust's *À la recherche du temps perdu* published; Stravinsky's *Rite of Spring* premiered in Paris
1914–18	World War I
1915–23	Schönberg experimenting with twelve-note scale
1918	Abdication of Kaiser William

La Belle Époque 235

chies and their traditional hereditary support groups
('hereditary' spells 'land') and their symbolisms of traditional authority are still in place—in Germany they
are even reinforced by a great military system; and with
growing incongruity they seek, with the aid of the
bureaucratic state, to control the tensions and stresses of
new change, to which they are utterly unsympathetic.
This too will have multiple repercussions.

It remains broadly true, however, that 'progress' has
been widely implanted into the culture of the nation-
state. And since both political and administrative
change may, under the symbol of the sovereign state,
realize liberal, even democratic, ideals, the impetus of
these ideals is not easily dispersed. Liberalism has for
example tended to look on the extension of education as
an absolute good; often this has been reinforced by
hostility to an anti-liberal Catholic Church exercising
its traditional teaching mission: and the state sets up
secular education systems and opens schools to meet
the need for literate employees in modern society. But
like the soul of John Brown, ideals tend to go marching
on irrespective of such political cruces. Life can *and
should* be enhanced by public health and medicine, by
cheap manufactured goods; merit *should* be rewarded;
talent *should* find its opportunity. 'Progress' survives,
whatever the intentions of rulers or the customary outlook of the elderly. The growing organs of the state
itself—schools, state railways, public hospitals—these
too are after all symbols of progress, implanted by the
unmoved authority. This is not at all the same
framework that suited the earlier 'self-help' English
liberals; it has an enhanced, and rather different, mystique. *Vaterland, Patrie,* are credited by the authorities
with transcendental values; these (or rather the rulers
who manipulate them) exert claims on loyalty that
would disconcert English free trade liberals. Public officials enjoy a dignity somewhat greater than the private citizen; they also tend to vote at elections in ways
generally supportive of authority: again something undreamt of in the 'classic' model of liberal society.

The mystic national entities also acquire a new
strength of appeal through becoming—in some cases—
empires, with a 'mission' to control a string of colonies
and numberless 'natives' far away. The older overseas
empires of Portugal and Spain (much reduced), of the
Netherlands, France, and Britain (much extended), are
joined by three new ones: those of Belgium, Germany,
and Italy. In the 1880s all these European states proceed
in a rush to 'carve up' Africa; then turn to jostling for
'concessions' and trading posts on the coast of China.
Away in the east, Russia has long since accumulated the
largest empire of all and now confronts the Chinese
empire across the Amur; her government broods on
plans to swallow Korea and Manchuria . . . The
motives of imperial expansion are extremely diverse,
varying from country to country. In the eyes of some,
there is a duty to spread the influence of Christian
missions or other benefits (medicine, the rule of law,
literacy, 'civilization'). For others, the aims are less
altruistic: advancement of trade; capture of raw materials (the dream of gold stimulated by sagas of California, the Yukon, the Transvaal, Australia); export markets to support employment at home; outlets for excess
population; openings for direct investment; strategic
points for defending trade or existing colonies; reserves
of colonial manpower in case of war. To the demagogue, annexing a colony is a mark of national virility;
to the politician, it offers plums and pickings for loyal
supporters—or adventurers. Such varied motives, both
real and imagined, show that the whole movement
expresses a by no means simple pattern of interests in
the European states. The chief beneficiary is the state
itself, which enlarges its range of action in response to
the lobbies which beset it.

There is also, in the background, a more sombre
rationalization; that of 'Social Darwinism'. This now
forgotten doctrine has its origins in the popularization
by Haeckel and others of Darwin's evolution theory; it
consists in the proposition that in the jungle of the
world survival goes to the fittest species, or 'race'—be
that the (European) white man as against others, or
(among Europeans) the Teuton, Latin, Anglo-Saxon,
or Slav. Quite grown-up and seemingly responsible
persons embroider this curious 'science': in 1875 a
German writer, Albert Schäffler, popularizes the idea of
an international 'struggle for existence'; in Austria F.
Hellwald echoes the doctrine. In 1901 F. Ratzel brings
the term *Lebensraum* (living-space) before the same
public. Colonies are, of course, *Lebensraum*—in a
general sense—and proof of 'fitness'. These ideas come
handy to dynamic or demagogic governments: mass
elementary education has produced a large (and mainly
urban) public eager to pick up snatches of jejune
'theory' of this kind. There is little difference between
aggressive patriotism and the ideology of empire, expressed in the respective countries by voluntary or
state-patronized organizations: German Leagues, Pan-
slav Movements, Primrose Leagues, and so on. What is
characteristic is the hold of these fantasies on large
numbers of people, and their deep irrationality. The
man in the street can read in his newspaper of wars in
Ashantiland or Tonkin, the exchange of Zanzibar, the
siege of the Peking legations; he has little idea where
these places are, but his heart beats a little faster when

**172   Wassily Kandinsky,
Couple on Horseback, 1906.
Oil on canvas, 21⅝ × 19⅞ in
(55 × 50.5 cm). Munich,
Städtische Galerie
im Lenbachhaus**

*In the remarkable career of
Kandinsky, this quite early
work stands on the edge of a
striking transition from
decorative book-illustration* art
nouveau *– almost a fairy
romanticism – to the artist's
decomposition of subjects into
the entirely abstract and
suggestively symbolic patterns of
shapes and colours that he has
mastered barely six years later.*

news comes of the dispatch of a gunboat, the sack and
looting of the Summer Palace, the triumph of 'our'
soldiers . . . The foreign correspondent's story is read
as something only a step removed from exotic fiction,
sent in from a land of strange-sounding names whose
inhabitants are no doubt not 'real' people: but this conjunction of the known and the exotic fortifies belief in
the transcendent State, which has asserted its existence,
planted the national flag.

If only the world were endlessly large, there could
continue to be an endless stream of such adventures in
distant places. And then perhaps no dangers need arise
for imperialism—no dangers, that is to say, for the
European states. But the annexable world is not large

enough; indeed by 1900 it is nearly 'full'. The Moroccan
crisis of 1904 occurs over the last remaining African
territory where an important new protectorate might
be set up. Dangers are visible, at least in foreign ministries and General Staff map-rooms. A long rivalry between Russia and Britain has taken on a new character:

**173   Gustav Klimt, *The Kiss*, 1908. Oil on canvas,
70⅞ × 70⅞ in (180 × 180 cm). Vienna, Österreichische
Galerie**

Gustav Klimt's Kiss *has been carried completely out of reality
and, via its rich mosaics, into a world of erotic symbols: an overall
phallic shape, the Art Nouveau character of what little is shown
of the ecstatic figures, the insistent patterning of rectangles (male)
and rounds (female), form not a message but a kind of poetic icon.*

it has become global, its pressure points stretch from the Baltic, eastern Mediterranean, Persia, Afghanistan, Tibet, all the way round to the China Sea. A new kind of discourse, geopolitics, begins to be expounded by the geographer Halford Mackinder and the American Admiral Mahan. Are sea routes decisive in struggles for world power? Or control of the central Asian land mass?

For the time being debates of this kind are seen as theoretical, not quite real. The German Reich, late to arrive on the scene, is demanding colonies, a 'place in the sun': but public opinion has already been excited by Anglo-French rivalries over the Nile valley and all there has ended well; the new demands are not felt to be specially dangerous. Threats of an Anglo-Russian war, fears of conflict over Morocco, or over the Balkans, fill newspapers. Yet the European order seems so solid, so indestructible, that neither statesmen nor citizens are unduly alarmed. The power ploys by which right up to the summer of 1914 ministers lightly juggle with alliances, naval programmes, threats, *démarches*, or—ultimately—mobilization, patriotic hysteria, and all-out war, simply do not arouse a wide sense of foreboding. War, yes: 'bright and jolly' ('*frisch fröhlich*' in the Prince's immortal phrase), a big new adventure, a change from boring worries, almost a public holiday.

We are not here concerned with the impact of European empires upon the world at large, though this is the time when they are massively implanted. But what of influences the other way? Influences of the world upon European societies at the height of their colonial expansion? It is evident that opportunities abroad, by merely existing, affect in an obscure way the lives of more and more people. The cadres of empire, administrators and soldiers, retire home bringing picturesque turns of phrase, a few vices. We should not overlook them: for ideas taken out decades earlier, and hardened under distant skies, become set in a mould and then return into circulation. In a very few cases, the overseas experience is destabilizing, either because administrators, like the French commander Lyautey, learn unusual lessons and frame novel ideals of paternal responsibility, or because expatriates, like Cecil Rhodes in South Africa, are prone to become freebooters, severed from close surveillance by a home government. But whether a Lyautey or a Rhodes, the lessons of far away make little impression in Europe, receive little attention, except when (as in the case of Rhodes) they lead to an odious and embarrassing war. The diligent efforts of overseas Christian missions, similarly, have little apparent feedback. Though they are supported by congregations of every creed, no perceptible impact results in European

religious sensibility or even in theology; the 'modernist' controversy of the 1900s shows no sign of contacts with non-Christian belief systems, being only a new stage in the domestic crisis of faith and scholarship, authority and critical awareness unfolding within the old continent.

Why such imperviousness? Everything seems to hinge upon the movement of peoples. Up to 1880 there has been emigration out of Europe on a large scale, mainly, but not only, from Sweden and Germany, Italy and Ireland, to the new worlds of the U.S.A. (especially), Canada, South Africa, Australia, New Zealand, a scatter also to Latin America; some of these flows continue, but there is very little emigration to the new 'colonies'. Furthermore, quite large movements of overseas peoples are also being encouraged as part of the economic development of the world (Indian 'indented' labour to Africa, Chinese to California, etc.). But there is no migration *whatever* from the colonies into the European states; even colonial élites (where they exist) are held at arm's length. The human beings who might rather cogently symbolize contrasted patterns of belief or customs or styles of life are simply not there to be seen in the streets of Europe.

It is not surprising then that the symbolic fruits of empire (as distinct from the economic ones) are almost all in a sense trivial: carved ivory objects, Shantung silks, Chinese ceramics designed for 'European' taste, ebony cudgels, Benares brass-ware, a bric-à-brac of trophies adorning middle-class life in much the same way as bananas and pineapples are set out on the dining-room console (the English novelist H. G. Wells, a self-made man, contracts the habit of keeping a pineapple on display in his fruit-bowl as a symbol of success after hard times in the 1900s). At most these objects convey a vague message of superiority—of class, of nationality, of race. The Paris Colonial Exhibition of 1901, even while it exhibits 'native' crafts and introduces to European eyes West African sculpture, confirms the point of view. So too with ethnographic museums. If we ask what new perceptions of value, what enlargement of the sense of humanity, arise from this dizzy European hegemony, the answer supplied by the evidence is quite unambiguous: none.

And it is borne out by the commonplaces of popular journalism: assertions of a 'civilizing mission', self-congratulatory odes ('the White Man's Burden'), nightmares (the 'Yellow Peril' evoked by Kaiser Wilhelm, among others), and from time to time misgivings as to ultimate success ('East is East and West is West', in the jingle of Rudyard Kipling). An immense popular literature in every language, of travel, adventure, conquest, all appealing by its exotic settings, tells the same tale. Jules Verne's *Around the World in Eighty Days* has the originality that, over and above the fascinating glimpses of outlandish ('backward') customs, its great connecting theme is for once the triumph of modern (European) transportation—steamship, railway, balloon—in place of that more usual symbol, the Maxim gun. It also betrays its French author's incomplete familiarity with English society by having its clubman hero gallantly marry a Hindu widow: such a union is, in imperial Britain as in every other European country, absolutely excluded by powerful cultural taboos.

In short, for the whole of *la Belle Époque*, when Europe is riding high, we can point to few inputs crucial to national cultures coming from outside the continent. The exceptions—among intellectuals—are either on the boundaries of the expressive arts (Japanese prints influencing decorative arts, African masks noted in Paris by Picasso); or eccentric (theosophy, the 'wisdom of the east', Rudolf Steiner's attention to *karma*); or else at such a depth that their effects lie far in the future (the painstaking fieldwork of ethnographers in Brazil, India, Africa, Australasia). Imperial Europe triumphs through a world-conquering technology—steam engines, dynamite, metallurgy, artillery, gunboats, and other one-way communications. To the world which it believes it has come to dominate it remains, on the whole, massively insensitive.

Cosmopolitanism

It may seem odd then to speak of a cosmopolitan European culture in 1900. The word certainly cannot mean anything that a Stoic philosopher of antiquity would expect; for Europe is, bluntly speaking, *not* cosmopolitan with respect to Japan or China, India or Islam.

Moreover, the economic geography of the continent has become more diversified than at almost any time since the collapse of Rome. Industrial societies in regions of Germany, Britain, France, Belgium, flourish alongside much more traditional scenes everywhere in the crescent between Baltic and Black Sea, in the southern peninsulas, in the simpler world of Scandinavia; but they have come into existence at different times, also, and in different ways: the textile industries of Lyons, Manchester, Vienna, have quite distinct forms, as different as the varieties of agricultural life between large estates and small-holdings, or the differences between market towns and industrial cities. And superimposed on these variegated regions is the new grid of national states. Certainly scientists, engineers, art historians, musicians, have all the appearance of cros-

174   Kaiser Franz Josef, 1910

The Kaiser Franz Josef has reigned over the Hapsburg dominions since 1848; in 1910 his photograph still portrays the stolid and unimaginative personality who holds together an Empire on the verge of dissolution.

sing the grid for their strictly professional exchanges. Also, in 1889 in Paris delegates from socialist groups set up a new 'International', with ambitious aims. But how much is there really in common between these patchworks of communities of every shape and size? How can one speak of a European culture transcending such a multiplicity of old and new divisions? Surely this Europe is *less* cosmopolitan (within its own confines) than in earlier times?

If we pick up a vintage Wilhelmine or Edwardian 'society' magazine, we receive an exactly opposite impression. Here the world on display *is* cosmopolitan, if in a limited sense. Beginning with the national symbols themselves: the crowned heads are for a large part re-

175   Franz Marc (1880–1916), *Red and Blue Horses*, 1912. Mixed media, 10⅜ × 13⅜ in (26.5 × 34 cm). Munich, Städtische Galerie im Lenbachhaus

That colour has significance is no doubt an idea as old as Homo Sapiens. Socrates has conjectured that simple colours can be beautiful. Why then should they not express mood or feeling, regardless of how they appear in nature? And why should not forms, abstracted from nature, do likewise? All that remains is to recombine them in exploratory compositions—a programme shared by Marc, Kandinsky, Schönberg, and others around the Blue Rider group.

lated by marriage or descended from one or other prolific dynasty, Hapsburg or Bourbon or Saxe-Coburg. The life-style of a monarch is everywhere shaped by identical requirements. Public appearances are (as they always have been) the key to his role. Every year in summer there are visits to watering places or health resorts or cruising on the sea (this last being suitable for kings with large navies); in the season from autumn onwards, hunting, ceremonial openings of the legislature, opera, balls, receptions, parades; with the coming of spring grave crises are overcome, charities patronized, race meetings attended, state visits exchanged.

Ceremonial rites, political signals, and personal caprice too are woven into the year-round pageant of performing monarchs. Edward VII, travelling home from a holiday in the sun, charms an uncertain Paris street crowd in the interest of a diplomatic *entente* (Paris happens to be the city where he most enjoys himself); Kaiser Wilhelm, to underline a close Austro-German alliance, exchanges uniforms with Kaiser Franz Josef at a public parade (Wilhelm has a mania for uniforms). Monarchs are not as interchangeable as uniforms (one is tempted to wonder whether their daughters are), and dynastic links are a convenience only, not a force in international relations; nevertheless, at this summit level there is undoubtedly a pronounced if fragile confraternity among the living symbols of separate sovereign identities.

The same is even more apparent when we consider the gilded cohorts surrounding the monarch, and 'high society' in general. A majority of ambassadors and diplomats come from titled families, and are chosen to represent with brilliance; even republican France finds it wise to choose many of her ambassadors from families ennobled under previous régimes. This world maintains attitudes formed before the arrival of nationalism. Its lingua franca is French, the language of diplomacy. Cross-frontier marriages are normal; confessional barriers raise no more obstacle than national frontiers for an élite travelling with servants and a cartload of luggage—both kinds of formalities lack reality for them. (We might bear in mind that by 1900, unlike a quarter of a century earlier, communication has been greatly eased by the first-class railway compartment and the *wagon-lit*; in 1881 the St. Gotthard tunnel is opened; in the 1880s the first international railway timetables are published.) We see all the signs of a cosmopolitan Europe in the national capitals, in the fashionable holiday spots. At every centre luxury hotels cater for its needs—the Savoy, Ritz, Crillon, Gritti . . . A short step away is the glittering casino. It matters very little where the money comes from to speed the roulette wheel; it may be rents from peasants, royalties from coal, income from government stock, the nest egg of a dynasty. To all, the casino is equally hospitable (as also to any stray Russian 'prince' who wanders in—on the supposition that he is as rich as Croesus, which occasionally he is). But the casino is not of course an arbiter of rank or status. It is one thing to be seen in the haunts of the great and the rich; quite another to be recognized or greeted. This millionaire's daughter or that chorus girl may become a duchess and wear her emeralds at Monte Carlo; even so, society is jealous of its membership rights and pecking order, the more so because

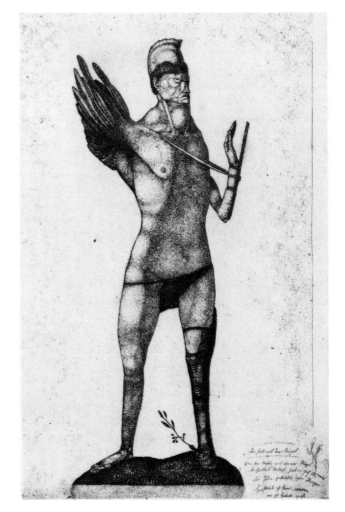

176   Paul Klee, *Hero with a Wing*, 1905. Etching, 9⅞ × 6¼ in (25 × 16 cm). Bern, Kunstmuseum

An artist whose intelligent inventiveness will span a whole half century has, in this early emblematic etching, linked fantasy from the past to surrealism in the future. It takes no exceptional penetration to decipher the elaborate and disobliging critique of senescent militarism in the reign of Kaiser Wilhelm II.

in the century just ended its members have mushroomed through the gratitude of successive monarchs for services rendered, the spread of wealth, and the pretensions of the *nouveau riche*. Little wonder that, alongside the international railway timetable, there now proliferate those useful directories, almanacs, peerages, which help the hostess to avoid solecism and preserve some remnant of order in the codification of manners.

The 'upper classes', or a few sections of them, supply the walk-on parts for the brilliant occasions of *la Belle Époque*: the state receptions and gala performances, the audiences for Diaghileff's brilliant *Ballets russes*, the clientèle of the Orient Express. But in truth their more practical functions in the community are hard to detect. The sociologist Pareto rather pointedly discusses the rotation of *élites*, not of *aristocracies* (though himself of aristocratic descent). His American contemporary Thorstein Veblen publishes his *Theory of the Leisure Class* (1899), a pioneer exercise in corrosive sociological debunking. Henry James is a kindlier moralist and explores the human predicaments of these leisured classes without judging them too hardly; but another contemporary novelist, the still youthful Marcel Proust, gazes first in wonder and then in profound disillusion at the intricacies of protocol, ritual, elegance, exhibitionism, affectation, and, in the last resort, futility, in a social round whose only asset is arrogant exclusiveness, whose only ethos an aimless charade.

In fact, we would look in vain in *la Belle Époque* for any profound or philosophic justification of the upper classes to match Edmund Burke's apology against the French Revolution. Four generations is all it has taken for any active belief in inherited superiority to fade away, leaving only custom and sufferance. These too are about to be swept away, together with the monarchs and empires of central Europe. Till then, the Establishments hold firm, and a tenacious rearguard action is fought by at any rate the landed interests. In Vienna Franz Josef presides over a reform of the archaic Austrian franchise (1907), eliminating an entrenched class of 'constitutional landed proprietors' in the lower parliamentary chamber: the upper house reacts by insisting that its own ranks should not in future be diluted, nor its powers weakened, by further elevations to the peerage. In London only a few years later a bitter political battle is won by the ruling Liberal Party, which threatens to do exactly what the Austrian nobility has dreaded—create a large number of new peers to force its measures through the House of Lords. This last political battle, and its outcome, may be seen as the final twitch of a once-dominant order of European society.

Vienna

Of all the capitals of Europe before the Great War none is more brilliant and alluring than the city of the Hapsburg monarchs. To the observer, Vienna is a prosperous, gracious, easy-going metropolis, whose theatres and operettas and crowded cafes and restaurants, Sunday afternoon parade of aristocracy, fashion, middle classes, taking an airing in carriages along the Ringstrasse or to the Prater, betoken all that history conjures up by the term *la Belle Époque*. An unshakeable social order? A rich cultural life? Cream cakes and Johann Strauss? Undoubtedly. Vienna has more than its share of public grandeur, aristocracies, officialdoms, high culture. Its whole musical tradition is unsurpassed: there are the remoter echoes of Haydn, Mozart, Beethoven, Schubert; the home of the waltz, it has continuing ties with a now independent Italy, is close to the birthlands of Liszt, of Dvořák; there has been Bruckner, and now there is Gustav Mahler, the State Opera's brilliant conductor; the latter is also a controversial song-writer, and author of symphonies of a vehemence and elaborateness that take that form to its limits and repel most listeners of the day. A completely new chapter is about to be opened by a young composer, Arnold Schönberg, even more innovative. Together, Vienna's favourite art exhibits an abundant stream of native genius and a cosmopolitan breadth not found anywhere else: this is partly because of the peculiar history of the city, the empire, the monarchy, but also partly—now—because of the curious stasis, not unpleasing, which has settled on it by comparison with energetic Berlin to the north or prosperous Budapest down the Danube.

Yet oddly, if we review the most original cultural achievements of this decade in the life of Vienna, what strikes us is not a testimony of happiness, contentment, order, optimism, but . . . precisely the opposite. The imposing backcloth itself, the central monuments of the city, contribute to a paradoxical scene. The baroque imperial palace, the Hofburg, faces out from the edge of the old inner city and across the broad Ringstrasse. This latter feature is just a generation old, being nearly contemporary with Haussmann's reshaping of imperial Paris in the 1860s; along it are grouped the great public buildings of the state. Unlike the Napoleonic redevelopments of Paris, these monuments, each in its suitable style—Gothic town hall, classical parliament, Renaissance university—commemorate a brief age of liberal dominance of the state and the levers of power: the *Bürgerministerium* and its successors from 1867 to 1879. The neo-baroque Burgtheater is a temple for cultural pomps and, as C. E. Schorske puts it, 'a meeting-ground for old noble and new bourgeois élites'. Such symbols also recall other liberal 'improvements' of a quite recent past: a state education system secularized and extended, measures for public health, museums, universities, water-supplies, railways, expansion of industry, partial enfranchisement of the Jews. But the momentum inspiring these changes is now over: the liberals' power base in banking, trade, and industry has been overshadowed by an immensely more dynamic German neighbour, and sapped by economic depression (see above, p. 230); their politicians face an indifferent, at times a hostile old Establishment; and they lose electoral support and power for reasons peculiarly Austrian.

Crucial to the defeat of Austrian liberalism has been the fact that it cannot harness an ideal of nationhood to the appeal of 'progress'. In Vienna, unlike other capital cities, 'nation' is not a rallying cry but a disruptive slogan—it spells Hungarian independence, Czech separatism, the dissolution of an ancient empire which also includes Rumanians, Poles, Slovaks, Slovenes, Croats, Serbs, Italians. Moreover it calls to mind the newly (1871) united Germany, to which many of the emperor's German subjects in Bohemia and Austria are greatly attracted. Liberal leadership in Vienna is actually undone by the clash of nationalisms; by the creation of popular movements—Czech and pro-German nationalists, added to an anti-liberal, Catholic Social movement, and a small but growing Social Democratic Party. This fragmentation not only causes the eclipse of liberalism, it brings about the collapse of the Austrian parliament and the crippling of government, disrupted by violence from Czech and German nationalists. The latter introduce strong-arm gang tactics and intimidation, not only into the streets but also into the legislative chamber; antagonisms reach such a pitch that the president of the lower house is physically assaulted, besieged in his office. Parliamentary majorities cannot be found. For several years at the turn of the century the emperor rules by decree; and after that his introduction of universal suffrage produces electoral stalemates as intractable as before. The empire faces constitutional impasse, uncontrollable tensions. Incapable of joining the colonial race, it does the next best thing in annexing Bosnia in 1908; but instead of proving a distraction, this serves only to increase anxiety at the sight of a sabre-rattling foreign policy.

These are not the only sources of worry and dismay to men of goodwill and liberal sentiment. The new Christian Social movement is a populist coalition of small landowners, 'tailors and greengrocers', and minor public servants under a plausible demagogue, Karl Lueger; it is anti-big-business, anti-Prussian, and anti-Semitic. In this last feature, it shares the honours with the more violent German nationalists in making a pitch for popular support—racialism being an easy enough appeal in a city where a tenth of the population are Jews, many of them recent immigrants from backward Galicia. Against the opposition of the emperor

and the Catholic bishops (but without condemnation from Rome) Lueger's party captures control of the city council, and Lueger is installed as mayor (1897); anti-Semitism is promoted to a feature of political life. To be sure, it is only one of a number of ethnic frictions, but it is marked by peculiarly odious violence and irrationalism. It is not surprising that Vienna is the birthplace of Zionism: the brilliant young journalist of the city's *Neue Freie Presse*, Theodor Herzl, covering the Dreyfus trial in France, is so concerned by the tide of hostility, all too familiar, that he writes *Der Judenstaat* (*The Jewish State*, 1898): a first step only towards a future Israel, but a reminder of Austrian tensions in 1900. And while we are about it, we might recall that in 1906 a young provincial drop-out, under the name of Adolf Hitler, comes to Vienna and in its suburbs learns from nationalist propaganda and Jew-baiting some of the lessons he needs for the future.

La Belle Époque? Life goes on in Vienna, with or without a parliament; the imperial regime is studiously benign and the Emperor Franz Josef deeply respected as a symbol. (But he is very old—what happens when he dies?) Below the surface, even beneath the threshold of attention, there are premonitions of the eventual dissolution of his empire. Foreign newspapers speculate freely on it. Moreover, even the most unpolitical person must be aware of the impasse of a society so unable to solve any of its major problems: nationalists, separatists, patriots, liberals, conservatives, democrats, Social Catholics, socialists, all at odds, government largely paralysed. With the old liberal faith in reason and progress to all intents and purposes stultified, what remains? Men of the highest distinction duck the question. Plener, the liberal ex-leader, displays a loyal sense of duty to stick it out honourably, helping with advice when asked; the sharp-eyed journalist Karl Kraus plies a restless *feuilleton* in the cause of uncomfortable truths, humane to the last—and beyond . . . The goodwill of honourable men is not enough, though.

Disillusion

One important key to central European avant-garde expressive arts lies not in political but in social revolt: revolt against what Stefan Zweig calls 'the steady bourgeois world'. Not just any bourgeois world: specifically that of central European middle strata which have grown up in a political society—Hohenzollern and Hapsburg—where the state still reflects an age-old pattern of 'estates of the realm'—nobility, bourgeois, farmer—a *Ständestaat* (state of the social orders), which has been largely dismantled but not lost sight of even so, and in which there is peculiar virtue in living one's life *in the right and proper way*. Not quite the Victorian cascade of cultural imitation, therefore, but proper deference and, inevitably, complacency; showing proper behaviour at weddings and funerals, reading the *right* newspaper, wearing the *right* clothes, appreciating the *right* masterpieces, living at the *right* address, acting out one's role in conformable ways; all this has an immeasurably deeper importance than individual self-realization. There are similarities, here, with Victorian suburbia, but profound differences also. It catches the eye that around 1900 a number of German and Austrian writers—Thomas Mann, Heinrich Mann, Wedekind, Musil—each in his own way depicts the experience of schooling as a brutal clash between adolescent sensitivity and the peremptory demands of an institution. Adolescence, not education, is the awakening: nature, not nurture. The school is a microcosm of society; in his novel *Buddenbrooks* Thomas Mann even calls it 'a state within a state': a system existing for its own sake, therefore, one which can bruise or crush the sensitive prisoner with total indifference, and not in any sense a liberating experience. The Brontës and Thackeray too, not to mention Dickens, have had harsh things to say about schooling, but have not made it the image of a tyrannical society. And after school, the adult world is waiting with a similar lesson: an oppressive pattern of conformities, firmly wedged within what remains of the *Ständestaat*. The bureaucrat, the army officer, the lawyer, doctor, professor, and so on down the list, have their allotted parts to play, their titles, grades, and so on, plainly set out. Within these constraints, paradoxically, the middle classes yet believe themselves to be defenders of individualism. They even expect to be reminded of the fact in the arts and literatures to which they piously devote a proportion of their attention (*Bildung*, culture, being a sphere of peculiarly individual responsibility, perhaps also a consolation).

How then in this society should the artist prove his worth by being *original*, individual, creative? What happens if he sets out to seek, for example, 'the truth', as in the matter of adolescent feeling, and finds it different from the stereotypes current around him? That is what Friedrich Nietzsche has actually done. Insisting on a new slant for 'truth', and beginning with the self and its impulses, he is driven to repudiate the attitudes and well-graded satisfactions of the German bourgeoisie, the 'culture-philistines' (*Unzeitgemässe Betrachtungen—Thoughts out of Season*—1873–76). The contrast with Matthew Arnold, who in *Culture and Anarchy* (1869) also points an accusing finger at middle-class 'Philistines', is very striking. Arnold mourns in his poem

177   Edvard Munch (1863–1944), *August Strindberg,* **1895. Oil on canvas, 47¼ × 35⅜ in (120 × 90 cm). Stockholm, Nationalmuseum**

The Norwegian forerunner of Expressionism portrays with sympathy the cosmopolitan writer Strindberg, whose plays are destined to evolve from what literary historians call 'naturalism' into something very much more akin to the (later) Expressionist theatre.

'Dover Beach' over the 'darkling plain . . . Where ignorant armies clash by night'. Nietzsche is more ferocious: a 'transvaluation of all values', he proclaims, ending in denunciation of German culture *en bloc*, a *Götzendämmerung* (*Twilight of the Idols*) in the very decades when a new and powerful German Reich embraces and endows its middle classes (on its own authoritarian terms, of course) as never before.

This clash, triggered off in Germany, is central. It has been prefigured by Ibsen; is already clear in the Swedish writer August Strindberg, and in the artistic evolution of the Norwegian Edvard Munch. In Germany it becomes deafening, and in Austria hardly less so. Experimental artists seek a new 'humanism', that of man in his nakedness, the *Awakening of Spring*, or the agony of death; and to proclaim it they flay the stereotypes of right-thinking society almost as vehemently as Nietzsche has done.

And that is in fact the message of those artists who, around 1892, 'secede' from academism in Munich, to open their doors to all that is new in France and Germany; and then again the message of a similar coming-together of Austrian 'Secession' artists several years later. Fastening especially on the forms of Art Nouveau (*Jugendstil*), they fuse them in a programme—Naked Truth—which would look gauche and curious in Paris or London, but has a powerful impact in Vienna. Why *Art Nouveau*? Perhaps because a style which seeks renewal in decorative idioms can be peculiarly suitable for breaking away from the enormous weight of academic tradition, 'grocers' art' (see p. 222). Gustav Klimt, having gratified 'bourgeois' taste with some neo-classical murals at the Burgtheater, sets out in his next commissioned work (1900) to tell 'the truth' in the university, citadel of respectability. Three large compositions represent philosophy, medicine, and law: three faculties, three central ideals of a comfortable and self-regarding liberal culture. But what a commemoration! For philosophy, Klimt sketches a vast and empty space and suspends in it a mute and shadowy sphinx, a swirl of drifting ghosts . . . Medicine? a pillar of dissolving, intertwining, maimed, obscure, or dying forms streaming up behind a priestly hieratic figure of cold indifference . . . Law? in a nameless nether region a misshapen, naked, bowed, humiliated prisoner in the toils of an octopus-like shape, under the eye of the Furies, while Justice and Truth, tiny figures far away on another plane, turn their eyes elsewhere. Allegories indeed, they carry messages of denunciation as intense as any Nietzschean outburst. Even in tolerant Vienna, such messages produce a storm of protest. But the great optimistic liberal aspirations are quite flaccid and unexciting. Why not reveal the vacuity that remains, the illusoriness, and the uncontrolled, and ferociously inhumane, forces that confront man's intuition of the real world? Such forces have not the pleasantly familiar and well-tamed shapes handed down by the art school: they call for new forms—forms to delineate the present. They may not be alluring, and are certainly not modest or comforting, but they are 'truthful' and therefore release the artist from the worst of his bondage.

With Oskar Kokoschka, a young Viennese who (exceptionally) is a graduate of the workshop and not of middle-class family background, art begins at the point to which the Secession movement brings it: readiness to

178   Josef Maria Olbrich (1867–1908), poster for the Second Secession Exhibition, 1898. Vienna, Graphische Sammlung Albertina

For their 1898 exhibition, the Austrian 'Secession' artists produce a poster featuring the edifice purpose-built to house displays of the Viennese movement, bearing on it the portentous statement 'To the Age, its Art: to Art, its Freedom', and on the wall the title of their avant-garde periodical, Ver Sacrum (Holy Spring).

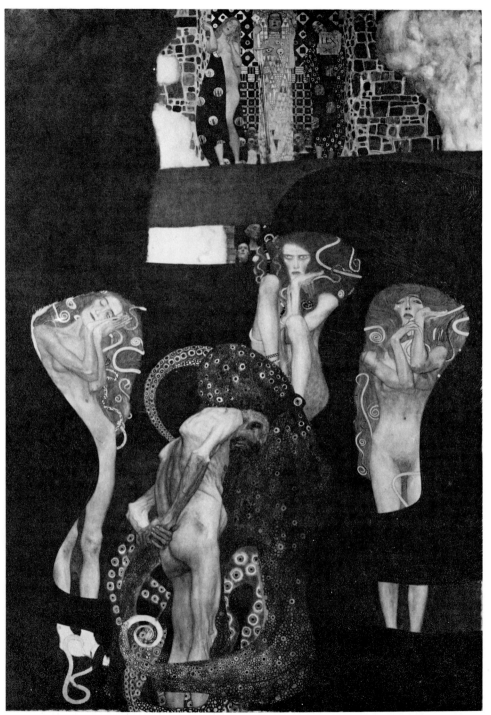

179   Gustav Klimt (1862–1918), decoration for the University of Vienna's Great Hall: *Jurisprudence* **(destroyed), 1903. Oil on canvas, 192⅞ × 118⅛ in (430 × 300 cm).**

Heroic painting, and painting on the heroic scale, offer insuperable difficulties for modern art (and for that matter, poetry too): at least for so long as academic tradition stands close behind. It remains possible to fracture space, however; and Klimt's huge allegory, without explicitly evoking Hell, is assembled in a decorative manner uniquely upsetting to his staid university clients. No doubt they would have preferred something more in the vein of Raphael (compare plate 69).

180 (right)   Josef Hoffmann (1870–1956), 'Hoffmann's Room'— interior for the School of Decorative Art in Vienna, shown at the Paris World Exhibition, 1900

'Hoffmann's Room', designed by the architect for the Vienna School of Decorative Art, is a kind of boudoir painted by Gustav Klimt in magisterially Art Nouveau idiom—an undulating decorative style, austere and precious together, and nicely suited to the mannerist proportions of the room.

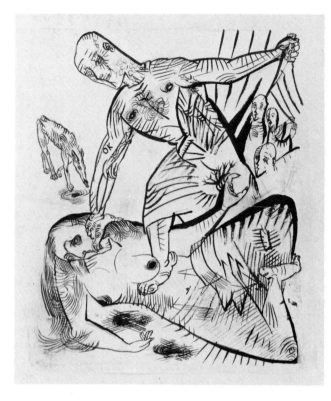

181 Oskar Kokoschka (1886–1980), Illustration for
Mörder, Hoffnung der Frauen, c. **1908. Pen and ink,**
8½ × 6⅞ in (21.6 × 17.5 cm). Stuttgart, Staatsgalerie

Kokoschka's abrasive little drama is supplied by its author with
an illustration of surprising ferocity, both primitive and
sophisticated. He has not forgotten to include a fascinated (but
presumably shocked) opera-box group and an animal-figure at its
watering-hole: a piece of artful symmetry?

shock, the inventive use of line, the resources of Art
Nouveau, and a false (or even mocking, satirical) naïve-
ty. And in his very first work, *Die träumenden Knaben*,
(*The Dreaming Boys*, 1908), an illustrated poem, we are
into something half-way between a horrific Struw-
welpeter children's book and a quite sadistic strip-
cartoon; acidulated, brilliant, outrageous. Moving to
Berlin, where he falls in with the dissident group
around the magazine *Der Sturm* (*Storm*), his next offering is an even more disconcerting mini-play, *Mörder,
Hoffnung der Frauen* (*Assassin, Hope of Women*, 1910)—a
nasty little business of sadism, sexual provocation, and
stabbing, with Greek choruses in attendance, 'cruelty
on cruelty, wheels turning in the void . . .' From that
point, Kokoschka is in the stream of 'Expressionism'.

Expressionism

This extremely loose designation is applied first to
artists (at any rate) who group themselves in *die Brücke*
(the Bridge) around Ernst Ludwig Kirchner and a few
friends in Dresden in 1905. What is being 'bridged'?
Frontiers and generations, to begin with. We find there
the Norwegian Munch, the Belgian Ensor, the Swiss
Hodler; but also sympathy for earlier styles and experiments elsewhere—Symbolism, Van Gogh, Art
Nouveau, Gauguin; in due course for Fauvism and
Cubism also. But such eclecticism misses the essential,
if there is such a thing, in Expressionism, which is its
mood of protest. Protest against what? Not anything so
easily defined as a political regime (though Kurt Pinthus later bids us not to forget the German Reich and its
'megalomaniac Kaiser' with his 'terrifying metal hel-
met and bristling moustache', and the reigning 'scorn
for and suppression of all critical spirit' . . . 'only he
who has known this empire of William the Charlatan
can understand . . . the exultant cry, the destructive
nihilism ,the messianic aspiration and the universal ecstatic love which marks expressionism; only thus can
one understand the presence and union of such opposed
styles'). Rather it is a protest against the way *things are.*
Across nearly the whole of its range, whether in painting, in poetry, or, presently, in drama, we confront in
Expressionism a passionate note that defies easy classification. Personal anguish, obsessional neuroses undoubtedly; but the anguish seems to stretch out to
cosmic and terrible dimensions, and the protest
embraces every kind of human predicament—relations
between the sexes, oppression, threats of violence,
humiliation—a universal denunciation of all things
morbidly smug and sterile. Nature, seen through new
eyes, becomes hostile, violent: Nolde indulges in the
most thorough 'desacralization' of it. Kirchner rehabili-
tates the woodcut, to carry forward a sixteenth-century
tradition in its starkest, most jagged, and shocking
forms . . . And always, alongside this protest, the
anguish of difficulty, of an empty universe which no
amount of inner self-exploration will restructure.

Slightly different is the character of a second small
group movement, *Der Blaue Reiter* the (*Blue Rider*),
formed by Franz Marc and Wassily Kandinsky, in Berlin from 1911. No less a revolt, and no less cosmopolitan, it takes in Secession painters, Cubists, some of *die
Brücke* . . . and most importantly, it frames Marc's own
anti-naturalist dream images and Kandinsky's path-
breaking *abstract* expressionism.

Theatre in Germany and Austria comes late to Expressionism; but already in Vienna in 1905 Karl Kraus

presents a private performance of a highly original play, *Pandora's Box* by Franz Wedekind, with Wedekind himself acting the rather central role of Jack the Ripper. It is a kind of 'Carmen among the rich', but different in this respect, that it is less easy to shrug off the moral deviance of Wedekind's characters than it is of cigarette-factory girls and common soldiers. This first version of what eventually becomes Alban Berg's opera *Lulu* (Berg and his teacher Arnold Schönberg attend the performance) is too subversive of morality to pass the censor, or even find a publisher for the time being; but it heralds a trend of a rather particular kind—one in which 'naturalism' shades off into the macabre, even the grotesque, the shocking, Grand Guignol, which will recur in expressionist drama (and cinema) as a potent arm in 'revolt' against middle-class morality. And is there not even a son of one of the crowned heads of Europe to whom rumour attaches a Jack-the-Ripperish association? . . .

Curiously, the most revolutionary intrusion of Expressionism comes not on the acting stage, yet, but through music; and in the work of Schönberg. Less well known than the early *Gurrelieder*, or *Erwartung*, or the symbolistic *Pierrot Lunaire*, his peculiar composition *Die Glückliche Hand* (*The Lucky Hand*, 1908–13) takes the form of a semi-operatic charade for baritone, mimes, a kind of Greek chorus (again!), and a very large orchestra. At one leap it epitomizes much of what we associate with Expressionism: half-articulated protest, embarrassing crudity, abrasive offence to decorum, 'all-too-human' truths. Beginning with its compressed and disconcerting stage business, which goes somewhat as follows: a central figure, personifying the Artist, appears on the scene bleeding, in rags, exhausted, haunted by his dream, a chimera. The chorus exhorts him to pull himself together, and a vulgar noisy orchestral passage heralds the arrival of Woman, who hands him a chalice, receives his adoration. Almost at once appears a wealthy Suitor, who seduces her; remorseful, she implores the Artist's pardon, and the scene ends with his ecstatic cry that he 'possesses her for ever'. In the next scene we see him arrive at a workmen's grotto and forge; with his 'lucky left hand' he creates a precious diadem and throws it scornfully to the (hostile) artisans; after which gesture a musical climax of prodigious volume (wind, tempest) effects the transition to a final, pathetic, tableau. Here, Woman's robe is found to be missing a large patch; Suitor throws the patch to Artist, who attempts to climb to a second grotto on stage and restore it to her. Woman, however, disdains his grovelling offer, pushes a chimera-shaped rock at him, and with a final choral comment and

182   Edvard Munch, *The Kiss*, 1895. Drypoint and aquatint, 13½ × 11 in (34.3 × 27.8 cm). Vienna, Albertina

The lovers' passionate embrace is framed by dark curtains and backed by a prison-like wall seen through the window. Is this then the typical setting for a 'Spring Awakening'? Are raptures merely pathetic? Compare plate 173.

orchestral storm, the curtains close on his ultimate discomfiture.

The Lucky Hand attracts our attention not so much as a masterpiece of the musical stage, which it is not (for that we must wait for Berg's *Wozzeck* and *Lulu*, and Schönberg's own *Moses and Aaron*), but rather as an early synthesis of half-a-dozen 'Expressionisms'. This grotesque, angular, crude, *brief* action: what more violent rejection of the comfortable 'realism' which presides over the lengthier operatic rites of *Bohème* or *Meistersinger*? Then in the music itself: while there are echoes of *Tristan* and *Siegfried*, and clamours and climaxes reminiscent of both Wagner and Mahler, Schönberg has left tonality quite behind; as he is writing, he is also inventing a twelve-tone system which is a

183 Oskar Kokoschka, *Portrait of Arnold Schönberg*, 1924. Oil on canvas, 37¾ × 29⅛ in (96 × 74 cm). Private collection

An 'expressive' portrait of the most controversial composer of the 1900s by his almost equally controversial fellow-countryman. Academic convention and the pretentious values it enshrines have no place in this encounter; Kokoschka is creating his own means to replace both.

finally, when it comes to staging, in Berlin in 1913 Schönberg, who has established close ties in the *Blue Rider* movement (he is also a not uninteresting expressionist painter), designs the stark sets himself, and has the benefit of discussion on colours and lighting with his friend Kandinsky. (Together they agree on two hundred lighting changes to be woven into the thirty-minute performance.) Not only are composer and artist convinced that sight and sound can fuse here in a 'total' work of art, but they agree on the reason for this: Schönberg's music is, at last, an absolutely 'direct' expression of the 'subjective'—this goes for colour too—without reference to any 'external reality' (that is, any conventionally appreciated one).

Forms of alienation

The striking examples of artistic disaffection that we have been observing, and particularly the last, show the particularly aggressive artistic trends in central Europe around 1900. But they are only the culmination of a much wider phenomenon, unprecedented: that of self-accredited specialists in the creative arts beginning to detach themselves radically from the service of what one might call mainstream culture. The phenomenon is too large and varied and nuanced to be described here in all its aspects; but it is so peculiar, and so insistent, that we can hardly disregard it or take it for granted. Some of its general features might be set out in the following way.

1   The size of the world of all the arts has multiplied along with other dimensions of culture in the nineteenth century: both as a market (for reading-matter for leisure or improvement, for domestic decoration, for public monuments, for social rituals, for concerts and music in the home, for art collections, etc.) and in terms of the population of producers. One result of the latter is the proliferation of little circles or chapels of mutually supportive writers or artists in large cities; this begins even before 1800, and an artistic free-state 'Bohemia' is a myth in Paris by 1840. In these self-selecting environments creative spirits come to produce almost primarily with an eye to the critical appraisal of their fellows.

2   While an artistic vocation is not yet as highly institutionalized as it is later to be (nor as commercialized), 'art for art's sake' becomes in one form or another a self-conscious stance; it is fortified by large amounts of writing on aesthetics (in Germany), of 'criticism' (an almost new literary genre at the service of magazine

radical break with accepted musical languages. Also, the singing voice explores his new 'speaking-song', reminding us of *Pierrot Lunaire*, that other allegory of the alienated artist. For both, dream is the 'real' world; but the dreams can take strange shapes—chimeras—and Schubert's melodious comforts, even in the developments that we find in Mahler's songs or in Richard Strauss's or Schönberg's own early vocal music (all remarkably close in idiom) have simply no place in evoking the new disconcerting immediacy. Then again, the whole work is totally, puerilely, ego-centred: only the Artist sings, the other figures mime—truth is what *I* feel; *my* anguish, *my* frustrations. And

readers everywhere), and manifestos by innovative groups themselves (this reaches a climax by 1900). Art claims its own 'autonomy', more and more emphatically.

3   Pressure to innovate marks the very concept of art from the outset of this expansion; it is inseparable from a (liberal) ideal of individual self-fulfilment, and also to some extent merges with a consumer expectation of something (slightly) new all the time. The emphasis of novelty may fall on forms, on the creator's personal feeling and testimony, or on relations with an audience, these things being not fully separable: an artist may be being an 'uncrowned legislator', or denouncing wrongs, or locked in his ivory tower, or wearing a dandy's costume, or 'shocking the bourgeois' (who buys it half the time), or shaking his fist at heaven, or slyly rediscovering the earthy realities of peasant life . . . Is he a professional (like the doctor)? A supplier (like the pharmacist)? Or a dilettante or a visionary or a tramp or a militant reformer or an anarchist revolutionary? He may be any one of these: there is room for all, and more. Yet all the time his audience remains predominantly a middle-class one whose tastes go to make up (involuntarily—another 'hidden hand') sets of 'right' consensual standards: and whatever role he chooses will derive a part of its meaning from that presence and those standards.

4   The outcome is, overall, a permanent tension: between on the one hand new critically expressive forms being offered (already in the German romantic experiments of the 1800s, the English *Lyrical Ballads*, the French 'romanticism' of literature and painting in the 1820s, the Pre-Raphaelite Brotherhood . . .) and on the other hand the range of expectations of society at large (always lagging, and reliably displayed in many of its public monuments). By the late nineteenth century, around the huge mass of conventional literatures and arts being supplied (much of it of course highly professional) there is a moving fringe of experimental work, of which virtually the only category to attract a large public—and that chiefly by way of scandal—is that of 'naturalist' writers unmasking disagreeable novelties about contemporary society in their plays or novels: Ibsen, Strindberg, Zola, Schnitzler, Wedekind, Shaw, Hauptmann . . . There is usually only a tiny public for the more daring adventures of aestheticism or preciosity, 'symbolist' or 'decadent' writing, the astonishing achievements of Impressionists, Symbolists, Post-Impressionists, 'Nabis', etc. in France, and for the experimental theatre, Expressionism, Cubism,

and so on. Zola's painstaking novel *L'Oeuvre* (*The Work of Art*) is built around the huge discrepancy between a (modern) artist's total commitment to an avant-garde masterpiece that will not be recognized and the impossibility of a tolerable social adjustment. But the theme appears in all manner of forms and disguises: if an all but unknown poet in France, Jules Laforgue, and the little-known composer Arnold Schönberg in Austria, both find the image of Pierrot to be a compulsive symbol of frustrated idealism, of condemned artistic endeavour, they are putting into an 'expressionistic' mode the futility (in a sense) of their decisions to *be* Pierrots. It is their existential 'project'. And *Die Glückliche Hand* is, in its own terms, simply a very condensed and elaborate formulation of the artist's 'cry'.

The unconscious

Into the Vienna of empire and authority, insouciance and *douceur de vivre*, respectability and bourgeois proprieties, but also political unease, nationalism, social stress, and artistic experimental 'revolt' on the margin, history may now be allowed to introduce one of its better ironies.

   Mental disorder has not always been regarded as a form of illness. In antiquity, possession by the god has been a 'natural', if not always a helpful, diagnosis. The diagnosis of the Christian Middle Ages hovers between diabolical possession and a recognition of derangements not obviously perverse. In an age of puritanism, fears of diabolic conspiracy (and a virulent propensity to look for witches) gradually recede, and in an age of Enlightenment attempts begin to be made to look for natural 'causes'. Thereafter, the growth of psychological medicine, just like physics or evolutionary biology, has its own 'paradigm', its conditional logic. (Not least significant among the conditions is the sheer number of mentally disturbed persons who, with the growth of hospital services in the nineteenth century, are brought under professional supervision in institutions.) By the end of the century several generations of medical and biological scientists and 'alienists', mostly centred in hospital clinics, have an archive of case-lore, a vocabulary to discuss it, and a will to explain it; alongside, and in a largely unrelated fashion, philosophers have also opened an annexe, 'the Unconscious', for phenomena which seem to fall outside the accepted processes of mind. E. von Hartmann's *Philosophy of the Unconscious* (1869) is almost a classic, known widely to writers and to the general public. Less well known are the learned published papers of professional alienists; yet Strindberg is 'into' the clinical writings of

184   Edvard Munch, *Chamber of Death*, 1894–5. Casein colours on canvas, 59 × 66 in (150 × 167.5 cm). Oslo, Nasjonalgalleriet

In a corner of the 'Chamber of Death', respectable Ibsen-like figures stand or sit in poses appropriate to the august but invisible event in their midst. A scene evacuated of all meaning, in the conventional sense at least. It is the 'unreality' of just such conventional scenes and poses which has begun to be oppressive – not only in Ibsen's world but in Berlin, London, Paris . . . Vienna – and it is this world of middle-class proprieties that Freud will shortly begin to devastate with 'scientific' candour.

Charcot and Ribot in France, 'into' hysteria and 'neurasthenia', a decade before psycho-analysis even takes shape in Vienna. The subject is 'in the air'.

Sigmund Freud, the intensely ambitious son of a Moravian Jewish family, enters medicine in Vienna because that career, like teaching but unlike the army or the civil service, is open to men of his community. His first interest is in physiology and the nervous system, but attending Charcot's clinic in Paris he encounters the use of hypnosis for hysterical patients; he also hears Charcot remark, 'Sex is always at the bottom of the trouble.' It takes him some time, back in Vienna, to arrive at his own method of free association to gain access to the 'Unconscious' (whatever that may be) of his mental patients, and in the process he antagonizes some colleagues by his invariably searching after sexual causes of disorder; for a time he presumes that all his patients are suppressing memories of childhood rape, until it occurs to him that he himself may be putting such ideas into their heads. In a circle formed in 1902 with like-minded investigators (they include Alfred Adler and Carl Jung from Zürich), there is general agreement that unconscious processes in the mind have little direct relation to society's explicit values and rules, though the participants' opinions differ as to what the processes are. Freud himself is a 'materialist' and would like to show that organic causes shape our actions absolutely and explain mental disorders too; the means to do this escape him, however, and in any case he has a clinical activity within which to apply his other conjectures. So he settles for a less mechanical determinism. By 1900, in his book *The Interpretation of Dreams*, followed in 1901 by the *Psychopathology of Everyday Life*, something clearly identifiable as Freudian psychoanalytical theory is offered to the world.

No human acts, no mental happenings, are on Freud's view accidental or capricious; all are *determined* (his word) ultimately by 'Darwinian' principles: the drive to survive, the drive to procreate. All our recognized cultural values and imperatives and social standards are very fine (and it may be we cannot do without them); but men are animals before they are citizens, and when we look into the child's first experiences we encounter the family unit; it is a biological device, but it is also the source of frightful dangers. Infant desire is bound to develop in ways which are shocking (Freud is insistent on the very broad nature of sexuality); it is therefore repressed, very early, and this gives rise to burdens of 'guilt', to all sorts of mental processes of evasion, and to subsequent disorders of apparent irrationality. All humans are in this predicament, neurosis lurks around the corner for everyone; therapy must take the form of a cathartic process; it cures by making sufferers reconstitute and face the origins of their disorders, even at the cost of outrage to cherished taboos.

It is hardly necessary to underline the very subversive and disruptive potentialities of psycho-analytical theories of the unconscious, especially in Freud's version. His theory claims 'scientific' status, but it is a debunking science. It unmasks hypocrisies, dismisses 'rationalizations', lies in wait to pounce on pudor, respects neither persons nor institutions, makes the emperor into a symbolic dummy father-figure, puts God rather pointedly among what the *Psychopathology* calls 'mythological inventions' of an unquiet fantasy. In Freud's teaching it also invites every man to regard himself as an involuntary Oedipus, and in the most humdrum affairs makes every slip tell a discreditable story. On the surface, our acts and words may have all the meanings we have joined others in agreeing they should have; but now there is another level of reference, deeper, in some sense more decisive, 'natural', a level into which only the therapist can peek and poke and explore, the machine-code level of operations of a by no means integrated actor. In another dozen years, Freud will have supplied his new science with a map, marked out with id, ego, super-ego, libido, and the rest (*Totem and Taboo*, 1913).

Two projects

How much does this kind of theory rely on promptings from contemporary art and literature in Vienna, as well as upon those more obvious sources which have already been partly alluded to (the whole build-up of clinical speculation in France and Vienna, Freud's own clinical practice)? And likewise, in the other direction, how much does Freud's own work feed in by way of encouragement to the expressive symbolisms of the early 1900s?

Disconcertingly, the answer to the first question must be 'not much'; and certainly less than would be expected from the fact that psychoanalysts and the avant-garde artists and musicians are both living in the same city (not even a very big city: Vienna, for all its imperial brilliance, has only one and a half million inhabitants). There are, in effect, two rather dissimilar sets of 'projects' proceeding alongside one another: those of the professional clinicians and those of the intellectuals. Freud, on his side, has everything to gain by pursuing *his* project under the guise of total respectability; he adorns his writing and his leisure with the most solidly bourgeois display of tastes and points of reference: the 'safe' Greek and Latin literatures, Shakespeare, Goethe, Schiller, Roman remains, Renaissance art, tourism in Italy . . . Long hours of clinical sessions and writing up notebooks are framed in an impeccably 'normal' life. Out of the corner of his eye he is very well aware of outside events: Lueger's and others' anti-Semitism, for instance (being a Jew seriously delays his promotion to professor). The writer Arthur Schnitzler has, some time back, reviewed Freud's early, and extremely injudicious, monograph on cocaine (1888); presently Freud returns the compliment by professing surprise at the uncanny insights into human nature in Schnitzler's play *Paracelsus*. But it would be more interesting to know what he thinks of the same writer's *La Ronde* (1895), that jarring study of libido, of Eros dissolving society by its implacable incitements to death. Wedekind's *Awakening of Spring* (already referred to), with its picture of adolescent repression, is also much to his purpose (though published in 1891, it is not performed in public until 1906). In the *Psychopathology*, along with case stories and references to the classics, Freud *adds* an excerpt from Strindberg's *Gothic Rooms* which he reads in 1913;

but there is no other intrusion of contemporary example. Freud reads Karl Kraus's review *Die Fackel* (*The Torch*) and even writes (1906) polite notes to Kraus, from whom he would very much like favourable attention. But that brilliant journalist seems to despise psychoanalysis. That the problems of artists occupy him is certain: apart from Gustav Mahler's approach for a consultation (abortive, however), Freud works on what later becomes a famous case-study ('Gradiva') where artistic creation is touched on. But that is in 1907. Tellingly, it is not Freud but Jung who will become a collector of Expressionist art works. There is no evidence that for Freud the artistic quest for raw soul, for the unalloyed human impulse, distinctively sharpens his understanding of patients and their inhibitions and disabilities, or influences the thrust of his inquiry.

And in the opposite direction? Strindberg, whose plays open up even more agonizing vistas than Ibsen's, and who moreover is an omnivorous reader, has, we know, satisfied his own morbid introspective curiosities by feasting on the repertory of speculation on the Unconscious, dream, hysteria, the enigmas of human motivation, that are coming into sight in the 1880s. That is to say, Strindberg has not had to wait for Freud; and indeed there is no evidence of his ever coming upon Freud's writings at all. This directs our attention to the curious fact that, although *The Interpretation of Dreams* looks to us now a milestone in psychoanalysis, its publication in 1900 goes almost completely unremarked by the public in Austria or abroad; it is dismissed in one or two unflattering reviews, and hardly any copies are sold. Yet what might it not have offered to a Schönberg, or a Kokoschka! 'The phantoms that lurk in depths where no human being before [has] dared to tread'; Oedipus, the pleasure principle, repression, anxiety, dream transformations . . . Tantalizingly, when Schönberg writes his first monodrama, *Erwartung* (*Awaiting*), his librettist is a local poetess, Marie Pappenheim, who happens to be an acquaintance of Dr. Freud; nothing comes of the coincidence. In *Die Glückliche Hand* the chimera is not a Freudian haunting but a symbol of the artist's impossible ambition—by now something approaching a *topos* of avant-garde poetry. Young Kokoschka's shocking early outrages to decorum are similarly innocent of commerce with the subversions of the analyst. Whether Freud is or is not attentive to the eroticism which is a constant feature of Austrian *Jugendstil* (and he appears not to have been), there is no doubt that its practitioners have not had to wait for *him* to fix on a sensitive link in 'bourgeois' morality, any more than Ibsen, or Zola, or Wedekind, or Schnitzler have.

Perverse as it may look, the artist's 'project' is totally distinct from Freud's. Indeed, it is facing in a contrary direction. Freud seeks to push rational explanation down into new depths and discover mechanisms, regularities, causes, determinisms; to be a great scientist (he has already had several false starts). He has the truth, has psychoanalysed himself exhaustively, is reconciled with himself. Artists too are seeking new depths of personal reality, authentic 'humanity', in sensation, impulse, reflex; but they have their own discovery processes, their own fight against stereotypes—a different fight. Sexuality is only one field for demystification of 'bourgeois' prudery; whether it be young Klimt or young Schönberg, there are many other idols (Nietzsche's *Götzen*) to demolish as well. Vienna is, by and large, no more prudish than any other great European capital (it is in Berlin that Strauss's wonderfully self-indulgent *Rosenkavalier* incurs imperial displeasure); its middle classes have their (small) movements for women's emancipation, for combating prostitution, a climate of *moeurs* less ferociously hypocritical than London, less propensity, so far as one can judge, to be furtive about reading Krafft-Ebing's *Psychopathia sexualis* (twelve editions between 1886 and 1903) than Londoners are about even mentioning Havelock Ellis's *Psychology of Sex* (1897–1928). Against a common background, art and therapy go separate ways for the time being.

What then of the characteristic feature of Expressionism already noted, the highlighting of neurosis, or alternatively hysteria, which marks a prevailing style, even the choice of great idols—Strindberg, Van Gogh, Munch? Are we in the presence of a real wave of mental instability passing over Europe, some sort of invisible contagion testified to by artists and especially encouraging to a Freud? There is, I think, a degree of optical illusion here. On the one hand there are some intellectuals, those named, and others, whose original and creative work retains our attention. Some of them are sharing a *fashion*—of the same nature as that which in the wake of *Werther* (1774) makes suicide interesting in some corners of German society, or that which around 1830 makes the pale, consumptive young poet into a specially interesting image, or that which makes literary mysticism (and the Unconscious) modish in Paris around 1890. Such images and fashions can sometimes be quite tenacious; but they are also apt to be very localized. Gauguin's retreat from Paris, or indeed Van Gogh's tortured canvasses, arouse no special reverberations in France in 1891. And the Expressionist pose or posture for which these things acquire great significance in 1905 has almost no hold, even no meaning—

185   Otto Wagner, Post Office Savings Bank, Vienna, 1904–6

The novelty of Otto Wagner's Post Office Savings Bank is in its unprecedented simplicity and extremely careful use of untraditional materials (in this modern photograph some features – e.g., the furniture, the loudspeaker on the wall – are clearly not part of Wagner's original conception). Today we accept it without difficulty as a 'functional' place of business. At the outset though it shocks many, even if it cannot be faulted on technical grounds (the lighting is helpful, the heating works . . .).

or at least a very different one—in Paris, in Rome, in London. That is no evidence of there being fewer neurotic or anguished persons in those cities than in Vienna or Dresden or Berlin (something we simply do not know). Nor is it relevant whether in one city or another, Vienna or Berlin, mental instability is the object of more (or of less) general public attention or sympathy or reprobation. It is simply that artistic testimonies of a highly confrontational nature characterize the central European scene (both Vienna and Berlin) and not elsewhere. In Paris, Debussy can be nearly as revolutionary as young Schönberg (and far more so than Mahler) without screaming or throwing fits at all; Matisse, even if called a '*fauve*', can convey a wonderful serenity; van Dongen, a Dutch *fauve* who gravitates to Paris, can be as much as Debussy the darling of a 'high society'; and none of these is taking up a tragic, 'cosmic' pose . . .

Two separate kinds of project, then, unfold in Vienna; and it would be as frivolous to suggest that their conjuncture defines the city's culture or determines its future as it is to suppose that Freud on his own is a symptom of bourgeois decay or Schönberg a symptom of musical collapse. Each project is decidedly eccentric (in the strict sense of the word), and what we can reasonably ascribe to each is its small contribution to an enormously involved scene of shifting strains and values experienced by quite small and rather marginal groups. The background of exasperation with no longer imposing official sterotypes, contempt for outworn symbolisms, conflicts of ideals between an old official order and newer groups (ethnic frictions, nationalisms under Hapsburg rule, even working-class socialists, including a few Marxists), this background is shared: it *suits* the artist's self-imposed retreat from public complicities, whether into aestheticism or into anguish; it is also an inescapable background to Freud's career. It is as natural that Schönberg should take the step of inventing an absolutely new language of the twelve tones of music in the name of a superior inner truthfulness, as it is that Kandinsky should proceed (in Germany) to an absolutely new visual language of what the English poet Hopkins is already calling 'inscape'. And equally natural that Sigmund Freud should embark on that massive subversion of a complacent society—but in the name of science.

Modernism

In a banal sense, anything new is modern. Mahler's symphonies are modern—at any rate more so than those of Brahms. But in another sense, which would absolutely exclude Mahler, Modernism (like Expressionism) has a narrower connotation; interestingly this comes to us first from the hand of the architect. Otto Wagner, publishing *Modern Architecture* (1895), is an inaugurator: not in a technical sense, for iron-frame buildings and non-traditional structures have been making their way for several decades; not even in a stylistic sense, for in America Louis H. Sullivan has already in the 1880s introduced the steel-frame office block, of which no examples exist at that time in Europe; but in an ideological sense, in calling for a new

186   Pablo Picasso (1881–1973), *Les Demoiselles d'Avignon*, 1907. Oil on canvas, 96 × 92 in (243.8 × 233.6 cm). New York, Museum of Modern Art, Lillie P. Bliss Collection
Out of the profusion of movements and styles and schools that mark the amiable Parisian world of art, Picasso's Demoiselles d'Avignon *is one landmark at least in the fanning-out of European modernisms. Nothing here is 'expressionistic', everything is reduction, construction; down to the two masks (right) introduced from African carving. See p. 256.*

truthfulness in the application of modern materials to modern tasks—railways, factories—this time in a spirit of 'tough' functionalism. 'Truthfulness' again! And again linked to revolution in the techniques of an art. No more grocers' ornamentation and fussiness: if at the start Wagner accommodates *Jugendstil* ceramics and metalwork to the allegedly functional needs of low-cost housing, he really does exhibit modernity in his design for the Viennese Postal Savings Bank (1904–06), which is not only free from clutter, but lacks even that minimum of ornamentation which Sullivan has wished to preserve. By the time another architect, Adolf Loos, has handed on the fruits of his own experience in the United States, denouncing not only echoes of historical styles but also all forms of architectural ornament whatever (so much for the symbolic edifices on the Ringstrasse, the baroque Hofburg . . .), building structures can begin to be seen in terms of pure geometry,

187   Marcel Duchamp (1887–1968), *Nude Descending a Staircase No. 2*, 1912. Oil on canvas, 58 × 35 in (147.3 × 88.9 cm). Philadelphia, Museum of Art, Louise and Walter Arensberg Collection

Duchamp, a migrant from France to America, experiments on the fringes of half-a-dozen 'isms' when he evolves this study—in its day notorious—with its synthetic view of what the title invites us to see as bodily movement down a spiral stair.

abstraction in question is manifest in Loos's resounding essay *Ornament and Crime* (1908) and in his first Viennese commission, for a large department store, in 1910; it is also to be seen in Germany in P. Behrens's factory buildings (from 1908), and Walter Gropius's steel and glass Fagus factory (1911). And if modernism is at its most conspicuous in large buildings, it is at the same moment making a sensational appearance elsewhere, under a different guise, in the pure arts. In 1909 in France, Picasso and Braque present a radical novelty—Cubism. Three years later they 'abstract' still further from the idea of a pictorial art by sticking on the canvas, along with the paint, bits of other materials—collages. And in the same years (1910–13) in Germany, Kandinsky makes his way forward to a fully 'abstract' Expressionist painting idiom.

In case one were to be tempted today to underrate the force of this wave of innovations, it is instructive to glance at a book which in 1908, the year of Loos's essay, receives in Germany a good deal of attention: *Abstraktion und Einfühlung* (*Abstraction and Empathy*) by the German aesthetician Wilhelm Worringer. Worringer is anything but a grocer's art historian; yet his argument makes curious reading. Of the two principles announced in his title, empathy ('feeling one's way into' representational art) is claimed to be typical of advanced, confident, well-rounded cultures, where men are not afraid to open their minds to the attractions of subtlety and a range of variety in artists' insights and allusions; abstraction, on the contrary, is typical of primitive and backward cultures, at a low level of sophistication—that low evolutionary stage at which art is presumed to begin. Primitive man, according to Worringer, is fearful, 'life-denying'; he cannot control the world, *therefore* he traces rigid, geometrical forms, and finds in them shelter and relief from 'the great inner unrest inspired in man by the phenomena of the outside world'. Also, seeking to represent nothing, he observes nothing. In a word, abstraction is defensive, anti-life, *primitive*. There is no doubt whatever that Worringer is in a peculiar manner aligning his theory with some rather gross prejudices of public opinion, in this decade of noisily aggressive expansion of the German Reich in colonial Africa. It is not only a Karl Peters, the ruthless boss of German South West Africa, who has difficulty in seeing colonial populations as anything but backward, not yet 'evolved', peoples. Worringer himself suggests in a foreword, 'I was the medium of the necessities of the period. The compass of my instinct had pointed in a direction inexorably pre-ordained by the dictates of the spirit of the age.' In other words, African carvings or masks, and modern artists attracted by

announcing in their volumes and surfaces the functional requirements for which they have been commissioned. They are no longer echoes of something else out of the past, emerging from a welter of tradition and reminiscence. Something modern has been *abstracted*. The

188 Wassily Kandinsky (1866–1944), *Improvisation 'Deluge',* **1913. Oil on canvas, 37½ × 59 in (95 × 150 cm). Munich, Städtische Galerie im Lenbachhaus**

By the time of his association with the Blue Rider group, Kandinsky is arriving at a repertory of entirely abstract ways of expression in painting; this Improvisation *exhibits one of his lines of advance.*

abstract forms, are both equally 'primitive', inferior. Worringer's thesis illustrates something of the feeling with which modernism of the abstract sort will be— indeed *is*—received by many. (Of course his argument can be stood on its head: say simply that 'primitive' can mean life-*affirming*, and abstraction need then encounter no ideological hindrance.)

Architecture is the sphere in which the instrumental values of economic society intersect with its expressive symbolisms; and therefore 'modern' architecture will be most readily accepted in an industrial scene where 'function' is expected to dominate. Acceptance is more gradual elsewhere. If the expert eye detects that the architect's design and use of materials are rational, even sophisticated, the general public is still liable to see its simplicities as a mark of regression, or brutality, or indecency. In the 'pure' arts, functional purpose is not available as an excuse or saving grace; here abstraction from the expected shapes and representations is purely gratuitous, and what its creator is aiming to do in the name of truthfulness (or in the case of Cubism, real invention) is turned around by a large proportion of the public and seen instead as primitive! In the whole scatter of impulses for renewal and innovation briefly surveyed here, from Nietzsche to the collage, it is true that there is invariably something 'primal'—whether in feeling or form or function—whatever may be the case regarding 'primitive'; and it is always challenging, disturbing. That is to say, virtually all the most innovative

art in the 1900s, as distinct from the humdrum ceremonial rehearsal of safe symbolisms, is in one sense or another revolutionary, disquieting; and this is not the least interesting feature of *la Belle Époque*—even in the most gracious of its pre-war settings, imperial Vienna.

Memorial of an age

It would be wrong to home in on the revolt of selected intellectuals and the experiments of a very few creative minds and offer these, and only these, as the ultimate expression of *la Belle Époque*: wrong, because misleadingly narrow. There are other ways in which we can see Vienna in a more balanced perspective as part of a European context on the eve of the Great War. One of these is to take note of the musical scene—not simply through the work of Mahler and Schönberg, but in a much wider array of masterpieces.

The 1890s and 1900s offer in their music a spectacle that has not been equalled at any time known to history for its brilliance and lavishness. Whether because music is by its nature an art of public performance, akin to ritual, or for whatever other reason, it seems at this period to typify an age as nothing else does. Not all music-lovers are equally devoted to it, just as not everyone sees in the Baroque the most congenial climate of European art. Yet it is futile to dismiss Rubens, and it would be equally futile to turn one's back on the music of imperial Europe. The first and obvious point is that this music is large—imperial sized. The symphonies of Bruckner, and then those of Mahler, are grandiose, and they cannot be this without being long, sometimes gigantic. The same is true of those of Saint-Saëns, of Elgar: the limits of form recognized by a Brahms or a Dvořák have simply been pushed aside, impatiently.

The orchestra, too, has reached an unprecedented size, and with it the resources of scoring: we have only to think of a Rimsky-Korsakov, of Mahler, of the young Stravinsky, of Debussy and the more melli-fluous Ravel, of Richard Strauss in his tone poems and operas. It is impossible not to see the great impresario Diaghileff as in some sense a focal point in these tremendous mobilizations: offering to élite audiences a series of unprecedented ballet spectaculars, drawing on Ravel for *Daphnis and Chloe*, on Stravinsky for *The Firebird* and the sensational and scandalous (because primitive) *Rite of Spring*, each with equally un-precedented orchestration.

Undoubtedly societies are rich—they can afford the enlargement of the (relatively low-paid) orchestral force, the musical extravaganzas. At a much later date (1932) Schönberg, who is no mean exploiter of sheer orchestral virtuosity, will write his long-delayed *Moses and Aaron*, which really belongs to *la Belle Époque*: its performance in modern times raises real economic problems . . . But given that the resources are there, it

remains that the achievements are colossal. *Is* music in any way a faithful image of the world as pre-war society feels it *should* be? The world of *Ein Heldenleben* and *Rosenkavalier*, of Mahler's Eighth Symphony and *Song of the Earth*, of Stravinsky's *Petroushka* (another Pier-rot!), of Debussy's *La Mer*? If so, it tells a story of misgivings, undoubtedly, but also of extraordinary beauties and adventures; of strident protest and gloom, but also of overflowing *joie de vivre*; of individual de-spair, but also of collective raptures. And perhaps its epitaph is Elgar's Second Symphony (dedicated to the memory of that very *Belle Époque* monarch Edward VII, but gathering up a much broader feeling for the age that collapses in 1918): with its moments of empty horror, but also its noble, even stoic, elegiac gran-deur—the nostalgic funeral oration over a great, if vanished, world. That at least is one testimony to set alongside others which we have encountered.

189   Peter Behrens (1868–1940), AEG Turbine Factory, Berlin, 1908

A factory is liable not to be brought within the range of traditional expectations in 'architecture'. Hence the scope for function and form to come together in a work of modern integrity, as in Behrens's forthright AEG building—one of a number of pioneering structures built in the years immediately preceding the Great War.

Chapter 9
A Crisis of Modernity

The Great War of 1914–18 brings about the collapse of three empires (German, Austo-Hungarian, Russian), a Bolshevik revolution, the death of millions in the trenches of northern France and on the battlefields of eastern Europe and Italy, and after that by famine and diseases, and cultural earthquakes across the whole continent. The decades that follow exhibit a most complex mixture of 'back to normal' and 'brave new world' trends; attempts not to notice irreversible changes and attempts to carry those changes much further; new states and independent nations, but also collapsing old ones (Italy, Turkey, Spain); dreams of an international order for peace, but also fresh outbreaks of national aggressiveness on half a dozen frontiers. These last are a great deal more marked than the lofty debates of a new League of Nations at Geneva; they arise in states whose governments press for some sort of reward for their victory, or in states which feel balked of their victory, or in states which have 'lost'. The years between the two world wars are overtly 'politicized' because of tensions between the states, because of the mobilization of peoples by mass media and propaganda, because of nationalism and internationalism, because of the huge and uncontrollable fluctuations of destruction, recovery, then economic disaster (depression in 1929–33), and because, overall, these are not years of general expansion. Their close is darkened by the shadow of approaching war, which few doubt will soon be upon them. As indeed it is. A second catastrophe then puts an end to any surviving belief in the world supremacy of Europe.

Apart from two waves of overwhelming destruction, do these twenty years mark any notable additions to the experience of European culture? The answer seems to be yes: two notable additions. One is the introduction of a spirit of democracy to a mass society; the other is its spectacular overthrow. And both are best seen by stationing ourselves in Germany.

Mass society

Although the streets of post-war Berlin, or for that matter any other part of Germany, may not look dramatically different from a generation before, the society that goes about its business in them is different; both in its perceptions of itself and in its symbolisms.

The dethroning of the Kaiser and the collapse of the curiously frozen social system of Bismarck's Reich has led to the disappearance of the most 'brilliant' part of society, its uniforms and displays and equipages. Motor cars have in any case displaced horse-drawn carriages, though status can still be conveyed by horse-power under a shiny bonnet (it is almost past belief to be told that in far-away Detroit American factory-hands ride to work in the morning in their own automobiles). In place of the curious pre-war trinity of aristocracy, generals, and industrialists, there is now one ruling class only—a plutocracy. The left-wing cartoonist George Grosz represents it as cosmopolitan, smug, sensual, and depraved: definitely not a ruling class to be proud of. Is it even 'ruling'? Another way of expressing this shift is to view the post-war order of things as *desacralized*; the world of 1918 and after is missing some indefinable sanctity in its images. Very suddenly, it is dominated by a *demos* lumped together in a mass society. (It makes no odds that in Germany at any rate the demographic reality is at variance with the image, and that in terms of sheer number the numerous small towns and rural communities still preponderate; after all, Russia too is credited with becoming an 'industrial' society when, as everyone knows, most of its inhabitants are peasants.)

What then does 'mass' signify? The answer is not plain, though the expression is on everyone's lips. For a long time 'the masses' have been seen, or shunned, by their superiors as a population of the 'lower' orders or classes, waiting in the wings: a flood to overwhelm the

Chronology for Chapters 9 and 10

1919	Treaty of Versailles; Mussolini forms Fasci di Combattimento (Blackshirts); Gropius establishes Bauhaus; *The Cabinet of Dr Caligari* filmed
1919–33	Weimar Republic in Germany
1920	First meeting of League of Nations; German Workers' Party renamed National Socialist (Nazi) Party
1922	Blackshirts' March on Rome brings Mussolini to power; T. S. Eliot's *The Waste Land* published
1922–53	Stalin in power in Russia
1923	Hyper-inflation in Germany; Hitler's abortive 'Beer Hall Putsch' in Munich; Frankfurt Institute for Social Research founded
1924	Death of Lenin; Chaplin films *The Gold Rush*; Thomas Mann's *The Magic Mountain* published
1925	Berg's *Wozzeck* produced in Berlin; Bauhaus moves to Dessau; Kafka's *The Trial* published
c. 1925	*Neue Sachlichkeit* movement beginning in German art
1927	Lindbergh flies the Atlantic; Al Jolson's *The Jazz Singer* ushers in sound movies
1928	Brecht and Weill's *Threepenny Opera* produced
1929	Wall Street crash causes worldwide economic collapse
1930	Marlene Dietrich stars in *The Blue Angel*
1932	Aldous Huxley's *Brave New World* published
1933	Bauhaus dissolved
1933–45	Hitler rules in Germany; F. D. Roosevelt president of the USA
1934	Death of Hindenburg; Hitler assumes title of 'Führer'
1935	Hoare-Laval Pact; Mussolini invades Ethiopia; Nuremberg Laws promulgated against Jews
1936	Accession and abdication of Edward VIII of England; Berlin-Rome Axis formed; Keynes's *General Theory of Employment, Interest, and Money* published

1936–9	Spanish Civil War
1936–52	George VI king of England
1938	Germany annexes Austria
1939–45	World War II
1940	Chaplin films *The Great Dictator*
1945	United Nations founded; Le Corbusier's *Unité d'Habitation* at Marseilles
1945–6	Nuremberg trials of Nazi war criminals
1945–53	Harry S. Truman president of the USA
1948–9	Berlin airlift
1948–51	Marshall Plan
1949	NATO founded; Orwell's *1984* published
1951	Festival of Britain
1952	Elizabeth II become queen
1953–61	Eisenhower president of the USA
1954	Beckett's *Waiting for Godot* produced
1956	Suez crisis
1958	European Economic Community formed
1958–69	De Gaulle president of France
1959–75	War in Vietnam
1961	Building of Berlin Wall
1961–3	J. F. Kennedy president of the USA
1962–5	Second Vatican Council
1962–70	Beatles dominate pop music scene
1963–9	L. B. Johnson president of the USA
1964	Pasolini films *The Gospel according to St. Matthew*; Marcuse's *One-Dimensional Man* published; Mods fight Rockers in British holiday resorts
1968	Student revolt in Paris; Russians occupy Prague
1969–74	Nixon president of the USA
1970	Death of De Gaulle

190   A demonstration by massed student leagues in Berlin, August 1932

After the Armistice, the Versailles Treaty: the former has been mourned, but the latter provokes angry demonstrations. In this Berlin protest meeting, massed student Leagues (Verbände) in their varied uniforms display a form of patriotism by no means friendly to the regime which signs the peace.

191   John Heartfield (1891–1968), *Ten Years After, Fathers and Sons*, 1924. Photo-montage, East Berlin, Academy of Arts (John Heartfield Archive)

The photo-montage comes into its own in the inter-war years; here, the revolutionary 'dada' artist John Heartfield uses it to blunt effect. Just two years later, Hindenburg is elected President of the Republic.

**192   George Grosz (1893–1959), *At Five in the Morning.*
Illustration from *Das Gesicht der herrschenden Klasse*
(*The Face of the Ruling Class*), 1921. Berlin (West),
Staatliche Museen**

*The left-wing artist George Grosz leaves inhibition behind
when he presents what he sees as the 'ruling class' (or plutocracy)
at the end of a long night's recreation; outside, the virtuous but
exploited 'masses' turn out for the early morning shift.*

old gods (in Wagernian-style scenarios), Caliban about
to take over from Prospero (the French scholar Renan's
version), a problem in 'crowd psychology' (Gustave le
Bon), or the class which is to usher in the fully classless
society (Marx). Generally speaking they are undiffer-
entiated, a kind of formless residue. And that too is how
'their' spokesmen on the Left have insistently sought to
portray them: by talk of unity identity is lost, and

something undefined confronts us: a fertile ground for
mysticism. Where do we actually *see* the 'masses'?
Streaming in and out of large factories, crowding the
public places, pouring out of housing estates around the
big city, assembling for great public occasions or sporting events or political processions. Also the imagination fills in its idea from abstract data—voting figures,
demographics, a housing problem . . . They have been
there, these urban populations, constantly growing in
number for generations. Now they are on-stage, prominent, an enormous chorus. The cobbler, the miner, the
tram-driver, the office-clerk, have little enough in
common, but they are part of a mass—a mass which the
press-photographer, a new witness, can show to the
mass-readership of his newspaper—for whatever purpose. The film producer, inspired by Russian depiction
of the People as Hero, develops a taste for crowd
scenes, and *Metropolis* attests the new collective actor.
On occasion, some groups within this mass are separately identifiable: in a parade, a politician's audience, a
trade union demonstration. Some sections, and notably
in Germany, identify themselves by a uniform; in Italy
too, the intended character of a Fascist movement is
promoted by a black shirt. For the first time in European history, organized propaganda dominates political action, and borrows more and more from the
methods of 'mass' advertising—the systematic coverage, the message simplified to the 'lowest' common
appeal, the pushing aside of 'respectability'. Where
numbers have come to be decisive in democracy's political confrontations, 'mass' acquires an almost physical
meaning, becomes the irresistible force in motion. The
lesson of the war is carried into peace: big battalions
count, and their purpose is to roll back other big battalions. Mass politics, in the German Republic, as elsewhere, comes to *look* extraordinarily like war carried on
by other means. In sum, the concept of the masses,
except to the manipulative politician (be he Baldwin or
Mussolini, Briand or Hitler), is an irrational and confusing concept; how mass society should or can
advance is a question of impenetrable ambiguity. One
thing only is clear: it is unstable, problematic.

To face its problematics, however, this modern
world of masses is, endowed with the means of its own
salvation, at least in the material sense of *mass* production. If pre-war futurists and prophets of the machine
have been vaguely ridiculous, their dreams now appear
trivial because in the intervening four years the gigantic
labours of armament have supervened: industry can
produce. And it now continues to produce practical reminders of this power. Traditional silver and plated
metals tarnish: but chromium plate is a striking arrival,

shiny, impersonal, much prized for artefacts and decoration. Wood and leather and metal are joined by new synthetic resins, of which the first to achieve wide use is called after its inventor Baekeland: precursor of the plastics universe, bakelite appears in ash-trays and insulation, toys and industrial components. The future is now! And a higher technology is announcing that future: speeded in their development by war, the motor car supersedes the carriage, the aeroplane and seaplane and airship supplement the railway and the ship; Lindberg flies across the Atlantic; the tractor appears in the fields; the phonograph and wireless set make their way into a million homes; the telephone, the loudspeaker, the cinematograph become a part of everyday life. For the intellectual who wants to see it that way, industrial society gives every indication of being able to save itself and ride above the problematics of the mass (whatever they are) by sheer technology. Such is the tenacious optimism of an H. G. Wells; alongside it, his fellow-countryman Aldous Huxley entertains the other view—in which industrial marvels, far from liberating, are devices of enslavement and serve a mass society of totalitarian control, with humans themselves graded and classed as totally standard objects (*Brave New World*, 1932).

What is common to both points of view, and indeed to the symbolism of chromium plate and bakelite and all the other fruits of mass-production industry, is the presumption of *uniformity*. Mass society, modern society, is the age of mass production of uniform things and of the mass compresence of uniform people; expectations regarding the one colour expectations regarding the other. Thus both liberal individualism and the craft movement are being edged out of the modern world in the making. If there is a 'mass civilization', will a 'minority culture' also survive?

There is one further new ingredient in the modernity of Europe in the 1920s: an American presence. We are not talking of international politics or trade or finance, important though these are to the problems of post-war settlement: we are referring to jazz, and the products of the movie cinema, and to a very sketchy frieze of knowledge—or misinformation—about the great democracy across the ocean. The latter comes largely by way of the movie screen, which in the 1920s, and much more in the next decade, comes to be the regular source of weekly entertainment for town populations; on the screen, 'U.S.A.' stands for tycoons, a land of opportunity, Yankee slickers, bustling business, and a moderately wholesome vulgarity.

In several ways this American presence confuses the perceived values of mass society. Jazz, for example, is

193   Käthe Kollwitz (1867–1945), *Bread! Soup!* 1924. Lithograph. Berlin (West), Staatliche Museen

Another passionately committed left-wing German artist, haunted by scenes of starvation and soup-kitchens in the last year of the Great War and in its immediate aftermath, focuses on the suffering of the poor and under-privileged in a most striking image directed to strictly ideological ends.

not at first identified at all as a 'popular' idiom (which is how it originates), but as an add-on to the tastes of 'young sets' in the middle classes (their dance tunes are at the same time acquiring, like their emancipated clothing, a character of singular, even flippant, inanity). Crooning, when it comes, will much more promptly attract a large popular following. But what of the rich vein of comic movie actors, from Harold Lloyd to Charlie Chaplin, whom American studios introduce along with their cosmetic film stars? Since all are performing against a backcloth which is somewhat unrelated to the day-to-day experience of their German (or

194   Film still from Charles Chaplin's *Gold Rush*, 1925

The 'little man' is gripped by an all-too-human dream of striking lucky and making it quick; at the same time Chaplin's incomparable gift consists in decking out the Klondike odyssey with every grotesque predicament through which the clown reveals virtues quite other than greed. Cowardice? But fortitude also. Bravado? But also misgivings about self.

French, or English, etc.) spectators, there is no question of their addressing closely vital topics: in their astounding new forms of clowning what they do exhibit is, simply, clowning. That already is not a little. But in the case of Chaplin there is slightly more to be said. Chaplin does, as it happens, have a message for 'modern times'; like clowns through the ages, he is absolutely not the man of the masses (whatever that is) but a kind of encyclopaedic Everyman, and more particularly the 'little man', ridiculous but indomitable, compounded of the most ordinary and fallible human clay, but with his self-respect; battered by every kind of mishap but surviving still on a diet of low-key optimism. He might indeed be a yardstick for sanity; it is the case, sadly, that all too many 'little men' in Europe will in the 1930s be looking for sterner ways to greatness than those of a clown, and that, when the time comes, no one inside Hitler's Germany will set eyes on Chaplin's *Great Dictator*.

Democracy in doubt

Of all the European nations, Germany undergoes the most violent shock in November 1918. Up to the last moment of hostilities the Kaiser's subjects are entirely confident of victory: in fact the war in the east *is already won*, and truly vast annexations have been secured from Russia at the treaty of Brest-Litovsk (1917/18). Then suddenly the world is upside down: an armistice is being sought in the west, the Kaiser abdicates, his war chiefs resign, strikes and mutinies break out, a new 'progressive' government is formed, a republic proclaimed, a revolt in Berlin by extreme socialists ('Spartakists') is put down by the army, and volunteers (*Freikorps*) are fighting the Poles and repressing further uprisings in the cities. The country is not yet restored to peace when elections are held and a constitution drawn up; the first meeting of deputies, for safety, is held not in the Berlin Reichstag, but at Weimar—which is how the regime gets its name. All this is in the space of three months. The Reich, with its authoritarian glitter, Prussian supremacy, 'world power' policies, great armed might, imminent hegemony in Europe—all this is gone. In place of it? Something dramatically different and totally unexpected: a democratic republic, modern and secular, with civil rights for all, no barriers to stop any citizen (including Jews) attaining the highest offices of state; votes for women; an eight-hour working day; actual parliamentary control of government. A number of other countries within the next year or two achieve a similar mutation into democratic nationhood, but Ger-

195   Al Jolson, film still from Crosland's *The Jazz Singer*, 1927

The first sound movie features Al Jolson 'blacked-up'. To European audiences unfamiliar with the transatlantic background of jazz or Negro or pseudo-Negro music, the spectacle is exotic: welcomed by the bright young generation of Weimar, but to nationalist sentiment as much a symptom of 'degeneracy' as any shady Berlin night-club or the transvestites in it. Hitler's followers will brand French occupation of the Rhineland (where African units appear) as a 'Negerbesatzung': the ultimate indignity.

many is by far the largest and also the most spectacular, having regard to her character as a recent military power dominating central Europe.

It is not our concern to follow in all their details the extreme difficulties faced by the republic in its early years: the responsibility laid upon it for the loss of territories and German subjects and colonies; the odium incurred for signing at pistol-point a peace treaty which allocates 'war guilt' and imposes disarmament and reparations on a huge scale; the government's apparent inability to prevent local uprisings, or *putsches*, by Left or Right extremists; the hyper-inflation which ruins millions of small people in 1923. All these things are held against the new regime, relentlessly, throughout its existence—even if many of them are the fault of the outgoing management or due to the shaping of the peace by other powers.

There is in fact a democratic republic for no better reason than that in 1914 the Social Democrats have had enough votes to constitute the largest single party in the pre-war Reichstag. They face violent antagonism on the extreme Right, and now on the extreme Left as well. A Communist party is being built on the old Spartakist foundations, as in every other European country, and under guidance from new rulers in Moscow sees as its first task to destroy its comrades of yesterday, soon to be labelled 'social fascists'. Social democracy, despite the massive support of trade unions, never comes to be seen as the 'natural party of government'. Though it has a 'Marxist' programme, it settles for justice, progress, welfare, because of its dependence on 'centre' party support; it presides over policies of compromise, unguided industry, international finance, orthodox budgets. Strangely inarticulate, too, relying on brilliant allies from the smaller parties of the centre—Schacht to restore financial health, Stresemann for its foreign policy—it has not even any considerable public figures of its own: after the death of Ebert in 1925, an election to the presidency produces, of all people, the incongruous Hindenburg, a retired pillar of the army. So long as recovery and prosperity last, the country is no doubt quite adequately led by an assortment of unexciting and conscientious politicians. However, when economic crisis and slump and mass unemployment again break over Europe (1929–33), the political weakness becomes a disaster: a tiny abrasive National Socialist Party leaps with the aid of national-

196 Socialist Workers' Sports International, Mass Display, Frankfurt am Main, April 1924

A 'Red Sports International' with headquarters in Moscow and supporters in a number of western countries musters a large turn-out in Germany. The supporters here go on to open their own training centres (1926) with state subsidies: as their manifesto of that year puts it, the movement can now go purposefully forward – 'Frei Heil!' It takes little to replace that greeting by the 'Sieg Heil!' of Nazi usage.

ists in industry and the press from having a handful of deputies to being the largest single party in the Reichstag, crushing the centre groupings with its white-collar and artisan (and especially its rural) vote; no majority alignment of parties, and therefore no government, can be found without support of either Communists or Nazis; and as a reckless expedient the Catholic politician Papen persuades Hindenburg to summon Adolf Hitler to take office as a 'cat's-paw' chancellor of the republic.

Until that black day at the end of January 1933, therefore, the Weimar Republic is an enlightened and moderate regime, but one which has all the appearance of being execrated, or at best despised, by everyone in the country except a handful of 'internationalists'. The enemies of autocracy, old radicals or new radicals of the Left, have the same view of the socialist leaders Ebert and Scheidemann that Brecht presently expresses about Communism in 1926: 'the crowd (*Menge*) on the left is fine, while it fights; when it wins it has to be replaced.' Unlimited freedom of expression earns no gratitude from those who enjoy it. Patriots of the Right, old or new imperialists or nationalists or authoritarians, declaim against the republic's record of defeat, lack of noble purpose; the republican kind of political life (trade-offs, compromise, the pork-barrel) is 'corruption'. The creative symbols of art and literature, pat-

ternings of idealism or hope offered to the age, and mostly of a Left complexion, have little to do with the humdrum pursuit of a liveable world; if they had, the 'humanity' (*Menschheit*) they preach would very likely be less vapid, the satire less shrill, the longings less ineffable, and 'alienation' less of a discovery.

This polarizing of values exactly reflects the peculiar origins of Weimar: a makeshift patching-up exercise, not willed, not the act of a 'nation in arms'. It is absolutely crucial that only the constitution is new: the rules for high policy-making and civic rights. These of course should lead on to a cascade of 'democratic' adjustments in a whole range of social values, a gradual reshaping of institutions and orientations; but that cascade occurs only in a few patches and segments, being absolutely blocked in others. The army, for example, a social microcosm of the Reich, supports the republic in the crisis of its birth—on condition it is left free from political interference. No nonsense about 'democracy' there! And the same then happens with the other great institutions of society and state: they survive intact from the old Reich. The Churches, Evangelical and Catholic, have, first, no reason to rally to a godless state; they are more exercised by the dangers of militant atheism than attracted by the merits of democracy. They successfully stop abortion being legalized in the 'modern' constitution; their pastors and priests oppose, openly and often, the presumed relaxation of decorum and standards of morality; their conservatism is addressed, massively, to the past. Or again, the civil service moves, *en bloc*, and with no changes, from serving the Kaiser to serving the republic—equally without enthusiasm. The Prussian pre-war bureaucracy has been conservative and formalist: it remains so. It is notorious that judges in the new republic show themselves meticulously stern in punishing left-wing law-breakers, but are swayed by sentiment, even compassion, when sentencing nationalist bravos or thugs whose love of fatherland may somehow have led them astray. The writer Ernst Toller is caught up in the Bavarian 'soviet' uprising of 1919: he serves a rigorous five-year gaol sentence. Four years later, the agitator Adolf Hitler attempts a different kind of *putsch* in Munich; he serves barely a year of his sentence. More shockingly, the prominent Catholic politician Erzberger (a signatory of the armistice) is murdered in 1919, and in 1922 the same fate befalls foreign minister Rathenau (equally culpable in nationalist eyes—and a Jew): the assassins go unpunished. In the end, such bias is an incitement to right-wing violence.

It is very surprising indeed to find the same thing in the world of learning. In their own way, the state universities too advertise open hostility to the regime. Their leaders have a new paymaster but old allegiances. Conservative, self-important, they have been pampered under the Reich; with status upheld alongside that of government and army, they remain guardians of *Bildung*; and they act accordingly. *Bildung* serves the state. But what state? Great scholars and historians of the past—Ranke, Treitschke, Droysen—have taught patriotism as well as the pursuit of truth; sometimes the patriotism has seemed to outside eyes intemperate (as when Treitschke lends the authority of his Berlin professorship to 'patriotic' anti-Semitism). But that is nothing compared with the 1920s. Today's professors publicly mourn the armistice and devote their lectures to denouncing Versailles and refuting the infamous 'war guilt' clause (accepted by the republic); in adversity, a firm belief in a German 'cultural mission' is all the more important, and respect for the nation's glories—the Lutheran Bible, Bach, Schiller, Kleist, Wagner—and the greatness of the founding fathers—medieval emperors, Luther, the Great Elector, Frederick the Great, Bismarck. The genealogy and greatness of the pre-war Reich continue to be offered as the German tradition; defiantly, and as a symbolic resistance to present apostasy. National culture is either a matter of household gods or else a problem, we might say; the concept of the state is even more problematic; twined

197   Cover picture of the magazine *AIZ*, 1932

The younger postwar generation takes to the open in costumes steadily more 'enfranchised' than those of its parents; and, of course, more practical. The postwar press also changes its appearance with the advance of photography and printing technology, to capture 'living' images and mass circulations. We are just one generation away from the 'pin-up' image, and even more ambiguous discords of values.

together, they form a mystique, a cult, an inexhaustible fount of irrationalism. The time will come when Professor J. Haller, in his *Epochs of German History*, tells the tale in such a manner that all past glories and monuments, including those of the late Kaiser, will seem to lead inevitably to consummation in a Third Reich, under a new leader. That time is not quite yet, because in the early 1920s the National Socialists are too small and crude a faction to merit attention; only when ten million voters turn to the N.S.D.A.P., and its public demonstrations become thoroughly alarming, will might command the respect which *Mein Kampf* fails at

198   Film still from Fritz Lang's *Metropolis*, 1925

Fritz Lang puts strikingly on the screen the disparities between an 'ordinary' scale of human existence and that of a mass society. And though his factory plant is scaled up to science fiction dimensions (what wrench could ever loosen those titanic nuts?), the science fiction here is very much anchored in the twenties, not a far-away allegory.

first to receive. Meanwhile the universities are digging the grave of the republic.

This is not a trivial matter. Universities have a kind of standing, a quasi-independent authoritativeness. Moreover, we are not looking just at the pronouncements of a thousand or so ineffectual pedagogues who regret the military parades and see themselves repeating the patriotic heroics of Fichte and the university of Berlin in 1810. Students, their parents, alumni, contribute to a campus nationalism; the old *Burschenschaften* (student fraternities) survive, except that they are now Francophobe as well as anti-Semitic; the clusters of *Wandervögel* (nature trail adepts), tramping on holiday through the countryside, are turning their backs on a hateful reality to seek communion with the Wagnerian *Urwald* (primal forest). Students are radical, to be sure: some have answered the call to join a *Freikorps* and save the country from the despised *Polacken*; they now reject the norms of tolerance implied in the constitution, exclude Jews from their associations, hound out pacifist lecturers (there are some), make no difficulty about scorning the 'foreign', 'utilitarian', 'rationalist', 'un-German' regime which their teachers tell them has been foisted by treachery on the nation. In 1933, under Nazi inspiration, they will take a hand in the public burning of 'un-German' books. But who in the meanwhile has encouraged them to think any differently?

The answer is that of course there is a minority of less 'reactionary' spirits in the faculties. A young patristics scholar, Aloys Dempf, can recall another German tradition, that of the good patriot but also *liberal* Goerres, whose views in the early nineteenth century might have relevance still today; Aby Warburg's new cultural institute in Hamburg attracts the flower of liberal scholarship in art and cultural studies, unaffected by chauvinism. Several hundred lecturers actually form a *pro*-republic academic association. The weakness of all these voices is shown, however, in the attitudes of the most eminent of the Republic's supporters. P. Gay's profound study of Weimar culture puts two such in the centre of the picture: the history professor Friedrich Meinecke and the novelist Thomas Mann. Each is a thoughtful 'liberal' from pre-war days, each becomes a reluctant convert to the Republic, each publishes a famous and revealing book in 1924. Thomas Mann we shall come to presently; but it is doubly significant that Meinecke's great work of scholarship is on Machiavelli and *The Idea of the Reason of State*—a burning issue—and that to our eyes it reads very strangely.

He asks, in effect, 'Must the State be as ruthless as the Florentine said the Prince should be?' and his answer, however veiled, is 'yes'. The State is an 'organic' unity; it has a duty to survive; its morality is bound to be different from that of individuals because of the 'tragic'

199 Film still from G. W. Pabst's *Westfront 1918*, 1930

The grim reality of the Flanders trenches, their massive outrage to human decencies, are recorded by poets and novelists—more than in censored journalism—even before the 1918 armistice; and feed into the current of pacifism that runs through interwar politics. 'Never again'. Thanks largely to Remarque's Im Westen nichts Neues (All quiet on the Western Front), a best-seller at the time of Locarno peace diplomacy, the witness of a 'Front Generation' is revived on the cinema screen; its viewers are still under the shadow of the terrible carnage, and many of them will remain so as war-clouds gather ten years later.

nature of history ('tragic' here means conflicts of interest). A Bismarck cannot be criticized; indeed, if more recent statesmen make 'mistakes', even that should arouse 'our respect'. In the 'over-cultivated and unclear relations of modern civilization' the recent invasion of Belgium was simply one such mistake 'which harmed us more than it helped us'. All very understandable. But what are we to make of Meinecke's further conjecture: 'would not the extinction of power conflicts (i.e., war) *also extinguish the inner vitality and strength of the State?*' And what of his endorsement of Treitschke, and of Oswald Spengler now, in their belief that 'all culture requires *a certain nutritive basis of barbarism*'?

The case is instructive. Weimar, for Meinecke, can justify itself only by toughness, by *virtù*, not by those other (secondary) ideals enshrined in its constitution. He is, in fact, under the spell of the 'power state' (*Machtstaat*). Against such nostalgia for the formidable ghost, what liberal traditions can make an effective stand? Only those (we should say at once) which exist on the margin of the state's system, or actually outside it.

But before coming to these, it is interesting to see where public opinion is tending in the broader arena of journalistic debate.

German nationalism in the 1920s shares most of its characteristics with the rest of Europe—everywhere it is nostalgic, more or less irrational, unwilling to face

real problems, but longing to suppress them. Its tone in Berlin only differs by being a little more outspoken. To the national culture heritage and the state, the two central idols, there attaches a whole constellation of typical values and obsessions: the dream of an *organic* community, where all individuals fit into a scheme inspired by a single—and explicit—harmonizing ideal; the *unity* of the nation, free from outside intrusion; the *coherence* of its symbolisms (language, art, cults, 'heritage'); the *energy* of its collective purposes, in which all concur. Then more concrete values: the *superiority* of a people, against (say) recent foes, Slav or Latin; an *ethnic identity*, however defined; *integrity* (recovery of stolen territory); finally, *enemies* (atheism, Jews, international conspiracies of Bolshevism or capitalism or freemasons or improbable alliances of these) and the tactics imputed to such enemies—corruption, encirclement, infiltration by false gospels (of psychology or economics or sexual emancipation or jazz or in the last resort any 'modern' foreign ideas at all). At the limit nationalism is hard to distinguish from paranoia, and in Weimar Germany there is no limit offered or imposed: Othmar Spann denounces Freud and modern films; Hans Grimm expounds the strangulation of the nation in his best-selling novel *Volk ohne Raum* (*People without Space*); anti-Semitic journalists revive the grotesque 'Protocols of the Elders of Zion'; critics flay the decadence of art.

200   Stage set for Walter Hasenclever's *The Son*, 1919. Sketch by Otto Reigbert. Munich, Deutsches Theatermuseum

Hasenclever's The Son, *written pre-war, comes into its own in a Weimar setting, where a disturbing and spluttering action can be matched by this Expressionist stage set.*

The 'Western' ex-allies are denounced equally with the 'bolshevik' East.

One of the most arresting figures of the day, however, is a prophet who unlike most nationalists does have something new of his own to say. Oswald Spengler is probably the most pretentious and (in his time) overrated writer of the inter-war years; the fact of his celebrity is a sign of the general uncertainties, and of the spread of irrationalism. His huge *Decline of the West* (1918–22), turgid and unreadable as it is, is a best-seller; it conveys prophetic warnings in sibylline terms; its title has precisely the kind of doom-laden note which confirms anxiety; apocalypse is fascinating; and its writer dares to think the unthinkable.

Spengler's argument is, moreover, a heady blend of pseudo-science and learned mystification. He announces that civilizations are no different from organisms: they are born, and they die. They may last a thousand years, but none can escape its ultimate fate. As organisms, also, they can be identified—there have been eight—and classified; a general 'morphology' can be observed in them; all very 'scientific'! The West has been a 'Faustian' civilization, dynamic and restless; now as it approaches its natural term, it has begun to show signs of decay, breakdown, loss of direction, wars. What awaits it now? This is less clear. But decline, decadence, doom, are not things to be complacent about.

Spengler's big book is translated, admired, commented, criticized, demolished, upheld, all over the world. It comes of course at the right time: it coincides with Bolshevik uprisings, Dadaism, the great 'flu epidemic, the poet T. S. Eliot's writing of *The Waste Land*, a host of testimonies of weariness, disillusion, exhaustion, all over the West. But its irrational fascination in Germany has a more urgent quality: the fall of the Reich is easy to equate with the end of civilization. Success at home therefore is immense, and its author is emboldened to produce a further though shorter study: *Prussianism and Socialism* (1920). In contrast to the big picture, this is about Germany: after the diagnosis, the cure. And in a way Spengler shows himself now more perceptive than other patriots, though again he supplies a perverse mixture of the obvious and the inconceivable. Essentially, he recognizes that the 'old' conservatism of aristocracy and landowner and officer caste is a thing of the past. There does survive a 'bureaucratic' conservatism, however, at the service of Germany, and what is needed is to preserve this tradition and apply it widely to the modern age of industrial mass society. Failure in this has been the Achilles heel of the Reich—hence the growth of the socialist party, the 'stab in the back', and indeed the republic now. But there is still a Prussian tradition: discipline, efficiency, control. This could be the path of salvation; a substitute for the destructive 'mass' ideology of class conflict which has overwhelmed the East. *In some way* industry, labour, the whole community, should be brought under it, and conflict abolished. A new 'socialism', indeed, but organic—without strikes or lock-outs. Where all obey, all may be said to share in the 'power of the whole': how then could problems of freedom arise? These ideas are not a prefiguration of National Socialism as understood by Hitler. They are however the first example of an attempt to imagine a state less antipathetic than the republic, an order more in line with national tradition. (In the same year the sociologist Max Weber, with much deeper understanding of public affairs, has recorded his doubt whether a constitutional republic can survive at all in Germany, and goes on to suggest that a charismatic mass-leader would be a safer option.)

Prussianism in its turn is read, debated, applauded on the Right; Spengler becomes a very great sage. Nothing comes of his proposals because they reflect no real political possibilities, but many others (with no more practicality but always the same urgency) follow in presenting their own ideas for a different kind of Germany—formulae which range from a restored monarchy to a 'national' Bolshevism. Always, at the centre, the problem of the state. Ironically, the day will be won by a movement which has nothing to say about the state, but puts all its money on the nation, the German *Volk*. That too will be no less irrationalist and absolute than its rivals.

Modernism unchained?

So long as the rebel can tug on his chains, cry defiance, curse the gods, he has no problem. What happens when the chains come off?

The disdain shown to the avant-garde by imperial society has never seriously checked the revolt of 'expressionist' artists. If anything, in palmy days, the Kaiser's outbursts against modern art are a stimulus. Since then, in the war, the formless cry of anguish is supplied with a huge object, greater than any dreamed of, and many avant-garde artists and writers take up revolutionary attitudes that only a few have adopted before: Hans Johst's early play *The Hour of the Dying* (1914) is a pacifist tract; Walter Hasenclever's pre-war drama of parricide, *The Son*, published in 1914 and performed privately in 1916 (officially it is banned), is a 'cry of alarm addressed to all Mankind'; the painter Max Beckmann faces the collapse of 1918 with the words 'we must surrender our heart and our nerves to the dreadful screams of pain of the poor disillusioned people.' In Berlin the 1918 *Novembergruppe* is a group of intellectuals approaching the new regime with a manifesto, a mixture of exhortation and self-interest, from 'Cubist, Futurist, Expressionist artists conscious of their vocation': the government, which really has more urgent things to attend to, replies that old prejudices are a thing of the past—there are to be no chains any more. When it comes to practicalities, the public galleries now may—and do—buy and exhibit contemporary canvases; controversial artists—Beckmann, Klee, Kokoschka—are appointed to posts in art schools; censorship becomes to all intents and purposes invisible, and dramatists may shock anyone they please. Beyond that, Weimar politicians have little enough interest in avant-garde activities: but that is enough.

Chains off, intellectuals can set about the work of transforming mankind. Their most energetic efforts are

201   Max Beckmann (1884–1950), *Carnival,* **1920. Oil on canvas, 73¼ × 36 in (186 × 91.5 cm). London, Tate Gallery**

If the artist has indeed pictured himself, masked, in the bottom right-hand corner, and figured two close friends more centrally, this panel drifts between pseudo-allegory and decorative topsy-turvydom; 'Carnival' is a moment's interlude from the artist's more typical mood of vehement protest.

202   Max Ernst (1891–1976), *The Teetering Woman,*
1923. Oil on canvas, 51⅛ × 38¼ in (130 × 97 cm).
Düsseldorf, Kunstammlung Nordrhein-Westfalen

The systematically irrational stance of Surrealism is, at the very
least, a means for manufacturing new hybrid images—if that
resource is not yet abundantly available in the post-war world.
Even before the publication in Paris of André Breton's Surrealist
Manifesto (1924), Ernst has headed toward cryptic, smoothly
disturbing, visions of an alternative (but always momentary)
reality, or 'surreality'.

203   Kurt Schwitters (1887–1954), *Dislocated Forces,*
1920. Collage, 41½ × 34⅛ in (105.5 × 86.7 cm). Bern,
Kunstmuseum

Alongside adepts of anarchic Dadaism and (presently)
Surrealism, Schwitters at the end of the Great War has begun to
assemble scraps and rags and bits of objects into exhibits for which
he invents a generic (but meaningless) name—Merz. Austere in
the example shown, Schwitters's Merz-objects will range between
the epic and the genuinely witty.

seen in the theatre. The Berlin stage, and to a lesser
extent that of Frankfurt and other centres, not only
springs to life with the arrival of peace, it becomes the
experimental workshop of all Europe, dominated at
first by 'Expressionists' (Hasenclever, Georg Kaiser,
Ernst Toller), but welcoming every cosmopolitan interest (Ibsen, Strindberg) and brilliant revivals of
national hero-figures (Kleist, Schiller), with daring sets
by liberated artists of the day; an extraordinary effervescence. The ambitions and dreams of the generation
of 1900 are put to a severe test: what are their promises

worth? The answer is, not a great deal. Their work is
diffuse, vague; even Toller's new satires on nationalism
and Hitler (*Wotan Unchained*) and on communist agitators (*Hinkemann*) are stronger on sentiment than on
structure; while in the end total liberty to explore the
disconcerting, the macabre, the odious or discordant,
the painful unmasking of old hypocrisies, parricide
(fashionable), Grand Guignol, last gasps of romanticism, sermons, stark silences, *tableaux*, begin to evoke
yawns. One can have too much of 'the artist is the
conscience of humanity' (Kornfield, 1918). This,

204 Set design by Otto Reigbert for Bertholt Brecht's *Drums in the Night*, 1922. Staged at Munich, Kammerspiele

Otto Reigbert's design for a set for Drums in the Night *makes it pretty clear how much Brecht's early years are saturated by Expressionistic theatre interests. But likewise, it suggests—as does all Expressionist art—how urgent a need is felt to strip away the 'good manners' (usually referred to as 'bourgeois') of conventions which are outworn—whether in the street or on the stage.*

however is the most visible contribution of intellectuals to the spirit of Weimar.

It is from this total fluidity and anarchy of theatrical tradition that one considerable dramatist, the young Brecht, emerges, 'distancing' himself by turns from each successive allegiance that he contracts, and fashioning a highly personal *oeuvre* with its own disciplines. He has something new to offer; specifically, a gift of rhythm and dialogue, not dependent on effusions of the ineffable 'Oh Mankind' type. The run of the mill Expressionist may be worth reading: *he* is worth seeing. Is Brecht Expressionist or not? Yes, if one considers the numerous echoes of others' work, a certain radical truculence, grating parody, close association with Bronnen and other writers 'in the swim'; no, if one sees his very first play *Baal* as an anti-Expressionist gibe, or considers his later rewritings and exculpations. What, anyway, is Expressionism now? Is it stage lighting? Inarticulacy? Horror? Anything definable at all? *Drums in the Night* (1922) is Brecht's first step away, *In the Jungle* (1924) the second. But the adaptation of Marlowe's *Edward II* (1924) is a third, and then he is away to study Marx for a play on Chicago capitalism; finally to join a 'straight' revolutionary school . . .

Even more typical of the post-war climate of experiment is the transfer of Expressionist values to other media: and first to the operatic stage. Not surprisingly, the process has links with Vienna; also with experimental theatre production. In 1921 the still youthful Paul Hindemith has composed a setting for Kokoschka's equally juvenile (and strident) *Assassin, Hope of Women*; Kurt Weill, after achieving glory in another direction, adapts the Expressionist Yvan Goll's *Royal-*

205   Set design by P. Avarantinos for the first production of Alban Berg's *Wozzeck* at the Berlin Staatstheater, 1925

Büchner's grim drama of a simple and none too articulate soldier who pathetically kills his mistress and then drowns himself provides Berg with the material for an operatic masterpiece, Wozzeck, *first offered to the public in 1925. This stark set makes clear the affinities with Schoenberg and Expressionism (compare plate 183).*

Place (1924) with an orchestral score of the most abstract, atonal, shapeless aridity. And then just a year later, Alban Berg's setting of Büchner's *Woyzeck* (composed in 1922) causes a sensation at the Berlin Opera itself: whether accepted or not, *this* is undoubtedly the masterpiece which gives some sort of lasting consecration both to the Expressionist stage and to the laborious stridency of atonal music-writing which has its origin in the Austrian master, Schönberg. In 1928 Berg returns with *Lulu*, adapted from Wedekind (another Austrian echo). Along with the twelve-tone idiom, Berg again pays homage to his master in his extraordinary

use of the human voice (for cantando, rhythmic speaking, *Sprechgesang*, even integrated howls), in the enormously elaborate and virtuoso matching of musical forms with each slice of Wedekind's scenes, in the tightness of construction. If Büchner's and Wedekind's texts date from the previous century, their subjects are absolutely within the range of an Expressionist stage: the first, the tragedy of the inarticulate, groping soldier-victim; the second a tragedy of sexual infatuation and scandal, suicide and murder, trivial and unedifying—a commentary of course on 'bourgeois morality', but not without its gruesome transcendental little something hovering about the fatal charms of Lulu herself. But these affinities are unimportant; the exigencies of opera compel in Berg's works a far more terse and concentrated discipline than is imposed upon writers for the acting stage; and this concentration is one of the chief features that lift them high above the theatre of the age and its all-too-successful renderings of 'authentic' incoherence.

There is another musical masterpiece of inter-war German opera, very different from those just men-

206   Ernst Toller's *Masses and Man*, staged at the Stadttheater, Nuremberg, 1921

The young anarchist Ernst Toller has his Masses and Man *performed while he is still in prison; in contrast to* The Son, *it merges Expressionistic social revolt and mass mythology—a fable for the 1920s, and strangely* passé *to a later age with less of a sense of their novelty.*

tioned: Brecht's and Weill's *Dreigroschenoper* (*Threepenny Opera*, 1923). In going back two hundred years to John Gay's satirical *Beggar's Opera* for his starting-point, Brecht has by no means abandoned modernity; he has found a way, simply, to get away from its by now embarrassing clichés. *Old* clichés are an alibi. This work is satirical, farcical, sinister, and savage all in one: an entertainment, not a sermon. Unquestionably it catches better than any other work of the decade a certain level of complicity that can be established between the Left-infected (but not too serious) writer and his public—emancipated now of course, worldly-wise, with more than a taste for the spivvish, and delightfully tickled by Brecht's memorable pseudo-proletarian aphorism: '*Erst kommt das Fressen, dann kommt die Moral*' ('Grub comes first and Morals after').

Kurt Pinthus points out with great seriousness that in literature the whole drift of German Expressionist protest against the condition of man is entirely 'middle class': in a mini-sociological review of his friends and acquaintances, all the chief exponents, he shows that with hardly an exception they come from professional families—their fathers are doctors, bureaucrats, lawyers—and most of them have diligently completed university studies. In perspective, there is nothing very surprising in this; where else in the republic would young writers come from? To the east, in the new revolutionary Russian state, exactly the same is true of the experimental art and literature which flourishes there until 1924. Nor should too much be made of post-war 'generation gap' tension. We know that the 'front-generation' despises the generals; the Kaiser is a bogy man; the new society has no time for the old. *But* the carrier-themes of revolt have all been explored

207   Cesare on the rooftops, a film still from Wiene's *Cabinett des Dr Caligari*, 1919

Caligari's zombie-like Cesare kidnaps the heroine. What prodigious possibilities this offers for a chase across the roof-tops: angular, distorted, impossible, mad. But who—or what—is mad? Is it a psychotic narrator-hero? Or is it the world at large?

already in experimental writing *before* Weimar (father-hatred, revolt against school discipline, pacifism, anti-authoritarian attitudes); these themes have become 'respectable' in literature, even dominant; all that is left is to explore them in greater depth; they will very soon be hackneyed. Thus from Wedekind and Heinrich Mann to the memorable and seemingly original film *Mädchen in Uniform* (1931), the essential theme is oppression in school; all that is added is an equivocal treatment of personal relationships in an all-female society: 'daring' even in Berlin's emancipated climate to be sure, but basically not new; the subject is a worn-out one. In an even more visible way, *The Blue Angel* enacts for its generation a theme similarly established by Heinrich Mann (*Professor Unrat*, 1905) and with echoes of Wedekind—and now of course of *Lulu*. What gives *this* film its epoch-making character is very little more than its sound-track and the sight of Marlene Dietrich's long legs. A star is born . . . Is it surprising to find Brecht 'distancing' himself from these clichés (in a sense different from that which he later turns into an artistic principle)?

It is, even so, the cinema which adds a brand-new dimension to the cultural symbolism of the post-war world, and for a time enlivens Expressionist art. Like all the great media alongside which it takes its place (live stage, print, painting) it eventually supplies *all* levels of sophistication in society, and acquires its own universe of artistic specialists, promoters, critics, followers. But

in the 1920s it is constantly interwoven with literature and the visual arts; and therefore, in the early Weimar Republic, with Expressionism.

The Cabinet of Doctor Caligari (1919) is a milestone. Silently of course (and therefore the more spookily, disconnectedly) its macabre subject takes us through murder, abduction, hypnotism, suspense of every kind. Shots of unreal street-corners, fairground scenes, pursuits over slanting rooftops, vertigo and claustrophobia, are what it is all about; the psychosis on which the story rests, and which gives a consistent sense to its disturbing sequences, should be enough to satisfy the most extreme craving for alienation. *Doctor Caligari* is a straight (or relatively straight) horror film: which is undoubtedly not what its authors intended it to be. The first script of Mayer and Jannowitz has a perfectly sane hero pursuing the mysteries through to the shocking discovery that Doctor Caligari, director of an asylum, is *himself* the crazed and murderous source of all the evil—an undoubted allegory of the mad criminality of those in authority, an unmasking of the political dislocation of the world. In the version as shot, director Robert Wiene has made the smiling doctor sane, and the hero a psychotic victim of delusions: tidier, certainly, since the 'mysteries' can now be accounted for rationally, and the sanity of the world is upheld. Either way, the artist Reimann and his painter colleagues supply for this strange and wayward script a truly vertiginous décor—painted flats, leaning walls,

**208   Marlene Dietrich as the Blue Angel, film still
from Josef Von Sternberg's *Blaue Engel*, 1930**

*Marlene Dietrich displaying her underwear on the screen takes
Blue Angel a long way beyond Heinrich Mann's literary account
of respectability infatuated with a harlot: to each generation its
'daring', be it verbal or visual. The 'story' though is still the
same.*

jagged obsessive angles, harsh shadows, a distorted
unstable world—an Expressionist triumph. A fashion
once created, it is followed up vigorously: looming
threats, menacing shadows, broken images of the
world, enigma, characterize the output of the next few
years in *The Golem, Raskolnikoff, The Waxwork Cabinet*,
and a dozen other productions quite distinct from anything being produced abroad at the same period for the
cinema. Grand Guignol and horror feature as major
attractions (*Nosferatu*, Jack the Ripper sequences in *The
Waxwork Cabinet, Doctor Mabuse* . . .)—and by no
means solely as a means of attracting audiences. The
cinema, in one sense so obviously an extension of the
business of supplying photographic images of ordinary
reality, is very deliberately being used *as a means of doing
precisely the opposite*.

There are in fact limits to what can be quarried from
any mine—even a seemingly unlimited one, even 'expression' of the subjective. Before the middle of the
decade the intensity of its seriousness is exhausted.
Perhaps this can be related to Germany's return to
economic prosperity during 1924 (the two things are
certainly synchronous). The restlessness of mere
fashion is certainly not to be underrated, though: the
quest for new forms and the luxury of new attitudes.
When the cinema broadens out into satisfying all demands (sentimental, epic, documentary) it is also moving into line with literature, and the arts.

209   Ernst Fritsch (1892–), *Jeunesse Dorée,* **1926. Oil on canvas, 41⅛ × 58⅞ in (104.5 × 149.5 cm). Private collection**

Sachlichkeit (factuality—see below) covers a rather large range of experimental art in the mid-1920s; Fritsch's painting is a clear example of retreat from Expressionism. The 'young things' shown here, their attire, their mode of dancing, are all up-to-date; but Fritsch is not exulting in this, nor offering any message of judgement (compare Grosz, plate 192); he offers simply a presentation—a spectacle of his painterly satisfactions.

Ideology and confrontation

A *neue Sachlichkeit* (new factuality) as a direction for artists to bend their attention is first announced not in cinema but in painting. It features as the title of an exhibition at Mannheim in 1925, and G. E. Hartlaub, its begetter there, calls for an art which shall 'remain loyal or rediscover a loyalty to a positive, tangible reality'. Is this, as he also suggests, only a sign of 'resignation'? And is it a more or less disgraceful and sterile opting out from political conflict, from ideological debate on the way the world should go, from active interpretation of the meaning of things? Its critics, especially those on the Left, have said so: George Lukács calls *Sachlichkeit* 'mere reportage', instead of an interpretation of reality. That may be to underrate the tenacious appeal of a straightforward artistic perception and rendering of what is perceived. Why should men *not* paint what they see, if they want to, without having to relate their art to cosmic suffering or revolutionary class-consciousness or the salvation of the state?

Such underrating is nevertheless another example of the pressure to *politicize* all possible issues by the extremes of political Left and Right in the Weimar Republic. Fervent ideology allows nothing to be neutral or non-committal; it makes every act contentious; and this is so oppressively borne in on the sociologist Karl Mannheim that he is at this moment seeking a theoretical escape from its predicament, the predicament of

210   Walter Gropius (1883–1969), Bauhaus, Dessau, 1925–6

The Bauhaus at Dessau looks to us much like thousands of commonplace structures erected much later on green-field sites. That, however, is a tribute to Gropius, not a reproach: in its time this careful but unassuming functional simplicity is the more cogent for not being aggressive.

'either-or' with which men of goodwill are being beset (an attempted solution to the problem is at the heart of his *Ideology and Utopia*, 1929). In fact the *Neue Sachlichkeit* has a necessarily unheroic and inconclusive career in Germany, though we see its products and derivatives all over Europe; and this is because most of it *is* undoubtedly a disengagement from 'commitment'—perhaps even a quite emphatic and committed disengagement, more so than a Lukács would like to think possible; but foredoomed.

In truth, the big casualty of the Weimar Republic is 'fact'. Atonality, Expressionism, Surrealism, are *not* groundless trends and adventures, but symptoms. The same is true of the extraordinary reputation now acquired by the novels and tales of Kafka, where fear of unknown processes or dangers, bafflement, impenetrable allegory, are the basis of existential disorientation, endlessly repeated. Fact, the simple (?) building-block of everyday experience, which is also the necessary common ground for shared communication, is being attacked, undermined, put in doubt from a dozen angles at the same time. We cannot closely interrelate them, but here are some. The popularization of modern physics, to begin with: this is a field of discourse which may be trivial; nevertheless it has a myth-making force of its own. Heisenberg's recently evolved 'uncertainty principle' can be fastened on to 'show' that the world of science is not deterministic after all; garbled versions of Einstein's relativity theory can be worked up (by popu-

larizers) into a general thesis that nothing can ever be 'what it is', but only what you care to say it is from your own corner. Or again, the rapid spread of psychoanalysis in post-war Germany (a Freudian institute under Karl Abraham is set up in Berlin with an active clinic): despite the disagreements between the sects of Freud, Jung, and presently the committed left-winger Reich, it is at least common ground that ordinary acts and beliefs never mean what they seem to, but always something else. Or, in a different vein, the findings of the new school of Gestalt psychology (notably Koffka) which affirm that even simple perception is a complex and, for the time being, controversial process. There is the pervasive clash of ideologies (already referred to), each of which—'old' conservative, conservative-bureaucratic, liberal, Marxist, nationalist—purports to explain everything from a standpoint which must be 'right' because it is coherent, and also to unmask the unavowed motives of its rivals in terms consistent with its own preferred reading of the facts: this is the climax of 'relativism', above which Mannheim is struggling to climb. There is the attack on 'positivism' or crude scientism conducted by the Frankfurt-based Institute for Social Research, a private foundation where the left-wing intellectuals Max Horkheimer, Theodor Adorno, then Herbert Marcuse, seek to rethink Marx and Freud in their own ways and elaborate a new 'critical philosophy'. And, finally, and not yet obtrusive, there is the abdication of mainstream German philo-

**211 Walter Gropius,
Bauhaus hall and bar.
Werkbund exhibition,
Paris, 1930**

*Disregard the tea-urn; look
instead at the furniture,
light-fittings (top left) and
wall-cladding in the Bauhaus
hall and bar on display in Paris
in 1930. This international,
'modern' style (alongside other
versions) will filter slowly in
the following decade, at first via
élite circles, into Western
applied arts.*

**212   Theodor Bogler,
Bauhaus porcelain, 1923**

*The porcelain coffee-machine
is not a mass-production
percolator; apart from anything
else, the (half-hidden)
spirit-lamp heater belongs to a
time when 'convenience' is not
yet a market-place imperative.
But this Bauhaus product, once
again, points the way to
genuinely industrial applications
of design a generation later.*

sophy: Husserl searches for a necessary and universal system ('phenomenology') which bypasses 'mere' empirical knowledge—at least provisionally—in the hope of a future science of 'essences' (but 'essences' are extremely elusive, and not in the least concerned with what ordinary people understand by real things 'out there'); his ex-disciple, the other new path-breaker Martin Heidegger, opaquely eloquent, seems to be drifting into a species of nihilism, death-centred and tinged with poetic intuition, with more than a hint that firm grounding for a rational theory of knowledge need not concern adult beings any longer.

About the one trend of thinking that arouses no passionate interest in Germany in the 1920s is empiricism. In Vienna there is a brilliant circle of 'logical positivism': not here. In whichever direction we turn, we seem to confront an avant-garde (or a rearguard) intent on demolishing every one of our comfortable shared or naïve views of the world (what Heidegger calls 'the public interpretation of reality'); and promising new battles and the imposition of sectional views by one or another passionate minority.

There is one illustrous exception to the foregoing; not central, indeed, not a flaming beacon claiming universal attention, but nevertheless an exception so notable that its effects spread visibly around the world and confer on Weimar, in retrospect, an aura of positive direction which is more than a little misleading. This has to be, evidently, the Bauhaus movement.

Function and Design

When, at the close of the Great War, the architect Walter Gropius conceives the idea of an interdisciplinary school of design, his concept is more far-reaching than earlier *craft* movements (William Morris, the prewar *Werkbund*) because it looks towards an integral approach, a coherent purpose, and a collaborative achievement. The ingredients of it are in fact mostly to hand already. Gropius has himself pioneered new architectural idioms—in the Fagus factory they are functional, clean, unfussy—and we recall that he is not alone in such pioneering work. But he does not wish to see architecture isolated, any more than any other particular skill or vocation. In the town of Weimar in 1919 he takes over the local arts and crafts school, and assembles a team which is the first *deliberate* bringing together of 'pure' and 'applied' arts. It is not lacking in distinction: it attracts Kandinsky, Paul Klee, the American painter Lyonel Feininger, the artist-sculptor Schlemmer (shortly to have a place in *Sachlichkeit*), the metal-worker and photographer Moholy-Nagy, and a stream of other practitioners no less remarkable. Harassed by local jealousies, the school moves in 1925 to premises at Dessau purpose-built by Gropius—they are a visible symbol of what it stands for. One unified vision (*Gestaltung*) embraces building construction, decoration, furniture, fittings; other crafts, painting, sculpture, graphic arts, typography, are no less integral. Design has to do with how we can live: it is sensitive to function, to the properties of materials (especially new materials), to living use; it pushes aside irrelevant conventions and shapes and techniques which may have meant something in a distant age but do so no longer; it is an education because it arises out of, and is applied to, realities. The realities of the modern world are not traditional: the craftsman must come to terms with mass production, cities require large-scale housing projects. We are at a point in time when Gropius, like his former associate Le Corbusier, gives attention to problems of large blocks of low-cost modern housing, and Mies van der Rohe (presently his successor as head of the Bauhaus) is designing high-rise structures in steel and concrete and glass which, twenty years later,

213   Ludwig Mies van der Rohe (1886–1969), apartment block, Stuttgart, 1927

The simplicity of line in Mies van der Rohe's early apartment block is a reminder that modern design belongs to an industrial urban culture, where human values are all too easily submerged by technical (and ultimately, financial) ones. Compare plates 185 and 223.

have ceased to be futuristic dreams and instead confront us in any big city. But as well as construction projects there come from Dessau modern furniture (which breaks with the laborious hierarchies of nineteenth-century forms) and new type-faces for the printing industry, equally 'functional' and free from pretentiousness (in the sense that the sanserif forgets about the handwriting of Petrarch and shows that it is for use in a leaner, differently stylized world). Page lay-outs in two dimensions, no less than the interior lay-out of a building in three, carry deliberately into daily life the constructive impulse hitherto sterilized in exhibits on the walls of art galleries or in monuments for special occasions. Why should our surroundings not fit, and therefore express, the reality of the lives we lead, instead of the irrelevant accumulation of lives led by generations of ancestors? And why should the standards of craftsmen not be maintained and reflected everywhere, in a practical and not an exotic sense?

Half a century after its demise we take for granted much of the spirit of the Bauhaus and many of the forms it generates; it is not easy to recapture the feeling of their original impact. We forget that in a Weimar world stuffed full with yesterday's objects and dreams and ideas, even a Bauhaus chair is a shock and a challenge. What Gropius and his friends put before their society is more disconcerting than what Frank Lloyd Wright or Sullivan have already been doing, in something of the same spirit, in the United States. It is, in every aspect and even more in its overall programme, a threat to those who make a cult of old-established ways. National Socialists after 1933 will attempt to reimpose an age-old Gothic script throughout Germany in place of Roman: this 'un-German' Bauhaus sanserif is facing in precisely the opposite direction. Gropius—and most of his colleagues—have strong views on the social implications of their work; but he himself is in no doubt as to the risks that surround him. It is highly significant that he imposes on his colleagues a strict ban on any political discussion. All to no avail: the school is very soon being accused of (variously) un-German, bolshevistic, regressive, Jewish, or subversive tendencies. Eventually, Nazi attacks drive it from Dessau to Berlin (1932), and there it dissolves.

The Bauhaus is an exemplary model of that hybridizing which at certain moments can lead to astonishing creation through bringing together previously unrelated skills and ideas. We have seen something of the kind occurring in every preceding chapter of this study. Gropius's example offers a lesson very widely attended to in schools of art and design a generation later (to such an extent indeed that inevitably it leads to the further discovery that an interdisciplinary formula on its own is not sufficient to guarantee startling new advances). But the fortunate opportunity grasped by the Bauhaus venture is unique to Weimar Germany. It marks a vital adjustment of cultural values at a privileged conjuncture—a constellation that includes design and the repertory of forms (possibility of integration), definition of roles (pure and applied 'arts' on an equal footing, craft 'masters' not art pedagogues or professors), newly adaptable techniques and prospects for technology (why not steel tubes indoors?), social opportunity (in an ambiguous but not absolutely deterrent republic), and motivation (furthering a realistic society).

A symbol of plurality?

A modern society is under all circumstances a segmented affair. It may share a single language, but breaks it into a multiplicity of jargons. Its various classes and professions have their own orientations and sectional values; even if not in dispute, they see common laws in different lights. On top of that, however, the Weimar society we are looking at is also deeply fissured and fragmented by the fate of the preceding régime and the trials of the new republic—so much so that it is hard to imagine any single monument able to reflect its overall character, if it has one. Weimar has neither a Dante nor a Dickens. The best chance, perhaps, would be to look for something not too closely matched to the idiosyncrasies, even the idiom, of the day: not explicitly or obviously reflecting any part, since no part is going to be even vaguely representative of the whole. And since the years after 1918 witness a remarkable flowering of experimental novels of unprecedented size and complexity (James Joyce's *Ulysses*, Proust's *A la recherche du temps perdu*, André Gide's *Les Faux-monnayeurs*, Aldous Huxley's *Point Counter-Point*), it would not be too surprising to find our monument in this class of writing.

Thomas Mann establishes his standing as a major writer under the old Reich; perfectly aware of its abnormalities, he protects himself from them by a massive system of irony and artistic detachment. Unlike his brother Heinrich he is conservative enough to opt for conformism in the Great War; the Versailles treaty he sees as a sad victory of 'rationalism' and 'utilitarianism' over cultural idealism; and when the republic is set up he has real difficulty in bringing himself to accept its inglorious humdrum nature. Yet, like Meinecke, he does swing over to being a *Vernunftrepublikaner* (reasoned republican); perhaps the spectacle of ferocious nationalism loose in the streets has something to do with it—he testifies on behalf of Ernst Toller when the latter is put on trial in 1919. Then in *The German Republic* (1922) he proclaims a high and ideal 'humanism' (*Humanität*), which he would like to see inspiring society, as a balance to its necessary social arrangements; indeed, the two things, the ideal and the expedient, must converge and blend. As the years pass, he continues to elaborate this idea: in *Culture and Socialism* (1928) he wants to see 'the conservative cultural idea and the revolutionary concept of society' finding a middle way, or as he defines it, a cross between Marx and

Hölderlin (the latter is a singularly gnomic symbol of whatever it is that 'humanism' is meant to be—the rarefied and unhappy poet, a favourite of Heidegger). Unfortunately, if the ideal is dark its execution is elusive . . . But then National Socialism begins to sweep the country, and Mann is forced to change his tune and express much simpler thoughts, calling for 'rationality', 'decency', 'a human meaning for the world'; and in 1933, consistently anti-Nazi, he goes into exile. He has taken 'an expressly rationalistic' position, he says, 'only under pressure of that irrationalism and political anti-humanism now spreading over Europe, but particularly over Germany'.

Thomas Mann is thus a kind of self-constructed *eupatrid* in the democracy, a by no means instinctive or sentimental citizen: not a democratic idealist like his brother Heinrich or other pro-Weimar writers, such as Feuchtwanger or the amiable Kästner, but not capable of disregarding society either.

In a year of major convulsions—the breakdown of reparations payments, the French and Belgian military occupation of the Ruhr, Hitler's Munich *putsch*, and the hyper-inflation—he is at work completing a new novel; in 1924 it is published: *Der Zauberberg* (*The Magic Mountain*). Periphrastic, complex, and vast, it presents the arrival of a young consumptive Hans Castorp in a Swiss Alpine sanatorium; in that strangely rarefied and remote microcosm, all sorts of things then happen. What holds the novel together, and indeed dominates every stage of it, is the confrontation, in endless dialogues, of half-a-dozen or more human standpoints and *Weltanschauungen*, each expressed by a different character in the sanatorium, either in action or in words. Aristocratic, nihilist, liberal, practical, blustering, or whatever—no single one is central or privileged. A florid and faintly embarrassing character, Settembrini, personifies an old-fashioned vein of liberal democracy—an extremely wordy personification, as it happens; but is he, or anyone else for that matter, a person in his own right, or simply an ingredient in the hero's experience? The detached voice of the 'narrator' gives no hint of partiality for this kind of humanism; or for any other. Nor do we even know if that 'narrator' should be identified with Thomas Mann himself. In the closing chapter, however, young Hans leaves the sanatorium, the mountain fastness, to make his way back to the 'real world', now at war, and disappears from view into the gloom and confusion of the battlefield. That at least is an act of commitment—but to what? To life? To death? And what would either of these signify? In the last analysis the 'meaning' of The Magic Mountain might be no more than this: 'it is valuable that a novelist should be able to rehearse, and we to read, a profound and searching meditation on different attitudes to life and death and destiny.' More natural would be to see it as a vast kind of parable of the conscious and deliberative search for rational commitment. But under all circumstances this *is* a picture of a pluralistic world, a world by no means univocal or 'organic'—an array of alternative attitudes, problematic for the hero, incapable of integration other than by the purely formal design of the novel, held together by the precarious artifice of a sanatorium. And in this perspective it is undoubtedly reminiscent of the Weimar Republic itself, even if Mann takes care to set it in the pre-war world. *Der Zauberberg* is both immensely topical and frighteningly detached; but it is the nearest thing to a work of art reflecting (in the terms of *Humanität*, of course) a whole moment of European culture; and to do that there is only one place in Europe where it could be written and acclaimed at once as a masterpiece: Weimar Germany.

Society or community?

To call Weimar a 'republic' is to expect more than its political constitution in fact achieves. With so much unchanged from the old regime, a deep acculturation is simply not effected. Germany does not have its Cleisthenes. And if we look at its intellectuals and its artists, we perceive the signs of this. Sadly, or angrily, many of them are aware that their labours are accepted but not vital, that they are ineffectual. In the short term this is certainly true: the big gods who do battle are all pre-war ones. Over a short time, major systems of thought may have little direct impact on decision-makers, though over one or two generations they are certainly apt to influence élites. But the Weimar Republic does not enjoy the luxury of waiting one or two generations.

The obliteration of a political symbol (the Hohenzollern dynasty) has eliminated the central focus in a customary geography of values. It is of secondary importance that these values are in part overlaid by others in a massive industrial society; a particular authority may be tolerated, or its agents resisted—the pattern beneath remains. Loyalty to a pattern may even be thought of as the nostalgic loyalty of an individual or group to the centre, and this in turn may be represented, even felt, as 'community' (*Gemeinschaft*), 'organic', sanctioned by tradition. To replace it overnight by a 'society' (*Gesellschaft*) implying a far more intricate network of formal interconnections, a radical change in the geography of values and in the personal orientation of millions of citizens, is a venture of breath-taking presumptuousness. Not entirely without reason, it is denounced by the critics of Weimar as introducing an artificial system, repugnant to German *Kultur*; or alternatively as a rickety *bourgeois* device to put off 'the Revolution'. 'Pluralism' being alien, the classes and castes and the great collectivities of state and society conduct their political relations in a manner as unsettling and provocative as possible. A mere *modus operandi* is not regarded as ground for rational optimism. On the contrary: bafflements and frustrations feed a taste for irrationalism and are all eventually distilled into an extraordinary brew by an unexpectedly powerful enemy of the regime.

Until that tide engulfs the country, the Weimar Republic makes Germany an intellectual centre of Europe. Not only is Berlin the most exciting city, with its theatres, cinema, *avant-garde* opera, and controversial night-life. The country's thinkers, or some of them, are further into adventurous problematics than those of anywhere else. The human condition, the crisis of modern man, his alienation, destiny, perhaps downfall; the limits of historicism, of relativism, the critique of psychoanalysis, of Nietzsche, of Marx, of phenomenology, are best studied there. Existentialism is reborn: not from the Christian despair of Kierkegaard, or the pagan fervour of Nietzsche, but from the morose anguish of Heidegger. Along with a certain professionalism (very 'German' to the foreign observer—but it is grounded in an old pattern of social stratification), there is an unmistakable intensity, even a feverishness, not encountered further west: and it is impossible to dissociate these from the polarities and the misfits of an unprepared adventure in pluralism.

Into darkness

The eclipse of the Weimar Republic in 1933 is not a unique event; but just as its constitution has been the most momentous innovation, so too its end is the most exemplary. The National Socialist German Workers' Party (Nazi Party for short) has lesser parallels in other European countries, marked more or less by extreme nationalism after 1918; nowhere else is the growth of such a party so enormously facilitated by circumstance, by the regime it comes to replace, by the impact of economic crisis, slump and unemployment between 1929 and 1932, and by the hopes and expectations of those who put it into power—the mass electorate—among whom all classes are represented, even if these electors amount to less than half the voting population.

In seeking the support of this electorate, the Nazis produce a movement of a certain originality, but the first thing to notice about it is that *all* its ingredients are copied and taken up from existing features of the Weimar Republic and its life. It is a movement addressed to the 'masses'—like the German Nationalists of pre-war Austria, like the major parties of Weimar, especially the Socialists and the Communists (its nearest rival); it promises to break the mould of custom, that is to say the formal structures now forced together in a mixed democracy, which we have seen so widely execrated; it plays on a wide range of irrationalisms—of which we have seen no lack—the mystique of a People (*Volk*), the dream of a Community (*Gemeinschaft*), the enemies without. Race, superiority, destiny, revenge, *Lebensraum*, anti-Semitism, anti-Bolshevism, discipline: these are already commonplaces, either left over from the pre-war Reich or stridently adapted to present humiliations; while protection of the small man, of agriculture, of jobs, is a stock-in-trade of the hustings, mere promises. The sight of other party parades and military bands and mass spectacles in the 1920s is a reminder that the Nazi groups are not in the least eccentric in putting on uniforms and parading as paramilitary formations—the neglect of such things, rather, would require justification; strong-arm brutalities are no departure from the violence of the *Freikorps* in 1919 and *putsches* later (to say nothing of those tactics once observed by young Hitler in Vienna).

The famous Nazi programme of twenty-five points, which appeals to so many voters in the crisis years, is a compilation easily identified by the symbolic swastika on the front (other mass organizations have had their symbols too); within, there is no way of differentiating it from any other compilation of extreme nationalism, save only the paranoid violence with which Jews are denounced on almost every page. All this, taken together, suggests that we can in no way regard Nazism as an excrescence imposed on the republic. Its imitators in other countries will look in varying degree exotic or foreign; not so the Nazis themselves in Germany. From the start down to 1929 it is a small movement, just one particular form of extremism battening on the ideas of others, an alliance of toughs and misfits and deviants and adventurers. Gaining the support of Hugenberg's press and a fraction of industry, it is then put in a position to offer instant salvation to all; and Hitler's accession to power takes place in strict conformity with the letter of the Weimar constitution. *Corruptio optimi pessima . . .*

What happens *after* that is a different matter. The unloved regime is at once replaced by a totalitarianism as violent as any the world has seen (though not of course the only one).

Totalitarianism as we perceive it now is arbitrary rule of a special kind. It is a withdrawal of accountabil-

214   Adolf Hitler meeting the public

It is idle to seek to establish the 'true' character of a professedly 'charismatic' leader: heading a populist movement, his public images alone matter. There is no evidence that Hitler had any particular fondness for little girls.

ity on the part of the ruler to the ruled, but superimposed on a large industrial society. It involves, first, the absolute outlawing of every ideology but one: its own. All the numerous forms of association between individuals must be accredited, or reorganized, and policed; information must be controlled. Secondly, to affirm power and announce the ideology, symbolic acts and messages and monuments must be run as a monopoly, frequent, standardized, and massive. For these tasks a large force of agents of the regime is needed. Third, no limit is assigned to the control of individuals in society: for they are a part of the resources now to be deployed according to a sovereign decision. The Nazi minister Ley is on record that 'the private citizen has ceased to exist' (*Soldiers of Work*, 1938); this is untrue as it happens, but it states an ideal. Fourthly, although collective leadership is possible, a single powerful leader is likely to have featured in a mass movement's formative stages; his charismatic identity is of high symbolic usefulness even if (as in all political systems) there are aspirants for the succession. Fifthly, since leadership is unaccountable, it can do no wrong; or at the least, subjects have greatly reduced chances of redress against a wrong, as always in an absolutist state. And finally, to

the extent that such a society can be *totally* organized, it becomes a 'closed' one; not incapable of change, no doubt, but with vastly reduced means of innovation and at the limit only able to bring about requisite change by the application of threats.

Accordingly, as the prince in his heyday creates new organs of power and recruits new servants, so now the totalitarian state requires its own outsize agencies: of espionage, of coercive police, of punishment. For some of this, mass parties may be used, alongside new bureaucracies; in Nazi Germany both systems are adopted, from the moment that Heinrich Himmler becomes head of police as well as party boss in charge of Nazi storm-troops (S.S.)—an early measure of Hitler's Third Reich, and prodigiously suggestive. The people's élite—or at least its power élite—begins to create a 'community', an 'organic' structure of control: not quite in the way dreamed of before.

This brief typology fits rather closely the extremely barbarous regime that follows the Weimar Republic. But with one restriction: the Third Reich lasts so short a time that the system is one of perpetual improvisation with hardly a moment for thoughtful integration. Also its orientation is frankly and openly warlike. Assuming office in 1933, the Nazis under Hitler abolish democracy, opposition parties, trade unions, resistance, in three months flat; within a year the leader has set up concentration camps for his enemies, and then liquidated by mass murder his more radical supporters (the Storm Detachment hearties of Ernst Röhm). In 1935 the Nuremberg Laws unleash a reign of terror for the large population of Jews; serious rearmament begins; mass unemployment is eliminated. In the following three years the nation is brought under a 'New Order' and made ready for aggressive world policies; then Austria is annexed, and in the succeeding eighteen months Czechoslovakia is dismembered, Poland attacked, and a general war begun. Thereafter the Third Reich fulfils a purely destructive self-appointed destiny of annexation, predation, and genocide, ending with its own annihilation in 1945.

In consequence of this breathless tempo, some parts of the totalitarian project are much more sketchy than others. The army stands largely aside from the Nazis' embrace, while executing their orders. The direction of the economy is less brilliant than a Four-Year Plan suggests. By contrast, the *bureaucratization of terror* is overwhelmingly successful: in this field at least Spengler's intuitions bear fruit. No wartime campaign will be more thoroughly planned and punctiliously carried through than the horrifying programme for simply killing millions upon millions of Jews in an aimless holocaust. Alongside the machinery of repression, the other triumph of National Socialism is its propaganda. It helps, of course, to have a ministry without inhibitions; but now the leader's voice can be relayed into millions of homes (at about the same time that the voice of F. D. Roosevelt is also heard across another continent—but in 'fireside chats'); party rallies can be followed on screens by those unable to attend them; a controlled press effects an absolutely novel conditioning of the public. Its efficacy may be judged by the lack of new opposition once the regime's main opponents have been silenced, and the terrifying docility with which brutality against the scapegoat Jew is countenanced, to the extent that it is known or rumoured.

It is not easy to see National Socialism as anything other than a systematic cowing and brutalization of a whole people, with various complicities. Among the less horrifying gestures by which this is announced is the hounding out of all dissonant voices or figures in the country, liberal or leftist or Jewish, in the name of national purity. There is a spectacular exodus of talent and eminence, and no replacement for it: among those whose names we have lately encountered, the emigration includes Grosz, Hindemith, Zweig, Gropius,

Mannheim, Lukács, Klee, Kandinsky; among many distinguished scientists Einstein, Oppenheimer, Krebs; whole centres of learning disperse or emigrate—the Bauhaus, the Institute for Social Research, the Warburg Institute. Other symbolic 'cultural' gestures include the public burning of 'un-German' books by stormtroopers and students, and the derisive dispersal of 'un-German' (or Jewish, or decadent, or bolshevist, or 'negroid') art from public galleries in 1935. A few of Weimar's luminaries offer their services to the régime or the party: Spengler, the Expressionists Gottfried Benn and Edgar Jung; the first two are cold-shouldered, the third shot. The Reich has no need for 'intellectuals', and we recall the words of Goering's admirer Johst (the former Expressionist and pacifist of 1914!): 'When I hear the word culture [*Kultur*] I unfasten [*entsichere*] my Browning.'

This is one aspect of a seeming contradiction at the heart of Nazi policies. The régime is brash, uninhibited, making a break with old customs, and its political 'style' is in a sense studiously 'modern': Hitler-salutes, uniforms, media, symbols, rallies. This in fact gives it an enormous enhancement of power, as does any confident display of purpose previously not expected from a government. But it has actually no use for contemporary arts, and no wish to look for new forms. The leader himself has petit-bourgeois tastes; the failed architect and 'artist', he knows what he likes in buildings (grandiose, imperial, a sort of updated neoclassical); for his great rallies the same; for the rest, art must be 'German', and this takes a little time to define. As for literature, Hitler has a nod for the aged race theorist H. S. Chamberlain (a keen Wagnerite!), and allows Nietzsche, suitably adjusted, to be used as prophet of the Aryan superman. But it is notorious that when his loyal follower Alfred Rosenberg produces a slightly more worked out than usual ideology of Nazism (*The Myth of the Twentieth Century*, 1930) Hitler does not bother about it. It remains that 'modernism' as hitherto exhibited is in all respects 'Jewish' and 'culture-bolshevistic': the truthfulness or otherwise of such assertions is hardly material.

The Third Reich leaves behind it absolutely no significant memorial other than the technical achievements of its engineers and scientists: missile rockets (eagerly scrambled for by victorious enemies to improve *their* rocketry), the concept of the *Autobahn*, a string of synthetic pharmaceuticals and substitute products required by an 'autarkic' economy, and the *Volkswagen* designed to order for the regime by the engineer Dr. Porsche. (As this last-named item shows, objects can change their meaning; had the famous 'Beetle' been in

215   Publicity still for Leni Riefenstahl's _Triumph of the Will_, 1936

Not only are Nuremberg rallies an important Nazi ritual; they must also be fed into the propaganda system. Leni Riefenstahl (stooping by the camera) captures in a brilliant film images of implacable power, absolute unity, and also the diversity of uniformed groups—soldiers, storm-troops, police, labour corps—brought together in huge numbers to celebrate the Will of the Leader.

general use already in 1939 as a People's Car, it is not so obvious that its unmistakable profile would have been so happily accepted in a post-war world.) The general point stands. It is not a case here of victors blotting out memories of the losers' achievements; it is simply that Hitler's 'populism' contains no original orientations but only reactionary ones: militarism, anti-feminist 'back to the kitchen', chauvinism, racism. An American journalist of the time, E. Mowrer, accurately defines this scenario in the title of his book *Germany Puts the Clock Back*. And though Hitler and some of his associates would be happy to see cultural reflections of the revived 'organic' society they direct, under the swastika nothing results which today would seem to have the faintest positive merit; the swastika itself survives as not much more than a symbol of deviance among young persons whom one presumes ignorant of what it has actually presided over. Much the same can be said of other attempts at totalitarian regimes of the twentieth century; worshipping them has produced no great human memorials, and hankering for them only curiosities. Is this Black Hole in European culture very surprising? Germany, at any rate in 1933, has the extraordinary ill-fortune to fall under the rule of a movement which glorifies brutality, derides reason and humanity, outlaws the 'alien', the hybrid, and the cosmopolitan, takes leave of reality, declares war on the world, and with all controls jammed plunges into the Void. National Socialist culture is a rather successful case of collective suicide.

This chapter bears the title 'A Crisis in Modernity'. What is the nature of that crisis?

At the root of the matter is the suddenness with which democracy arrives in Germany. As shown, it is not a 'natural' pattern of political relations, and it has no time to strike root. There is a conspicuous disjointedness in the way institutions old and new are bidden to coexist. At the political level the tensions are manifest. But at the level of intellectual activity—which is very intense—the same is also true; and it is cruel to see the way in which pre-war, pre-republican battles continue to be fought in the arts, even in *Doctor Caligari*! Those whose vocation is to give expression to values, even, if they wish, in extreme and unadulterated form, seem often to be talking about the problems of a world which is not in the last resort their world: no bad thing, to be sure, and indeed that may be an important task of the expressive arts; yet the curious time-lag of Expressionism is disturbing. One swallow does not make a summer: neither the Bauhaus nor *The Magic Mountain* is representative, even if each is in its way typical of a powerful drive for meaningfulness—against the odds. The crisis, as we see it, has to do with a profound failure—at this point in time—to anchor creative activity either in a vision of the present or indeed in any perception of direction (other than the sinister fragmentation of the ideologies, black or red). Individual achievement is not enough. All that freedom . . . and to what purpose? One is sorely tempted to wonder whether the abortive adventure in freedom is not a melancholy experience, part of the décor for looking back and seeing the past as indeed *La Belle Époque*.

216   Volkswagen, 1938

The most famous profile, perhaps, of any automobile ever made. Yet who remembers that 'Volk' is in its name only because the Leader of the Third Reich was determined to supply his People with a spectacular token of his regime's achievement? Thanks to a World War, this vehicle ends up as a symbol of postwar economic recovery and mass-consumption society.

Chapter 10
Yesterday

The broken picture

The starting-point of yesterday is 1945, the end of a second great war in Europe, a scene of devastation and terrifying uncertainties: hecatombs of war dead and missing persons; cities gutted, bridges broken, factories wrecked. All over central Europe deportees or refugees are crowded into camps or wander in directions where home may no longer be. Alien armies administer 'relief' in shattered communities. There are oceans of anomaly—victims and ex-predators in the same bread queue, black markets, deft identity changes, this hero acclaimed and that imprisoned, *sauve-qui-peut*. And then as new or restored governments settle into place and life resumes, a picture of what has happened begins to take shape; it brings home, even to those in untroubled corners of the countryside, something of the precariousness of civil society, and of the unimaginable which has happened and may not in fact be at an end. The widely publicized war-crimes trials, news photographs of nameless horror—Belsen, Auschwitz, Buchenwald, Mauthausen—reprisals on Lidice and Oradour, populations wiped out in giant air raids, the calvary of a Warsaw uprising. Ten million Germans have been turned out on to roads westward from Prussia and Bohemia with a brutality little different from the preceding reign of terror; elsewhere quislings are brought to account, and 'resisters' settle old scores with 'collaborators' (the reckoning is less edifying, less morally simple, than the dream cherished in a long night of oppression). In the east, a red terror quickly follows the black one, this time not covered by the world's press; it feeds a more distant archipelago of slavery and humiliation, revealed only later as part of the same nightmare landscape.

It takes a whole generation for this dawn scene of 1945 to lose an obsessive power. Peace is not the millennium.

Revulsion from the hated Nazism is a common starting-point agreed by all. Dictators, totalitarian control, militarism, arbitrary oppression, are absolute evils that must never return. But what is now to replace those evils? Far away, and at a level high above the streets and camps and soup-kitchens, a preamble to the United Nations Charter proclaims a shape for things to come, great commonplaces which now are *not* to be taken for granted. They are peace, fundamental human rights—the equality of men and women, of nations large and small—and the application of wealth to 'social progress' and greater 'freedom'. Such terms, drafted by officials, reflect compromises made between allies in war, specifically between Roosevelt and Stalin. To one superpower (the U.S.A.) the programme spells open societies everywhere, commercial expansion; to the other (the U.S.S.R.) it points to new communist regimes and wholly collectivist societies. Both superpowers read into the U.N. Charter the demise of old colonial empires and scope for their own modes of expansion in the future. It becomes a major fact for post-war Europe that the U.S.A. has just *doubled* its economic power, for which reason expanding trade is a policy imperative; another major fact is that the U.S.S.R. has turned itself into a vast military-industrial monolith. The partition of Europe by an 'iron curtain' follows inevitably.

In Western societies the democratic ideals of the U.N. Charter are accepted with little comment, but even so, in a way which is peculiarly European; this is particularly as regards the interpretation of 'social progress'. In virtually every one of the restored or surviving states of western Europe this term is read to mean not simply a New Deal but something rather more: a 'welfare state'. Is it that memories survive of bad old *laissez-faire* in the pre-war years? In most communities this is certainly the case; also in occupied Germany there is a need to do better than Hitler, in Italy to surpass by

217   Professor Fritz Cremer and others, DDR war memorial, Austrian war memorial park, Mauthausen

A memorial to the victims of a mass-extermination camp raises severe problems of symbolism. All earlier commemorative forms are, almost by definition, inappropriate. A text by Brecht, engraved on a wall, announces the expiatory nature of the monument; and there has *to be a haunting memory of barbed wire, that most inhuman of motifs. Even so, the artist keeps the latter in its place – behind the desolate solemn figure.*

deeds the rhetoric of fascism. The decision is at all events unanimous. 'Society' must assume responsibility for providing work, also for the realities of 'charity', concern for one's neighbour, the weak, and the poor; these things are too big to be left in future to private Samaritans, and have therefore to be the object of state policy, control, and administration. (Going further, governments with a socialist leaning carry the same argument into economic policy and 'nationalize' coal-mines, railways, airlines, steel industries, major banks, and public utilities, to varying degrees.) With variations in detail from country to country, the easiest and most obvious method is followed for the new welfare services: state bureaucracies are created for comprehen-

sive health provision, pensions, employment, poor relief, and education; and these things are paid for (mostly) via the tax-collector.

A whole new sector of economic and social life thus becomes recognized, along with a range of expanded or upgraded or newly structured professions—health administrator, social worker and the like—and the occupational structure of western Europe takes a massive tilt towards 'service' jobs (this coincides with the equally massive resumption of a drift into towns). So long as this adjustment is actually taking place, and new bureaucracies are being brought into being at the same time as post-war reconstruction is being pursued and six years of housing neglect caught up on, 'full employment' is no problem.

The welfare state may look to us such a humdrum, even trite, concept that it is not easy to recognize the very large transformations that its arrival triggers off at every level of cultural institution. We shall presently come upon some of the less obvious aspects of this; here we may simply note that once introduced (broadly, by the early 1950s), the growth of public services gives government—'big' government—a momentum and an appetite that continues for at least three decades. The new institutions have value-loadings: for example, expanded and reformed systems of education are meant to further the ideals of personal freedom and equality (of opportunity), comprehensive social insurance removes degrading fear, transfer payments and graduated taxes are to erase the more obvious signs of inequality. Following the same trail, big government intervenes to provide or control minimum wages, statutory holidays, safety at work, subsidized housing, care for the aged, protection for children in problem families, concessionary prices, and a hundred other features of daily life. All these unpoetical measures serve the ideal of 'human', not merely civil, rights: they are quite different from the nineteenth century's more legalistic idea of freedom, and also different in their impact from millenarian talk of (instant and absolute) equality.

In surprisingly little time, in fact, each and all come to be taken for granted; that is to say absorbed into general patterns of expectation. They also arouse an expectation of yet *more* intervention; and at the same time they generate a backlash, a demand for *less*. They also set the scene for unprecedented economic problems: the symbols of a rising standard of living are almost always physical objects (bought by citizens) or immediate enjoyments (leisure), while the 'service' realities are often invisible or even merely stand-by insurance for a rainy day, yet paid for by (rising) taxation. Who wants to temper his enjoyment of the visible

218 Basil Spence, entrance screen of the Crown of Thorns Chapel, Coventry Cathedral, 1962

As part of a great church erected alongside the bombed ruins of its predecessor, the Crown of Thorns motif echoes most explicitly the barbed wire of the concentration camps (and of battlefields in a previous war); and as though to underline the architect's intention here, his design is executed by the hands of army engineers.

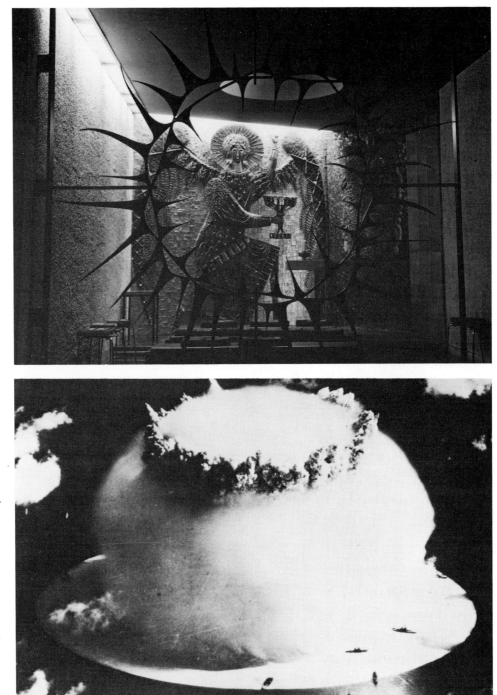

219 A nuclear bomb explosion at Bikini Atoll in the Pacific, 1946

The enormous mushroom cloud is first seen by the world in 1945 over Hiroshima and Nagasaki. Shown here is the subsequent explosion of a test nuclear device (the mushroom about to burst forth upwards); such experiments, carried out for a score of years by five states, cast a formidable shadow over international relations; and partly explain the power-eclipse of the historical nation-states of Europe.

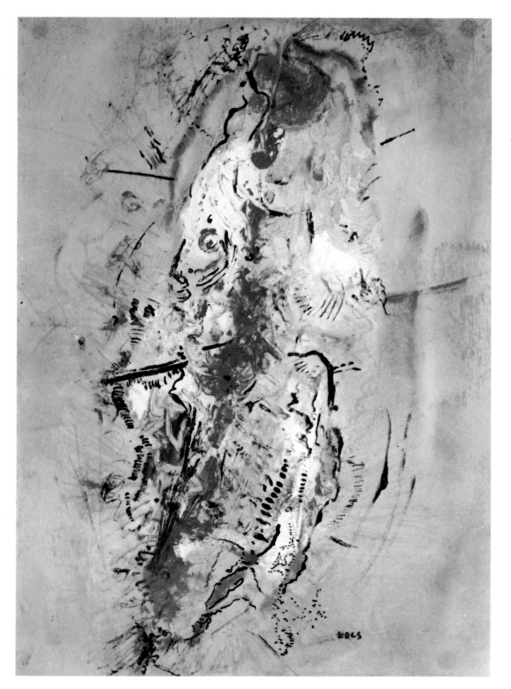

220   Wols (Alfred Otto Wolfgang Schulze), *Gouache*, **1949.** $8\frac{1}{4} \times 6$ **in (21 × 15 cm). Private Collection**

The complete liberation of painting from preconceived ideas about communication – subject or message, mood or rhetoric – follows from the endless 'modern' pursuit of the artist's unique statement; it has come to leave only form (in the most general sense) as a common ground. With this, Western art at last inherits a limitless vein of intuition: in which any future 'styles' will be arbitrary and not 'natural' languages.

221   Film still from Vittorio De Sica's *Umberto D*, 1951

Umberto D (with his older, 'liberal' values) seeks to escape into a hospital from the world as it has come to seem to him. The seedy guest-house and its clutter symbolize a pre-war order of society that has fallen to pieces – without the Brave New reconstructed Italy being ready yet to supply his welfare.

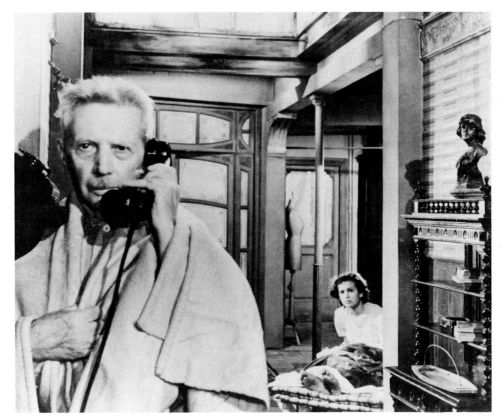

in order to provide for more of the invisible? The Protestant ethic begins to look quite old-fashioned.

By its nature, then, the welfare state as actually created leads to large bureaucracies, floods of laws and regulations, impersonal adjudications, form-filling, registration, licensing, declarations, encroachments on privacy. Within a decade paradox appears: is the 'caring' society edging towards one of the hated characteristics of totalitarianism, intrusion into the citizen's private affairs? George Orwell's *1984* is an allegory, a very early warning of wider import than is recognized in 1949. Presently *any* elaborate public system begins to be seen as harbouring an Orwellian threat, or at the least it is a re-run of Kafka's *The Trial*; any social environment built up from gigantic organizations can be as threatening as a tyranny. It is also as demoralizing: the condition of loneliness is not abolished by administration.

There are further handicaps to be faced in developing the society which is both caring and free. Thus, democratic pluralism depends on large political organizations which are in business to compete with each other; they offer conflicting ideologies, diagnoses, and recommendations. Which to believe? Even in learning to mistrust them *all* (and at the same time discount the rhetoric of governments), a citizen does not escape from ignorance or inadequacy. In an age which sets out to create a welfare society, and elevates 'economic performance' to pay for it into a kind of materialist *machismo*, it is amazing to reflect that nearly every man in the street is completely vague about economic realities, which in truth are no longer simple. That is not the only form of blinkering. In an age given to redoubled promises, policies, planning, confidence in social action, a persistent *failure to deliver* is also baffling. A sober Italian film, *Umberto D*, captures the predicament of a lonely old man in a post-war society where democracy has *not* introduced kindness, rationality, purpose, or hope for all. On the contrary, the landscape around him is quite explicit: empty lots, crumbling tenements, hostile raw concrete buildings, roads petering out . . .

Post-war Europe has therefore a kitbag of disparate ideals, and problems reflecting just that. Freedom, but a growing web of bureaucratic, depersonalized imperatives; democracy, but the threat of alienation at every turn; respect for the individual, but increasingly a disregard for real persons; a 'caring' society, but the very words 'society', 'social', coming to be overworked so obsessively that they lose their sense altogether. One thing at any rate is plain: the idea of progress, decisively discredited in the horrors of war, has now lost any power to inspire. National pride, too, is under a cloud; no other great inspiration breaks the surface; surviving ideologies—liberalism, socialism, communism—continue rather as organizational habits than as sources of new insight into the predicaments of the day. 'Economic growth', offered as an ideal, is no substitute, for it does not deign to vouchsafe a view on the lineaments of the Good Life; it is, of course, a programme of ways and means for enabling that desirable (but undefined) end to be made possible, assuming it calls for the deployment of enhanced wealth.

The absurd

It is no surprise that the symbolisms and arts of the post-war world do not celebrate the achievement of an extraordinary new set of social standards or the convalescence of ordinary life (at any rate in any direct or explicit way). Instead, they begin by rehearsing conflict, frustrations, the continuing protest of idealism—but robbed now of its convenient 'fascist' bogyman. A new cultural map rapidly takes shape: its centre-piece is, first, a debate on 'stripped-down' man; and then within the decade, as memories of war recede, more surprising trends branch out.

The thoughts of intellectuals in 1945 focus to begin with on Existentialism. In an occupied Europe atrocious dilemmas have been common. 'Whose side am I on?' 'Who do I choose to be?' 'What am I prepared to pay for being who I am?' The society which has undergone both disturbing convulsions in war and then the most rapid return to normality is that of France. Almost predictably, therefore, these questions, the *anguish* associated with them, the *absurdity* of a world which offers not one single helpful clue towards an answer, are most passionately explored in Paris, at least by its progressive 'mandarins': by the heavy-weight philosophic J.-P. Sartre in a series of plays and novels, by the more humane A. Camus in tales and essays, by Christian philosophers—E. Mounier, Gabriel Marcel. Camus' *Outsider*, indeed 'the Outsider', acquires dominant status. From the existential problems of political allegiance (*Dirty Hands*) or of cities under siege (*The Plague*), a new 'theatre of the absurd' quickly moves on from war echoes to the more general predicament of man. *Waiting for Godot* is a play enacted in a setting quite without social co-ordinates, and without any location in time either: simply two tramps in a void. What

makes Samuel Beckett's first play remarkable is not simply the stripped-down allegory of whatever we may wish to read into its strange riddle. It is that the two tramps who hold the stage, Vladimir and Estragon, are also *clowns*: in their modulated pattern, their misunderstanding, inelegant hernias and odours, and fumbling stage business. And clowns are above all else images of the little man. They echo Charlie Chaplin, and behind him the clown in tatters, *Pierrot Lunaire*, the scarecrow, the endlessly contemptible outcast, the image of a humanity stripped of feathers and medals, standing naked, twisted, twitching—but *hanging on*. And at the start of that very long road, the Man of Sorrows. (Vladimir and Estragon have no ancestors in Greek or Roman comedy. That is one reason why we sometimes find the latter so oddly lacking in what we sense to be 'ordinary' humanity. *Waiting for Godot* is not necessarily a Christian allegory; but it cannot escape being set in a tradition which has been quickened by Christianity somewhere along the line.)

These clowns, we have said, are not in historical time; yet they have been pulled out of *a* time, and it is a rather recent one. Their existential choice—for it is that—is to 'hang on'; and in that they remind us, however distantly, of moral traces left by the holocaust of war. Can we speak of 'progress' in such matters? Very likely not; even so, something has changed between the aftermath of 1918 and that of 1945. In the former, Europe has commemorated her heroes and her dead in *noble figures*: statues of generals or idealized long-suffering soldiers from the trenches, or else in strident totems (eagles struck down, statues of the victorious *Latin Genius*). Even the tomb of the Unknown Soldier (no one knows which side he was on) has been the scene for patriotic bugle calls and ceremonies. And those writers who between the wars attempt to tell it like it was—Barbusse, Robert Graves, Remarque—have not made very much of a dent in the conventional attitudes to heroism. But in 1945 grandiloquent symbols have no longer any place in recording what is to be commemorated: which is not victory and triumph but loss—not forgetting the heroism of some, true, but with overwhelmingly greater awareness of wanton massacres, an ocean of unrecorded suffering, the pathetic extinction of millions of quite unheroic persons. A repeat of 1919 is unthinkable. Stripped and humiliated, the dead and the missing *cannot* be idealized in hackneyed ways. And therefore the expression of loss must take other forms. The abstractions of anatomy convey realism in a new mode, an angular wreckage of barbed wire, a detritus of the battlefield or the shattered town. Barbed wire . . . a Crown of Thorns . . . even in a

222   Henry Moore (1898–), *Falling Warrior*, 1956–7. Bronze, 23¼ × 57¾ × 30 in (59.1 × 146.7 × 76.2 cm). Washington, Smithsonian Institution, Hirshhorn Museum and Sculpture Garden

For Henry Moore the 'falling warrior' theme, so long established and widely recognized already, no longer conveys (in the mid-50s) any poignant reference at all, but rather a grand and timeless monumentality.

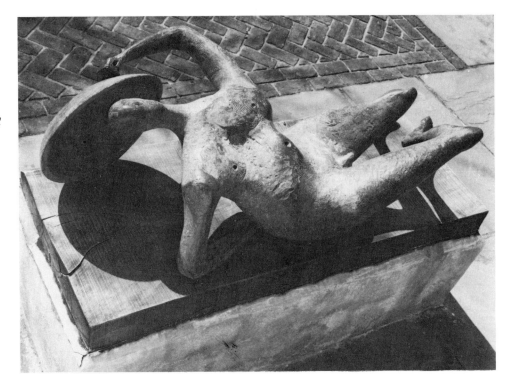

rebuilt Coventry Cathedral the ubiquitous barbed wire finds an echo.

Heroes are out; they have no place in post-war symbolism. In their place, the little man is the norm: he has no style, no panache, no grandiloquence. What could be his authentic pose? A resister? His resistance is blind, his fortitude looks something like a tetanus spasm, his death a spectacle of disgust and ignominy. Merely to cling to being, against all the odds, that is his supreme defiance; the unclear no-man's-land between being and not-being, the limits of existence when the human cry is not even unambiguously human any longer—*that*, not rhetorical defiance, is the obsessive focus of innumerable war stories and memoirs; no doubt of recollections, too (and again, all Beckett's plays and writings after *Godot* probe at the thin, frayed edge of life, on the point of disappearance).

Contemplation of near extinction cannot go on for ever, even so. The 'theatre of the absurd', to begin with, branches out, from either the historically anchored or the existential to either the abstract or the general. The absurd can take so many forms! Eugène Ionesco picks up earlier strands of surrealist fantasy; some are simple exercises in virtuosity, grotesqueries; but *Rhinoceros* takes the atrocious image of a whole township which succumbs little by little to the epidemic of Rhinoceritis (even the girl-friend welcomes turning into a rhinoceros), leaving the 'little man' Béranger at the end entirely alone, shut up in his room, preparing to sell his life dearly. This curious fantasy has been staged as though it were an allegory of the inexorable Nazi take-over of men's minds. But it could equally well stand for any other irrational—or, if it comes to that, rational—take-over: a single image with a multitude of references, this (as its author would state) is not surrealism but realism. But personal relations too can be absurd: Harold Pinter's *The Caretaker* in a more homespun English idiom offers an exploration of their totally capricious dislocations (not the less influentially for being pleasantly accessible to amateur theatricals). And social conventions can, once again, be assaulted; but now head-on, from the viewpoint of confirmed criminality, as Jean Genet exhibits (with enthusiastic philosophical support from Sartre).

In a word, post-war theatre, building on common traumatic experiences in a recent past, offers little promise of agreeable 'rationality' in human affairs. We are, of course, used by now to seeing the collective discomforts of intellectuals in their imaginings, their fear of trite sentiment, their reliance on effects of shock to prove authenticity. For all that, they are supplying the rituals of the tribe.

223   Le Corbusier
(1887–1966), Unité
d'Habitation, Marseilles,
1947–53

*An early—and
famous—example of post-war
city building, Le Corbusier's
contribution to the townscape of
Marseilles gives no warning of
what will prove to be socially
disruptive in 'mass' housing
projects: effects in fact unrelated
to, and unaffected by, this
architect's interest in adapting
his building 'module' to a
human scale.*

Engineering society

There is so much to plan in the years after 1945! So
much scope for rationality! Recovery and aid programmes, new or modernized administrations, industrial
infra-structures, economic and social futures, all the
new welfare systems, and all the housing needs of tens
of millions of homeless persons, new households, new
cities.

Planning goes with the ambition to achieve big
things against the clock; with 'socialism'; with
'growth'; with the vindication of bureaucracies; with
new and self-important specialisms; with the architect's
dream of constructing on a large scale—whole environments sprouting from the ground, cities remodelled,
new uses for bombed lots, technologies and materials
put to work, *social engineering.*

Looking back, we can judge with a moderate
amount of dispassion the visible monuments of a hectic
period: some grandiose, some practical, some clumsily
contemptuous of the realities of day-to-day living,
almost all failing to supply cities where hugely expanding urban populations can feel at one with their surroundings without the gratuitous insult of social dislocation. It takes half a generation for the urban scene to
take on its new characteristic landmarks—for earlier

pioneering in concrete or steel or glass to spawn the
high-rise downtown office block or suburban mass
housing. By the time this has happened, the city centres
of Europe are beginning to look very like one another;
large buildings have become engineering projects for
populations, not for people.

And not too much attention has been paid to human
perceptions or to the feelings of the troglodytes secreted
in the cliffs of concrete or funnelled to and from their
work or play. It has proved quite easy to design and
erect a complete 'precinct'; less easy to coax a 'living'
community into existence in it. Great design achievements display in use another face: call it inhumanity—in
Le Corbusier's vaunted showpieces, beginning in
Marseilles (*la Cité Radieuse* becoming the less glamor-

224   L. S. Lowry (1887–1976), *Industrial Scene with
Monument*, 1972. Oil on board, 30 × 25 in (76.2 ×
63.5 cm). Private Collection

*That every moment of history is a tangle of anachronism has
been obvious in earlier pages. Nowhere is this more forcibly
shown than in works such as this, where an industrial landscape at
least a hundred years old has been built into a composition which
is interesting in itself ('socially' too) but which also owes
something to studiously 'naive' paintings and to twentieth-century
abstraction.*

ous 'unit of habitation'), in the intimidating cliff-like structures zigzagging around the perimeter of great metropolitan centres, or in the hundreds of like developments which are the means for turning Europe from a dominantly rural into a largely urban environment for a majority of its citizens. The planner's dream, the science fiction image, preside at the start; but dreams and images are treacherous. From an early date, in some of these structures, the other face declares itself: loneliness, neglected upkeep, prostitution, other uncovenanted worries, are reported from the new Elysiums. The break-up of more 'natural' communities, no doubt insalubrious, the increasing isolation of the nuclear family in its allotted pigeonhole, neglect of schoolchildren by mothers out at work, separation from other members of the larger family network; truancy; vandalism; all these productions of the planner (who else?) call for multiplied exertions on the part of the welfare officer and the policeman to stem the human reactions which come into prominence (they are called 'social problems'). One bureaucratic service creating work for another: what work of science fiction could have contrived better?

The 'social problems' are absorbed into the fabric of dulled hopes and disappointments. Significantly, the old concept of 'anomie', coined by the sociologist Durkheim at the turn of the century (in his investigations into suicide rates), comes into fashion after long disuse. Not only does it preoccupy a new generation of sociologists; it finds echoes in a popular musical hit, the Beatles' *Eleanor Rigby*. The refuse on a windy lot may have caught an earlier poet's eye, and Leonardo da Vinci has recommended looking at stains on walls: but now rubbish and art come much closer together. The abstract rationale in the planner's diagram is one thing—unfortunately, no one gets much artistic elation from it; it is not the rationale but the physical reality on the sidewalk, the slum not yet cleared away, the new slum in the making, the debris, and the derelicts—that is where drama and poetry and the visual arts actually find their images.

And of course the mass 'consumer society', surfacing in the 1950s, the fruit of huge labours of clearing and reconstruction and investment and urban sprawls and twenty million new households and surging markets to supply all that goes into them, is—with its concomitant welfare systems—not exactly a subject for song, or exultant fictions. At least, it gets none, after J. B. Priestley's maudlin anticipatory film, *They Came to a City*: but if we care to look we can see that it too is reflected, both directly and indirectly, in the symbolisms of the time.

A culture of leisure?

Within one generation from 1945, what is loosely called 'youth' takes on an identity in Europe that it has never had before. (The same is evidently true in the U.S.A. and in most other consumer-oriented industrialized service societies). What distinguishes it most is that, unlike earlier identifications of youth as a kind of respectful preparation for being grown up (catered for by Boy Scouts, Boys' Brigades, Hitler Youth, Young Socialists, or Komsomol organizations), Yesterday discovers Youth as a category in its own right, and with what appear to be its own values. It is no longer anyone's apprentice.

In strict chronology, the first door to open on the way, the first condition to be satisfied, is economic: rising disposable incomes in the urban community, wage packets and pocket-money which bring independence nearer to teenagers. The first sign that this shift has occurred is when retail traders begin to supply a large market with clothing more and more distinctively for *young* people (the first inspiration seems to have come from wartime California, where cheeky civil attire can provoke the uniformed serviceman on shore leave; with peace and wages the idea crosses the Atlantic). There are several starts in European youth-styles: zoot-suits, teddy-boy or spiv gear—these catering for the 'sharp' tastes of a working-class minority with money to spare. A much more significant breakthrough comes with a new range of symbols which are distinctive and yet also democratic. And for this, again, there are transatlantic inspirations: the informal wear and casual bearing of the G.I. off duty in Europe has not gone unnoticed by young observant eyes. But the process is a gradual one; mid-1950s prosperity supplies Milanese boys with Vespas and Lambrettas, but the girl-friend perched on the pillion still wears a pretty frock and rides side-saddle. Five years later both are in jeans.

The welfare society, for which the new urban landscape is rising up, is (as we have noted) also affecting the habits and norms of its basic social unit, the family, especially in the largest cities. Not only are family cohesions eroded, with growing employment of women; schooling is extended—one result being to accentuate the transition of young people to the status of 'earner', by making it coincide more with growing up. The household head finds his authority slipping away, at least in some of its traditional forms. A pillar of Victorian society, nearly a century earlier, has stated flatly that 'there is no greater uncertainty about the duty of obedience to parents and to the laws of the land than about the properties of triangles' (B. Jowett). Who in 1950 can make that confident claim?

In proportion as older links are blurred, there is a gain in peer-group identity; and this is rooted neither in encounters at home, nor at work, but essentially in leisure pursuits, whether centred on the street, around the football match, the club, the bar, the café, or that even more informal focal point, the 'disco'. In all these places, two features spring to the eye. First, that as never before in history, leisure becomes a *repudiation* of work and functional relationships (in contrast with older customs associated with membership of craft guilds, particular groupings, etc.). And secondly, in sharp contrast with the disciplined tasks imposed by 'official' society (school classes, work in large organizations, bowing the neck to bureaucracy, military service, religious observances) the relationships of leisure are informal, local, casual in style. To emphasize the point, new dance movements are likewise 'unstructured': 'classical' steps may still be practised on occasion, but they are a dying art; in the club or disco, jiving and rock'n'roll (again an American inspiration) allow a more personal easiness, more 'spontaneity'. As with clothing: jeans, originally a symbol of liberation, are prone to become a uniform; therefore they have to be re-casualized by frayed ends, long turn-ups, brand labels, patches, embroidered figures, messages, bagginess, tight hips, or simply encrusted layers of neglect. Entirely symptomatic is the fate of badges or buttons: originally marks of identity, categorizers, their use becomes related either to proclaiming emancipation in one or other witty or subversive form, or purely gratuitous, 'meaningless'. After all, Goering covered himself with medals . . . And so too with the introduction on clothing of written messages (originally indications of club membership): as the practice becomes generalized, so too the 'meanings' deteriorate, become unreliable, are displayed indiscriminately—just as tourists buy labels of places they have never been to to stick on their luggage . . . This indeed is an absolute novelty, because it is a sign of a literate age that can now afford to treat written messages, literacy itself, as a throw-away.

While clothing and dance sketch something of a 'revolt' of youth against conformity, discipline, tidy categories, it is pop music which really delineates the new culture of leisure. Impressive is the fact that for a decade and a half it appears to transcend boundaries, to unite all classes of young people, in an extraordinary fashion. Displacing the older outputs of dance bands (typically depicted in *uniforms*) or jazz groups or sentimental crooners, there is a quite sudden discovery of swing, then rock'n'roll. Its music celebrates a com-

prehensive range of 'youth' ideals: at the risk of pedantry they can be listed as togetherness, abolition of artificial barriers, revolt against old oppressions (thus betraying folksy American inspiration), but above all the call to be, to feel, *to do one's own thing*—whatever it may be; and this is mediated by the excitement and escape of rhythm, dance, presently loud music, hypnotic psychedelic lights, ecstasy or trance or sexual impulsion or drug-induced 'trips'. From the first and rather limited rock there comes Elvis; from the expanding world of pop, Bob Dylan, then the Beatles and the Rolling Stones: that is to say, groups of highly advertised suppliers of song and a style.

Among the multitude of young singers and groups who clutch a microphone and ply the guitar or the drums, the Beatles are a phenomenon. Not for outstanding talent or wit—but certainly for reiterated effort of invention, from an extremely narrow basis in musical competence. Typically, their name is meaningless but catchy. They sing for a pittance in clubs and bars in Liverpool, Glasgow, Hamburg, big cities with a limited but 'popular' music culture; endless gigs on the road to fame. Whatever the appearances, this 'scene' is not in any of the older senses of the word 'working-class'; three of their number and much of their audience represent that now quite large segment of an age group for which an ambiguous social mobility is both a liberation of a sort and a bit of a threat; with more than a touch of *anomie* thrown in. They are most warmly applauded in societies which have been most affected by the kinds of social change mentioned above: the north-western crescent of Europe, and Anglo-Saxon countries.

Once they take off, that is to say once commercial interests enter into alliance with newspaper media to generate extraordinary 'scenes', crowds of screaming teenage girls, near-riots, an irrational and escapist frenzy, the Beatles become something like the Voice of Youth. Sometimes a quite unusual voice, not really pop at all. Sometimes a voice of assured inanity (yet with lurking ambiguities). '*We all live in a Yellow Submarine*': this opaque and zany phrase is taken up, literally around the world; chanted over and over again; almost a mantra; not formless, but without end. '*And our friends are all aboard.*' Who? Anyone or everyone, pop star, drummer, fan, art student, the lad from the next street, bum, guru . . . Up to this point the Beatles stand at a point where the tastes of 'working-class' youth and all other youth can approximately merge.

This is no longer the case with the semi-surreal cartoon fantasy film which commercial studios produce to ride on the back of *Yellow Submarine*; nor indeed with

John Lennon's *Sergeant Pepper*, the first 'acid rock' advertisement of artificial paradise (the illegal drug L.S.D.) and other subversions. Enrichment of psyche and musical range by a futile stay in India (another breaking-down of barriers) marks a further shift towards the bohemian. By the time John Lennon is struck down by a crazy assassin's bullet in America (1980)—

and briefly mourned as a saint or great teacher—a more sophisticated pop, through endless diversification, is no longer quite the animal of the 1950s.

In the intervening two decades pop music stands for the ideals noted above; it can also be intertwined with certain kinds of protest. Protest against the world of routine, of discipline, of predestined careers (in pros-

228   The Beatles, a film still from Richard Lester's *Hard Day's Night*, 1964

The best-known of all pop groups puts on a show of high-spirited (and unrehearsed) insolence for the benefit of a camera-man. The interest of this youthful Beatles shot lies principally, no doubt, in the glimpse of urban neglect and decay—so essential a backcloth to this particular brand of insolence.

pect . . .), and class stratification; protest against the aspiring society and meritocracy and yardsticks of success (except that the commercial success of Elvis or the Beatles or the Rolling Stones is itself a grave paradox), against the materialism of the previous generation's satisfactions, and the insanities of established things in general. Against that despised (or allegedly despised) nexus it proclaims that only sincerity counts—and sincerity does *not* imply a deep search for quality or beauty or any other excellence. Sincerity can easily have to do with drifting around; it does not exclude contrived or dangerous experiences; its hallmark seems to be 'letting go'—which makes it look escapist to one of the severest critics of the age (Theodor Adorno), if not to the vast following it has attracted.

If it is a rather complicated exercise to prove that listening to the Beatles is escapist while listening to Mozart is not (and in fact outside the scope of our present inquiry), there is one further, and rather obvious, feature of pop which may be noted, since it marks a rather abrupt divergence from earlier traditions of European music. It is that the song is inseparable from the performer—as much a part of him as his hair. There is not a singer *here* and a song *there*, able to be considered separately on its own. Hundreds of thousands of young ladies in an earlier century have

given their own renderings of one and the same Schubert song; but who ever heard of any self-respecting major pop group singing the hit song of another group? That would not be 'their thing'. Conveniently to this ethos, the gramophone has all but replaced sheet music; it makes little difference if the Beatles can hardly read a score; the unique can be replicated—not a hundred thousand times but several million times.

Alternative

The youth culture whose readiest symbols are in clothing and pop music is much less homogeneous than the symbols suggest. In large industrial communities, small prominent groups on the streets have the most *déclassé* and least 'bourgeoisified' backgrounds: 'mods', tough gangs, *blousons noirs*, Hell's Angels for whom money means a motorcycle, a black leather jacket, boots, a clasp knife, emancipation with a nasty streak of violence, 'for kicks'. A larger segment of the population is busy with its own present rise in well-being and status, and this is true of the stratified working classes—there are still numerous 'working classes', whatever the ideologists proclaim—and among their young a majority are indeed on the 'educational conveyor-belt': that is

229   Film still from Wadleigh's *Woodstock*, 1970

For some, an all but unbelievably squalid spectacle; for others, an experience of escape, freedom, togetherness, fulfilment—the pop festival, and camping out for its tens or hundreds or thousands of followers. Here, clearly, is peaceful if momentary demolition of 'boundaries'; one more widely followed (both in Europe and America) than its complementary alternative the active terrorist group.

where the largest following of the Beatles is found. By contrast, from families of all strata which regard themselves as 'middle class', a different current flows, not always converging; that of the young or adolescent 'bohemian', often in revolt against parental standards, fostered by 'progressive' education and by a tenfold expansion in tertiary education. In the new service society, especially in its largest cities, bohemianism takes shape in the 1950s in the figure of the drop-out and the hippie, the more or less peaceable follower of radical non-conformity, the strolling guitarist, the pathetic drug addict; and by the end of the 1950s, certainly, in sufficient numbers for a collective identity to be detected, and a distinctly different life-style to take shape—in short, an *alternative culture.*

'Alternative'—or 'counter'—cultures are at the extreme limit of youth innovation: their adherents form loose groups to bring into reality the ideals rehearsed in their songs, to ask very earnestly the question 'Who am I?' but not trouble much with the answer (unlike existentialists). They elude the bondage of official institutions and official 'caring', they 'squat' in empty buildings, share necessities, migrate to rock festivals in summer, pick up cast-offs, play the welfare system, reject all sorts of routines that have been invented without *their* advice being asked. Alongside mass pop festivals

some have their own 'rave-ins', their own understanding of flower-power. The serious drop-out aims to squat permanently in a Yellow Submarine: not just call in for a trip. 'Paradise NOW.' 'Everything free for everybody.' Here and there a group sets to to create a genuinely *alternative*—that is, self-supporting, relatively non-parasitical—way of life, though as the fate of gipsy communities has begun to make plain there is not much room left in Europe for pioneering experiment, unlike nineteenth-century America; and there are not the motivations.

The ideals of the drop-out world are familiar enough, if vague. Tolerance is an absolute value. A kind of secular holiness is manifest in the respected image of the guru; if the Churches are fossilized, Buddhism or drugs or meditation are worth a try. Among the more literate the *names* of Marcuse, Nietzsche, Kropotkin, Ivan Illich, Sade, are definitely 'O.K.'; these are prophets, or guides, though their writings may be unread. Detachment from the nexus of capitalist conformity and 'order', detachment from formal institutions such as schooling and medicine, from the dogmas of European Christianity and its ethical and especially its sexual constraints: all that goes without saying. But also detachment from any determinate ideology, or any positive schemes for the future, or any

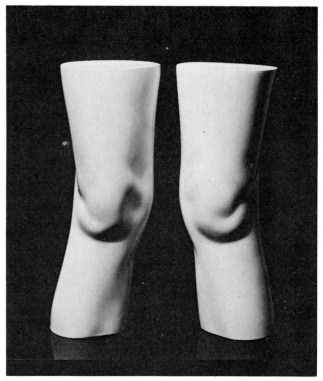

231   Claes Oldenburg (1929–), *London Knees*, 1966. Plastic, height 14¾ in (37.6 cm). Cologne, Museum Ludwig

The attractions of the mini-skirt, for wearer and beholder, need no comment; it takes pop art, in poker-faced mood, to highlight a lurking totemism.

230   Film still of Marlon Brando from Laslo Benedek's *The Wild one*, 1953

Moving shadows on a screen provide American images for a postwar generation seeking fantasy roles and badges – leather jacket, hot rod . . . A new avatar for Brighton Rock. *But the 'he-man' film-star with his animal endowments is not yet fully brutalized: that grass-roots refinement enters the repertory of urban youth with ostentatious gang violence in the following decade.*

definite messages from the past (history is dumped, which is why you don't need to read the masters, unless you want to). The heart-searching and debate which go on in mainstream society around such issues as abortion, single-parent families, homosexual tolerance, or ethnic conflict, can be dismissed with a shrug: if 'bourgeois society' promotes alcohol and tobacco yet bans hallucinogenic drugs, how can its moral agonizing be taken seriously?

The *scale* of hippie drop-out is hard to estimate

because its borders are hard to define. 'Communes' are usually unstable, with a short life-cycle; after which the participants drift elsewhere, or abroad, or 'back in'. Scattered around a dozen or so large European cities maybe several scores of thousands of individuals would form an unambiguous 'core' in the early 1960s. Perhaps the nearest thing to a European forerunner of this phenomenon would be the marginal sub-culture of spoiled priests and drop-out clerks in the later Middle Ages, whom we know of today only from a few surviving 'liberated' or smutty Latin lyrics. Both examples are, quantitatively, less than nothing when set alongside the vagrancy and banditry of the late sixteenth century, which is also in its way an alternative culture, and equally hard to circumscribe.

And yet the 'alternative cultures' of 1960 vintage, marginal and transient as they are, excercise a quite inordinate influence through their fringe of semi-adherents, sympathizers, echoes. Not only do 'smart sets' have affinities for Bohemia: *all* sets incline towards an increasing tolerance for symptoms of eccentricity and non-conformism. Bohemianism itself is no longer identified solely with avant-garde artists. The edges of convention are blurred, the outlandish in costume loses much of its power to shock, just as pop songs through endless repetition cease to convey a message and become simply an accepted background noise. And in this shifting of the economy of values and meanings, status symbols either disappear (bowler hats) or else are recast as ostentatious signs of affluence (shiny motor-cars, expensive hair-styling) or become ceremonial fancy dress (traditional formal wear).

Would the 'deformalizing' of social relations and their symbols have occurred anyway—through the varied impacts of democratized education, social promotion, changes in the pattern of urban life, and perhaps a few left-over memories of wartime dislocations? Obviously yes. But deformalizing has to look like something; and the lineaments actually taken over are largely those supplied by youth, and pop, and up to a point adolescent 'revolt'. 'It's child's play: Mum and Dad are learning fast.' What after all is more natural? Where else would a new set of lineaments come from? From the nostalgia of ex-servicemen? That has been tried before; to the extent that anything has come of it, it has been black shirts and military boots. But ex-servicemen in 1945 are less keen on glory than their fathers.

Christ without God?

It is centrally important to the reverberations of youth culture, and then of 'alternative' cultures, that post-war society with its welfare ideal generates a new prominence for the large categories of people in service functions already mentioned. The sociologist B. Martin has called them 'communicators'; in France something of the same sort is covered by the expression *'animateurs'* (animators): the teacher, the welfare worker, the priest, or active Church laity, those whose calling has to do with contact with people. They have existed before; what gives them importance now is their very great increase in numbers, their arrival at a large collective identity. All are deeply 'into' the ideals of the new society; not many have had either a rigorous educational formation or a serious intellectual commitment; they are widely recruited into an indeterminate and certainly not a high-visibility status; and they are loth to regard as 'deviant' the behaviour of any of those with whom they 'communicate' (one might almost

say, those with whom they *side* against the rigidities of 'society'). To be sure, there is no one standard profile of the 'communicator'; but the field in which their 'style' is most sharply profiled is that of upheaval in religious practice and in belief in the Christian Churches.

'De-Christianization' is the background, a challenge which has been faced between the two wars, notably by Catholic Action, attempting missionary tasks *within* Europe. In the 1950s the same challenge is more insistent, and the response much more thoroughgoing. The 'worker-priest', assigned to live and undertake work among the 'urban masses', to merge into the life of the latter and share their attitudes and hardships, sets aside his cassock and plays down the separateness of his calling; he comes also to incline to a new view of his inspiration, a new Christology, a view of Jesus as a radical; and even, sometimes, as more than a radical—a militant, a revolutionary. By 1960 the Gospel teachings are being rethought in terms of the political Left; St. Augustine's 'Love, and do what you will' seems to authorize extreme experiment; St. Paul's 'folly' becomes a call to plunge into social confrontation. Along with the worker-priest, the missionary in the Third World (ex-colonies) or the Italian Christian Democrat calling for an *apertura a sinistra* (political alliance with the Left) similarly testify to new inspirations.

In these various initiatives one issue within the Catholic Church comes repeatedly to the fore: the embarrassment of forms of the sacred which because they are traditional have become out of tune with 'reality', or suspect from association with earlier 'class structures'. In Catholic Europe this condemns the pomps and formalities of the Church, its liturgy, its reserved sacraments, old practices of veneration, and the uniforms which set the clergy aside, *outside*; also the clergy's doctrinally inspired separateness—the supernatural meaning of priesthood. Despite the canon of the Mass, why not bring in concelebration to symbolize brotherliness? Why not strip altar rails out of churches? Sacramental rites can then become like any other 'celebrations'. At any rate pop concerts and 'happenings' are brought into the churches, since solidarity and compassion and sincerity are the themes of such events. From there it is only a step to the question: 'What need at all of special, archaic, rites?' And after that, to the more portentous question: 'Do we even need the old meanings?' In short, the 'desacralization' of the Church is part of a process for making Christianity 'relevant': relevant to a new humanism of youth, and through that a revised vision of humanity. On those terms it is possible for a concerned laity to join hands with a 'religious Underground' by 1960, with its determined rejection of all sorts of marks of separation and distinction, vestments, and so forth, and a decidedly 'do-it-yourself' approach to the transmission of the Gospel of Love.

The demolition of barriers, the down-grading of forms of the sacred, open the way to adventures in relevance far more radical than those of previous generations of 'Christian Socialism'. It is no longer inconceivable to write and publish a Marxist commentary on St. Mark's Gospel. 'Theology of liberation', 'theology of revolution' are attempts by fringe groups to fuse materialism and religion, violence and love. In Paris and Louvain it is vigorously argued that the historical Jesus has foreseen class war and the violent denouement of history's Marxist dialectic (a denouement still in the future); in Germany, the Baader-Meinhof terrorist group issues from similarly concerned Lutheran opinion. Why wait for a Last Judgement?

And retreat from authority and its 'boss' roles (not only the epitome of injustice but now also darkened by recent memories of Hitler as the authoritarian leader) is mirrored both in attitudes towards a Church hierarchy and in the revision of belief. The radical Christian prefers to turn to Christ as the despised, the brother, the sufferer, the disturber, rather than (if the choice be faced) to the authoritarian Father, the Creator of a misshapen world, the God of Job and the atom, the Judge in his own cause. The echoes are plain: Existentialism with its flat denial of any 'meaning' built into the universe, socialism as an ideal of generalized mutual responsibility and respect, pop testifying to spontaneity and unlimited catholicity, and—perhaps not least—a sensitivity sharpened to the idea of an extreme suffering not only as manifested in one crucifixion and sacrifice but also in a more recent agony of millions, regardless of their creed. All these strands are interwoven.

In bringing them together—not of course an exclusive achievement of Catholics—the central arguments of Christian theology are in effect torn up: beginning with a belief in a transcendental order traceable to Providence. There is a very marked convergence here with the Protestant Churches. Lutheran, Calvinist, or Anglican, traditions are, to be sure, fairly familiar with desacralization because each in coming into existence has defined itself by desacralizing a part of earlier beliefs; and they have been on the whole less suspicious of erratic operations of the Holy Spirit. Even so, it marks a certain evolution when, in the years after 1945, Protestant theologians in considerable numbers are found taking to heart the anguished questionings of what thirty years before have been regarded as eccentric thinkers. In the case of Bultmann, a century of critical

232   Film still from Pier Paolo Pasolini's *Il Vangelo Secondo Matteo*, (The Gospel according to St. Matthew), 1964

A friendly young man surrounded by admiring children with bunches of flowers: viewed simply as an image, is this even so very far removed from the sentimental decencies of an earlier age? As a version of the Gospel, however, the shadows on the screen put in question once again the supernatural or sacred person of Jesus. And, as always, with a new topicality. For instance, those flowers—what should 'flower-power' mean?

German scholarship has led him to the point where he feels he must 'demythologize' (that is, reject) *all* the historical claims of the gospel, one after another, stopping short only at the one central acknowledged fact of a crucifixion. To identify with that sacrifice then remains the one supreme existential choice open to Bultmann as a believer; and he leaves himself no way of seeing the crucified as other than human. Such too is the message of Dietrich Bonhoeffer, the Lutheran pastor whose theology may be abstruse, but whose resolute anti-Nazism—and death—brings him wide admiration. He again has discovered his religion *only* in accepting the 'great risk' of Jesus; and by the manner in which he arrives at this he is forced into the paradox of a religion without reference to a transcendental deity. In like manner, the Anglican bishop John Robinson presently affirms in *Honest to God* (1963) the death of the God of Abraham ('old Nobodaddy up aloft' as William Blake has long since called him), 'demythologizes' heaven, creation, the incarnation, the resurrection . . . What is left? Jesus as the 'Son of Man', abandoned on the cross, and in that fact teaching 'the God within'.

These are developments of Christology which sit comfortably with the new pop imagery of *Jesus Christ Superstar* (or Pasolini's film rendering of St. Matthew's Gospel): that imagery, needless to say, marks an almost total annihilation of supernatural faith, let alone faith in a divine order or Providence. Who now could say that Christianity is 'reactionary'?

We are looking at extreme positions; some would again say, the self-indulgence of parasitical élites. Not everyone is a theologian, nor are whole congregations suddenly 'changed' by theologians of liberation or tracts such as Robinson's *Honest to God*. Yet other intellectuals are at any rate aware of what the theologians write; and more importantly, 'intellectuals' are ceasing to be quite the small separate fraction that they have been, addressing 'bourgeois' readerships through books and magazines and other innocuously serious performances. They are sprawling far more widely; *their* boundaries too are shifting and blurring. The difficulty of mapping with tidy precision a step-by-step movement of ideas and attitudes in the post-war decades stems quite largely from the fact that the traditional intelligentsia, the mandarins and stars and statesmen, undoubtedly survive but are now partly submerged by the large category of 'communicators'. A really very large population of these latter, not all geniuses but certainly not passive traditionalists, are growing up on a new diet of paperbacks and digests, weaving together a network of cultural reference in which theology and pop, ecological horror stories, demythologizing and wholesale destructuring, liturgical reform and social revolution, sex emancipation and criminal law reform, 'gay' liberation and every other imaginable 'liberation', are apt to fuse together in a half-digested (but thereby the more compelling) magma of feelings, hints, and half-articulated gestures. What is represented may or may not be the ideals of what older generations would argue over as a 'classless' society, but it certainly spells an erosion of boundaries, and it suits the recent great enhancement of social mobility. No doubt the two are not really separable from one another.

Even without benefit of a long perspective, this has to be seen as the working out of unprecedented syncretisms: new tolerances, new patterns of social relationship and concern (very much simplified overall), new accommodations of the tastes previously segmented in more primly stratified societies, new hybrids, new *styles*, however subdivided and fragmented internally or subject to rapid changes of fashion at the margin. It distinguishes post-1945 Europe very sharply from the inter-war years.

Interestingly it is the Catholic Church, not any other (perhaps more ephemeral) organization for communicators, which in 1962 boldly confronts this ocean of novelty. Ninety-two years after the adjournment of the last General Council, what is popularly called Vatican II faces the need both to preserve tradition and to recognize the present, and to accommodate its universal mission with cultural trends which are European but by no means universal. It is easy to point to its topicality, its adjustment: from it is promulgated a pastoral constitution which speaks of 'community spirit', 'the cult of man', 'solidarity', 'active participation', and introduces the device of a 'collegiality of bishops' alongside the affirmation of pontifical authority. This council, unlike its predecessors, is very much in key with democracy and aware of the equal *civil* dignity of every single one of the 'People of God'. It is also concerned to ease some of the rigidities of its rite; for example, to forgo the Latin liturgy, since Latin is no longer taught to educated élites, but is confined to a few scholars and trained clergy . . .

Yet along with this appreciation of change in the world, the (Second) Vatican Council is at pains also to promulgate a theological doctrine of unwavering and traditional orthodoxy. In this respect its final pronouncements in no way suggest that faith requires support from modern Existentialism: on the contrary, we might almost imagine Thomas Aquinas drafting the affirmation that 'God, the beginning and end of all things, can be known with certainty from created reality by the light of human reason', or the assurance that revelation can 'complete the effort of reason' to acquire a firm certainty. And so too with those doctrinal statements which cover the principal articles of Catholic belief; not least as regards the divine personality of Christ, incarnate Word, or the mystic nature of the Church and its authority, hierarchy, priesthood. Neither in the pontificate of John XXIII nor in those of his predecessors and successors is it customary to move with precipitation; and least of all in a world where the peculiarities of a European experience represent only a fraction of what the Church seeks to embrace.

**233 (left)   Mark Rothko,
No. 8, 1952. Oil on canvas,
80½ × 68 in (204.5 × 172.7
cm). Meriden, Conn.,
collection of Mr and Mrs
Burton Tremaine**

*Late in the long evolution of
abstraction, but still anchored
firmly in pure painterly values,
we show here a relatively early
work by an American, but deeply
cosmopolitan, master. In the
'60s the search for this kind of
achievement will pass over into
something importantly different,
however superficially akin—a
'minimalist's' concern with
suppression of boundary or of any
significant communication
whatever—and with that change
the artistic vocation as such will
have turned a corner.*

**234   Andy Warhol
(1930–), *Marilyn Monroe*,
1967. Silk-screen print on
paper, 36 × 36 in (91 × 91
cm). London, Tate Gallery**

*It has taken just one
generation for the image of the
film star (compare plate 208),
the 'sacred monster' of the
1930s, to be replaced by the
more elusive image constructed
out of a lively 'show-business'
personality. Once Marilyn
becomes a 'pin-up', though, pop
art can go to work.*

Alienation and revolt

'Alienation' is a concept by no means original. It is rediscovered in the early writings of Karl Marx by the Frankfurt group of critical philosophers and, relaunched by them with gusto in the post-war world, it comes to occupy an important place in progressive thinking. Marx originally fixed his attention upon the disaffection of industrial workers when severed from ownership of their own craft tools and made into 'wage-slaves': they are 'alienated' from what he has regarded as the central cultural determination, namely work. By 1960 alienation has become a cult word, covering most occasions when a circumstance of life is found to be distasteful. Lonely? Miserable at school? Unhappy in your surroundings? Repelled by mass advertising? By boring people around you? By a duty to be conscripted for military service in an unpopular cause? Alienation! The opposite is an ideal condition in which we have *no* misgivings about these things, or about any of our social relations, and are *not* forced to delude ourselves ('false consciousness') or shrug our shoulders at the absence of Utopia. When the world *is* as it should be, when 'the rational is real and the system delivers the goods', then indeed we can enjoy 'a happy consciousness'. But when is that? Not here and now, says Herbert Marcuse: capitalist society is the *contrary* of rational. And yet, transplanted from Nazified Germany to California, he is impressed by the sheer effectiveness of these same capitalist societies, modern and affluent, in 'delivering the goods'; he is forced to recognize that revolution is not around the corner; and in *One-Dimensional Man* (1964) he resigns himself to the prospect of a culture permanently dominated by alienation. All that is left is the hope that 'universal' ideals such as beauty may continue to provoke revolutionary feelings

235   Paris, May 1968, photograph by Bruno Barbey

Modern techniques of 'grass-roots' revolt take as a starting point any mundane grievances against a rigid authority, presented as aggressively as possible, then escalate to violence—here, against an unpopular riot police—with maximum exposure to media cameras. But except in the case of terrorism, peaceable and 'activist' roles co-exist comfortably enough.

because they lie tantalizingly beyond our grasp. They invite revolt against our alienation. Marcuse's resignation in this book appears in some ways premature.

Analysis of typical youth-culture groupings in North America and in Europe in the mid-1960s shows that among individuals who more or less consciously elect to regard themselves as alienated there tends to be a polarity of attitudes along an axis which we may call passive-active. 'Passive' would be characterized by drop-out, retreat, peaceable communes, smoking pot, enjoyment of 'aesthetic' values—or, if pessimistic, anomie, listlessness, like Camus's *Outsider*; 'active' by aggressive attitudes towards institutions judged hostile (property, law, prohibitions, etc.—in short, 'bound-

aries'), and consequent protest, overt challenges to power. Both can be displayed side by side, and neither is exclusive of the other; which is one reason for the chameleon-like appearance of some of the more extreme happenings of alternative culture, where an 'active' project is being concerted but at the same time is joined by 'passive' practitioners.

It is interesting in this regard to compare the impact of two unpopular wars which impinge within the space of a decade on general awarenesses in Europe. In the first, the French attempt to suppress nationalism in Algeria (1954–62), opposition at home takes quite straightforward forms of radical protest, demonstrations, 'martyrs' duly incarcerated; and it is still possible for a Marxist Sartre to proclaim that the 'Revolution' (the tactics and interpretations of a Moscow-led communist party) cannot be outflanked on the Left, that is, upstaged by even more radical attitudes. In the second case, U.S. involvement in Vietnam generates by 1966/7 a far more complex pattern of disturbance, both in America and in Western Europe, which ends up by having little relation to the reasons for which the old French colony of Indo-China is being torn in pieces. To begin with, ceremonial burning of draft-cards, and other confrontational tactics on campuses in America from coast to coast, are not packaged tidily into a set of political issues able to be contained within existing conventions for political action: with echoes of inner-city crises (Watts riots) and human rights movements drumming in its ears, 'revolt' spills over into squats, occupations, improvised resistance to the forces of law; with its rehearsals of alternative and loosely structured communities, a quite unscheduled style of action ventilated by pop and folk-song and adorned with one or two stars of its own (movie stars, singers), it draws on the dynamics of assorted 'liberation': open and mutable personal relations ('sleep with a stranger'), pure food cultism, open communications (that is, obscenity), drugs, ecstasy. The surprising surrealist 'naturalism' of Buñuel's film *Viridiana* is left far behind in the scenic displays of a Californian campus at that point in time.

It is an open question whether the 'active' pole of alternative cultures in Europe would have taken all the forms which it does in fact adopt without the well-advertised American examples that boil over by 1967, or without the missionary efforts of Eastern Seaboard draft-dodgers (relatively numerous) seeking refuge on European campuses in the ensuing year. In effect 1968 presents a subtle picture of Euro-American hybridization in revolt—specifically *student* revolt (this hybridizing also becomes prominent, under a slightly different guise, in Tokyo in 1969). The most spectacular European focus of the impact—not of course by any means the only one—is in the happenings at the University of Paris, in May 1968.

The events of that month have been studied and analysed repeatedly, not least by former participants, because they have something of the status of a political crisis (in a regime identified with the authoritarian figure of General de Gaulle as head of state); or at least a pseudo-political crisis. In the background also are paradoxes of a by no means 'democratic' national education system: ultra-selective *grandes écoles* (special colleges) for training state technocrats and captains of industry (three-quarters of the entry to the French National School of Administration comes from just *one* such school), alongside universities leading nowhere very much for the 'democratically' expanded secondary school graduations. The performance starts with a large number of students on-stage, 'alienated' by the nature of their studies, but complaining initially of the conditions in which those studies are pursued; they are led by a quite small fraction of activists, including junior teachers, articulate 'communicators', first to defy authority, then to occupy buildings, resist repossession

attempts, take on the forces of the state (riot police), and turn their occupation of the Sorbonne into an embryo 'alternative society'.

What makes this happening memorable is not the deployment of force on either side, but the uniting of 'passive' and 'active' features on the barricades. Surrealist eccentricity is felt to be breaking down age-old convention when students carry a piano into the courtyard of a venerable university to play round-the-clock *jazz*: the trumpeter J. Coltrane declares, 'I want to be the force which is really for good', and this is done by a 'surrealist exploring of contents *and* boundaries'— 'Man, there's no boundary-line to art.' Other students claim to have replaced the Bible by the Tao of Lao-Tse. Such gestures, recalled fourteen years after the event, may well look light-hearted and juvenile. What is more interesting is the underlying theme: unlike demonstrations a decade earlier, these are initiatives for enacting not so much a political battle as a *cultural revolution* (in the background, echoes of the largely unknown and unseen 'cultural revolution' under Chairman Mao in China). A 'Sino-political' overthrow of culture and *therefore* of society—'instinctive, sexual, emotional, artistic'—leading to the Utopia of flexibility, 'non-crystallization', 'constant renewal', 'permanent mobility'; rejection of established and 'fossilized' hierarchies of bourgeois thought, the 'defeat of identification'; endless talk, rambling consultation, day-and-night indoctrination (Fidel Castro may have set the example for eight-hour conferences); in short, anarchism. 'Leninism is dead' (i.e., the Bolshevists' disciplined procedure for violent action *now* and Utopia *later*): on the contrary, it is Utopia Now—Paradise Now. Communism is indeed outflanked.

An event, an effervescence of this kind, can sometimes lead to a dramatic change in the organization of society, through the oversetting of political power. This is particularly so in France, where it would not be fanciful to call the revolutions of 1789, of 1830, of 1848, and of 1871 *all* cultural revolutions. But that the mass student occupation of university buildings should trigger a revolution in 1968 is in fact inconceivable, despite its actors' confident hopes. They believe that a startling victory could result from a merger of their movement with a contemporary industrial strike movement in the suburbs of the capital: quite overlooking the fact that in the latter there is no trace of a wish to abolish 'boundaries', introduce 'permanent mobility', or operate an alternative society.

May 1968, for all its legendary qualities, is therefore not a 'revolution'. But how then are we to see it in terms of the culture of the 1960s? Undoubtedly it is a kind of

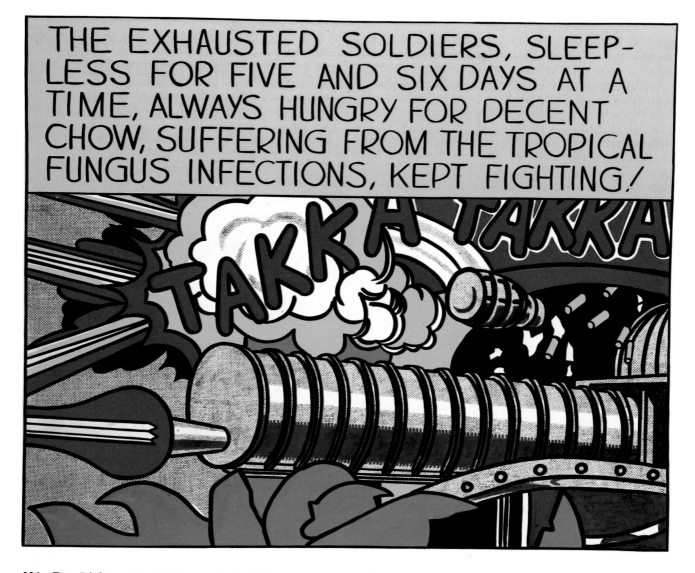

236   Roy Lichtenstein (1923–   ), *Takka Takka*, 1962. Acrylic on canvas, 68¼ × 56¼ in (173 × 143 cm). Cologne, Museum Ludwig

In Yesterday's world the strip-cartoon, which used to be strictly for children, is brought to adult readers – or at any rate semi-adult, semi-literate readers. And its intellectual level is kept rather low (for the connoisseur there are more sophisticated cartoons). To catch and retain a large market, the usual ingredients are violent adventure, supermen heroes, and the clash of Good and Evil: the uniform triviality of this last being in strong contrast with the great variety of forms in which the heroes appear. In Lichtenstein's take-off of the genre we are however looking at vulgarity of a more subtle and critical order.

achievement, a unique experience for its participants; a piece of collective 'op art' on a large scale. This analogy with art is not frivolous, but draws attention to what the reader may throughout this book have regarded as peculiar: that we define culture in terms of regularities, and then proceed to illustrate it by works of art or literature which are not themselves regularities but particular occurrences—often unique or unusual ones. The only way to 'realize' an emergent set of values is in fact to enact or express it or them in language or in action; at the same time the unique 'happenings' or pictures or books which most triumphantly record them are bound to be unusual, a little larger than life, a little more accentuated, even (on occasion) caricatural. The student occupation of the Sorbonne is an eminent example taken from a quite large epidemic of occupations, squats, confrontations; it is marked by exceptional size, verve, outbursts of wit and humour, in contrast to other more sordid or furtive breakdowns of boundaries, by no means all of which are judged worthy of media coverage, let alone crisis treatment. The more lasting effects, though, traced in undoubtedly revised roles and statuses in the corporation of learning itself, or reflected more faintly in other walks of life, are precisely the 'regularities' of attitude and expectation which make up the continuities (the changing continuities) of culture.

American voices

No greater contrast can be imagined than that which in cultural terms separates Western from Eastern Europe in the 1950s and 1960s. The two spheres correspond to the dominance of two super-powers, victors of the post-war world: Russia in the east, America in the west, separated by an 'iron curtain' down the middle of the lands of the old Central Powers. On the vicissitudes of cold wars, North Atlantic Treaty Organizations, Warsaw Pacts, airlifts, Berlin Walls, we need not dwell: but in contradistinction to these showy symptoms of intercontinental power struggle we may usefully turn to the one theme which throughout all previous chapters has had our attention—innovation.

In terms of this theme, the division of Europe throws up one quite remarkable and peremptory fact: that Western culture derives from what is now its Eastern neighbour no major original inputs *whatever*.

It is not that the 'iron curtain' interrupts flows of information in the same way that it arrests the movement of people. There is plenty of information regarding resistance to the unpopular regimes brought into being by a victorious Red Army—resistance in what is now East Germany, in Poland, Hungary, Czechoslovakia; resistance confirmed in uprisings, repression, tanks, and bloodshed; in an underground of writings that by the late 1960s has become very copious in Russia itself, virtually an 'alternative' institution. The death of Stalin (1953) and denunciation of his rule by Khrushchev (1956) leads to a particularly destabilizing sequence of revolts. Yet however the spectacle is interpreted, one thing is certain: it contains no novel lessons, offers no suggestive *new* values, exhibits only a familiar sight of struggle against tyranny and totalitarianism. It is extraordinary that in a model Soviet system the private citizen *is* as far as possible eliminated, exactly on the lines dreamt of by the Nazi Ley (see above, p. 285):

that even a modest initiative to found a local sports club or 'do one's own thing' must in practice either be sanctioned by the Party or viewed with grave suspicion; that the merely lyrical *Doctor Zhivago*, or a piece of abstract art, constitute acts of subversion. Neither such rules and norms nor the laborious construction of bureaucratic public agencies governing all functions of shared daily life have the power to kindle dreams of a new ideal. Official Soviet export displays of 'culture' (opera, ballet, circuses, acrobatics, athletics) are a part of modern cultural diplomacy; they unfailingly exhibit high proficiency and technique, along with a conspicuous absence of something else—adventure? daring? *risk*? These latter qualities are reserved for underground protest, the marginal and strictly unofficial wit of Warsaw or Prague (until the uprising of 1968), the wry sallies of millions of unrecognized Charlie Chaplins, or the furtive scribbling of the Gulag . . . We are back in a nineteenth-century world of national revolt against Metternich's police or the Tsar's autocracy; a world seeking to rediscover humanism. These are serious and moving *reminders*; but not keys to new problems in the West.

By contrast, it is impossible to delineate post-war Western Europe without drawing attention to a sustained two-way flow of novelty across the Atlantic.

The scene opens with the reality of aid in the immediate post-war years; and thereafter the implantation of an U.S. industrial and commercial presence without equal at any time in the past. With this comes the introduction of cultural examples of a rugged and functional nature—in the management of large, or very large, industries, the design and marketing of consumer goods, the techniques of mass advertising, and on the back of these things (inevitably) the image of an American Way of Life. That such an image and its local imitations can be derided and caricatured by Günter Grass or Jacques Tati in their respective idioms (novel, film); that the native critique of the *Status Seekers* or the *Organization Man* (denouncing artifice and unreal standars in the 'right' style of living of the American corporate executive) can itself be exported from America to Europe with great success; that the 'American Challenge' (meaning 'threat') can become a bogy word under the pen of a restless French politician—such reactions are simply a tribute to its very wide power. The European country whose nationalist fibres appear most strongly developed to resist that power is France; yet at the very time when Charles de Gaulle as head of state (1958–69) is intent on hustling the NATO headquarters and American soldiers out of France, and French academicians pore over ways of getting rid of 'franglais'

237   Claes Oldenburg, *Building in the Form of an English Extension Plug*, 1967. Pencil, 22 × 30 in (55.9 × 76.2 cm). Toronto, collection of Mr James Fleck
Nonsense images of buildings are not new to Western entertainment; what is noteworthy in this sketch is its amiable mockery of 'inter-disciplinary' study in post-war design schools.

industrial guru (or corporate guru) to emerge from California or New England—the heavyweight business consultant, the expert in advising how to set things up so that they work, the prophet of technological marvels and communications, the specialist in refashioning government or business or other large organizations, the quintessential technocrat. Bending new behavioural sciences to the deliberate engineering of group effectiveness, developing elaborate programmes to analyse the outcomes of bureaucratic action and point the way to rational improvement—whether in programmes of (American) nuclear missiles, the routines of a central bank, or aid to African or Central American republics—this profession is not in fact startlingly original; but it attains its majority, an eminent status, becomes a vogue. It holds a new Black Box of wonder-tricks. Whether it is the Rand Corporation or the Ford Foundation or the Brookings Institution or McKinsey Associates, or merely last year's near-bankrupt who prints 'consultant' on his business-card and sets out to con his acquaintances into giving him a livelihood for another year or two in a new role, this quasi-magical activity seems to bring a dimension of fresh hope and excitement into the administrative round. It lures governments no less than corporate clients with promises of squaring the circle (for instance, keeping welfare states solvent). It stands of course for the absolute pinnacle, the *nec plus ultra*, of that 'rationality' which Max Weber has attributed to Western capitalism; and it places an unprecedented weight of emphasis upon the orderliness and predictability of human behaviours. By 1970 the shine has begun to wear off, and in 1974 an oil crisis deals it a very hard blow; its detritus survives in the numerous business schools implanted in all Western European countries in emulation of American practice—building up a new scholasticism for the age of corporate planning and multinational expansion.

It will not have escaped the reader's notice that this big push of 'consultancy', this crowning development of the multi-bureaucratic state coincides, somewhat exactly, with the visible progress of all those *other* ideals which have to do with its cultural polar opposite—*dis*organization. The super-rationality imposed on planning requires the most exacting definition of boundaries, and nowhere is this more visible than in the requirements of that (often indispensable) tool, the computer; at the same time it appears entirely devoid of that 'idealism' which leads men to act freely, even surprisingly, instead of under constraint. (Again, this is something on which Max Weber has speculated in the closing pages of his *Protestant Ethic*.) And now, on the other side of the street, confronting super-rationality, is

from their idioms, the new suburbs that have sprung up around Paris are full of young businessmen who (for all that they style themselves 'cadres' and not 'executives') are intent on pursuing just that life of the Organization Man, with all its new stresses and many of its abrasive values, and talk freely of 'le manager' and 'le cash-flow'. And for all the much talked-of Challenge or threat the French government encourages the take-over of a prestigious native computer company by the multinational Honeywell, and plans ways of acquiring American nuclear reactor know-how.

The perceived impact (as distinct from the intensity) of this Americanization of the economies and managerial outlooks of European society reaches its height in or about the year 1966. At that moment not only is the 'affluent society' a widely heralded dream ('in ten years' time what shall we want to do with all that leisure?'), but there is a climax of reverence for the latest species of the busker with his guitar, the hippie, the Yellow Submarine: idealism without boundaries, slogans for a counter-rationalism. There are *two* gurus.

Both these highly characteristic trends of an age, along with their conflict, are copiously nourished, if not solely inspired, by North American inputs. Even at times it would appear that all the going is being made by American voices in the loud dialogue of contested values: the initial chorus of economic growth (Keynesian economics and welfare interpretations serving as the European ground-bass), and the subsequent follow-up of management sciences and consultancy and multinational offices—*and also* the related streams of criticism and hostility—*Organization Man, Status Seekers, The Affluent Society, The Cultural Contradictions of Capitalism,* the ('anonymous') *Report from the Iron Mountain* (on the industrial-military complex, its sinister interest, and imperatives); or again, the apologia of the automobile-plus-TV consumer society, *and also* its most vehement and uninhibited protest voices—on human rights, inner-city deprivation, anti-puritanism, consumerism (Nader's raiders being a louder version of analogous private lobbies which powerfully influence legislation in European countries), *as well as* the swelling thunder of pop music (Bob Dylan), youth emancipation, female and homosexual and bohemian liberation and protest in general (Joan Baez, Jane Fonda, Ginsburg, Leary) . . . Across the Atlantic is the place where the debate is trenchant, heroic, *epic*: and it is a *debate*, not a monotonous one-dimensional stereotype (*pace* Marcuse), that reaches the shores of Europe.

A first comment, by way of reflection: the character of this debate, a free and unrehearsed debate, is itself enough to distinguish American dialogue with Western Europe from Russian tutoring of Eastern states (or any spill-over from East into West). And it is not a one-way phenomenon. The American critique of affluent society owes a great deal to the indigenous nature of American Ways of Life (still largely unfamiliar to most Europeans) and to their commercial intensity; but the ideas behind it are in almost every sense commonplaces of a European welfare society and its antecedents. It is thus a natural (European) reflex to wonder, for example, what the well-known economist J. K. Galbraith is so steamed up about when he denounces the villainies of a materialistic capitalistic world in seemingly unoriginal terms; and similarly very little or no curiosity is aroused in Europe by J. F. Kennedy heralding, or L. B. Johnson inaugurating, the dream of a 'Great Society' in America with components not obviously different in nature from those of the welfare state. The rediscovery of the wheel, even on a very large scale, is not exciting.

A second comment relates to a less obvious fact: if *words* on either side of the Atlantic seldom mean precisely the same thing ('liberal' in twentieth-century Europe meaning something like 'benignly conservative', but in the U.S.A. of the 1960s, 'progressive', 'unreliable', and so on) something similar is true also of an almost indefinitely vast range of other conventions and assumptions. In particular, the *size* of the U.S.A., the compulsions of collective activity as experienced almost everywhere in that country, the highly competitive (not to say professionalized) character of even quite mild leisure activities—in short, the consummation of those attitudes to which a J. S. Mill has been seen to show such aversion (see p. 226)—all bring it about that an 'American style' whether in marketing or in cultural revolt conveys in a European setting a quality of stridency, of peculiarly intense dedication; when what it connotes in its native environment is a more or less obligatory adaptation to media exposure. Were the time to come when the armies of European communicators were similarly adapted, then no doubt a very noticeable cultural re-orientation would have occurred (as it undoubtedly has done in many branches of commerce or charity fund-raising). In the meanwhile though (and certainly in the 1960s) the Euro-American debate is carried on on a basis of almost continuous slight misunderstanding—creative misunderstanding, no doubt—and thus opens the way to possible further novelty—but misunderstanding for all that. 'Small is beautiful' means one thing in Texas, but quite another in Ireland or Sicily.

In consequence, rather than attempt to review in a compressed space all the cultural impacts of an American presence, it may be wise to propose only a statement that must under all circumstances be true: namely that American exchanges and inputs have the effect of adding *a very large amplifier* to the circuits of cultural change in Europe. This amplifier has a peculiar nature, however; on occasion it procures the unsynchronized recall of quite old signals, such as nineteenth-century optimisms; at others it doubles a signal with what seems to be a boosted replica but in fact is subtly different; at others it amplifies with remarkable distortion; finally, on a few occasions it supplies a tonality entirely novel. We have chanced on a few instances of all of these already. One further example is however not without interest.

The beginnings of pop art are no easier to fix with precision than its precise boundaries. Do they go back to the pre-1914 *collage*? To Surrealism? To the amusing later collages of Kurt Schwitters? Or to eccentric jokes scattered through the ages? At all events pop art is invented, or re-invented, simultaneously in the 1950s in London and New York. In each place the pressure on the eye of advertising, commercial photography, public slogans, branded products, ready-mades, is not to be ignored; likewise the ubiquity of a junk-culture, throwaway objects, disposable artefacts. Where once it was the Victorian living-room that was over-crowded, now it is the whole consumer society environment that is stuffed full of not very desirable *things*. In the 1950s already the advertisement jostles to catch your whim, the neon sign to guide your steps or your preferences. Even when you throw the can or the packaging away the garbage goes on shouting. But there are strategies for defence or sanity: you can try to run away, or you can kick the garbage, or you can enter into its 'spirit' with some zest; though to do the latter implies *some* kind of appropriation—that is, choice or act or assemblage or invention.

So it comes about that pop art, in the hands of Richard Hamilton or Peter Blake or Andy Warhol or Jasper Johns, spreads across an enormous zone between 'art' and 'not-art'—another rubbing-out of boundaries. Sometimes it operates by putting quote-marks round objects, sometimes by copying them much larger, or by placing them into unwonted collocation with other materials or things. Ideology can be primary, or secondary, or nowhere. The product may carry denunciation, or a joke, or a visual adventure. Pop art works *precede* the allocation of them to a category ('still life', 'landscape'), just as in existentialist philosphy 'existence *precedes* essence'. There is no evidence for pop art's being associated with existentialist doctrine—but then there is no evidence either of post-atonal experimental music of the 1960s generating its own 'languages' in the spirit of existentialist commitment: yet in either instance the practice of creative art has cut loose, absolutely, from two thousand years of formal pre-definition of what its operations are intended to be aiming towards.

But the operative point for our argument is that in this adventure, American example is for European artists not the original source of an idea but simply the much more conspicuous big partner; not even the more sophisticated or subtle or annunciatory partner, but certainly the more zestful and aggressive, for reasons that are plain when one compares New York with any European city.

And this raises in an acute form the question how far in the post-war age it is any longer very meaningful to attach a dominant *geographical* sense to the expression 'European' in relation to culture. This question we reserve for a final chapter.

A new break?

It might easily look as though the cultural pointers of post-war Europe, of Yesterday, are all facing more resolutely away from a traditional and recognizable past than any we have come upon in previous chapters.

It is not only that the framework of values of the welfare society as such ('caring', 'providential' . . . it has many synonyms) represents a very determined break with all earlier societies that we have encountered, in its manifest purpose of doing away with the ugliest signs of oppression or neglect of one man by another. Or that, as part of this process, it begins to make a very extraordinary change in an age-old split between 'urban' and 'rural' by having a majority of its citizens in towns, and gradually transforming agriculture from a timeless peasant servitude into a quasi-industrial process carried on by fewer, and therefore less disadvantaged, specialists. It is not only the bureaucratization that is a part of this scene, or for that matter the changes in quantitative standards of many sorts: life expectancy, length of working hours, 'living standards', plenitude of goods, holidays, education, travel, and the rest.

It is—much more—that by its urbanized setting and 'service' character it brings into immediate conjunction (again as never before) articulate cultural expression on a number of different levels; in the process it greatly blurs the dividing line between 'élites' and 'the rest', to the point where it begins to be no longer very satisfactory to use that simplified disjunction. Granted that the agricultural populations of the past, like the industrial working classes of the nineteenth century, have always had their own cultures and folklore alongside those of the more influential (and more leisured) orders or classes. It still remains that the leakage from one to the other has been, until this century, very limited indeed. This massive fact is hardly disproved by pointing to ancient Greek mysteries, Roman saturnalia and circuses, medieval mass pilgrimages and guild ceremonies, the shared experiences of war (in which as a matter of fact the distinctions of social order or class are maintained strictly); or, nearer our own times, to such features as interests in folk poetry or race meetings or great sporting events or other deliberate affirmations of an 'organic' group identity. 'Élite' cultures have always been fundamentally independent of a large substratum which they know of but take for granted. Even in the Weimar Republic between the two wars we have seen that to be still basically true; 'the masses' being, among other things, a highly divisive expression.

But now no longer. The leakage becomes a flood. In

large cities it is hardly possible to speak of *an* élite, or the manifestations of *its* identity, or even of a particularly conspicuous or dominant one; at the least we must recognize a plurality, or so to say an *Olympus* of élites (though without Zeus), among which the pop star of the 1960s has a status different in kind from that of his predecessor the film star (another celebrity based on mass sales). And away from urban centres, the radio and television and the record-player are still great democratizers, and not to be escaped from.

At the centre of the scene we now find the immensely tangled cat's-cradle of communicators. We have only to list—if we can—the range of kinds of signal carried on the most prominent media (screen, loudspeaker, press) to perceive that from the rarefied aesthetic minority interest replay to the most banal local news item this is a range without precedent; and although each kind of communication may be directed to a fairly determinate group, in principle each is on tap for all. And the prominent media in fact reflect at best only about half the significant ongoing cultural communications, the rest being at what one might call 'cottage industry' or 'do-it-yourself' level. And the 1960s are an age of more and more 'do-it-yourself'. Or again, we have only to compare the output of seven or eight *hundred* book titles published annually in Britain six generations ago with the thirty-five *thousand* produced in that country in 1970 to perceive a very extraordinary enlargement of (at any rate) curiosities percolating through a service society: an enlargement in no way unique to that country. 'Everything free for everybody?' By no means: but the climate is not far off from 'Everybody who wants is free to communicate with everyone else.' And with hindsight we know that this trend has not subsequently been arrested.

In this setting the 'communicators' are on the way to a kind of cultural presence for which history has no analogy; Pareto's élites are overshadowed and Gramsci's Marxian analysis of them is superseded. And at the same time, older projections of 'mass society' and its uniform trends become less convincing with every year that passes. The progressive outnumbering of compact industrial populations (following the disappearance of peasantries) by service populations has implications of the widest scope. It may be premature to endorse a saying of the 1960s, 'Isms are Wasms', because technocracy has not in fact 'taken over'. Nevertheless, in a multiplicity of vigorous 'Isms' (ideologies, or their derivatives) there does not appear to be too much threat of incipient suicide. The pluralist society bids fair to have simply *too many* equally known about and more or less recognized standpoints and worldviews and attitudes to be able to go down the same road as the Weimar Republic. Or seen from another angle, it is the polar opposite of that absolutism or 'monarchy' which permits of only *one* authorized perspective. And by the same token, it becomes more and more difficult to identify forms of hegemony or ideological aspiration of a given regime with patronage in the expressive arts leading to any one determinate 'style'. The pluralist society has a plurality of 'styles', of tastes, of values—disorderly, no doubt, but not obviously shaping up for collapse.

That is as far as Yesterday takes us. And we stop here. Not because Today lacks interest—how could that be imaginable?—nor because history stops at the end of the 1960s—manifestly it does not. But because *most* of the perceived ingredients of Today have already

238   The Atomium, Brussels, 1958

The Brussels international trade fair of 1958 provides occasion to erect yet another visionary structure. But there is more to this one than commercial zest. The Atomium captures a local mood of hopeful optimism as the Treaties of Rome come into existence – one of them establishing a European Atomic Energy Community. No one has ever yet gone to the chemistry lab. to find inspiration in its explanatory models for the shape of a building: now that the thing has been done, and drawn crowds, no one need trouble again. Besides, its symbolism is not unclouded. . . .

been seeded by Yesterday adding its quota to those of more distant cultural innovations. To be encyclopaedic, it is true, we should have had to include mention of other concerns which the next decade will bring into prominence—the ecology movement, for example, or nuclear protestors, or gathering clouds over the question of employment (in the 1960s it is foreseen, but only in terms of a future problem of *leisure*), or the growth of tensions over ethnic assimilation (which in the 1960s affects mainly Britain, rather than the 'guest-workers' of the rest of Western Europe), or perhaps trans-national terrorism. In the years we have been looking at, these features are not yet so large as to be representative. And in any event, it is the duty of an author to choose what he judges most central to record.

Among truly central issues, there is no question but that the challenging of 'boundaries' is conducted more vigorously in the 1960s than in any recent comparable age—this is no optical illusion. The phenomenon accompanies the enactment into law of many real cultural shifts, or reforms—regarding sex equality, ethnic rights, economic opportunity, penal codes, a host of lesser items variously mixed together in the different states of Europe; this undoubtedly stimulates the imagination of idealists and others thirsting for 'more'. And moral debate is sharpened by public media exposure and, without question, by science fiction. Yet there have been previous ages also of great boundary shifts, each time accompanied by their visionary extremists. They have not in fact caused the end of the world. Furthermore, it would not even be easy to argue

that over the long view the radical transformations of European value-systems from time to time in the past have necessarily resulted in a general degradation of standards, whether of morality (for which even Christianity has kept on changing its yardsticks) or of those more extended ranges of sensibility for which we have no word, but whose opposite is 'vulgarity'. In all ages since Homer, sages have been recording their regret at the late erosion of some particular standards; while their successors have tended to find compensatory virtues alongside what the sages before them have been regretting. On the evidence of what we have been reviewing here, it would seem that Yesterday's European culture, so far from being dealt a mortal blow by its experiences in World War II, has exhibited in the wake of that disaster a rather notable flurry of liveliness; and if not all of it has been congenial to persons of mature years and set preferences, we can only remark once again that something like that kind of disrelish has featured in one way or another *in every single one of the preceding chapters of this study*.

239   Richard Rogers (1933–) and Renzo Piano (1937–), Pompidou Centre, Paris, 1974–6

Paris already possesses one unmistakable 'fun' monument, the nineteenth-century Eiffel Tower. In a later age, influenced by the experience of great airports, government patronage of 'cultural' activities brings into existence a different but no less original edifice: structural engineering is again prominent but with more attention this time to function and logistics.

Conclusion

'Quo teneam voltus mutantem Protea nodo?'

Horace, *Epistles*

At this point in the performance, it is usual for the conjuror to invite his audience to watch very closely while he brings a white rabbit out of the hat. Or, in an exploration of the past, the philosophic historian is apt to disclose the hidden principle which all along has been organizing the thread of his argument and the meaning of his story. What, then, is the overall 'meaning' of these European scenes, each so varied and so idiosyncratic?

In the past, Europeans themselves have not been slow or backward in producing white rabbits. In fact they have bequeathed us, as part of our heritage, rather a wide choice. Christian philosophers have built upon St. Augustine's majestic pattern of interpretation, and Bishop Bossuet has summed it up for Louis XIV in a *Discourse on Universal History* which traces the finger of Providence in a great span from first to last things—much as the medieval schoolman could accept it. A rationalizing Enlightenment has offered us instead its vision of human progress—in civility, in morality, in rationality itself, in the 'Education of Mankind': quite a family of interpretations, but still a family. The idealist Hegel discovers in place of this that an Absolute Spirit has been unfolding itself; for which Karl Marx substitutes the unfolding of social 'productive relations'. An impatient Nietzsche derides all these ideas and invites us to consider an endless round of intrinsically meaningless situations recurring in new forms. Scientists of the nineteenth century prefer an even more impersonal spectacle of process or evolution (process forward in time, none the less); their successors outline an ecological system to constrain our ant-like choices. Around us in the 1980s we see adherents of each and every one of these standpoints; and hybrids of them too—Teilhard's

God evolving through mankind, a Marxist pageant advancing through Nietzschean choices, an intrinsically aimless chronicle punctured by the Christian's cross, or humankind generating garbage in a galactic space impervious to our tiny messes. Each puts the European saga under the lighting and perspective of his choice. *So far* there have been no further notable additions to the repertory. Accordingly, we may fumble among them as we wish: indeed we cannot easily ignore them, for these viewpoints taken all together do in effect *define* (that is, put a boundary around) the possibilities created for themselves by Europeans. We operate within the boundary.

I see no particular advantage in allowing any of these frames of vision (or any of the ideologies they may imply) to dictate to us our picture of European culture. Especially since we have still the rare privilege of being aware of them all, and also of non-Europeans' views of them. What of that culture *as a whole*? Can we stand in the middle and ask ourselves, for example, whether anything at all has featured constantly in it?

There is, without a doubt, a setting, which is constant, but ambiguous. It is the curious geography of peninsulas and islands at the extremity of a Eurasian land-mass, stretching from the Arctic Circle to the Mediterranean, bounded by water on three sides and on the fourth by a large space which for a very long time has offered only shifting and transient challenges (migrating tribes, war hordes flowing and ebbing, a Mongol empire, Seljuk invaders, sketchy trading routes, a Golden Horde, a great Ottoman empire, more latterly a huge but precarious Russian empire). Until getting on for 1492, this western peninsula has been virtually a cul-de-sac; thereafter something rather different. The characteristic feature of its geography has been that it both unites and divides: unites by virtue of the sea and of passes through great mountain-chains; divides by those same seas and mountains. And it also divides by juxtaposing half-a-dozen other great contrasting features: the differences between an Atlantic and a Mediterranean, between a climate with two hundred days of winter and one with two hundred days of summer; between formations rich in minerals and others with broad or narrow belts of cultivable land or pasture . . . Such concentrated variety is unique.

In case the reader supposes this to be the moment for producing a geographical white rabbit, let us insist a little on the word 'ambiguous'. If barriers isolate, they can with effort be made into channels of communication: it all depends on what we wish them to be, what use we can put them to, what meaning we elect to give them. For the Romans, the Rhine and the Danube are deliberate frontiers, but later they are made into waterways; the English Channel, Skagerrak, Hellespont, Straits of Taranto, of Gibraltar, can each do duty as a moat, but also as a temptingly convenient surface for ferries; frontier towns are fortresses but also cosmopolitan meeting-places; frontier districts are defensible 'marches' but also the setting for cultural encounters (Sicily, the Val d'Aosta, Granada); mountain passes let through a trickle of pilgrims or traders, but also trace the line for railway tunnels or motorway arteries. There is no other theatre of the world so densely marked with these ambiguous natural features, so fertile in the possibilities for powerfully divergent ways of life, for uncomfortable encounters, for changes in interpretation, for cultural novelty. And in its outward boundaries too: from the time when the Hellenes changed their conception of 'barbarian' (see p. 27), there has been a perpetual sequence of upheavals in the definition of what is a barbarian, a pagan, a 'foreigner', an 'outsider'; alternating with long stretches of more settled explorations of a *status quo*. It is not reasonable to suppose that this process is now at an end. Thus if Europe has at least a definite physical setting, it is not a closed one; within it, Europeans have constantly encountered occasions to change their boundaries, making what they will of the scene.

'What they will'? Are there no limits to 'will'? Assuredly: and first of all, those supplied by nature—geography, and all within it. There is a *praxis* or 'state of the art' which at a moment in time has its definition of nature, rather closely identified with the (culturally) recognized ways of interacting with it. It is *known* that the seasons recur every year; that only four seeds will be harvested just *here* for every one sown; that you only dig out silver where there is silver to dig; that a man, a horse, a wagon, a barge, a ship, a railway, or an aeroplane take not less than a certain time to pass from A to B; that iron can be reduced at 800 degrees (or under whatever perceived conditions may antedate the important invention of a standard temperature measurement); that the speed of light is a limit—and a constant . . . Always there are constraints, and the greater the mastery the more numerous they are known to be; natural, and also logical (you cannot make that journey from A to B without passing through all intermediate points on *some* trajectory—until you come to quantum physics which invites a different logic). We may leave it to the specialists to decide whether all natural constraints should in the last analysis be seen as simply 'logical' ones; if so, then we shall have to stretch our idea of logic and accept that the *physical geography of Europe*, so untidy, so utterly irregular, is no less logical than the subatomic structure of matter.

But as well as nature's constraints, there are those lurking in the actors themselves, seen as actors. Through every preceding chapter we have been referring to these constraints; and for much of the time we have called them 'social' factors.

If we take a single example, that of population as such, we are already into constraints which, when defined, are plainly seen to be 'logical'. For a given aggregation and grouping of people, social science arrives at insights about certain relations among its actors; insights which for the most part have not been clearly reckoned with in the past—that is, they are not shared, transmitted, cultural traditions. There are absolutely formal patterns of relation between a 'centre' and a 'periphery', between 'earlier' and 'later'; there are formal patterns of distribution (whether in the relative size of human settlements clustered in a region, or in the distribution of income in a given kind of society, as in the old Pareto distribution); there are all the formal constraints that can be mapped out to define a given economic system; and for a given society, organized in a particular way and provided with its peculiar resources, there are rigorous constraints on communication (and in this respect of this last factor, Periclean Athens is closer to Amsterdam than to Alexandria, and the twentieth century is unique). Or again, in a very large city of a million mouths (Alexandria, imperial Rome, nineteenth-century London) there is no way in which subsistence can rely on local sources of supply—the metropolis is always doomed to be a parasite. None of these types of constraint dictates *how* we must act; yet each narrows our choice, and its neglect opens the way to another set of entailments, and another . . .

Alongside such factors, the regularities of culture themselves are subject to a slightly different kind of logic, but for the sake of the similarities we will continue to call it a logic.

First, we are into a world of perpetual interactions, in all directions: Cleisthenes' Athens adjusting the deeply-rooted cults of tribes to fit a new society, 'genius' being adjusted to Rousseau's audience, and so on in every chapter of our outline. But if there is this straining towards consistency, this *nisus* (to give it a Latin name), we may yet ask how it comes about—what *is* crucial to the process? The answer offered here is both simple and extremely general. The process can only occur as one of change, of change in meanings and values; and for a start then it implies that there are already present at least two more or less coherent, but different, sets of values in the awareness of men (themselves participating in collective action, in institutions). In other words, even the *nisus* of cultural coherence has to do with the creation of something new out of previously unrelated elements; with hybridizing. The constraint is evident: you can only hybridize from what is there.

This pattern of affairs recurs in every example of cultural novelty, whether unobtrusive or prominent, simple or involved: Mozart bringing the (military-band) clarinet into symphonic writing; Darwin bringing Malthus into evolution; Suger's architect bringing together the elements of Gothic into a coherent structure; thirteenth-century shipbuilders merging the technology of their Baltic and Mediterranean crafts (overlapping planks, square *and* triangular sails, the rudder) to produce what can become one day an ocean-going vessel; teachers inventing an institution of learning—the university—which combines the conventions of the city trades with the tasks of the Church; Dante fusing memories of Virgil with the theologies of Aquinas and Bonaventura and a picture gallery of history; Newton mathematizing the heavens, and Mendel the breeding of plants; the men of 1789 fusing Roman citizenship with liberal ideology; Dutch entrepreneurs combining the forms of venture capital with the objects of a state monopoly; St. Paul and no doubt other early Christians combining diverse elements into a universal religion (seen, that is, as a cultural institution) . . .

The list, need we say, is endless; it includes every single work of expressive symbolism in all the arts, all science and technical innovation, all shifts in moral, social, political, ideological, religious, philosophical attitudes.

There have also been cases, and these not the least interesting, where hybridizing has been painful, or impossible. Of these, one clear European example is associated with the name of Machiavelli. In his ruthless analysis of *The Prince* there is a confrontation of two sets of moral values: that which is taught to all and that which alone (in his view) can satisfy the constraints imposed upon the absolute ruler by the nature of his project; this results in a whole problematic of communication (or mis-communication) and of violence. We have observed it baffling acute minds in a great twentieth-century republic (see p. 268 above).

What we are calling hybridization is widely known under one or another name as a feature of creativeness in individuals ('bisociation' for A. Koestler, 'lateral thinking' for E. de Bono); it is a commonplace of educational psychology and of parlour-games for businessmen. But it applies not only to individuals, but to collectivities too, and to institutions changing over time; it is very apparent in the natural sciences of ancient Ionia or seventeenth-century Europe, more still in their accelerated gallop of the last ninety years. And it applies to the fortunes of whole societies.

Always where we come upon it we observe also pre-conditions; and, of course, constraints. In each of the examples mentioned three paragraphs back the pre-conditions include existing traditions, and sometimes (but by no means always) an input from outside: most of all, among the latter, Europe has used inputs from the ancient world, but also algebra, cotton, potatoes, tulips, global discoveries to break down parochial complacency (in the end) . . . and such other circumstances as permit or favour the emergence of novelty.

Among these, undoubtedly, is the coming-together of widely—but not too widely—divergent cultures. Another is perceived opportunity or need; and one of the more insistent favourable conditions is unquestionably the social factor of population increase, as we repeatedly observe (more hands and minds addressing tasks)—though even that is not an imperative. History is apt to make set formulae look silly. It is not obviously the case that a blueprint for economic development and take-off (*à la* Rostow) supplies a model for all kinds of cultural change, any more than an (equally suggestive and controversial) Kuhn 'paradigm' for scientific revolution. Or again, we must take seriously T. Parsons's conjecture that in concentrated industrial societies conditions of work favour nuclear rather than extended family units, with all that this may imply in post-1945 Western Europe's resumption of rapid urbanization; it does not follow that intense industrialization and a resulting fragmentation of earlier kinship institutions must *necessarily* lead to anomie, youth cultures, dropout (if only because in nineteenth-century Britain no such thing occurred). No boundary has yet been successfully traced to limit the pre-conditions of cultural change.

If there is one single feature of European culture that links together all the scenes we have looked in on (as well as other intermediate scenes omitted), it is this unending flow of originality. There is no white rabbit. It is simply a fact that no other cultural story has exhibited so much hybridizing (or, as the anthropologist C. Lévi-Strauss calls it, 'coalitions'); nowhere else has the idea of an 'open society' (open to the future) in fact been stumbled upon and pursued until it becomes the heritage of the world; nowhere else has such restless 'evolution'—desired or undesired—been effected. And from no other source has come an agenda of problems so entirely without precedent for solution tomorrow, shared now with all the world.

By the side of this, in cultural terms, all other generalizations we could frame about Europe are merely contingent or trivial. They would include the fact of a steady increase of population (not unique); the more conspicuous fact of advancing *per capita* energy appropriation through technology; the progressive secularization attendant upon growth and specialization (but are bureaucracy and corporate forms of activity an unconditional good?); even the many-sided mastery over nature (is wealth an unconditional value? is great prolongation of life an unconditional good?); or again, the contention that there is a kind of 'rationality' exhibited in science and trade and government and even mysticism that is uniquely European (but is this really true?); or that other contention, that all our heritage is either classical or Christian or both (but are we certain that there is any longer one Christianity, or that the classical heritage, so long a presence, is still there).

We have no need to brood with Spengler upon a downfall of the West, or with Alfred Weber upon the end of Europe, as we might do if we had pinned our flag to one or other of these general features. At least, in the terms in which this study has been framed, there is nothing in the track record of European culture which need predispose us to gloom.

Similarly, if a profound thinker of the twentieth century were right in his affirmation that the whole of European philosophy, the quintessence of a cast of mind, comes down to a set of footnotes on Plato, and if we took narrowly the drift of this assertion, we might be disposed to worry. But we have no good grounds for that. It is one thing to say there are four cardinal points of the compass, and not more; so long as we crawl upon the surface of the globe this is good enough for anybody. Likewise in an exercise called philosophy, one set of metaphysical intuitions may indeed have been offered which, suitably interpreted, embrace all those zones of reasoning that philosophers might in the sequel be disposed to explore. But in the perspective of culture, as a whole, A. N. Whitehead's assertion about

Plato could seem either interesting (as if it told us about the points of the compass) or profoundly wrong-headed. For if there is one thing to be associated with Plato, it is his dismissal of *all that changes* as unreal, at best an intimation of a more permanent, and superior, Reality for which it is proper to yearn: *Alles Vergängliche ist nur ein Gleichniss* (all things that pass are only semblances) . . . We have come upon plenty of echoes of this Platonism—Christian, mystic, pagan, decorative, escapist, fashionable, or metaphysical; they can hardly be ignored. Of course, Platonism itself only comes to be there at all by a process of change which Plato himself has had a hand in; even a platonizing Christianity cannot do without the claim of a unique historical event in time to give it meaning.

But in any case, and in all circumstances, there have also been quite unplatonic, indeed massively anti-Platonic, currents in European thought; and it is grotesque to ignore their significant presence. Thus, if we urgently require to relate our story to the ideals of an ancient past, there are *also* the quite different claims to our attention of Zeno the Stoic and his lengthy following in Athens and Rome: why should *they* not suggest a central strand in our traditions? Challenged by the paradoxes of the arrow in flight, of Achilles and the Tortoise, of an earlier Zeno and by the confusions of dialectic that perplex the Hellenes, Stoics insist upon the inescapable *fact* of change; they too uphold the presence of law in Nature and in man's condition—indeed, they uphold the unity of these two realms of law; they insist upon the *Logos* which we are wise to know; upon universal brotherhood (or more exactly, upon the common humanity of all men *and* women) and the obliteration of tribal boundaries; a freed slave, Epictetus, can typify the highest attainment of the soul without too much bother about citizenship or status. Through the Stoics' effect on Roman law, on Christian ethics, their colouring of European culture might be adjudged quite as deep and pervasive as that of Plato; somewhat more open-ended too . . .

But why should we be under any duty to recommend one strand or another as 'the key' to Europe, when in fact there has been not one but a multitude, and not one eminent form of society but a dozen? How, behind all these changing forms, should we presume to detect anything but the massive actuality of unceasing change, of societies diversifying and combining, a panorama of adventure (to do justice to Whitehead, he too perceives a value in 'adventure', unsanctioned of course by Plato, but in the end much the same thing as our innovation and change)—a process both of organization *and* disturbance? In such a sense, European culture may come to be seen not as a set piece, or even as a repertory, but simply as cultural process carried on with a peculiar intensity.

It must be plain that in arriving at this view there are more assumptions being made than can conveniently be set out in the rather compressed arguments with which this book begins and ends.

For example, what about *people*? Individual people, that is to say: some of the individuals who have been mentioned—Hadrian, for example, or Charlie Chaplin, or Thomas Aquinas. Is there nothing to be said about *their* lives, their growing-up and their personal experiences and whims, what made them tick, how precisely they came to leave their mark on history? Is culture not about humans, and is not European culture particularly concerned with the values of individual experience, and personal choice, and freedom?

Alas, yes: there would be no culture without people, nor could Hadrian be a pawn, or something more than a pawn, in the great game of the Roman Empire unless he were also a man—a man first—with all the characteristics from which a biographer or novelist could make a fascinating tale. Unfortunately an outline of Europe cannot *also* be that tale, nor yet the tale of any one of a million other Great Men, or of the billions of perhaps lesser men, whose personal existences and experiences have shaped, and been shaped by, the great cultural regularities they have shared in. For that reason too we have not attempted either to bring individual psychology as a theme into the discussion of cultural patterns (where in the author's opinion it has in fact no influential place) or to allot pages to considering how any particular individual—Hadrian, or any other—comes to be *able* to sustain his singular role in the large situations we are concerned to glimpse. And yes, European culture has indeed always placed emphasis upon the values and worth of individuals—of *some* individuals at any rate, not always of all. That valuation, to the extent that it has been shared among many, has in fact been the subject of endless debate, an ingredient in an almost indefinite range of ideologies. It would be tiresome to give a re-run here of the preceding ten chapters. It so happens though that our view of the achievements of persons places them under several orders of constraints and pre-conditions. That after all is how they 'actually' operate.

That has not always been a fashionable position to take up. Only one hundred and fifty years ago it would have been much more proper to hold that Great Men determined the great shape of things to a far greater extent than we are nowadays prepared to concede. On that view, it would seem that they were able to act decisively and freely—almost as it were in a void—so that Shakespeare could conjure all dramatic technique into existence with a magician's wand, Cosimo de' Medici invent a Renaissance pretty well on his own, Rousseau hoist France into a revolution single-handed. To our way of thinking, such beliefs are simplistic; but they are consistent with a sense of history and a general world-view prevalent at a moment in time—in a corner of Victorian society where a premium is placed on individualism, where Carlyle extols the heroes of history, and where (as a matter of record) very many *fewer* people than today took a significant part in public affairs. By the same token, eighty years before Carlyle, we find Voltaire producing a quite different, 'Enlightenment', philosophy of culture in which only four great ages are worthy of attention, dominated by four great *rulers*—Pericles, Augustus, Lorenzo de' Medici, and Louis XIV—since these individuals and these alone have the qualities of wisdom and benevolence (!) to conjure up high civility and patronage of artists and writers. The examples could be multiplied. The perception of 'the individual's role' varies in a context. Our own experience today leads us to see exceptional opportunities seized upon by those outstanding enough (or lucky enough—or unlucky enough) to perceive them, whether Mozart or Henry Ford, but always in a context which has led up to that opportunity; and this forces us not to overlook the large numbers of *other* individuals, and groups, and trends, and surrounding expectations, which go to define those opportunities. We do not rest our culture on miracles, though we expect surprises.

And this in turn dictates the way in which we pick out those of our antecedents that appear worth remembering. A different standpoint would entail giving attention to periods quite different from those on which we have dwelt. Morbid pre-occupation with breakdowns of society would concentrate our thoughts in other directions; a glorification of nations (from the horde to totalitarianism) would have a quite different menu card; out-and-out apologies for an 'alternative culture' would not call for any choice at all, on the grounds that the past is no part of 'now'.

What then lies behind the choices in this book? What presumed world-view, what ideology, what 'project', can be inferred from them? To answer this question takes us back to the Introduction (p. 10), where it is emphasized that only large objects can interest us, since only they cast a long enough shadow (or project a light strong enough) to reach us today. After seven hundred years, for example, the scholastic theology of Aquinas is still a presence in the mid-1960s; if that is a personal judgement, it is also one for which there appears to be public evidence, and it is no part of our argument to express satisfaction or otherwise at the facts of the matter. More generally, it is not the purpose of an 'outline' to offer a display of personal preferences, nor indeed an ideological slant, but so far as possible a selection likely to recommend itself to as large a number of points of view as can be accommodated within narrow limits of space. And, to speak frankly, the needs of compression rule out much that it would be agreeable to dwell on if our intention were simply to exhibit the illimitable *variety* of forms in European culture. Our selection is therefore unashamedly eclectic; it is limited by the limitations of any single observer or selector, more than by the store of knowledge accumulated by a century of modern scholarship (another indicator of the plurality of European culture); and if it is not innocent of *contemporary* debate on what we mean by 'culture' it does not point to any one argument about the identity or essence of Europe, or Western culture, beyond the characteristics set out above. Yet even sacrificing an infinity of detail, and passing over a multitude of areas of historic interest and exemplary value, it may still be hoped that the panorama that remains will have conveyed something of the *resourcefulness* of the diverse and Protean phenomenon that much braver men have never to this day quite pinned down and immobilized to the satisfaction of their fellows.

Suggestions for further reading

The reader interested in looking further into matters touched on in this book may welcome a few indications of where to turn. The lists that follow are arranged mainly to back up the argument of each chapter to which they relate: they make no claim to 'cover' the sum of European culture, any more than the chapters themselves do. Even so, they embody various compromises. Some of the books suggested cover a much wider canvas than anything I have attempted to discuss—but that can have its uses. Some span more than one chapter. Nearly all are in English or English translation, but from the nature of my theme it is inevitable that one or two are not. I have tried to give preference to works that are thoroughly up-to-date—it is astonishing what a large proportion of the literature on European cultures has been renewed or rewritten in the last thirty or so years—and for that reason some well-known older authors do not appear (e.g. Gibbon, Burckhardt, Fustel de Coulanges). In some cases a book listed has plainly influenced my own presentation, but in many others its inclusion serves the aim of offering a quite different angle of approach. In general, I have not hesitated to recommend anything valuable, whether it is 'tough' or extremely simple.

In the last analysis the selection is a personal one—with all the very serious limitations that that implies. And it is extremely condensed: to proceed otherwise would be to risk swamping the reader with a virtually limitless catalogue. Nevertheless, to temper the disadvantages of this arrangement, I have marked with a dagger (†) some works which contain a valuable further reading list, or an unusual wealth of reference, around their subject.

Chapter 1: Roots

LEVI, P., *Atlas of the Greek World*, Oxford 1980

CORNELL, T., AND MATTHEWS, J., *Atlas of the Roman World*, Oxford 1982

The Cambridge Ancient History, 3rd ed., vols. II and III, Cambridge 1970–7 (†)

KITTO, H. D. F., *The Greeks*, Harmondsworth 1951

NICOLET, C., *The World of the Citizen in Republican Rome*, Eng. transl., London 1980 (†)

CARCOPINO, J., *Daily Life in Ancient Rome: the People and the City at the Height of the Empire* (1941), 2nd ed., London 1975

DÖRRIES, H., *Constantine the Great* (1958), Eng. transl., N.Y. and London 1972

BURY, J. B., *The Invasion of Europe by the Barbarians* (1928), N.Y. 1963

LOT, F., *The End of the Ancient World*, Eng. transl., London 1931

VERNANT, J. P., *Myth and Society in Ancient Greece*, Eng. transl., London 1980

NORTH, H., *Sophrosyne: Self-Knowledge and Self-Restraint in Greek Literature*, Ithaca (N.Y.) 1966

FRÄNKEL, H., *Early Greek Poetry and Philosophy*, Eng. transl., Oxford 1975

ARNOTT, P. D., *The Ancient Greek and Roman Theatre*, N.Y. 1971 (†)

ADRADOS, F. R., *Festival, Comedy and Tragedy: the Greek Origins of Theatre* (1972), Eng. transl. Leiden 1975

GUTHRIE, W. K. C., *A History of Greek Philosophy*, 6 vols., Cambridge 1962–81 (esp. vol. 2 for Anaxagoras, vols. 3–5 for sophists, Socrates, Plato, and vol. 6 for Aristotle) (†)

RANKIN, H. D., *Sophists, Socrates and Cynics*, London 1983

FIELD, G. C., *The Philosophy of Plato*, reprint, Oxford 1969

ROSS, W. D., *Aristotle*, 5th ed., London 1960

OGILVIE, R. M., *Roman Literature and Society*, Brighton 1980 (†)

CURRIE, H. MACL., *The Intellectual Life of Rome*, London 1983

GLOTZ, G., *The Greek City and its Institutions*, N.Y. 1951

GRANT, M., *From Alexander to Cleopatra: the Hellenistic World*, London 1982 (†)

ROSTOVTZEFF, M. I., *The Social and Economic History of the Hellenistic World*, Oxford 1941

CHADWICK, H., *The Early Church*, Harmondsworth 1967 (†)

KEE A., *Constantine versus Christ: the Triumph of Ideology*, London 1982

DECARREAUX, J., *Monks and Civilization*, Eng. transl., London 1964

HAUSSIG, H. W., *A History of Byzantine Civilization*, Eng. transl., London 1971

HALPHEN, L., *Charlemagne and the Carolingian Empire*, Eng. transl., Amsterdam and Oxford 1977

BULLOUGH, D. A., *Age of Charlemagne*, London 1965

RICHTER, G. M. A., *A Handbook of Greek Art*, 8th ed., Oxford 1983

HENIG, M., *A Handbook of Roman Art*, Oxford 1983

SWIFT, E. H., *Roman Sources of Christian Art*, N.Y. 1951

MOREY, C. R., *Early Christian Art*, Princeton 1953

Chapter 2: A Medieval Crossroads

SOUTHERN, R. W., *The Making of the Middle Ages*, London 1953

The Cambridge Medieval History, vol. 6, Cambridge 1929

PIRENNE, H., *A History of Europe from the Invasions to the XVI Century*, Eng. transl., London 1939

BLOCH, M., *Feudal Society*, Eng. transl., Chicago 1964 (†)

BAUTIER, R. H., *The Economic Development of Medieval Europe*, Eng. transl., London 1971

RUNCIMAN, S., *A History of the Crusades*, 3 vols., Cambridge 1952

TILLMANN, H., *Pope Innocent III*, Eng. transl., Amsterdam and Oxford 1980

CAZALLES, R., *Nouvelle Histoire de Paris*, vol. 1, Paris 1972

DUBY, G., *The Age of the Cathedrals: Art and Society 980–1420*, Eng. transl., London 1981

PAINTER, S., *French Chivalry: Chivalric Ideas and Practices in Medieval France*, Baltimore 1940

ARTZ, F. B., *The Mind of the Middle Ages*, 2nd ed., N.Y. 1954 (†)

LADURIE, E. Le ROY, *Montaillou* (1975), Eng. transl., London 1978 (documentary insight into rural society)

RASHDALL, H., *The Universities of Europe in the Middle Ages*, new edn., by Powicke, F. M. and Emden, A. B., 3 vols., Oxford 1936 (†)

GILSON, E., *History of Christian Philosophy in the Middle Ages* (1932), Eng. transl., London 1955 (†)

KRETZMANN, N., KENNY, A., and PINBORG, J. (eds.), *Cambridge History of Later Medieval Philosophy*, Cambridge 1982 (†)

CURTIUS, E. R., *European Literature and the Latin Middle Ages* (1948), Eng. transl., London 1955 (†)

ROUGEMONT, D. DE, *Passion and Society*, Eng. transl., London 1962 (embraces medieval courtly love)

JACKSON, W. T. H., *The Literature of the Middle Ages*, N.Y. 1960 (†)

KELLY, D., *Medieval Imagination: Rhetoric and the Poetry of Courtly Love*, Madison 1978 (†)

PARÉ, G., *Les idées et les lettres au 13e. siècle: Le Roman de la Rose*, Montreal 1947

COOKE, T. D., *The Old French and Chaucerian Fabliaux*, N.Y. and London 1978 (†)

Chronicles of the Crusades, transl. and intro. by Shaw, M. R. B., Harmondsworth 1963 (Villehardouin's *Conquest of Constantinople* and Joinville's *Life of Saint Louis*)

FOCILLON, H., *The Art of the West; Volume 2: Gothic*, Oxford 1980 (†)

PANOFSKY, E., *Gothic Architecture and Scholasticism*, London 1957

Chapter 3: The Renaissance in Florence

BURKE, P., *Civilization and Society in Renaissance Italy, 1420–1540*, London 1972

The New Cambridge Modern History, vols. I (the Renaissance) and II (the Reformation), Cambridge 1957–8 (†)

MARTIN, A. VON, *A Sociology of the Renaissance*, Eng. transl., London 1944

HUIZINGA, J., *The Waning of the Middle Ages*, London 1968

HAY, D., *The Italian Renaissance in its Historical Background*, Cambridge 1966

ORIGO, I., *The Merchant of Prato*, London 1957

ANTAL, F., *Florentine Painting and its Social Background*, London 1947

LAVEN, P., *Renaissance Italy 1464–1534*, London 1966

HIGHET, G., *The Classical Tradition*, N.Y. 1957

ROBB, N. A., *Neoplatonism of the Italian Renaissance*, London 1969

GILMORE, M. P., *The World of Humanism*, N.Y. 1962

KRISTELLER, P. O., *Renaissance Thought*, N.Y. 1961

WIGHTMAN, W. P., *Science and the Renaissance*, Aberdeen 1962

WOODWARD, W. H., *Studies in Education during the Age of the Renaissance, 1400–1600*, Aberdeen 1962

GARIN, E., *L'Educazione in Europa, 1400–1600*, Bari 1957 (also in French transl., *L'éducation de l'homme moderne. La pédagogie de la Renaissance, 1400–1600*, Paris 1968)

NELSON, F. C., *Renaissance Theory of Love*, N.Y. 1958

CHASTEL, A., *The Age of Humanism, 1480–1530*, Eng. transl., London 1963

WEISS, R., *The Spread of Italian Humanism*, London 1964

DICKENS, A. G., *Reformation and Society in Sixteenth-Century Europe*, London 1966

DICKENS, A. G., *The German Nation and Martin Luther*, London 1974

HAILE, H. G., *Luther, a Biography*, London 1980

SOWARDS, J. K., *Desiderius Erasmus*, Boston (Mass.) 1975

PANOFSKY, E., *Renaissance and Renascences in Western Art*, London 1970

GOMBRICH, E., *Norm and Form: Studies in the Art of the Renaissance, I*, Oxford 1978

WITTKOWER, R., *Architectural Principles in the Age of Humanism*, 3rd ed., London 1962

BLUNT, A., *Artistic Theory in Italy, 1450–1600*, Oxford 1962

FREEDBERG, S., *Painting of the High Renaissance*, 2 vols., Cambridge (Mass.) 1961

MURRAY, L., *The High Renaissance*, London 1967

MURRAY, L., *The Late Renaissance and Mannerism*, London 1967

STECHOW, W., *Northern Renaissance Art, 1400–1600*, New Jersey 1966

KRAUTHEIMER, R., *Lorenzo Ghiberti*, 2 vols., Princeton 1970

BATTISTI, E., *Brunelleschi*, Eng. transl., London 1981

JANSEN, H. W., *The Sculpture of Donatello*, Princeton 1963

BERTI, E., *Masaccio*, Penn. State U.P. 1967

BORSI, E., *Leon Battista Alberti*, Eng. transl., Oxford 1977

ETTLINGER, L. D. AND H. S., *Botticelli*, London 1976

CLARK, K., *Leonardo da Vinci*, Harmondsworth 1959

WILDE, J., *Michelangelo: Six Lectures*, Oxford 1978

ETTLINGER, L. D. and H. S., *Raphael*, Oxford 1983

Chapter 4: The Prince

The New Cambridge Modern History, vols. 2–5, Cambridge 1958–61 (†)

BRAUDEL, F., *The Mediterranean and the Mediterranean World in the Age of Philip II* (1949), 2 vols., Eng. transl., London and N.Y. 1972 (†)

BRANDI, K., *The Emperor Charles V*, Eng. transl., London 1939

PIERSON, P., *Philip II of Spain*, London 1975

THOMPSON, I. A. A., *War and Government in Habsburg Spain, 1560–1620*, London 1976

GRIERSON, E., *The Fatal Inheritance: Philip II and the Netherlands*, London 1969

SCHURZ, W. L., *The Manila Galleon*, N.Y. 1939

ELLIOTT, J. H., *Europe Divided: 1559–1598*, London 1968

DICKENS, A. G., *The Counter-Reformation*, London 1968

HATTON, R. (ed.), *Louis XIV and Absolutism*, London 1976

CHURCH, W. F. (ed.), *Louis XIV in Historical Thought*, N.Y. 1976

SABINE, G. H., *History of Political Theory*, 4th ed., London 1973

MEINECKE, FR., *Machiavellism: the Doctrine of Raison d'état and its Place in Modern History* (1924), Eng. transl., London 1957

BLOCH, M., *The Royal Touch* (1924), Eng. transl., London 1973

REBHORN, W. A., *Courtly Performances: Masking and Festivities in Castiglione's Book of the Courtier*, Detroit 1978

WOODHOUSE, J. R., *Baltasar Castiglione: a Reassessment of the Courtier*, Edinburgh 1978

YATES, F. A., *The French Academics of the Sixteenth Century*, London 1946

MANDROU, R., *From Humanism to Science, 1480–1700* (1973), Eng. transl., Harmondsworth 1978 (†)

KRAILSHEIMER, A. J. (ed.), *The Continental Renaissance, 1500–1600* (Pelican Guide to European Literature), Harmondsworth 1971 (†)

ROUSSET, J., *La Littérature de l'âge baroque en France: Circe et le paon*, Paris 1954

LAZARO CARRETER, F., *Estilo barroco y personalidad creadora: Gongora, Queveda, Lope de Vega*, Salamanca 1966

MARAVALL, J. A., *La Cultura del Barroco*, 2nd ed., Madrid 1980

ALEWYN, R., *Deutsche Barockforschung*, Köln 1965

CRUTTWELL, P., *The Shakespearian Moment*, London 1970

WÖLFFLIN, H., *Renaissance and Baroque*, Eng. transl., London 1964

POPE-HENNESSY, J., *Italian High Renaissance and Baroque Sculpture*, 3 vols., London 1963

WATERHOUSE, E. K., *Italian Baroque Painting*, 2nd ed., London 1968

ROBERTS, K., *Rubens*, Oxford 1977

JAFFÉ, M., *Rubens and Italy*, Oxford 1977

LAVIN, I., *Bernini and the Unity of the Visual Arts*, 2 vols., N.Y. 1980

BLUNT, A., *Art and Architecture in France, 1500–1700*, Harmondsworth 1953
WITTKOWER, R., AND JAFFÉ, I. B., *Baroque Art: the Jesuit Contribution*, N.Y. 1972

Chapter 5: A Reformed Culture

GEYL, P., *The Revolt of the Netherlands, 1555–1609*, London 1958
GEYL P., *The Netherlands in the Seventeenth Century*, 2 vols., London 1961–4
BRAUDEL, F., *Material Civilization and Capitalism*, vol. II, *The Wheels of Commerce*, Eng. transl., London 1982 (†)
BRUGMANS, H., *Geschiedenis van Amsterdam*, 6 vols., 2nd ed., Utrecht 1972–3 (especially vol. 3)
WILSON, C., *The Dutch Republic*, London 1968
PRICE, J. L., *Culture and Society in the Dutch Republic during the Seventeenth Century*, London 1974 (†)
BOXER, C. R., *The Dutch Seaborne Empire, 1600–1800*, London 1965.
ISRAEL J., *The Dutch Republic and the Hispanic World*, Oxford 1982
TEX, J. DEN, *Oldenbarnevelt* (1960–70), 2 vols., Eng. transl., Cambridge 1973
NOBBS, D., *Theocracy and Toleration*, Cambridge 1938
DAVIES, D. W., *The World of the Elzeviers*, The Hague 1954
COHEN, G., *Écrivains français en Hollande dans la première moitié du XVIIe siècle*, Paris 1920 (†)
CLARKE, D. M., *Descartes' Philosophy of Science*, Manchester 1982
BELL, A. E., *Christian Huygens and the Development of Science in the Seventeenth Century*, London 1947
WEBER, M., *The Protestant Ethic and the Spirit of Capitalism* (1905), Eng. transl., London 1930
LARSEN, E., AND DAVIDSON, J. P., *The Calvinistic Economy and Seventeenth-Century Dutch Art*, Kansas 1979
DUMBAULD, E., *The Life and Legal Writings of Hugo Grotius*, Norman (Okla.) 1969
FUCHS, R. H., *Dutch Painting*, London 1978
BROWN, C., *Dutch and Flemish Painting: Art in the Netherlands in the Seventeenth Century*, Oxford 1977
STECHOW, W., *Dutch Landscape Painting of the Seventeenth Century*, Oxford 1981
CLARK, K., *An Introduction to Rembrandt*, London 1978
KITSON, M., *Rembrandt*, Oxford 1982
GOLDSCHEIDER, L., *Johannes Vermeer. The Paintings. Complete edition*, London 1958

Chapter 6:

ANDERSON, M. S., *Europe in the Eighteenth Century, 1713–1783*, London 1961
ROBERTS, P., *The Quest for Security 1715–1740*, N.Y. and London 1947 (the early 'Enlightenment', politics and culture) (†)
GERSHOY, L., *From Despotism to Revolution, 1763–1789*, N.Y. 1944
MOUSNIER, R., *The Institutions of France under the Absolute Monarchy, 1598–1789* (1974), Eng. transl., Chicago and London 1979 (†)
HUFTON, O. H., *Europe: Privilege and Protest 1730–1789*, Brighton 1980
ROBERTS, J., *Revolution and Improvement. The Western World, 1775–1847*, London 1976
HAMPSON, N., *A Social History of the French Revolution*, London 1963 (†)
GAY, P., *The Enlightenment*, 2 vols., London 1966–70 (†)
HAZARD, P., *European Thought in the Eighteenth Century: from Montesquieu to Lessing*, Eng. transl., London 1954 (†)
MARSHALL, P. J., AND WILLIAMS, G., *The Great Map of Mankind: British Perceptions of the World in the Age of Enlightenment*, London 1982
VARTANIAN, A., *Diderot and Descartes: a Study of Scientific Naturalism*, Princeton 1953
MASON, H. T., *Voltaire*, London 1975
STARK, W., *Montesquieu, Pioneer of the Sociology of Knowledge*, London 1960
MOSSNER, E., *The Life of David Hume*, Edinburgh 1954

BROOME, J. H., *Rousseau: a Study of his Thought*, London 1963
CRANSTON, M., *Jean-Jacques: The Early Life and Works of Jean-Jacques Rousseau, 1712–1754*, London 1983
WILSON, A. M., *Diderot (Part I: the Testing Years, 1713–1759)*, New York 1972
BURTT, E. A., *The Metaphysical Foundations of Modern Physical Science* (1932), reprint, London 1951
DOODY, M. A., *A Natural Passion: a Study of the Novels of Samuel Richardson*, Oxford 1974
BLUNT, A. (ed), *Baroque and Rococo: Architecture and Decoration*, London 1978
CONISBEE, P., *Painting in Eighteenth-Century France*, Oxford 1981
ROSENBLUM, R., *Transformations in Late Eighteenth-Century Art*, Princeton 1967
BRAHAM, A., *The Architecture of the French Enlightenment*, London 1980
SUMMERSON, J., *Georgian London*, London 1945
MIDDLETON, R., AND WATKIN, D., *Neo-Classical and Nineteenth-Century Architecture*, N.Y. 1980
WINTER, J., *Industrial Architecture*, London 1970
WINCKELMANN, J. J. *Writings on Art*, selected and ed. by D. Irwin, London 1972
LANDON, H. C. R., *Haydn at Eszterháza, 1766–1790*, London 1978
EINSTEIN, A., *Mozart: his Character, his Work*, Eng. Transl. 4th ed., London 1959
HILDESHEIMER, W., *Mozart*, Eng. transl., London 1983
ROSEN, C., *The Classical Style: Haydn, Mozart, Beethoven*, London 1971

Chapter 7: The Triumph of Progress

RUGGIERO, G. DE, *History of European Liberalism* (1927), Eng. transl., Gloucester (Mass.) 1980 (†)
PERKIN, H., *The Origins of Modern English Society, 1780–1880*, London 1969
HENDERSON, W. O., *Britain and Industrial Europe, 1750–1870*, London 1954
MATTHIAS, P., *The First Industrial Nation*, London 1969
BRIGGS, A., *The Nineteenth Century: the Contradictions of Progress*, London 1970
THOMPSON, F. M. L., *English Landed Society in the Nineteenth Century*, London 1963
READER, W. J., *Professional Men: the Rise of the Professional Classes in the Nineteenth Century*, London 1966
SHEPPARD, F. H. W., *London 1808–1870*, London 1971
CHADWICK, O., *The Victorian Church*, 2 vols., London 1966–70
INGLIS, K. S., *Churches and the Working Classes in Victorian England*, London 1963
BARNARD, H. C., *A History of English Education from 1760*, 2nd ed., London 1961
ALTICK, R. D., *The English Common Reader: a Social History of the Mass Reading Public 1800–1900*, Chicago 1957
HEYCK, T. W., *The Transformation of Intellectual Life in Victorian England*, London 1982
CAZAMIAN, L., *The Social Novel in England, 1830–1850* (1903), Eng. transl., London 1973 (†)
CAMPBELL, I. M., *Thomas Carlyle*, London 1974
HENDERSON, P., *Tennyson, Poet and Prophet*, London 1978
WEBER, W., *Music and the Middle Classes*, London 1975
RADCLIFFE, P., *Mendelssohn*, London 1957
SUNDERLAND, J., *Constable*, Oxford 1981
GAUNT, W., *Turner*, Oxford 1981
ROSE, A., *The Pre-Raphaelites*, Oxford 1981
LEON, D., *Ruskin: the Great Victorian*, London 1949
EVANS, J., *The Lamp of Beauty: Writings on Art by John Ruskin*, Oxford 1980
HAMBURGER, J., *Intellectuals in Politics: J. S. Mill and the Philosophical Radicals*, New Haven (Conn.) 1965
DUNCAN, G., *Marx and Mill: Two Views of Social Conflict and Social Harmony*, Cambridge 1973
McLELLAN, D. S., *Karl Marx: his Life and Thought*, London 1973

KOLAKOWSKI, L., *Main Currents of Marxism*, 3 vols., Eng. transl., Oxford 1978 (esp. vol. 1) (†)
DARWIN, C. R., *The Autobiography of Charles Darwin*, ed. N. Barlow, London 1958

Chapter 8: La Belle Epoque

MAY, A. J., *The Habsburg Monarchy 1867–1914*, N.Y. 1968
MAYER, A. J., *The Persistence of the Old Regime: Europe to the Great War*, London 1981
MAY, A. J., *Vienna in the Age of Franz Josef*, Norman (Okla.) 1966
MASUR, G., *Imperial Berlin*, London 1971
JOHNSTON, M., *The Austrian Mind: an Intellectual and Social History, 1848–1938*, Berkeley 1972
SCHORSKE, C. E., *Fin de Siècle Vienna: Politics and Culture*, N.Y. and London 1980 (†)
MASUR, G., *Prophets of Yesterday: Studies in European Culture, 1890–1914*, N.Y. 1961
FUCHS, A., *Geistige Strömungen in Österreich, 1867–1918*, Vienna 1949
JANIK, A., AND TOULMIN, S., *Wittgenstein's Vienna*, N.Y. 1973 (†)
ZWEIG, S., *The World of Yesterday: an Autobiography*, Eng. transl., N.Y. 1943
PULTZER, P. G. J., *The Rise of Political anti-Semitism in Germany and Austria*, N.Y. and London 1964
KELLY, A., *The Descent of Darwin*, Chapel Hill 1981 (on 'Social Darwinism')
IGGERS, W. A., *Karl Kraus, a Viennese Critic of the Twentieth Century*, The Hague 1967
STROMBERG, R. N. (ed.), *Realism, Naturalism and Symbolism: Modes of Thought in Europe, 1848–1914*, N.Y. 1968
PASCAL, R., *From Naturalism to Expressionism: German Literature and Society*, London 1972
BRADBURY, M. AND MCFARLANE J. (eds.), *Modernism 1890–1930*, Harmondsworth 1976 (†)
WEISSTEIN, U. (ed.), *Expressionism as an International Literary Phenomenon*, Budapest and Paris 1973 (†)
SOKEL, W. E. (ed.), *Anthology of German Expressionist Drama*, N.Y. 1963 (includes early work by Kokoschka)
HAYMAN, R., *Nietzsche: a Critical Life*, London 1980
JASPERS, K., *Nietzsche: an Introduction to the Understanding of his Philosophical Activity*, Eng. transl., Tucson 1965
REICH, W., *Schoenberg: a Critical Biography*, Eng. transl., London 1971
NEWLIN, D., *Bruckner, Mahler, Schoenberg*, London 1976
VERGO, P., *Art in Vienna, 1898–1918*, 2nd ed., Oxford 1981 (†)
POWELL, N., *The Sacred Spring*, London 1974 (Secession Art)
SCHMALENBACH, F., *Oskar Kokoschka*, Eng. transl., Greenwich (Conn.) 1967
ROETHEL, H. K., *The Blue Rider*, N.Y. 1971
JONES, E., *S. Freud, Life and Works*, 3 vols., London 1953–7
BRANDELL, G., *Freud, a Man of his Century* (1961), Eng. transl., London 1979
FORSYTH, A., *Buildings for the Age (1900–1939)*, London 1982
GERETSEGGER, H. AND PEINTNER, M., *Otto Wagner*, London 1970
MUNZ, L. AND KUNSTLER, G., *Adolf Loos: Pioneer of Modern Architecture*, N.Y. 1966
WORRINGER, W., *Abstraction and Empathy* (1908), Eng. transl., London 1953

Chapter 9: A Crisis of Modernity

PAXTON, R. O., *Europe in the Twentieth Century*, N.Y. 1975
BIDDISS, M. D., *The Age of the Masses*, Harmondsworth 1977 (†)
CARR, E. H., *The Twenty Years' Crisis*, London 1939
CRAIG, G. A., *Germany 1866–1945*, Oxford 1978
LAQUEUR, W., *Weimar: a Cultural History 1918–1933*, London 1974 (†)
BREITMAN, R., *German Socialism and Weimar Democracy*, Chapel Hill 1981

BESSEL, R. J. AND FEUCHTWANGER, E. J., *Social Change and Political Development in Weimar Germany*, London 1981
GAY, P., *Weimar Culture: the Outsider as Insider*, London 1968 (†)
WAGER, W. W. (ed.), *Science, Faith and Man: European Thought since 1914*, N.Y. 1968
SPENGLER, O., *Decline of the West*, Eng. transl., London 1926–9
MANNHEIM, K., *Ideology and Utopia*, Eng. transl., London 1933
JAY, M., *The Dialectical Imagination: a History of the Frankfurt School*, London 1973
WILLETT, J., *Expressionism*, N.Y. 1970
PIERRE, J., *Futurism and Dada*, London 1967
Centre National de la Recherche scientifique, 'L'expressionisme dans le théâtre allemand', *Colloquium*, Paris 1971
WILLETT, J., *The Theatre of Bertold Brecht*, 3rd ed., London 1967
REED, T. J., *Thomas Mann: the Uses of Tradition*, Oxford 1974
BANHAM, R., *Theory and Design in the First Machine Age*, London 1960
LUCIE-SMITH, E., *A History of Industrial Design*, Oxford 1983 (†)
GROPIUS, W. A. G., *The New Architecture and the Bauhaus*, Eng. transl., London 1935
GLASER, H., *The Cultural Roots of National Socialism*, London 1982
BRACHER, R., *The German Dictatorship: Origins, Structure and Effects of National Socialism*, Eng. transl., Harmondsworth 1973
NICOLLS, A. J., *Weimar and the Rise of Hitler*, 2nd ed., London 1979 (†)
CECIL, R., *The Myth of the Master Race: Alfred Rosenberg and the Nazi Ideology*, London 1972

Chapter 10: Yesterday

URWIN, D. W., *Western Europe since 1945: a Short Political History*, London 1962
HALLE, L. J., *The Cold War as History*, London 1967
BARTLETT, C. J., *A History of Post-War Britain, 1945–1974*, London 1977
MARWICK, A., *British Society since 1945*, London 1982 (†)
SAMPSON, A., *The New Anatomy of Britain*, London 1971
HOFFMAN, F. J., *The Mortal No: Death and the Modern Imagination*, Princeton 1964
KOGAN, E., *The Theory and Practice of Hell* (1946), Eng. transl., N.Y. n.d.
CRUICKSHANK, J., *Albert Camus and the Literature of Revolt*, London 1959
SYPHER, W., *Loss of the Self, in Modern Literature and Art*, Westport 1962
STEINER, G., *Language and Silence*, Harmondsworth 1969
CRUICKSHANK, J. (ed.), *Aspects of the Modern European Mind*, London 1969 (†)
BELL, D., *The Cultural Contradictions of Capitalism*, London 1967
INGE, M. T. (ed.), *Concise Histories of Popular American Culture*, Westport 1982
GANS, H. J., *Popular Culture and High Culture*, N.Y. 1974
BIGSBY, C. W. E. (ed.), *Approaches to Popular Culture*, London 1976
MUSGROVE, F., *Youth and the Social Order*, London 1964
MUSGROVE, F., *Ecstasy and Holiness*, London 1975
HALL, S., AND JEFFERSON, T., *Resistance through Rituals: Youth Sub-Cultures in Post-War Britain*, London 1977
MARTIN, B., *A Sociology of Contemporary Cultural Change*, Oxford 1981 (†)
BECKER, J., *Hitler's Children*, London 1978 (on terrorism)
WILLENER, A., *The Action Image of Society*, Eng. transl., London 1970 (French student attitudes in May 1968)
MARCUSE, H., *One-Dimensional Man*, London 1964
ILLICH, I., *Deschooling Society*, N.Y. 1970
OGILVY, J., *Many-Dimensional Man: Decentralizing Self, Society and the Sacred*, N.Y. 1977
WILSON, B. R., *Contemporary Transformations of Religion*, Oxford 1976
GIDAL, A., *Andy Warhol: Films and Paintings*, London 1971
CURTIS, W. J. R., *Modern Architecture since 1900*, Oxford 1982

Index

Italic numbers refer to plates